15th Annual Meeting of the Special Interest Group on Discourse and Dialogue

(SIGDIAL 2014)

Philadelphia, Pennsylvania, USA
18 – 20 June 2014

ISBN: 978-1-63266-752-6

Printed from e-media with permission by:

Curran Associates, Inc.
57 Morehouse Lane
Red Hook, NY 12571

CURRAN ASSOCIATES INC.
proceedings.com

Some format issues inherent in the e-media version may also appear in this print version.

Printed by Curran Associates, Inc. (2014)

For permission requests, please contact the Association for Computational Linguistics at the address below.

Association for Computational Linguistics
209 N. Eighth Street
Stroudsburg, Pennsylvania 18360

Phone: 1-570-476-8006
Fax: 1-570-476-0860

acl@aclweb.org

Additional copies of this publication are available from:

Curran Associates, Inc.
57 Morehouse Lane
Red Hook, NY 12571 USA
Phone: 845-758-0400
Fax: 845-758-2634
Email: curran@proceedings.com
Web: www.proceedings.com

SIGDIAL 2014

15th Annual Meeting of the Special Interest Group on Discourse and Dialogue

Proceedings of the Conference

18-20 June 2014
Philadelphia, PA
USA

In cooperation with: Association for Computational Linguistics (ACL)
International Speech Communication Association (ISCA)
Association for the Advancement of Artificial Intelligence (AAAI)

We thank our sponsors:

Educational Testing Service (ETS) Microsoft Resarch Amazon.com Yahoo! Labs
Honda Research Institute (HRI) Linguistic Data Consortium (LDC)
Mitsubishi Electric Research Laboratories University of Pennsylvania Linguistics Department
AT&T Labs Research PARLANCE project SENSEI project

Association for Computational Linguistics (ACL)
209 N. Eighth Street
Stroudsburg, PA 18360
USA
Tel: +1-570-476-8006
Fax: +1-570-476-0860
acl@aclweb.org

Introduction

Welcome to the SIGDIAL 2014 Conference, the 15th Annual Meeting of the Special Interest Group on Discourse and Dialogue. The conference is held in Philadelphia, PA, USA on June 18-20th, jointly with the 8th International Natural Language Generation (INLG) conference and immediately preceding the 52nd Annual Meeting of the Association for Computational Linguistics (ACL).

SIGDIAL continues to serve as a publication venue for research that spans many aspects of discourse and dialogue. This year, the program included oral presentation and poster sessions on discourse, semantics, generation, situated and multi-modal dialogue, dialogue system control and evaluation, models of dialogue and spoken discourse and speech processing technology in dialogue. SIGDIAL 2014 also hosted a special session on the Dialogue State Tracking Challenge (DSTC), organized by Matt Henderson, Blaise Thomson and Jason Williams. The papers related to the challenge that appear in the proceedings were submitted and reviewed as regular SIGDIAL papers. Papers not accepted through the regular review process are not included in the proceedings, but were still invited to present posters in the special session. This is the first year SIGDIAL has issued a general call for special sessions.

We received 67 submissions—43 long papers, 20 short papers and 4 demo descriptions—from all around the world. All papers received 3 reviews. The members of the Program Committee did a superb job in reviewing the submitted papers. We thank them for their advice in selecting the accepted papers and for helping to maintain the high quality of the program. In line with the SIGDIAL tradition, our aim has been to create a balanced program that could accommodate as many favorably rated papers as possible.

Of the 43 long paper submissions: 13 were accepted as long papers for oral presentation, 9 were accepted as long papers for poster presentation. Of the 20 short paper submissions, 8 were accepted for poster presentation, for a total of 17 posters. There were 4 demonstration papers accepted. 9 papers were accepted for publication to appear in the DSTC Special Session (7 long and 2 short). This year's SIGDIAL conference runs 2.5 days as it did in 2013 with the special session being on the final half day.

We particularly thank the two keynote speakers, Lillian Lee (Cornell University) and Steve Young (Cambridge University) and for their contributions to research on discourse and dialogue systems.

We thank Svetlana Stoyanchev, Mentoring Chair for SIGDIAL 2014, for her dedicated work on coordinating the mentoring process. The goal of mentoring is to assist authors of papers that contain important ideas but lack clarity. Mentors work with the authors to improve English language usage or paper organization. This year, 9 of the accepted papers were mentored. We thank the Program Committee members who served as mentors: Timo Baumann, Giuseppe Di Fabbrizio, Jens Edlund, Annie Louis, Vincent Ng, Antoine Raux, Kristina Striegnitz, Nigel Ward and Jason Williams.

We extend special thanks to Keelan Evanini, the local arrangements chair, and his team Heather Blackman (administrative support) and Denise Maurer (event planning). SIGDIAL 2014 would not have been possible without Keelan and his team, who invested much effort in arranging the hotel venue and accommodation, handling registration, making banquet arrangements and handling numerous other preparations for the conference. We also thank the student volunteers for on-site assistance.

We thank Giuseppe Di Fabbrizio, Sponsorships Chair, for recruiting and liaising with our conference sponsors. The sponsorship program enables valuable aspects of the program, such as the invited speakers, conference reception and dinner. We gratefully acknowledge the support of our sponsors: Educational Testing Service, Microsoft Research, Amazon.com, Yahoo! Labs, Honda Research Institute, Linguistic Data Consortium, Mitsubishi Electric Research Laboratories, University of Pennsylvania Linguistics Department, AT&T Labs Research, PARLANCE project and SENSEI project. We also thank Priscilla

Rasmussen at the ACL for handling the financial aspects of sponsorship for SIGDIAL 2014.

We would also like to thank the INLG organizing committee, in particular Aoife Cahill and Margaret Mitchell, for the smooth running of the joint INLG/SIGDIAL session.

We also thank the SIGdial board, especially officers Kristiina Jokinen, Amanda Stent and Jason Williams, for their advice and support. Amanda's guidance and direct help in all aspects of organization have been most valuable. We thank Jason Williams and Barbara Di Eugenio for providing continuity and passing on advice derived from their experience as program chairs for SIGDIAL 2013. We appreciate Jason's prompt and patient replies to all our questions.

Finally, we thank all the authors of the papers in this volume, and all the conference participants for making this event such a great opportunity for new research in dialogue and discourse.

Kallirroi Georgila and Matthew Stone
General Co-Chairs

Helen Hastie and Ani Nenkova
Technical Program Co-Chairs

SIGDIAL 2014

General Co-Chairs:

Kallirroi Georgila, University of Southern California, USA
Matthew Stone, Rutgers, The State University of New Jersey, USA

Technical Program Co-Chairs:

Helen Hastie, Heriot-Watt University, Edinburgh, UK
Ani Nenkova, University of Pennsylvania, USA

Local Chair:

Keelan Evanini, Educational Testing Service, USA

Mentoring Chair:

Svetlana Stoyanchev, AT&T Labs Research, USA

Sponsorship Chair:

Giuseppe Di Fabbrizio, Amazon.com, USA

SIGdial Officers:

President: Amanda Stent, Yahoo! Labs, USA
Vice President: Jason D. Williams, Microsoft Research, USA
Secretary/Treasurer: Kristiina Jokinen, University of Helsinki, Finland

Program Committee:

Jan Alexandersson, DFKI GmbH, Germany
Masahiro Araki, Kyoto Institute of Technology, Japan
Yasuo Ariki, Kobe University, Japan
Ron Artstein, University of Southern California, USA
Timo Baumann, Universitat Hamburg, Germany
Frederic Bechet, Aix Marseille Universite - LIF/CNRS, France
Steve Beet, Aculab plc, UK
Jose Miguel Benedi, Universitat Politecnica de Valencia, Spain
Luciana Benotti, Universidad Nacional de Cordoba, Argentina
Nicole Beringer, 3SOFT GmbH, Germany
Nate Blaylock, Nuance Communications, Canada
Dan Bohus, Microsoft Research, USA
Johan Boye, KTH, Sweden
Boyer, North Carolina State University, USA
Asli Celikyilmaz, Microsoft, USA
Christophe Cerisara, CNRS, France
Joyce Chai, Michigan State University, USA
Mark Core, University of Southern California, USA
Paul Crook, Microsoft, USA
Heriberto Cuayáhuitl, Heriot-Watt University, Edinburgh, UK
Xiaodong Cui, IBM T. J. Watson Research Center, USA
Marie-Catherine de Marneffe, Ohio State University, USA

David DeVault, University of Southern California, USA
Barbara Di Eugenio, University of Illinois at Chicago, USA
Giuseppe Di Fabbrizio, Amazon.com, USA
Dimitrios Dimitriadis, AT&T Labs Research, USA
Myroslava Dzikovska, University of Edinburgh, UK
Jens Edlund, KTH Speech Music and Hearing, Sweden
Mauro Falcone, Fondazione Ugo Bordoni, Italy
Benoit Favre, Aix-Marseille Universite - LIF/CNRS, France
Raquel Fernández, ILLC, University of Amsterdam, Netherlands
Claire Gardent, CNRS/LORIA, Nancy, France
Kallirroi Georgila, University of Southern California, USA
Panayiotis Georgiou, University of Southern California, USA
Agustin Gravano, Universidad de Buenos Aires, Argentina
Nancy Green, University of North Carolina Greensboro, USA
Curry Guinn, University of North Carolina at Wilmington, USA
Dilek Hakkani-Tur, Microsoft Research, USA
Mark Hasegawa-Johnson, University of Illinois at Urbana-Champaign, USA
Helen Hastie, Heriot-Watt University, Edinburgh, UK
Peter Heeman, Oregon Health and Sciences University, Center for Spoken Language Understanding, USA
Keikichi Hirose, University of Tokyo, Japan
David Janiszek, Universite Paris Descartes, France
Kristiina Jokinen, University of Helsinki, Finland
Arne Jonsson, Linkoping University, Sweden
Pamela Jordan, University of Pittsburgh, USA
Tatsuya Kawahara, Kyoto University, Japan
Simon Keizer, Heriot-Watt University, Edinburgh, UK
Norihide Kitaoka, Nagoya University, Japan
Kazunori Komatani, Nagoya University, Japan
Stefan Kopp, Bielefeld University, Germany
Ian Lane, Carnegie Mellon University, USA
Romain Laroche, Orange Labs, France
Alex Lascarides, University of Edinburgh, UK
Sungjin Lee, Language Technologies Institute, Carnegie Mellon University, USA
Gary Geunbae Lee, POSTECH, South Korea
Fabrice Lefevre, University of Avignon, France
Oliver Lemon, Heriot-Watt University, Edinburgh, UK
James Lester, North Carolina State University, USA
Diane Litman, University of Pittsburgh, USA
Eduardo Lleida Solano, University of Zaragoza, Spain
Ramon Lopez-Cozar, University of Granada, Spain
Annie Louis, University of Edinburgh, UK
Hugo Meinedo, INESC-ID Lisboa, Portugal
Helen Meng, The Chinese University of Hong Kong, Hong Kong Special Administrative Region of China
Florian Metze, Carnegie Mellon University, USA
Wolfgang Minker, Ulm University, Germany
Teruhisa Misu, Honda Research Institute, USA
Mikio Nakano, Honda Research Institute Japan, Japan
Ani Nenkova, University of Pennsylvania, USA
Vincent Ng, University of Texas at Dallas, USA

Elmar Noeth, Friedrich-Alexander-University Erlangen-Nuremberg, Germany
Douglas O'Shaughnessy, INRS-EMT (University of Quebec), Canada
Paul Piwek, The Open University, UK
Andrei Popescu-Belis, Idiap Research Institute, Switzerland
Matthew Purver, Queen Mary, University of London, UK
Antoine Raux, Lenovo Labs, USA
Norbert Reithinger, DFKI GmbH, Germany
Verena Rieser, Heriot-Watt University, Edinburgh, UK
Carolyn Rose, Carnegie Mellon University, USA
Alexander Rudnicky, Carnegie Mellon University, USA
David Schlangen, Bielefeld University, Germany
Gabriel Skantze, KTH Speech Music and Hearing, Sweden
Manfred Stede, University of Potsdam, Germany
Georg Stemmer, Intel Corp., Germany
Amanda Stent, Yahoo! Labs, USA
Matthew Stone, Rutgers, The State University of New Jersey, USA
Svetlana Stoyanchev, AT&T Labs Research, USA
Kristina Striegnitz, Union College, USA
Marc Swerts, Tilburg University, Netherlands
Antonio Teixeira, University of Aveiro, Portugal
Joel Tetreault, Yahoo! Labs, USA
Takenobu Tokunaga, Tokyo Institute of Technology, Japan
Isabel Trancoso, INESC-ID / IST, Portugal
David Traum, University of Southern California, USA
Gokhan Tur, Microsoft Research, USA
Renata Vieira, PUCRS, Brazil
Marilyn Walker, University of California Santa Cruz, USA
Hsin-Min Wang, Academia Sinica, Taiwan
Nigel Ward, University of Texas at El Paso, USA
Jason Williams, Microsoft Research, USA
Steve Young, Cambridge University, UK
Kai Yu, Shanghai Jiao Tong University, China
Jian Zhang, Dongguan University of Technology and the Hong Kong University of Science and Technology, China

Additional Reviewers:

Rob Abbott, UC Santa Cruz, USA
Hendrik Buschmeier, Bielefeld University, Germany
Chen Chen, UT Dallas, USA
Layla El Asri, Orange Labs, France
Artur Freitas, PUCRS, Brazil
Roger Granada, PUCRS, Brazil
Hatim Khouzaimi, Orange Labs, France
Lihong Li, Microsoft Research, USA
Wencan Luo, University of Pittsburgh, USA
Amita Misra, UC Santa Cruz, USA

Invited Speakers:

Professor Lillian Lee, Cornell University, USA
Professor Steve Young, University of Cambridge, UK

Table of Contents

Keynote: Statistical Approaches to Open-domain Spoken Dialogue Systems
Steve Young 1

Crowdsourcing Street-level Geographic Information Using a Spoken Dialogue System
Raveesh Meena, Johan Boye, Gabriel Skantze and Joakim Gustafson 2

Out-of-Domain Spoken Dialogs in the Car: A WoZ Study
Sven Reichel, Jasmin Sohn, Ute Ehrlich, André Berton and Michael Weber 12

Situated Language Understanding at 25 Miles per Hour
Teruhisa Misu, Antoine Raux, Rakesh Gupta and Ian Lane 22

Information Navigation System Based on POMDP that Tracks User Focus
Koichiro Yoshino and Tatsuya Kawahara 32

Adapting to Personality Over Time: Examining the Effectiveness of Dialogue Policy Progressions in Task-Oriented Interaction
Alexandria Vail and Kristy Boyer 41

Probabilistic Human-Computer Trust Handling
Florian Nothdurft, Felix Richter and Wolfgang Minker 51

Learning Non-Cooperative Dialogue Behaviours
Ioannis Efstathiou and Oliver Lemon 60

Improving Classification-Based Natural Language Understanding with Non-Expert Annotation
Fabrizio Morbini, Eric Forbell and Kenji Sagae 69

User Modeling by Using Bag-of-Behaviors for Building a Dialog System Sensitive to the Interlocutor's Internal State
Yuya Chiba, Masashi Ito, Takashi Nose and Akinori Ito 74

Alex: Bootstrapping a Spoken Dialogue System for a New Domain by Real Users
Ondřej Dušek, Ondřej Plátek, Lukáš Žilka and Filip Jurčíček 79

InproTKs: A Toolkit for Incremental Situated Processing
Casey Kennington, Spyros Kousidis and David Schlangen 84

Back to the Blocks World: Learning New Actions through Situated Human-Robot Dialogue
Lanbo She, Shaohua Yang, Yu Cheng, Yunyi Jia, Joyce Chai and Ning Xi 89

An Easy Method to Make Dialogue Systems Incremental
Hatim Khouzaimi, Romain Laroche and Fabrice Lefevre 98

Free On-line Speech Recogniser Based on Kaldi ASR Toolkit Producing Word Posterior Lattices
Ondřej Plátek and Filip Jurčíček 108

Combining Task and Dialogue Streams in Unsupervised Dialogue Act Models
Aysu Ezen-Can and Kristy Boyer 113

Dialogue Act Modeling for Non-Visual Web Access
Vikas Ashok, Yevgen Borodin, Svetlana Stoyanchev and IV Ramakrishnan 123

Extractive Summarization and Dialogue Act Modeling on Email Threads: An Integrated Probabilistic Approach
Tatsuro Oya and Giuseppe Carenini . . . 133

Keynote: Language Adaptation
Lillian Lee . . . 141

Addressing Class Imbalance for Improved Recognition of Implicit Discourse Relations
Junyi Jessy Li and Ani Nenkova . . . 142

The Role of Polarity in Inferring Acceptance and Rejection in Dialogue
Julian Schlöder and Raquel Fernández . . . 151

In-depth Exploitation of Noun and Verb Semantics to Identify Causation in Verb-Noun Pairs
Mehwish Riaz and Roxana Girju . . . 161

Identifying Narrative Clause Types in Personal Stories
Reid Swanson, Elahe Rahimtoroghi, Thomas Corcoran and Marilyn Walker . . . 171

Evaluating a Spoken Dialogue System that Detects and Adapts to User Affective States
Diane Litman and Katherine Forbes-Riley . . . 181

Initiative Taking in Negotiation
Elnaz Nouri and David Traum . . . 186

Knowledge Acquisition Strategies for Goal-Oriented Dialog Systems
Aasish Pappu and Alexander Rudnicky . . . 194

Reducing Sparsity Improves the Recognition of Implicit Discourse Relations
Junyi Jessy Li and Ani Nenkova . . . 199

Interaction Quality Estimation in Spoken Dialogue Systems Using Hybrid-HMMs
Stefan Ultes and Wolfgang Minker . . . 208

Learning to Re-rank for Interactive Problem Resolution and Query Refinement
Rashmi Gangadharaiah, Balakrishnan Narayanaswamy and Charles Elkan . . . 218

Aspectual Properties of Conversational Activities
Rebecca J. Passonneau, Boxuan Guan, Cho Ho Yeung, Yuan Du, Emma Conner . . . 228

Detecting Inappropriate Clarification Requests in Spoken Dialogue Systems
Alex Liu, Rose Sloan, Mei-Vern Then, Svetlana Stoyanchev, Julia Hirschberg and Elizabeth Shriberg 238

Using Ellipsis Detection and Word Similarity for Transformation of Spoken Language into Grammatically Valid Sentences
Manuel Giuliani, Thomas Marschall and Amy Isard . . . 243

SAWDUST: A Semi-Automated Wizard Dialogue Utterance Selection Tool for Domain-Independent Large-Domain Dialogue
Sudeep Gandhe and David Traum . . . 251

A Demonstration of Dialogue Processing in SimSensei Kiosk
Fabrizio Morbini, David DeVault, Kallirroi Georgila, Ron Artstein, David Traum and Louis-Philippe Morency . . . 254

MVA: The Multimodal Virtual Assistant
Michael Johnston, John Chen, Patrick Ehlen, Hyuckchul Jung, Jay Lieske, Aarthi Reddy, Ethan Selfridge, Svetlana Stoyanchev, Brant Vasilieff and Jay Wilpon 257

The PARLANCE Mobile Application for Interactive Search in English and Mandarin
Helen Hastie, Marie-aude Aufaure, Panos Alexopoulos, Hugues Bouchard, Catherine Breslin, Heriberto Cuayáhuitl, Nina Dethlefs, Milica Gašić, James Henderson, Oliver Lemon, Xingkun Liu, Peter Mika, Nesrine Ben Mustapha, Tim Potter, Verena Rieser, Blaise Thomson, Pirros Tsiakoulis, Yves Vanrompay, Boris Villazon-Terrazas, Majid Yazdani, Steve Young and Yanchao Yu 260

The Second Dialog State Tracking Challenge
Matthew Henderson, Blaise Thomson and Jason D Williams 263

Optimizing Generative Dialog State Tracker via Cascading Gradient Descent
Byung-Jun Lee, Woosang Lim, Daejoong Kim and Kee-Eung Kim 273

Web-style Ranking and SLU Combination for Dialog State Tracking
Jason D Williams 282

Word-Based Dialog State Tracking with Recurrent Neural Networks
Matthew Henderson, Blaise Thomson and Steve Young 292

Comparative Error Analysis of Dialog State Tracking
Ronnie Smith 300

Extrinsic Evaluation of Dialog State Tracking and Predictive Metrics for Dialog Policy Optimization
Sungjin Lee 310

The SJTU System for Dialog State Tracking Challenge 2
Kai Sun, Lu Chen, Su Zhu and Kai Yu 318

Markovian Discriminative Modeling for Dialog State Tracking
Hang Ren, Weiqun Xu and Yonghong Yan 327

Sequential Labeling for Tracking Dynamic Dialog States
Seokhwan Kim and Rafael E. Banchs 332

Conference Program

Wednesday 18th June 2014

9:00	Welcome and conference overview
9:15	*Keynote: Statistical Approaches to Open-domain Spoken Dialogue Systems* Steve Young
10:15	Break
	Oral Session 1: Situated Spoken Dialog Systems in Motion Chair: Michael Johnston
10:45	*Crowdsourcing Street-level Geographic Information Using a Spoken Dialogue System* Raveesh Meena, Johan Boye, Gabriel Skantze and Joakim Gustafson
11:10	*Out-of-Domain Spoken Dialogs in the Car: A WoZ Study* Sven Reichel, Jasmin Sohn, Ute Ehrlich, André Berton and Michael Weber
11:35	*Situated Language Understanding at 25 Miles per Hour* Teruhisa Misu, Antoine Raux, Rakesh Gupta and Ian Lane
12:00	Lunch
	Oral Session 2: Adaptive Dialog Systems Chair: Kai Yu
13:00	*Information Navigation System Based on POMDP that Tracks User Focus* Koichiro Yoshino and Tatsuya Kawahara
13:25	*Adapting to Personality Over Time: Examining the Effectiveness of Dialogue Policy Progressions in Task-Oriented Interaction* Alexandria Vail and Kristy Boyer
13:50	*Probabilistic Human-Computer Trust Handling* Florian Nothdurft, Felix Richter and Wolfgang Minker

Wednesday 18th June 2014 (continued)

14:15 **Poster Madness Session** Chair: Rebecca Passonneau

14:35 **Poster Session with Coffee**

Learning Non-Cooperative Dialogue Behaviours
Ioannis Efstathiou and Oliver Lemon

Improving Classification-Based Natural Language Understanding with Non-Expert Annotation
Fabrizio Morbini, Eric Forbell and Kenji Sagae

User Modeling by Using Bag-of-Behaviors for Building a Dialog System Sensitive to the Interlocutor's Internal State
Yuya Chiba, Masashi Ito, Takashi Nose and Akinori Ito

Alex: Bootstrapping a Spoken Dialogue System for a New Domain by Real Users
Ondřej Dušek, Ondřej Plátek, Lukáš Žilka and Filip Jurčíček

InproTKs: A Toolkit for Incremental Situated Processing
Casey Kennington, Spyros Kousidis and David Schlangen

Back to the Blocks World: Learning New Actions through Situated Human-Robot Dialogue
Lanbo She, Shaohua Yang, Yu Cheng, Yunyi Jia, Joyce Chai and Ning Xi

An Easy Method to Make Dialogue Systems Incremental
Hatim Khouzaimi, Romain Laroche and Fabrice Lefevre

Free On-line Speech Recogniser Based on Kaldi ASR Toolkit Producing Word Posterior Lattices
Ondřej Plátek and Filip Jurčíček

Wednesday 18th June 2014 (continued)

Oral Session 3: Dialog Act Modelling Chair: Wolfgang Minker

16:15 *Combining Task and Dialogue Streams in Unsupervised Dialogue Act Models*
Aysu Ezen-Can and Kristy Boyer

16:40 *Dialogue Act Modeling for Non-Visual Web Access*
Vikas Ashok, Yevgen Borodin, Svetlana Stoyanchev and IV Ramakrishnan

17:05 *Extractive Summarization and Dialogue Act Modeling on Email Threads: An Integrated Probabilistic Approach*
Tatsuro Oya and Giuseppe Carenini

17:30 Announcements and business meeting
18:30 End of business meeting

Thursday 19th June 2014

9:00 *Keynote: Language Adaptation*
Lillian Lee

10:00 Break

Oral Session 4: Discourse Chair: Diane Litman

10:20 *Addressing Class Imbalance for Improved Recognition of Implicit Discourse Relations*
Junyi Jessy Li and Ani Nenkova

10:45 *The Role of Polarity in Inferring Acceptance and Rejection in Dialogue*
Julian Schlöder and Raquel Fernández

11:10 *In-depth Exploitation of Noun and Verb Semantics to Identify Causation in Verb-Noun Pairs*
Mehwish Riaz and Roxana Girju

11:35 *Identifying Narrative Clause Types in Personal Stories*
Reid Swanson, Elahe Rahimtoroghi, Thomas Corcoran and Marilyn Walker

Thursday 19th June 2014 (continued)

12:00 Lunch and sponsor talks

13:50 **Poster and Demo Madness Session** Chair: Amy Isard

INLG Joint Session Talks (see separate proceedings) Chair: Kathy McCoy

14:15 *Crowdsourcing Language Generation Templates for Dialog Systems*
Margaret Mitchell, Dan Bohus and Ece Kamar

14:40 *Generating Effective Referring Expressions Using Charts*
Nikolaos Engonopoulos and Alexander Koller

15:05 *Modeling Blame to Avoid Positive Face Threats in Natural Language Generation*
Gordon Briggs and Matthias Scheutz

15:30 **INLG Joint Session - Panel**

16:00 **Poster and Demonstration Session with Coffee**

Evaluating a Spoken Dialogue System that Detects and Adapts to User Affective States
Diane Litman and Katherine Forbes-Riley

Initiative Taking in Negotiation
Elnaz Nouri and David Traum

Knowledge Acquisition Strategies for Goal-Oriented Dialog Systems
Aasish Pappu and Alexander Rudnicky

Reducing Sparsity Improves the Recognition of Implicit Discourse Relations
Junyi Jessy Li and Ani Nenkova

Interaction Quality Estimation in Spoken Dialogue Systems Using Hybrid-HMMs
Stefan Ultes and Wolfgang Minker

Learning to Re-rank for Interactive Problem Resolution and Query Refinement
Rashmi Gangadharaiah, Balakrishnan Narayanaswamy and Charles Elkan

Aspectual Properties of Conversational Activities
Rebecca J. Passonneau, Boxuan Guan, Cho Ho Yeung, Yuan Du, Emma Conner

Detecting Inappropriate Clarification Requests in Spoken Dialogue Systems
Alex Liu, Rose Sloan, Mei-Vern Then, Svetlana Stoyanchev, Julia Hirschberg and Elizabeth Shriberg

Using Ellipsis Detection and Word Similarity for Transformation of Spoken Language into Grammatically Valid Sentences
Manuel Giuliani, Thomas Marschall and Amy Isard

Thursday 19th June 2014 (continued)

SAWDUST: A Semi-Automated Wizard Dialogue Utterance Selection Tool for Domain-Independent Large-Domain Dialogue
Sudeep Gandhe and David Traum

A Demonstration of Dialogue Processing in SimSensei Kiosk
Fabrizio Morbini, David DeVault, Kallirroi Georgila, Ron Artstein, David Traum and Louis-Philippe Morency

MVA: The Multimodal Virtual Assistant
Michael Johnston, John Chen, Patrick Ehlen, Hyuckchul Jung, Jay Lieske, Aarthi Reddy, Ethan Selfridge, Svetlana Stoyanchev, Brant Vasilieff and Jay Wilpon

The PARLANCE Mobile Application for Interactive Search in English and Mandarin
Helen Hastie, Marie-aude Aufaure, Panos Alexopoulos, Hugues Bouchard, Catherine Breslin, Heriberto Cuayáhuitl, Nina Dethlefs, Milica Gašić, James Henderson, Oliver Lemon, Xingkun Liu, Peter Mika, Nesrine Ben Mustapha, Tim Potter, Verena Rieser, Blaise Thomson, Pirros Tsiakoulis, Yves Vanrompay, Boris Villazon-Terrazas, Majid Yazdani, Steve Young and Yanchao Yu

18:00 **Poster session ends**

19:00 **Banquet**

Friday 20th June 2014

DSTC Special Session Chair: Alan Black

8:45 *The Second Dialog State Tracking Challenge*
Matthew Henderson, Blaise Thomson and Jason D Williams

9:07 *Optimizing Generative Dialog State Tracker via Cascading Gradient Descent*
Byung-Jun Lee, Woosang Lim, Daejoong Kim and Kee-Eung Kim

9:23 *Web-style Ranking and SLU combination for dialog state tracking*
Jason D Williams

9:39 *Word-Based Dialog State Tracking with Recurrent Neural Networks*
Matthew Henderson, Blaise Thomson and Steve Young

9:55 *Comparative Error Analysis of Dialog State Tracking*
Ronnie Smith

10:15 *Extrinsic Evaluation of Dialog State Tracking and Predictive Metrics for Dialog Policy Optimization*
Sungjin Lee

Friday 20th June 2014 (continued)

10:35 **Poster Session with coffee**

The SJTU System for Dialog State Tracking Challenge 2
Kai Sun, Lu Chen, Su Zhu and Kai Yu

Markovian Discriminative Modeling for Dialog State Tracking
Hang Ren, Weiqun Xu and Yonghong Yan

Sequential Labeling for Tracking Dynamic Dialog States
Seokhwan Kim and Rafael E. Banchs

Dialog State Tracking by Decomposing the States
Wencan Luo and Diane Litman

12:00 Best paper award ceremony and closing

Keynote: Statistical Approaches to Open-domain Spoken Dialogue Systems

Steve Young
Cambridge University, UK
sjy@eng.cam.ac.uk

In contrast to traditional rule-based approaches to building spoken dialogue systems, recent research has shown that it is possible to implement all of the required functionality using statistical models trained using a combination of supervised learning and reinforcement learning. This approach to spoken dialogue is based on the mathematics of partially observable Markov decision processes (POMDPs) in which user inputs are treated as observations of some underlying belief state, and system responses are determined by a policy which maps belief states into actions.

Virtually all current spoken dialogue systems are designed to operate in either a specific carefully defined domain such as restaurant information and appointment booking, or they have very limited conversational ability such as in Siri and Google Now. However, if voice is to become a significant input modality for accessing web-based information and services, then techniques will be needed to enable conversational spoken dialogue systems to operate within open domains.

This talk will discuss methods by which current statistical approaches to spoken dialogue can be extended to cover much wider domains. It will be argued that unlike many other areas of machine learning, spoken dialogue systems always have a user on-hand to provide supervision. Hence spoken dialogue systems provide a unique opportunity to automatically adapt on large quantities of speech data without the need for costly annotation.

Crowdsourcing Street-level Geographic Information Using a Spoken Dialogue System

Raveesh Meena **Johan Boye** **Gabriel Skantze** **Joakim Gustafson**
KTH Royal Institute of Technology
School of Computer Science and Communication
Stockholm, Sweden
{raveesh, jboye}@csc.kth.se, {gabriel, jocke}@speech.kth.se

Abstract

We present a technique for crowdsourcing street-level geographic information using spoken natural language. In particular, we are interested in obtaining first-person-view information about what can be seen from different positions in the city. This information can then for example be used for pedestrian routing services. The approach has been tested in the lab using a fully implemented spoken dialogue system, and has shown promising results.

1 Introduction

Crowdsourcing is increasingly being used in speech processing for tasks such as speech data acquisition, transcription/labeling, and assessment of speech technology, e.g. spoken dialogue systems (Parent & Eskenazi, 2011). However, we are not aware of any attempts where a dialogue system is the *vehicle* for crowdsourcing rather than the object of study, that is, where a spoken dialogue system is used to collect information from a large body of users. A task where such crowdsourcing dialogue systems would be useful is to populate geographic databases. While there are now open databases with geographic information, such as OpenStreetMap (Haklay & Weber, 2008), these are typically intended for map drawing, and therefore lack detailed street-level information about city landmarks, such as colors and height of buildings, ornamentations, facade materials, balconies, conspicuous signs, etc. Such information could for example be very useful for pedestrian navigation (Tom & Denis, 2003; Ross et al., 2004). With the current growing usage of smartphones, we might envisage a community of users using their phones to contribute information to geographic databases, annotating cities to a great level of detail, using multi-modal method including speech. The key reason for using speech for map annotation is convenience; it is easy to talk into a mobile phone while walking down the street, so a user with a little experience will not be slowed down by the activity of interacting with a database. This way, useful information could be obtained that is really hard to add offline, sitting in front of one's PC using a map interface, things like: Can you see X from this point? Is there a big sign over the entrance of the restaurant? What color is the building on your right?

Another advantage of using a spoken dialogue system is that the users could be asked to freely describe objects they consider important in their current view. In this way, the system could learn new objects not anticipated by the system designers, and their associated properties.

In this paper we present a proof-of-concept study of how a spoken dialogue system could be used to enrich geographic databases by crowdsourcing. To our knowledge, this is the first attempt at using spoken dialogue systems for crowdsourcing in this way. In Section 2, we elaborate on the need of spoken dialogue systems for crowdsourcing geographic information. In Section 3 we describe the dialogue system implementation. Section 4 presents our in-lab crowdsourcing experiment. We present an analysis of crowd-sourced data in Section 5, and discuss directions for future work in Section 6.

2 The pedestrian routing domain

Routing systems have been around quite some time for car navigation, but systems for pedestrian routing are relatively new and are still in their nascent stage (Bartie & Mackaness, 2006; Krug et al., 2003; Janarthanam et al., 2012; Boye et al., 2014). In the case of pedestrian navigation, it is preferable for way-finding systems to base their instructions on *landmarks*, by which we understand distinctive objects in the city environment. Studies have shown that the inclusion of landmarks into system-generated instructions for a pedestrian raises the user's confidence in the system, compared to only left-right instructions (Tom & Denis, 2003; Ross et al., 2004).

Basing routing instructions on landmarks means that the routing system would, for example, generate an instruction "Go towards the red brick building" (where, in this case, "the red brick building" is the landmark), rather than "Turn slightly left here" or "Go north 200 meters". This strategy for providing instructions places certain requirements on the geographic database: It has to include many landmarks and many details about them as well, so that the system can generate clear and un-ambiguous instructions. However, the information contained in current databases is still both sparse and coarse-grained in many cases.

Our starting point is a pedestrian routing system we designed and implemented, using the landmark-based approach to instruction-giving (Boye et al., 2014). The system performs visibility calculations whenever the pedestrian approaches a waypoint, in order to compute the set of landmarks that are visible for the user from his current position. OpenStreetMap (Haklay & Weber, 2008) is used as the data source. Figure 1 shows a typical situation in pedestrian routing session. The blue dot indicates the user's position and the blue arrow her direction. Figure 2 shows the same situation in a first-person perspective. The system can now compute the set of visible landmarks, such as buildings and traffic lights, along with distances and angles to those landmarks. The angle to a building is given as an interval in degrees relative to the direction of the user (e.g. 90° left to 30° left). This is exemplified in Figure 1, where four different buildings are in view (with field of view marked with numbers 1–4). Landmarks that are not buildings are considered to be a single point, and hence the relative angle can be given as a single number.

When comparing the map with the street view picture, it becomes obvious that the "SEB" bank office is very hard to see and probably not very suitable to use as a landmark in route descriptions. On the other hand, the database does not contain the fact that the building has six stories and a façade made of yellow bricks, something that would be easily recognizable for the pedestrian. This is not due to any shortcoming of the OpenStreetMap database; it just goes to show that the database has been constructed with map drawing in mind, rather than pedestrian routing. There are also some other notable omissions in the database; e.g. the shop on the corner, visible right in front of the user, is not present in the database. Since OpenStreetMap is crowd-sourced, there is no guarantee as to which information will be present in the database, and which will not. This also highlights the limitation of existing approaches to crowd-sourcing geographic information: Some useful information is difficult to add off-line, using a map interface on a PC. On the other hand, it would be a straightforward matter given the kind of crowd-sourcing spoken dialogue system we present next.

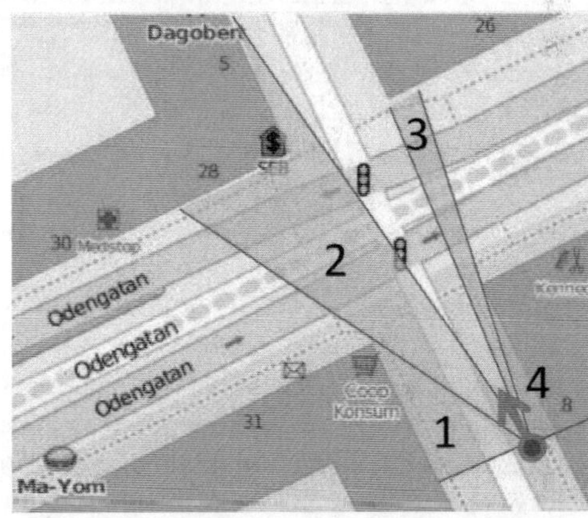

Figure 1: A pedestrian routing scenario

Figure 2: The visual scene corresponding to the pedestrian routing scenario in Figure 1

3 A dialogue system for crowd-sourcing

To verify the potential of the ideas discussed above, we implemented a spoken dialogue system that can engage in spoken conversation with users and learn details about landmarks in visual scenes (such as Figure 2). To identify the kind of details in a visual scene that the system could potentially ask the users, we first conducted a preliminary informal crowd-sourcing dialogue: one person (the receiver), was instructed to seek information that could be useful for pedestrian navigation from the other person (the giver). The receiver only had access to information available in the maps from OpenStreetMap, as in Figure 1, but without any marking of field of views, whereas the giver only had access to the corresponding visual scene (as in Figure 2). Interaction data from eight such dialogues (from four participants, and four different visual scenes) suggested that in a city environment, buildings are prominent landmarks and much of the interaction involves their properties such as color, number of stories, color of roof, signs or ornamentations on buildings, whether it has shops, etc. Seeking further details on mentioned signs, shops, and entities (whether mapped or unmapped) proved to be a useful strategy to obtain information. We also noted that asking for open-ended questions, such as "*Is there anything else in this scene that I should be aware of?*" towards the end has the potential of revealing unknown landmarks and details in the map.

Obtaining specific details about known objects from the user corresponds to slot-filling in a dialogue system, where the dialogue system seeks a value for a certain slot (= attribute). By engaging in an open-ended interaction the system could also obtain general details to identify new slot-value pairs. Although slots could be in some cases be multi-valued (e.g., a building could have both color red and yellow), we have here made the simplifying assumption that they are single valued. Since users may not always be able to specify values for slots we treat *no-value* as a valid slot-value for all type of slots.

We also wanted the system to automatically learn the most reliable values for the slots, over several interactions. As the system interacts with new users, it is likely that the system will obtain a range of values for certain slots. The variability of the answers could appear for various reasons: users may have differences in perception about slot-values such as colors, some users might misunderstand what building is being talked about, and errors in speech recognition might result in the wrong slot values. Some of these values may therefore be in agreement with those given by other users, while some may differ slightly or be in complete contradiction. Thus the system should be able to keep a record of all the various slot-values obtained (including the disputed ones), identify slot-values that need to be clarified, and engage in a dialogue with users for clarification.

In view of these requirements, we have designed our crowd-sourcing dialogue system to be able to (1) take and retain initiative during the interactions for slot-filling, (2) behave as a responsive listener when engaging in open-ended dialogue, and (3) ask *wh–* and *yes–no questions* for seeking and clarifying slot-values, respectively. Thus when performing the slot-filling task, the system mainly asks questions, acknowledges, or clarifies the concepts learned for the slot-values. Apart from requesting repetitions, the user cannot ask any questions or by other means take the initiative. A summary of all the attributes and corresponding system prompts is presented in Appendix A.

The top half of Figure 3 illustrates the key components of the dialogue system. The Dialogue Manager queries the Scene Manager (SM) for slots to be filled or slot-values to be clarified, engages in dialogue with users to learn/clarify slot-values, and informs the SM about the values obtained for these slots. The SM manages a list of scenes and the predefined slots – for each type of landmark in visual scenes – that need to be filled, maintains a record of slot-values obtained from all the users, and identifies slot-values with majority vote as the current reliable slot-value. To achieve these objectives, the scene manager uses an XML representation of visual scenes. In this representation, landmarks (e.g., buildings, junctions, etc.) – automatically acquired through the OpenStreetMap database and the visibility computations mentioned in Section 2 – are stored as *scene-objects* (cf. Figure 4).

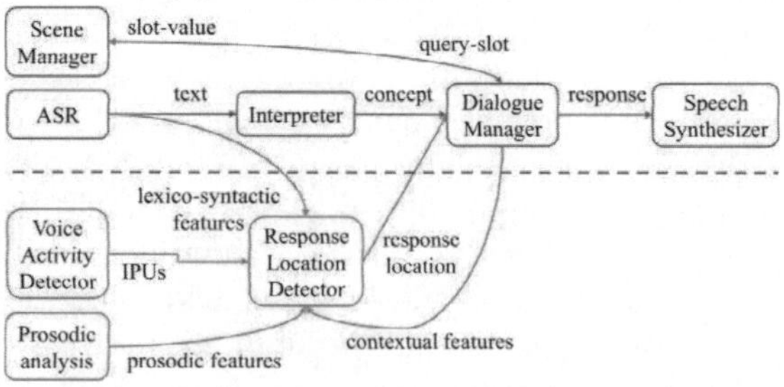

Figure 3: Dialogue system architecture

The Dialogue Manager (DM) uses scene-object attributes, such as type, angle or interval of a building, to generate referential expressions, such as "Do you see a *building* on the *far left*?"

or "Do you see a *shop* on the *left*?" to draw the users' attention to the intended landmark in the scene. During the course of interaction, the Scene Manager (SM) extends scene-objects with a set of predefined attributes (= slots) that we identified in the preliminary study, along with their various slot-values (cf. Figure 5). For each slot, the SM keeps a record of slot-values obtained through wh– questions as well as the ones disputed by the users in yes–no questions (cf. `obtained` and `disputed` tags in the XML), and uses their tally to identify the slot-value in majority. The system assumes this slot-value (or one of them in case of a tie) as its best estimate of a slot-value pair, which it could clarify with another user using a yes–no query. During the slot-filling mode the DM switches to open-ended interaction mode to seek general details (using prompts such as "*Could you describe it/them?*"), if the user suggests/agrees that there are signs on/at a scene-object, or a building has shops or restaurants. Once all the slots for all the scene-objects in a visual scene have been queried, the DM once again switches to the open-ended interaction mode and queries the users whether there are any other relevant signs or landmarks that the system may have missed and should be aware of. On completion of the open-ended queries the SM selects the next visual scene, and the DM engages in a new dialogue.

```
<scene xmlns="cityCS.scene" name=" view7.jpg" lat="59.34501"
lon="18.0614" fovl="-60" fovr="60" bearing="320" dist="100">
    <scene-object>
        <id>35274588</id> <type>building</type>
        <from>-60</from> <end>-39</end>
    </scene-object>
    <scene-object>
        <id>538907080</id> <type>shop</type>
        <distance>34.82</distance>
        <angle>-39</angle> <bearing>281</bearing>
    </scene-object>
    <scene-object>
        <id>280604</id> <type>building</type>
        <from>-38</from> <end>6</end>
    </scene-object>
    <scene-object>
        <id>193906</id> <type>traffic_signals</type>
        <distance>40.77</distance>
        <angle>-14</angle> <bearing>306</bearing>
    </scene-object>
    ...
</scene>
```

Figure 4: XML representation of visual scenes

For speech recognition and semantic interpretation the system uses a context-free grammar with semantic tags (SRGS[1]), tailored for the domain. The output of semantic interpretation is a concept. If the concept type matches the type of the slot, the dialogue manager informs the scene manager about the obtained slot-value. If the concept type is inappropriate the DM queries the user once more (albeit using different utterance forms). If still no appropriate concept is learned the DM requests the SM for the next slot and proceeds with the dialogue. For speech synthesis, we use the CereVoice system developed by CereProc[2]. The dialogue system has been implemented using the IrisTK framework (Skantze & Al Moubayed, 2012).

```
<scene-object>
    <id>35274588</id> <type>building</type>
    <from>-60</from> <end>-39</end>
    <slot slotName="VISIBLE">...    </slot>
    <slot slotName="COLOR">
     <obtained>
       <value slotValue="Green">
         <userlist>
           <usrDtls uid="u01" asrCnf="0.06" qType="WH"/>
         </userlist>
       </value>
       <value slotValue="no-value">
         <userlist>
           <usrDtls uid="u02" asrCnf="0.46" qType ="WH"/>
         </userlist>
       </value>
       <value slotValue="Gray">
         <userlist>
           <usrDtls uid="u03" asrCnf="0.19" qType ="WH"/>
         </userlist>
       </value>
     </obtained>
     <disputed>
       <value slotValue="Green">
         <userlist>
           <usrDtls uid="u02" asrCnf="0.92" qType ="YN"/>
         </userlist>
       </value>
     </disputed>
    </slot>
    <slot slotName="STORIES">...    </slot>
    <slot slotName="ROOF_COLOR">...    </slot>
    ...
</scene-object>
```

Figure 5: Every slot-value is recorded

In contrast to the slot-filling mode, when engaging in an open-ended interaction, the system leaves the initiative to the user and behaves as a responsive listener. That is, the system only produces feedback responses, such as backchannels (e.g., *okay*, *mh-hmm*, *uh-huh*), repetition requests for longer speaker turns (e.g., *could you repeat that?*), or continuation prompts such as "*anything else?*" until the user is finished speaking. Unless the system recognized an explicit closing statement from the user (e.g., "I can't"), the system encourages the user to continue the descriptions for 2 to 4 turns (chosen randomly).

To detect appropriate locations in users' speech where the system should give feedback response, the system uses a trained data-driven model (Meena et al., 2013). When the voice activity detector detects a silence of 200 ms in users' speech, the model uses prosodic, contextual and lexico-syntactic features from the preceding speech segment to decide whether the system

[1] http://www.w3.org/TR/speech-grammar/

[2] https://www.cereproc.com/

should produce a feedback response. The lower half of Figure 3 shows the additional components of the dialogue system used in open-ended interaction mode. In this mode, the ASR system uses a language model that is trained on interactions from a related domain (verbal route descriptions), in parallel to the SRGS grammar.

4 In-lab crowd-sourcing experiment

Nine visual scenes (wide-angle pictures in first-person perspective and taken in Stockholm city, cf. Figure 2) were used for the task of crowdsourcing. Fifteen human participants (4 females and 11 males) participated in the crowdsourcing exercise. All participants either studied or worked at the School of Computer Science and Communication, KTH, Stockholm.

Participants were placed in front of a computer display and were told that the system will engage them in a spoken conversation to seek or clarify details about landmarks and other objects in visual scenes. They were told that the details would be used for pedestrian routing and therefore they are free to choose and specify details (in open-ended questions) that they thought would be useful when giving route instructions to another person.

Each participant did the nine visual scenes in the same order, with a 1 minute pause between each of them. The first visual scene was used as a trial in order to familiarize participants with the interaction scenario. For this reason, the trial interaction was specifically designed to engage the participants in both wh– and yes–no type questions. We also wanted to investigate whether the use of wh– or yes–no questions alone has any impact on the interactions. For the remaining eight interactions, the dialogue system therefore alternatively used wh– and yes–no questions throughout the whole dialogue. The order of query types was switched for each successive participant. Thus visual scenes presented with wh– queries to a participant p_i were presented to participant p_{i+1} with only yes–no queries, and vice-versa. After each interaction participants were asked (1) whether the system appeared to be familiar with the visual scene; and (2) whether the interactions went smoothly.

An example of a conversation with wh–type queries is presented in Table 1. The second column indicates the various types of utterances (dialogue acts) used by the system during this interaction. Note that during the slot-filling mode, the system has the initiative, whereas in the open-ended queries (cf. rows 15–22 in Table 1) the system gives the initiative to the participant and only produces feedback responses. Table 2 presents a conversation with yes–no queries following the conversation in Table 1. In a conversation with only yes–no queries, a wh– query may be presented if a slot has been observed with *no-value* (cf. rows 9–10 in Table 1) or when the participant disputes the system's current best estimate (cf. rows 6–9 in Table 2).

S	Introduction	Could you help me with some details about this view?
P		Yes
S	wh– query	Do you see a building on the far left?
P		Yes
S	Backchannel	Mh-hmm
S	wh– query	What color does the building have?
P		Cream color [Green color]
S	Reprise	Green
S	wh– query	How many floors is this building?
P		I don't know [I do no]
	...	
S	wh– query	Are there any important signs in this scene that I may have missed?
P		No
S	Backchannel	Uh-huh
S	wh– query	Is there anything peculiar in this scene that I should be familiar with
P		There is a bike painted on street just in front of me [is the right pink university in front of may]
S	Backchannel	Anything else?
P		Yeah its white paint [Yes light pink]
S	Backchannel	Mh-hmm
P		That's it [that that]
S	Backchannel	Ehm
P		I am done [okay]
S	Ending	Okay, thanks

Table 1: An example interaction with wh– queries for the visual scene in Figure 2. S: system, P: participant (here, u01 from Figure 5). ASR results are shown within square brackets.

S	Introduction	Could you help me with some details about this view?
P		Yes
S	yes–no query	Is the building on the far left visible to you?
P		Yes
S	Backchannel	Mh-hmm
S	yes–no query	Does this building have green color?
P		No
S	Backchannel	Uh-huh
S	wh– query	But than what color is the building?

P		white [light]
S	Repeat	Sorry, what color did you say?
P		white [light]
S	wh– query	How many stories is this building?
P		I don't know [I do rental]
S	Backchannel	Ehm
	...	
S	wh– query	Are there any important signs in this scene that I may have missed?
P		Ehm no [nine no]
S	Backchannel	Ehm
S	yes–no query	I am informed that there are other important landmarks or structures in this scene that I should be aware of, is it true?
P		No
S	Backchannel	uh-huh
S	Ending	Okay, thanks

Table 2: An example interaction with yes–no queries corresponding to the visual scene in Figure 2. S: system, P: participant (here u02 from Figure 5). ASR results are shown within square brackets.

5 Data analysis

We analyzed the data (15×8 interactions) collected from the experiment along the following tracks: first, we compare the majority value of the slots to the ground truth as given by a human annotator; second, we explore how the ground truth of slot-values could be estimated automatically; third, we also analyzed the instances where the participants disputed the system's current estimate of slot values; and fourth, we examined the post-experimental questionnaires.

5.1 Rate of learning slot-values

A total of 197 slots were learned in the experiment. We analyzed how many slot-values had been correctly retrieved after 1, 2… 15 users. In Figure 6, the curve "Majority" illustrates the fraction of slot-values correctly learned with each new user, under the assumption that the slot-values with majority votes – from all the 15 users – constitute the ground truth. Thus after interacting with the first user the system had obtained 67.0% of slot-values correctly (according to the majority) and 96.4% of slot-values after interacting with the first six users. Another eight users, or fourteen in total, were required to learn all the slot-values correctly. The progression curve thus provides an estimate of how many users are required to achieve a specific percentage of slot-values correctly if majority is to be considered the ground truth. The curve "Not-in-Majority" indicates the number of slot with values that were not in the majority. Thus after interacting with the first user 20.8% of slot-values the system had obtained were not in majority and could be treated as incorrect. Note that the curves Majority and Not-in-Majority do not sum up to 100%, this is because we consider *no-value* as a valid slot-value, and treat the slot as unfilled. For example, 12.2% of the slots remained unfilled after interacting with the first user.

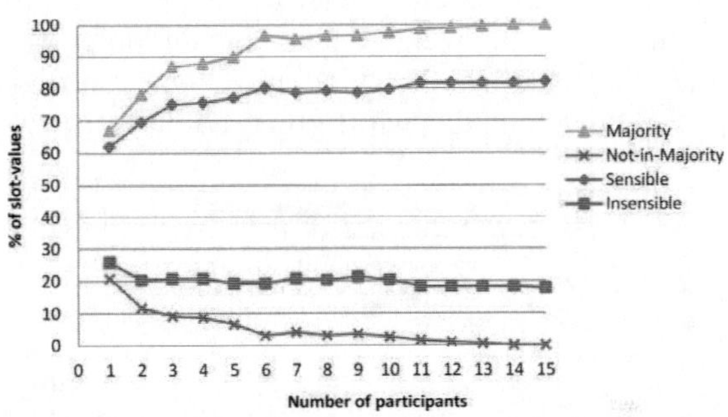

Figure 6: Rate of learning slot-values with two different estimates of ground truth

We also investigated how close the majority is to the actual truth. A human annotator (one of the coauthors) labeled all the obtained slot-values as either sensible or insensible, based on the combined knowledge from the corresponding maps, the visual scenes, and the set of obtained values. Thus a slot could have many sensible values. For example, various parts of a building could be painted in different colors. The progression curves "Sensible" and "Insensible" in Figure 6 illustrate the fraction of total slots for which the learned values were actually correct and incorrect, respectively. While the curve for sensible values follows the same pattern as the progression curve for majority as the estimate of ground truth, the percent of slot-values that were actually correct is always lower than the majority as ground truth, and it never reached 100%. The constant gap between the two curves suggests that some slot-values learned by the majority were not actually the ground truth. What led the majority into giving incorrect slot-values is left as a topic for future work.

As mentioned earlier, much of the slot-filling interaction involved buildings and their properties. Figure 7 illustrates that sensible values for most slots, pertaining to whether a building is visible, whether it is residential, whether it has shops, and the color of roof were obtained by interacting with only few participants. In contrast, properties such as color of the building and number of stories required many more participants. This could be attributed to the fact that participants may have differences in perception about slot-values. As regards to whether there are signs on buildings, we observed that the recall is relatively low. This is largely due to lack of common ground among participants about what could be considered a sign. Our intentions with designing this prompt was to retrieve any peculiar detail on the building that is easy to locate: for us a sign suggesting a name of restaurant is as useful as the knowledge that the building has blue sunshade on the windows. Some participants understood this while other didn't.

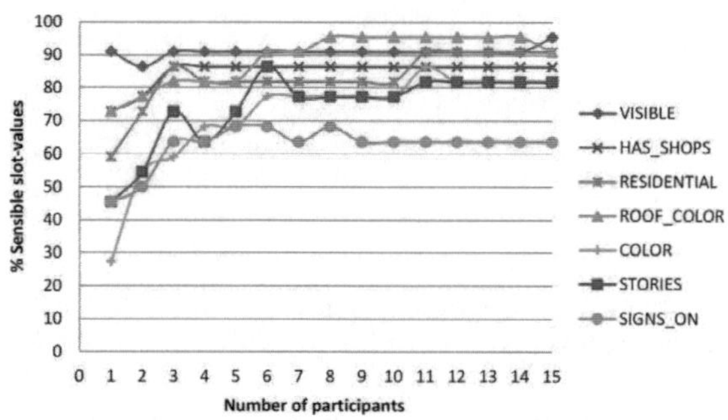

Figure 7: Learning rate of various slots for landmark type *building*

5.2 Estimated ground truth of slot-values

The 15 subjects in the in-lab experiment were all asked for the same information. In a real application, however, we want the system to only ask for slots for which it has insufficient or conflicting information. If the ground truth of a certain slot-value pair can be estimated with a certainty exceeding some threshold (given the quality requirements of the database, say 0.8), the system can consider the matter settled, and need not ask about that slot again. We therefore want to estimate the ground truth of slot-values along with a certainty measure. To this end, we use the CityCrowdSource Trust software package (Dickens & Lupu, 2014), which is based on the probabilistic approach for supervised learning when we have multiple annotators providing labels (possibly noisy) but no absolute gold standard, presented in Raykar et al. (2009).

Using this approach, a question concerning the color of a building, say with ID 24, (e.g. "What color is the building?") would be translated into several binary predicates COLOR_Red(24), COLOR_Brown(24), COLOR_Orange(24), etc. The justification for this binary encoding is that the different color values are not mutually exclusive: A building might of course have more than one color, and in many cases more than one color name might be appropriate even though the building has only one dominating color (e.g. to describe the color either as "brown" and "red" might be acceptable to most people). Figure 8 shows the incremental estimates for different colors for a certain building (OpenStreetMap ID 163966736) after 1, 2... 15 subjects had been asked. The answer from the first subject was erroneously recognized as "pink". The next 9 subjects all referred to the building as "brown". Among the final subjects, 3 subjects referred to building as "red", and 2 subjects as "brown". The final truth estimates are 0.98 for "brown", 0.002 for "red", and 0.00005 for "pink". The diagram shows that if the certainty threshold is set to 0.8, the value "brown" would have been established already after 4 subjects.

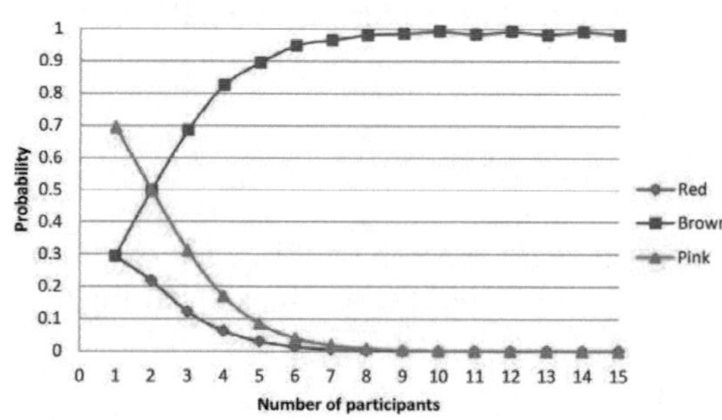

Figure 8: Probabilities of different estimated ground truth values for the color of a certain building

5.3 Disputed slot-values

We also examined all system questions of yes–no type that received negative answers, i.e. instances where the participants disputed the system's current best estimate (based on majority vote) of a slot-value. Among the 95 such instances, the system's current best estimate was actually insensible only on 43 occasions. In 30 of these instances the participants provided a rectified slot-value that was sensible. For the remaining 13 instances the new slot-values proposed by the participant were actually insensible. There were 52 instances of false disputations, i.e. the system's current estimate of a slot-value was sensible, but the participants disputed it. 6 of these occurrences were due to errors in speech recognition, but for the remaining 46 occasions, error in grounding the intended landmark (15), users' perception of slot-values (3), and ambiguity in what the annotator terms as sensible slot-values (28), (e.g. whether there are signs on a building (as discussed in Section 5.1)) were identified as the main reasons. This suggests that slots (i.e. attributes) that are often disputed may not be easily understood by users.

5.4 Post-experimental questionnaire

As described above, the participants filled in a questionnaire after each interaction. They were asked to rate the system's familiarity with the visual scene based on the questions asked. A Mann–Whitney *U* test suggests that participants' perception of the system's familiarity with the visual scene was significantly higher for interactions with yes–no queries than interactions with wh– queries (U=1769.5, p= 0.007). This result has implications for the design choice for systems that provide as well as ask for information from users. For example, a pedestrian routing system can already be used to offer routing instructions as well as crowdsourcing information. The system is more likely to give an impression of familiarity with the surrounding, to the user, by asking yes–no type questions than wh–questions. This may influence a user's confidence or trust in using the routing system.

Since yes–no questions expect a "yes" or "no" in response, we therefore hypothesized that interactions with yes–no questions would be perceived smoother in comparison to interactions with wh– questions. However, a Mann–Whitney *U* test suggests that the participants perceived no significant difference between the two interaction types (U=1529.0, p= 0.248). Feedback comments from participants suggest that abrupt ending of open-ended interactions by the system (due to the simplistic model of detecting whether the user has anything more to say) gave users an impression that the system is not allowing them to speak.

6 Discussion and future work

We have presented a proof-of-concept study on using a spoken dialogue system for crowd-sourcing street-level geographic information. To our knowledge, this is the first attempt at using spoken dialogue systems for crowdsourcing in this way. The system is fully automatic, in the sense that it (i) starts with minimal details – obtained from OpenStreetMap – about a visual scene, (ii) prompts users with wh– questions to obtain values for a predefined set of attributes; and (iii) assumes attribute-values with majority vote as its beliefs, and engages in yes–no questions with new participants to confirm them. In a data collection experiment, we have observed that after interacting with only 6 human participants the system acquires more than 80% of the slots with actually sensible values.

We have also shown that the majority vote (as perceived by the system) could also be incorrect. To mitigate this, we have explored the use of the CityCrowdSource Trust software package (Dickens & Lupu, 2014) for obtaining the probabilistic estimate of the ground truth of slot-values in a real crowd-sourcing system. However, it is important not only to consider the ground truth probabilities per se, but also on how many contributing users the estimate is based and the quality of information obtained. We will explore these two issues in future work.

We have observed that through open-ended prompts, the system could potentially collect a large amount of details about the visual scenes. Since we did not use any automatic interpretation of these answers, we transcribed key concepts in participants' speech in order to obtain an estimate of this. However, it is not obvious how to quantify the number of concepts. For example, we have learned that in Figure 2, at the junction ahead, there is: a *traffic-sign*, a *speed-limit* sign, a sign with *yellow* color, a sign with *red* color, a sign with *red boarder*, a sign that is *round*, a sign with some *text*, the *text* says *50*. These are details obtained in pieces from various participants. Looking at Figure 2 one can see that these pieces when put together refer to the speed-limit sign mounted on the traffic-signal at the junction. How to assimilate these pieces together into a unified concept is a task that we have left for future work.

Acknowledgement

We would like to thank the participants of the in-lab crowd-sourcing experiment. This work is supported by the EIT KIC project "*CityCrowdSource*", and the Swedish research council (VR) project *Incremental processing in multimodal conversational systems* (2011-6237).

Reference

Bartie, P. J., & Mackaness, W. A. (2006). Development of a Speech-Based Augmented Reality System to Support Exploration of Cityscape. *Transactions in GIS, 10*(1), 63-86.

Boye, J., Fredriksson, M., Götze, J., Gustafson, J., & Königsmann, J. (2014). Walk This Way: Spatial Grounding for City Exploration. In Mariani, J., Rosset, S., Garnier-Rizet, M., & Devillers, L.

(Eds.), *Natural Interaction with Robots, Knowbots and Smartphones* (pp. 59-67). Springer New York.

Dickens, L., & Lupu, E. (2014). *Trust service final deliverable report*. Technical Report, Imperial College, UK.

Haklay, M., & Weber, P. (2008). OpenStreetMap: User-Generated Street Maps. *IEEE Pervasive Computing, 7*(4), 12-18.

Janarthanam, S., Lemon, O., Liu, X., Bartie, P., Mackaness, W., Dalmas, T., & Goetze, J. (2012). Integrating Location, Visibility, and Question-Answering in a Spoken Dialogue System for Pedestrian City Exploration. In *Proceedings of the 13th Annual Meeting of the Special Interest Group on Discourse and Dialogue* (pp. 134-136). Seoul, South Korea: Association for Computational Linguistics.

Krug, K., Mountain, D., & Phan, D. (2003). Webpark: Location-based services for mobile users in protected areas.. *GeoInformatics*, 26-29.

Parent, G., & Eskenazi, M. (2011). Speaking to the Crowd: Looking at Past Achievements in Using Crowdsourcing for Speech and Predicting Future Challenges. In *INTERSPEECH* (pp. 3037-3040). ISCA.

Raykar, V. C., Yu, S., Zhao, L. H., Jerebko, A., Florin, C., Valadez, G. H., Bogoni, L., & Moy, L. (2009). Supervised Learning from Multiple Experts: Whom to Trust when Everyone Lies a Bit. In *Proceedings of the 26th Annual International Conference on Machine Learning* (pp. 889-896). New York, NY, USA: ACM.

Ross, T., May, A., & Thompson, S. (2004). The Use of Landmarks in Pedestrian Navigation Instructions and the Effects of Context. In Brewster, S., & Dunlop, M. (Eds.), *Mobile Human-Computer Interaction - MobileHCI 2004* (pp. 300-304). Springer Berlin Heidelberg.

Skantze, G., & Al Moubayed, S. (2012). IrisTK: a statechart-based toolkit for multi-party face-to-face interaction. In *Proceedings of ICMI*. Santa Monica, CA.

Tom, A., & Denis, M. (2003). Referring to Landmark or Street Information in Route Directions: What Difference Does It Make?. In Kuhn, W., Worboys, M., & Timpf, S. (Eds.), *Spatial Information Theory. Foundations of Geographic Information Science* (pp. 362-374). Springer Berlin Heidelberg.

Appendix A

The table below lists slots (= landmark attributes) and the corresponding wh– and yes–no system questions. For attributes marked with * the dialogue manager switches to open-ended interaction mode.

Slot (=attribute)	System wh– questions	System yes–no questions
Visible: whether a particular landmark is visible from this view.	• Do you see a building on the far left? • Do you see another building in front of you? • Is there a junction on the right? • Do you see a traffic-signal ahead?	• Is the building on the far right visible to you? • I think there is another building in front of you, do you see it? • Can you see the junction on the right? • Are you able to see the traffic-signal ahead?
Color of the building	• What color does the building have? • What color is the building?	• I think this building is *red* in color, what do you think? • Does this building have *red* color?
Size of the building (in number of stories)	• How many floors do you think are there in this building • How many stories is this building	• I think there are *six* floors in this building, what do you think? • Is this building *six* storied?
Color of the building's *roof*	• What color does the roof of this building have? • What color is the roof of this building?	• I think the roof of this building is *orange* in color, what do you think? • Do you think that the roof of this building is *orange*?
Signs or ornamentation on the building	• Do you see any signs or decorations on this building?	• I think there is a sign or some decoration on this building, do you see it? • There may be a sign or a name on this building, do you see it?
Shops or restaurants in the building	• Are there any shops or restaurants in this building?	• I am informed that there are some shops or restaurants in this building, is it true? • I think there are some shops or restaurants in this building, what do you think?
Signs at landmarks	• Are there any important signs at the junction/crossing?	• I believe there is a sign at this junction/crossing, do you see it? • Do you see the sign at this junction/crossing?
**Description* of sign	• Could you describe this sign? • What does this sign look like? • Does the sign say something?	• Could you describe this sign? • What does this sign look like? • Does the sign say something?
**Signs* in the visual scene	• Are there any important signs in this scene that I may have missed? • Have I missed any relevant signs in this scene?	• There are some important signs in this scene that could be useful for my knowledge, am I right? • I am informed that there are some signs in this scene that are relevant for me, is it true?
**Landmarks* in the visual scene	• Are there any other important buildings or relevant structures in this scene that I should be aware of? • Is there anything particular in this scene that I should be familiar with? • Have I missed any relevant buildings or landmarks in this scene?	• I am informed that there are some important landmarks or structures in this scene that I should be aware of, is it true? • I have been told that there are some other things in this scene that I are relevant for me, is it true? • I believe I have missed some relevant landmarks in this scene, am I right?
**Description* of unknown *landmarks* e.g. shop, restaurant, building, etc.	• Could you describe it? • Could you describe them? • How do they look like?	• Could you describe it? • Could you describe them? • How do they look like?

Out-of-Domain Spoken Dialogs in the Car: A WoZ Study

Sven Reichel, Jasmin Sohn,
Ute Ehrlich, André Berton
Speech Dialogue Systems
Daimler AG, Ulm, Germany
sven.reichel@daimler.com

Michael Weber
Institute of Media Informatics
Ulm University
Germany
michael.weber@uni-ulm.de

Abstract

Mobile Internet access via smartphones puts demands on in-car infotainment systems, as more and more drivers like to access the Internet while driving. Spoken dialog systems (SDS) distract drivers less than visual/haptic-based dialog systems. However, in conversational SDSs drivers might speak utterances which are not in the domain of the SDS and thus cannot be understood. In a Wizard of Oz study, we evaluate the effects of out-of-domain utterances on cognitive load, driving performance, and usability. The results show that an SDS which reacts as expected by the driver, is a good approach to control in-car infotainment systems, whereas unexpected SDS reactions might cause severe accidents. We evaluate how a dialog initiative switch, which guides the user and enables him to reach his task goal, performs.

1 Introduction

The acceptance of smartphones is a success story. These devices allow people to access the Internet nearly anywhere at anytime. While driving, using a smartphone is prohibited in many countries as it distracts the driver. Regardless of this prohibition, people use their smartphone and cause severe injuries (National Highway Traffic Safety Administration (NHTSA), 2013). In order to reduce driver distraction, it is necessary to integrate the smartphones functionality safely into in-car infotainment systems. Since hands and eyes are involved in driving, a natural and intuitive speech-based interface increases road safety (Maciej and Vollrath, 2009). There are already infotainment systems with Internet applications like e.g. weather, music streaming, gas prices, news, and restaurant search.

However, conversational spoken dialog systems (SDS) to control all these applications and the car's functionality, are still missing. Current SDSs operate mostly in specific domains and they understand user utterances which are related to these domains. While using natural language, users are not restricted to specific domains. Thus one crucial problem for them is to know which utterances the system is able to understand. People use different approaches to solve this problem, for example by reading the manual, using on-screen help, or relying on their mental model of the SDS. In multi-domain SDSs, utterances can be quite complex and remembering all of them or displaying them on screen would not be possible. As a result, as long as conversational SDSs are not able to operate in much wider domains, sooner or later the user will speak an utterance which is in his mental model of the SDS, but cannot be processed. Such utterances can be divided into out-of-domain and out-of-application-scope (Bohus and Rudnicky, 2005). We induce errors in domain switches and not within one domain, thus only out-of-domain utterances are considered.

In this paper, we present results from a **W**izard **o**f **O**z (WoZ) study on multi-domain interaction with an in-car SDS to evaluate the effects of out-of-domain utterances on driver performance. We considered four different system reactions: successful domain switch, misunderstanding, non-understanding, and a dialog initiative switch. By analyzing them concerning driver distraction and usability, we are able to evaluate whether a dialog initiative switch is an appropriate response to an out-of-domain utterance or not. The results offer valuable clues for the development of multi-domain in-car SDSs.

The remainder is structured as follows: Section 2 provides an overview of studies in this context. Section 3 describes the domain of the study which is shown in Section 4. Data analysis methods are defined in Section 5. We present and discuss the results in Section 6 and conclude in Section 7.

2 Related Work

Driver distractions, due to secondary tasks, are evaluated in many studies (a good overview provides Ei-Wen Lo and Green (2013)). The driver's performance is generally better when using speech interfaces than manual or visual interfaces, however, interacting with an SDS is often worse than just driving (Barón and Green, 2006). Most studies consider specific domains and do not evaluate how to handle domain switches. Kun et al. (2013) evaluated multi-threaded dialogs between humans while driving. By interrupting a dialog, they observed an increase of cognitive load, which affected the driving performance negatively. The participants were prepared that an interruption will be initiated at some time. This means they might be surprised, however, it won't be as unexpected as system reactions in response to out-of-domain utterances. In this work, we evaluate a dialog initiative switch, as a possible reaction to out-of-domain utterances.

In a driving simulator study, Kun et al. (2007) showed that low SDS recognition accuracy affects the steering wheel angle variance negatively. This is first evidence that in-car SDSs need to handle speech recognition or language understanding errors intelligently. In preliminary work to this study, we analyzed a dataset containing dialog errors in relation to driving performance, measured by the lane change task (Mattes, 2003). This showed slight evidence that dialog errors, such as responses to out-of-domain utterances, have an influence on driving performance. However, the lane change task is not the right driving task for such a fine granular analysis, as drivers are only occupied during a lane change and thus not constantly at the same level. Therefore, we analyze driving performance with the **Cont**inuous **T**racking and **Re**action (ConTRe) task (Mahr et al., 2012).

3 User Tasks

In a user experiment it is crucial to set real tasks for users, since artificial tasks will be hard to remember and can reduce their attention. We analyzed current in-car infotainment systems with Internet access and derived eight multi-domain tasks from their functionality (see Table 1). Since only few natural use cases involve more than three domains, every user task is a story of three subtasks. In task number 5 for example, a user has to start a subtask, which navigates him to Berlin. Then he would like to search an Italian restaurant at the destination. Finally, he adds the selected restaurant to his address book.

No	Domain 1	Domain 2	Domain 3
1	POI Search	Restaurant	Call
2	Knowledge	Ski Weather	Navigation
3	Weather	Hotel Search	Address book
4	Play Artist	News Search	Forward by eMail
5	Navigation	Restaurant	Save Address
6	News Search	Play Artist	Share on Facebook
7	News Search	Knowledge	Convert Currency
8	Navigation	Gas Prices	Status Gas Tank

Table 1: Multi-domain user tasks.

At the beginning of a task and during a subtask, the SDS always reacts as it is expected by the users, which means it answers their requests. This increases the stress when the system suddenly starts to react unexpectedly. After presenting the final answer of a subtask, the user has to initiate a domain switch. In response to domain switching utterances four different system reactions were used (see Section 4.2.2).

4 User Experiment

Developing an SDS includes specifying a grammar or training statistical language models for speech recognition. These steps precede any real user test. In system-initiated dialogs, with a few possible utterances, specifying a grammar is feasible. However, in strictly user-initiative dialogs covering multiple domains, this is rather complicated. A WoZ study does not require to develop speech recognition and language understanding as this is performed by a human (Fraser and Gilbert, 1991). In addition, the system reaction is controlled and not influenced by recognition errors. Our study requires such a controlled environment, as an unexpected system reaction, due to a recognition error, would influence the results negatively.

Driver distraction and usability ratings vary among people and depend on age, personality, experience, context, and many more. Therefore, it is essential to conduct a user study with people who might use the SDS later on. A study by the NHTSA (National Highway Traffic Safety Administration (NHTSA), 2013) showed that 73% of the drivers involved in fatal crashes due to cell phone use in 2011, were less than 40 years old. For this reason, our study considers drivers between 18 and 40 years who are technically affine and are likely to buy a car equipped with an infotainment system with Internet access.

4.1 Set-Up of the Experiment

When designing a user interaction experiment, it is important that it takes place in a real environment. As driving on a real road is dangerous, we used a fixed-base driving simulator in a laboratory. A screen in front of the car covers the driver's field of view (see Figure 1). Steering and pedal signals are picked from the car's CAN bus.

It is important that the user assumes he is interacting with a computer as "human-human interactions are not the same as human-computer interactions" (Fraser and Gilbert, 1991). The wizard, a person in charge of the experiment, was located behind the car and mouse clicks or any other interaction of the wizard was not audible in the car. To ensure a consistent behavior of the wizard, we used SUEDE (Klemmer et al., 2000) to define the dialog, which also provides an interface for the wizard. SUEDE defines a dialog in a state machine, in which the system prompts are states and user inputs are edges between them. The content of system prompts was synthesized with NUANCE Vocalizer Expressive[1] version 1.2.1 (Voice: anna.full). During the experiment, the wizard clicks the corresponding edge after each user input and SUEDE plays the next prompt.

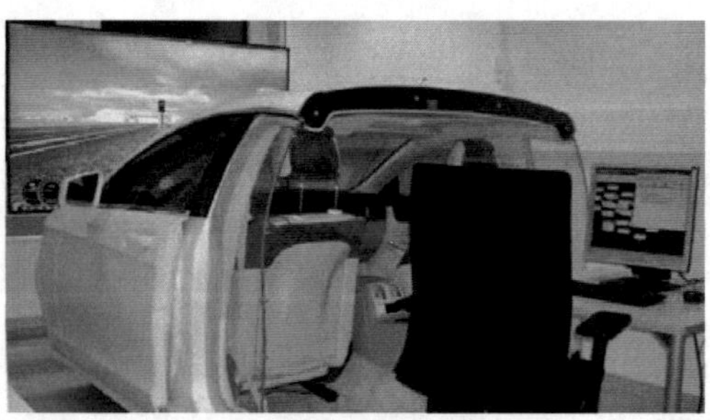

Figure 1: Set-up of the experiment

4.2 Design of the Experiment

Driving a car requires the driver to focus on the road and react appropriately to sudden events. However, if drivers are occupied with a secondary task, such as controlling an infotainment system, their attention to the road might suffer. This is due to the fact that the human's performance is reduced when human resources overlap (Wickens, 2008). In this experiment, a dual task scenario is used by driving in a simulator and interacting with an SDS at the same time. There is no visual display in the car, as this would require additional human resources and it would increase the driver distraction (Young and Regan, 2007).

4.2.1 Primary Task: Driving Simulator

One major requirement for the driving simulator is to ensure a controlled and comparable driver distraction measure over all interaction variants and participants. The open-source driving simulator OpenDS provides a driving environment and extensive logging facilities (Math et al., 2012). As explained in Section 2, it is essential to keep the driver occupied at a constant level all the time. Therefore, we used the ConTRe task (Mahr et al., 2012), which consists of a continuous steering task and a reaction task.

Figure 2 shows the ConTRe task with steering cylinders and a traffic light. The yellow steering cylinder moves unpredictably right and left at a constant distance from the driver. The driver has to steer the blue cylinder to superpose it with the middle section of the yellow one. This is similar to driving on a curved road. Sometimes a driver needs to react to sudden events to prevent an accident. A traffic light shows randomly red and green and requires the driver to push the throttle or brake pedal. As the car drives constantly at 50km/h, the pedals are only pushed in response to the traffic light. The movement of the yellow cylinder and the appearance of the traffic light can be controlled by manipulating OpenDS' control variables. We used the "hard driving" condition as described by Mahr et al. (2012).

Figure 2: Continuous tracking and reaction task

4.2.2 Secondary Task: Responses to Domain Switching Requests

A task in our experiment consists of three subtasks and each subtask requires two to four semantic concepts. For a user it is possible to insert multiple concepts at once:

U: "Search an Italian restaurant at my destination"

[1] http://www.nuance.com/for-business/mobile-solutions/vocalizer-expressive/index.htm

or as single utterances in a dialog:

U: "Search an Italian restaurant"

S: "Where do you search an Italian restaurant?"

U: "At my destination"

Prompts were created for all possible combinations. SUEDE provides a GUI for the wizard to select which semantic concepts a user input contains. Depending on the selection, either another concept is requested or the answer is provided. Within one subtask, the system always reacts as expected by the user. An answer for the presented example might look like:

S: "There is one Italian restaurant: Pizzeria San Marco."

After this, the user has to initiate a domain switch to save the pizzeria's address into his personal address book. Such user-initiated domain switches challenge current SDSs as language models increase and thus speech recognition as well as language understanding is error prone (Carstensen et al., 2010). Furthermore, the user could request a functionality which is not supported by the system. In case of such a request, SDSs react differently and could apply error recovery strategies if the error is recognized. To analyze the impact of error recovery strategies in the car, we use four different kinds of responses to domain switching requests.

Figure 3 shows the study's conditions. Detailed dialogs that corresponds to them can be found in the Appendix. First of all, we consider the **E**xpected **R**eaction (ER) condition, in which the SDS reacts as expected by the user and switches the domain. As the speech is recognized by a wizard, this is an optimal system without any errors.

Miscommunication can be distinguished between misunderstanding and non-understanding (Skantze, 2007). In the **M**is**U**nderstanding (MU) condition, the SDS does not recognize the domain switch request and it responses in context of the current domain. On the contrary, in the **N**on-**U**nderstanding (NU) condition, it recognizes an out-of-domain utterance and refuses the action by apologizing and encouraging the user to rephrase his utterance (a combination of Bohus and Rudnicky (2005)'s Notify and AskRephrase error handling strategies). The only way to proceed with a MU or NU task in our experiment is to use an explicit domain switching command, such as "start radio application". As we have shown in Reichel et al. (2014), participants do not use such commands naturally in a speech-only infotainment system and only use them after trying numerous unsuccessful utterances. Another approach is a **D**ialog **I**nitiative **S**witch (DIS) to guide the user after recognizing an out-of-domain utterance (Notify and YouCanSay strategy (Bohus and Rudnicky, 2005)). Therefore, the SDS proposes a choice of four possible domains to interact with. Users have to select the first option which was followed by four possible actions within this domain. By selecting the desired action, the SDS reads out four examples of possible utterances. After that, the dialog initiative is given back to the user.

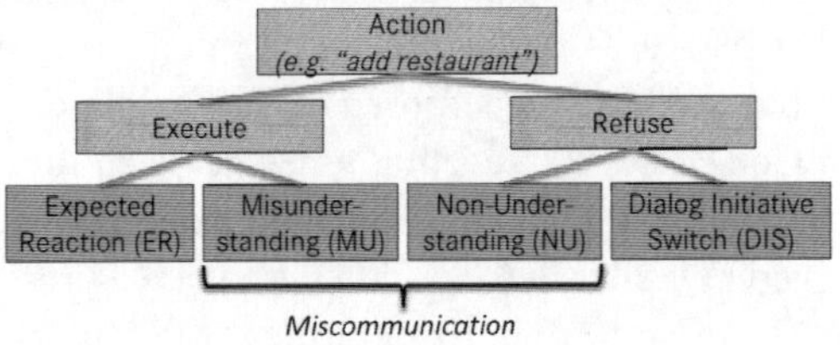

Figure 3: Domain switching response conditions

4.3 Procedure of the experiment

The experiment starts with an initial questionnaire to create a profile of the participant, concerning age, experience with smartphones, infotainment systems and SDSs. Then participants are introduced to the driving task and they have time to practice till being experienced. After completing a baseline drive, they start to use the SDS. For each spoken dialog task users get a story describing in prose what they like to achieve. To minimize priming effects, they have to remember their task and are not allowed to keep the description during the interaction. There is no explanation or example of the SDS, apart from a start command for activation. After the start command, the system plays a beep and the user can say whatever he likes to achieve his task. The exploration phase consists of four tasks, in which the system reacts as it is expected by the user. This enables the user to get used to the SDS while driving. In the second part of the experiment, one task for each condition was completed (ER, MU, NU, and DIS). The conditions were assigned randomly to a task and each one was rated by a **S**ubjective **A**ssessment of **S**peech **S**ystem **I**nterfaces (SASSI) (Hone and Graham, 2000) and **D**river **A**ctivity **L**oad **I**ndex (DALI) (Pauzié et al., 2007) questionnaire. At end of the experiment, each participant completed a second baseline drive without using the SDS to analyze whether the driving performance changed to the first baseline drive or not.

After that, the four conditions were compared in a questionnaire.

5 Evaluation Metrics and Hypotheses

The goal of this study is to evaluate four SDS response conditions concerning driver distraction and usability. Therefore, we used four kinds of measurements (see Table 2): objective driving performance logged by OpenDS, subjective driver distraction with DALI questionnaires, usability scores measured by SASSI questionnaires, and dialog performance. The steering deviation value measures the driver's performance to keep the blue cylinder superposed to the yellow one in the ConTRe task. Reaction times between the appearance of a traffic light and the pedal press are logged as well as wrong and missed pedal presses. The DALI questionnaire consists of 7 questions which are assigned to 7 domains to evaluate the driver's cognitive load. We did not ask for visual or haptic demand, as the system does not have visual output or haptic input. A 7-point Likert scale was used: *low* cognitive load (-3) to *high* cognitive load (+3). SASSI is widely used to measure the usability of an SDS covering 6 dimensions with 34 questions. We used a 7-point Likert scale from *strong disagree* (-3) to *strong agree* (+3). High values mean good usability, except for annoyance and cognitive demand ratings, which are opposed.

objective driving performance (OpenDS)	steering deviation reaction time missed reaction wrong reaction
cognitive load (DALI)	global attention auditory demand interference temporal demand
usability (SASSI)	system response accuracy (SRA) likeability (Like) cognitive demand (Cog Dem) annoyance (Ann) habitability (Hab) speed
dialog performance	task success user response delay system turn duration user turn duration

Table 2: Evaluation metrics

Obviously, we expect that drivers perform best during the baseline drives without controlling the SDS. As ER does not stress or frustrate drivers and they do not need much cognitive power to think what to say, there won't be huge differences between ER and baseline drives. On the contrary, if the system does not react as expected (MU and NU), we expect a worse driving performance and poor usability ratings. NU should be rated better than MU, as the SDS explains the problem. The interesting part is how a DIS will perform as an error handling strategy to out-of-domain utterances. We assume that it is rated better than MU and NU and worse than ER. As the help dialogs in DIS are long, DIS might tend towards MU and NU in terms of driver distraction. However, it will be rated better in terms of usability because the task success is expected to be higher.

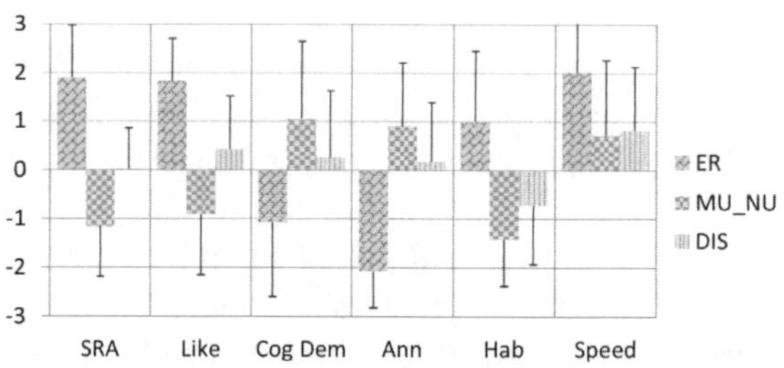

Figure 4: Usability ratings, all of them are significant (p<.001) except of: speed between DIS and MU_NU

6 Results

In the following, evaluation results of the four domain switching responses are shown. We analyzed data from 30 participants (16m/14f), with average age of 26.65 (SD: 3.32). Their experience with SDS is little (6-Likert Scale, avg: 3.06, SD: 1.48) as well as the usage of SDSs (5-Likert Scale, avg: 2.04, SD: 1.16). We asked them how they usually approach a new system to learn its interaction schema and scope of operation. All 30 of them try a new application on their smartphone without informing themselves how it is used. Concerning infotainment systems, trying is also the most used learning approach, even while driving (26 people). This means, people do not read a manual, but the system has to be naturally usable. In terms of driving experience, all participants have a driver license for average 8.6 (SD: 3.5) years and most of them use their car daily. Considering the objective driving performances of the two baseline drives, there are no significant differences, which means the participants performed at a constant level over the entire experiment. Figure 4, 5 and 6 show a detailed overview of the evaluation results, which will be explained in this Section.

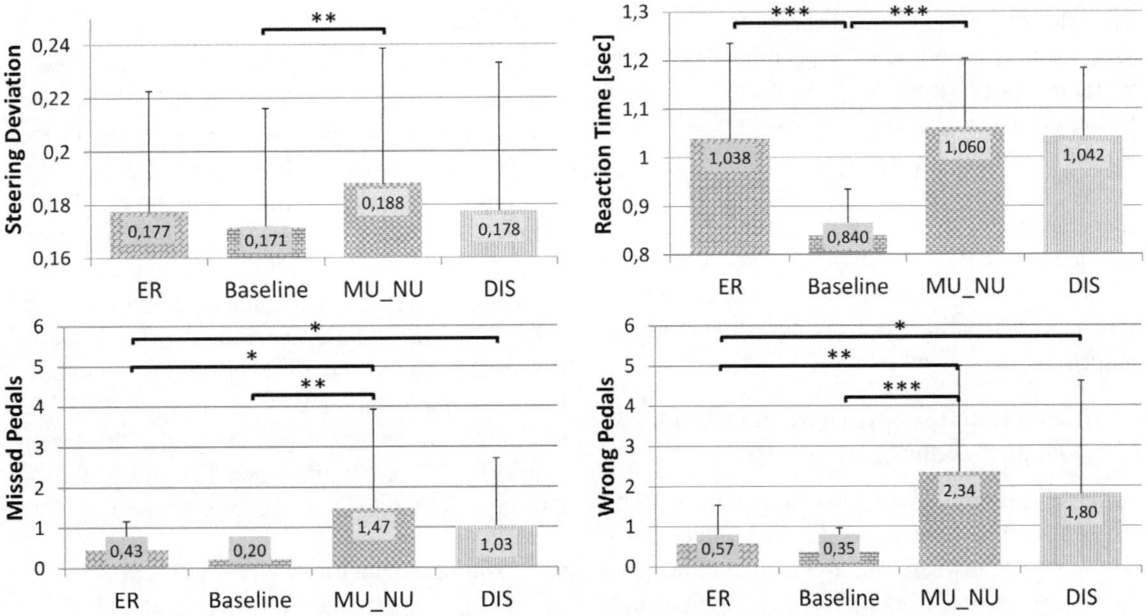

Figure 5: Objective driving performance (OpenDS), significance levels: p<.05(*), p<.01(**), p<.001(***)

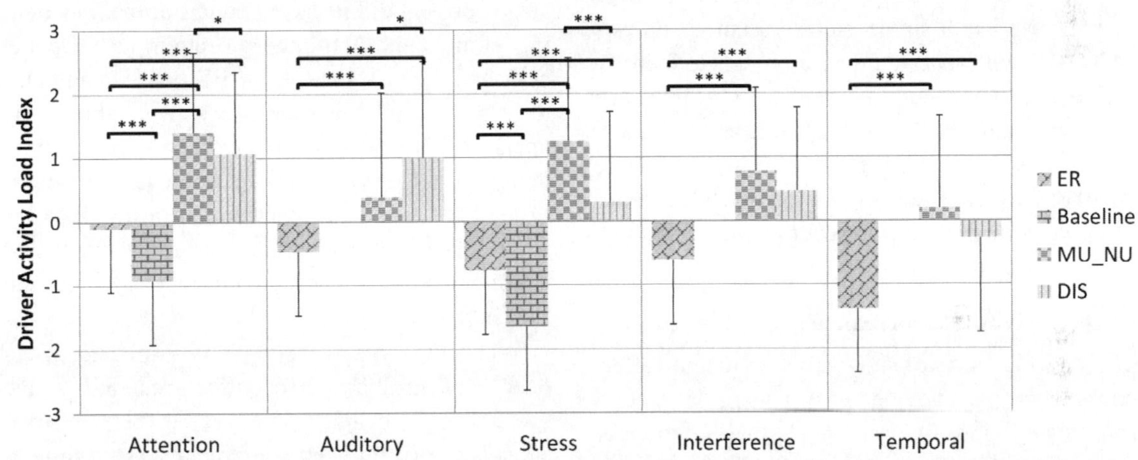

Figure 6: Cognitive load: driver activity load index (DALI), significance levels: p<.05(*), p<.01(**), p<.001(***)

6.1 SDS which Reacts as Expected (ER)

First of all, results of an optimal SDS (ER), which reacts as expected and does not make any mistakes, are presented. The objective driver performance (see Figure 5) is slightly worse than the baseline drives in terms of steering and pressing the right pedals, but not significantly. However, reaction times are worse than without interacting with an SDS. This corresponds to the results from Patten et al. (2004), who observed an increase in reaction times when drivers talk to someone on the phone. The cognitive load (see Figure 6) caused by an optimal SDS is negative in all dimensions, which means an optimal SDS does not put high demands on the driver. In general, ER was rated very good in terms of usability (see Figure 4) and would most likely be accepted by young drivers.

6.2 Mis- and Non-Understanding (MU, NU)

The results of MU and NU do not show significant differences in any dimension. Therefore, the mean value of MU and NU is used. As shown in Figure 6, the driver's cognitive load is high in all dimensions for MU_NU. In terms of stress and attention, it is significantly higher than during baseline drives (other DALI dimensions are not assessed for baseline drives). Due to the increased cognitive load, the driver's performance (see Figure 5) concerning steering, reaction times, and pedal presses decreases significantly compared to baseline drives. Especially the number of times drivers do not react to external events at all (missed pedal), or they do not react appropriately (wrong pedal), increases strongly. The usability ratings provide evidence how users rate an SDS which is not usable.

As expected, ER performs better than MU_NU. An unexpected system reaction causes higher cognitive load in all dimensions. However, in contrast to what one might expect, the driver's steering performance and reaction times are not better than for ER ($p_{steering}$=.083 and $p_{reaction}$=.215).

6.3 Dialog Initiative Switch as an Out-Of-Domain Handling Strategy (DIS)

Previous Sections have shown that it is important to minimize misunderstandings and non-understandings in a safe and usable in-car infotainment system. Comparing DIS with an optimal and a worst-case SDS shows whether it is a reasonable approach to handle out-of-domain utterances or not. We use a single factor variance analysis (ANOVA) with repeated measurements to identify the best (Helmert contrast) and worst (difference contrast) condition out of ER, DIS, and MU_NU. If DIS lays between ER and MU_NU, we analyze whether DIS tends towards ER or MU_NU. Therefore, we compare the differences of ER-DIS with MU_NU-DIS and use a one sample t-test.

6.3.1 Driving Performance

The ANOVA did not show any significant differences in drivers' steering performances or reaction times (see Figure 5). Using a Helmert contrast to determine the best response, the ANOVA identified ER as the condition with significantly fewest missed and wrong reactions. There is no difference between DIS and MU_NU, thus DIS tends in terms of objective driver distraction more towards MU_NU than to ER.

6.3.2 Cognitive Load

Analyzing the cognitive load of ER, DIS, and MU_NU (see Figure 6), the ANOVA identifies ER as the significant best condition ($p<.002$). The significant worst one in terms of attention, stress, and interference is MU_NU, which means DIS lays in between for these dimensions. However, no evidence is found for stress or interference whether DIS tends towards ER or MU_NU. In global attention, DIS tends slightly ($p<.031$) towards MU_NU. Furthermore, the long prompts in DIS put high auditive demands on the driver.

6.3.3 Usability

As task success of MU_NU dialogs is poor (see Section 6.4), it is obvious that ER is the best ($p<.001$) and MU_NU is the worst condition ($p<.001$) in terms of usability (see Figure 4). All DIS ratings, except of speed, are between ER and MU_NU ($p<.001$). Speed is basically identical to the MU_NU rating, which is due to the long prompts. There is a slight tendency of DIS towards ER in system response accuracy ($p<.051$) and in habitability ($p<.077$), however, this is not significant. In annoyance DIS tends towards MU_NU ($p<.002$), which might be due to the three step help dialog. For cognitive demand and likability, DIS lays exactly between ER and MU_NU.

6.4 Dialog Performance

The task success is pretty low in MU (29.03%) and NU (19.35%) as the task was aborted by the wizard, if drivers did not use explicit domain switching commands after multiple attempts. On the contrary, the task success for ER (96.8%) and DIS (93.6%) is good, however, 3 tasks were aborted by users. Figure 7 shows the average user response delay, system turn duration, and user turn duration. The rectangular bars drawn in line patterns show successful interactions during a subtask and the ones drawn in checked pattern dialogs between two subtasks.

When the system responds as expected, users need between 2 and 3 seconds to respond. If the system does not react as expected (between two subtasks), drivers need significantly more time to respond, as they need to think what to say. In DIS, they only need to repeat the proposed term, thus they respond faster. In MU_NU, the system turns in dialogs between subtasks are shorter, whereby the user turns are longer (user turn duration does not include the user's response time). So either drivers speak slower or provide longer sentences, if the SDS does not react as expected. Due to the four proposed utterances in DIS, system turn durations are longer in dialogs between subtasks.

6.5 Summary and Discussion

In general, if an SDS reacts as expected by the user, it will be a good approach to control the in-car infotainment system. Except for the driver's reaction time, an optimal SDS does not influence the driving performance. However, a delayed reaction of 200ms might be better than glancing at a

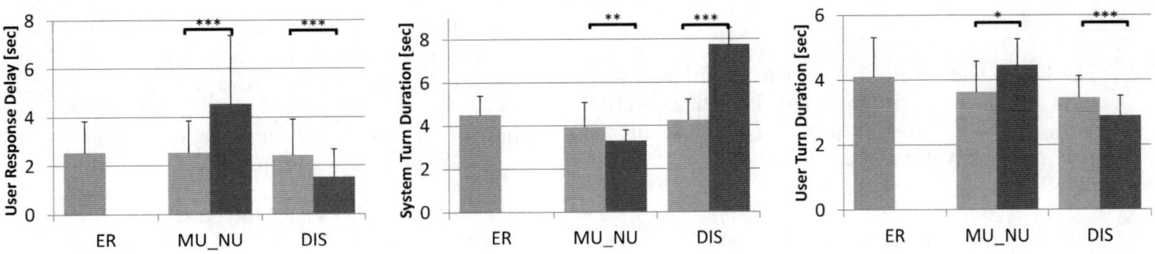

Figure 7: Dialog performance (light color: interaction during subtasks, dark color: dialog between two subtasks), significance levels: p<.05(*), p<.01(**), p<.001(***)

display. For example, the Driver Focus-Telematics Working Group (2006) states in their guidelines to visual distraction: "single glance durations generally should not exceed 2 seconds".

As long as conversational SDSs are not able to operate in much wider domains, sooner or later the user will provide an utterance the system is not able to respond to. Comparing the MU and NU conditions shows that an out-of-domain recognition with a simple rephrase error recovery strategy does not work. This is understandable, as both conditions increase the cognitive load, which influences the driving performance negatively. Especially the reaction to external events, such as traffic lights, suffers. In our experiment, the traffic light was in the middle of the screen. According to Victor et al. (2005), drivers concentrate their gaze on the road center at the expense of peripheral glances during auditory or complex driving tasks. Thus we would expect even worse results if the traffic light occurs in the driver's peripheral vision. This means an intelligent handling strategy for out-of-domain utterances needs to be established, which informs drivers of the system's capabilities.

We evaluated a dialog initiative switch as a response to out-of-domain utterances. Mostly, this strategy performed somewhere between the optimal and worst-case SDS. Due to long narrative system prompts, the auditive demand is rated high by drivers and thus the driving performance tends towards the worst-case SDS. The dialog initiative switch was rated as usable, but different variants need to be developed and evaluated in the future.

After the experiment, the participants rated the four conditions with two questions from ITU-T P.851 (ITU, 2003) on a 7-point Likert scale from *strong disagree* (-3) to *strong agree* (+3):

Q1: "Would you have expected more help from the system?"

Q2: "You feel adequately informed about the system's possibilities?"

	ER (SD)	MU (SD)	NU (SD)	DIS (SD)
Q1	-1.73(1.78)	1.47(1.81)	2.1(1.32)	-1.1(1.58)
Q2	0.43(2.13)	-1.53(1.36)	-1.7(1.49)	0.73(1.66)

Table 3: Adequate system help

Table 3 shows the results, whereby DIS tends towards ER in Q1 (p<.004) and is even better than ER in Q2. This means the drivers felt informed adequately of the SDS, however, further research is necessary to evaluate how to present this information. Shorter helping prompts might be better. Furthermore, multimodal aspects needs to be considered. For example, head-up displays are able to present information, such as possible utterances, right in the driver's view. This might reduce the auditive demand.

7 Conclusions

In this paper, we showed results from a WoZ study on user-initiated multi-domain SDSs in the car. If an in-car SDS cannot fulfill a user's request due to, for example, missing functionality, the driver's cognitive load and distraction will increase. Therefore, out-of-domain utterances need to be identified and handled adequately by in-car SDSs. Switching the dialog initiative is a good approach to guide users to the task goal and reduce their cognitive load. However, if drivers need to process any information, some mental activity will be required. Therefore, the design and implementation of a dialog initiative switch strategy need further efforts to minimize the driver's distraction and to make it enjoyable for the user. Other modalities than speech-only SDSs, such as head-up displays, need to be evaluated in future studies.

Acknowledgments

The work presented here was funded by GetHomeSafe (EU 7th Framework STREP 288667).

References

Adriana Barón and Paul Green. 2006. Safety and usability of speech interfaces for in-vehicle tasks while driving: A brief literature review. Technical report, University of Michigan Transportation Research Institute.

Dan Bohus and Alexander I. Rudnicky. 2005. Sorry, i didnt catch that! an investigation of non-understanding errors and recovery strategies. In *Proceedings of SIGdial*, Lisbon, Portugal.

Kai-Uwe Carstensen, Christian Ebert, Cornelia Ebert, Susanne Jekat, Ralf Klabunde, and Hagen Langer. 2010. *Computerlinguistik und Sprachtechnologie*. Spektrum, Akad. Verl.

Driver Focus-Telematics Working Group. 2006. Statement of principles, criteria and verification procedures on driver interactions with advanced in-vehicle information and communication systems.

Victor Ei-Wen Lo and Paul A. Green. 2013. Development and evaluation of automotive speech interfaces: Useful information from the human factors and the related literature. *Int. Journal of Vehicular Technology*, 2013:13.

Norman M. Fraser and G.Nigel Gilbert. 1991. Simulating speech systems. *Computer Speech & Language*, 5(1):81 – 99.

Kate S Hone and Robert Graham. 2000. Towards a tool for the subjective assessment of speech system interfaces (sassi). *Natural Language Engineering*, 6(3&4):287–303.

International Telecommunication Union (ITU). 2003. Subjective quality evaluation of telephone services based on spoken dialogue systems (itu-t rec. p.851).

Scott R. Klemmer, Anoop K. Sinha, Jack Chen, James A. Landay, Nadeem Aboobaker, and Annie Wang. 2000. Suede: a wizard of oz prototyping tool for speech user interfaces. In *Proc. of the 13th annual ACM symposium on User interface software and technology*, New York. ACM.

Andrew L. Kun, Tim Paek, and Zeljko Medenica. 2007. The effect of speech interface accuracy on driving performance. In *INTERSPEECH*, pages 1326–1329, Antwerp, Belgium.

Andrew L. Kun, Alexander Shyrokov, and PeterA. Heeman. 2013. Interactions between humanhuman multi-threaded dialogues and driving. *Personal and Ubiquitous Computing*, 17(5):825–834.

Jannette Maciej and Mark Vollrath. 2009. Comparison of manual vs. speech-based interaction with in-vehicle information systems. *Accident Analysis and Prevention*, 41(5):924 – 930.

Angela Mahr, Michael Feld, Mohammad Mehdi Moniri, and Rafael Math. 2012. The contre (continuous tracking and reaction) task: A flexible approach for assessing driver cognitive workload with high sensitivity. In *Adjunct Proceedings of the 4th AutomotiveUI*, Portsmouth. ACM.

Rafael Math, Angela Mahr, Mohammad M Moniri, and Christian Müller. 2012. Opends: A new open-source driving simulator for research. *Adjunct Proceedings of the 4th AutomotiveUI*.

Stefan Mattes. 2003. The lane-change-task as a tool for driver distraction. In *Proceedings of IGfA*, Dearborn.

National Highway Traffic Safety Administration (NHTSA). 2013. Distracted driving 2011. Technical report.

Christopher J.D Patten, Albert Kircher, Joakim stlund, and Lena Nilsson. 2004. Using mobile telephones: cognitive workload and attention resource allocation. *Accident Analysis & Prevention*, 36(3):341 – 350.

Annie Pauzié, J Manzan, and Nicolas Dapzol. 2007. Driver's behavior and workload assessment for new in-vehicle technologies design. In *Proceedings of the 4th International Driving Symposium on Human Factors in Driver Assessment, Training, and Vehicle Design.*, Stevenson, Washington.

Sven Reichel, Ute Ehrlich, André Berton, and Michael Weber. 2014. In-car multi-domain spoken dialogs: A wizard of oz study. In *EACL Workshop Dialog in Motion*, Gothenburg, Sweden.

Gabriel Skantze. 2007. *Error Handling in Spoken Dialogue Systems*. Ph.D. thesis, KTH Computer Science and Communication.

Trent W. Victor, Joanne L. Harbluk, and Johan A. Engstrm. 2005. Sensitivity of eye-movement measures to in-vehicle task difficulty. *Transportation Research Part F: Traffic Psychology and Behaviour*, 8(2):167 – 190. The relationship between distraction and driving performance: towards a test regime for in-vehicle information systems In-vehicle information systems.

Christopher D Wickens. 2008. Multiple resources and mental workload. In *Human factors*, volume 50, pages 449–55. USA.

Kristie Young and Michael Regan. 2007. Driver distraction: A review of the literature. *Distracted Driving*.

Appendix

ER:
U: Navigation
S: Navigation, what do you want?
U: City Berlin
S: To what address or place of interest do you want?
U: Brandenburger Tor
S: Brandenburger Tor in Berlin was set as your destination
U: Italian restaurant near Brandenburger Tor?
S: There is one Italian restaurant in Berlin: Pizzeria San Marco
U: Save the address
S: Alright, the address was added

DIS:
U: I would like to go to the Brandenburger Tor in Berlin
S: Brandenburger Tor in Berlin was set as your destination.
U: Italian restaurant nearby?
S: Action unknown, you can say: restaurant, navigation, hotel, or radio
U: Restaurant
S: You can: search a restaurant, order a table, rate a restaurant, request opening times
U: Search a restaurant
S: Say for example: Search a restaurant at the destination, I search a Chinese restaurant, "Die Krone" in Stuttgart, or Mexican restaurant
U: I search an Italian restaurant
S: Where do you search an Italian restaurant
U: Near Brandenburger Tor in Berlin
S: There is one Italian restaurant in Berlin: Pizzeria San Marco
U: Save the address
S: Action unknown, you can say: address book, restaurant, navigation, or hotel
U: address book
S: You can: add a contact, remove a contact, access contact details, or delete address book
U: Add a contact
S: Say for example: I'd like to add a contact, add an address, add Paul to my address book, save the number 0165332
U: Add San Marco to my address book
S: Alright, the address was added

MU:
U: Navigation to Berlin, Brandenburger Tor
S: Brandenburger Tor in Berlin was set as your destination.
U: Italian restaurant at the destination
S: Italian restaurant could not be set as a destination
U: Navigate to a restaurant in Berlin
S: The address restaurant in Berlin was not found
U: I would like to search a restaurant
S: Sorry?
U: Start restaurant application
S: Restaurant search, what do you want?
U: An Italian restaurant in Berlin
S: There is one Italian restaurant in Berlin: Pizzeria San Marco
U: Add the address to my address book
S: The address of Pizzeria San Marco is Mainstreet 1, Berlin
U: Save that to my address book
S: Sorry?
U: Save Pizzeria San Marco
S: Pizzeria San Marco is famous for its delicious Italian dishes
U: Address book
S: Address book, what do you want?
U: Save the address of San Marco
S: Alright, the address was added

NU:
U: Drive me to the Brandenburger Tor in Berlin
S: Brandenburger Tor in Berlin was set as your destination.
U: Is there an Italian restaurant near Brandenburger Tor?
S: Action unknown, please say something else
U: Give me an Italian restaurant along the route
S: Action unknown, please say something else
U: Italian restaurant
S: Action unknown, please say something else
U: Restaurant in Berlin
S: Action unknown, please say something else
U: I'd like to search a restaurant
S: Action unknown, please say something else
<aborted by the wizard>

Appendix 1: Detailed dialog examples of the four response conditions. Translated from German and based on real experiment data. Red rectangles identify the domain switching dialogs between two subtasks.

Situated Language Understanding at 25 Miles per Hour

Teruhisa Misu, Antoine Raux*, Rakesh Gupta
Honda Research Institute USA
425 National Avenue
Mountain View, CA 94040
tmisu@hra.com

Ian Lane
Carnegie Mellon University
NASA Ames Research Park
Moffett Field, CA 93085

Abstract

In this paper, we address issues in situated language understanding in a rapidly changing environment – a moving car. Specifically, we propose methods for understanding user queries about specific target buildings in their surroundings. Unlike previous studies on physically situated interactions such as interaction with mobile robots, the task is very sensitive to timing because the spatial relation between the car and the target is changing while the user is speaking. We collected situated utterances from drivers using our research system, Townsurfer, which is embedded in a real vehicle. Based on this data, we analyze the timing of user queries, spatial relationships between the car and targets, head pose of the user, and linguistic cues. Optimized on the data, our algorithms improved the target identification rate by 24.1% absolute.

1 Introduction

Recent advances in sensing technologies have enabled researchers to explore applications that require a clear awareness of the systems' dynamic context and physical surroundings. Such applications include multi-participant conversation systems (Bohus and Horvitz, 2009) and human-robot interaction (Tellex et al., 2011; Sugiura et al., 2011). The general problem of understanding and interacting with human users in such environments is referred to as *situated interaction*.

We address yet another environment, where situated interactions takes place – a moving car. In the previous work, we collected over 60 hours of in-car human-human interactions, where drivers interact with an expert co-pilot sitting next to them in the vehicle (Cohen et al., 2014). One of the insights from the analysis on this corpus is that drivers frequently use referring expressions about their surroundings. (e.g. *What is that big building on the right?*) Based on this insight, we have developed Townsurfer (Lane et al., 2012; Misu et al., 2013), a situated in-car intelligent assistant. Using geo-location information, the system can answer user queries/questions that contain object references about points-of-interest (POIs) in their surroundings. We use driver (user) face orientation to understand their queries and provide the requested information about the POI they are looking at. We have previously demonstrated and evaluated the system in a simulated environment (Lane et al., 2012). In this paper, we evaluate its utility in real driving situations.

Compared to conventional situated dialog tasks, query understanding in our task is expected to be more time sensitive, due to the rapidly changing environment while driving. Typically, a car will move 10 meters in one second while driving at 25 mi/h. So timing can be a crucial factor. In addition, it is not well understood what kind of linguistic cues are naturally provided by drivers, and their contributions to situated language understanding in such an environment. To the best of our knowledge, this is the first study that tackles the issue of situated language understanding in rapidly moving vehicles.

In this paper, we first present an overview of the Townsurfer in-car spoken dialog system (Section 2). Based on our data collection using the system, we analyze user behavior while using the system focusing on language understanding (Section 3). Specifically, we answer the following research questions about the task and the system through data collection and analysis:

1. Is timing an important factor of situated language understanding?
2. Does head pose play an important role in language understanding? Or is spatial distance information enough?

* Currently with Lenovo.

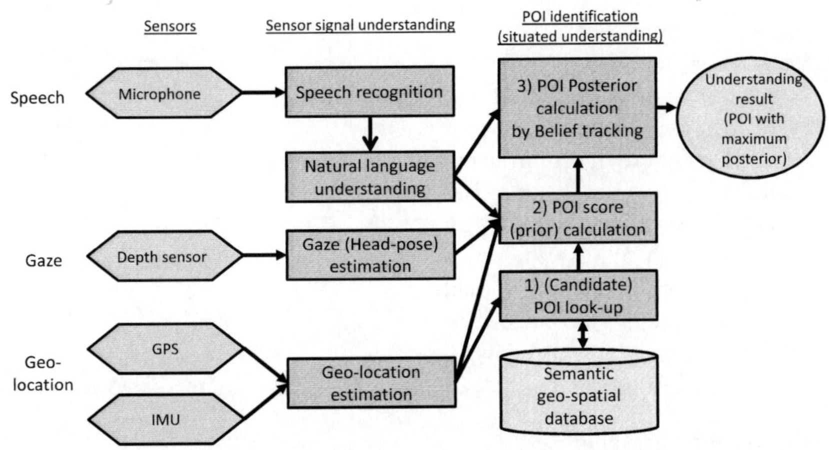

Figure 1: System overview of Townsurfer

Table 1: Example dialog with Townsurfer

U1:	What is *that place*. (POI in gaze)
S1:	This is Specialty Cafe, a mid-scale coffee shop that serves sandwiches.
U2:	What is *its* (POI in dialog history) rating.
S2:	The rating of Specialty Cafe is above average.
U3:	How about *that one* on the left. (POI located on the left)
S3:	This is Roger's Deli, a low-priced restaurant that serves American food.

3. What is the role of linguistic cues in this task? What kinds of linguistic cues do drivers naturally provide?

Based on the hypothesis obtained from the analysis for these questions, we propose methods to improve situated language understanding (Section 4), and analyze their contributions based on the collected data (Sections 5 and 6). We then clarify our research contributions through discussion (Section 7) and comparison with related studies (Section 8).

2 Architecture and Hardware of Townsurfer

The system uses three main input modalities, speech, geo-location, and head pose. Speech is the main input modality of the system. It is used to trigger interactions with the system. User speech is recognized, then requested concepts/values are extracted. Geo-location and head pose information are used to understand the target POI of the user query. An overview of the system with a process flow is illustrated in Figure 1 and an example dialog with the system is shown in Table 1. A video of an example dialog is also attached.

In this paper, we address issues in identifying user intended POI, which is a form of reference resolution using multi-modal information sources[1]. The POI identification process consists of the following three steps (cf. Figure 1). This is similar to but different from our previous work on landmark-based destination setting (Ma et al., 2012).

1) The system lists candidate POIs based on geo-location at the timing of a driver query. Relative positions of POIs to the car are also calculated based on geo-location and the heading of the car.

2). Based on spatial linguistic cues in the user utterance (e.g. *to my right, on the left*), a 2D scoring function is selected to identify areas where the target POI is likely to be. This function takes into account the position of the POI relative to the car, as well as driver head pose. Scores for all candidate POIs are calculated.

3) Posterior probabilities of each POI are calculated using the score of step 2 as prior, and non-spatial linguistic information (e.g. POI categories, building properties) as observations. This posterior calculation is computed using our Bayesian belief tracker called DPOT (Raux and Ma, 2011).

The details are explained in Section 4.

System hardware consists of a 3D depth sensor (Primesense Carmine 1.09), a USB GPS (BU-353S4), an IMU sensor (3DM-GX3-25) and a close talk microphone (plantronics Voyage Leg-

[1]We do not deal with issues in language understanding related to dialog history and query type. (e.g. General information request such as U1 vs request about specific property of POI such as U2 in Table 1)

end UC). These consumer grade sensors are installed in our Honda Pilot experiment car. We use Point Cloud Library (PCL) for the face direction estimation. Geo-location is estimated based on Extended Kalman filter-based algorithm using GPS and gyro information as input at 1.5 Hz. The system is implemented based on the Robot Operating System ROS (Quigley et al., 2009). Each component is implemented as a node of ROS, and communications between the nodes are performed using the standard message passing mechanisms in ROS.

3 Data Collection and Analysis

3.1 Collection Setting

We collected data using a test route. The route passes through **downtown** Mountain View[2] and **residential area** around Honda Research Institute. We manually constructed our database containing 250 POIs (businesses such as restaurants, companies) in this area. Each database entry (POI) has name, geo-location, category and property information explained in Section 3.4. POI geo-location is represented as a latitude-longitude pair (e.g. 37.4010,-122.0539). Size and shape of buildings are not taken into account. It takes about 30 minutes to drive the route. The major difference between residential area and downtown is the POI density. While each POI in downtown has on average 7.2 other POIs within 50 meters, in residential area POIs have only 1.9 neighbors. Speed limits also differ between the two (35 mi/h vs 25 mi/h).

We collected data from 14 subjects. They were asked to drive the test route and make queries about surrounding businesses. We showed a demo video[3] of the system to the users before starting the data collection. We also told them that the objective is a data collection for a situated spoken dialog system, rather than the evaluation of the whole system. We asked subjects to include the full description of the target POI within a single utterance to avoid queries whose understanding requires dialog history information[4]. Although the system answered based on the baseline strategy explained in Section 4.1, we asked subjects to ignore the system responses.

As a result, we collected 399 queries with a valid target POI. Queries about businesses that do not exist on our database (typically a vacant store) were excluded. The data contains 171 queries in downtown and 228 in residential area. The queries were transcribed and the user-intended POIs were manually annotated by confirming the intended target POI with the subjects after the data collection based on a video taken during the drive.

[2]We assumed that a POI is in downtown when it is located within the rectangle by geo-location coordinates (37.3902, -122.0827) and (37.3954, -122.0760).

[3]not the attached one.

[4]Understanding including dialog history information is our future work.

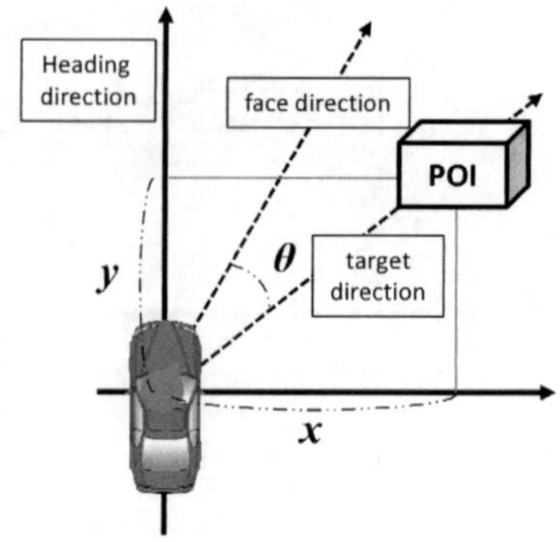

Figure 2: Parameters used to calculate POI score (prior)

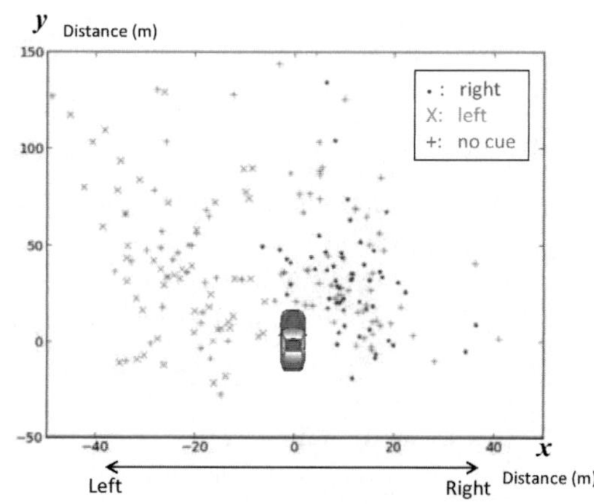

Figure 3: Target POI positions

3.2 Analysis of Spatial Relation of POI and Head Pose

We first analyze the spatial relation between position cues (right/left) and the position of the user-intended target POIs Out of the collected 399 queries, 237 (59.4%) of them contain either right or left position cue (e.g. *What is that on the left?*). The relation between the position cues (cf. Figure 2) and POI positions at start-of-speech timing [5] is plotted in Figure 3. The X-axis is a lateral distance (a distance in the direction orthogonal to the heading; a positive value means the right direction) and the Y-axis is an axial distance (a distance in the heading direction; a negative value means the POI is in back of the car.). The most obvious finding from the scatter plot is that right and left are pow-

[5]Specifically, the latest GPS and face direction information at that timing is used.

Table 2: Comparison of average and standard deviation of distance (in meter) of POI form the car

		ASR result timing		Start-of-speech timing	
Position cue	Site	Ave dist.	Std dist.	Ave dist.	Std dist.
Right/left	Downtown	17.5	31.0	31.9	28.3
	Residential	22.0	36.3	45.2	36.5
No right/left cue	Downtown	17.4	27.8	31.1	26.5
	Residential	38.3	45.9	52.3	43.4

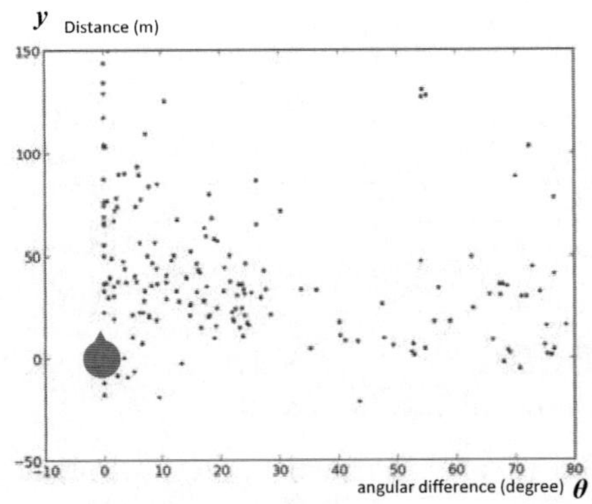

Figure 4: Relation between POI positions and head pose

erful cues for the system to identify target POIs. We can also see that the POI position distribution has a large standard deviation. This is partly because the route has multiple sites from downtown and residential area. Interestingly, while the average distance to the target POI in downtown is 37.0 meters, that of residential area is 57.4 meters.

We also analyze the relation between face direction and POI positions. Figure 4 plots the relation between the axial distance and the angular difference θ (between the user face direction and the target POI direction) (cf. Figure 2). The scatter plot suggests that the angular differences for distant target POIs is often small. For close target POIs the angular differences are larger and have a large variance[6].

3.3 Analysis of Timing

Referring expressions such as "the building on the right" must be resolved with respect to the context in which the user intended. However, in a moving car, such a context (i.e. the position of the car and the situation in the surroundings) can be very different between the time when the user starts speaking the sentence and the time they finish speaking it. Therefore, situated understanding must be very time sensitive.

To confirm and investigate this issue, we analyze the difference in the POI positions between the time the ASR result is output vs the time the user actually started speaking. The hypothesis is that the latter yields a more accurate context in which to interpret the user sentence. In contrast, our baseline system uses the more straightforward approach of resolving expressions using the context at the time of resolution, i.e. whenever the ASR/NLU has finished processing an utterance (hereafter "ASR results timing").

[6]We will discuss the reason for this in Section 6.2.

Table 3: User-provided linguistic cues

Category of linguistic cue	Percentage used (%)
Relative position to the car (right/left)	59.4
Business category (e.g. restaurant, cafe)	31.8
Color of the POI (e.g. green, yellow)	12.8
Cuisine (e.g. Chinese, Japanese, Mexican)	8.3
Equipments (e.g. awning, outside seating)	7.2
Relative position to the road (e.g. corner)	6.5

Specifically, we compare the average axial distance to the target POIs and its standard deviation between these two timings. Table 2 lists these figures broken down by position cue types and sites. The average axial distance from the car to the target POIs is often small at the ASR result timing, but the standard deviation is generally small at the start-of-speech timing. This indicates that the target POI positions at the start-of-speech timing is more consistent across users and sentence lengths than that at the ASR result timing. This result indicates the presence of a better POI likelihood function using the context (i.e. car position and orientation) at the start-of-speech timing than using the ASR result timing.

3.4 Analysis of Linguistic Cues

We then analyze the linguistic cues provided by the users. Here, we focus on objective and stable cues. We exclude subjective cues (e.g. *big, beautiful, colorful*) and cues that might change in a short period of time (e.g. *with a woman dressed in green in front*). We have categorized the linguistic cues used to describe the target POIs. Table 3 lists the cue types and the percentage of user utterances containing each cue type.

The cues that the users most often provided concern POI position related to the car (right and left). Nearly 60% of queries included this type of cue and every subject provided it at least once. The second most frequent cue is category of business, especially in downtown. Users also provided colors of POIs. Other cues include cuisine, equipments, relative position to the road (e.g. *on the corner*).

Another interesting finding from the analysis is that the users provided more linguistic cues with increasing candidate POIs in their field of view. Actually, the users provided 1.51 categories in average per query in downtown, while they provided 1.03 categories in residential area. (cf. POI density in Section 3.2: 7.2 vs 1.9) This indicates that users provide cues considering environment complexity.

4 Methods for Situated Language Understanding

4.1 Baseline Strategy

We use our previous version (Misu et al., 2013) as the baseline system for situated language understanding. The baseline strategy consists of the following three paragraphs, which correspond to the process 1)-3) in Section 2 and Figure 1.

The system makes a POI look-up based on the geo-location information at the time ASR result is obtained. The search range of candidate POIs is within the range (relative geo-location of POIs against the car location) of -50 to 200 meters in the travelling direction and 100 meters to the left and 100 meters to the right in the lateral direction. The ASR result timing is also used to measure the distances to the candidate POIs.

POI priors are calculated based on the distance from the car (= axial distance) based on "the closer to the car the likely" principle. We use a likelihood function inversely proportional to the distance. We use position cues simply to remove POIs from a list of candidates. For example "right" position cue is used to remove candidate POIs that are located on < 0 position in the lateral distance. When no right/left cue is provided, POIs outside of 45 degrees from the face direction are removed from the list of candidates.

No linguistic cues except right/left are used to calculate POI posterior probabilities. So, the system selects the POI with the highest prior (POI score) as the language understanding result.

4.2 Strategies Toward Better Situated Language Understanding

To achieve better situated language understanding (POI identification) based on the findings of the analysis in Section 3, we modify steps 1)-3) as follows:

1. Using start-of-speech timing for the POI prior calculation

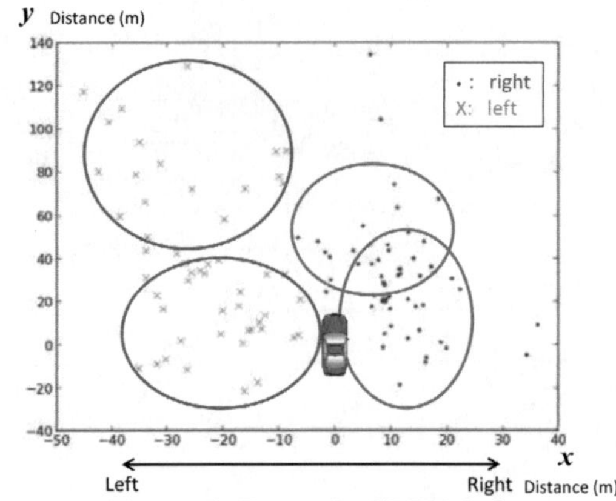

Figure 5: Example GMM fitting

2. Gaussian mixture model (GMM)-based POI probability (prior) calculation
3. Linguistic cues for the posterior calculation.

We use the start-of-speech timing instead of the time ASR result is output. Because the standard deviations of the POI distances are small (cf. Section 3.2), we expect that a better POI probability score estimation with the POI positions at this timing in the subsequent processes than the positions at the ASR result timing. The POI look-up range is the same as the baseline.

We apply Gaussian mixture model (GMM) with diagonal covariance matrices over the input parameter space. The POI probability (prior) is calculated based on these Gaussians. We use two input parameters of the lateral and axial distances for queries with right/left cue, and three parameters of the lateral and axial distances and the difference in degree between the target and head pose directions for queries without right/left cue. (The effect of the parameters is discussed later in Section 6.2.) We empirically set the number of Gaussian components to 2. An example GMM fitting to the POI positions for queries with right and left cues is illustrated in Figures 5. The center of ellipse is the mean of the Gaussian.

We use the five linguistic cue categories of Section 3.4 for the posterior calculation by the belief tracker. In the following experiments, we use either 1 or 0 as a likelihood of natural language understanding (NLU) observation. The likelihood for the category value is 1 if a user query (NLU result) contains the target value, otherwise 0. This corresponds to a strategy of simply removing candidate POIs that do not have the category values specified by the user. Here, we assume a clean POI database with all their properties annotated manually.

Table 4: Comparison of POI identification rate

Method	Success rate (%)
right/left linguistic cues, the-closer-the-likely likelihood, ASR result timing) (**Baseline**)	43.1
1) Start-of-speech timing	42.9
2) GMM-based likelihood	47.9
3) Linguistic cues	54.6
1) + 2)	50.6
1) + 3)	54.4
2) + 3)	62.2
1) + 2) + 3)	67.2

5 Experiments

We use manual transcriptions and natural language understanding results of the user queries to focus our evaluations on the issues listed in Section 1. We evaluate the situated language understanding (POI identification) performance based on cross validation. We use the data from 13 users to train GMM parameters and to define a set of possible linguistic values, and the data from the remaining user for evaluation. We train the model parameters of the GMM using the EM algorithm. Knowledge about the sites (downtown or residential area) is not used in the training[7].

We do not set a threshold for the presentation. We judge the system successfully understands a user query when the posterior of the target (user-intended) POI is the highest. The chance rate, given by the average of the inverse number of candidate POIs in the POI look-up is 10.0%.

6 Analysis of the Results

We first analyze the effect of our three methods described in Section 4.2. The results are listed in Table 4.

Simply using the POI positions at the start-of-speech timing instead of those of the ASR result timing did not lead to an improvement. This result is reasonable because the distances to target POIs are often smaller at the ASR result timing as we showed in Table 2. However, we achieved a better improvement (7.5% over the baseline) by combining it with the GMM-based likelihood calculation. The results supports our Section 3.3 hypothesis that the POI position is less dependent on users/scenes at the start-of-speech timing. The linguistic cues were the most powerful information for this task. The improvement over the baseline was 11.5%. By using these three methods together, we obtained more than additive improvement of 24.1% in the POI identification rate over the baseline[8]. The success rates per site were 60.8% in downtown and 71.9% in residential area.

[7]The performance was better when the knowledge was not used.

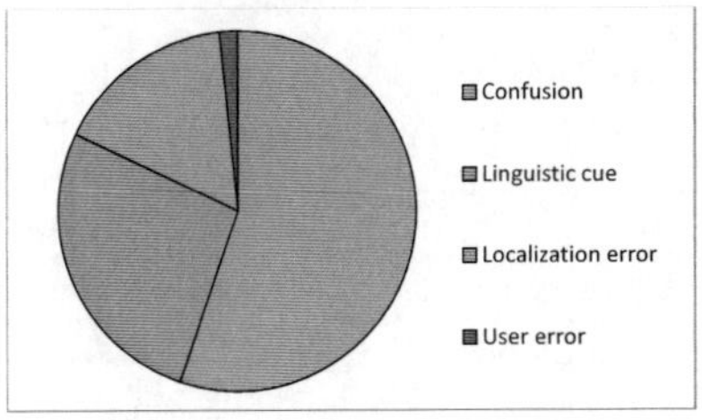

Figure 6: Breakdown of error causes

6.1 Error Analysis

To analyze the causes of the remaining errors, we have categorized the errors into the following four categories:

1. **Ambiguous references:** There were multiple POIs that matched the user query. (e.g. another *yellow building* sat next to the target)
2. **Linguistic cue:** The driver used undefined linguistic cues such subjective expressions or dynamic references objects (e.g. optometrist, across the street, colorful)
3. **Localization error:** Errors in estimating geo-location or heading of the car.
4. **User error:** There were errors in the user descriptions (e.g. user misunderstood the neighbor POI's outside seating as the target's)

The distribution of error causes is illustrated in Figure 6. More than half of the errors are due to reference ambiguity. These errors are expected to be resolved through clarification dialogs. (e.g. asking user *"Did you mean the one in front or back?"*) Linguistic errors might be partly resolved by using a better database with detailed category information. For dynamic references and subjective cues, use of image processing techniques will help. Localization errors can be solved by using high-quality GPS and IMU sensors. User errors were rare and only made in downtown.

6.2 Breakdown of Effect of the Spatial Distance and Head Pose

We then evaluate the features used for the POI prior calculation to investigate the effect of the input parameters of the lateral and axial distances

[8]For reference, the performances of "1) + 2) + 3)" were 62.9%, 67.2%, 66.1%, 67.2%, and 66.2% when the number of Gaussian components were 1, 2, 3, 4, and 5.

Table 5: Relation between the parameters used for the POI identification and success rates (%)

	query type	
parameters used	right/left	no cue
lateral (x) distance	58.6	51.2
axial (y) distance	59.5	53.7
face direction	43.3	44.4
lateral + axial ($x + y$)	73.8	54.3
lateral (x) + face direction	57.8	48.1
axial (y) + face direction	59.1	54.9
lateral + axial + face	68.4	57.4

and the difference in degree between the target and user face direction angles. Table 5 lists the relationship between the parameters used for the GMM-based likelihood calculation and the POI identification performances[9].

The results indicate that the axial distance is the most important parameter. We got a slight improvement by using the face direction information for the queries without right/left cue, but the improvement was not significant. On the other hand, use of face direction information for the right/left queries clearly degraded the POI identification performance. We think this is because the users finished looking at the POI and returned the face to the front when they started speaking, thus they explicitly provided right/left information to the system. However, we believe that using a long-term trajectory of the user face direction will contribute to an improve in the POI identification performance.

6.3 Breakdown of the Effect of Linguistic Cues

We then evaluate the effect of the linguistic cues per category. Table 6 lists the relationship between the categories used for the posterior calculation and the success rates. There is a strong correlation between the frequency of the cues used (cf. Table 3) and their contributions to the improvement in success rate. For example, business category information contributed the most, boosting the performance by 8.5%.

Another point we note is that the contribution of business category and cuisine categories is large. Because other categories (e.g. color) are not readily available in a public POI database (e.g. Google Places API, Yelp API), we can obtain reasonable performance without using a special database or image processing.

Table 6: Effect of linguistic cues

linguistic cue category used	Success rate (%)
No linguistic cues (*)	50.6
(*) + Business category (e.g. cafe)	59.1
(*) + Color of the POI (e.g. green)	57.6
(*) + Cuisine (e.g. Chinese)	54.1
(*) + Equipments (e.g. awning)	53.9
(*) + Relative position (e.g. corner)	51.4

We also found that linguistic cues were especially effective in downtown. Actually, while the improvement[10] was 20.0% in downtown that for residential area was 14.4%. This mainly would be because the users provided more linguistic cues in downtown considering the difficulty of the task.

6.4 Using Speech Recognition Results

We evaluate the degradation by using automatic speech recognition (ASR) results. We use Google ASR[11] and Julius (Kawahara et al., 2004) speech recognition system with a language model trained from 38K example sentences generated from a grammar. An acoustic model trained from the WSJ speech corpus is used. Note that they are not necessarily the best system for this domain. Google ASR uses a general language model for dictation and Julius uses a mismatched acoustic model in terms of the noise condition.

The query success rate was 56.3% for Julius and 60.3% for Google ASR. We got ASR accuracies of 77.9% and 80.4% respectively. We believe the performance will improve when N-best hypotheses with confidence scores are used in the posterior calculating using the belief tracker.

7 Discussion

The main limitation of this work comes from the small amount of data that we were able to collect. It is not clear how the results obtained here would generalize to other sites, POI density, velocities and sensor performances. Also, results might depend on experimental conditions, such as weather, hour, season. Hyper-parameters such as the optimal number of Gaussian components might have to be adapted to different situations. We therefore acknowledge that the scenes we experimented are only a limited cases of daily driving activities.

[9] Note that, we first determine the function to calculate POI scores (priors) based on the position cues, then calculate scores with the selected function.

[10] 1) + 2) vs 1) + 2) + 3).

[11] Although it is not realistic to use cloud-based speech recognition system considering the current latency, we use this as a reference system.

However, the methods we propose are general and our findings should be verifiable without loss of generality by collecting more data and using more input parameters (e.g. velocity) for the POI prior calculation.

In addition, much future work remains to realize a natural interaction with the system, such as taking into account dialog history and selecting optimal system responses. On the other hand, we believe this is one of the best platform to investigate situated interactions. The major topics that we are going to tackle are:

1. Dialog strategy: Dialog strategy and system prompt generation for situated environments are important research topics, especially to clarify the target when there is ambiguity as mentioned in Section 6.1. The topic will include an adaptation of system utterances (entrainment) to the user (Hu et al., 2014).
2. Eye tracker: Although we believe head pose is good enough to estimate user intentions because we are trained to move the head in driving schools to look around to confirm safety, we would like to confirm the difference in this task between face direction and eye-gaze.
3. POI identification using face direction trajectory: Our analysis showed that the use of face direction sometimes degrades the POI identification performance. However, we believe that using a trajectory of face direction will change the result.
4. Database: We assumed a clean and perfect database but we are going to evaluate the performance when noisy database is used. (e.g. A database based on image recognition results or user dialog log.)
5. Feedback: Koller et al. (2012) demonstrated referential resolution is enhanced by giving gaze information feedback to the user. We would like to analyze the effect of feedback with an automotive augmented reality environment using our 3D head-up display (Ng-Thow-Hing et al., 2013).

8 Related Work

The related studies include a landmark-based navigation that handles landmarks as information for a dialog. Similar system concepts have been provided for pedestrian navigation situations (Janarthanam et al., 2013; Hu et al., 2014), they do not handle a rapidly changing environment.

Several works have used timing to enhance natural interaction with systems. Rose and Horvitz (2003) and Raux and Eskenazi (2009) used timing information to detect user barge-ins. Studies on incremental speech understanding and generation (Skantze and Hjalmarsson, 2010; Dethlefs et al., 2012) have proved that real-time feedback actions have potential benefits for users. Komatani et al. (2012) used user speech timing against user's previous and system's utterances to understand the intentions of user utterances. While the above studies have handled timing focusing on (para-)linguistic aspect, our work handles timing issues in relation to the user's physical surroundings.

Recent advancements in gaze and face direction estimation have led to better user behavior understanding. There are a number of studies that have analyzed relationship between gaze and user intention, such as user focus (Yonetani et al., 2010), preference (Kayama et al., 2010), and reference expression understanding (Koller et al., 2012), between gaze and turn-taking (Jokinen et al., 2010; Kawahara, 2012). Nakano et al. (2013) used face direction for addressee identification. The previous studies most related to ours are reference resolution methods by Chai and Prasov (2010), Iida et al. (2011) and Kennington et al. (2013). They confirmed that the system's reference resolution performance is enhanced by taking the user's eye fixation into account. However, their results are not directly applied to an interaction in a rapidly changing environment while driving, where eye fixations are unusual activities.

Marge and Rudnicky (2010) analyzed the effect of space and distance for spatial language understanding for a human-robot communication. Our task differs with this because we handle a rapidly changing environment. We believe we can improve our understanding performance based on their findings.

9 Conclusion

We addressed situated language understanding in a moving car. We focused on issues in understanding user language of timing, spatial distance, and linguistic cues. Based on the analysis of the collected user utterances, we proposed methods of using start-of-speech timing for the POI prior calculation, GMM-based POI probability (prior) calculation, and linguistic cues for the posterior calculation to improve the accuracy of situated language understanding. The effectiveness of the proposed methods was confirmed by achieving a significant improvement in a POI identification task.

10 Acknowledgments

The authors would like to thank Yi Ma at Ohio State University for his contributions to the development of HRItk.

References

D. Bohus and E. Horvitz. 2009. Models for Multiparty Engagement in Open-World Dialog. In *Proc. SIGDIAL*, pages 225–234.

J. Chai and Z. Prasov. 2010. Fusing eye gaze with speech recognition hypotheses to resolve exophoric reference in situated dialogue. In *Proc. EMNLP*.

D. Cohen, A. Chandrashekaran, I. Lane, and A. Raux. 2014. The hri-cmu corpus of situated in-car interactions. In *Proc. IWSDS*, pages 201–212.

N. Dethlefs, H. Hastie, V. Rieser, and O. Lemon. 2012. Optimising incremental dialogue decisions using information density for interactive systems. In *Proc. EMNLP*, pages 82–93.

Z. Hu, G. Halberg, C. Jimenez, and M. Walker. 2014. Entrainment in pedestrian direction giving: How many kinds of entrainment? In *Proc. IWSDS*, pages 90–101.

R. Iida, M. Yasuhara, and T. Tokunaga. 2011. Multimodal reference resolution in situated dialogue by integrating linguistic and extra-linguistic clues. In *Proc. IJCNLP*, pages 84–92.

S. Janarthanam, O. Lemon, X. Liu, P. Bartie, W. Mackaness, and T. Dalmas. 2013. A multithreaded conversational interface for pedestrian navigation and question answering. In *Proc. SIGDIAL*, pages 151–153.

K. Jokinen, M. Nishida, and S. Yamamoto. 2010. On eye-gaze and turn-taking. In *Proc. EGIHMI*.

T. Kawahara, A. Lee, K. Takeda, K. Itou, and K. Shikano. 2004. Recent Progress of Open-Source LVCSR Engine Julius and Japanese Model Repository. In *Proc. ICSLP*, volume IV.

T. Kawahara. 2012. Multi-modal sensing and analysis of poster conversations toward smart posterboard. In *Proc. SIGDIAL*.

K. Kayama, A. Kobayashi, E. Mizukami, T. Misu, H. Kashioka, H. Kawai, and S. Nakamura. 2010. Spoken Dialog System on Plasma Display Panel Estimating User's Interest by Image Processing. In *Proc. 1st International Workshop on Human-Centric Interfaces for Ambient Intelligence (HCIAmi)*.

C. Kennington, S. Kousidis, and D. Schlangen. 2013. Interpreting situated dialogue utterances: an update model that uses speech, gaze, and gesture information. In *Proc. SIGDIAL*.

A. Koller, K. Garoufi, M. Staudte, and M. Crocker. 2012. Enhancing referential success by tracking hearer gaze. In *Proc. SIGDIAL*, pages 30–39.

K. Komatani, A. Hirano, and M. Nakano. 2012. Detecting system-directed utterances using dialogue-level features. In *Proc. Interspeech*.

I. Lane, Y. Ma, and A. Raux. 2012. AIDAS - Immersive Interaction within Vehicles. In *Proc. SLT*.

Y. Ma, A. Raux, D. Ramachandran, and R. Gupta. 2012. Landmark-based location belief tracking in a spoken dialog system. In *Proc. SIGDIAL*, pages 169–178.

M. Marge and A. Rudnicky. 2010. Comparing Spoken Language Route Instructions for Robots across Environment Representations. In *Proc. SIGDIAL*, pages 157–164.

T. Misu, A. Raux, I. Lane, J. Devassy, and R. Gupta. 2013. Situated multi-modal dialog system in vehicles. In *Proc. Gaze in Multimodal Interaction*, pages 25–28.

Y. Nakano, N. Baba, H. Huang, and Y. Hayashi. 2013. Implementation and evaluation of a multimodal addressee identification mechanism for multiparty conversation systems. In *Proc. ICMI*, pages 35–42.

V. Ng-Thow-Hing, K. Bark, L. Beckwith, C. Tran, R. Bhandari, and S. Sridhar. 2013. User-centered perspectives for automotive augmented reality. In *Proc. ISMAR*.

M. Quigley, K. Conley, B. Gerkey, J. Faust, T. Foote, J. Leibs, R. Wheeler, and A. Ng. 2009. ROS: an open-source Robot Operating System. In *Proc. ICRA Workshop on Open Source Software*.

A. Raux and M. Eskenazi. 2009. A Finite-state Turn-taking Model for Spoken Dialog Systems. In *Proc. HLT/NAACL*, pages 629–637.

A. Raux and Y. Ma. 2011. Efficient probabilistic tracking of user goal and dialog history for spoken dialog systems. In *Proc. Interspeech*, pages 801–804.

R. Rose and H. Kim. 2003. A hybrid barge-in procedure for more reliable turn-taking in human-machine dialog systems. In *Proc. Automatic Speech Recognition and Understanding Workshop (ASRU)*, pages 198–203.

G. Skantze and A. Hjalmarsson. 2010. Towards incremental speech generation in dialogue systems. In *Proc. SIGDIAL*, pages 1–8.

K. Sugiura, N. Iwahashi, H. Kawai, and S. Nakamura. 2011. Situated spoken dialogue with robots using active learning. *Advance Robotics*, 25(17):2207–2232.

Table 7: Example user utterances

- What is that blue restaurant on the right?
- How about this building to my right with outside seating?
- What is that Chinese restaurant on the left?
- Orange building to my right.
- What kind of the restaurant is that on the corner?
- The building on my right at the corner of the street.
- What about the building on my right with woman with a jacket in front
- Do you know how good is this restaurant to the left?
- Townsurfer, there is an interesting bakery what is that?
- Is this restaurant on the right any good?

S. Tellex, T. Kollar, S. Dickerson, M. Walter, A. Banerjee, S. Teller, and N. Roy. 2011. Understanding natural language commands for robotic navigation and mobile manipulation. In *Proc. AAAI*.

R. Yonetani, H. Kawashima, T. Hirayama, and T. Matsuyama. 2010. Gaze probing: Event-based estimation of objects being focused on. In *Proc. ICPR*, pages 101–104.

11 Appendix

Test route:

```
https://www.google.com/maps/
preview/dir/Honda+Research+
Institute,+425+National+Ave+
%23100,+Mountain+View,+CA+
94043/37.4009909,-122.0518957/
37.4052337,-122.0565795/37.
3973374,-122.0595982/37.4004787,
-122.0730021/Wells+Fargo/37.
4001639,-122.0729708/37.3959193,
-122.0539449/37.4009821,-122.
0540093/@37.3999836,-122.
0792529,14z/data=!4m21!4m20!
1m5!1m1!1s0x808fb713c225003d:
0xcf989a0bb230e5c0!2m2!
1d-122.054006!2d37.401016!
1m0!1m0!1m0!1m0!1m5!1m1!1s0x0:
0x86ca9ba8a2f15150!2m2!1d-122.
082546!2d37.388722!1m0!1m0!1m0!
3e0
```

Information Navigation System Based on POMDP that Tracks User Focus

Koichiro Yoshino **Tatsuya Kawahara**
School of Informatics, Kyoto University
Sakyo-ku, Kyoto, 606-8501, Japan
yoshino@ar.media.kyoto-u.ac.jp

Abstract

We present a spoken dialogue system for navigating information (such as news articles), and which can engage in small talk. At the core is a partially observable Markov decision process (POMDP), which tracks user's state and focus of attention. The input to the POMDP is provided by a spoken language understanding (SLU) component implemented with logistic regression (LR) and conditional random fields (CRFs). The POMDP selects one of six action classes; each action class is implemented with its own module.

1 Introduction

A large number of spoken dialogue systems have been investigated and many systems are deployed in the real world. Spoken dialogue applications that interact with a diversity of users are available on smart-phones. However, current applications are based on simple question answering and the system requires a clear query or a definite task goal. Therefore, next-generation dialogue systems should engage in casual interactions with users who do not have a clear intention or a task goal. Such systems include a sightseeing navigation system that uses tour guide books or documents in Wikipedia (Misu and Kawahara, 2010), and a news navigation system that introduces news articles updated day-by-day (Yoshino et al., 2011; Pan et al., 2012). In this paper, we develop an information navigation system that provides information even if the user request is not necessarily clear and there is not a matching document in the knowledge base. The user and the system converse on the current topic and the system provides potentially useful information for the user.

Dialogue management of this kind of systems was usually made in a heuristic manner and based on simple rules (Dahl et al., 1994; Bohus and Rudnicky, 2003). There is not a clear principle nor established methodology to design and implement casual conversation systems. In the past years, machine learning, particularly reinforcement learning, have been investigated for dialogue management. MDPs and POMDPs are now widely used to model and train dialogue managers (Levin et al., 2000; Williams and Young, 2007; Young et al., 2010; Yoshino et al., 2013b). However, the conventional scheme assumes that the task and dialogue goal can be clearly stated and readily encoded in the RL reward function. This is not true in casual conversation or when browsing information.

Some previous work has tackled with this problem. In a conversational chatting system (Shibata et al., 2014), users were asked to make evaluation at the end of each dialogue session, to define rewards for reinforcement learning. In a listening dialogue system (Meguro et al., 2010), levels of satisfaction were annotated in logs of dialogue sessions to train a discriminative model. These approaches require costly input from users or developers, who provide labels and evaluative judgments.

In this work, we present a framework in which reward is defined for the quality of system actions and also for encouraging long interactions, in contrast to the conventional framework. Moreover, user focus is tracked to make appropriate actions, which are more rewarded.

2 Conversational Information Navigation System

In natural human-human conversation, participants have topics they plan to talk about, and they progress through the dialogue in accordance with the topics (Schegloff and Sacks, 1973). We call this dialogue style "information navigation." An example is shown in **Figure 1**. First, the speaker

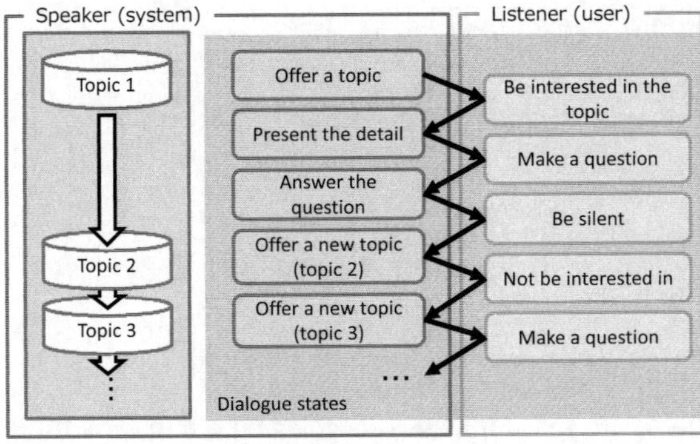

Figure 1: An example of information navigation.

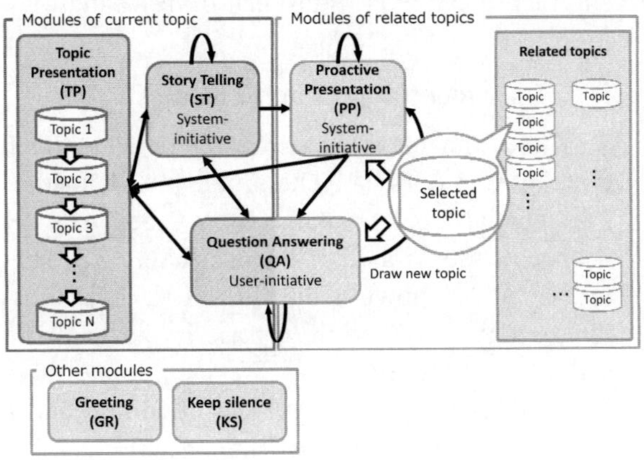

Figure 2: Overview of the information navigation system.

offers a new topic and probes the interest of the listener. If the listener shows interest, the speaker describes details of the topic. If the listener asks a specific question, the speaker answers the question. On the other hand, if the listener is not interested in the topic, the speaker avoids the details of that topic, and changes the topic. Topics are often taken from current news.

In our past work, we have developed a news navigation system (Yoshino et al., 2011) based on this dialogue structure. The system provides topics collected from Web news texts, and the user gets information according to his interests and queries.

2.1 System overview

An overview of the proposed system is depicted in **Figure 2**. The system has six modules, each of which implements a class of actions. Each module takes as input a recognized user utterance, an analyzed predicate-argument (P-A) structure and the detected user focus.

The system begins dialogues by selecting the "topic presentation (TP)" module, which presents a new topic selected from a news article. The system chooses the next module based on the user's response. In our task, the system assumes that each news article corresponds to a single topic, and the system presents a headline of news in the TP module. If the user shows interest (positive response) in the topic without any specific questions, the system selects the "story telling (ST)" module to give details of the news. In the ST module, the system provides a summary of the news article by using lead sentences. The system can also provide related topics with the "proactive presentation (PP)" module. This module is invoked by system initiative; this module is not invoked by any user request. If the user makes a specific question regarding the topic, the system switches to the "question answering (QA)" module to answer the question. This module answers questions on the presented topic and related topics.

The modules of PP and QA are based on a dialogue framework which uses the similarity of P-A structures (Yoshino et al., 2011). This framework defines the similarity of P-A structures between user queries and news articles, and retrieves or recommends the appropriate sentence from the news articles. This method searches for appropriate information from automatically parsed documents by referring to domain knowledge that is automatically extracted from domain corpus.

Transitions between the modules are allowed as shown in Figure 2. The modules "greeting (GR)" and "keep silence (KS)" are also implemented. GR module generates fixed greeting patterns by using regular expression matching. In terms of dialogue flow, these modules can be used at any time.

2.2 User focus in information navigation

"Focus" in discourse is "attentional state (that) contains information about the objects, properties, relations, and discourse intentions that are most salient at any given point." (Grosz and Sidner, 1986). The user has specific attention to an object if the user utterance contains the focus. In this work, we define the user focus as "the main piece of information of interest to the user." It makes a central component when making a reply or selecting relevant topics at the current dialogue state. For example, given "Did Ichiro perform bril-

```
SYS, tp, "Matsui, a part-time coach for the Giants, demonstrated 5 homeruns. The Giants president
         told him "Come back as a player!"
USR, st, 0, " Give me the detail?", "Give:me/0 the:detail/0"
SYS, st, "Matsui joined the extra batting training in the Giants' camp, and demonstrated his batting
         to young players."
USR, qa, 1, "Will Matsui become the Giants' manager in the future?", "Matsui/0 will:become/0
             the Giants' manager/1 in the future/0"
SYS, qa, "The director of Giants told him "Come back as a player!""
USR, tp, 0, "Next news, please.", "Next:news/0 please/0"
SYS, tp, " To be a ace pitcher, has Fujinami improved from the rookie year?
...
```

Figure 3: An example of annotation for collected dialogue. System utterances have a tuple of three elements separated by a comma: speaker, called module and utterance. User utterances have a tuple of four elements: speaker, the module the user request falls in, binary information of user focus, utterance and user focus annotation on each phrase or P-A element. (This example is translated from Japanese)

liantly?," user focus is "Ichiro" because the system reply should include information on Ichiro. This information is annotated on content words or named entities in a user utterance. In the POMDP, decisions are made based on whether any user focus was detected in the user's utterance.

3 Spoken Language Understanding (SLU)

In this section, we present the spoken language understanding components of our system. It detects the user's focus and intention and provides these to the dialogue manager. These spoken language understanding modules are formulated with a statistical model to give likelihoods which are used in POMDP.

3.1 Dialogue data

We collected 606 utterances (from 10 users) with a rule-based dialogue system (Yoshino et al., 2011). We annotated two kinds of tags: user intention (6 tags defined in Section 3.3), and focus information defined in Section 2.2. An example of annotation is shown in **Figure 3**. We highlighted annotation points in the bold font.

To prepare the training data, each utterance was labeled with one of the six modules, indicating the best module to respond. In addition, each phrase or P-A elements is labeled to indicated whether it is the user's focus or not. The user focus is determined by the attributes (=specifications of words in the domain) and preference order of phrases to identify the most appropriate information that the user wants to know. For example, in the second user utterance in Figure 3, the user's focus is the phrase "the Giants' manager". These tags are annotated by one person.

3.2 User focus detection based on CRF

To detect the user focus, we use a conditional random field (CRF) [1]. The problem is defined as a sequential labeling of the focus labels to a sequence of the phrases of the user utterance. Features used are shown in the **Table 1**. ORDER features are the order of the phrase in the sequence and in the P-A structure. We incorporate these features because the user focus often appears in the first phrase of the user utterance. POS features are part-of-speech (POS) tags and their pairs in the phrase. P-A features are semantic role of the P-A structure. We also incorporate the domain-dependent predicate-argument (P-A) scores that are defined with an unsupervised method (Yoshino et al., 2011). The score is discretized to 0.01, 0.02, 0.05, 0.1, 0.2, 0.5.

Table 2 shows the accuracy of user focus detection, which was conducted via five-fold cross-validation. "Phrase" is phrase-base accuracy and "sentence" indicates whether the presence of any user focus phrase was correctly detected (or not), regardless of whether the correct phrase was identified. This table indicates that WORD features are effective for detecting the user focus, but they are not essential for in the sentence-level accuracy. In this paper, we aim for portability across domains; therefore the dialogue manager only uses the sentence-level feature, so in our system we do not user the WORD features.

3.3 User intention analysis based on LR

The module classifies the user intention from the user utterance. We define six intentions as below.

- *TP*: request to the TP module.

[1] CRFsuite (Okazaki, 2007).

Table 1: Features of user focus detection.

feature type	feature
ORDER	Rank in a sequence of phrases Rank in a sequence of elements of P-A
POS	POS tags in the phrase POS tag sequence
POSORDER	Pair of POS tag and its order in the phrase
P-A	Which semantic role the phrase has Which semantic roles exist on the utterance
P-AORDER	Pair of semantic role and its order in the utterance
P-A score	P-A templates score
WORD	Words in the phrase Pair of words in the phrase Pair of word and its order in the phrase

Table 2: Accuracy of user focus detection.

	Accuracy
phrase	86.7%
phrase + (WORD)	90.3%
sentence (focus exist or not)	99.8%
sentence (focus exist or not) + (WORD)	99.8%

- *ST*: request to the ST module.
- *QA*: request to the QA module.
- *GR*: greeting to the GR module.
- *NR*: silence longer than a threshold.
- *II*: irrelevant input due to ASR errors or noise.

We adopt logistic regression (LR)-based dialogue act tagging approach (Tur et al., 2006). The probability of user intention o given an ASR result of the user utterance h is defined as,

$$P(o|h) = \frac{\exp(\omega \cdot \phi(h,o))}{\Sigma_o \exp(\omega \cdot \phi(h,o))}. \quad (1)$$

Here, ω is a vector of feature weights and $\phi(h,o)$ is a feature vector. We use POS, P-A and P-A templates score as a feature set. In addition, we add a typical expression feature (TYPICAL) to classify *TP*, *ST* or *GR* tags. For example, typical expressions in conversation are "Hello" or "Go on," and those in information navigation are "News of the day" or "Tell me in detail." Features for the classifier are shown in the **Table 3**.

The accuracy of the classification in five-fold cross-validation is shown in **Table 4**. The TYPICAL feature improves the classification accuracy while keeping the domain portability.

Table 3: Features of user intention analysis.

feature type	feature
POS	Bag of POS tags Bag of POS bi-gram
P-A	Bag of semantic role labels Bag of semantic role labels bi-gram Pair of semantic role label and its rank
P-A score	P-A templates score
TYPICAL	Occurrence of typical expressions

Table 4: Accuracy of user intention analysis.

	All features	without TYPICAL
TP	100%	100%
ST	75.3%	64.2%
QA	94.1%	93.5%
GR	100%	100%
II	16.7%	16.7%
All	92.1%	90.2%

3.4 SLU for ASR output

ASR and intention analysis involves errors. Here, s is a true user intention and o is an observed intention. The observation model $P(o|s)$ is given by the likelihood of ASR result $P(h|u)$ (Komatani and Kawahara, 2000) and the likelihood of the intention analysis $P(o|h)$,

$$P(o|s) = \sum_h P(o,h|s) \quad (2)$$

$$\approx \sum_h P(o|h)P(h|u). \quad (3)$$

Here, u is an utterance of the user. We combine the N-best ($N = 5$) hypotheses of the ASR result h.

4 Dialogue Management for Information Navigation

The conventional dialogue management for task-oriented dialogue systems is designed to reach a task goal as soon as possible (Williams and Young, 2007). In contrast, information navigation does not always have a clear goal, and the aim of information navigation is to provide as much relevant information as the user is interested in. Therefore, our dialogue manager refers user involvement or engagement (=level of interest) and the user focus

(=object of interest). This section describes the general dialogue management based on POMDP, and then gives an explanation of the proposed dialogue management using the user focus.

4.1 Dialogue management based on POMDP

The POMDP-based statistical dialogue management is formulated as below. The random variables involved at a dialogue turn t are as follows:

- $s \in I_s$: user state
  User intention.
- $a \in K$: system action
  Module that the system selects.
- $o \in I_s$: observation
  Observed user state, including ASR and intention analysis errors.
- $b_{s_i} = P(s_i|o^{1:t})$: belief
  Stochastic variable of the user state.
- π: policy function
  This function determines a system action a given a belief of user b. π^* is the optimal policy function that is acquired by the training.
- r: reward function
  This function gives a reward to a pair of the user state s and the system action a.

The aim of the statistical dialogue management is to output an optimal system action $\hat{a}^t$ given a sequence of observation $o^{1:t}$ from 1 to t time-steps.

Next, we give the belief update that includes the observation and state transition function. The belief update of user state s_i in time-step t is defined as,

$$b^{t+1}_{s'_j} \propto \underbrace{P(o^{t+1}|s'_j)}_{\textbf{Obs.}} \sum_{s_i} \underbrace{P(s'_j|s_i,\hat{a_k})}_{\textbf{Trans.}} b^t_{s_i}. \quad (4)$$

Obs. is an observation function which is defined in Equation (3) and **Trans.** is a state transition probability of the user state. Once the system estimates the belief $b^t_{s_i}$, the policy function outputs the optimal action $\hat{a}$ as follows:

$$\hat{a} = \pi^*(b^t). \quad (5)$$

4.2 Training of POMDP

We applied Q-learning (Monahan, 1982; Watkins and Dayan, 1992) to acquire the optimal policy π^*. Q-learning relies on the estimation of a Q-function, which maximizes the discounted sum of future rewards of the system action a^t at a dialogue turn t given the current belief b^t. Q-learning is performed by iterative updates on the training dialogue data:

$$\begin{aligned} Q(b^t, a^t) &\Leftarrow (1-\varepsilon)Q(b^t, a^t) \\ &+ \varepsilon[R(s^t, a^t) + \gamma \max_{a^{t+1}} Q(b^{t+1}, a^{t+1})], \end{aligned} \quad (6)$$

where ε is a learning rate, γ is a discount factor of a future reward. We experimentally decided $\varepsilon = 0.01$ and $\gamma = 0.9$. The optimal policy given by the Q-function is determined as,

$$\pi^*(b^t) = \operatorname*{argmax}_{a^t} Q(b^t, a^t). \quad (7)$$

However, it is impossible to calculate the Q-function for all possible real values of belief b. Thus, we train a limited Q-function given by a Grid-based Value Iteration (Bonet, 2002). The belief is given by a function,

$$b_{s_i} = \begin{cases} \eta & \textbf{if } s = i \\ \frac{1-\eta}{|I_s|} & \textbf{if } s \neq i \end{cases}. \quad (8)$$

Here, η is a likelihood of $s = i$ that is output of the intention analyzer, and we selected 11 discrete points from 0.0 to 1.0 by 0.1. We also added the case of uniform distribution. The observation function of the belief update is also given in a similar manner.

4.3 Dialogue management using user focus

Our POMDP-based dialogue management chooses actions based on its belief in: the user intention s and the user focus f (0 or 1 $\in J_f$). The observation o is controlled by hidden states f and s that are decided by the state transition probabilities,

$$P(f^{t+1}|f^t, s^t, a^t), \quad (9)$$
$$P(s^{t+1}|f^{t+1}, f^t, s^t, a^t). \quad (10)$$

We constructed a user simulator by using the annotated data described in Section 3.1.

Equation (10) is also used for the state transition probability of the belief update. The equation of the belief update (4) is extended by introducing the previous user focus f_l and current user focus f'_m information,

$$\begin{aligned} b^{t+1}_{s'_j} &= \underbrace{P(o^{t+1}|s'_j)}_{\textbf{Obs.}} \\ &\times \sum_i \underbrace{P(s'_j|f'_m, f_l, s_i, \hat{a_k})}_{\textbf{Trans.}} b^t_{s_i, f_l}. \end{aligned} \quad (11)$$

Table 5: Rewards in each turn.

state s	focus f	action a: TP	ST	QA	PP	GR	KS
TP	0 1	+10	-10	-10	-10	-10	-10
ST	0 1	-10	+10	-10	0	-10	-10
QA	0	-10	**+10**	+10	-10	-10	-10
	1		-10	**+30**	**+10**		
GR	0 1	-10	-10	-10	-10	+10	-10
NR	0	**+10**	-10	-10	-10	-10	0
	1	-10			**+10**		
II	0 1	-10	-10	-10	-10	-10	+10

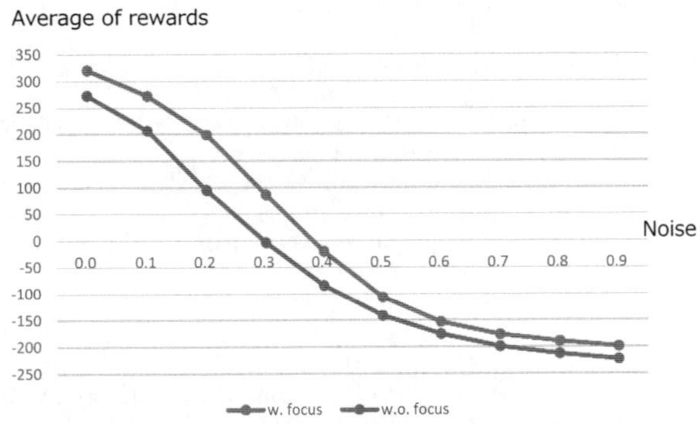

Figure 4: Effect of introduction of the user focus in simulation.

The resultant optimal policy is,

$$\hat{a} = \pi^*(b^t, f_l). \tag{12}$$

4.4 Definition of rewards

Table 5 defines a reward list at the end of a each turn. The reward of +10 is given to appropriate actions, 0 to acceptable actions, and -10 to inappropriate actions.

In Table 5, pairs of a state and its apparently corresponding action, *TP* and TP, *ST* and ST, *QA* and QA, *GR* and GR, and *II* and KS, have positive rewards. Rewards in bold fonts (**+10**) are defined for the following reasons. If the user asks a question (*QA*) without a focus (e.g. "What happened on the game?"), the system can continue by story telling (ST). But when the question has a focus, the system should answer the question (QA), which is highly rewarded (**+30**). If the system cannot find an answer, it can present relevant information (PP). When the user says nothing (*NR*), the system action should be decided by considering the user focus; present a new topic if the user is not interested in the current topic (f=0) or present an article related to the dialogue history (f=1).

Reward of +200 is given if 20 turns are passed, to reward a long continued dialogue. The user simulator terminates the dialogue if the system selects an inappropriate action (action of $r = -10$) five times, and a large penalty -200 is given to the system.

5 Evaluations of Dialogue

We evaluated the proposed system with two experiments; dialogue state tracking with real users and average reward with a user simulator. For the evaluation, we collected an additional 312 utterances (8 users, 24 dialogues) with the proposed dialogue system.

5.1 Evaluation of dialogue manager with user simulator

First, we evaluated the dialogue manager with user simulation that is constructed from the training corpus (Section 3.1). In this evaluation, the system calculated average reward of 100,000 dialogue sessions between the system and the user simulator given a fixed noise rate. **Figure 4** shows the effect of the user focus. By introducing the user focus, the system receives higher rewards than the model without the user focus. Especially, the proposed model is more robust with a noise level of 10–30% that spoken dialogue systems often encounter (Yoshino et al., 2013a).

5.2 Evaluation of dialogue state tracking with real users

Dialogue state tracking (DST) is a task of tracking the correct user state with a noisy input (e.g. ASR and NLU errors) (Williams et al., 2013). It tries to maximize the probability of the belief of the correct states, but we evaluated the accuracy of the 1-best result of the belief update. We also evaluated the average reward of each dialogue. The baseline system is a rule-based dialogue manager which we previously implemented. The baseline system is operated by a score of the question-answering module using predicate-argument structures (Yoshino et al., 2011) and regular expressions for TP and GR modules.

The DST accuracy and average reward are shown in **Table 6**. This result shows that the proposed method tracks the dialogue state of the user with a high accuracy. Our statistical framework

Dialogue 1

Sys: Hello.
Usr: Hello. Tell me today's news.
Sys: Tanaka showed a crazy split. His colleague Sabathia was stunned.

$s=TP$, $P(o|s)=0.8$, $b(s=TP)=0.800$, $f=0$
$a=$TP, $b(s=TP\ f=0)=0.8$

Usr: What is the crazy split?
Sys: His split comes just like a four-seam, but it drops quickly in front of the home plate.

$s=QA$, $P(o|s)=0.4$, $b(s=QA)=0.934$, $f=1$
$a=$QA, $b(s=QA, f=1)=0.9$

Usr: Where was he training?
Sys: Tanaka practiced at the bullpen in the New York Yankees' camp on Feb. 20th.

$s=QA$, $P(o|s)=0.8$, $b(s=QA)=0.973$, $f=1$
$a=$QA, $b(s=QA, f=1)=1.0$

Usr: (pause)
Sys: By the way, he also practiced a drop two-seam on Feb. 18.

$s=NR$, $P(o|s)=1.0$, $b(s=NR)=1.00$, $f=1$
$a=$PP, $b(s=NR, f=1)=1.0$

Usr: Does his two-seam drop?
Sys: The catcher said "Tanaka's two-seam not only slides, but also drops."

$s=QA$, $P(o|s)=0.6$, $b(s=QA)=0.867$, $f=1$
$a=$QA, $b(s=QA, f=1)=0.9$

Usr: OK, any other news?
Sys: Yankees' Ichiro is training strenuously!

$s=TP$, $P(o|s)=0.8$, $b(s=TP)=0.984$, $f=0$
$a=$TP, $b(s=TP, f=0)=1.0$

Usr: Tell me more.
Sys: Ichiro came to the field an hour earlier than usual and trained strenuously.
...

$s=ST$, $P(o|s)=0.9$, $b(s=ST)=0.871$, $f=0$
$a=$ST, $b(s=ST, f=0)=0.9$

Dialogue 2

Sys: Hello.
Usr: Hello. Tell me today's news?
Sys: Matsui, a part-time coach for the Giants, demonstrated 5 homeruns. The Giants president told him "Come back as a player!"

$s=TP$, $P(o|s)=0.8$, $b(s=TP)=0.800$, $f=0$
$a=$TP, $b(s=TP\ f=0)=0.8$

Usr: What happened?
Sys: The godzilla cannon came back to the Giants' spring camp in Miyazaki.

$s=QA$, $P(o|s)=0.8$, $b(s=QA)=0.532$, $f=0$
$a=$ST, $b(s=QA, f=0)=0.5$

Usr: What is the Godzilla cannon?
Sys: The Godzilla coach demonstrated his home-run batting to young players.

$s=QA$, $P(o|s)=0.8$, $b(s=QA)=0.806$, $f=1$
$a=$QA, $b(s=QA, f=1)=0.8$

Usr: Next please.
Sys: To be a ace pitcher, has Fujinami improved from the rookie year?
...

$s=TP$, $P(o|s)=0.8$, $b(s=TP)=0.986$, $f=0$
$a=$TP, $b(s=TP, f=0)=1.0$

Figure 5: A dialogue example. (This example is translated from Japanese)

Table 6: Accuracy of dialogue state tracking.

	rule	focus POMDP
Accuracy of tracking (1-best)	0.561 (=175/312)	0.869 (=271/312)
Average reward	-22.9	188.6

improved SLU accuracy and robustness against ASR errors, especially reducing confusions between question answering (*QA*) and topic presentation (*TP*). Moreover, belief update can detect the *TP* state even if the SLU incorrectly predicts *QA* or *ST*.

5.3 Discussion of trained policy

An example dialogue is shown in **Figure 5**. In the example, the system selects appropriate actions even if the observation likelihood is low. At the 4th turn of Dialogue 1 in this example, the system with the user focus responds with an action of proactive presentation a=PP, but the system without the user focus responds with an action of topic presentation a=TP. At the 2nd turn of Dialogue 2, the user asks a question without a focus. The confidence of $s=QA$ is lowered by the belief update, and the system selects the story telling module a=ST. These examples show that the training result (=learned policy) reflects our design described in Section 4.4: It is better to make a proactive presentation when the user is interested in the topic.

6 Conclusions

We constructed a spoken dialogue system for information navigation of Web news articles updated day-by-day. The system presents relevant information according to the user's interest, by tracking the user focus. We introduce the user focus detection model, and developed a POMDP framework which tracks user focus to select the appropriate action class (module) of the dialogue system. In experimental evaluations, the proposed dialogue management approach determines the state of the user more accurately than the existing system based on rules. An evaluation with a user simulator shows that including user focus in the dialogue manager's belief state improves robustness to ASR/SLU errors.

In future work, we plan to evaluate the system with a large number of real users on a variety of domains, and optimize the reward function for the information navigation task.

Acknowledgments

We thank Dr. Jason Williams for his valuable and detailed advice to improve this paper on SIGDIAL mentoring program. This work was supported by Grant-in-Aid for JSPS Fellows 25-4537.

References

Dan Bohus and Alexander I. Rudnicky. 2003. Ravenclaw: Dialog management using hierarchical task decomposition and an expectation agenda. In *Proceedings of the 8th European Conference on Speech Communication and Technology*, pages 597–600.

Blai Bonet. 2002. An e-optimal grid-based algorithm for partially observable Markov decision processes. In *Proceedings of International Conference on Machine Learning*, pages 51–58.

Deborah A. Dahl, Madeleine Bates, Michael Brown, William Fisher, Kate Hunicke-Smith, David Pallett, Christine Pao, Alexander Rudnicky, and Elizabeth Shriberg. 1994. Expanding the scope of the ATIS task: the ATIS-3 corpus. In *Proceedings of the workshop on Human Language Technology*, pages 43–48.

Barbara J. Grosz and Candace L. Sidner. 1986. Attention, intentions, and the structure of discourse. *Computational Linguistics*, 12(3):175–204.

Ryuichiro Higashinaka, Katsuhito Sudoh, and Mikio Nakano. 2006. Incorporating discourse features into confidence scoring of intention recognition results in spoken dialogue systems. *Speech Communication*, 48(3):417–436.

Tatsuya Kawahara. 2009. New perspectives on spoken language understanding: Does machine need to fully understand speech? In *Proceedings of IEEE workshop on Automatic Speech Recognition and Understanding*, pages 46–50.

Kazunori Komatani and Tatsuya Kawahara. 2000. Flexible mixed-initiative dialogue management using concept-level confidence measures of speech recognizer output. In *Proceedings of the 18th conference on Computational linguistics*, pages 467–473.

Esther Levin, Roberto Pieraccini, and Wieland Eckert. 2000. A stochastic model of human-machine interaction for learning dialog strategies. *IEEE Transactions on Speech and Audio Processing*, 8(1):11–23.

Toyomi Meguro, Ryuichiro Higashinaka, Yasuhiro Minami, and Kohji Dohsaka. 2010. Controlling listening-oriented dialogue using partially observable markov decision processes. In *Proceedings of the 23rd International Conference on Computational Linguistics*, pages 761–769.

Teruhisa Misu and Tatsuya Kawahara. 2010. Bayes risk-based dialogue management for document retrieval system with speech interface. *Speech Communication*, 52(1):61–71.

George E. Monahan. 1982. State of the art? a survey of partially observable Markov decision processes: Theory, models, and algorithms. *Management Science*, 28(1):1–16.

Naoaki Okazaki. 2007. CRFsuite: a fast implementation of Conditional Random Fields (CRFs).

Yi-Cheng Pan, Hung yi Lee, and Lin shan Lee. 2012. Interactive spoken document retrieval with suggested key terms ranked by a markov decision process. *IEEE Transactions on Audio, Speech, and Language Processing*, 20(2):632–645.

Emanuel A. Schegloff and Harvey Sacks. 1973. Opening up closings. *Semiotica*, 8(4):289–327.

Tomohide Shibata, Yusuke Egashira, and Sadao Kurohashi. 2014. Chat-like conversational system based on selection of reply generating module with reinforcement learning. In *Proceedings of the 5th International Workshop Series on Spoken Dialog Systems*.

Gokhan Tur, Umit Guz, and Dilek Hakkani-Tur. 2006. Model adaptation for dialog act tagging. In *Proceedings of IEEE workshop on Spoken Language Technology*, pages 94–97. IEEE.

Christopher JCH Watkins and Peter Dayan. 1992. Q-learning. *Machine learning*, 8(3):279–292.

Jason D. Williams and Steve Young. 2007. Partially observable Markov decision processes for spoken dialog systems. *Computer Speech & Language*, 21(2):393–422.

Jason D. Williams, Antoine Raux, Deepak Ramachandran, and Alan Black. 2013. The dialog state tracking challenge. In *Proceedings of the 14th Annual Meeting of the Special Interest Group on Discourse and Dialogue*, pages 404–413.

Koichiro Yoshino, Shinsuke Mori, and Tatsuya Kawahara. 2011. Spoken dialogue system based on information extraction using similarity of predicate argument structures. In *Proceedings of the 12th Annual Meeting of the Special Interest Group on Discourse and Dialogue*, pages 59–66.

Koichiro Yoshino, Shinsuke Mori, and Tatsuya Kawahara. 2013a. Incorporating semantic information to selection of web texts for language model of spoken dialogue system. In *Proceedings of IEEE International Conference on Acoustic, Speech and Signal Processing*, pages 8252–8256.

Koichiro Yoshino, Shinji Watanabe, Jonathan Le Roux, and John R. Hershey. 2013b. Statistical dialogue management using intention dependency graph. In *Proceedings of the 6th International Joint Conference on Natural Language Processing*, pages 962–966.

Steve Young, Milica Gašić, Simon Keizer, François Mairesse, Jost Schatzmann, Blaise Thomson, and Kai Yu. 2010. The hidden information state model: A practical framework for POMDP-based spoken dialogue management. *Computer Speech & Language*, 24(2):150–174.

Adapting to Personality Over Time: Examining the Effectiveness of Dialogue Policy Progressions in Task-Oriented Interaction

Alexandria Katarina Vail and Kristy Elizabeth Boyer
Department of Computer Science
North Carolina State University
Raleigh, North Carolina, USA
{akvail, keboyer}@ncsu.edu

Abstract

This paper explores dialogue adaptation over repeated interactions within a task-oriented human tutorial dialogue corpus. We hypothesize that over the course of four tutorial dialogue sessions, tutors adapt their strategies based on the personality of the student, and in particular to student introversion or extraversion. We model changes in strategy over time and use them to predict how effectively the tutorial interactions support student learning. The results suggest that students leaning toward introversion learn more effectively with a minimal amount of interruption during task activity, but occasionally require a tutor prompt before voicing uncertainty; on the other hand, students tending toward extraversion benefit significantly from increased interaction, particularly through tutor prompts for reflection on task activity. This line of investigation will inform the development of future user-adaptive dialogue systems.

1 Introduction

Throughout dialogue interactions, humans adapt to each other in a variety of ways (Cohen et al., 1981; Power, 1974; Wahlster and Kobsa, 1989). Some recent studies suggest that dialogue systems that mirror these adaptations to the user, e.g., by adopting the user's vocabulary (Niederhoffer and Pennebaker, 2002) or linguistically aligning to the user's context (Pickering and Garrod, 2004), may be more effective than those that do not. For supporting human dialogue, it has been demonstrated that tutorial dialogue systems improve in effectiveness when they adapt to user uncertainty (Forbes-Riley and Litman, 2007) or perform 'small talk' to increase the user's trust in the system (Cassell and Bickmore, 2003). Some studies have provided evidence that adapting to the user at the personality level also increases effectiveness; for example, users may become more agreeable when systems mirror their personality (Reeves and Nass, 1997), and varying levels of encouragement may help users of extraverted or introverted personalities accomplish a task more effectively (Tapus and Mataric, 2008).

With this substantial evidence that adapting to user personality may improve the effectiveness of a dialogue system, there is little investigation of how personality affects repeated interactions. For supporting human learning in particular, we hypothesize that taking personality into account may enhance outcomes by providing a more tailored experience. To explore this hypothesis, this paper presents an analysis that uses the change in human tutorial dialogue policies over repeated interaction with introverted and extraverted students to predict the effectiveness of the tutoring. We utilize a widely-used and validated questionnaire, the Big Five Inventory, to determine a personality profile for each student. We hypothesize that introverted and extraverted students learn more effectively under different dialogue policies. The results suggest dialogue policy progressions that could aid in the future development of personality-based user-adaptive tutorial dialogue systems.

2 Related Work

Humans adapt to their dialogue partner in a variety of ways: for example, using knowledge acquired through the dialogue to inform subsequent utterances (Carberry, 1989), maintaining a set of subdialogues (Litman and Allen, 1987), and structuring dialogue to achieve a common goal (Power, 1974), including asking particular sorts of questions (Cohen et al., 1981), reaching dialogue convergence (Mitchell et al., 2012), and understanding context-specific vocabulary (Grosz, 1983). It has been strongly suggested by a number of studies that dialogue systems would benefit greatly from mirroring this sort of adaptation, e.g., by adopting the user's syntax (Niederhoffer and Pennebaker, 2002), goal-oriented language (Brennan, 1996), and dialogue structure (Levelt and Kelter, 1982).

Some of these factors have been successfully applied to task-oriented dialogue systems. For example, 'entrainment' (the alignment between partners at various linguistic levels) has been shown to be predictive of task success in telephone conversation (Nenkova et al., 2008) and of less misunderstanding in personality-matching systems (Mairesse and Walker, 2010).

In order to gauge user personality, we utilize the Big Five Factor model, which was developed to objectively measure five particular aspects of a person's personality (Goldberg, 1993). This personality model has been widely implemented in a number of studies of personality in dialogue systems, including recommender systems (Dunn et al., 2009) and conversational systems (Mairesse and Walker, 2010). The investigation of personality as it pertains to tutorial dialogue systems is a natural step for user-adaptive dialogue systems.

3 Tutorial Dialogue Corpus

The corpus under examination in this study consists of computer-mediated human-human textual dialogue (Mitchell et al., 2013; Ha et al., 2013). For each dialogue session, participants included one tutor and one student who cooperated with the goal of creating a working software artifact, a text-based adventure game, by the end of the repeated interactions. Students were first-year university students from an introductory engineering course who volunteered in exchange for course credit. No previous computer science knowledge was assumed or required. The tutors were primarily graduate students with previous experience in tutoring or teaching Java programming.

The tutorial sessions were conducted within a web-based textual dialogue interface for introductory programming in Java. The tutorial dialogue interface, displayed in Figure 1, consists of four panes in which the student interacts: the task description, the compilation and execution output, the student's Java source code, and the textual dialogue messages between the tutor and the student. The student could modify, compile, and execute Java code from within the interface, in addition to conversing with the tutor via the textual dialogue pane. The content of the interface was synchronized in real time between the student and the tutor; however, the tutor's interactions with the environment were constrained to the textual dialogue with the student and the progression between tasks.

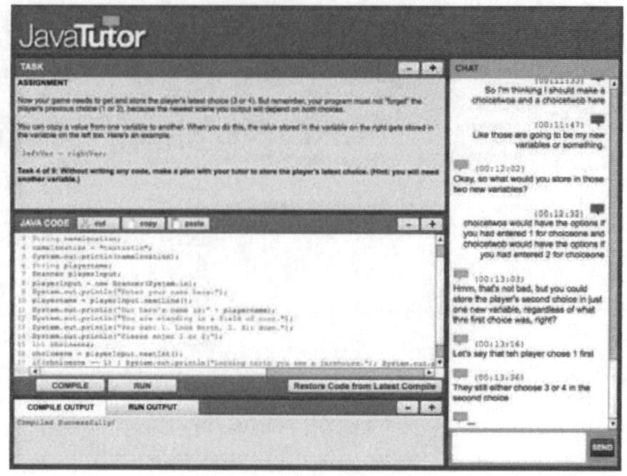

Figure 1: The task-oriented tutorial dialogue interface.

The corpus was collected during two university semesters in Fall 2011 and Spring 2012. A total of $N = 67$ students interacted with one of seven tutors to complete the series of interactions during this time frame. The tutoring curriculum was composed of six task-based lessons completed over four weeks, each constrained to forty minutes in duration. Each lesson consisted of multiple subtasks, with each lesson concluding at a milestone. This paper considers only the first four of the six lessons, because the fifth lesson suffered from significant data loss due to a database connectivity error, and the sixth lesson consisted of an unstructured review of the previous five lessons, and is therefore a different type of dialogue than the prior lessons. The structure of the corpus is illustrated in Table 1.

The sessions under consideration contained 67 students, with a total of $45,904$ utterances: $13,732$ student utterances and $32,172$ tutor utterances. There were an average of 117 utterances per session: 82 tutor utterances (652 words) and 35 student utterances (184 words). Introverted students averaged 36 utterances and 172 words per session, while extraverted students averaged 34 utterances and 187 words per session. There was no statistically significant difference between in-

Tutor	Student	Lessons					
1	1	L1	L2	L3	L4	L5	L6
1	2	L1	L2	L3	L4	L5	L6
			⋮				
2	15	L1	L2	L3	L4	L5	L6
			⋮				
3	18	L1	L2	L3	L4	L5	L6
3	19	L1	L2	L3	L4	L5	L6
			⋮				

Table 1: A diagram of the structure of the corpus. Gray cells indicate dialogue sessions that were not considered in the present analysis.

troverts and extraverts on these counts. The possible extraversion score on the questionnaire ranges from -10 (highly introverted) to 25 (highly extraverted), and the mean extraversion score of the students in our corpus was 6.40 (standard deviation 6.42). The distribution of scores across the sample was comparable to a normal distribution, as demonstrated by the histogram in Figure 2.

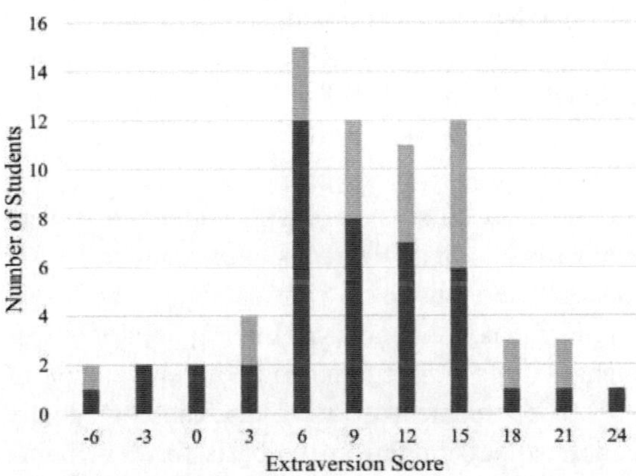

Figure 2: Histogram of extraversion scores across students in the corpus. Lighter bars indicate female students, while darker bars indicate male students.

3.1 Learning Gain

Students completed an identical pretest and posttest for each lesson. The average pretest and posttest scores for students scoring above and below the median extraversion score in the four lessons are detailed in Table 3 (determination of extraversion is detailed in Section 3.2). There was no statistically significant difference between the scores of extraverted and introverted students. The tutoring was statistically significantly effective overall and within each student group ($p \ll 0.0001$, on all accounts).

Lesson	Pretest		Posttest	
	Introvert	*Extravert*	*Introvert*	*Extravert*
L1	50.69%	47.42%	71.63%	68.18%
L2	43.70%	38.96%	71.01%	73.59%
L3	55.88%	54.55%	67.65%	64.85%
L4	68.79%	65.66%	80.56%	79.97%

Table 3: Average pretest and posttest scores for each lesson.

This equation adjusts for negative learning gain in the rare cases that posttest score is less than pretest score (Marx and Cummings, 2007).

$$norm\_gain = \begin{cases} \frac{post-pre}{1-pre} & post > pre \\ \frac{post-pre}{pre} & post \leq pre \end{cases} \quad (1)$$

Since pretest and posttest scores for introverts and extraverts were not identical, normalized learning gain was standardized within each group before developing models to predict learning (Section 4).

3.2 Extraversion vs. Introversion

One of the standard frameworks for identifying personality traits is the Big Five Factor model of personality (Goldberg, 1993). The standard method of testing for the Big Five personality traits is by questionnaire (John and Srivastava, 1999; Gosling et al., 2003). The students under consideration in this study were administered a Big Five Inventory survey, a type of self-assessment of personality, prior to any interaction with the tutorial dialogue system. The Big Five Inventory consists of 44 items to measure an individual on the Big Five Factors of personality: Openness, Conscientiousness, Extraversion, Agreeableness, and Neuroticism (Goldberg, 1993). This study focuses on a student's responses to the items reflective of extraversion and introversion. These items are identified in Table 4. Extraversion is defined as the part of the Big Five Factors that identifies gregariousness, assertiveness, activity, excitement-seeking, positive emotions, and warmth (John and Srivastava, 1999).

3.3 Dialogue Act Annotation

As described in the previous section, the corpus being considered consists of 268 dialogues, four

Extraverted Student Dialogue Excerpt
STUDENT: So do we need an `else` statement for each one? *[QI]*
TUTOR: That wouldn't actually work. *[AWH]*
STUDENT: Really? *[FNU]*
TUTOR: See, because it's testing them each independently. *[E]*
TUTOR: So when it gets to 2 and 4, any other combination goes to its `else`. *[E]*
Pause for 29 seconds.
TUTOR: If we added an `else` clause for each statement, we'd end up with 3 of them printing out for every valid input. *[E]*
STUDENT: Oh. *[ACK]*
Pause for 44 seconds.
TUTOR: What else do you think we could try? *[QP]*
Pause for 49 seconds.
STUDENT: Well the first one worked last time because it was checking only `playerChoice` ... maybe `currentChoice` has something to do with this case. *[AWH]*

Introverted Student Dialogue Excerpt
STUDENT: The `else` applies no matter what because it doesn't have an `else if` to combine with? *[QI]*
TUTOR: Well, it's a little different than that. *[AWH]*
TUTOR: Each `if` statement applies no matter what. *[I]*
TUTOR: So, instead of checking the values as mutually exclusive conditions, each `if` is checked in sequence. *[I]*
Pause for 22 seconds.
TUTOR: Your `else` occurs only with the final `if`, regardless of what happened with the previous `if` statements! *[E]*
Pause for 31 seconds.
TUTOR: Let's fix it by doing the change that you started much earlier. *[D]*
Pause for 50 seconds.
TUTOR: Much better. :) *[FP]*
STUDENT: Thanks! *[ACK]*
Pause for 22 seconds.
TUTOR: Do you have any issues with the input checking as it is now? *[QP]*
Pause for 46 seconds.
STUDENT: I do not! *[AYN]*

Table 2: Excerpts of similar dialogue between an extraverted and an introverted student.

I see myself as someone who ...
... is talkative.
... is reserved.*
... is full of energy.
... generates a lot of enthusiasm.
... tends to be quiet.*
... has an assertive personality.
... is sometimes shy, inhibited.*
... is outgoing, sociable.

Table 4: Items of the Big Five Inventory reflective of a student's extraversion traits. Asterisks represent items negatively associated with extraversion.

for each of 67 students, with $45,904$ utterances total. As described in this section, a portion of these dialogues were manually annotated, and then a supervised dialogue act classifier was trained on them and was used to tag the remaining dialogues.

The annotation scheme applied to the corpus consisted of 31 dialogue act tags grouped into four high-level categories (Statement, Question, Answer, Feedback) (Vail and Boyer, In press). This tagset represents a refinement of previous dialogue act tagsets developed for task-oriented tutoring (Ha et al., 2013). During this refinement, emphasis was placed on decomposing frequent tags that tended to be broad, such as STATEMENT and QUESTION, in order to capture more fine-grained pedagogical and social phenomena in the dialogues. The annotation scheme is detailed in Table 5.

A total of 30 sessions ($4,035$ utterances) were manually annotated by a single annotator. Of those 30 sessions, 37% were annotated by a second independent annotator. Inter-annotator agreement on this subset reached a Cohen's kappa of κ=0.87 (agreement of 89.6%). These manually annotated sessions form the basis for developing an automated classifier.

The automated classifier was trained using the WEKA machine learning software (Hall et al., 2009). We used a J48 decision tree classifier, which has a low running time (Verbree et al., 2006) and as we will see, performed very well for this task. The classifier was provided the features listed in Table 6.

Before the construction of the classifier, the 30 sessions of the manually annotated corpus were systematically split into a training and a test set, consisting of 24 and 6 sessions, respectively; the test set contained the first three sessions with students identified as introverts and the first three sessions with students identified as extraverts. Utterances were defined as single textual messages.

Tag	Example	Session Type		κ
		Introvert	Extravert	
ACKNOWLEDGE (**ACK**)	*Okay.*	10.46%	10.36%	0.872
EXTRA-DOMAIN ANSWER (**AEX**)	*I'm doing great.*	1.33%	1.42%	0.813
READY ANSWER (**AR**)	*I'm ready.*	2.75%	3.08%	0.963
WH-QUESTION ANSWER (**AWH**)	*Line 9.*	8.14%	8.10%	0.819
YES/NO ANSWER (**AYN**)	*No, sir.*	2.99%	3.73%	0.839
CORRECTION (**CO**)	**exclamation*	0.43%	0.41%	0.700
DIRECTIVE (**D**)	*Test what you have.*	6.01%	5.97%	0.888
EXPLANATION (**E**)	*Your code stops on line 2.*	31.48%	26.70%	0.822
NEGATIVE FEEDBACK (**FN**)	*No, that's wrong.*	0.02%	0.02%	0.615
ELABORATED NEGATIVE FEEDBACK (**FNE**)	*You're using the wrong function.*	0.21%	0.14%	0.689
NOT UNDERSTANDING FEEDBACK (**FNU**)	*I'm not sure.*	0.05%	0.04%	0.749
OTHER FEEDBACK (**FO**)	*That's okay.*	0.17%	0.16%	0.614
ELABORATED OTHER FEEDBACK (**FOE**)	*What you had was fine.*	0.29%	0.27%	0.665
POSITIVE FEEDBACK (**FP**)	*Very good!*	6.78%	5.45%	0.927
ELABORATED POSITIVE FEEDBACK (**FPE**)	*That's a very good approach.*	0.05%	0.12%	0.705
UNDERSTANDING FEEDBACK (**FU**)	*Ohh, I see!*	0.76%	0.92%	0.804
GREETING (**GRE**)	*Hello!*	2.59%	3.03%	0.941
INFORMATION (**I**)	*Variable names must be one word.*	4.55%	5.33%	0.859
OBSERVATION (**O**)	*As you see, we have a bug.*	0.25%	0.31%	0.760
EXTRA-DOMAIN OTHER (**OEX**)	*Calculus is difficult.*	1.49%	2.22%	0.789
CONFIRMATION QUESTION (**QC**)	*Does that work?*	0.16%	0.16%	0.857
DIRECTION QUESTION (**QD**)	*What do I do now?*	0.68%	0.58%	0.758
EVALUATIVE QUESTION (**QE**)	*Does that make sense?*	0.87%	0.83%	0.763
EXTRA-DOMAIN QUESTION (**QEX**)	*How are you today?*	0.42%	0.45%	0.781
FACTUAL QUESTION (**QF**)	*What line is it waiting on?*	4.10%	5.12%	0.832
INFORMATION QUESTION (**QI**)	*How do you add spaces?*	4.06%	4.91%	0.820
OPEN QUESTION (**QO**)	*How can you fix it?*	0.15%	0.14%	0.725
PROBING QUESTION (**QP**)	*Do you think that looks correct?*	4.99%	4.76%	0.731
QUESTION PROMPT (**QQ**)	*Any questions?*	2.49%	2.24%	0.978
READY QUESTION (**QR**)	*Are you ready to move on?*	2.47%	2.75%	0.989
REASSURANCE (**R**)	*We have plenty of time left.*	0.12%	0.15%	0.763

Table 5: Dialogue act tags comprising the annotation scheme, the average composition of a Lesson 4 session with introverted and extraverted students, and the Cohen's kappa achieved by the automated classifier.

Feature Description	Number of Features	
	Initial	Selected
TUTOR or STUDENT	1	1
Two-step tag history	2	2
Two-step category history	2	2
Number of tokens in the utterance	1	1
Existence of a question mark	1	1
Existence of word unigrams	1459	160
Existence of word bigrams	8959	150
Existence of POS unigrams	50	31
Existence of POS bigrams	928	152

Table 6: Features provided to the J48 automatic dialogue act classifier.

Feature selection was performed on the features occurring more than three times in the training set using the WEKA machine learning software: various top-N cut-offs were examined for performance on tenfold cross-validation after ranking the features by information gain. A peak in performance during cross-validation on the training set was observed at N=500 features.

The final dialogue act classifier includes the following features: speaker role, two-step dialogue act history (category and tag), utterance length, existence of the '?' token, existence of 160 unigrams and 150 bigrams, and existence of 31 part-of-speech unigrams and 152 part-of-speech bigrams.

The part-of-speech tagger used in this analysis was an n-gram tagger within the Natural Language Tool Kit for Python, trained on the NPS chat corpus (Bird et al., 2009; Forsyth and Martell, 2007). The classifier performance on the held-out test set consisting of 714 utterances was 80.11% accuracy, Cohen's kappa of 0.786. This classifier was then used to tag dialogue acts in the remaining 41,869 utterances.

4 Extraversion and Dialogue Policy

With the annotated corpus in hand, the goal is to examine how *dialogue policy progression*, as represented by tutors' contextualized dialogue acts, occurs over time with students tending toward extraversion or introversion. We hypothesize that tutors adapt differently to introverted and extraverted students, and that students of different extraverted or introverted tendencies learn more effectively from different dialogue policies.

Students were binned into two groups, the 'introverts', consisting of the students scoring below or equal to the median extraversion score of 7, and the 'extraverts', consisting of the students scoring above the median score[1]. These groups included 34 and 33 students, respectively.

We describe tutor dialogue policy by identifying the conditional probabilities of a tutor move following a student move (i.e., the probabilities $Pr(T_n|S_{n-1})$) during each session. In other words, we compute bigram probabilities over dialogue acts, where the second dialogue act of the bigram is a tutor move. Because the task-oriented nature of the dialogue allows for extended periods of dialogue silence while the student is working on the task, a WAIT tag was added to the corpus when there was a pause in the dialogue for more than twenty seconds. This threshold was chosen based upon qualitative inspection of the corpus. To identify the changes in this policy over time, we calculated the difference in the probability of each dialogue act bigram between the first and fourth lessons of each student-tutor pair. Finally, in order to allow for directly comparing parameter values across models, each column of predictors was standardized by subtracting the mean and dividing by the standard deviation.

After all of the bigram probabilities were standardized, we split the students into two groups based on median extraversion score: those tending toward extraversion and those tending toward introversion. A feature selection algorithm was then applied to each of these sets in order to identify the most relevant dialogue act bigram features for predicting learning. Any feature that provided non-positive information gain was eliminated from consideration. A stepwise linear regression model was then applied using the SAS statistical modeling software, resulting in the models displayed in Tables 7 and 8. Subscripts indicate the speaker of the dialogue act, student or tutor. Note that in each of these tables, the predictors are not just bigram probabilities, but *change* in that particular bigram probability from the *first to the fourth* dialogue within repeated-interactions tutoring.

Students Tending Toward Extraversion

Normalized Learning Gain =	Partial R^2	p
$1.244 * OEX_S \rightarrow FP_T$	0.228	< 0.001
$-0.445 * AYN_S \rightarrow R_T$	0.169	< 0.001
$0.440 * E_S \rightarrow QE_T$	0.139	0.001
$0.359 * QI_S \rightarrow QF_T$	0.092	0.002
$-0.298 * AWH_S \rightarrow QO_T$	0.081	0.013
$0.207 * WAIT \rightarrow QP_T$	0.050	0.037
$-0.226 * QI_S \rightarrow I_T$	0.038	0.041
0.000 (intercept)		1.000
RSME = 50.97% of range in Normalized Learning Gain		

Table 7: Stepwise linear regression model for standardized Normalized Learning Gain in students scoring above the median in extraversion.

Students Tending Toward Introversion

Normalized Learning Gain =	Partial R^2	p
$-0.447 * QI_S \rightarrow R_T$	0.262	0.003
$0.371 * QI_S \rightarrow QP_T$	0.125	0.007
$-0.331 * QI_S \rightarrow QQ_T$	0.092	0.015
$-0.278 * WAIT \rightarrow FPE_T$	0.083	0.018
$0.384 * AYN_S \rightarrow QQ_T$	0.067	0.010
$0.288 * ACK_S \rightarrow E_T$	0.067	0.022
0.000 (intercept)		1.000
RSME = 60.89% of range in Normalized Learning Gain		

Table 8: Stepwise linear regression model for standardized Normalized Learning Gain in students scoring below the median in extraversion.

[1]We split on the median introversion/extraversion score as observed in our student sample rather than splitting on a larger population median because the range of personality traits differs significantly based on the sample. To date, no large study has examined university students in order to establish personality norms.

Several tutorial dialogue policy progressions were identified as statistically significantly associated with learning gain in both extraverted and introverted students. An increase in factual questions following extra-domain statements was associated with increased learning in students scoring above the median in extraversion, as was an increase in evaluative questions after explanations, an increase in the number of factual questions following information questions, and an increase in probing questions initiated after the conclusion of a sub-dialogue. On the other hand, extraverted students achieved a lower learning gain when tutors offered increasing reassurance after yes/no answers, asked more open questions after answers to WH-questions, or gave increasing instruction after an information question.

A similar number of tutorial dialogue policy progressions were identified as statistically significantly correlated with learning gain in introverted students. For these students, a higher learning gain was achieved when tutors followed more information questions with a probing question, more yes/no answers with a prompt for questions, or offered increasing explanation after acknowledgements. Students scoring below the median in extraversion achieved a lower learning gain when tutors offered more reassurance after information questions, more prompts for questions after information questions, or increasing elaborated positive feedback after pauses in the dialogue.

5 Discussion

This section examines the tutorial dialogue policy progressions that were identified as statistically significant to learning gain in these groups of students; recall that each feature represents a change over time in the probability that the second dialogue act follows the first. First we examine the extraverted student model, and then we examine the introverted student model. Dialogue excerpts illustrating these dialogue interactions are displayed in Appendix 1.

5.1 Extraverted Students

Students scoring higher in extraversion tend to be assertive, outgoing, and energetic (Goldberg, 1993). As the models show, these characteristics likely influence the extent to which particular dialogue policies are effective for supporting learning for extraverted students. For example, the high energy nature of the extraversion personality trait may influence how dialogues transition. The model shows that students learned more when tutors progressed over time toward more positive feedback following extra-domain statements (*Extra-Domain Statement*$_S$ $\rightarrow$ *Positive Feedback*$_T$) and toward more probing questions following pauses (*Wait* $\rightarrow$ *Probing Question*$_T$). Both of these bigrams indicate important transition points within dialogue. For the former, extra-domain statements represent off-topic utterances, whereas tutor positive feedback can only be task-related (if it were a positive response to an extra-domain statement, the response would also have been tagged extra-domain). For tutor probing questions following pauses, it is likely that extraverted students benefited from this adaptation over time because in being asked to reflect and explain their current understanding or goals, they may have been re-engaged. It should be noted that in general, asking students to self-explain can support learning (VanLehn et al., 1992).

Another example of a dialogue policy progression that emerged in the model and illustrates a widely known fact about tutoring is reflected in the *Information Question*$_S$ $\rightarrow$ *Information*$_T$ bigram, which when tutors progressed more toward this approach, is associated with decreased learning. Our prior work has shown that directing students what to do, even if they have just asked for such direction, is strongly associated with decreased learning (Mitchell et al., 2013).

Extraverted students tend to be assertive, and this characteristic influences how they make and interpret particular dialogue moves. An example of this can be seen within the model: when tutors progressed toward providing more reassurance after student yes/no answers, students learned less. This *Yes/No Answer*$_S$ $\rightarrow$ *Reassurance*$_T$ policy is likely a form of indirect feedback or politeness, both of which have been shown to be unhelpful, and sometimes harmful, to learning (Johnson and Rizzo, 2004), and this seems to be a particularly marked effect for extraverted students who may benefit more from direct evaluations of their answers. Another example of this indirect approach may be within the *WH-Question Answer*$_S$ $\rightarrow$ *Open Question*$_T$ tutor policy, whose increasing use over time was associated with lower student learning. Like reassurance, a follow-up question may be interpreted by extraverted students as an indirect indication that the previous answer was incorrect, and a more direct approach may have been more helpful.

Finally, extraverted students tend to be talkative. This tendency is consistent with two of the model's findings regarding the helpfulness of particular types of tutor questions. Students tended to learn more when tutors progressed toward following student explanations with evaluative questions (*Explanation*$_S$ $\rightarrow$ *Evaluative Question*$_T$). Although students' responses to evaluative questions (e.g., *'Do you understand?'*) are frequently considered to be inherently inaccurate, especially when students are first introduced to material, it may be the case that as students work on a task for an extended period of time, evaluative questions may become increasingly helpful. Another tutor questioning policy was also positively associated with learning gain for extraverted students: *Information Question*$_S$ $\rightarrow$ *Factual Question*$_T$ involves the tutor answering a question with a question, potentially a very helpful strategy for talkative or highly social students.

5.2 Introverted Students

Students scoring lower in extraversion tend to be less talkative, more reserved, and more shy (Goldberg, 1993). This may result in introverted students being less outspoken about their understanding, and less likely to ask questions about misunderstandings. These characteristics affect the way that tutor choices impact student learning during tutoring. For example, when less talkative students ask information questions and tutors tend to provide more reassurance as time goes on, this *Information Question*$_S$ $\rightarrow$ *Reassurance*$_T$ pair is associated with decreased student learning. It is possible that since introverts are less likely to speak up with a question, the "stakes" or importance of providing a direct answer may be higher for these students. Another dialogue policy progression that is not helpful for student learning is to provide elaborated positive feedback after a pause in dialogue (*Wait* $\rightarrow$ *Elaborated Positive Feedback*$_T$). Because pauses in the dialogue typically correspond to student task actions, it is possible that introverted students who are on the right track would benefit more from the tutor allowing them to continue working.

Introverted students also tend to describe themselves as shy or inhibited, which may be influential in the apparent helpfulness of tutors' increasing their question prompts following student answers (*Answer Yes/No*$_S$ $\rightarrow$ *Question Prompt*$_T$). This could be due to the fact that introverted students are prone to giving terse responses, and may need extra encouragement to ask questions if they are uncertain. Increasing the number of these prompts could increase the likelihood that more of the student's questions are voiced. Another helpful type of question for introverted students seems to be probing questions, even when they follow a student question (*Question Information*$_S$ $\rightarrow$ *Probing Question*$_T$). A probing question is an indirect request for reflection, prompting the student to reconsider her approach; this has previously been shown to have a positive effect on learning gain (VanLehn et al., 1992).

6 Conclusion and Future Work

Adapting to personality during dialogue may substantially improve the effectiveness of both human-human interactions as well as interactions with dialogue systems. We have investigated the ways in which human tutorial dialogue policy progressions are associated with learning within a repeated-interactions dialogue study. The models indicate that depending on a student's tendencies toward introversion or extraversion, different dialogue policy progressions support higher learning. In particular, introverts may benefit from additional prompting and encouragement to speak their mind, while extraverts may benefit from being given opportunities to discuss their thoughts with a tutor.

While this study has focused on the extraversion facet of personality, future work may benefit from examining the other facets of the Big Five Factors: Neuroticism, Openness, Conscientiousness, and Agreeableness. How we may best design a tutorial dialogue policy around a more fully-featured model of the student's personality is an important research area. It will also be important to examine task actions closely in future analyses, as this may have significant effects on task-oriented dialogue system design in particular. Additionally, analyzing the intermediate sessions in order to capture a fuller picture of the interaction over time is a promising direction. Finally, examining tutor personality may also reveal important insight for the design of tutorial systems. It is hoped that these lines of investigation will lead to a next generation of user-adaptive dialogue systems with increased effectiveness facilitated by their adaptation to personality traits.

Acknowledgements

The authors wish to thank the members of the LearnDialogue group at North Carolina State University for their helpful input. This work is supported in part by the Department of Computer Science at North Carolina State University and the National Science Foundation through Grant DRL-1007962 and the STARS Alliance, CNS-1042468. Any opinions, findings, conclusions, or recommendations expressed in this report are those of the participants, and do not necessarily represent the official views, opinions, or policy of the National Science Foundation.

References

Steven Bird, Ewan Klein, and Edward Loper. 2009. *Natural language processing with Python*. O'Reilly Media, Inc.

Susan E Brennan. 1996. Lexical entrainment in spontaneous dialog. In *Proceedings of ISSD*, pages 41–44.

Sandra Carberry. 1989. Plan recognition and its use in understanding dialog. In *User Models in Dialog Systems*, pages 133–162. Springer.

Justine Cassell and Timothy Bickmore. 2003. Negotiated collusion: Modeling social language and its relationship effects in intelligent agents. *User Modeling and User-Adapted Interaction*, 13(1-2):89–132.

Philip R Cohen, C Raymond Perrault, and James F Allen. 1981. Beyond Question-Answering. Technical report, DTIC Document.

Greg Dunn, Jurgen Wiersema, Jaap Ham, and Lora Aroyo. 2009. Evaluating interface variants on personality acquisition for recommender systems. In *User Modeling, Adaptation, and Personalization*, pages 259–270. Springer.

Kate Forbes-Riley and Diane Litman. 2007. Investigating human tutor responses to student uncertainty for adaptive system development. In *Affective Computing and Intelligent Interaction*, pages 678–689. Springer.

Eric N Forsyth and Craig H Martell. 2007. Lexical and discourse analysis of online chat dialog. In *Semantic Computing, 2007. ICSC 2007. International Conference on*, pages 19–26. IEEE.

Lewis R. Goldberg. 1993. The structure of phenotypic personality traits. *American Psychologist*, 48(1):26–34.

Samuel D Gosling, Peter J Rentfrow, and William B Swann Jr. 2003. A very brief measure of the Big-Five personality domains. *Journal of Research in personality*, 37(6):504–528.

Barbara J. Grosz. 1983. TEAM: A Transportable Natural-language Interface System. In *Proceedings of the First Conference on Applied Natural Language Processing*, pages 39–45, Santa Monica, California. Association for Computational Linguistics.

Eun Young Ha, Christopher M Mitchell, Kristy Elizabeth Boyer, and James C Lester. 2013. Learning Dialogue Management Models for Task-Oriented Dialogue with Multiple Communicative Channels. In *Proceedings of the 14th Annual SIGDIAL Meeting on Discourse and Dialogue*, pages 204–213, Metz, France.

Mark Hall, Eibe Frank, Geoffrey Holmes, Bernhard Pfahringer, Reutemann, and Ian H. Witten. 2009. The WEKA Data Mining Software: An Update. *SIGKDD Explorations*, 11(1).

Oliver P. John and Sanjay Srivastava. 1999. The Big Five trait taxonomy: History, measurement, and theoretical perspectives. *Handbook of personality: Theory and research1*, 2:102–138.

W Lewis Johnson and Paola Rizzo. 2004. Politeness in tutoring dialogs: "Run the factory, thats what Id do". In *Intelligent Tutoring Systems*, pages 67–76. Springer.

Willem JM Levelt and Stephanie Kelter. 1982. Surface form and memory in question answering. *Cognitive psychology*, 14(1):78–106.

Diane J Litman and James F Allen. 1987. A plan recognition model for subdialogues in conversations. *Cognitive Science*, 11(2):163–200.

Francois Mairesse and Marilyn A Walker. 2010. Towards personality-based user adaptation: psychologically informed stylistic language generation. *User Modeling and User-Adapted Interaction*, 20(3):227–278.

Jeffrey D. Marx and Karen Cummings. 2007. Normalized change. *American Journal of Physics*, 75(1):87.

Christopher M Mitchell, Kristy Elizabeth Boyer, and James C Lester. 2012. From strangers to partners: examining convergence within a longitudinal study of task-oriented dialogue. In *Special Interest Group on Discourse and Dialogue*, pages 94–98.

Christopher M Mitchell, Eun Young Ha, Kristy Elizabeth Boyer, and James C Lester. 2013. Learner characteristics and dialogue: recognising effective and student-adaptive tutorial strategies. *International Journal of Learning Technology (IJLT)*, 8(4):382–403.

Ani Nenkova, Agustin Gravano, and Julia Hirschberg. 2008. High frequency word entrainment in spoken dialogue. In *Proceedings of the 46th Annual Meeting of the Association for Computational Linguistics on Human Language Technologies*, pages 169–172. Association for Computational Linguistics.

Kate G Niederhoffer and James W Pennebaker. 2002. Linguistic style matching in social interaction. *Journal of Language and Social Psychology*, 21(4):337–360.

Martin J Pickering and Simon Garrod. 2004. Toward a mechanistic psychology of dialogue. *Behavioral and brain sciences*, 27(2):169–190.

Richard Power. 1974. A computer model of conversation.

Byron Reeves and C Nass. 1997. *The Media equation: how people treat computers, television, and new media*. Cambridge University Press.

Adriana Tapus and Maja J Mataric. 2008. Socially Assistive Robots: The Link between Personality, Empathy, Physiological Signals, and Task Performance. In *AAAI Spring Symposium: Emotion, Personality, and Social Behavior*, pages 133–140.

Alexandria Katarina Vail and Kristy Elizabeth Boyer. In press. Identifying Effective Moves in Tutorial Dialogue: On the Refinement of Speech Act Annotation Schemes. In *Proceedings of the 12th International Conference on Intelligent Tutoring Systems*, Honolulu, Hawaii, USA.

Kurt VanLehn, Randolph M Jones, and Michelene TH Chi. 1992. A model of the self-explanation effect. *The Journal of the Learning Sciences*, 2(1):1–59.

Daan Verbree, Rutger Rienks, and Dirk Heylen. 2006. Dialogue-act tagging using smart feature selection; results on multiple corpora. In *Spoken Language Technology Workshop*, pages 70–73. IEEE.

Wolfgang Wahlster and Alfred Kobsa. 1989. *User models in dialog systems*. Springer.

Extraverted Student Dialogue Excerpt	
Extra-Domain Other → Positive Feedback	STUDENT: I haven't really done this before. TUTOR: You're doing well!
Yes/No Answer → Reassurance	STUDENT: Yes. TUTOR: Actually, I was wording the question incorrectly...
Explanation → Evaluative Question	STUDENT: But it still prompts for 3 or 4... TUTOR: Yes; does that make sense from what you learned about sequential program flow?
Information Question → Factual Question	STUDENT: What did I do wrong? TUTOR: What is your `Scanner`'s name?
WH-Question Answer → Open Question	STUDENT: Previous. TUTOR: Why did `previousChoice` get assigned a value?
Wait → Probing Question	TUTOR: What do you think about your program's behavior?
Information Question → Instruction	STUDENT: There wouldn't have been any output? TUTOR: Yeah, but more than that, the program would report an error.
Introverted Student Dialogue Excerpt	
Information Question → Reassurance	STUDENT: So the previous answer needs to be stored as a part of `PlayerInput2`? TUTOR: That would work fine.
Information Question → Probing Question	STUDENT: That's not what I want? TUTOR: Do you really want 'or'?
Information Question → Question Prompt	STUDENT: So I need an `else if` for every `if` statement? TUTOR: Do you have any questions?
Wait → Elaborated Positive Feedback	TUTOR: Nice, you compiled the code.
Yes/No Answer → Question Prompt	STUDENT: No, I got it. TUTOR: Any questions so far?
Acknowledgement → Explanation	STUDENT: Okay. TUTOR: When Java gets to the `nextLine()`, it will stop.

Appendix 1: Dialogue excerpts illustrating the dialogue interactions emergent as significant in the analysis. All excerpts originate from Lesson 4, at the end of the series of dialogue sessions.

Probabilistic Human-Computer Trust Handling

Florian Nothdurft*, **Felix Richter**† **and Wolfgang Minker***
*Institute of Communications Engineering
†Institute of Artificial Intelligence
Ulm University
Ulm, Germany
florian.nothdurft, felix.richter, wolfgang.minker@uni-ulm.de

Abstract

Human-computer trust has shown to be a critical factor in influencing the complexity and frequency of interaction in technical systems. Particularly incomprehensible situations in human-computer interaction may lead to a reduced users trust in the system and by that influence the style of interaction. Analogous to human-human interaction, explaining these situations can help to remedy negative effects. In this paper we present our approach of augmenting task-oriented dialogs with selected explanation dialogs to foster the human-computer trust relationship in those kinds of situations. We have conducted a web-based study testing the effects of different goals of explanations on the components of human-computer trust. Subsequently, we show how these results can be used in our probabilistic trust handling architecture to augment pre-defined task-oriented dialogs.

1 Introduction

Human-computer interaction (HCI) has evolved in the past decades from classic stationary interaction paradigms featuring only human and computer towards intelligent agent-based paradigms featuring multiple devices and sensors in intelligent environments. For example, ubiquitous computing no longer seems to be a vision of future HCI, but has become reality, at least in research labs and prototypical environments. Additionally, the tasks a technical system has to solve cooperatively with the user have become increasingly complex. However, this change from simple task solver to intelligent assistant requires the acceptance of and the trust in the technical system as dialogue partner and not only as ordinary service device.

Especially trust has shown to be a crucial part in the interaction between human and technical system. If the user does not trust the system and its actions, advices or instructions the way of interaction may change up to complete abortion of future interaction (Parasuraman and Riley, 1997). Especially those situations in which the user does not understand the system or does not expect the way how the system acts are critical to have a negative impact on the human-computer trust (HCT) relationship (Muir, 1992). Those situations do occur usually due to incongruent models of the system: During interaction the user builds a mental model of the system and its underlying processes determining system actions and output. However, if this perceived mental model and the actual system model do not match the HCT relationship may be influenced negatively (Muir, 1992). This may, for example, be due to a mismatch in the expected and the actual system action and output.

For example, if a technical system would assist the user in having his day scheduled in a time effective manner, the user would be in a vulnerable situation of relying on the reasoning capabilities of the system. However, when the user-expected time schedule does not match the system-generated, the question arises if the user will trust the system, despite lacking the knowledge if the schedule is correct. If the user trusts the automated day scheduling capability of the system, he will probably attend the appointments exactly as scheduled. However, if he does not trust this automated outcome he won't rely on it and will question the plan.

Therefore, the goal should be to detect those critical situations in HCI and to react appropriately. If we take a look at how humans detect and handle critical situations, we can conclude that they use contextual information combined with interpreted multimodal body analysis (e.g., facial expression, body posture, speech prosody) for detection and usually some sort of explanation to

Goals	Details
Transparency	How was the systems answer reached?
Justification	Explain the motives of the answer?
Relevance	Why is the answer a relevant answer?
Conceptualization	Clarify the meaning of concepts
Learning	Learn something about the domain

Table 1: Goals of explanation after (Sørmo and Cassens, 2004). These goals subsume different kinds of explanation as e.g., why, why-not, what-if, how-to explanations

clarify the process of reasoning (i.e. increasing transparency and understandability). As even humans are sometimes insecure about judging the dialog partner and to decide whether and which type of reaction would be appropriate, it seems valid that a technical system will not overcome this issue of uncertainty. Therefore, we assume that the transfer of this problem to a technical system can only be handled effectively by incorporating uncertainty and thus using a probabilistic model. In the remainder of this paper, we will first elaborate how to react to not understandable situations and secondly present how to incorporate these findings into a multimodal dialogue system using a probabilistic model.

2 Coping with Incomprehensible Situations

Analogous to human-human interaction providing explanations in not understandable situations in HCI can reduce the loss of trust (Glass et al., 2008). However, HCT is not a one-dimensional simple concept. It may be devided into several components, which all have to be well-functioning to have the user trust a technical system. Existent studies concentrated on showing that explanations or different kinds of explanations can influence HCT in general (Lim et al., 2009). So, what is lacking currently is which explanations do influence which bases of human-computer trust.

2.1 Explanations

In general, explanations are given to clarify, change or impart knowledge. Usually the implicit idea consists of aligning the mental models of the participating parties. The mental model is the perceived representation of the real world, or in our case of the technical system and its underlying processes. In this context explanations try to establish a common ground between the parties in the sense that the technical system tries to clarify its actual model to the user. This is the attempt of aligning the user's mental model to the actual system. However, explanations do not always have the goal of aligning mental models, but can be used for other purposes as well. Analogous to human-human interaction, in human-computer interaction the sender of the explanation pursues a certain goal, with respect to the addressee, which should be achieved. The question remains, how these different goals of explanation (see table 1) map to HCT, meaning, how they influence HCT or components of it.

2.2 Human-Computer Trust

Mayer et al. (1995) define trust in human-human interaction to be "the extent to which one party is willing to depend on somebody or something, in a given situation with a feeling of relative security, even though negative consequences are possible". For HCI trust can be defined as "the attitude that an agent will help achieve an individual's goals in a situation characterized by uncertainty and vulnerability" (Lee and See, 2004). Technical Systems which serve as intelligent assistants with the purpose of helping the user in complex as well as in critical situations seem to be very dependent on an intact HCT relationship. However, trust is multi-dimensional and consists of several bases. For human relationships, Mayer et al. defined three levels that build the bases of trust: ability, integrity and benevolence. The same holds for HCI, where HCT is a composite of several bases. For human-computer trust Madsen and Gregor (2000) constructed a hierarchical model (see figure 1) resulting in five basic constructs or so-called bases of trust, which can be divided in two general components, namely cognitive-based and affect-based bases. In short-term human-computer interaction, cognitive-based HCT components seem to be more important, because it will be easier to influence those. Perceived understandability can be seen in the sense that the human supervisor or observer can form a mental model and predict future system behavior. The perceived reliability of the system, in the usual sense of repeated, consistent functioning. And technical competence means that the system is perceived to perform the tasks accurately and correctly based on the input information. In this context it is important to mention, that as Mayer already stated, the bases of trust are separable, yet related to one another. All bases must be perceived highly for the trustee to be

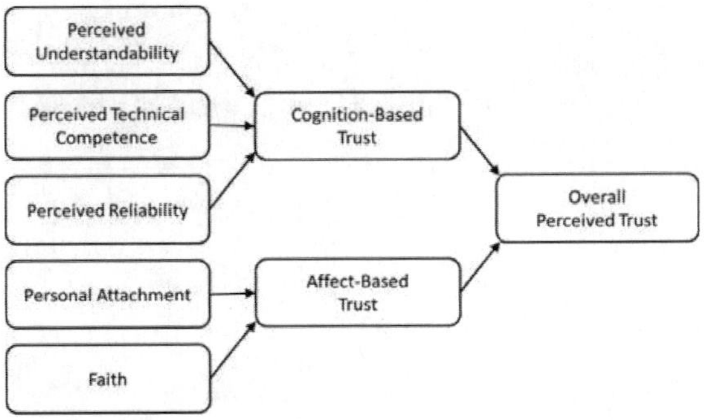

Figure 1: Human-computer trust model: Personal attachment and faith build the bases for affect-based trust. Rerceived understandability, technical competence and reliability for cognition-based trust.

deemed trustworthy. If any of the bases does not fulfill this requirement, the overall trustworthiness can suffer (Madsen and Gregor, 2000).

3 Related Work

Previous work on handling trust in technical systems was done for example by Glass et al. (2008). They investigated factors that may change the level of trust users are willing to place in adaptive agents. Among these verified findings were statements like "provide the user with the information provenance for sources used by the system", "intelligently modulating the granularity of feedback based on context- and user-modeling" or "supply the user with access to information about the internal workings of the system". However, what is missing in Glass et al.'s work is the idea of rating the different methods to uphold HCT in general and the use of a complex HCT model. Other related work was for example done by Lim et al. (2009) on how different kinds of explanations can improve the intelligibility of context-aware intelligent systems. They concentrate on the effect of Why, Why-not, How-to and What-if explanations on trust and understanding system's actions or reactions. The results showed that Why and Why-not explanations were the best kind of explanation to increase the user's understanding of the system, though trust was only increase by providing Why explanations. Drawbacks of this study were that they did only concentrate on understanding the system and trusting the system in general and did not consider that HCT is on the one hand not only influenced by the user's understanding of the system and on the other hand that if one base of trust is flawed, the HCT in general will be damaged (Mayer et al., 1995).

Regarding the issue of trusting a technical system or its actions and reactions related work exists for example on "credibility" (Fogg and Tseng, 1999). However, this term developed in the web community focusing on the believability of external sources. The term trust is used in the web research community as well as in work on "trust in automation". However, as Fogg stated himself later (Tseng and Fogg, 1999) credibility should be called believability and trust-in-automation should be called dependability to reduce the missunderstandings. In this work we use the term human-computer trust and its model by Madsen and Gregor (2000) subsuming both terms.

4 Experiment on Explanation Effectiveness

The insight that human-computer trust is not a simple but complex construct and the lack of directed methods to influence components of HCT motivated us to conduct an experiment which tried to overcome some of these issues. The use of explanations to influence HCT bases in a directed and not arbitrary way, depends on whether an effective mapping of explanation goals to HCT bases can be found. This means, that we have to identify which goal of explanation influences which base of trust in the most effective way. Therefore, the goal was to change undirected strategies to handle HCT issues into directed and well-founded ones, substantiating the choice and goal of explanation.

For that we conducted a web-based study inducing events to create not understandable or not expected situations and then compared the effects of the different goals of explanations on the HCT-bases. For our experiment we concentrated on justification and transparency explanations. Justifications are the most obvious goal an explanation can pursue. The main idea of this goal is to provide support for and increase confidence in given system advices or actions. The goal of transparency is to increase the users understanding in how the system works and reasons. This can help the user to change his perception of the system from a black-box to a system the user can comprehend. Thereby, the user can build a mental model of the system and its underlying reasoning processes.

The participants in the experiment where acquired by using flyers in the university as well as through facebook. The age of the participants was in a range from 14 to 61, with the mean being 24,1. Gender wise, the distribution was 59% (male) to 41% (female), with most of the participants being students. For the participation the students did receive a five euro voucher for a famous online store. However, this was only granted when finishing the complete experiment. Therefore, participants dropping out of the experiment would waive the right on the voucher.

4.1 Set-Up

The main objective of the participants to organize four parties for friends or relatives in a web-based environment. This means that they had to use the browser at home or the university to organize for example, the music, select the type and amount of food or order drinks. Each party was described by an initial screen depicting the key data for the party. This included which tasks had to be accomplished and how many people were expected to join (see figure 2). Each task was implemented as a single web-page, with the goal to organize one part of the party (i.e., dinner, drinks, or champagne reception). The user had to choose from several drop-down menus which item should be ordered for the party and in what number. For example, the user had to order the components of the dinner (see figure 3). When an entry inside a drop-down menu was chosen, the system gave an advice on how much of this would be needed to satisfy the needs of one guest. Additionally, before the participant could move on to the next task, the orders were checked by the system. The system would output whether the user had selected too much, too little or the right amount and only if everything was alright could proceed to the next task. The experiment consisted in total of four rounds. The first two rounds were meant to go smoothly and were supposed to get the subject used to the system and by that building a mental model of it. After the first two rounds a HCT questionnaire was presented to the user. As expected the user has built a relationship with the system by gaining an understanding of the systems processes. The next two rounds were meant to influence the HCT-relationship negative with unexpected external events. These unexpected, and incongruent to the user's mental model, system events were influencing pro-actively the decisions

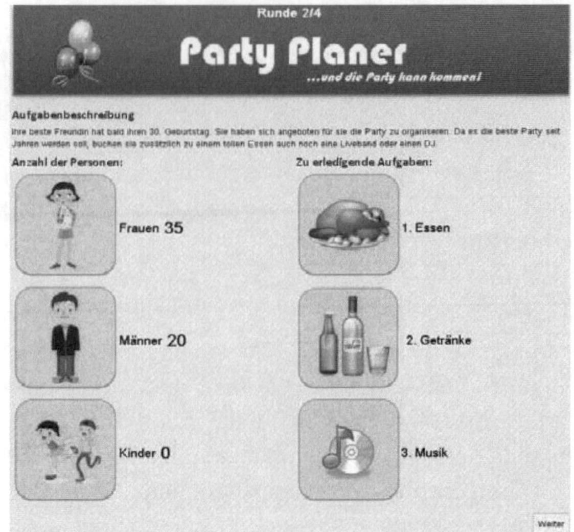

Figure 2: General information on the party. How many people plan to attend the event and what type of tasks have to be accomplished.

and solutions the user made to solve the task. This means, without warning, the user was overruled by the system and either simply informed by this change, or was presented an additional justification or transparency explanation as seen in figure 3. In this figure we can see that the user's order ('Bestellungsliste') was changed pro-actively because of an external event. Here the attendance of some participants was cancelled in the reservation system, thus the system did intervene. This pro-active change was explained at the bottom of the web-page by, in this case, providing a justification ('The order was changed by the system, because the number of attending persons decreased'). The matching transparency explanation would not only provide a reason, but explain how the system answer was reached ('Due to recent events the order was changed by the system. The order volume has been reduced, because several persons canceled their attendance in the registration system.'). Events like this occurred several times in the rounds 3 and 4 of the party planning.

4.2 Results

139 starting participants were distributed among the three test groups (no explanation, transparency, justifications). 98 accomplished round 2, reaching the point until the external events were induced and 59 participants completed the experiment. The first main result was that 47% from the group receiving no explanations quit during

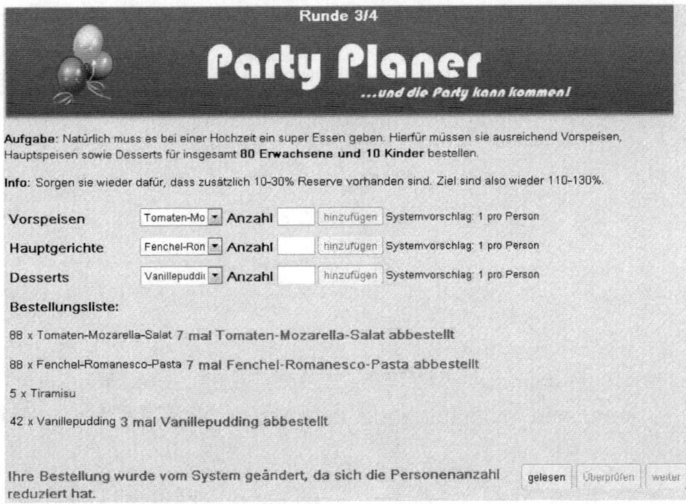

Figure 3: This screenshot shows one of the tasks the user has to accomplish. In this case dinner ('Hauptgerichte') including entree ('Vorspeisen') and desserts has to be ordered.

the critical rounds 3 and 4. However, if explanations were presented only 33% (justifications) and 35% (transparency) did quit. This means that eventhough the participants would encounter negative consequences of losing the reward money, they did drop out of the experiment. Therefore, we can state that the use of explanations in incomprehensible and not expected situations can help to keep the human-computer interaction running. The main results from the HCT-questionnaires can be seen in figure 4. The data states that providing no explanations in rounds three and four resulted in a decrease in several bases of trust. Therefore, we can conclude that the external events did indeed result in our planned negative change in trust. *Perceived understandability* diminished on average over the people questioned by 1.2 on a Likert scale with a range from 1 to 5 when providing no explanation at all compared to only 0.4 when providing *transparency* explanations (no explanation vs. transparency $t(34)=-3.557$ $p<0.001$), and on average by 0.5 with *justifications* (no explanation vs. justifications $t(36)=-2.023$ $p<0.045$). Omitting explanations resulted in an average decrease of 0.9 for the *perceived reliability*, with transparency explanations in a decrease of 0.4 and for *justifications* in a decrease of 0.6 (no explanation vs. transparency $t(34)=-2.55$ $p<0.015$).

These results support our hypotheses that transparency explanations can help to reduce the negative effects of trust loss regarding the user's perceived understandability and reliability of the system in incomprehensible and unexpected situations. Especially for the base of understandability, meaning the prediction of future outcomes, transparency explanations fulfill their purpose in a good way. Additionally, they seem to help with the perception of a reliable, consistent system. The results show that it is worthwhile to augment ongoing dialogs with explanations to maintain HCT.

While analyzing the data we did not find any statistically significant differences between providing transparency and justification explanations. However, this could be due to limited differences in the goals of explanation. Usually, the transparency explanations in the experiment were including more information on what happened inside the system, and how the system did recognize the external event (e.g., the reduction of attending persons). In future experiments we will try to distinguish those two goals of explanations more from each other. For example, the justification for reduce attendance to an event can be changed to something like 'The order was changed by the system, because otherwise you would have too much food' instead of 'The order was changed by the system, because the number of attending persons decreased' and by that making it more different from the transparency explanation ('Due to recent events the order was changed by the system. The order volume has been reduced, because several persons canceled their attendance in the registration system.'). In the following, we will describe how this is used in our developed explanation aug-

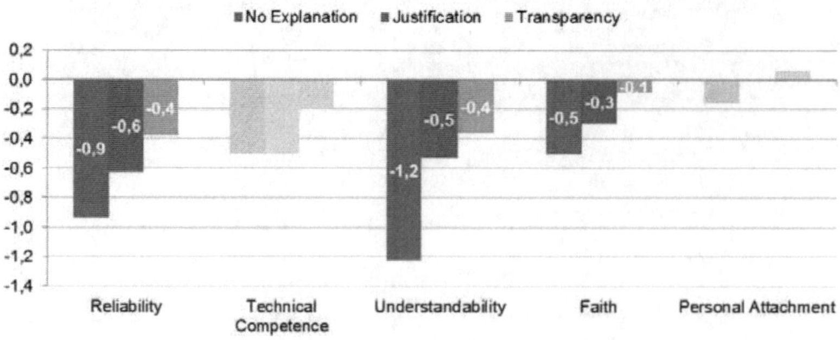

Figure 4: This figure shows the changes of HCT bases from round 2 to round 4. The scale was a 5 point likert scale with e. g., 1 the system being not understandable at all and 5 the opposite.

mentation architecture (see figure 5).

5 Implementation

The augmentation of the dialog is done using two different kinds of dialog models. On the one hand we are using a classic dialog model based on a finite-state machine approach for the task-oriented part of the dialog. On the other hand a planner (Müller et al., 2012) is used to generate from a POMDP a decision tree. This POMDP is used only for the augmentation of the task-oriented part of the dialog with explanations. The communication between each module of the architecture is controlled by a XML-based message-oriented middleware (Schröder, 2010), using a publish-subscribe system to distribute the XML-messages. In order to decide when to induce additional explanations, on one hand critical situations in HCI have to be recognized and on the other hand, if necessary the appropriate type of explanation has to be given. Obviously, recognizing those situations cannot be done solely by using information coming from interaction and its history. Multimodal input as speech recognition accuracy, facial expressions or any other sensor information can help to improve the accuracy of recognizing critical moments in HCI. However, mapping sensor input to semantic information is usually done by classifiers and those classifiers convey a certain amount of probabilistic inaccuracy which has to be handled. Therefore, a decision model has to be able to handle probabilistic information in a suitable manner.

5.1 Probabilistic Decision Model

For the problem representation when and how to react, a so-called partially observable Markov decision process (POMDP) was chosen and formalized in the Relational Dynamic Influence Diagram Language (RDDL) (Sanner, 2010). RDDL is a uniform language which allows an efficient description of POMDPs by representing its constituents (actions, observations, belief state) with variables. Formally, a POMDP consists of a set S of world states, a set A of system actions, and a set O of possible observations the system can make. Further, transition probabilities $P(s'|s,a)$ describe the dynamics of the environment, i.e., the probability of the successor world state being s' when action a is executed in state s. The observation probabilities $P(o|s',a)$ represent the sensors of the system in terms of the probability of making observation o when executing a resulted in successor world state s'. Each time the system executes an action a, it receives a reward $R(s,a)$ which depends on the world state s the action was executed in. The overall goal of the system is to maximize the accumulated reward it receives over a fixed number of time steps. (For more information on POMDPs, see Kaelbling et al. (1998).)

A POMDP is then used by a planner (Silver and Veness, 2010; Müller et al., 2012) to search for a policy that determines the system's behavior. This policy is, e.g., represented as a decision tree that recommends the most suitable action based on the system's previous actions and observations. For example, a policy for a POMDP that models HCI with respect to HCT, can thus represent a decision tree which represents a guideline for a dialog flow which ensures an intact HCT-relationship.

The RDDL model is a probabilistic representation of the domain, which determines when and how to augment the dialog with explanations at run-time. Each observation o consists of the du-

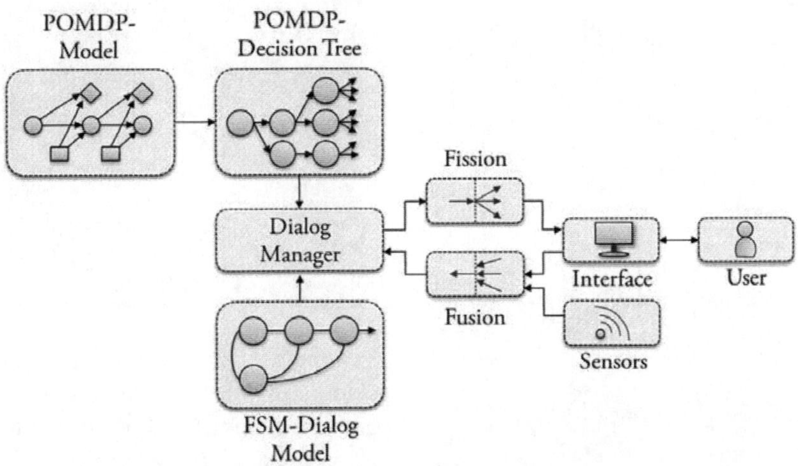

Figure 5: The architecture consists of two dialog models, a fission and fusion engine, sensors as well as the multimodal interface representation to interact with the user. The dialog models can be seperated in a task-oriented FSM-dialog model and into a POMDP-based decision tree for explanation augmentation. This decision tree is generated from a POMDP-model by a planner.

ration of interaction for each dialog step as well as the semantic information of the input (i.e., which action in the interface was triggered by speech, touch or point-and-click interaction). Those types of interaction can bring along uncertainty (e.g., speech recognition rate). The state s in terms of HCT is modeled by its respective bases, namely understandability, technical-competence, reliability, faith and personal attachment. The system actions A are the dialogs presented to the user. These are the different goals of explanations (justification, transparency, conceptualization, relevance and learning) as well as the task-oriented part of the dialog represented by a so-called *communicative function(c)* with c from set C (e.g., question, inform, answer, offer, request, instruct). This means, that in the POMDP only the communicative function of the task-oriented dialogs is represented without the specific content.

The transition probabilities are defined as *conditional probability functions* (CPFs) and model user behavior dependent on the system's actions and the user's current HCT values. Basically, conditional functions are defined using *if else* for all wanted cases. For example, we defined that the user's understanding in s' will probably be high if a transparency explanation was the last system action. When the user's understanding is indeed high in s', the observation will probably be that the user clicked *okay*, and the time he took for the interaction was around his usual amount taken for explanations. From this observation, a planner can infer that the transparency explanation indeed increased the user's understanding.

Now, the quest is to define the reward function $R(s, a)$ in a way that it leads to an optimal flow of actions. I.e., the system should receive a penalty when the bases of trust do not remain intact, and actions should incur a cost so that the system only executes them when trust is endangered. However, because POMDPs tend to be become very quick very complex, we chose to seperate the task-oriented dialog from the additional dialog augmentation with explanations when needed.

5.2 Dialog Augmentation Process

The task-oriented dialog is modeled as a classic finite-state machine (FSM). Each dialog action has several interaction possibilities, each leading to another specified dialog action. Each of those dialog action is represented as POMDP action a as part of C (*communicative function(c)*). As already mentioned, only the communicative function is modeled to reduce the complexity in the POMDP.

The HCI is started using the FSM-based dialog model approach and uses the POMDP to check whether the user's trust or components of the user's trust are endangered. At run-time the next action in the FSM is compared to the one determined by the POMDP (see figure 6). This means, that if the next action in the FSM is not the same as the one planned by the POMDP, the dia-

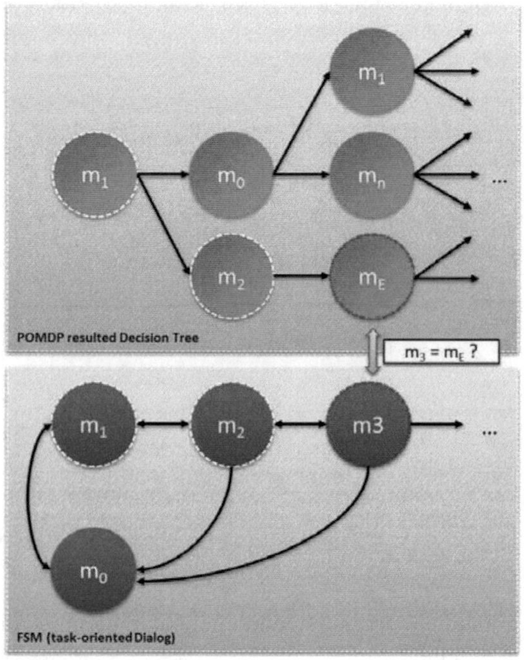

Figure 6: This figure shows the comparison of FSM to Decision Tree. The next action m_3 in the FSM does not correspond to the one endorsed by the POMDP Decision Tree. Therefore, the dialog will be augmented by explanation action m_E.

log flow is interrupted, and the ongoing dialog is augmented by the proposed explanation. For example, if the user is presented currently a communicative function of type *inform* and the decision tree recommends to provide a transparency explanation, because the understanding and reliability are probably false, the originally next step in the FSM is postponed and first the explanation is presented. The other way around, if the next action in the FSM is subsumed by the one scheduled by the POMDP, the system does not need to intervene. For example, if the next FSM-action is to instruct the user about how to connect *amplifier* and *receiver* and the POMDP would recommend an action of type communicative function *instruct*, no dialog augmentation is needed.

6 Dialog Interface

Each dialog action in the FSM as well as the explanation dialogs are represented by a so-called dialog goal, which is allocated on the one hand a type of communicative function c. On the other hand the dialog content is composed of multiple information objects referencing so-called *information IDs* in the information model. Each information object can consist of different types (e.g., text, audio, and pictures). For interface presentation the dialog goal is passed to the fission which selects and combines the information objects at runtime by a fission sub-component to compose the user interface in a user- and situation-adaptive way (Honold et al., 2012). In figure 7 we can see a typical interface for a transmitted dialog goal in which the user can interact via speech, touch or GUI.

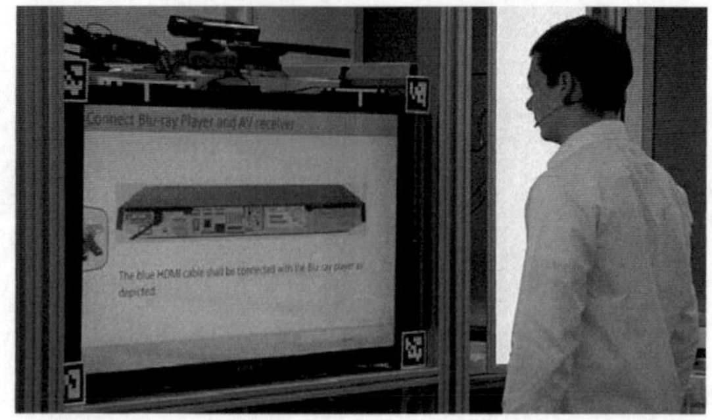

Figure 7: A typical output presentation of the fission component of a dialog goal. Here the user gets instruction on how to connect the *BluRay-Player* with an *HDMI* cable.

7 Conclusion and Future Work

In this paper we showed the necessity to deal with critical situations in HCI in a probabilistic approach. The advantage of our approach is that the designer still can define a FSM-based task-oriented dialog. Usually most commercial systems are still based on such approaches. However, expanding the dialog by a probabilistic decision model seems to be a valuable choice. Our experiment on the influence of explanations on HCT has clearly shown, that it is worthwhile to augment the ongoing dialog by transparency or justification explanations for an intact HCT relationship. In the future we will run experiments on how effective the hybrid FSM-POMDP approach is compared to classic as well as POMDP dialog systems.

Acknowledgment

This work was supported by the Transregional Collaborative Research Centre SFB/TRR 62 "Companion-Technology for Cognitive Technical Systems" which is funded by the German Research Foundation (DFG).

References

B. J. Fogg and Hsiang Tseng. 1999. The elements of computer credibility. In *Proceedings of the SIGCHI conference on Human Factors in Computing Systems*, CHI '99, pages 80–87, New York, NY, USA. ACM.

Alyssa Glass, Deborah L. McGuinness, and Michael Wolverton. 2008. Toward establishing trust in adaptive agents. In *IUI '08: Proceedings of the 13th international conference on Intelligent user interfaces*, pages 227–236, NY, USA. ACM.

Frank Honold, Felix Schüssel, and Michael Weber. 2012. Adaptive probabilistic fission for multimodal systems. In *Proceedings of the 24th Australian Computer-Human Interaction Conference*, OzCHI '12, pages 222–231.

L. P. Kaelbling, M. L. Littman, and A. R. Cassandra. 1998. Planning and acting in partially observable stochastic domains. *Artificial Intelligence*, pages 99–134.

John D. Lee and Katrina A. See. 2004. Trust in automation: Designing for appropriate reliance. *Human Factors*, 46(1):50–80.

Brian Y. Lim, Anind K. Dey, and Daniel Avrahami. 2009. Why and why not explanations improve the intelligibility of context-aware intelligent systems. In *Proceedings of the SIGCHI Conference on Human Factors in Computing Systems*, CHI '09, pages 2119–2128, NY, USA. ACM.

Maria Madsen and Shirley Gregor. 2000. Measuring human-computer trust. In *Proceedings of the 11 th Australasian Conference on Information Systems*, pages 6–8.

Roger C. Mayer, James H. Davis, and F. David Schoorman. 1995. An Integrative Model of Organizational Trust. *The Academy of Management Review*, 20(3):709–734.

B M Muir. 1992. Trust in automation: Part i. theoretical issues in the study of trust and human intervention in automated systems. In *Ergonomics*, pages 1905–1922.

Felix Müller, Christian Späth, Thomas Geier, and Susanne Biundo. 2012. Exploiting expert knowledge in factored POMDPs. In *Proceedings of the 20th European Conference on Artificial Intelligence (ECAI 2012)*, pages 606–611.

Raja Parasuraman and Victor Riley. 1997. Humans and automation: Use, misuse, disuse, abuse. *Human Factors: The Journal of the Human Factors and Ergonomics Society*, 39(2):230–253, June.

Scott Sanner. 2010. Relational dynamic influence diagram language (rddl): Language description. http://users.cecs.anu.edu.au/ ssanner/IPPC2011/RDDL.pdf.

Marc Schröder. 2010. The semaine api: Towards a standards-based framework for building emotion-oriented systems. *Advances in Human-Machine Interaction*, (319406):21.

D. Silver and J. Veness. 2010. Monte-carlo planning in large POMDPs. In *NIPS*, pages 2164–2172.

F. Sørmo and J. Cassens. 2004. Explanation goals in case-based reasoning. In *Proceedings of the 7th European Conference on Case-Based Reasoning*, pages 165–174.

Shawn Tseng and B. J. Fogg. 1999. Credibility and computing technology. *Commun. ACM*, 42(5):39–44, May.

Learning non-cooperative dialogue behaviours

Ioannis Efstathiou
Interaction Lab
Heriot-Watt University
ie24@hw.ac.uk

Oliver Lemon
Interaction Lab
Heriot-Watt University
o.lemon@hw.ac.uk

Abstract

Non-cooperative dialogue behaviour has been identified as important in a variety of application areas, including education, military operations, video games and healthcare. However, it has not been addressed using statistical approaches to dialogue management, which have always been trained for co-operative dialogue. We develop and evaluate a statistical dialogue agent which learns to perform non-cooperative dialogue moves in order to complete its own objectives in a stochastic trading game. We show that, when given the ability to perform both cooperative and non-cooperative dialogue moves, such an agent can learn to bluff and to lie so as to win games more often – against a variety of adversaries, and under various conditions such as risking penalties for being caught in deception. For example, we show that a non-cooperative dialogue agent can learn to win an additional 15.47% of games against a strong rule-based adversary, when compared to an optimised agent which cannot perform non-cooperative moves. This work is the first to show how an agent can learn to use non-cooperative dialogue to effectively meet its own goals.

1 Introduction

Research in automated conversational systems has almost exclusively focused on the case of cooperative dialogue, where a dialogue system's core goal is to assist humans in particular tasks, such as buying airline tickets (Walker et al., 2001) or finding a place to eat (Young et al., 2010). Gricean cooperative principles have been shown to emerge from multi-agent decision theory, in a language task modelled using Decentralised Partially Observable Markov Decision Processes (Vogel et al., 2013a), and in related work conversational implicature was argued to be a by-product of agents who maximise joint utility (Vogel et al., 2013b).

However, non-cooperative dialogues, where an agent may act to satisfy its own goals rather than those of other participants, are also of practical and theoretical interest (Georgila and Traum, 2011), and the game-theoretic underpinnings of non-Gricean behaviour are actively being investigated (Asher and Lascarides, 2008). For example, it may be advantageous for an automated agent not to be fully cooperative when trying to gather information from a human, and when trying to persuade, argue, or debate, when trying to sell them something, when trying to detect illegal activity (for example on internet chat sites), or in the area of believable characters in video games and educational simulations (Georgila and Traum, 2011; Shim and Arkin, 2013). Another arena in which non-cooperative dialogue behaviour is desirable is in negotiation (Traum, 2008), where hiding information (and even outright lying) can be advantageous. Furthermore, deception is considered to be an essential part of successful military operations. According to Sun Tzu "All warfare is based on deception" and Machiavelli clearly states in *The Discourses* that "Although deceit is detestable in all other things, yet in the conduct of war it is laudable and honorable"(Arkin, 2010). Indeed, Dennett argues that deception capability is required for higher-order intentionality in AI (Dennett, 1997).

A complementary research direction in recent years has been the use of machine learning methods to automatically optimise *cooperative* dialogue management - i.e. the decision of what dialogue move to make next in a conversation, in order to maximise an agent's overall long-term expected utility, which is usually defined in terms of meeting a user's goals (Young et al., 2010; Rieser and Lemon, 2011). This research has shown how robust and efficient dialogue management strategies can be learned from data, but has only addressed the case of cooperative dialogue. These approaches use Reinforcement Learning with a reward function that gives positive feedback to the agent only when it meets the user's goals.

An example of the type of non-cooperative dialogue behaviour which we are generating in this work is given by agent B in the following dialogue:

A: "I will give you a sheep if you give me a wheat"
B: "No"
B: "I really need rock" [B actually needs wheat]
A: "OK... I'll give you a wheat if you give me rock"
B: "OK"

Here, A is deceived into providing the wheat that B actually needs, because A believes that B needs rock rather than wheat. Similar behaviour can be observed in trading games such as Settlers of Catan (Afantenos et al., 2012).

1.1 Non-cooperative dialogue and implicature

Our trading dialogues are linguistically cooperative (according to the Cooperative Principle (Grice, 1975)) since their linguistic meaning is clear from both sides and successful information exchange occurs. Non-linguistically though they are non-cooperative, since they they aim for personal goals. Hence they violate Attardo's Perlocutionary Cooperative Principle (PCP) (Attardo, 1997). In our non-cooperative environment, the manipulative utterances such as "I really need sheep" can imply that "I don't really need any of the other two resources", as both of the players are fully aware that three different resources exist in total and more than one is needed to win the game, so therefore they serve as scalar implicatures (Vogel et al., 2013b). Hence we will show that the LA learns how to include scalar implicatures in its dialogue to successfully deceive its adversary by being cooperative on the locutionary level and non-cooperative on the perlocutionary level.

1.2 Structure of the paper

In this paper we investigate whether a learning agent endowed with non-cooperative dialogue moves and a 'personal' reward function can learn how to perform non-cooperative dialogue. Note that the reward will not be given for performing non-cooperative moves themselves, but only for winning trading games. We therefore explore whether the agent can learn the advantages of being non-cooperative in dialogue, in a variety of settings. This is similar to (Vogel et al., 2013a) who show how cooperativity emerges from multi-agent decision making, though in our case we show the emergence of non-cooperative dialogue behaviours.

We begin with the case of a simple but challenging 2-player trading game, which is stochastic and involves hidden information.

In section 2 we describe and motivate the trading game used in this work, and in section 3 we describe the Learning Agent. In section 4 we explain the different adversaries for experimentation, in section 5 we provide results, and in section 6 we conclude and discuss areas for future work.

2 The Trading Game

To investigate non-cooperative dialogues in a controlled setting we created a 2-player, sequential, non-zero-sum game with imperfect information called "Taikun". Motivated by the principle of Occam's razor we shaped this game as simply as possible, while including the key features of a resource trading game. The precise goal was also to implement mechanics that are not restrictive for the future of this research and therefore can be flexibly extended to capture different aspects of trading and negotiation. We call the 2 players the "adversary" and the "learning agent" (LA).

The two players can trade three kinds of resources with each other sequentially, in a 1-for-1 manner, in order to reach a specific number of resources that is their individual goal. The player who first attains their goal resources wins. Both players start the game with one resource of each type (wheat, rock, and sheep). At the beginning of each round the game updates the number of resources of both players by either removing one of them or adding two of them, thereby making the opponent's state (i.e. the cards that they hold) unobservable. In the long run, someone will eventually win even if no player ever trades. However, effective trading can provide a faster victory.

2.1 "Taikun" game characteristics

Taikun is a sequential, non-cooperative, non-zero-sum game, with imperfect information, where:

- The goal is to reach either 4 or 5 of two specific resources (4 wheat and 5 rocks for the learning agent and 4 wheat and 5 sheep for the adversary). The players share a goal resource (wheat).
- Each round consists of an update of resources turn, the learning agent's trading proposal turn (and adversary's acceptance or rejection), and finally the adversary's trading proposal turn (and LA's acceptance or rejection).
- The update turn, which is a hidden action, changes one of the resources of each player at random by +2 or -1.
- When a resource is "capped", that is if its number is 5 or more, then no update rule can be applied to it. Trading can still change its quantity though.

2.2 Actions (Trading Proposals)

Trade occurs through trading proposals that may lead to acceptance from the other player. In an agent's turn only one '1-for-1' trading proposal may occur, or nothing (7 actions in total):

1. I will do nothing
2. I will give you a wheat if you give me a rock
3. I will give you a wheat if you give me a sheep
4. I will give you a rock if you give me a wheat
5. I will give you a rock if you give me a sheep
6. I will give you a sheep if you give me a wheat
7. I will give you a sheep if you give me a rock

Agents respond by either saying "No" or "OK" in order to reject or accept the other agent's proposal.

2.3 Non-cooperative dialogue moves

In our second experiment three manipulative actions are added to the learning agent's set of actions:

1. "I really need wheat"
2. "I really need rock"
3. "I really need sheep"

The adversary believes these statements, resulting in modifying their probabilities of making certain trades.

Note that in the current model we assume that only these 3 manipulative actions potentially have an effect on the adversary's reasoning about the game. An alternative would be to allow all the trading utterances to have some manipulative power. For example the LA's uttering "I will give you a wheat if you give me a rock" could lead the adversary to believe that the LA currently needs rock. For the present work, we prefer to separate out the manipulative actions explicitly, so as to first study their effects in the presence of non-manipulative dialogue actions. In future work, we will consider the case where all trading proposals can cause adversaries to change their game strategy.

3 The Learning Agent (LA)

The game state can be represented by the learning agent's set of resources, its adversary's set of resources, and a trading proposal (if any) currently under consideration. We track up to 19 of each type of resource, and have a binary variable representing whose turn it is. Therefore there are 20 x 20 x 20 x 2 = 16,000 states.

The learning agent (LA) plays the game and learns while perceiving only its own set of resources. This initial state space can later be extended with elements of history (previous dialogue moves) and estimates of the other agent's state (e.g. beliefs about what the adversary needs).

The LA is aware of its winning condition (to obtain 4 wheat and 5 rocks) in as much as it experiences a large final reward when reaching this state. It learns how to achieve the goal state through trial-and-error exploration while playing repeated games.

The LA is modelled as a Markov Decision Process (Sutton and Barto, 1998): it observes states, selects actions according to a policy, transitions to a new state (due to the adversary's move and/or a update of resources), and receives rewards at the end of each game. This reward is then used to update the policy followed by the agent.

The rewards that were used in these experiments were 1,000 for the winning case, 500 for a draw and -100 when losing a game. The winning and draw cases have the same goal states and that would initially suggest the same reward but they can be achieved through different strategies. Experiments that we have conducted using either the above rewards or the same rewards for win and draw have verified this. The learning agent's performance is slightly better when the reward for a win is 1000 and 500 for a draw.

The LA was trained using a custom SARSA(λ) learning method (Sutton and Barto, 1998) with an initial exploration rate of 0.2 that gradually decays to 0 at the end of the training games. After experimenting with the learning parameters we found that with λ equal to 0.4 and γ equal to 0.9 we obtain the best results for our problem and therefore these values have been used in all of the experiments that follow.

4 Adversaries

We investigated performance with several different adversaries. As a baseline, we first need to know how well a LA which does not have non-cooperative moves at its disposal can perform against a rational rule-based adversary. Our hypothesis is then that a LA with additional non-cooperative moves can outperform this baseline case when the adversary becomes somewhat gullible.

A 'gullible' adversary is one who believes statements such as "I really need rock" and then acts so as to restrict the relevant resource(s) from the LA. Our experiments (see experiments 3.1-3.3) show that this gullible behaviour may originate from sound reasoning. The adversary confronts in this case a very important dilemma. It suddenly does not know if it should stay with its goal-oriented strategy (baseline) or instead it should boycott the LA's stated needed resources. A priori, both of these strategies might be equally successful, and we will show that their performances are indeed very close to each other.

4.1 Rule-based adversary: experiment 1

This strategy was designed to form a challenging rational adversary for measuring baseline performance. It cannot be manipulated at all, and non-cooperative dialogue moves will have no effect on it – it simply ignores statements like "I really need wheat".

The strict rule-based strategy of the adversary will never ask for a resource that it does not need (in this case rocks). Furthermore, if it has an available non-goal resource to give then it will offer it. It only asks for resources that it needs (goal resources: wheat and sheep). In the case where it does not have a non-goal resource (rocks) to offer then it offers a goal resource only if its quantity is more than it needs, and it asks for another goal resource if it is needed.

Following the same reasoning, when replying to the LA's trading proposals, the adversary will never agree to receive a non-goal resource (rock). It only gives a non-goal resource (rock) for another one that it needs (wheat or sheep). It also agrees to make a trade in the special case where it will give a goal resource of which it has more than it needs for another one that it still needs. This is a strong strategy that wins a significant number of games. In fact, it takes about 100,000 training games before the LA is able to start winning more games than this adversary, and a random LA policy loses 66% of games against this adversary (See Table 1, LA policy 'Random').

4.2 Gullible adversary: experiment 2

The adversary in this case retains the above strict base-line policy but it is also susceptible to the non-cooperative moves of the LA, as explained above. For example, if the LA utters "I really need rock", weights of actions which transfer rock from the adversary will decrease, and the adversary will then be less likely to give rock to the LA. Conversely, the adversary is then more likely to give the other two resources to the LA. In this way the LA has the potential to mislead the adversary into trading resources that it really needs.

4.3 The restrictive adversaries: experiments 3.1, 3.2, 3.3

Here we investigate performance against adversaries who cannot be manipulated, but their strategy is to always restrict the LA from gaining a specific type of resource. We need to explore how well a manipulated adversary (for example one who will no longer give rocks that only its opponent needs) performs. This will show us the potential advantage to be gained by manipulation and most important, it will generalise our problem by showing that the restriction (boycott) of a resource that only the opponent needs, or of a resource that both of the players need, are actually reasonably good strategies compared to the baseline case (Experiment 1). Hence, the manipulated adversary has indeed a reason for choosing to restrict resources (Experiment 2) rather than staying with its rule-based strategy. In other words it has a rational reason to become gullible and fall in the learning agent's trap.

4.4 Gullible-based adversary with risk of exposure: experiments 4.1, 4.2

Here we extend the problem to include possible negative consequences of manipulative LA actions. The adversary begins each game with a probability of detecting manipulation, that exponentially increases after every one of the LA's manipulative actions. In more detail, every time the LA performs a manipulation, there is an additional chance that the adversary notices this (starts at 1-in-10 and increases after every manipulative move, up to 100% in the case of the 10th manipulative attempt). The consequence of being detected is that the adversary will refuse to trade with the LA any further in that game (experiment 4.1), or that the adversary automatically wins the game (experiment 4.2). In these two cases there is always a risk associated with attempting to manipulate, and the LA has to learn how to balance the potential rewards with this risk.

5 Results

The LA was trained over 1.5 million games against each adversary for the cases of the rule-based (experiment 1), gullible (experiment 2) and restrictive adversaries (experiments 3.1, 3.2, 3.3). The resulting policies were tested in 20 thousand games.

For reasons of time, the LA was trained for only 35 thousand games for the case of the gullible adversary who stops trading when the LA becomes exposed (experiment 4.1), and 350 thousand games for the gullible adversary who wins the game when the LA becomes exposed (experiment 4.2). In the former case we used 2 thousand testing games and in the latter 20 thousand.

5.1 Baseline performance: Experiment 1

The LA scored a winning performance of 49.5% against 45.555% for the adversary, with 4.945% draws (Table 1), in the 20 thousand test games, see Figure 1. This represents the baseline performance that the LA is able to achieve against an adversary who cannot be manipulated at all. This shows that the game is 'solvable' as an MDP problem, and that a reinforcement learning agent can outperform a strict hand-coded adversary.

Here, the learning agent's strategy mainly focuses on offering the sheep resource that it does not need for the rocks that does need (for example $action7 > action2 > action6 > action3$ Table 2). It is also interesting to notice that the LA learnt not to use action 3 at all (gives 1 wheat that they both need for 1 sheep that only the adversary needs). Hence its frequency is 0. The actions 4 and 5 are never accepted by the adversary so their role in both of the experiments is similar to that of the action 1 (do nothing). The rejections of the adversary's trades dominate the acceptances with a ratio of 94 to 1 as our learning agent learns to become negative towards the adversarial trading proposals and therefore to prohibit its strategy.

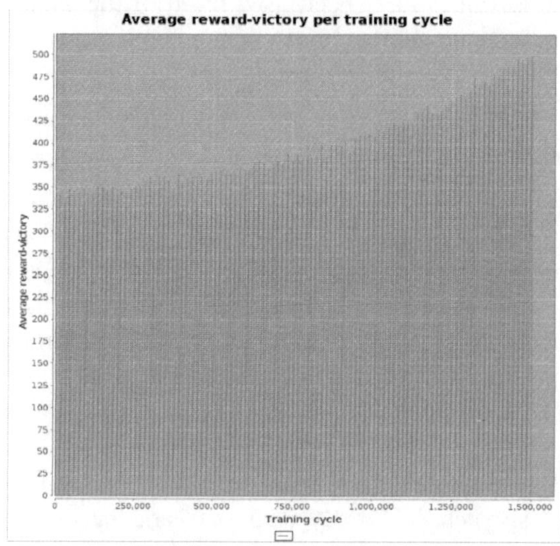

Figure 1: *Learning Agent's reward-victory graph over 1.5 million training games of Experiment 1.*

5.2 Non-cooperative actions: Experiment 2

In Experiment 2 the learning agent scored a winning performance of 59.17% against only 39.755% of its adversary, having 1.075% draws (Table 1), in the 20 thousand test games, see Figure 2.

Similarly to the previous experiment, the LA's strategy focuses again mainly on action 7, by offering the sheep resource that it does not need for rocks that it needs (Table 2). However in this case we also notice that the LA has learnt to use action 2 very often, exploiting cases where it will win by giving the wheat resource that they both need for a rock that only it needs. This is a result of its current manipulation capabilities. The high frequency manipulative actions 8 ("I really need wheat") and 9 ("I really need rock") assist in deceiving its adversary by hiding information, therefore significantly reinforcing its strategy as they both indirectly result in gaining sheep that only the adversary needs (experiment 3.2).

Rejections to adversarial trading offers over the

acceptances were again the majority in this experiment. However in this case they are significantly fewer than before, with a ratio of only 2.5 to 1, as our learning agent is now more eager to accept some trades because it has triggered them itself by appropriately manipulating its adversary.

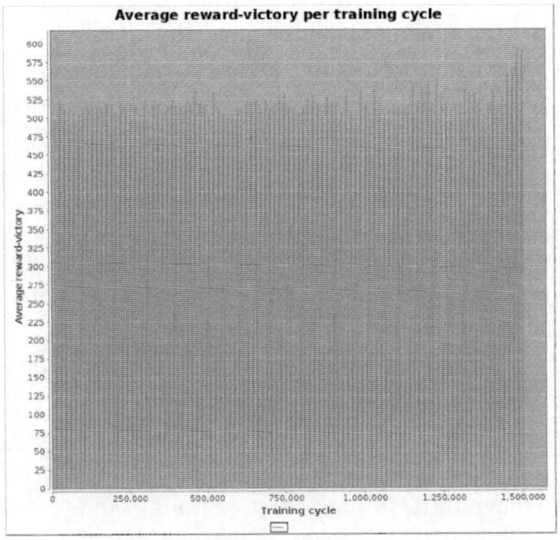

Figure 2: *Learning Agent's reward-victory graph in 1.5 million training games of Experiment 2.*

In Experiment 1 the LA's dominating strategy (mainly based on requiring the rocks resource from its adversary) provides it with a difference in winning performance of $+3.945\%$. In Experiment 2 the adversary, further being deceived by the learning agent's hiding information actions, loses 19.415% more often than the learning agent.

Action number	**Exp. 1** frequency	**Exp. 2** frequency
1. Do nothing	81969	144727
2. Give wheat for rock	8077	46028
3. Give wheat for sheep	**0**	10358
4. Give rock for wheat	80578	62874
5. Give rock for sheep	78542	55627
6. Give sheep for wheat	6429	24687
7. Give sheep for rock	**23888**	31132
8. I really need wheat	-	**68974**
9. I really need rock	-	**87123**
10. I really need sheep	-	18

Table 2: *Frequencies of LA actions.*

Table 2 shows that the LA's strategy in Experiment 1 mainly focuses on requiring rocks from the adversary by offering sheep (for example action 7 > action 2 or 6). In Experiment 2 the agent's strategy is similar. However, it is now enhanced by the frequent use of the manipulative actions 8 and 9 (both hide information). The LA gathers mainly sheep (8 and 9) through its manipulation and then wheat (9 > 8) that the adversary needs to win. It also offers them 'selectively' back (2 and 7) for rock that only it needs in order to win.

5.3 Restrictive adversaries: Experiment 3

In experiment 3 the LA uses no manipulative actions. It is the same LA as that of Experiment 1. It is trained and then tested against 3 different types of restrictive adversaries. The first one (Experiment 3.1) never gives wheat, the second one (Experiment 3.2) never gives rocks, and the third one never gives sheep (Experiment 3.3). They all act randomly regarding the other 2 resources which are not restricted. In the first case (adversary restricts wheat that they both need), the LA scored a winning performance of 50.015% against 47.9% of its adversary, having 2.085% draws in the 20 thousand test games. In the second case (adversary restricts rocks that the LA only needs), the LA scored a winning performance of 53.375% against 44.525% of its adversary, having 2.1% draws in the 20 thousand test games. In the third case (adversary restricts sheep that only itself needs), the LA scored a winning performance of 62.21% against 35.13% of its adversary, having 2.66% draws in the 20 thousand test games. These results show that restricting the resource that only the opponent needs (i.e. LA only needs rocks) and especially the resource that they both need (i.e. wheat) can be as effective as the strategy followed by the rule-based adversary (see Table 1). The difference in the performances for the former case (rock) is +8.85% and for the latter (wheat) only +2.115%. That means the adversary has indeed a reason to believe that boycotting its opponent's resources could be a winning opposing strategy, motivating its gullibility in experiment 2 (section 5.2).[1]

5.4 Non-cooperative actions and risk of exposure: Experiment 4.1 (adversary stops trading)

In this case when the LA is exposed by the adversary then the latter does not trade for the rest of the

[1] Further experiments showed that having the same number of goal resources (i.e. both need 4 of their own goal resources, rather than 5) still produces similar results.

Exp.	Learning Agent policy	Adversary policy	LA wins	Adversary wins	Draws
	Random	Baseline	32%	66%	2%
1	SARSA	Baseline	49.5%	45.555%	4.945%
2	SARSA + Manipulation	Baseline + Gullible	59.17%*	39.755%	1.075%
3.1	SARSA	Restrict wheat	50.015%*	47.9%	2.085%
3.2	SARSA	Restrict rock	53.375%*	44.525%	2.1%
3.3	SARSA	Restrict sheep	62.21%*	35.13%	2.66%
4.1	SARSA + Manipulation	Basel. + Gull. + Expos.(no trade)	53.2%*	45.15%	1.65%
4.2	SARSA + Manipulation	Basel. + Gull. + Expos.(win game)	36.125%	61.15%	2.725%

Table 1: *Performance (% wins) in testing games, after training. (*= significant improvement over baseline,* $p < 0.05$*)*

game. The LA scored a winning performance of 53.2% against 45.15% for this adversary, having 1.65% draws in the 2 thousand test games, see Figure 3. This shows that the LA managed to locate a successful strategy that balances the use of the manipulative actions and the normal trading actions with the risk of exposure (Table 3). In more detail, the strategy that the LA uses here makes frequent use of the manipulative actions 8 ("I really need wheat") and 9 ("I really need rock") again which mainly result in the collection of sheep that only its adversary needs to win. Restriction of a resource that the opponent only needs is a good strategy (as our experiment 3.2 suggests) and the LA managed to locate that and exploit it. The next highest frequency action (excluding actions 4 and 5 that mostly lead to rejection from the adversary as it also follows its rule-based strategy) is 7 ("I will give you a sheep if you give me a rock") that is exclusively based on the LA's goal and along with 6 they 'selectively' give back the sheep for goal resources. Rejections to adversary's proposals over the acceptances were in a ratio of approximately 4 to 1. The LA is quite eager (in contrast to the baseline case of experiment 1) to accept the adversary's proposals as it has already triggered them by itself through deception.

5.5 Non-cooperative actions and risk of exposure: Experiment 4.2 (adversary wins the game)

In this case if the LA becomes exposed by the adversary then the latter wins the game. The LA scored a winning performance of 36.125% against 61.15% of its adversary, having 2.725% draws in 20 thousand test games, see Figure 4. It is the only case where the LA so far has not yet found a strategy that wins more often than its adversary, and therefore in future work a larger set of training games will be used. Note that this was only trained for 350 thousand games – we expect better performance with more training. In fact, here we would expect a good policy to perform at least as well as experiment 1, which would be the case of learning never to use manipulative actions, since they are so dangerous. Indeed, a good policy could be to lie (action 10) only once, at the start of a dialogue, and then to follow the policy of experiment 2. This would lead to a winning percentage of about 49% (the 59% of experiment 2 minus a 10% loss for the chance of being detected after 1 manipulation).

The LA has so far managed to locate a strategy that again balances the use of the manipulative actions and that of the normal ones with the risk of losing the game as a result of exposure (Table 3). According to Figure 4 we notice that the LA gradually learns how to do that. However its performance is not yet desirable, as it is still only slightly better than that of the Random case against the Baseline (Table 1). It is interesting though to see that the strategy that the LA uses here makes frequent use of the action 10 ("I really need sheep") that lies. On the other hand, the actions 8 and 9 are almost non-existent. That results in accepting wheat that they both need and rocks that it only needs, showing that the main focus of the manipulation is on the personal goal. The LA has learned so far in this case that by lying it can get closer to its personal goal. Rejections to adversary's proposals over the acceptances resulted in a ratio of approximately 1.7 to 1, meaning that the LA is again quite eager to accept the adversarial trading proposals that it has triggered already by itself through lying.

We report further results on this scenario in an updated version of this paper (Efstathiou and

Lemon, 2014).

Action number	Exp. 4.1 frequency	Exp. 4.2 frequency
1 Do nothing	8254	74145
2 Give wheat for rock	2314	3537
3 Give wheat for sheep	1915	4633
4 Give rock for wheat	5564	46120
5 Give rock for sheep	4603	57031
6 Give sheep for wheat	2639	2737
7 Give sheep for rock	3132	3105
8 I really need wheat	**7200**	4
9 I really need rock	**7577**	7
10 I really need sheep	548	**19435**

Table 3: *Frequencies of LA actions.*

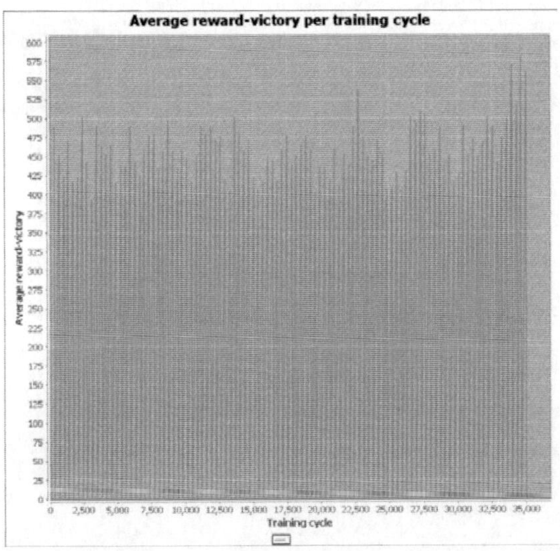

Figure 3: *Learning Agent's reward-victory graph in 35 thousand training games of Experiment 4.1.*

6 Conclusion & Future Work

We showed that a statistical dialogue agent can learn to perform non-cooperative dialogue moves in order to enhance its performance in trading negotiations. This demonstrates that non-cooperative dialogue strategies can emerge from statistical approaches to dialogue management, similarly to the emergence of cooperative behaviour from multi-agent decision theory (Vogel et al., 2013a).

In future work we will investigate more complex non-cooperative situations. For example a real dialogue example of this kind is taken from

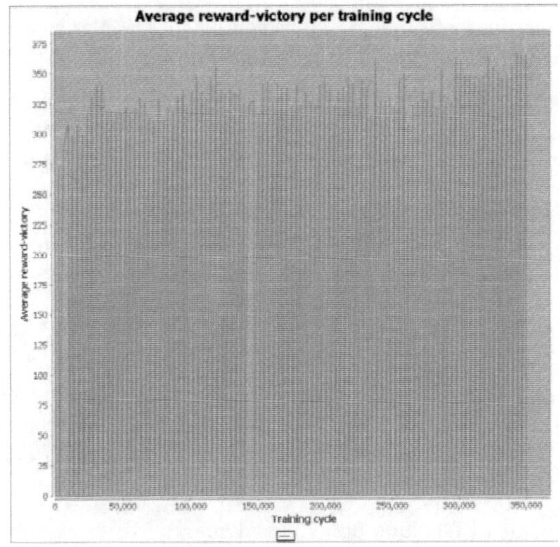

Figure 4: *Learning Agent's reward-victory graph in 350 thousand training games of Experiment 4.2.*

the "Settlers of Catan" game corpus (Afantenos et al., 2012):

- A: Do you have rock?
- B: I've got lots of wheat [in fact, B has a rock]
- A: I'll give you 2 clay for a rock
- B: How about 2 clay for a wheat?
- A: I'll give 1 clay for 3 wheat
- B: Ok, it's a deal.

In future more adversarial strategies will also be applied, and the learning problem will be made more complex (e.g. studying 'when' and 'how often' an agent should try to manipulate its adversary). Alternative methods will also be considered such as adversarial belief modelling with the application of interactive POMDPs (Partially Observable Markov Decision Processes) (Gmytrasiewicz and Doshi, 2005). The long-term goal of this work is to develop intelligent agents that will be able to assist (or even replace) users in interaction with other human or artificial agents in various non-cooperative settings (Shim and Arkin, 2013), such as education, military operations, virtual worlds and healthcare.

References

Stergos Afantenos, Nicholas Asher, Farah Benamara, Anais Cadilhac, Cedric Degremont, Pascal Denis, Markus Guhe, Simon Keizer, Alex Lascarides, Oliver Lemon, Philippe Muller, Soumya Paul, Verena Rieser, and Laure Vieu. 2012. Developing a corpus of strategic conversation in The Settlers of Catan. In *Proceedings of SemDial 2012*.

R. Arkin. 2010. The ethics of robotics deception. In *1st International Conference of International Association for Computing and Philosophy*, pages 1–3.

N. Asher and A. Lascarides. 2008. Commitments, beliefs and intentions in dialogue. In *Proc. of SemDial*, pages 35–42.

S. Attardo. 1997. Locutionary and perlocutionary cooperation: The perlocutionary cooperative principle. *Journal of Pragmatics*, 27(6):753–779.

Daniel Dennett. 1997. When Hal Kills, Who's to Blame? Computer Ethics. In *Hal's Legacy:2001's Computer as Dream and Reality*.

Ioannis Efstathiou and Oliver Lemon. 2014. Learning to manage risk in non-cooperative dialogues. In *under review*.

Kallirroi Georgila and David Traum. 2011. Reinforcement learning of argumentation dialogue policies in negotiation. In *Proc. INTERSPEECH*.

Piotr J. Gmytrasiewicz and Prashant Doshi. 2005. A framework for sequential planning in multi-agent settings. *Journal of Artificial Intelligence Research*, 24:49–79.

Paul Grice. 1975. Logic and conversation. *Syntax and Semantics*, 3.

Verena Rieser and Oliver Lemon. 2011. *Reinforcement Learning for Adaptive Dialogue Systems: A Data-driven Methodology for Dialogue Management and Natural Language Generation*. Theory and Applications of Natural Language Processing. Springer.

J. Shim and R.C. Arkin. 2013. A Taxonomy of Robot Deception and its Benefits in HRI. In *Proc. IEEE Systems, Man, and Cybernetics Conference*.

R. Sutton and A. Barto. 1998. *Reinforcement Learning*. MIT Press.

David Traum. 2008. Exrended abstract: Computational models of non-cooperative dialogue. In *Proc. of SIGdial Workshop on Discourse and Dialogue*.

Adam Vogel, Max Bodoia, Christopher Potts, and Dan Jurafsky. 2013a. Emergence of Gricean Maxims from Multi-Agent Decision Theory. In *Proceedings of NAACL 2013*.

Adam Vogel, Christopher Potts, and Dan Jurafsky. 2013b. Implicatures and Nested Beliefs in Approximate Decentralized-POMDPs. In *Proceedings of ACL 2013*.

M. Walker, R. Passonneau, and J. Boland. 2001. Quantitative and qualitative evaluation of DARPA Communicator spoken dialogue systems. In *Proc. of the Annual Meeting of the Association for Computational Linguistics (ACL)*.

Steve Young, M. Gasic, S. Keizer, F. Mairesse, J. Schatzmann, B. Thomson, and K. Yu. 2010. The Hidden Information State Model: a practical framework for POMDP-based spoken dialogue management. *Computer Speech and Language*, 24(2):150–174.

Improving Classification-Based Natural Language Understanding with Non-Expert Annotation

Fabrizio Morbini and **Eric Forbell** and **Kenji Sagae**
Institute for Creative Technologies
University of Southern California
Los Angeles, CA 90094, USA
{morbini,forbell,sagae}@ict.usc.edu

Abstract

Although data-driven techniques are commonly used for Natural Language Understanding in dialogue systems, their efficacy is often hampered by the lack of appropriate annotated training data in sufficient amounts. We present an approach for rapid and cost-effective annotation of training data for classification-based language understanding in conversational dialogue systems. Experiments using a web-accessible conversational character that interacts with a varied user population show that a dramatic improvement in natural language understanding and a substantial reduction in expert annotation effort can be achieved by leveraging non-expert annotation.

1 Introduction

Robust Natural Language Understanding (NLU) remains a challenge in conversational dialogue systems that allow arbitrary natural language input from users. Although data-driven approaches are now commonly used to address the NLU problem as one of classification, e.g. (Heintze et al., 2010; Leuski and Traum, 2010; Moreira et al., 2011), where input utterances are mapped automatically into system-specific categories, the dependence of such approaches on training data annotated with semantic classes or dialogue acts creates a chicken and egg problem: user utterances are needed to create the annotated training data necessary for NLU by classification, but these cannot be collected without a working system that users can interact with.

Common solutions to this problem include the use of Wizard-of-Oz data collection, where a human expert manually provides the functionality of data-driven modules while data is collected from users, or the use of scenario authors who attempt to anticipate user input to create an initial set of training data. While these options offer practical ways around the training data acquisition problem, they typically require substantial work from system experts and provide suboptimal solutions: data-driven approaches work best when utterances in the training data are drawn from the same distribution as those encountered in actual system use, but the conditions under which training data is collected (a human expert filling in for systems modules, or a human expert generating possible user utterances) are quite different from those where users interact with the final system. High quality results are often obtained through an iterative process where an initial training set is authored by a scenario designer, but NLU resources are gradually updated based on real user data over time (Gandhe et al., 2011). Although this can ultimately produce training data composed primarily of real user utterances, and therefore result in better performance from data-driven models, an expert annotator is required to perform manual classification of user utterances. This is a laborious process that assumes availability and willingness of the annotator for as long as it takes to collect enough user utterances, which may range from weeks to months or even years, depending on the size of the domain and the number and type of utterance categories.

The main question we address is whether annotation by non-experts can be leveraged to speed up utterance classification and lower its cost. We present a technique that frames the annotation of training data as a human intelligence task suitable for crowdsourcing. Although there are similarities between our technique and active learning (e.g. see (Gambck et al., 2011)), an important difference is that our technique does not reduce the annotation effort by reducing the size of the data to be labeled, but by casting the annotation task into a simpler problem. This allows us to take advantage of the entire data generated by the users. Through an experiment with a conversational dialogue system deployed on the web, we show that a dramatic improvement in the quality of NLU can be achieved with non-expert data annotation, reducing the time required of an expert annotator by 70%.

2 Improving understanding with data

Our approach for creating accurate utterance classifiers for NLU in conversational dialogue systems is based on a simple strategy, which we describe next in general terms. NLU is assumed to be performed through multiclass classification.

The first step is to create a small initial training dataset T_0 either through Wizard-of-Oz data collection or by generation of utterances by a system developer or content author. This training set is used to train a NLU model M_0. Although this model is likely to be inadequate, it allows users to interact with an initial version of the system. As input utterances are collected from real users, these utterances are annotated with their desired NLU output labels. Periodically, at time i, we add to the initial training dataset T_0 the annotated user utterances accumulated up to that point. We train a new NLU model M_i using this augmented training set, T_i.[1] We also keep aside a small fraction of utterances to test the performance of the NLU models, that is, at each time i we also have an evaluation set E_i and the union of E_i and T_i is the entire set of user utterances collected up to time i. As more utterances are added and annotated, an NLU model M_i is expected to surpass the initial model M_0. In general, we replace the running NLU model M_r whenever we have a better performing M_i model. This straightforward process can be used to obtain increasingly more accurate language understanding, at the cost of data annotation in the form of labelling utterances with categories that are defined according to the needs of the specific system and the specific domain. The categories may be based on dialogue acts, e.g. (Core and Allen, 1997; Bunt et al., 2010), user information needs, e.g. (Moreira et al., 2011), or stand in for entire semantic frames, e.g. (DeVault and Traum, 2013). The technical nature of the task of categorizing utterances in schemes such as these usually means that substantial time is required of an expert annotator.

2.1 Annotation as a human intelligence task

Although the task of annotating NLU training data involves assigning categories with technical definitions to utterances, and therefore would appear to require knowledge of these technical definitions, in fact the task requires primarily the type of language understanding that is common to all native speakers of a given language. Our main hypothesis is that this annotation can be structured as a trivial task that requires no specific expertise, and that annotations performed this way can have a substantial impact on the quality of utterance classification. We define the NLU annotation task as follows.

Before annotation begins, each utterance category in the system is associated with one or more canonical utterance(s) that capture the meaning and communicative intent of that category. These canonical utterances allow for trivial generation of surface text from NLU categories by simple lookup.

Given a set of dialogues between the system and individual users, each dialogue is split into segments. Segments are typically composed of a user utterance and the preceding system utterance. In cases where users produce multiple utterances without intervening system utterances, segments may consist of a system utterance followed by consecutive user utterances, so that there is exactly one segment corresponding to each user utterance u in the dialogue and each segment starts with a system utterance and ends with u.

Annotators work on one dialogue at a time, and within a dialogue they are presented with one segment at a time, following the order in which the utterances appear in the dialogue. Assignment of a system category to the utterance targeted in a segment is a multiple choice task, involving n choices, one of which is *none of the above*. The remaining $n-1$ choices are generated automatically by running the current NLU utterance classifier on the target utterance, and generating the canonical surface realizations of each of the $n-1$ highest scoring categories. The annotator is then asked to choose the option containing language that means the same as the targeted utterance in the segment. The choice of n depends on the quality of the current NLU model, and must be made to balance the length of the list of options with the expected number of times the appropriate choice is not in the list of options. The more *none of the above* annotations are performed, the less effective the annotation exercise will be in reducing the effort required by an annotation expert.

The utterances annotated as *none of the above* are given to an expert for annotation. The impact

[1] For every time i and j with $i < j$ it holds that $T_i \subseteq T_j$.

System Hello and welcome.

...

User Are you married?

System Yeah, forty-four years this September. I can't believe Linda's stuck with me this long.

System Okay, let's get to it. Why are you here today?

User I've been having trouble sleeping lately.

System This must be hard for you.

System Are you feeling stressed at all?

User Yes, quite a bit

System So, I've got some questions I need to ask you, to get to know you better.

System Just double checking, you haven't been sleeping good. Is that right?

User That's right

System Have you been having any nightmares?

User Every once in a while, but mostly I can't stay asleep

...

Figure 1: Excerpt of a sample interaction with a Simcoach character over the web. User input is typed into a text box on a web page.

of this procedure on how quickly user utterances are annotated as training examples for the NLU and how much expert time is saved depends on the quality of the initial classification model and the choice of n. These are practical factors that are expected to vary greatly from one dialogue system to another. In the next section, we present one application of this procedure to an existing conversational dialogue system deployed on the web, and show examples of dialogue segments and annotation options.

3 Experiment

To test our hypothesis that language understanding can be improved with much reduced expert effort, we applied the framework described above to a system that implements a conversational character that talks with users about issues relating to mental and behavioral disorders and presents health care options. The system is publicly accessible at http://www.simcoach.org, and receives traffic on the order of one hundred users per week. Of these, about one quarter engage the system in a meaningful dialogue with multiple turns, with the dialogues containing on average 16 user utterances. Because our process depends crucially on user traffic to generate data for annotation, a web-accessible system is ideally suited for it. An excerpt from a typical interaction with the system is shown in Figure 1. The system and the NLU classifier based on Maximum Entropy models (Berger et al., 1996) are described respectively in (Rizzo et al., 2011) and (Sagae et al., 2009).

3.1 Data collection

Starting with an initial system deployed with an NLU model trained with data generated by an author attempting to anticipate user behavior, we applied the approach described in section 2 to improve NLU accuracy over a period of approximately five months. The initial accuracy of the NLU classifier was 62%, measured as the number of utterances classified correctly divided by the total number of user utterances. This accuracy figure was obtained only after the five months of data annotation, using the heldout set of manually annotated dialogues.

Although the data annotation procedure as described in section 2 could in principle be performed continuously as user data come in, we instead performed all of our annotation in three rounds, the first consisting of approximately 2,000 user utterances, the second one month later, consisting of an additional 1,000 utterances. The last round, collected about two months later, contained about 2,000 utterances. We used five annotators[2] working in parallel, and the average speed of each annotator exceeded 500 utterances per hour.

The total number of NLU utterance classes in the system is 378, although only 120 classes were used by annotators in all rounds of annotation to cover all of the utterances collected[3]. In our annotation exercise we set the number of multiple choice items at $n = 6$, including 5 choices generated from categories chosen by the NLU classifier, and one *none of the above* choice. Figure 2 shows a sample dialogue segment with the corresponding multiple choice items. During annotation, clicking on a multiple choice item advances the annotation by presenting the next segment containing a user utterance to be annotated.

3.2 Results

Of the utterances in the three rounds of data collection, respectively 29%, 34% and 17% were marked by annotators as *none of the above*. These were given to a developer of the NLU system who assigned a category to each of them. In this expert annotation step the choice is not restricted to a small set of options, and may be any of the categories in the system. Given this rate of use of

[2]The non-expert annotators belonged to the same team that developed the system but did not participate in the development of the NLU module and the NLU classes used in the particular dialogue system used.

[3]This difference is a further evidence of the difficulty of correctly anticipating how the end users will interact with the dialogue system.

System Okay, let's get to it. Why are you here today?

User I've been having trouble sleeping lately.

Which of the following options correspond most closely to the last user utterance? If none of them have the same general meaning as the user utterance, select "none of the above."

(a) I have been in a bad mood lately
(b) I have nightmares often
(c) I haven't been sleeping well
(d) My family is worried about me
(e) I eat too much
(f) None of the above

Figure 2: Example of a dialogue segment with corresponding multiple choice items. The annotation task consists of choosing the item that has approximately the same meaning and communicative intent as the targeted utterance (the user utterance).

the *none of the above* category, the need for expert annotation is not eliminated, but the amount of expert effort necessary is reduced by over 70%.

The NLU classification accuracy figures obtained after each round of annotation are shown in Table 1. In the table, *Our Approach* represents the results obtained by the technique described here. A large improvement is observed after the first round of annotation, with a more modest improvement observed after the other two rounds. The initial jump in accuracy after round 1 is explained by the fact that the initial model based on a system author's expectation of what users may say to the system (approximately 3,000 utterances) is improved using utterances that users did in fact produce in real interactions with the system. Clearly, a more well-matched distribution of utterances in the training data produces higher accuracy.

To assess the value of our approach, we compare it with two other reasonable experimental conditions: a baseline where only expert annotation is used (*Expert Only*), and a condition where no expert annotation is used (*No Expert*). The *Expert Only* condition is meant to represent what can be achieved with the same workload for the expert used in *Our Approach*. This is achieved by random selection of user utterances to create a set with the same number of utterances set aside for expert annotation in *Our Approach*. The expert then annotates each of these utterances to create training data. For the *No Expert* condition, we used only utterances annotated by non-experts, leaving out completely utterances labeled as *none of the above*. Both *Expert Only* and *No Expert* conditions achieve significantly lower performance than the approach described here. This indicates that expert annotation is important, but also that cheap and fast non-expert annotation can provide substantial improvements to NLU.

	NLU accuracy after each annotation round [%]			
	Base	1st round	2nd round	3rd round
Our Approach	62	**70**	**73**	**78**
Expert Only	62	64	68	70
No Expert	62	64	65	71

Table 1: NLU accuracy obtained using the initial training dataset T_0, after one round of annotation with T_1 (2,013 utterances), after two rounds of annotation with T_2 (additional 948 utterances), and after three rounds with T_3 (additional 1806 utterances). Accuracy is estimated on the same heldout set of dialogues E_3 for all conditions, accounting for roughly 10% of the annotated data.

4 Conclusion

We described a framework for annotation of training data by non-experts that can provide dramatic improvements to natural language understanding in dialogue systems that perform NLU through utterance classification. Our approach transforms the annotation NLU training data into a task that can be performed by anyone with language proficiency. Annotation is structured as a simple multiple choice task, easily delivered over the web.

Using our approach with a conversational character on the web, we improved NLU accuracy from 62% to 78% using only less than 30% of the effort it would be required of an expert to annotate data without non-expert annotation.

Acknowledgments

We thank Kelly Christoffersen, Nicolai Kalisch and Tomer Mor-Barak for data annotation and updates to the SimCoach system, David Traum for insightful discussions, and the anonymous reviewers. The effort described here has been sponsored by the U.S. Army. Any opinions, content or information presented does not necessarily reflect the position or the policy of the United States Government, and no official endorsement should be inferred.

References

Adam L. Berger, Vincent J. Della Pietra, and Stephen A. Della Pietra. 1996. A maximum entropy approach to natural language processing. *Comput. Linguist.*, 22(1):39–71, March.

Harry Bunt, Jan Alexandersson, Jean Carletta, Jae-Woong Choe, Alex Chengyu Fang, Koiti Hasida, Kiyong Lee, Volha Petukhova, Andrei Popescu-Belis, Laurent Romary, Claudia Soria, and David Traum. 2010. Towards an iso standard for dialogue act annotation. In Nicoletta Calzolari (Conference Chair), Khalid Choukri, Bente Maegaard, Joseph Mariani, Jan Odijk, Stelios Piperidis, Mike Rosner, and Daniel Tapias, editors, *Proceedings of the Seventh International Conference on Language Resources and Evaluation (LREC'10)*, Valletta, Malta, may. European Language Resources Association (ELRA).

Mark G. Core and James F. Allen. 1997. Coding dialogues with the DAMSL annotation scheme. In David Traum, editor, *Working Notes: AAAI Fall Symposium on Communicative Action in Humans and Machines*, pages 28–35, Menlo Park, California. AAAI, American Association for Artificial Intelligence.

David DeVault and David Traum. 2013. A method for the approximation of incremental understanding of explicit utterance meaning using predictive models in nite domains. In *Conference of the North American Chapter of the Association for Computational Linguistics: Human Language Technologies*, Atlanta, GA, June.

Bjrn Gambck, Fredrik Olsson, and Oscar Tckstrm. 2011. Active learning for dialogue act classification. In *INTERSPEECH*, pages 1329–1332. ISCA.

Sudeep Gandhe, Michael Rushforth, Priti Aggarwal, and David Traum. 2011. Evaluation of an integrated authoring tool for building advanced question-answering characters. In *12th Annual Conference of the International Speech Communication Association (InterSpeech 2011)*, Florence, Italy, August.

Silvan Heintze, Timo Baumann, and David Schlangen. 2010. Comparing local and sequential models for statistical incremental natural language understanding. In Raquel Fernández, Yasuhiro Katagiri, Kazunori Komatani, Oliver Lemon, and Mikio Nakano, editors, *SIGDIAL Conference*, pages 9–16. The Association for Computer Linguistics.

Anton Leuski and David R. Traum. 2010. Practical language processing for virtual humans. In *Twenty-Second Annual Conference on Innovative Applications of Artificial Intelligence (IAAI-10)*.

Catarina Moreira, Ana Cristina Mendes, Luísa Coheur, and Bruno Martins. 2011. Towards the rapid development of a natural language understanding module. In *Proceedings of the 10th International Conference on Intelligent Virtual Agents*, IVA'11, pages 309–315, Berlin, Heidelberg. Springer-Verlag.

Albert A. Rizzo, Belinda Lange, John G. Buckwalter, E. Forbell, Julia Kim, Kenji Sagae, Josh Williams, Barbara O. Rothbaum, JoAnn Difede, Greg Reger, Thomas Parsons, and Patrick Kenny. 2011. An intelligent virtual human system for providing healthcare information and support. In *Studies in Health Technology and Informatics*.

Kenji Sagae, Gwen Christian, David DeVault, and David R. Traum. 2009. Towards natural language understanding of partial speech recognition results in dialogue systems. In *Short Paper Proceedings of the North American Chapter of the Association for Computational Linguistics - Human Language Technologies (NAACL HLT) 2009 conference*.

User Modeling by Using Bag-of-Behaviors for Building a Dialog System Sensitive to the Interlocutor's Internal State

Yuya Chiba, Takashi Nose, Akinori Ito
Graduate School of Engineering,
Tohoku University, Japan

Masashi Ito
Faculty of Engineering
Tohoku Institute of Technology, Japan

Abstract

When using spoken dialog systems in actual environments, users sometimes abandon the dialog without making any input utterance. To help these users before they give up, the system should know why they could not make an utterance. Thus, we have examined a method to estimate the state of a dialog user by capturing the user's non-verbal behavior even when the user's utterance is not observed. The proposed method is based on vector quantization of multi-modal features such as non-verbal speech, feature points of the face, and gaze. The histogram of the VQ code is used as a feature for determining the state. We call this feature "the Bag-of-Behaviors." According to the experimental results, we prove that the proposed method surpassed the results of conventional approaches and discriminated the target user's states with an accuracy of more than 70%.

1 Introduction

Spoken dialog systems have an advantage of being a natural interface since speech commands are less subject to the physical constraints imposed by devices. On the other hand, if the system accepts only a limited expression, the user need to learn how to use the system. If the user is not familiar with the system, he/she cannot even make an input utterance. Not all users are motivated to converse with the system in actual environments, and sometimes a user will abandon the dialog without making any input utterance. When the user has difficulty to make the utterance, conventional systems just repeat the prompt at fixed interval (Yankelovich, 1996) or taking the initiative in the dialog to complete the task (Chung, 2004; Bohus and Rudnicky, 2009). However, we think that the system has to cope with the user's implicit requests to help the user more adequately. To solve this problem, Chiba and Ito (2012) proposed a method to estimate two "user's states" by capturing their non-verbal cues. Here, the state A is when the user does not know what to input, and the state B is when the user is considering how to answer the system's prompt. These states have not been distinguished by the conventional dialog systems so far, but should be handled differently.

The researchers of spoken dialog systems have focused on the various internal states of users such as emotion (Forbes-Riley and Litman, 2011a; Metallinou et al., 2012), preference (Pargellis et al., 2004) and familiarity with the system (Jokinen and Kanto, 2004; Rosis et al., 2006) to build natural dialog system. In particular, the user's "uncertainty" is assumed to be the nearest user's states that we wish to study. Forbes-Riley and Litman (2011b) and Pon-Barry et al. (2005) introduced a framework for estimating the user's uncertainty to a tutor system.

The above-mentioned researches have a certain result by employing linguistic information for the estimation, but it remains difficult to assist a user who does not make any input utterance. By contrast, the method by Chiba and Ito (2012) estimated the target user's state by only using the user's non-verbal information. In their work, the user's multi-modal behaviors were defined empirically, and the labels of the behaviors were annotated manually. Based on this result, the present paper proposes the method that does not use manually-defined labels nor manual annotation. The multi-modal behaviors are determined automatically using the vector quantization, and the frequency distribution of the VQ code is used for estimation of the user's state. Because this approach expects to construct clusters of the speech events or behaviors of the user, we called it as Bag-of-Behaviors approach.

2 Data collection

The experimental data (video clips) were the same as those used in the experiment by Chiba et al. (Chiba and Ito, 2012; Chiba et al., 2012). The video clips contained the frontal image of the user and their speech, which were recorded with a web camera and a lapel microphone, respectively. The task of the dialog was a question-and-answer task to ask users to answer common knowledge or a number they remembered in advance, such as "Please input your ID." 16 users (14 males and 2 females) participated in the dialog collection.

Recorded clips were divided into sessions, where one session included one interchange of the system's prompt and the user's response. The total number of sessions was 792. Then we employed evaluators to label each video clip as either state A, B or C, where state A and B were that described in the previous section, and state C is the state where the user had no problem answering the system. We took the majority vote of the evaluators' decisions to determine the final label of a clip. Fleiss' κ among the evaluators was 0.22 (fair agreement). Finally, we obtained 59, 195 and 538 sessions of state A, B and C, respectively.

3 Discrimination method by using Bag-of-Behaviors

In the work of Chiba et al. (2013), the user's state was determined using the labels of the multi-modal events such as fillers or face orientation, which were estimated from the low-level acoustic and visual features.

Here, inventory of multi-modal events was determined empirically. There were, however, two problems with this method. The first one was that the optimality of the inventory was not guaranteed. The second one is that it was difficult to estimate the events from the low-level features, which made the final decision more difficult. Therefore, we propose a new method for discriminating the user's state using automatically-determined events obtained by the vector quantization.

First, a codebook of the low-level features (which will be described in detail in the next section) is created using k-means++ algorithm (Arthur and Vassilvitskii, 2007). Let a low-level feature vector at time t of session s of the training data be $\boldsymbol{x}_t^{(s)}$. Then we perform the clustering of the low-level feature vectors for all of t and s, and create a codebook $\mathcal{C} = \{\boldsymbol{c}_1, \ldots, \boldsymbol{c}_K\}$, where $\boldsymbol{c}_k$ denotes the k-th centroid of the codebook.

Then the input feature vectors are quantized frame-by-frame using the codebook. When a session for evaluation s_E is given, we quantize the input low-level feature vectors $\boldsymbol{x}_1^{(s_E)}, \ldots, \boldsymbol{x}_T^{(s_E)}$ into $q_1, \ldots, q_T$, where

$$q_t = \arg\min_q ||\boldsymbol{x}_t^{(s_E)} - \boldsymbol{c}_q||. \quad (1)$$

Then we calculate the histogram $\boldsymbol{Q}_0(s_E) = (Q_1, \ldots, Q_K)$ where

$$Q_k = \sum_{t=1}^{T} \delta(k, q_t) \quad (2)$$

$$\delta(x, y) = \begin{cases} 1 & x = y \\ 0 & x \neq y \end{cases} \quad (3)$$

Then $\boldsymbol{Q}(s_E) = \boldsymbol{Q}_0(s_E)/||\boldsymbol{Q}_0(s_E)||$ is used as the feature of the discrimination. The similar features based on the vector quantization were used for image detection and scene analysis (Csurka et al., 2004; Jiang et al., 2007; Natarajan et al., 2012) and called "Bag-of-Features" or "Bag-of-Keypoints." In our research, each cluster of the low-level features is expected to represent some kind of user's behavior. Therefore, we call the proposed method the "Bag-of-Behaviors" approach.

After calculating the Bag-of-Behaviors, we employ an appropriate classifier to determine the user's state in the given session. In this research, the support vector machine (SVM) is used as a classifier.

4 The low-level features

In this section, we describe the acoustic and visual features employed as the low-level features.

The target user's states are assumed to have similar aspects to emotion. Collignon et al. (2008) suggested that emotion has a multi-modality nature. For example, Wöllmer et al. (2013) showed that the acoustic and visual features contributed to discriminate arousal and expectation, respectively. Several other researches also have reported that recognition accuracy of emotion was improved by combining multi-modal information (Lin et al., 2012; Wang and Venetsanopoulos, 2012; Paulmann and Pell, 2011; Metallinou et al., 2012). Therefore, we employed similar features as those used in these previous works, such as the spectral features and intonation of the speech, and facial feature points, etc.

4.1 Audio features

To represent spectral characteristics of the speech, MFCC was employed as an acoustic feature. We used a 39-dimension MFCC including the velocity and acceleration of the lower 12th-order coefficients and log power. In addition, a differential component of log $F0$ was used to represent the prosodic feature of the speech, and zero cross (ZC) was used to distinguish voiced and unvoiced segments. Therefore, total number of audio features was 3. The basic conditions for extracting each feature are shown in Table 1. Here, five frames (the current frame, the two previous frames and two following frames) were used to calculate the Δ and $\Delta\Delta$ components of MFCC and Δ component of log $F0$.

4.2 Face feature

Face feature (Chiba et al., 2013) was extracted by the Constraint Local Model (CLM) (Saragih et al., 2011) frame by frame. The coordinates of the points relative to the center of the face were used as the face features. The scale of the feature points was normalized by the size of the facial region. The number of feature points was 66 and the dimension of the feature was 132.

4.3 Gaze feature

The evaluators of the dialogs declared that movement of the user's eyes seems to express their internal state. The present paper used the Haar-like feature which has a fast calculation algorithm using the integral image to represent the brightness of the user's eye regions. This feature was extracted by applying filters comprehensively changed the size and location to the image (eye regions in our case). The eye regions were detected by the facial feature points. Because this feature had large dimensions, the principal component analysis (PCA) was conducted to reduce the dimensionality. Finally, gaze feature had 34 dimensions and the cumulative contribution rate was about 95%.

4.4 Feature synchronization

The audio features were calculated every 10 ms (see Table 1) while the visual features were extracted every 33 ms. Therefore, the features were synchronized by copying the visual features of the previous frame in every 10 ms.

5 Discrimination examination

5.1 Conditions of the Bag-of-Behaviors construction

We built the Bag-of-Behaviors under two conditions described below.

Let $\boldsymbol{x}_{at}^{(s)}, \boldsymbol{x}_{ft}^{(s)}$ and $\boldsymbol{x}_{et}^{(s)}$ represent the audio feature, face feature and gaze feature of the session s at time t, respectively.

Table 1: Conditions of audio feature extraction

	MFCC	log $F0$	ZC
Frame width	25.0 ms	17.0 ms	10.0 ms
Frame shift	10.0 ms	10.0 ms	10.0 ms

Table 2: Experimental conditions

# of sessions		State A(59), State B(195)
Codebook size	K	4, 8, 16, 32, 64
	K_a	4, 8, 16, 32, 64
	K_f	4, 8, 16, 32, 64
	K_e	4, 8, 16, 32, 64

In Condition (1), the three features are combined to single feature vector $\boldsymbol{x}_t^{(s)}$:

$$\boldsymbol{x}_t^{(s)} = (\boldsymbol{x}_{at}^{(s)}, \boldsymbol{x}_{ft}^{(s)}, \boldsymbol{x}_{et}^{(s)}) \quad (4)$$

Then, the low-level feature vectors $\boldsymbol{x}_t^{(s)}$ are clustered to construct one codebook $\mathcal{C}$ with size K. When an input session s_E is given, we calculate the combined feature vector $\boldsymbol{x}_t^{(s_E)}$, and generate the Bag-of-Behaviors $\boldsymbol{Q}(s_E)$. This method is a kind of the feature-level fusion method.

In Condition (2), the three features are used separately. First, we generate three codebooks $\mathcal{C}_a, \mathcal{C}_f$ and $\mathcal{C}_e$ using the audio, face and gaze features, respectively. Size of those codebooks were K_a, K_f and K_e. When an input session s_E is given, we generate three Bag-of-Behaviors feature vectors $\boldsymbol{Q}_a(s_E), \boldsymbol{Q}_f(s_E)$ and $\boldsymbol{Q}_e(s_E)$ using the three codebooks. Finally, we combine those features as

$$\boldsymbol{Q}(s_E) = (\boldsymbol{Q}_a(s_E), \boldsymbol{Q}_f(s_E), \boldsymbol{Q}_e(s_E)). \quad (5)$$

5.2 Experimental condition

We employed the SVM with RBF-kernel as a classifier. The experimental conditions are summarized in Table 2. The hyperparameters of the classifier were decided by grid-searching. Since the session of state C and the other states (state A and state B) were clearly distinguished by the duration of the session, we used only the session of state A and state B for the experiments. Hence, each experiment was a two-class discrimination task.

As explained, the experimental data were unbalanced. Since it is desirable that the system can discriminate the user's state without deviation, the harmonic mean H of the accuracy of the two states was used for measuring the performance. This is calculated by

$$H = \frac{2C_A C_B}{C_A + C_B}, \quad (6)$$

where C_A and C_B represent the discrimination accuracy of state A and state B, respectively. The experiments were conducted based on a 5-fold cross validation.

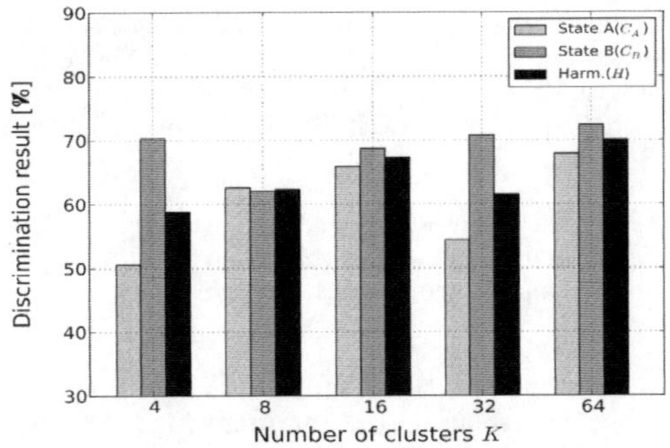

Figure 1: Discrimination results of condition (1)

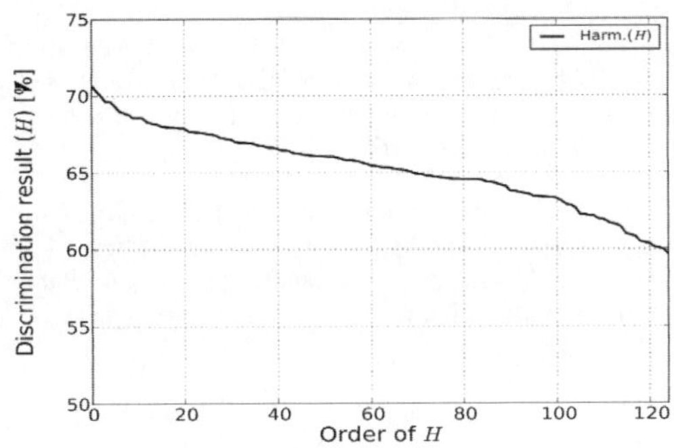

Figure 2: Discrimination results of condition (2) arranged in descending order

5.3 Experimental results

The results of condition (1) are shown in Figure 1. The figure shows the best H of each number of clusters. In condition (1), the best result ($H = 70.0\%$) was obtained when the number of clusters K was 64. Figure 2 shows the results of condition (2). In this figure, the results are shown in descending order of the harmonic mean for all combination of codebook size of the three codebooks (there were $5^3 = 125$ conditions). The best $H = 70.7\%$ was obtained when $K_a = 8, K_f = 8$ and $K_e = 64$.

The best results of the tested methods are summarized in Table 3. Here, "Baseline + NN" in the table denotes the result in Chiba et al. (2013), where the visual events and acoustic events were annotated manually, and the manual labels were used as input for a neural network for the classification. The gaze feature was not used in "Baseline + NN." We added the result when including the gaze feature, shown as "Baseline + Gaze + NN." As shown in Table 3, the performance of the method proposed in this paper surpassed the baseline methods. Therefore, the proposed method could not only automatically determine the inventory of the audio-visual events, but also achieved better discrimination accuracy. One of the reasons of the improvement is VQ can construct the clusters in proper quantities.

Table 3: Comparison of estimation methods

	State A	State B	Harm.
Baseline + NN	52.5	65.1	58.2
Baseline + Gaze + NN	64.5	59.5	61.9
Condition (1) + RBF-SVM	67.9	72.3	70.0
Condition (2) + RBF-SVM	67.7	73.8	70.7
Condition (2) + MKL-SVM	**68.0**	**76.4**	**72.0**

Comparing the two conditions of feature combination, H of condition (2) (denoted as "Condition (2) + RBF-SVM") was slightly higher than that of condition (1) (denoted as "Condition (1) + RBF-SVM"). This result was similar to Split-VQ (Pariwal and Atal, 1991) where a single feature vector split into subvectors and the input vector was quantized subvector by subvector.

We conducted additional experiments for condition (2) by using SVM with combined kernel trained by Multiple Kernel Learning (MKL) (Sonnenburg et al., 2006). The combined kernel is represented as a linear combination of several subkernels. The distinct kernel was employed for the speech, face feature and gaze feature, respectively. This paper used the RBF-kernel having the same width as the sub-kernels . The best result was shown as "Condition (2) + MKL-SVM" in Table 3. As shown in the table, the MKL-SVM showed the highest performance of 72.0 %. The weights of the audio, face and gaze feature were 0.246, 0.005 and 0.749, respectively. This result suggested that the contribution of the face feature was weaker than the other features.

6 Conclusion

In this paper, we proposed a method to estimate the state of the user of the dialog system by using non-verbal features. We proposed the Bag-of-Behaviors approach, in which the user's multmodal behavior was first classified by vector quantization, and then the histogram of the VQ code was used as a feature of the discrimination. We verified that the method could discriminate the target user's state with an accuracy of 70% or more.

One of the disadvantages of the current framework is that it requires to observe the session until just before the user's input utterance. This problem makes it difficult to apply this method to an actual system, because the system has to be able to evaluate the user's state successively in order to help the user at an appropriate timing. Therefore, we will examine a sequential estimation method by using the Bag-of-Behaviors in a future work.

References

David Arthur and Sergei Vassilvitskii. 2007. k-means++: The advantages of careful seeding. In *Proc. the 18th annual ACM-SIAM symposium on Discrete algorithms*, pages 1027–1035.

Dan Bohus and Alexander I. Rudnicky. 2009. The ravenclaw dialog management framework: Architecture and systems. *Computer Speech & Language*, 23(3):332–361.

Yuya Chiba and Akinori Ito. 2012. Estimating a user's internal state before the first input utterance. *Advances in Human-Computer Interaction*, 2012:11, DOI:10.1155/2012/865362, 2012.

Yuya Chiba, Masashi Ito, and Akinori Ito. 2012. Effect of linguistic contents on human estimation of internal state of dialog system users. In *Proc. Feedback Behaviors in Dialog*, pages 11–14.

Yuya Chiba, Masashi Ito, and Akinori Ito. 2013. Estimation of user's state during a dialog turn with sequential multi-modal features. In *HCI International 2013-Posters' Extended Abstracts*, pages 572–576.

Grace Chung. 2004. Developing a flexible spoken dialog system using simulation. In *Proc. the 42nd Annual Meeting on Association for Computational Linguistics*, pages 63–70.

Olivier Collignon, Simon Girard, Frederic Gosselin, Sylvain Roy, Dave Saint-Amour, Maryse Lassonde, and Lepore Franco. 2008. Audio-visual integration of emotion expression. *Brain research*, 1242:126–135.

Gabriella Csurka, Christopher Dance, Lixin Fan, Jutta Willamowski, and Cédric Bray. 2004. Visual categorization with bags of keypoints. In *Proc. workshop on statistical learning in computer vision, ECCV*, pages 1–2.

Kate Forbes-Riley and Diane Litman. 2011a. Benefits and challenges of real-time uncertainty detection and adaptation in a spoken dialogue computer tutor. *Speech Communication*, 53:1115–1136.

Kate Forbes-Riley and Diane Litman. 2011b. Designing and evaluating a wizarded uncertainty-adaptive spoken dialogue tutoring system. *Computer Speech & Language*, 25(1):105–126.

Yu-Gang Jiang, Chong-Wah Ngo, and Jun Yang. 2007. Towards optimal bag-of-features for object categorization and semantic video retrieval. In *Proc. of the 6th ACM international conference on Image and video retrieval*, pages 494–501.

Kristiina Jokinen and Kari Kanto. 2004. User expertise modelling and adaptivity in a speech-based e-mail system. In *Proc. the 42nd Annual Meeting on Association for Computational Linguistics*, pages 88–95.

Jen-Chun Lin, Chung-Hsien Wu, and Wen-Li Wei. 2012. Error weighted semi-coupled hidden markov model for audio-visual emotion recognition. *IEEE Trans. Multimedia*, 14(1):142–156.

Angeliki Metallinou, Martin Wöllmer, Athanasios Katsamanis, Florian Eyben, Björn Schuller, and Shrikanth Narayanan. 2012. Context-sensitive learning for enhanced audiovisual emotion classification. *IEEE Trans. Affective Computing*, 3(2):184–198.

Pradeep Natarajan, Shuang Wu, Shiv Vitaladevuni, Xiaodan Zhuang, Stavros Tsakalidis, and Unsang Park, Rohit Prasad, and Premkumar Natarajan. 2012. Multimodal feature fusion for robust event detection in web videos. In *Proc. Computer Vision and Pattern Recognition*, pages 1298–1305.

Andrew Pargellis, Hong-Kwang Jeff Kuo, and Chin-Hui Lee. 2004. An automatic dialogue generation platform for personalized dialogue applications. *Speech Communication*, 42:329–351.

Kuldip Paliwal and Bishnu Atal. 1993. Efficient vector quantization of lpc parameters at 24 bits/frame. In *IEEE Trans. Speech and Audio Processing*, 1(1):3–14.

Silke Paulmann and Marc Pell. 2011. Is there an advantage for recognizing multi-modal emotional stimuli? *Motivation and Emotion*, 35(2):192–201.

Heather Pon-Barry, Karl Schultz, Elizabeth Owen Bratt, Brady Clark, and Stanley Peters. 2005. Responding to student uncertainty in spoken tutorial dialogue systems. *Int. J. Artif. Intell. Edu.*, 16:171–194.

Fiorella Rosis, Nicole Novielli, Valeria Carofiglio, Addolorata Cavalluzzi, and Berardina Carolis. 2006. User modeling and adaptation in health promotion dialogs with an animated character. *J. Biomedical Informatics*, 39:514–531.

Jason Saragih, Simon Lucey, and Jeffrey Cohn. 2011. Deformable model fitting by regularized landmark mean-shift. *Int. J. Computer Vision*, 91(2):200–215.

Yongjin Wang and Anastasios Venetsanopoulos. 2012. Kernel cross-modal factor analysis for information fusion with application to bimodal emotion recognition. *IEEE Trans. Multimedia*, 14(3):597–607.

Martin Wöllmer, Moritz Kaiser, Florian Eyben, Björn Schuller, and Gerhard Rigoll. 2013. Lstm-modeling of continuous emotions in an audiovisual affect recognition framework. *Image and Vision Computing*, 31(2):153–163.

Nicole Yankelovich. 1996. How do users know what to say? *Interactions*, 3(6):32–43.

Alex: Bootstrapping a Spoken Dialogue System for a New Domain by Real Users*

Ondřej Dušek, Ondřej Plátek, Lukáš Žilka, and **Filip Jurčíček**
Charles University in Prague, Faculty of Mathematics and Physics
Institute of Formal and Applied Linguistics
Malostranské náměstí 25, CZ-11800 Prague, Czech Republic
{odusek,oplatek,zilka,jurcicek}@ufal.mff.cuni.cz

Abstract

When deploying a spoken dialogue system in a new domain, one faces a situation where little to no data is available to train domain-specific statistical models. We describe our experience with bootstrapping a dialogue system for public transit and weather information in real-word deployment under public use. We proceeded incrementally, starting from a minimal system put on a toll-free telephone number to collect speech data. We were able to incorporate statistical modules trained on collected data – in-domain speech recognition language models and spoken language understanding – while simultaneously extending the domain, making use of automatically generated semantic annotation. Our approach shows that a successful system can be built with minimal effort and no in-domain data at hand.

1 Introduction

The Alex Public Transit Information System is an experimental Czech spoken dialogue system providing information about all kinds of public transit in the Czech Republic, publicly available at a toll-free 800 telephone number.[1] It was launched for public use as soon as a first minimal working version was developed, using no in-domain speech data. We chose an incremental approach to system development in order to collect call data and use them to bootstrap statistical modules. Nearly a year after launch, we have collected over 1,300 calls from the general public, which enabled us to train and deploy an in-domain language model for Automatic Speech Recognition (ASR) and a statistical Spoken Language Understanding (SLU) module. The domain supported by the system has extended from transit information in one city to ca. 5,000 towns and cities in the whole country, plus weather and time information. This shows that a even a very basic system is useful in collecting in-domain data and that the incremental approach is viable.

Spoken dialogue systems have been a topic of research for the past several decades, and many experimental systems were developed and tested with users (Walker et al., 2001; Gašić et al., 2013; Janarthanam et al., 2013). However, few experimental systems became available to general public use. Let's Go (Raux et al., 2005; Raux et al., 2006) is a notable example in the public transportation domain. Using interaction with users from the public to bootstrap data-driven methods and improve the system is also not a common practice. Both Let's Go and the GOOG-411 business finder system (Bacchiani et al., 2008) collected speech data, but applied data-driven methods only to improve statistical ASR. We use the call data for statistical SLU as well and plan to further introduce statistical modules for dialogue management and natural language generation.

Our spoken dialogue system framework is freely available on GitHub[2] and designed for easy adaptation to new domains and languages. An English version of our system is in preparation.

We first present the overall structure of the Alex SDS framework and then describe the minimal system that has been put to public use, as well as our incremental extensions. Finally, we provide an evaluation of our system based on the recorded calls.

*This work was funded by the Ministry of Education, Youth and Sports of the Czech Republic under the grant agreement LK11221 and core research funding, SVV project 260 104, and grants GAUK 2058214 and 2076214 of Charles University in Prague. It used language resources stored and distributed by the LINDAT/CLARIN project of the Ministry of Education, Youth and Sports of the Czech Republic (project LM2010013).

[1] Call 800-899-998 from the Czech Republic.

[2] http://github.com/UFAL-DSG/alex

2 Overall Alex SDS System Structure

The basic architecture of Alex is modular and consists of the traditional SDS components: automatic speech recognizer (ASR), spoken language understanding (SLU), dialogue manager (DM), natural language generator (NLG), and a text-to-speech (TTS) module.

We designed the system to allow for easy replacement of the individual components: There is a defined interface for each of them. As the interfaces are domain-independent, changing the domain is facilitated as well by this approach.

3 Baseline Transit Information System

We decided to create a minimal working system that would not require any in-domain data and open it to general public to collect call data as soon as possible. We believe that this is a viable alternative to Wizard-of-Oz experiments (Rieser and Lemon, 2008), allowing for incremental development and producing data that correspond to real usage scenarios (see Section 4).

3.1 Baseline Implementation of the Components

Having no in-domain data available, we resorted to very basic implementations using hand-written rules or external services:

- ASR used a neural network based voice activity detector trained on small out-of-domain data. Recordings classified as speech were fed to the the web-based Google ASR service.
- SLU was handcrafted for our domain using simple keyword-spotting rules.
- In DM, the dialogue tracker held only one value per dialogue slot, and the dialogue policy was handcrafted for the basic tasks in our domain.
- NLG is a simple template-based module.
- We use a web-based Czech TTS service provided to us by SpeechTech.[3]

3.2 Baseline Domain

At baseline, our domain only consisted of a very basic public transport information for the city of Prague. Our ontology contained ca. 2,500 public transit stops. The system was able to present the next connection between two stops requested by the user, repeat the information, or return several following connections. Connection search was based on Google Directions API.[4]

[3]http://www.speechtech.cz/

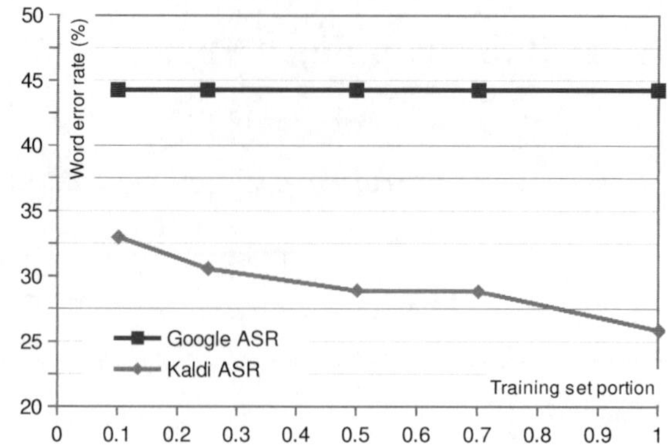

Figure 1: ASR word error rate depending on the size of in-domain language model training data
The full training set amounts to 9,495 utterances (30,126 tokens). The test set contains 1,187 utterances (4,392 tokens).

4 Collecting Data and Extending the System in Real Usage

We launched our system at a public toll-free 800 number and advertised the service at our university, among friends, and via Facebook. We also cooperate with the Czech Blind United association,[5] promoting our system among its members and receiving comments about its use. We advertised our extensions and improvements using the same channels.

We record and collect all calls to the system, including our own testing calls, to obtain training data and build statistical models into our system.

4.1 Speech Recognition: Building In-Domain Models

The Google on-line ASR service, while reaching state-of-the-art performance in some tasks (Morbini et al., 2013), showed very high word error rate in our specific domain (see Figure 1). We replaced it with the Kaldi ASR engine (Povey et al., 2011) trained on general-domain Czech acoustic data (Korvas et al., 2014) with an in-domain class-based language model built using collected call data and lists of all available cities and stops.

We describe our modifications to Kaldi for online decoding in Plátek and Jurčíček (2014). A performance comparison of Google ASR with

[4]https://developers.google.com/maps/documentation/directions/

[5]http://www.sons.cz

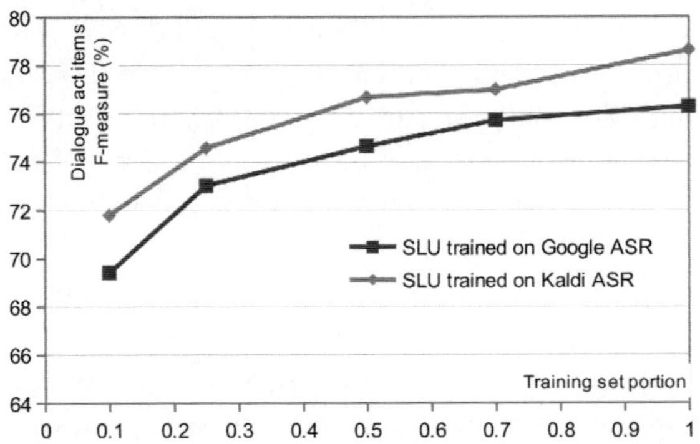

Figure 2: SLU performance (F-measure on dialogue act items) depending on training data size
The same data sets as in Figure 1 are used, with semantic annotations from handcrafted SLU running on manual transcriptions.

Kaldi trained on our data is shown in Figure 1. One can see that the in-domain language model brings a substantial improvement, even with very small data sizes.

4.2 Spoken Language Understanding

To increase system robustness, we built a statistical SLU based on a set of logistic regression classifiers and word n-gram features (Jurčíček et al., 2014). We train it on the output of our handcrafted SLU applied to manual transcriptions. We chose this approach over obtaining manual semantic annotation due to two main reasons:

1. Obtaining semantic annotation for Czech data is relatively slow and complicated; using crowdsourcing is not a possibility due to lack of speakers of Czech on the platforms.
2. As we intended to gradually extend our domain, semantic annotation changed over time as well.

This approach still allows the statistical SLU to improve on a handcrafted one by compensating for errors made by the ASR. Figure 2 shows that the performance of the statistical SLU module increases with more training data and with the in-domain ASR models.

4.3 Dialogue Manager

We have replaced the initial simplistic dialogue state tracker (see Section 3.1) by the probabilistic discriminative tracker of Žilka et al. (2013), which achieves near state-of-the-art performance while remaining completely parameter-free. This property allowed us to employ the tracker without any training data; our gradual domain extensions also required no further adjustments.

The dialogue policy is handcrafted, though it takes advantage of uncertainty estimated by the belief tracker. Its main logic is similar to that of Jurčíček et al. (2012). First, it implements a set of domain-independent actions, such as:

- dialogue opening, closing, and restart,
- implicit confirmation of changed slots with high probability of the most probable value,
- explicit confirmation for slots with a lower probability of the most probable value,
- a choice among two similarly probable values.

Second, domain-specific actions are implemented for the domain(s) described in Section 4.4.

4.4 Extending the Domain

We have expanded our public transit information domain with the following tasks:

- The user may specify departure or arrival time in absolute or relative terms ("in ten minutes", "tomorrow morning", "at 6 pm.", "at 8:35" etc.).
- The user may request more details about the connection: number of transfers, journey duration, departure and arrival time.
- The user may travel not only among public transport stops within one city, but also among multiple cities or towns.

The expansion to multiple cities has lead to an ontology improvement: The system is able to find the corresponding city in the database based on a stop name, and can use a default stop for a given city. We initially supported three Czech major cities covered by the Google Directions service, then extended the coverage to the whole country (ca. 44,000 stops in 5,000 cities and towns) using Czech national public transport database provided by CHAPS.[6]

We now also include weather information for all Czech cities in the system. The user may ask for weather at the given time or on the whole day. We use OpenWeatherMap as our data source.[7]

Furthermore, the user may ask about the current time at any point in the dialogue.

5 System Evaluation from Recorded Calls

We have used the recorded call data for an evaluation of our system. Figure 3 presents the num-

[6] http://www.idos.cz
[7] http://openweathermap.org/

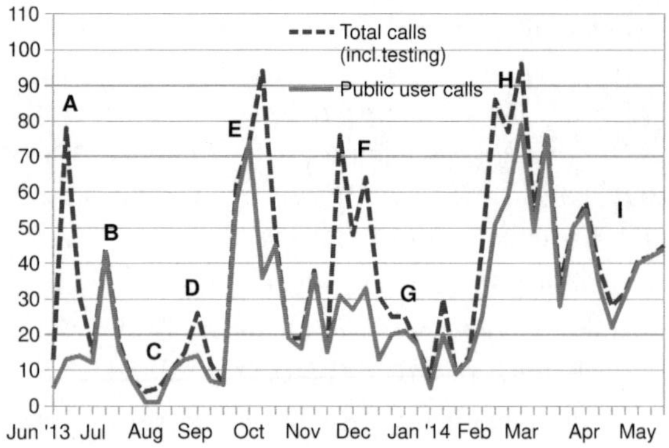

Figure 3: Number of calls per week

The dashed line shows all recorded calls, including those made by the authors. The full line shows calls from the public only.

Spikes: *A* – initial testing, *B* – first advertising, *C* – system partially offline due to a bug, *D* – testing statistical SLU module, *E* – larger advertising with Czech Blind United, *F* – testing domain enhancements, *G* – no advertising and limited system performance, *H* – deploying Kaldi ASR and nationwide coverage, *I* – no further advertising.

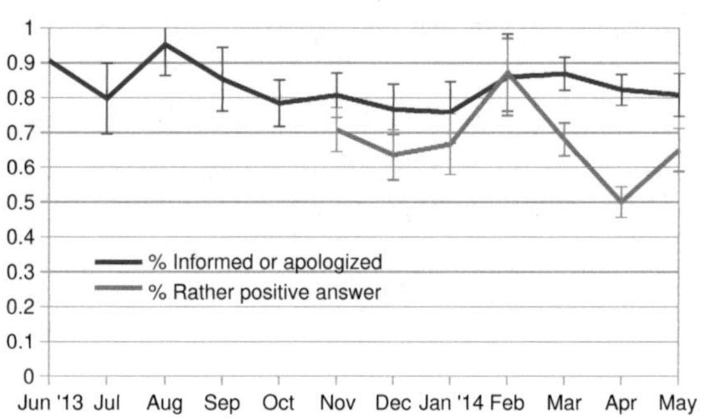

Figure 4: System success rates by month

Percentage of calls where the system provided information (or apology for not having one) and percentage of rather positive responses to the final question, both shown with standard error bars.

ber of calls to our system per week and reflects the testing and advertising phases, as well as some of our extensions and improvements described in Section 4. A steeper usage increase is visible in recent weeks after the introduction of Kaldi ASR engine and nationwide coverage (see Sections 4.1 and 4.4). The number of calls and unique users (caller phone numbers) grows steadily; so far, more than 300 users from the public have made over 1,300 calls to the system (cf. Figure 5 and Table 1 in the appendix).[8]

Figure 4 (and Table 1 in the appendix) give a detailed view of the success of our system. Information is provided in the vast majority of calls. Upon manual inspection of call transcripts, we discovered that about half of the cases where no information is provided can be attributed to the system failing to react properly; the rest is off-topic calls or users hanging up too early.

We have also introduced a "final question" as an additional success metric. After the user says good-bye, the system asks them if they received the information they were looking for. By looking at the transcriptions of responses to this question, we recognize a majority of them as rather positive ("Yes", "Nearly" etc.); the proportion of positive reactions seems to remain stable. However, the final question is not an accurate measure as most users seem to hang up directly after receiving information from the system.

6 Conclusions and Further Work

We use an iterative approach to build a complex dialogue system within the public transit information domain. The system is publicly available on a toll-free phone number. Our extensible dialogue system framework as well as the system implementation for our domain can be downloaded from GitHub under the Apache 2.0 license.

We have shown that even very limited working version can be used to collect calls from the public, gathering training data for statistical system components. Our experiments with the Kaldi speech recognizer show that already a small amount of in-domain data for the language model brings a substantial improvement. Generating automatic semantic annotation from recording transcripts allows us to maintain a statistical spoken language understanding unit with changing domain and growing data.

The analysis of our call logs shows that our system is able to provide information in the vast majority of cases. Success rating provided by the users themselves is mostly positive, yet the conclusiveness of this metric is limited as users tend to hang up directly after receiving information.

In future, we plan to add an English version of the system and further expand the domain, allowing more specific connection options. As we gather more training data, we plan to introduce statistical modules into the remaining system components.

[8] We only count calls with at least one valid user utterance, disregarding calls where users hang up immediately.

A System Evaluation Data

In the following, we include additional data from call logs evaluation presented in Section 5.

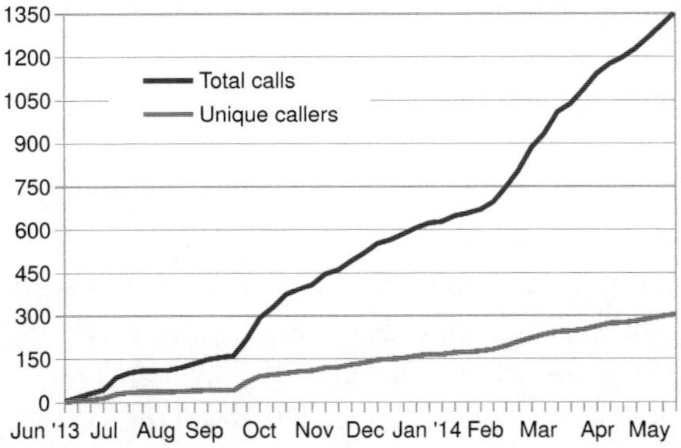

Figure 5: Cumulative number of calls and unique callers from the public by weeks

The growth rates of the number of unique users and the total number of calls both correspond to the testing and advertising periods shown in Figure 3.

Total calls	1,359
Unique users (caller phone numbers)	304
System informed (or apologized)	1,124
System informed about directions	990
System informed about weather	88
System informed about current time	41
Apologized for not having information	223
System asked the final question	229
Final question answered by the user	199
Rather positive user's answer	146
Rather negative user's answer	23

Table 1: Detailed call statistics

Total absolute numbers of calls from general public users over the period of nearly one year are shown.

References

M. Bacchiani, F. Beaufays, J. Schalkwyk, M. Schuster, and B. Strope. 2008. Deploying GOOG-411: early lessons in data, measurement, and testing. In *Proceedings of ICASSP*, page 5260–5263. IEEE.

M. Gašić, C. Breslin, M. Henderson, D. Kim, M. Szummer, B. Thomson, P. Tsiakoulis, and S. Young. 2013. On-line policy optimisation of bayesian spoken dialogue systems via human interaction. In *Proceedings of ICASSP*, page 8367–8371. IEEE.

S. Janarthanam, O. Lemon, P. Bartie, T. Dalmas, A. Dickinson, X. Liu, W. Mackaness, and B. Webber. 2013. Evaluating a city exploration dialogue system combining question-answering and pedestrian navigation. In *Proceedings of ACL*.

F. Jurčíček, B. Thomson, and S. Young. 2012. Reinforcement learning for parameter estimation in statistical spoken dialogue systems. *Computer Speech & Language*, 26(3):168–192.

F. Jurčíček, O. Dušek, and O. Plátek. 2014. A factored discriminative spoken language understanding for spoken dialogue systems. In *Proceedings of TSD*. To appear.

M. Korvas, O. Plátek, O. Dušek, L. Žilka, and F. Jurčíček. 2014. Free English and Czech telephone speech corpus shared under the CC-BY-SA 3.0 license. In *Proceedings of LREC*, Reykjavík.

F. Morbini, K. Audhkhasi, K. Sagae, R. Artstein, D. Can, P. Georgiou, S. Narayanan, A. Leuski, and D. Traum. 2013. Which ASR should i choose for my dialogue system? In *Proceedings of SIGDIAL*, page 394–403.

O. Plátek and F. Jurčíček. 2014. Free on-line speech recogniser based on kaldi ASR toolkit producing word posterior lattices. In *Proceedings of SIGDIAL*.

D. Povey, A. Ghoshal, G. Boulianne, L. Burget, O. Glembek, N. Goel, M. Hannemann, P. Motlicek, Y. Qian, P. Schwarz, et al. 2011. The Kaldi speech recognition toolkit. In *Proceedings of ASRU*, page 1–4, Hawaii.

A. Raux, B. Langner, D. Bohus, Alan W. Black, and M. Eskenazi. 2005. Let's go public! taking a spoken dialog system to the real world. In *Proceedings of Interspeech*.

A. Raux, D. Bohus, B. Langner, Alan W. Black, and M. Eskenazi. 2006. Doing research on a deployed spoken dialogue system: one year of Let's Go! experience. In *Proceedings of Interspeech*.

V. Rieser and O. Lemon. 2008. Learning effective multimodal dialogue strategies from Wizard-of-Oz data: Bootstrapping and evaluation. In *Proceedings of ACL*, page 638–646.

M. A. Walker, R. Passonneau, and J. E. Boland. 2001. Quantitative and qualitative evaluation of DARPA communicator spoken dialogue systems. In *Proceedings of ACL*, page 515–522.

L. Žilka, D. Marek, M. Korvas, and F. Jurčíček. 2013. Comparison of bayesian discriminative and generative models for dialogue state tracking. In *Proceedings of SIGDIAL*, page 452–456, Metz, France.

InproTK$_S$: A Toolkit for Incremental Situated Processing

Casey Kennington
CITEC, Dialogue Systems Group, Bielefeld University
ckennington[1]

Spyros Kousidis
Dialogue Systems Group
Bielefeld University
spyros.kousidis[2]

David Schlangen
Dialogue Systems Group
Bielefeld University
david.schlangen[2]

[1]@cit-ec.uni-bielefeld.de
[2]@uni-bielefeld.de

Abstract

In order to process incremental situated dialogue, it is necessary to accept information from various sensors, each tracking, in real-time, different aspects of the physical situation. We present extensions of the incremental processing toolkit INPROTK which make it possible to plug in such multimodal sensors and to achieve situated, real-time dialogue. We also describe a new module which enables the use in INPROTK of the Google Web Speech API, which offers speech recognition with a very large vocabulary and a wide choice of languages. We illustrate the use of these extensions with a description of two systems handling different situated settings.

1 Introduction

Realising incremental processing of speech in- and output – a prerequisite to interpretation and possibly production of speech concurrently with the other dialogue participant – requires some fundamental changes in the way that components of dialogue systems operate and communicate with each other (Schlangen and Skantze, 2011; Schlangen and Skantze, 2009). Processing situated communication, that is, communication that requires reference to the physical setting in which it occurs, makes it necessary to accept (and fuse) information from various different sensors, each tracking different aspects of the physical situation, making the system multimodal (Atrey et al., 2010; Dumas et al., 2009; Waibel et al., 1996).

Incremental situated processing brings together these requirements. In this paper, we present a collection of extensions to the incremental processing toolkit INPROTK (Baumann and Schlangen, 2012) that make it capable of processing situated communication in an incremental fashion: we have developed a general architecture for plugging in multimodal sensors whith we denote INPROTK$_S$, which includes instantiations for motion capture (via *e.g. via Microsoft Kinect* and *Leap Motion*) and eye tracking (*Seeingmachines FaceLAB*). We also describe a new module we built that makes it possible to perform (large vocabulary, open domain) speech recognition via the Google Web Speech API. We describe these components individually and give as use-cases in a driving simulation setup, as well as real-time gaze and gesture recognition.

In the next section, we will give some background on incremental processing, then describe the new methods of plugging in multimodal sensors, specifically using XML-RPC, the Robotics Service Bus, and the InstantReality framework. We then explain how we incorporated the Google Web Speech API into InproTK, offer some use cases for these new modules, and conclude.

2 Background: The IU model, INPROTK

As described in (Baumann and Schlangen, 2012), INPROTK realizes the *IU*-model of incremental processing (Schlangen and Skantze, 2011; Schlangen and Skantze, 2009), where incremental systems consist of a network of processing *modules*. A typical module takes input from its *left buffer*, performs some kind of processing on that data, and places the processed result onto its *right buffer*. The data are packaged as the payload of *incremental units* (IUs) which are passed between modules.

The IUs themselves are also interconnected via so-called *same level links* (SLL) and *grounded-in links* (GRIN), the former allowing the linking of IUs as a growing sequence, the latter allowing that sequence to convey what IUs directly affect it (see Figure 1 for an example). A complication particular to incremental processing is that modules can "change their mind" about what the best hypothe-

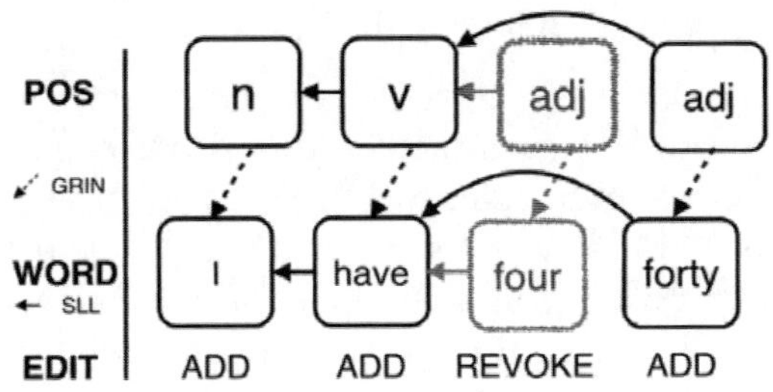

Figure 1: Example of IU network; part-of-speech tags are grounded into words, tags and words have same level links with left IU; *four* is revoked and replaced with *forty*.

sis is, in light of later information, thus IUs can be *added*, *revoked*, or *committed* to a network of IUs.

INPROTK determines how a module network is "connected" via an XML-formatted configuration file, which states module instantiations, including the connections between left buffers and right buffers of the various modules. Also part of the toolkit is a selection of "incremental processing-ready" modules, and so makes it possible to realise responsive speech-based systems.

3 InproTK and new I/O: InproTK$_S$

The new additions introduced here are realised as INPROTK$_S$ modules. The new modules that input information to an INPROTK$_S$ module network are called *listeners* in that they "listen" to their respective message passing systems, and modules that output information from the network are called *informers*. Listeners are specific to their method of receiving information, explained in each section below. Data received from listeners are packaged into an IU and put onto the module's right buffer. Listener module left buffers are not used in the standard way; left buffers receive data from their respective message passing protocols. An informer takes all IUs from its left buffer, and sends their payload via that module's specific output method, serving as a kind of right buffer. Figure 2 gives an example of how such listeners and informers can be used. At the moment, only strings can be read by listeners and sent by informers; future extensions could allow for more complicated data types.

Listener modules add new IUs to the network; correspondingly, further modules have to be designed in instatiated systems then can make use of these information types. These IUs created by the listeners are linked to each other via SLLs. As with audio inputs in previous version of INPROTK, these IUs are considered *basedata* and not explictly linked via GRINs in the sensor data. The modules defined so far also simply *add* IUs and do not revoke.

We will now explain the three new methods of getting data into and out of INPROTK$_S$.

3.1 XML-RPC

XML-RPC is a *remote procedure call* protocol which uses XML to encode its calls, and HTTP as a transport mechanism. This requires a server/client relationship where the listener is implemented as the server on a specified port.[1] Remote sensors (e.g., an eye tracker) are realised as clients and can send data (encoded as a string) to the server using a specific procedural call. The informer is also realised as an XML-RPC client, which sends data to a defined server. XML-RPC was introduced in 1998 and is widely implemented in many programming languages.

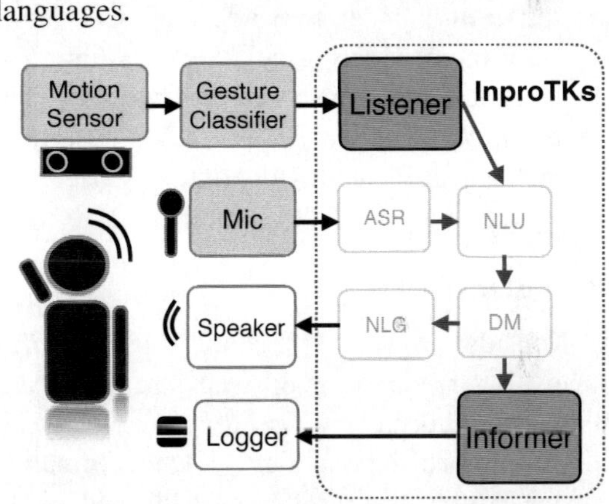

Figure 2: Example architecture using new modules: motion is captured and processed externally and class labels are sent to a listener, which adds them to the IU network. Arrows denote connections from right buffers to left buffers. Information from the DM is sent via an Informer to an external logger. External gray modules denote input, white modules denote output.

3.2 Robotics Service Bus

The *Robotics Service Bus* (RSB) is a middleware environment originally designed for message-passing in robotics systems (Wienke and Wrede, 2011).[2] As opposed to XML-RPC which requires

[1]The specification can be found at http://xmlrpc.scripting.com/spec.html

[2]https://code.cor-lab.de/projects/rsb

point-to-point connections, RSB serves as a *bus* across specified transport mechanisms. Simply, a network of communication nodes can either *inform* by sending events (with a payload), or *listen*, i.e., receive events. Informers can send information on a specific *scope* which establishes a visibility for listeners (e.g., a listener that receives events on scope /one/ will receive all events that fall under the /one/ scope, whereas a listener with added constants on the scope, e.g., /one/two/ will not receive events from different added constants /one/three/, but the scope /one/ can listen on all three of these scopes). A listener module is realised in INPROTK$_S$ by setting the desired scope in the configuration file, allowing INPROTK$_S$ seamless interconnectivity with communication on RSB.

There is no theoretical limit to the number of informers or listeners; events from a single informer can be received by multiple listeners. Events are typed and any new types can be added to the available set. RSB is under active development and is becoming more widely used. Java, Python, and C++ programming languages are currently supported. In our experience, RSB makes it particularly convenient for setting distributed sensor processing networks.

3.3 InstantReality

In (Kousidis et al., 2013), the *InstantReality* framework, a virtual reality environment, was used for monitoring and recording data in a real-time multimodal interaction.[3] Each information source (sensor) runs on its own dedicated workstation and transmits the sensor data across a network using the *InstantIO* interface. The data can be received by different components such as InstantPlayer (3D visualization engine; invaluable for monitoring of data integrity when recording experimental sessions) or a logger that saves all data to disk. Network communication is achieved via multicast, which makes it possible to have any number of listeners for a server and vice-versa.

The InstantIO API is currently available in C++ and Java. It comes with a non-extensible set of types (primitives, 2D and 3D vectors, rotations, images, sounds) which is however adequate for most tracking applications. InstantIO listeners and informers are easily configured in INPROTK$_S$ configuration file.

[3]http://www.instantreality.org/

3.4 Venice: Bridging the Interfaces

To make these different components/interfaces compatible with each other, we have developed a collection of bridging tools named *Venice*. Venice serves two distinct functions. First, *Venice*.HUB, which pushes data to/from any of the following interfaces: disk (logger/replayer), InstantIO, and RSB. This allows seamless setup of networks for logging, playback, real-time processing (or combinations; e.g, for simulations), minimizing the need for adaptations to handle different situations. Second, *Venice*.IPC allows interprocess communication and mainly serves as a quick and efficient way to create network components for new types of sensors, regardless of the platform or language. Venice.IPC acts as a server to which TCP clients (a common interface for sensors) can connect. It is highly configurable, readily accepting various sensor data outputs, and sends data in real-time to the InstantIO network.

Both Venice components operate on all three major platforms (Linux, Windows, Mac OS X), allowing great flexibility in software and sensors that can be plugged in the architecture, regardless of the vendor's native API programming language or supported platform. We discuss some use cases in section 5.

4 Google Web Speech

One barrier to dialogue system development is handling ASR. Open source toolkits are available, each supporting a handful of languages, with each language having a varying vocabulary size. A step in overcoming this barrier is "outsourcing" the problem by making use of the Google Web Speech API.[4] This interface supports many languages, in most cases with a large, open domain of vocabulary. We have been able to access the API directly using INPROTK$_S$, similar to (Henderson, 2014).[5] INPROTK$_S$ already supports an incremental variant of Sphinx4; a system designer can now choose from these two alternatives.

At the moment, only the Google Chrome browser implements the Web Speech API. When the INPROTK$_S$ Web Speech module is invoked, it creates a service which can be reached from

[4]The Web Speech API Specificiation: https://dvcs.w3.org/hg/speech-api/raw-file/tip/speechapi.html

[5]Indeed, we used Matthew Henderson's *webdial* project as a basis: https://bitbucket.org/matthen/webdialog

the Chrome browser via an URL (and hence, microphone client, dialogue processor and speech recogniser can run on different machines). Navigating to that URL shows a simple web page where one can control the microphone. Figure 3 shows how the components fit together.

While this setup improves recognition as compared to the Sphinx4-based recognition previously only available in INPROTK, there are some areas of concern. First, there is a delay caused by the remote processing (on Google's servers), requiring alignment with data from other sensors. Second, the returned transcription results are only 'semi-incremental'; sometimes chunks of words are treated as single increments. Third, n-best lists can only be obtained when the API detects the end of the utterance (incrementally, only the top hypothesis is returned). Fourth, the results have a crude timestamp which signifies the end of the audio segment. We use this timestamp in our construction of word IUs, which in informal tests have been found to be acceptable for our needs; we defer more systematic testing to future work.

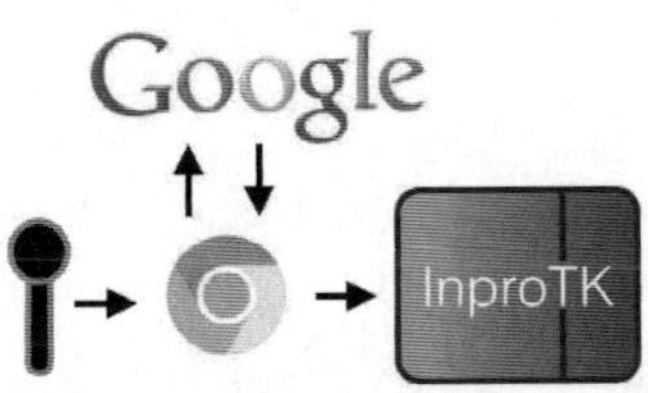

Figure 3: Data flow of Google Web Speech API: Chrome browser controls the microphone, sends audio to API and receives incremental hypotheses, which are directly sent to InproTK$_S$.

5 INPROTK$_S$ in Use

We exemplify the utility of INPROTK$_S$ in two experiments recently performed in our lab.

In-car situated communication We have tested a "pause and resume" strategy for adaptive information presentation in a driving simulation scenario (see Figure 4), using INPROTK$_S$ and OpenDS (Math et al., 2013). Our dialogue manager – implemented using OpenDial (Lison, 2012) – receives trigger events from OpenDS in order to update its state, while it verbalises calendar events and presents them via speech. This is achieved by means of InstantIO servers we integrated into OpenDS and respective listeners in INPROTK$_S$. In turn, InstantIO informers send data that is logged by Venice.HUB. The results of this study are published in (Kousidis et al., 2014). Having available the modules described here made it surprisingly straightforward to implement the interaction with the driving simulator (treated as a kind of sensor).

Figure 4: Participant performing driving test while listening to iNLG speech delivered by InProTK$_S$.

Real-time gaze fixation and pointing gesture detection Using the tools described here, we have recently tested a real-time situated communication environment that uses speech, gaze, and gesture simultaneously. Data from a *Microsoft Kinect* and a *Seeingmachines Facelab* eye tracker are logged in realtime to the InstantIO network. A Venice.HUB component receives this data and sends it over RSB to external components that perform detection of gaze fixation and pointing gestures, as described in (Kousidis et al., 2013). These class labels are sent in turn over RSB to INPROTK$_S$ listeners, aggregating these modalities with the ASR in a language understanding module. Again, this was only enabled by the framework described here.

6 Conclusion

We have developed methods of providing multimodal information to the incremental dialogue middleware INPROTK. We have tested these methods in real-time interaction and have found them to work well, simplifying the process of connecting external sensors necessary for multimodal, situated dialogue. We have further extended its options for ASR, connecting the Google Web Speech API. We have also discussed Venice, a tool for bridging RSB and InstantIO interfaces, which can log real-time data in a time-aligned manner, and replay that data. We also offered some use-cases for our extensions.

INPROTK$_S$ is freely available and accessible.[6]

[6]https://bitbucket.org/inpro/inprotk

Acknowledgements Thank you to the anonymous reviewers for their useful comments and to Oliver Eickmeyer for helping with InstantReality.

References

Pradeep K. Atrey, M. Anwar Hossain, Abdulmotaleb El Saddik, and Mohan S. Kankanhalli. 2010. *Multimodal fusion for multimedia analysis: a survey*, volume 16. April.

Timo Baumann and David Schlangen. 2012. The InproTK 2012 Release. In *NAACL*.

Bruno Dumas, Denis Lalanne, and Sharon Oviatt. 2009. Multimodal Interfaces : A Survey of Principles , Models and Frameworks. In *Human Machine Interaction*, pages 1–25.

Matthew Henderson. 2014. The webdialog Framework for Spoken Dialog in the Browser. Technical report, Cambridge Engineering Department.

Spyros Kousidis, Casey Kennington, and David Schlangen. 2013. Investigating speaker gaze and pointing behaviour in human-computer interaction with the mint.tools collection. In *SIGdial 2013*.

Spyros Kousidis, Casey Kennington, Timo Baumann, Hendrik Buschmeier, Stefan Kopp, and David Schlangen. 2014. Situationally Aware In-Car Information Presentation Using Incremental Speech Generation: Safer, and More Effective. In *Workshop on Dialog in Motion, EACL 2014*.

Pierre Lison. 2012. Probabilistic Dialogue Models with Prior Domain Knowledge. In *Proceedings of the 13th Annual Meeting of the Special Interest Group on Discourse and Dialogue*, pages 179–188, Seoul, South Korea, July. Association for Computational Linguistics.

Rafael Math, Angela Mahr, Mohammad M Moniri, and Christian Müller. 2013. OpenDS: A new open-source driving simulator for research. *GMM-Fachbericht-AmE 2013*.

David Schlangen and Gabriel Skantze. 2009. A General, Abstract Model of Incremental Dialogue Processing. In *Proceedings of the 10th EACL*, number April, pages 710–718, Athens, Greece. Association for Computational Linguistics.

David Schlangen and Gabriel Skantze. 2011. A General, Abstract Model of Incremental Dialogue Processing. *Dialoge & Discourse*, 2(1):83–111.

Alex Waibel, Minh Tue Vo, Paul Duchnowski, and Stefan Manke. 1996. Multimodal interfaces. *Artificial Intelligence Review*, 10(3-4):299–319.

Johannes Wienke and Sebastian Wrede. 2011. A middleware for collaborative research in experimental robotics. In *System Integration (SII), 2011 IEEE/SICE International Symposium on*, pages 1183–1190.

Back to the Blocks World: Learning New Actions through Situated Human-Robot Dialogue

Lanbo She[1], Shaohua Yang[1], Yu Cheng[2], Yunyi Jia[2], Joyce Y. Chai[1], Ning Xi[2]
[1]Department of Computer Science and Engineering
Michigan State University
East Lansing, MI 48824, USA
{shelanbo, jchai, yangshao}@cse.msu.edu
[2]Department of Electrical and Computer Engineering
Michigan State University
East Lansing, MI 48824, USA
{chengyu9, jiayunyi, xin}@egr.msu.edu

Abstract

This paper describes an approach for a robotic arm to learn new actions through dialogue in a simplified blocks world. In particular, we have developed a three-tier action knowledge representation that on one hand, supports the connection between symbolic representations of language and continuous sensorimotor representations of the robot; and on the other hand, supports the application of existing planning algorithms to address novel situations. Our empirical studies have shown that, based on this representation the robot was able to learn and execute basic actions in the blocks world. When a human is engaged in a dialogue to teach the robot new actions, step-by-step instructions lead to better learning performance compared to one-shot instructions.

1 Introduction

When a new generation of robots start to work side-by-side with their human partners in joint tasks (Christensen et al., 2010), they will often encounter new objects or are required to perform new actions. It is important for the robots to automatically learn new knowledge about the environment and the tasks from their human partners. To address this issue, this paper describes our recent work on action learning through dialogue. As a first step, we limit our investigation to a simple blocks world motivated by Terry Winograd's early work (Winograd, 1972). By using an industrial robotic arm (SCHUNK) in this small world, we are interested in addressing the following questions. First, human language has a discrete and symbolic representation, but the robot arm has a continuous representation for its movements. Where should the connections between the symbolic representation and the continuous representation take place so that human language can be used to direct the robot's movements? Second, when the robot learns new tasks from its human partner, how to represent the acquired knowledge effectively so that it can be applied in novel situations? Third, during human-robot dialogue, when the robot fails to perform the expected actions due to the lack of knowledge, how should the human teach the robot new actions? through step-by-step instructions or one-shot instructions?

With these questions in mind, we have developed a three-tier action knowledge representation for the robotic arm. The lower level connects to the physical arm and defines the trajectories of executing three atomic actions supported by the arm (i.e., *open_gripper*, *close_gripper*, *move*). The middle level defines primitive operators such as *Open_Grip*, *Close_Grip* and *MoveTo* in the fashion of the traditional AI planner (Fikes and Nilsson, 1971) and directly links to the lower level. The upper-level captures the high-level actions acquired by learning from the human. These high-level actions are represented as the desired goal states of the environment as a result of these actions. This three-tier representation allows the robot to automatically come up with a sequence of lower-level actions by applying existing planning algorithms.

Based on this representation, we implemented a dialogue system for action learning and further conducted an empirical study with human subjects. In particular, we compared the dialogue

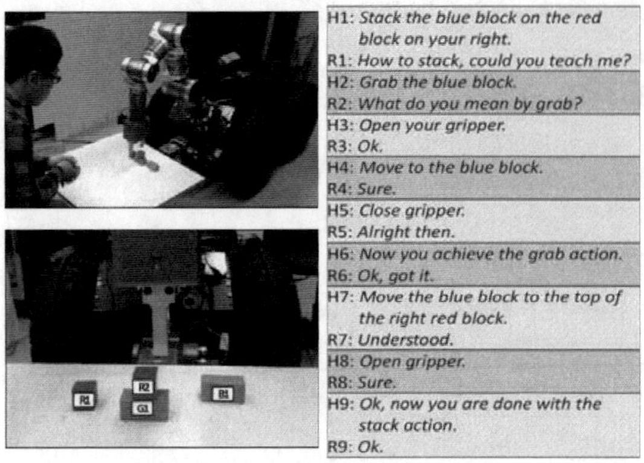

Figure 1: An example setup and dialogue. Objects are marked with labels only for the illustration purpose.

based on the step-by-step instructions (i.e., one step at a time and wait for the robot's response at each step before going to the next step) with the one-shot instructions (i.e., give the instruction with all steps at once). Our empirical results have shown that the three-tier knowledge representation can capture the learned new action and apply it to novel situations. Although the step-by-step instructions resulted in a lengthier teaching process compared to the one-shot instructions, they led to better learning performance for the robot.

2 Related Work

Over forty years ago, Terry Winograd developed SHRDLU (Winograd, 1972) to demonstrate natural language understanding using a simulated block-moving arm. One aspect he did not address, but mentioned in his thesis (Winograd, 1972) as an important aspect, was learning new actions through natural language. Motivated by Winograd's early work, we start our initial investigation on action learning in a physical blocks world and with a physical robotic arm. The blocks world is the most famous domain used for planning in artificial intelligence. Thus it allows us to focus on mechanisms that, on one hand, connect symbolic representations of language with lower-level continuous sensorimotor representations of the robot; and on the other hand, support the use of the planning algorithms to address novel situations.

Most previous work on following human instructions are based on supervised learning (Kollar et al., 2010; Tellex et al., 2011; Chen et al., 2010) or reinforcement learning (Branavan et al., 2012; Branavan et al., 2010). These types of learning may not be adequate in time-critical situations where only resources available to the robot is its human partners. Thus it is desirable that humans can engage in a natural language dialogue to teach robots new skills. Using natural language dialogue to learn new skills have been explored previously by (Allen et al., 2007) where an artificial agent was developed to acquire skills through natural language instructions (i.e., find restaurant). But this work only grounds language to symbolic interface widgets on web pages.

In the robotics community, previous work has applied learning by demonstration to teach robots new skills (Cakmak et al., 2010). To potentially allow natural language instructions, previous work has also explored connecting language with lower-level control systems (Kress-Gazit et al., 2008; Siskind, 1999; Matuszek et al., 2012). Different from these previous works, here we investigate the use of natural language dialogue for learning actions. Previous work described in (Cantrell et al., 2012; Mohan et al., 2013) is most similar to our work. Here we focus on both grounded learning and the use of planning for action learning.

3 Dialogue System

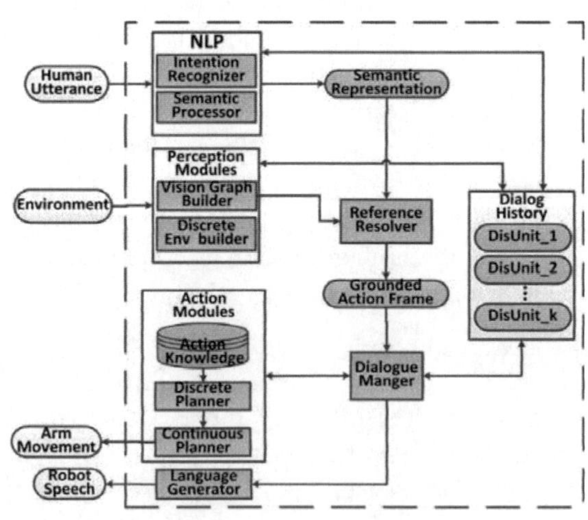

Figure 2: System Architecture

We developed a dialogue system to support learning new actions. An example setup is shown in Figure 1, in which a SCHUNK arm is used to manipulate blocks placed on a surface. In H_1, the human starts to ask the robot to stack the blue block (i.e., B_1) on top of the red block (i.e., R_1). The robot does not understand the action "stack", so it asks the human for instructions. Then the hu-

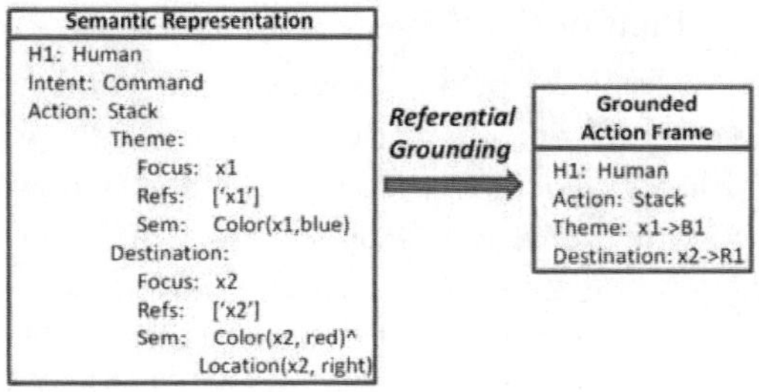

Figure 3: Example semantic representation and action frame for the human utterance *"stack the blue block on the red block on your right."*

man provides detailed steps to accomplish this action (i.e., H_2 to H_8) and also observes the robot's response in each step. Note that during this process, another unknown action (i.e., "grab" as in H_2) is encountered. The robot thus needs to learn this action first. The robot is able to keep track of the dialogue structure so that actions and subactions can be learned accordingly. Once the robot receives a confirmation from the human that the corresponding action is successfully performed (i.e., H_6 and H_9), it acquires the new action and explicitly represents it in its knowledge base for future use. Instead of representing the acquired knowledge as specific steps as illustrated by the human, the acquired action is represented by the expected final state, which represents the changes of environment as a result of the action. The new action can be directly applied to novel situations by applying planning algorithms. Figure 2 shows the system structure. Next we explain main system modules in detail.

Natural Languge Processing: Natural language processing modules capture semantic information from human language inputs. In particular, the `Intention Recognizer` is used to recognize human intent (e.g., *Command* and *Confirmation*). The `Semantic Processor`, implemented as *Combinatory Categorial Grammar (CCG)* [1], is used to generate semantic representation. Current semantic information includes the actions (e.g., stack) and their roles (e.g., *Theme* and *Destination*). The roles are further represented by objects' properties (*Color*, *Location* and *Spatial Relation*). An example semantic representation of "H1: *Stack the blue block on the red block on your right.*" is shown in Figure 3.

[1]We utilized *OpenCCG*, which could be found at: http://openccg.sourceforge.net/

Perception Modules: Besides interpreting human language, the robot also continuously perceives the shared environment with its camera. Objects in video frames are recognized through vision system (Collet et al., 2011), and further represented as a *Vision Graph* (computed by `Vision Graph Builder`), which captures objects and their properties (in the numerical form). The robot can also access to its own internal status, such as the location of the gripper and whether it's open or closed. Combining the robot's state and environment information, the `Discrete State Builder` can represent the entire environment as a conjunction of predicates, which will be later used for action planning.

Referential Grounding: To make the semantic representation meaningful, it must be grounded to the robot's representation of perception. We use the graph-based approach for referential grounding as described in (Liu et al., 2012)(Liu et al., 2013). Once the references are grounded, the semantic representation becomes a *Grounded Action Frame*. For example, as shown in Figure 3, *"the blue block"* refers to *B1* and *"the red block on your right"* refers to *R1*.

Dialogue Manager: The `Dialogue Manager` is used to decide what dialog acts the system should perform give a situation. It is composed by: a representation of dialogue state, a space of system activity and a dialogue policy. The dialogue status is computed based on the human intention a dialogue state captures (from semantic representation) and the `Grounded Action Frame`. The current space of system activities includes asking for instructions, confirming, executing actions and updating its action knowledge base with new actions. The dialogue policy stores the (dialogue state, system activities) pairs. During interaction, the `Dialogue Manager` will first identify the current dialogue state and then apply the dialogue acts associated with that state as specified in the dialogue policy.

Action Modules: The `Action Modules` are used to realize a high-level action from the `Grounded Action Frame` with the physical arm and to learn new actions. For realizing high-level actions, if the action in the `Grounded Action Frame` has a record in the `Action Knowledge`, which keeps track of all the knowledge about various actions, the

Discrete Planner will do planning to find a sequence of primitive actions to achieve the high-level action. Then these primitive actions will sequentially go through Continuous Planner and be translated to the trajectories of arm motors. By following these trajectories, the arm can perform the high-level action. For learning new actions, these modules will calculate state changes before and after applying the action on the focus object. Such changes of the state are generalized and stored as knowledge representation of the new action.

Response Generator: Currently, the Response Generator is responsible for language generation to realize the detail sentence. In our current investigation, the speech feedback is simple, so we just used a set of pre-defined templates to do language generation. And the parameters in the templates will be realized during run time.

4 Action Learning through Dialogue

To realize the action learning functionality we have developed a set of action related processes including an action knowledge base, action execution processes and action learning processes. Next we give detailed explanations.

4.1 Action Modules

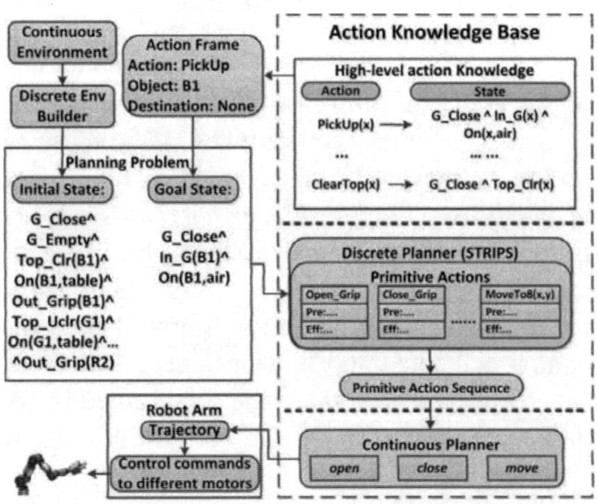

Figure 4: Execution example for "*Pick up the blue block*".

As shown in Figure 4, the action knowledge base is a three-level structure, which consists of *High-level action Knowledge*, *Discrete Planner* and *Continuous Planner*.

4.1.1 Continuous Planner

This lowest level planner defines three primitive actions: *open* (i.e., open gripper), *close* (i.e., close gripper) and *move* (i.e., move to the destination). Each primitive action is defined as a trajectory computing function, implemented as inverse kinematics. The outputs of these functions are control commands sendt to each arm motor to keep the arm following the trajectory.

4.1.2 Discrete Planner

The *Discrete Planner* is used to decompose a high-level action into a sequence of primitive actions. In our system, it is implemented as a *STRIPS* (Fikes and Nilsson, 1971) planner, which is defined as a quadruple $\langle P, O, I, G \rangle$:

- *P*: Set of predicates describing a domain.
- *O*: Set of operators. Each is specified by a set of preconditions and effects. An operator is applicable only when its preconditions could be entailed in a state.
- *I*: Initial state, the starting point of a problem.
- *G*: Goal state, which should be achieved if the problem is solved.

In our system, *O* set includes *Open_Gripper*, *Close_Gripper* and 8 different kinds of *MoveTo* (She et al., 2014). And the *P* set consists of two dimensions of the environment:

- *Arm States*: *G_Open/Close* (i.e., whether the gripper is open or closed), *G_Full/Empty* (i.e., whether the gripper has an object in it) and *G_At(x)* (i.e, location of the arm).
- *Object States*: *Top_Uclr/Clr(o)* (i.e., whether the block *o* has another block on its top), *In/Out_G(o)* (i.e., whether *o* is within the gripper fingers or not) and *On(o,x)* (i.e., *o* is supported by *x*).

The *I* and *G* are captured real-time during the dialogue interaction.

4.1.3 High-level action Knowledge

The high-level actions represent actions specified by the human partner. They are modeled as desired goal states rather than the action sequence taught by human. For example, the "*Stack(x,y)*" could be represented as "*On(x,y)*$\wedge$*G_Open*". If the human specifies a high-level action out of the action knowledge base, the dialogue manager will verbally request for instructions to learn the action.

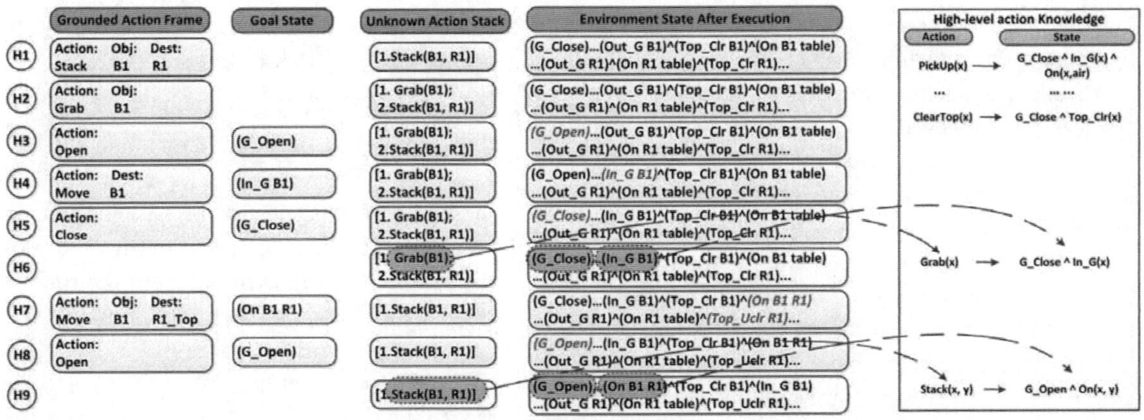

Figure 5: Learning process illustration. After hearing the stack action, the robot cannot perform. So the human gives step by step instruction. When the instruction is completed, new knowledge of *Grab(x)* and *Stack(x,y)* are learned in the high-level action knowledge base as the combination of the goal state of the robotic arm and the changes of the state for the involved objects.

4.2 Action Execution

Given a `Grounded Action Frame`, it is firstly checked with the high-level action knowledge base. If the knowledge base has its record (e.g., the *Pickup* and *ClearTop* in Figure 4.), a goal state describing the action effect will be retrieved. This goal state, together with the initial state captured from the current environment, will be sent to the `Discrete Planner`. And, through automated planning, a sequence of primitive actions will be generated to complete the task, which can be immediately executed by the arm.

Take the "*Pick up*" action frame in Figure 4 as an example. By checking the grounded action frame with the high-level action knowledge, a related goal state (i.e., "*G_Close*$\wedge$*Top_Clr(B1)* $\wedge$*In_G(B1)*$\wedge$*On(B1,air)*") can be retrieved. At the same time, the `Discrete Evn Builder` translates the real world environment as a conjunction of predicates, which serves as the initial state. Given the combination of initial state and goal state, the *STRIPS* planner can search for a path of primitive actions to solve the problem. For example, the *PickUp(B1)* in Figure 4 can be solved by *Open_Grip*, *MoveTo(B1)*, *Close_Grip* and *MoveTo(air)*.

The primitive actions are executed by the continuous planner and control process in the lower robotic system. For the "*open*" and "*close*", they are executed by controlling the position of the gripper fingers. For the "*move*", a task-space trajectory is first planned based on the minimum-time motion planning algorithm to move the robot end-effector from the current position to the final position. A kinematic controller with redundancy resolution (Zhang et al., 2012) is then used to generate the joint movements for the robot to track the planned trajectory. Achieving the end of the trajectory indicates the action completion.

4.3 Action Learning

Figure 5 illustrates the system internal process of acquiring action knowledge from the dialogue in Figure 1.

At the beginning of the dialogue, the grounded action frame *Stack(B1, R1)* captured from the first human utterance is not in the action knowledge, so it will be pushed to the top of the unknown action stack as a new action waiting to be learned. The environment state at this point is calculated as shown in the figure. Then the robot will verbally request instructions. During the instruction, it's possible that another unknown action *Grab(B1)* is referred. The same as the *Stack* action, it will be pushed to the top of unknown action stack waiting to be learned.

In the next instruction, the human says "*Open your gripper*". This sentence can be translated as action frame *Open* and the goal state "*G_Open*" can be retrieved from the action knowledge base. After executing the action sequence, the gripper state will be changed from "*G_Close*" to "*G_Open*", as shown in Figure 5. In the following two instructions, the human says "*Move to the blue block*" and "*Close gripper*". Similarly, these two instructions are translated as action frames *Move(B1)* and *Close*, then are executed accordingly. After executing these two steps, the state of *B1* is changed from "*Out_G(B1)*" to "*In_G(B1)*".

At this point, the previous unknown action *Grab(B1)* is achieved, so the human says "*Now you achieve the grab action*" as a signal of teaching completion. After acknowledging the teaching completion, the action learning module will learn the new action representation by combining the arm state with the state changes of the argument objects in the unknown action frame. For example, the argument object of unknown action *Grab(B1)* is *B1*. By comparing the original state of *B1*, [*(Out_G B1)*$\wedge$*(Top_Clr B1)*$\wedge$*(On B1 table)*] with the final state, [*(In_G B1)*$\wedge$*(Top_Clr B1)*$\wedge$*(On B1 table)*], *B1* is changed from *(Out_G B1)* to *(In_G B1)*. So, the learning module will generalize such state changes and acquire the knowledge representation of the new action *Grab(x)* as *G_Close*$\wedge$*In_G(x)*.

5 Empirical Studies

The objectives of our empirical studies are two folds. First, we aim to exam whether the current representation can support planning algorithms and execute the learned actions in novel situations. Second, we aim to evaluate how extra effort from the human partner through step-by-step instructions may affect the robot's learning performance.

5.1 Instruction Effort

Previous work on mediating perceptual differences between humans and robots have shown that a high collaborative effort from the robot leads to better referential grounding (Chai et al., 2014). Motivated by this previous work, we are interested in examining how different levels of effort from human partners may affect the robot's learning performance. More specifically, we model two levels of variations:

- **Collaborative Interaction:** In this setting, a human partner provides step-by-step instructions. At each step, the human will observe the the robot's response (i.e., arm movement) before moving to the next step. For example, to teach "stack", the human would issue "pick up the blue block", observe the robot's movement, then issue "put it on the red block" and observe the robot movement. By this fashion, the human makes extra effort to make sure the robot follows every step correctly before moving on. The human partner can detect potential problems and respond to immediate feedback from the robot.
- **Non-Collaborative Interaction:** In this setting, the human only provides a one-shot instruction. For example, to teach "stack", the human first issues a complete instruction "pick up the blue block and put it on top of the red block" and then observes the robot's responses. Compared to the collaborative setting, the non-collaborative setting is potentially more efficient.

5.2 Experimental Tasks

Similar to the setup shown in Figure 1, in the study, we have multiple blocks with different colors and sizes placed on a flat surface, with a SCHUNK arm positioned on one side of the surface and the human subject seated on the opposite side. The video stream of the environment is sent to the vision system (Collet et al., 2011). With the pre-trained object model of each block, the vision system could capture blocks' 3D positions from each frame. Five human subjects participated in our experiments [2]. During the study, each subject was informed about the basic actions the robot can perform (i.e., open gripper, close gripper, and move to) and was instructed to teach the robot several new actions through dialogue. Each subject would go through the following two phases:

5.2.1 Teaching/Learning Phase

Each subject was asked to teach the following five new actions under the two strategies (i.e., step-by-step instructions vs. one-shot instructions): {Pickup, Grab, Drop, ClearTop, Stack} Each time, the subject can choose any blocks they think are useful to teach the action. After finishing teaching one action (either under step-by-step instructions or under one-shot instructions), we would survey the subject whether he/she thinks the teaching is completed and the corresponding action is successfully performed by the robot. We record the teaching duration and then re-arrange the table top setting to move to the next action.

For the teaching/learning phase, we use two metrics for evaluation: 1) *Teaching Completion Rate*(R_t) which stands for the number of actions successfully taught and performed by the robot; 2)*Teaching Completion Duration* (D_t which measures the amount of time taken to teach an action.

[2]More human subjects will be recruited to participate in our studies.

5.2.2 Execution Phase

The goal of learning is to be able to apply the learned knowledge in novel situations. To evaluate such capability, for each action, we designed 10 additional setups of the environment which are different from the environment where the action was learned. For example, as illustrated in Figure 6, the human teaches the *pick Up* action by instructing the robot how to perform "*pick up the blue block(i.e., B1)*" under the environment in 6(a). Once the knowledge is acquired about the action "pick up", we will test the acquired knowledge in a novel situation by instructing the robot to execute "*pick up the green block(i.e., G1)*" in the environment shown in 6(b).

(a) Learning: the human teaches the robot how to "*pick up the blue block (i.e., B1)*" during the learning phase

(b) Execution: the human asks the robot to "*pick up the green block (i.e., G1)*" after the robot acquires the knowledge about "pick up"

Figure 6: Examples of a learning and an execution setup.

For the execution phase, we also used two factors to evaluate: 1) *Action Sequence Generation*(R_g) which measures how many high-level actions among the 10 execution scenarios where the corresponding lower-level action sequences are correctly generated; 2) *Action Sequence Execution*(R_{ge}) which measures the number of high level actions that are correctly executed based on the lower level action sequences.

5.3 Empirical Results

Our experiments resulted in a total of 50 action teaching dialogues. Half of these are under the step-by-step instructions (i.e., collaborative interaction) and half are under one-shot instructions (i.e., non-collaborative). As shown in Figure 7, 5 out of the 50 teaching dialogues were considered as incomplete by the human subjects and all of them are from the *Non-Collaborative* setting. For each of the 45 successful dialogues, an action would be learned and acquired. For each of these acquired actions, we further tested its execution under 10 different setups.

Action learning successful rate	User 1		User 2		User 3		User 4		User 5	
	Non	Col	Non	Col	Non	Col	Non	Col	Non	Col
Pickup	1	1	1	1	1	1	1	1	0	1
Grab	1	1	1	1	1	1	1	1	1	1
Drop	1	1	1	1	1	1	1	1	0	1
ClearTop	1	1	1	1	1	1	1	1	1	1
Stack	1	1	0	1	0	1	0	1	1	1
Total	5	5	4	5	4	5	4	5	3	5

Figure 7: The teaching completion result of the 50 teaching dialogues. "1" stands for the dialogue where the subject considers the teaching/learning as complete since the robot performs the corresponding action correctly; and "0" indicates a failure in learning. The total numbers of teaching completion are listed in the bottom row.

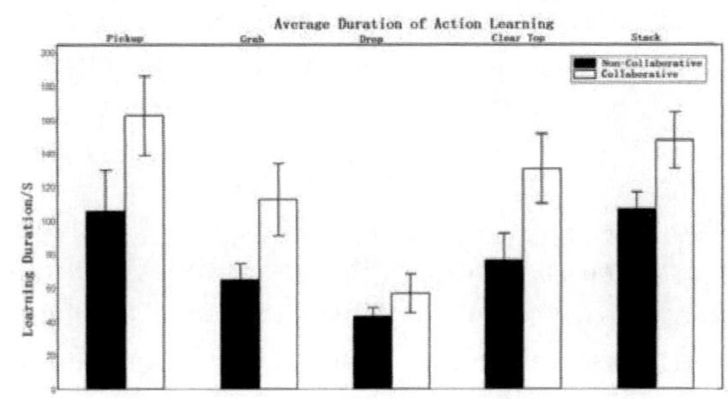

Figure 8: The teaching completion duration results. The durations under the non-collaborative strategy are smaller than the collaborative strategy in most cases.

5.3.1 Teaching Performance

The result of teaching completion is shown in Figure 7. Each subject contributes two columns: the "*Non*" stands for the *Non-Collaborative* strategy and the "*Col*" column refers to the *Collaborative* strategy. As the table shows, all the 5 uncompleted teaching are from the *Non-Collaborative* strategy. In most of these 5 cases, the subjects thought the actual performed actions were different from their expectations. For example, in one of the "*stack*" failures, the human one-shot instruction was "*move the blue block to the red block on the left.*". She thought the arm would put the blue block on the top of red block, open gripper and then move away. However, based on the robot's knowledge, it just moved the blue block above the red block and stopped there. So the subject considered this teaching as incomplete. On the other hand, in the *Collaborative* interactions, the robot's actual actions could also be different from the subject's expectation. But, as the instruction

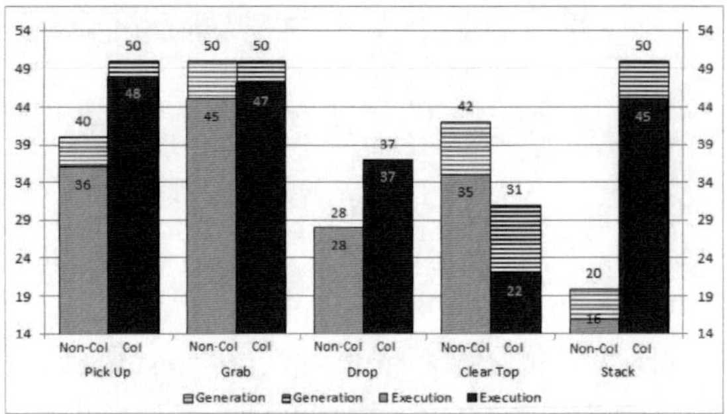

Figure 9: Each bar represents the number of successfully generated action sequences during testing. The solid portion of each bar represents the number of successfully executed action sequences. The number of successfully execution is always smaller than or equal to the generation. This is because we are dealing with dynamic environment, and the inaccurate real-time localization will make some correct action sequence fail to be executed.

was given step-by-step, the instructors could notice the difference from the immediate feedback and adjust their follow-up steps, which contributed to a higher completion rate.

The duration of each teaching task is shown in Figure 8. Bar heights represent average teaching duration, the ranges stand for standard error of the mean (SEM). The 5 actions are represented by different groups. As shown in the figure, the teaching duration under the *Collaborative* strategy tends to take more time. Because in the *Collaborative* case, the human needs to plan next step after observing the robot's response to a previous step. If an exception happens, a sub-dialogue is often arranged to do correction. But in the *Non-Collaborative* case, the human comes up with an entire instruction at the beginning, which appears more efficient.

5.3.2 Execution Performance

Figure 9 illustrates the action sequence generation and execution results in the execution phase.

As shown in Figure 9, testing results of actions learned under the Collaborative strategy are higher than the ones using *Non-Collaborative*, this is because teaching under the *Collaborative* strategy is more likely to be successful. One exception is the *Clear Top* action, which has lower generation rate under the *Col* setting. By examining the collected data, we noticed that our system failed to learn the knowledge of *Clear Top* in one of the 5 teaching phases using *Col* setting, although the human subject labeled it as successful. Another phenomenon shown in Figure 9 is that the generation results are always larger than or equal with the corresponding execution results. This is caused by inaccurate localization and camera calibration, which introduced exceptions during executing the action sequence.

6 Conclusion

This paper describes an approach to robot action learning in a simplified blocks world. The simplifications of the environment and the tasks allow us to explore connections between symbolic representations of natural language and continuous sensorimotor representations of the robot which can support automated planning for novel situations. This investigation is only our first step. Many issues have not been addressed. For example, the world is full of uncertainties. Our current approach can only either succeed or fail executing an action based on the acquired knowledge. There is no approximation or reasoning of the uncertain states which may affect potential execution. Also, when the robot fails to execute an action, there is no explanation why it fails. If the robot can articulate its internal representations regarding where the problem occurs, the human can provide better help or targeted teaching. These are the directions we will pursue in our future work.

7 Acknowledgment

This work was supported by IIS-1208390 from the National Science Foundation and N00014-11-1-0410 from the Office of Naval Research.

References

James F. Allen, Nathanael Chambers, George Ferguson, Lucian Galescu, Hyuckchul Jung, Mary D. Swift, and William Taysom. 2007. Plow: A collaborative task learning agent. In *AAAI*, pages 1514–1519. AAAI Press.

S. R. K. Branavan, Luke S. Zettlemoyer, and Regina Barzilay. 2010. Reading between the lines: Learning to map high-level instructions to commands. In *Proceedings of the 48th Annual Meeting of the Association for Computational Linguistics*, ACL '10, pages 1268–1277, Stroudsburg, PA, USA. Association for Computational Linguistics.

S.R.K. Branavan, Nate Kushman, Tao Lei, and Regina Barzilay. 2012. Learning high-level planning from text. In *Proceedings of the 50th Annual Meeting of the Association for Computational Linguistics (Volume 1: Long Papers)*, pages 126–135, Jeju Island, Korea, July. Association for Computational Linguistics.

Maya Cakmak, Crystal Chao, and Andrea Lockerd Thomaz. 2010. Designing interactions for robot active learners. *IEEE T. Autonomous Mental Development*, 2(2):108–118.

R. Cantrell, K. Talamadupula, P. Schermerhorn, J. Benton, S. Kambhampati, and M. Scheutz. 2012. Tell me when and why to do it! run-time planner model updates via natural language instruction. In *Human-Robot Interaction (HRI), 2012 7th ACM/IEEE International Conference on*, pages 471–478, March.

Joyce Y. Chai, Lanbo She, Rui Fang, Spencer Ottarson, Cody Littley, Changsong Liu, and Kenneth Hanson. 2014. Collaborative effort towards common ground in situated human robot dialogue. In *Proceedings of 9th ACM/IEEE International Conference on Human-Robot Interaction*, Bielefeld, Germany.

David L. Chen, Joohyun Kim, and Raymond J. Mooney. 2010. Training a multilingual sportscaster: Using perceptual context to learn language. *J. Artif. Int. Res.*, 37(1):397–436, January.

H. I. Christensen, G. M. Kruijff, and J. Wyatt, editors. 2010. *Cognitive Systems*. Springer.

Alvaro Collet, Manuel Martinez, and Siddhartha S. Srinivasa. 2011. The MOPED framework: Object Recognition and Pose Estimation for Manipulation.

Richard E. Fikes and Nils J. Nilsson. 1971. Strips: A new approach to the application of theorem proving to problem solving. In *Proceedings of the 2Nd International Joint Conference on Artificial Intelligence*, IJCAI'71, pages 608–620, San Francisco, CA, USA. Morgan Kaufmann Publishers Inc.

Thomas Kollar, Stefanie Tellex, Deb Roy, and Nicholas Roy. 2010. Toward understanding natural language directions. In *Proceedings of the 5th ACM/IEEE International Conference on Human-robot Interaction*, HRI '10, pages 259–266, Piscataway, NJ, USA. IEEE Press.

Hadas Kress-Gazit, Georgios E. Fainekos, and George J. Pappas. 2008. Translating structured english to robot controllers. *Advanced Robotics*, 22(12):1343–1359.

Changsong Liu, Rui Fang, and Joyce Chai. 2012. Towards mediating shared perceptual basis in situated dialogue. In *Proceedings of the 13th Annual Meeting of the Special Interest Group on Discourse and Dialogue*, pages 140–149, Seoul, South Korea.

Changsong Liu, Rui Fang, Lanbo She, and Joyce Chai. 2013. Modeling collaborative referring for situated referential grounding. In *Proceedings of the SIGDIAL 2013 Conference*, pages 78–86, Metz, France.

Cynthia Matuszek, Evan Herbst, Luke S. Zettlemoyer, and Dieter Fox. 2012. Learning to parse natural language commands to a robot control system. In Jaydev P. Desai, Gregory Dudek, Oussama Khatib, and Vijay Kumar, editors, *ISER*, volume 88 of *Springer Tracts in Advanced Robotics*, pages 403–415. Springer.

Shiwali Mohan, James Kirk, and John Laird. 2013. A computational model for situated task learning with interactive instruction. In *Proceedings of ICCM 2013 - 12th International Conference on Cognitive Modeling*.

Lanbo She, Yu Cheng, Joyce Chai, Yunyi Jia, Shaohua Yang, and Ning Xi. 2014. Teaching robots new actions through natural language instructions. In *RO-MAN*.

Jeffrey Mark Siskind. 1999. Grounding the lexical semantics of verbs in visual perception using force dynamics and event logic. *J. Artif. Int. Res.*, 15(1):31–90, February.

Stefanie Tellex, Thomas Kollar, Steven Dickerson, Matthew R. Walter, Ashis Gopal Banerjee, Seth J. Teller, and Nicholas Roy. 2011. Understanding natural language commands for robotic navigation and mobile manipulation. In Wolfram Burgard and Dan Roth, editors, *AAAI*. AAAI Press.

T. Winograd. 1972. Procedures as a representation for data in a computer program for understanding natural language. *Cognitive Psychology*, 3(1):1–191.

Huatao Zhang, Yunyi Jia, and Ning Xi. 2012. Sensor-based redundancy resolution for a nonholonomic mobile manipulator. In *IROS*, pages 5327–5332.

An easy method to make dialogue systems incremental

Hatim KHOUZAIMI
Orange Labs
Laboratoire Informatique d'Avignon
hatim.khouzaimi@orange.com

Romain LAROCHE
Orange Labs,
Issy-les-Moulineaux,
France
romain.laroche@orange.com

Fabrice LEFEVRE
Laboratoire Informatique d'Avignon,
Avignon, France
fabrice.lefevre@univ-avignon.fr

Abstract

Incrementality as a way of managing the interactions between a dialogue system and its users has been shown to have concrete advantages over the traditional turn-taking frame. Incremental systems are more reactive, more human-like, offer a better user experience and allow the user to correct errors faster, hence avoiding desynchronisations. Several incremental models have been proposed, however, their core underlying architecture is different from the classical dialogue systems. As a result, they have to be implemented from scratch. In this paper, we propose a method to transform traditional dialogue systems into incremental ones. A new module, called *the Scheduler* is inserted between the client and the service so that from the client's point of view, the system behaves incrementally, even though the service does not.

1 Introduction

An incremental compiler (Lock, 1965) processes each instruction irrespectively from the others so that local modifications of the source code do not affect the global result. This idea of incrementality has been adapted to the field of natural language analysis (Wirén, 1992): instead of feeding modules with full utterances, the input signal is delivered and processed chunk by chunk (word by word for example) and each new piece engenders a new output hypothesis.

Human beings behave similarly when interacting with each other (Levelt, 1989; Clark, 1996). They understand each other gradually when they speak, they can interrupt each other and the listener is able to predict the end of an utterance before it is fully pronounced by the speaker (Tanenhaus et al., 1995; Brown-Schmidt and Hanna, 2011; DeVault et al., 2011). Reading is also a task that we perform incrementally (Ilkin and Sturt, 2011).

Traditional dialogue systems[1] work in a turn-taking manner. The user pronounces his request and after a silence is detected, the systems starts processing the utterance and planning an answer. Some systems can even allow the user to barge in on them, however, they do not take the timing of the interruption into account nor try to link it with the system's utterance. On the other hand, incremental dialogue systems process the user's request chunk by chunk as the latter is divided in several *incremental units* (IU) (Schlangen and Skantze, 2011). They keep a hypothetical user request that evolves as new IUs arrive as input. The response to this hypothesis can be used to make live feedback to the user using voice or other modalities if available. As opposed to traditional systems, when the user interrupts the system, the content and the timing of its utterance are taken into account (Matsuyama et al., 2009; Selfridge et al., 2013) to determine how to act on it. Therefore, incremental systems have been shown to be more reactive, to offer a more human-like experience (Edlund et al., 2008) and to correct errors faster hence achieving better results in terms of user experience (Skantze and Schlangen, 2009; Baumann and Schlangen, 2013; El Asri et al., 2014) and task completion (Matthias, 2008; El Asri et al., 2014).

Many incremental architectures have already been proposed. Nevertheless, designing systems based on them requires an implementation from scratch as they are fundamentally different from traditional dialogue systems. The objective of this paper is to propose a method of transforming a traditional system into an incremental one at minimal cost. A new module called *the Scheduler* is inserted between the client and the service so that

[1] We will use the expression *traditional dialogue systems* to talk about non incremental ones.

from the client's point of view, the system behaves incrementally, even though the service works in a traditional way.

Section 2 draws a state-of-the-art concerning incremental dialogue systems. The architecture proposed here and the role of the Scheduler are presented in Section 3. In Section 4, two implementations of our method are presented: CFAsT and DictaNum. Then, a discussion is held in Section 5 before concluding the paper and presenting our next objectives in Section 6.

2 Related work

Dialogue systems can be split into four groups according to how they integrate incrementality in their behaviour. Traditional dialogue systems (Laroche et al., 2011) form the first category whereas the second one refers to systems that propose some incremental strategies among traditional others (El Asri et al., 2014). The architecture presented in this paper belongs to the third group which contains incremental systems based on a traditional inner behaviour (Hastie et al., 2013; Selfridge et al., 2012). The fourth category contains incremental systems where internal modules work incrementally (Dohsaka and Shimazu, 1997; Allen et al., 2001; Schlangen and Skantze, 2011). Figure 1 discussed later provides a list of the features that are available in each category.

Several dialogue strategies have been implemented in NASTIA (El Asri et al., 2014), a dialogue system helping the user to find a date and a time for an appointment with a technician (completing the work made during the European project CLASSiC (Laroche and Putois, 2010)). Among them, List of Availabilities is an incremental strategy where the system enumerates a list of alternatives for the appointment. The user is supposed to interrupt this enumeration when he hears an option that is convenient for him. An experiment showed that List of Availabilities produced better results than other traditional strategies in terms of task completion and user satisfaction.

PARLANCE (Hastie et al., 2013) is an example of a third category system (it was developed in the European project PARLANCE). Its architecture is similar to the traditional ones but it integrates a new module, called MIM (Micro-turn Interaction Manager), which decides when the system should speak, listen to the user and when it should generate back-channels. The closest approach to the method introduced in this paper is presented in (Selfridge et al., 2012) : the IIM (Incremental Interaction Manager) is an intermediate module between an incremental ASR and a TTS on the one hand and the service on the other hand. Instead of replicating the dialogue context as it is suggested in this paper, different instances of the service are run. Moreover, the IIM is introduced as preliminary work in order to simulate incremental dialogue whereas in this paper, the Scheduler approach is fully studied and placed into the context of the current state-of-the-art concerning incremental dialogue. It is also viewed as a new layer that can be extended later on, into a smart turn-taking manager.

The architecture proposed in (Dohsaka and Shimazu, 1997) contains eight modules that work in parallel: the Speech Recognizer, the Response Analyzer, the Dialogue Controller, the Problem Solver, the Utterance Planner, the Utterance Controller, the Speech Synthesizer and the Pause Monitor. The user asks the system to solve a problem. Then, his request is submitted incrementally to the Speech Recognizer which sends its output text to the Response Analyzer that figures out concepts to be sent to the Dialogue Controller. The latter interacts with the Problem Solver and the Utterance Planner in order to compute a solution that is communicated to the user through the Utterance Controller then the Speech Synthesizer. This system belongs to the fourth category as all its modules behave incrementally in order to start suggesting a solution to the user's problem before it is totally computed. In the same category, (Allen et al., 2001) proposes another architectures split in three main modules: the Interpretation Manager, the Behavioral Agent and the Generation Manager. The first module catches the user's request and broadcasts it incrementally inside the system. The second one manages the system's action plan and the third is in charge of the response delivery.

A general and abstract model is introduced in (Schlangen and Skantze, 2011). A dialogue system can be viewed as a chain of modules. Each module has a Left Buffer (LB) where its inputs are pushed, an Internal State (IS) and a Right Buffer (RB) where it makes its outputs available. Data (audio, text, concepts...) flows through these modules in the form of Incremental Units (IU). When an IU is put in the LB of a module, it can be processed immediately hence modifying its RB. For example, every 500 ms, a new IU in the form of a chunk of audio signal can be put into the LB of the ASR which can modify its output according to what the user said during this time window. All dialogue systems from the four categories can be viewed as instances of this general model: *we can now see that a non-incremental system can be characterised as a special case of an incremental system, namely one where IUs are always maximally complete [...] and where all modules update in one go.*

In this paper, we introduce an architecture that belongs to the third category. In comparison with the first two categories, these systems behave incrementally during the whole dialogue. On the other hand, they can be built at a lower cost than the systems from the fourth category.

3 Architecture

Traditional dialogue systems are generally composed of a client on the user's terminal and a service that is deployed on a remote machine. They work in a turn-taking manner as when the user speaks, the system waits until the end of his request before processing it and vice versa (except for some systems where the user can interrupt the system). To make such a system incremental, we suggest inserting a new module between the client and the service: the Scheduler (this denomination is taken from (Laroche, 2010)). This new architecture can be cast as an instance of the general abstract model of (Schlangen and Skantze, 2011). The client, the Scheduler and the service are the three modules that compose the system. The first two ones are incremental but the last one is not. We will not use the notions of LB and RB and will consider that these modules interact with each other through some channel (network in the case of our implementation, see Section 4).

3.1 The traditional architecture

In a traditional architecture, the client receives a stream of data (audio signal, string...). If it is not the case (a web interface where each button represents a request for example), it does not make sense to transform such a system in an incremental one, so they are out of the scope of this paper. The end of a request is determined by a condition $EndTurnCond$. It can be a long enough silence (Raux and Eskenazi, 2008; Wlodarczak and Wagner, 2013) in the case of vocal services or a carriage return for text systems. A *dialogue turn* is the time interval during which the user sends a request to the system and gets a response. These turns will be called T^1, T^2, ..., T^k... and each one of them can be split into a *user turn* $T^{k,U}$ and a *system turn* $T^{k,S}$: $T^k = T^{k,U} \cup T^{k,S}$. During the user turn, a request Req^k is sent and during the system turn, the corresponding response $Resp^k$ is received. The instant when a condition goes from $false$ to $true$ will be called its *activation time*. As a consequence, $T^{k,U}$ ends at the activation time of $EndTurnCond$ and $T^{k,S}$ is finished when the system gives the floor to the user.

The service is made up of three parts: the internal interface, the internal context and the external interface. The internal interface manages the interactions between the service and the client. The internal context handles the way the client's requests should be acted on and the external interface is in charge of the interactions with the external world (database, remote device...).

3.2 Incrementality integration

The way the client sends the user's request to the service should be modified in order to make the system incremental. A new sending condition is defined: $EndMicroTurnCond$ and it is less restrictive than $EndTurnCond$ (which makes the latter imply the former). Therefore, the new client sends requests more frequently than the traditional one. A user micro-turn is the time interval between two activation times of $EndMicroTurnCond$ so the user turn $T^{k,U}$ can be divided into $n^{k,U}$ user micro-turns $\mu T_i^{k,U}$: $T^{k,U} = \bigcup_{i=1}^{n^{k,U}} \mu T_i^{k,U}$. We also define the pth *sub-turn* of the user turn $T^{k,U}$ as: $T_p^{k,U} = \bigcup_{i=1}^{p} \mu T_i^{k,U}$. The union symbol is used as we concatenate time intervals. In general, $EndMicroTurnCond$ can be activated at a constant frequency or at each new input made by the user. Moreover, when $EndTurnCond$ is activated, the Scheduler is informed by the client thanks to a dedicated signal: *signal_ETC*. At each $T^{k,S}$, the user makes a new request but at the micro-turn $\mu T_i^{k,S}$ with $i < n^{k,U}$, the complete request is not available yet. Consequently, a temporary request which we will call *sub-request* (Req_i^k) is sent. Sending the whole request from the beginning of the turn at each micro-turn is called *restart incremental* processing (Schlangen and Skantze, 2011). Let us notice that if $i_1 < i_2$ then $Req_{i_1}^k$

is not necessarily a prefix of $Req^k_{i_2}$ (in spoken dialogue, a new input in the ASR can modify the whole or a big part of the output).

The Scheduler is an intermediate module between the client and the service whose aim is to make the combination {Scheduler + Service} behave incrementally from the client's point of view. We define $ServiceReqCond$ as the condition constraining the Scheduler to send a request to the system or not. At each user micro-turn $\mu T_i^{k,S}$, it receives a sub-request Req_i^k. If $ServiceReqCond$ is true, the latter is sent to the system and the corresponding response $Resp_i^k$ is stored so that the client can ask for it later. For example, $ServiceReqCond$ can be constantly true which makes the Scheduler send all the sub-requests that it receives or it can be activated only if the new sub-request is different from the previous one (if the client already behaves the same way through $EndMicroTurnCond$ it is redundant to do so in $ServiceReqCond$ too).

The end of a turn is determined by the Scheduler. This module decides when to validate the current sub-request and to no longer wait for new information to complete it. It engages the dialogue in the direction of this hypothesis as it is considered as the user's intent. The Scheduler is said to *commit* the sub-request (Schlangen and Skantze, 2011) (this notion is described in Section 3.3). We define $CommitCond$ as the condition for the Scheduler to commit a hypothesis. For example, in the case of a system that asks for a 10 digits phone number, $CommitCond = (length(num) == 10)$ where $length(num)$ is the number of digits in each sub-request. Hence, a user turn ends at the activation time of $CommitCond$ and not when a *signal_ETC* is received. However, $EndTurnCond$ implies $CommitCond$.

The client is made of two threads: the *sending thread* and the *recuperation thread*. The first one is in charge of sending sub-requests at each micro-turn and the second one gets the last response hypothesis available in the Scheduler. The recuperation thread is activated at the same frequency as micro-turns so that the client is always up to date. In the case of vocal services, it is the Scheduler's task to decide which intermediate responses should be pronounced by the system and which ones should be ignored. Therefore, a flag in the message must be set by this module to declare whether it has to be outputted or not. When the recuperation thread gets new messages from the Scheduler, it decides whether to send it to the Text-To-Speech module or not based on the value of this flag.

The service in our architecture is kept unchanged (apart from some changes at the applicative level, see Section 4.2). The only functional modification is that the context is duplicated: *the simulation context* (see Section 3.3) is added. When a new sub-request is received by the Scheduler and $ServiceReqCond$ is true, an incomplete request (sub-request) is sent to the service. Therefore, the system knows what would be the response of a sub-request if it has to be committed. As the service is not incremental and cannot process the request chunk by chunk, all the increments from the beginning of the turn have to be sent and that is what justifies the choice of the *restart incremental* mode.

The service can also order the Scheduler to commit. This behaviour is described in (Schlangen and Skantze, 2011) where the IUs in the RB of a module are *grounded in* the ones in the LB that generated them. Consequently, when a module decides to commit to an output IU, all the IUs that it is grounded in must be committed. In our architecture, when the service commits to the result of a request (if it already started delivering the response to the user for example), this request has to be committed by the Scheduler.

On the other hand, as we defined the user micro-turn, we can introduce the *system micro-turn*. In traditional systems, the service's response is played by the TTS during the system turn $T^{k,S}$. In incremental dialogue, this turn can be divided into n_S^k system micro-turns $\mu T_i^{k,S}$: $T^{k,S} = \bigcup_{i=1}^{n_S^k} \mu T_i^{k,S}$. Their duration depends on the way the service decides to chunk its response (for example, every item in an enumeration can be considered as a chunk). When the user interrupts the system, the timing of his interruption is given by the micro-turn during which he reacted. Moreover, when the user barges in, a new tour is started. Only vocal systems are concerned with this behaviour as textual systems cannot be interrupted (the whole service response is displayed instantly).

3.3 Commit, rollback and double context

The request hypothesis fluctuates as long as new increments are taken into account. However, at some point, the system has to take an action that is based on the last hypothesis and visible by the user. For example, a response may be sent to the TTS or a database can be modified. At that point, the system is said to *commit* to its last hypothesis which means that it engages the dialogue according to its understanding of the request at that moment. It no longer waits for other incremental units to complete the request as it can no longer change it. On the contrary, the system can decide to forget its last hypothesis and come back to the state it was in at the moment of the last commit. This operation is called *rollback* (both terms are taken from the database terminology).

Most of the requests sent by the Scheduler to the service are aimed to know what would the latter respond if the current hypothesis contains all the information about the user's intent. Consequently, these requests should not modify the current context of the dialogue. We suggest that the service maintains two contexts: the *real context* and the *simulation context*. The first one plays the same role as the classical context whereas the second one is a buffer that can be modified by partial requests.

In our architecture, committing to a hypothesis will be made by copying the content of the simulation context (generated by the current request hypothesis) into the real context. On the opposite, a rollback is performed by copying the real context into the simulation one, hence going back to the state the system was in right after the last commit.

Every user micro-turn, the client sends to the Scheduler the whole user's sub-request since the last commit. This incomplete request is then sent to the service and the answer is stored in the Scheduler. If during the next micro-turn, the Scheduler does not ask for a commit but needs to send a new sub-request instead, a rollback signal is sent first as the system works in a restart incremental way (in this paper, rollbacks are only performed in this case). Figures A.1 and A.2 represent the way our three modules interact and how the double context is handled. In Figure A.1, the conditions $EndTurnCond$, $EndMicroTurnCond$, $ServiceReqCond$ and $CommitCond$ are written on the left of the streams they generate. On the left of the figure, the times where the sending thread of the client is active and inactive are represented and dashed arrows represent streams that are received by the recuperation thread. They are not synchronized with the rest of the streams, even though they are in this figure (for more clarity). Also, the commit decision has been taken by the Scheduler after it received a *signal_ETC* which is not always the case.

We call $ctxt(T^k)$ the real context at the end of T^k ($ctxt(T^0)$ being the initial context at the beginning of the dialogue). The context is not modified during the system turn, hence, we may notice that $ctxt(T^{k,U}) = ctxt(T^k)$. During the commit at the end of $T^{k,U}$, the simulated context is copied into the real context: $ctxt(T^k) = ctxt(T^{k-1} + T^{k,U}_{n^{k,U}})$.

4 Implementations

We implemented our method in the case of two dialogue systems developed at Orange Labs. The first one is a text service where the client is a web interface and the second one is a vocal service designed to record numbers. With only a few modifications, these two systems have been made incremental, showing that our solution is easy to implement, and demonstrating the incremental behaviour of the transformed systems, in the limit of the implemented strategies and according to the modalities that have been used (text and vocal modes).

4.1 CFAsT: Content Finder AssitanT

CFAsT is an application developed at Orange Labs and which can be used to generate textual dialogue systems and whose objective is to help the user search for some specific content in a database.

The client is a web page with a text-box where the user can type a request using natural language (validated by a carriage return or by clicking on the `validate` button). This page also contains buttons representing keywords or content suggestions. In this implementation, the content base chosen is the list of accepted papers at the NIPS 2013 conference. A list of keywords is maintained through the interaction. It is initially empty and for each new request, if new keywords are detected, they are added to the list. The interaction ends when the user selects a unique content.

In our implementation[2], the client is made of two screens. The first one contains the same view as the classical system and the second one fluctuates incrementally. When the user is typing a request, the second view is updated

[2]http://dialogue.orange-labs.fr/CFAsTIncrEng/

each time the space button is hit: it shows the answer that the service would have given in case of a carriage return at that moment. When a request is validated, a commit is performed and the two views are identical. In this case: $EndMicroTurnCond$ is activated when the space button is hit ($ServiceReqCond$ does not filtrate any sub-request) and $EndTurnCond$ is $true$ if a carriage return is detected. In addition, $CommitCond = EndTurnCond$.

4.2 DictaNum

The second implementation is a vocal system called DictaNum and inspired by NUMBERS dialogue system (Skantze and Schlangen, 2009). It asks the user to dictate a number and then gives a feedback to confirm that it has been well understood. The client is an HTML web page that interacts with the Scheduler using AJAX[3]. It uses the Google web API for both the ASR and TTS tasks. Other existing systems ask the user to dictate a number (telephone, credit card...) such as *How may I help you?* (Langkilde et al., 1999). Here is an example of an interaction with the traditional version of DictaNum:

System: Welcome to the DictaNum service. Please dictate your number.
User: 01 45 65 79 98.
System: The dictated number is: 01 45 67 79 98. Is that correct?
User: No.
System: Sorry. Let us try again. Please dictate your number.
User: 01 45 65 79 98.
System: The dictated number is: 01 47 65 79 98. Is that correct?
User: No.
System: Sorry. Let us try again. Please dictate your number.
[...]
System: The dictated number is: 01 45 65 79 98. Is that correct?
User: Yes.
System: Thank you for using DictaNum. Bye.

If the user's request has not been understood correctly in one shot, he has to dictate it again. This is not an optimal strategy. DictaNum has been modified to support chunk by chunk dictation as in the following example:

[3]http://dialogue.orange-labs.fr/DictaNumEng/

System: Welcome to the DictaNum service. Please dictate your number.
User: 01 45
System: 01 45
User: 65 79
System: 67 79
User: No, 65 79
System: Sorry, 65 79
User: 98
System: 98
User: ...
System: The dictated number is: 01 45 65 79 98. Is that correct?
User: Yes.
System: Thank you for using DictaNum. Bye.

In order to generate feedbacks, the service has been modified at the applicative level. It maintains a string that is supposed to contain the complete number at the end of the interaction. Initially, this string is empty. When a silence is detected after a chunk is dictated, the system repeats the latter as a feedback to the user and concatenates it at the end of the number string. If the user begins a new chunk with *No*, the system understands that it has to correct the last one (starting the next feedback with *Sorry...*), otherwise, it keeps it and moves forward in the dictation. Finally, if after a feedback a silence is detected with nothing dictated, the system understands that the dictation is over and makes a general feedback over the whole number.

These modifications are not enough for the system to be used in an incremental way. It is not optimal for the user to insert silences in his dictation. Of course, he can, but it is not convenient nor natural. The client has been modified so that it no longer waits for a silence to send the user's request, instead, it sends a partial request every 500 ms ($EndMicroTurnCond$). The partial request is sent on a restart incremental mode.

Also, DictaNum can detect silences in a micro-turn level. We call Δ_s the silence threshold used to determine the end of a request in the traditional system and we introduce a new threshold δ_s such as $\delta_s \leq \Delta_s$. A silence whose duration is greater than δ_s is called *micro-silence*. The system has been modified in order to detect these shorter silences during the dictation, to commit ($EndTurnCond = CommitCond$) and deliver a feedback right after. Additionally, our system's response time is very short, the feedback message is available before the end of the micro-silence, so it is fed to the TTS without any delay. If $\delta_s = \Delta_s$, it is more convenient to dictate the number in one shot. Therefore, moving δ_s between zero and Δ_s creates a continuum between traditional systems and incremental ones. One may argue that these modifications are enough and no incremental behaviour is required, but the response delay will be higher, hence, the user will not wait for any feedback and will try to dictate his number in one shot.

If the user manifests a silence that is longer than Δ_s right after a feedback, the dictation ends and a general feedback is made to confirm the whole number. In our system, silences are determined by the number micro-turns during which there is no new input from the ASR but we could have used the VAD (Voice Activity Detection) (Breslin et al., 2013).

We set $EndMicroTurnCond$ to be activated by a 2 Hz clock and at every micro-turn, the Scheduler checks whether the new request is different from the previous one ($ServiceReqCond$). If that is the case, a rollback signal is sent followed by all the digits in the current number fragment. When a micro-silence is detected, a string *silence* is sent to the Scheduler (as *signal_ETC*) and that is when the Scheduler decides to commit. The recuperation thread requests the last message from the service with the same frequency as micro-turns, so when $CommitCond$ is activated, the feedback is already available and is delivered instantly to the TTS.

Finally, it is also possible for the user to interrupt the system during the final feedback. To do so, the service sends a feedback message in the following format: *The dictated number is: 01 <sep> 45 <sep> 65 <sep> 79 <sep> 98. Is that correct?*. The <sep> is a separator that is used to delimit the system micro-turns $\mu T_i^{k,S}$. They are pronounced one after another by the TTS. As a result, a dictation may end like this:

System: The dictated number is: 01 45 67 ...

User: No, 65.

System: Sorry. The dictated number is: 01 45 65 79 98. Is that correct?

User: Yes.

System: Thank you for using DictaNum. Bye.

After the interruption, a message sent to the service under the following format: {*part of the request that has been pronounced so far | barge-in content*}. In our example, this message is {*The dictated number is: 01 45 67 | No, 65*} which makes the service know how to perform the correction (or not, if the interruption is just a confirmation for example).

5 Discussion

Incremental dialogue systems present new features compared to traditional ones. In this section, we analyse the abilities of these systems given the way they integrate incrementality. To do so, we classify them as suggested in Section 2. Figure 1 summarizes the features discussed. These features are specific to incremental dialogue systems, so they do not exist in the first category. On the contrary, they have all been implemented in systems from the fourth category.

To interact with the NASTIA service, the user has to call a vocal platform which handles the ASR and TTS tasks. It has been configured in order to interrupt the TTS when activity is detected in the ASR. When using the List of Availabilities strategy, each item during an enumeration is a dialogue turn where the timeout duration is set to a low value (time to declare that the user did not answer) so that if he does not barge-in, the system moves to the next item of the list. If the user speaks, the TTS is stopped by the vocal platform and the user's utterance and its timing are communicated to the service. The latter can ignore the barge-in (if the user says *No* for example) or select an item in the list according to this input. Some traditional systems allow the user to interrupt them but they do not take the content of the utterance into account nor its timing (in order to make the link with the utterance of the TTS). Hence, these two features can be implemented in a dialogue system provided that it is permanently listening to the user and that it catches his utterance and its timing. These conditions are true for systems from the third category which make it possible for them to integrate these features.

Incremental dialogue systems can sometimes detect desynchronisations before the user has finished his utterance. Therefore, the dialogue would take less time if the system can interrupt the user asking him to repeat his request. Feedbacks are also a form of interrupt as it is the case for DictaNum because they are uttered after a short si-

Features	Category 1	Category 2	Category 3	Category 4
TTS interruption after input analysis	-	+	+	+
Link interruption time with TTS	-	+	+	+
User interruption by the system	-	-	+	+
Better reactivity	-	-	+	+
Optimal processing cost	-	-	-	+

Figure 1: Available features for dialogue systems given the way they integrate incrementality

lence (micro-silence). These features can only be implemented in systems from the third and the fourth group, as for the the first two ones, the system is only requested at the end of a user's utterance.

As far as reactivity is concerned, systems from the third and the fourth category process the user's request every time that a new increment is pushed into the system. Therefore, when the end of the request is detected (long enough silence), the service's response is already ready and can be delivered immediately. On the other hand, systems from group 1 and 2 wait until the end of the user's utterance to send the request to the service, hence, being less reactive. However, systems from the third group work on a restart incremental, reprocessing the whole request at each new increment. On the contrary, systems from the fourth category can process the request increment by increment hence optimizing the processing cost. Sometimes, a new increment can modify the whole request (or a part of it) and those systems are designed to handle this too by canceling some previous processing (*revoke* mechanism (Schlangen and Skantze, 2011)). While integrating incrementality in CFAsT and DictaNum, we noticed that the system responded so quickly that no efforts are necessary to optimise the processing time. However, systems from the fourth group can make the difference if the system needs to process tasks that create a delay (slow access to a remote database for example).

In our method, the service is not modified in a functional level (except from the double context management). However, as it is the case for DictaNum, some modifications at the applicative level might be compulsory. The Scheduler is not supposed to generate messages by himself or to perform traditional dialogue management tasks. As a consequence, when one needs to add some new feedback messages at the micro-turn level or the possibility to correct an utterance, these features must be implemented in the service.

Finally, in order for the Scheduler to decide when to commit and when to take the floor in an optimal way, it might need information coming from the back-end modules. Once again, this should be handled in the applicative level. A future paper, focused on how to implement systems using the Scheduler, will cover the ideas briefly described in the last two paragraphs.

6 Conclusion and future work

This paper describes a method for transforming a traditional dialogue system into an incremental one. The Scheduler is an intermediate module that is inserted between the client and the service. From the client's point of view, the system's behaviour is incremental despite the fact that the service works in a traditional turn-taking manner. Most requests that are sent by the Scheduler to the service are aimed to see what would be the answer if the current request hypothesis is the final one. In this case, the service's context should not be modified. Therefore, two context have to be maintained: the real context and the simulated one.

This solution has been implemented in the case of a textual dialogue system generated by the CFAsT application. It helps the user navigate through the NIPS 2013 proceedings titles. It has also been used to make a vocal system incremental: DictaNum. This service asks the users to dictate a number and confirms that it has been well understood.

In the future, we will explore how to make the Scheduler learn when to commit the current request hypothesis and when to take the floor. We will use reinforcement learning to figure out the optimal strategies.

References

James Allen, George Ferguson, and Amanda Stent. 2001. An architecture for more realistic conversational systems. In *6th international conference on Intelligent user interfaces*.

Timo Baumann and David Schlangen. 2013. Open-ended, extensible system utterances are preferred, even if they require filled pauses. In *Proceedings of the SIGDIAL 2013 Conference*.

Catherine Breslin, Milica Gasic, Matthew Henderson, Dongho Kim, Martin Szummer, Blaise Thomson, Pirros Tsiakoulis, and Steve Young. 2013. Continuous asr for flexible incremental dialogue. In *ICASSP*, pages 8362–8366.

Sarah Brown-Schmidt and Joy E. Hanna. 2011. Talking in another person's shoes: Incremental perspective-taking in language processing. *Dialogue and Discourse*, 2:11–33.

Herbert H. Clark. 1996. *Using Language*. Cambridge University Press.

David DeVault, Kenji Sagae, and David Traum. 2011. Incremental interpretation and prediction of utterance meaning for interactive dialogue. *Dialogue and Discourse*, 2:143–170.

Kohji Dohsaka and Akira Shimazu. 1997. A system architecture for spoken utterance production in collaborative dialogue. In *IJCAI*.

Jens Edlund, Joakim Gustafson, Mattias Heldner, and Anna Hjalmarsson. 2008. Towards human-like spoken dialogue systems. *Speech Communication*, 50:630–645.

Layla El Asri, Remi Lemonnier, Romain Laroche, Olivier Pietquin, and Hatim Khouzaimi. 2014. NASTIA: Negotiating Appointment Setting Interface. In *Proceedings of LREC*.

Helen Hastie, Marie-Aude Aufaure, et al. 2013. Demonstration of the parlance system: a data-driven incremental, spoken dialogue system for interactive search. In *Proceedings of the SIGDIAL 2013 Conference*.

Zeynep Ilkin and Patrick Sturt. 2011. Active prediction of syntactic information during sentence processing. *Dialogue and Discourse*, 2:35–58.

Irene Langkilde, Marilyn Anne Walker, Jerry Wright, Allen Gorin, and Diane Litman. 1999. Automatic prediction of problematic human-computer dialogues in how may i help you? In *ASRU99*.

R. Laroche and G. Putois. 2010. D5.5: Advanced appointment-scheduling system "system 4". Prototype D5.5, CLASSIC Project.

R. Laroche, G. Putois, et al. 2011. D6.4: Final evaluation of classic towninfo and appointment scheduling systems. Report D6.4, CLASSIC Project.

Romain Laroche. 2010. *Raisonnement sur les incertitudes et apprentissage pour les systemes de dialogue conventionnels*. Ph.D. thesis, Paris VI University.

Willem J. M. Levelt. 1989. *Speaking: From Intention to Articulation*. Cambridge, MA: MIT Press.

Kenneth Lock. 1965. Structuring programs for multiprogram time-sharing on-line applications. In *AFIPS '65 (Fall, part I) Proceedings of the November 30–December 1, 1965, fall joint computer conference, part I*.

Kyoko Matsuyama, Kazunori Komatani, Tetsuya Ogata, and Hiroshi G. Okuno. 2009. Enabling a user to specify an item at any time during system enumeration – item identification for barge-in-able conversational dialogue systems –. In *Proceedings of the INTERSPEECH 2009 Conference*.

Gary M. Matthias. 2008. Incremental speech understanding in a multimodal web-based spoken dialogue system. Master's thesis, Massachusetts Institute of Technology.

Antoine Raux and Maxine Eskenazi. 2008. Optimizing endpointing thresholds using dialogue features in a spoken dialogue system. In *SIGDIAL*.

David Schlangen and Gabriel Skantze. 2011. A general, abstract model of incremental dialogue processing. *Dialogue and Discourse*, 2:83–111.

Ethan O. Selfridge, Iker Arizmendi, Peter A. Heeman, and Jason D. Williams. 2012. Integrating incremental speech recognition and pomdp-based dialogue systems. In *Proceedings of the 13th Annual Meeting of the Special Interest Group on Discourse and Dialogue*, July.

Ethan Selfridge, Iker Arizmendi, Peter Heeman, and Jason Williams. 2013. Continuously predicting and processing barge-in during a live spoken dialogue task. In *Proceedings of the SIGDIAL 2013 Conference*.

Gabriel Skantze and David Schlangen. 2009. Incremental dialogue processing in a micro-domain. In *ACL*.

Michael K. Tanenhaus, Michael J. Spivey-Knowlton, Kathleen M. Eberhard, and Julie C. Sedivy. 1995. Integration of visual and linguistic information in spoken language comprehension. *Science*, 268:1632–1634.

Mats Wirén. 1992. *Studies in Incremental Natural Language Analysis*. Ph.D. thesis, Linköping University, Linköping, Sweden.

Marcin Wlodarczak and Petra Wagner. 2013. Effects of talk-spurt silence boundary thresholds on distribution of gaps and overlaps. In *INTERSPEECH Proceedings*.

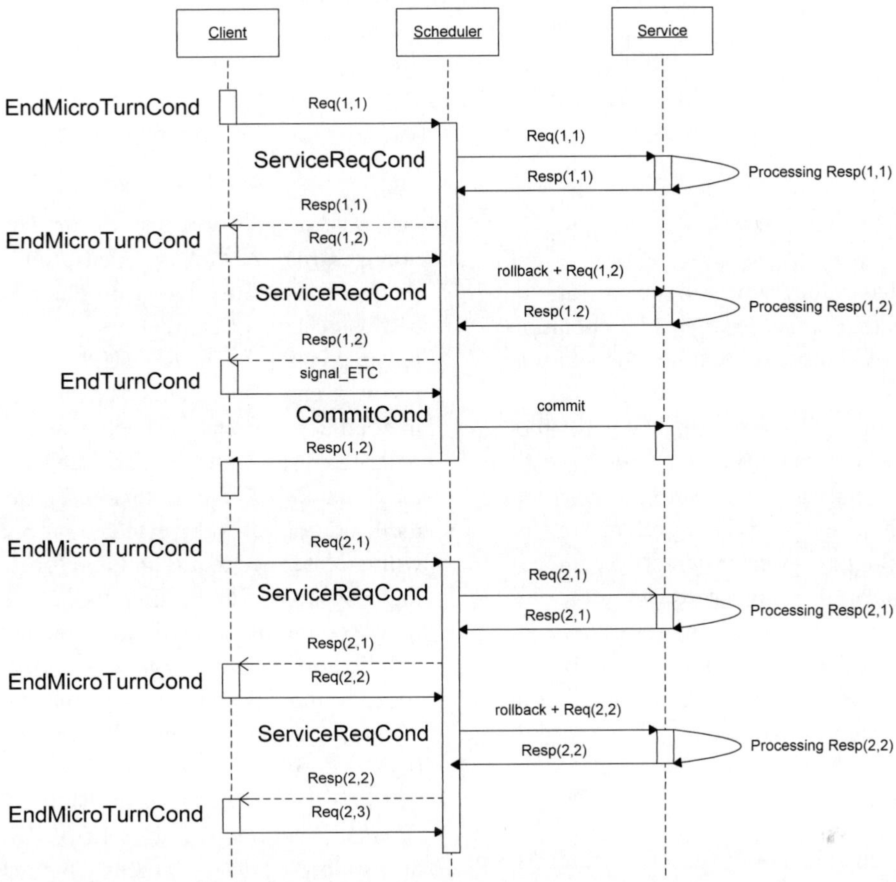

Figure A.1: The scheduler sub-requests management (The streams in dashed lines are received by the recuperation thread of the client).

Turn	**User sub-turn**	**Input**	**Real context**	**Simulation context**
T^1	$T_1^{1,U}$	Req_1^1	ctxt(T^0)	ctxt($T^0 + T_1^{1,U}$)
	$T_2^{1,U}$	Req_2^1	ctxt(T^0)	ctxt($T^0 + T_2^{1,U}$)
	...	...	ctxt(T^0)	...
	$T_{n^{1,U}}^{1,U}$	$Req_{n^{1,U}}^1$	ctxt(T^0)	ctxt($T^0 + T_{n^{1,U}}^{1,U}$)
	COMMIT: $ctxt(T^1) = ctxt(T^0 + T_{n^{1,U}}^{1,U})$			
T^2	$T_1^{2,U}$	Req_1^2	ctxt(T^1)	ctxt($T^1 + T_1^{2,U}$)
	...	...	ctxt(T^1)	...

Figure A.2: A double context: the real context and the simulation context.

Free on-line speech recogniser based on Kaldi ASR toolkit producing word posterior lattices

Ondřej Plátek and Filip Jurčíček
Charles University in Prague
Faculty of Mathematics and Physics
Institute of Formal and Applied Linguistics
{oplatek, jurcicek}@ufal.mff.cuni.cz

Abstract

This paper presents an extension of the Kaldi automatic speech recognition toolkit to support on-line recognition. The resulting recogniser supports acoustic models trained using state-of-the-art acoustic modelling techniques. As the recogniser produces word posterior lattices, it is particularly useful in statistical dialogue systems, which try to exploit uncertainty in the recogniser's output. Our experiments show that the on-line recogniser performs significantly better in terms of latency when compared to a cloud-based recogniser.

1 Introduction

There are many choices of speech recognisers, but we find no alternative with both a permissive license and on-line recognition suitable for a spoken dialogue system. The Google speech recognition service[1] provides state-of-the-art quality for many tasks (Morbini et al., 2013) and may be used for free; however, the licensing conditions are not clear, adaptation of acoustic and language models to a task at hand is not possible and the service is not officially supported.

Another option is Nuance cloud based recognition[2]; however, again adjustments to the system are not possible. Moreover, it is a paid service.

When considering local ASR systems, we found no viable alternatives either. The HTK toolkit does not provide on-line large vocabulary decoders suitable for real-time decoding. OpenJulius can be used with custom-built acoustic and language models and for on-line decoding (Akinobu, 2014). However, OpenJulius suffers from software instability when producing lattices and confusion networks; therefore, it is not suitable for practical use. The RWTH decoder is not a free software and a license must be purchased for commercial applications (Rybach et al., 2011).

As a result, we implemented a lightweight modification of the *LatticeFasterDecoder* from the Kaldi toolkit and created an on-line recogniser with an interface that is suitable for statistical dialogue systems. The Kaldi toolkit as well as the on-line recogniser is distributed under the Apache 2.0 license[3]. Our on-line recogniser may use acoustic models trained using the state-of-the-art techniques, such as Linear Discriminant Analysis (LDA), Maximum Likelihood Linear Transform (MLLT), Boosted Maximum Mutual Information (BMMI), Minimum Phone Error (MPE). It produces word posterior lattices which can be easily converted into high quality n-best lists. The recogniser's speed and latency can be effectively controlled off-line by optimising a language model and during decoding by beam thresholds.

In the next section, the Kaldi recognition toolkit is briefly described. Section 3 describes the implementation of the *OnlineLatgenRecogniser*. Section 4 evaluates the accuracy and speed of the recogniser. Finally, Section 5 concludes this work.

2 The Kaldi toolkit

The Kaldi toolkit[4] is a speech recognition toolkit distributed under a free license (Povey et al., 2011). The toolkit is based on Finite State Transducers, implements state-of-the-art acoustic modelling techniques, is computationally efficient, and is already widely adapted among research groups.

[1]The API is available at https://www.google.com/speech-api/v1/recognize, and its use described in a blog post at http://mikepultz.com/2013/07/google-speech-api-full-duplex-php-version/.

[2]http://www.nuancemobiledeveloper.com/

[3]http://www.apache.org/licenses/LICENSE-2.0

[4]http://sourceforge.net/projects/kaldi

Its only major drawback was the lack of on-line recognition support. Therefore, it could not be used directly in applications such as spoken dialogue systems. Kaldi includes an on-line recognition application; however, hard-wired timeout exceptions, audio source fixed to a sound card, and a specialised 1-best decoder limit its use to demonstration of Kaldi recognition capabilities only.

3 OnlineLatgenRecogniser

The standard Kaldi interface between the components of the toolkit is based on a batch processing paradigm, where the components assume that the whole audio signal is available when recognition starts. However, when performing on-line recognition, one would like to take advantage of the fact that the signal appears in small chunks and can be processed incrementally. When properly implemented, this significantly reduces recogniser output latency.

3.1 C++ implementation

To achieve this, we implemented Kaldi's *DecodableInterface* supporting incremental speech preprocessing, which includes speech parameterisation, feature transformations, and likelihood estimation. In addition, we subclassed *LatticeFasterDecoder* and split the original batch processing interface.

The newly implemented *OnlineLatgenRecogniser* makes use of our incremental speech preprocessing and modified *LatticeFasterDecoder*. It implements the following interface:

- *AudioIn* – queueing new audio for preprocessing,
- *Decode* – decoding a fixed number of audio frames,
- *PruneFinal* – preparing internal data structures for lattice extraction,
- *GetLattice* – extracting a word posterior lattice and returning log likelihood of processed audio,
- *Reset* – preparing the recogniser for a new utterance,

The C++ example in Listing 1 shows a typical use of the *OnlineLatgenRecogniser* interface. When audio data becomes available, it is queued into the recogniser's buffer (line 11) and immediately decoded (lines 12-14). If the audio data is supplied in small enough chunks, the decoding of queued data is finished before new data arrives. When the recognition is finished, the recogniser prepares for lattice extraction (line 16). Line 20 shows how to obtain word posterior lattice as an OpenFST object. The *getAudio()* function represents a separate process supplying speech data. Please note that the recogniser's latency is mainly determined by the time spent in the *GetLattice* function.

Please note that we do not present here the functions controlling the input stream of audio chunks passed to the decoder and processing the output because these differ according to use case. An example of a nontrivial use case is in a dialogue system through a thin Python wrapper (see Section 3.2).

```
1  OnlineLatgenRecogniser rec;
2  rec.Setup(...);
3
4  size_t decoded_now = 0;
5  size_t max_decoded = 10;
6  char *audio_array = NULL;
7
8  while (recognitionOn())
9  {
10   size_t audio_len = getAudio(audio_array);
11   rec.AudioIn(audio_array, audio_len);
12   do {
13     decoded_now = rec.Decode(max_decoded);
14   } while(decoded_now > 0);
15 }
16 rec.PruneFinal();
17
18 double tot_lik;
19 fst::VectorFst<fst::LogArc> word_post_lat;
20 rec.GetLattice(&word_post_lat, &tot_lik);
21
22 rec.Reset();
```

Listing 1: Example of the decoder API

The source code of the *OnlineLatgenRecogniser* is available in Kaldi repository[5].

3.2 Python extension

In addition, we developed a Python extension exporting the *OnlineLatgenRecogniser* C++ interface. This can be used as an example of bringing Kaldi's on-line speech recognition functionality to higher-level programming languages. This Python extension is used in the Alex Dialogue Systems Framework (ADSF, 2014), an open-source language and domain independent framework for developing spoken dialogue systems. The *OnlineLatgenRecogniser* is deployed in an application which provides information about public

[5] https://sourceforge.net/p/kaldi/code/HEAD/tree/sandbox/oplatek2/src/dec-wrap/

transport and weather in the Czech republic and is available on a public toll-free telephone number.

4 Evaluation

4.1 Acoustic and language model training

The *OnlineLatgenRecogniser* is evaluated on a corpus of audio data from the Public Transport Information (PTI) domain. In PTI, users can interact in Czech with a telephone-based dialogue system to find public transport connections (UFAL-DSG, 2014). The PTI corpus consist of approximately 12k user utterances with a length varying between 0.4 s and 18 s with median around 3 s. The data were divided into training, development, and test data where the corresponding data sizes were 9496, 1188, 1188 respectively. For evaluation, a domain specific the class-based language model with a vocabulary size of approximately 52k and 559k n-grams was estimated from the training data. Named entities e.g., cities or bus stops, in class-based language model are expanded before building a decoding graph.

Since the PTI acoustic data amounts to less then 5 hours, the acoustic training data was extended by an additional 15 hours of telephone out-of-domain data from the VYSTADIAL 2013 - Czech corpus (Korvas et al., 2014). The acoustic models were obtained by BMMI discriminative training with LDA and MLLT feature transformations. The scripts used to train the acoustic models are publicly available in ASDF (2014) as well as in Kaldi[6] and a detailed description of the training procedure is given in Korvas et al. (2014).

4.2 Experiments

We focus on evaluating the speed of the *OnlineLatgenRecogniser* and its relationship with the accuracy of the decoder, namely:

- Real Time Factor (RTF) of decoding – the ratio of the recognition time to the duration of the audio input,
- Latency – the delay between utterance end and the availability of the recognition results,
- Word Error Rate (WER).

Accuracy and speed of the *OnlineLatgenRecogniser* are controlled by the *max-active-states*, *beam*, and *lattice-beam* parameters (Povey et al., 2011). *Max-active-states* limits the maximum number of active tokens during decoding. *Beam* is used during graph search to prune ASR hypotheses at the state level. *Lattice-beam* is used when producing word level lattices after the decoding is finished. It is crucial to tune these parameters optimally to obtain good results.

In general, one aims for a setting RTF smaller than 1.0. However, in practice, it is useful if the RTF is even smaller because other processes running on the machine can influence the amount of available computational resources. Therefore, we target the RTF of 0.6 in our setup.

We used grid search on the development set to identify optimal parameters. Figure 1 (a) shows the impact of the *beam* on the WER and RTF measures. In this case, we set *max-active-states* to 2000 in order to limit the worst case RTF to 0.6. Observing Figure 1 (a), we set *beam* to 13 as this setting balances the WER, 95th RTF percentile, and the average RTF. Figure 1 (b) shows the impact of the *lattice-beam* on WER and latency when *beam* is fixed to 13. We set *lattice-beam* to 5 based on Figure 1 (b) to obtain the 95th latency percentile of 200 ms, which is considered natural in a dialogue (Skantze and Schlangen, 2009). *Lattice-beam* does not affect WER, but larger *lattice-beam* improves the oracle WER of generated lattices (Povey et al., 2012).

Figure 2 shows the percentile graph of the RTF and latency measures over the development set. For example, the 95th percentile is the value of a measure such that 95% of the data has the measure below that value. One can see from Figure 2 that 95% of development utterances is decoded with RTF under 0.6 and latency under 200 ms. The extreme values are typically caused by decoding long noisy utterances where uncertainty in decoding slows down the recogniser. Using this setting, *OnlineLatgenRecogniser* decodes the utterances with a WER of about 21%.

Please note that *OnlineLatgenRecogniser* only extends the batch Kaldi decoder for incremental speech processing interface. It uses the same code as the batch Kaldi decoder to compute speech parametrisation, frame likelihoods, and state-level lattices. Therefore, the accuracy of *OnlineLatgenRecogniser* is equal to that of the batch Kaldi decoder given the same parameters.

[6] http://sourceforge.net/p/kaldi/code/HEAD/tree/trunk/egs/vystadial_en/

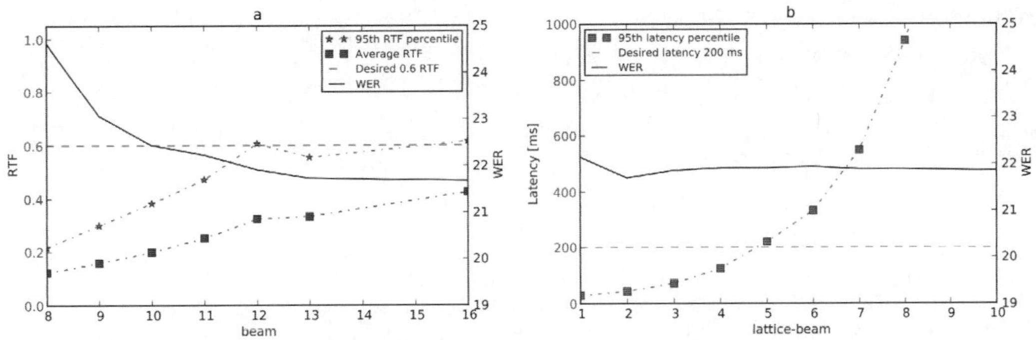

Figure 1: The left graph (a) shows that WER decreases with increasing *beam* and the average RTF linearly grows with the beam. Setting the maximum number of active states to 2000 stops the growth of the 95th RTF percentile at 0.6, indicating that even in the worst case, we can guarantee an RTF around 0.6. The right graph (b) shows how latency grows in response to increasing *lattice-beam*.

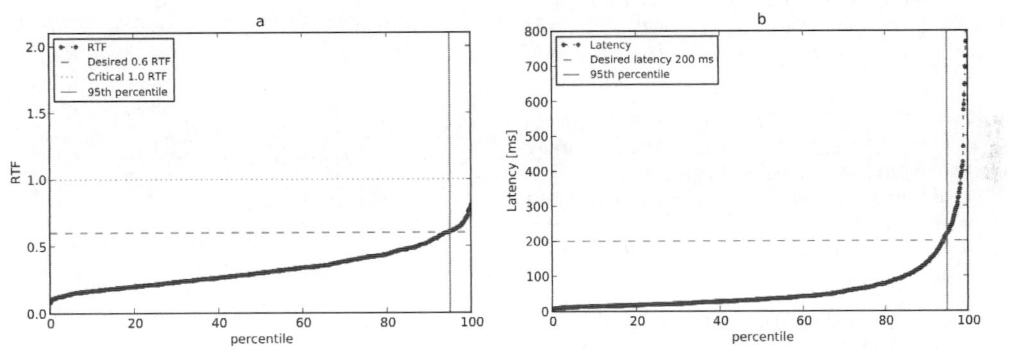

Figure 2: The percentile graphs show RTF and Latency scores for development data for *max-active-sates*=2000, *beam*=13, *lattice-beam*=5. Note that 95 % of utterances were decoded with the latency lower that 200ms.

In addition, we have also experimented with Google ASR service on the same domain. The Google ASR service decodes 95% of test utterances with latency under 1900 ms and WER is about 48%. The high latency is presumably caused by the batch processing of audio data and network latency, and the high WER is likely caused by a mismatch between Google's acoustic and language models and the test data.

5 Conclusion

This work presented the *OnlineLatgenRecogniser*, an extension of the Kaldi automatic speech recognition toolkit. The *OnlineLatgenRecogniser* is distributed under the Apache 2.0 license, and therefore it is freely available for both research and commercial applications. The recogniser and its Python extension is stable and intensively used in a publicly available spoken dialogue system (UFAL-DSG, 2014). Thanks to the use of a standard Kaldi lattice decoder, the recogniser produces high quality word posterior lattices. The training scripts for the acoustic model and the *OnlineLatgenRecogniser* code are currently being integrated in the Kaldi toolkit. Future planned improvements include implementing more sophisticated speech parameterisation interface and feature transformations.

Acknowledgments

We would also like to thank Daniel Povey and Ondřej Dušek for their useful comments and discussions. We also thank the anonymous reviewers for their helpful comments and suggestions.

This research was funded by the Ministry of Education, Youth and Sports of the Czech Republic under the grant agreement LK11221, by the core research funding of Charles University in Prague. The language resources presented in this work are stored and distributed by the LINDAT/CLARIN project of the Ministry of Education, Youth and Sports of the Czech Republic (project LM2010013).

References

ADSF. 2014. The Alex Dialogue Systems Framework. https://github.com/UFAL-DSG/alex.

Lee Akinobu. 2014. Open-Source Large Vocabulary CSR Engine Julius. http://julius.sourceforge.jp/en_index.php.

Matěj Korvas, Ondřej Plátek, Ondřej Dušek, Lukáš Žilka, and Filip Jurčíček. 2014. Free English and Czech telephone speech corpus shared under the CC-BY-SA 3.0 license. In *Proceedings of the Eigth International Conference on Language Resources and Evaluation (LREC 2014)*.

Fabrizio Morbini, Kartik Audhkhasi, Kenji Sagae, Ron Artstein, Doan Can, Panayiotis G. Georgiou, Shrikanth S. Narayanan, Anton Leuski, and David Traum. 2013. Which ASR should I choose for my dialogue system? In *Proc. SIGDIAL*, August.

Daniel Povey, Arnab Ghoshal, Gilles Boulianne, Lukas Burget, Ondrej Glembek, Nagendra Goel, Mirko Hannemann, Petr Motlicek, Yanmin Qian, Petr Schwarz, et al. 2011. The kaldi speech recognition toolkit. In *Proc. ASRU*, pages 1–4.

Daniel Povey, Mirko Hannemann, Gilles Boulianne, Lukas Burget, Arnab Ghoshal, Milos Janda, Martin Karafiát, Stefan Kombrink, Petr Motlicek, Yanmin Qian, et al. 2012. Generating exact lattices in the WFST framework. In *Acoustics, Speech and Signal Processing (ICASSP), 2012 IEEE International Conference on*, pages 4213–4216. IEEE.

David Rybach, Stefan Hahn, Patrick Lehnen, David Nolden, Martin Sundermeyer, Zoltan Tüske, Siemon Wiesler, Ralf Schlüter, and Hermann Ney. 2011. RASR-The RWTH Aachen University Open Source Speech Recognition Toolkit. In *Proc. IEEE Automatic Speech Recognition and Understanding Workshop*.

Gabriel Skantze and David Schlangen. 2009. Incremental dialogue processing in a micro-domain. In *Proceedings of the 12th Conference of the European Chapter of the Association for Computational Linguistics*, pages 745–753. Association for Computational Linguistics.

UFAL-DSG. 2014. The Alex Dialogue Systems Framework - Public Transport Information. https://github.com/UFAL-DSG/alex.

Combining Task and Dialogue Streams in Unsupervised Dialogue Act Models

Aysu Ezen-Can and Kristy Elizabeth Boyer
Department of Computer Science
North Carolina State University
aezen,keboyer@ncsu.edu

Abstract

Unsupervised machine learning approaches hold great promise for recognizing dialogue acts, but the performance of these models tends to be much lower than the accuracies reached by supervised models. However, some dialogues, such as task-oriented dialogues with parallel task streams, hold rich information that has not yet been leveraged within unsupervised dialogue act models. This paper investigates incorporating task features into an unsupervised dialogue act model trained on a corpus of human tutoring in introductory computer science. Experimental results show that incorporating task features and dialogue history features significantly improve unsupervised dialogue act classification, particularly within a hierarchical framework that gives prominence to dialogue history. This work constitutes a step toward building high-performing unsupervised dialogue act models that will be used in the next generation of task-oriented dialogue systems.

1 Introduction

Dialogue acts represent the underlying intent of utterances (Austin, 1975; Searle, 1969), and constitute a crucial level of representation for dialogue systems (Sridhar et al., 2009). The task of automatic dialogue act classification has been extensively studied for decades within several domains including train fares and timetables (Allen et al., 1995; Core and Allen, 1997; Crook et al., 2009; Traum, 1999), virtual personal assistants (Chen and Di Eugenio, 2013), conversational telephone speech (Stolcke et al., 2000), Wikipedia talk pages (Ferschke et al., 2012) and as in the case of this paper, tutorial dialogue (Serafin and Di Eugenio, 2004; Forbes-Riley and Litman, 2005; Boyer et al., 2011; Dzikovska et al., 2013).

Most of the prior work on dialogue act classification has depended on manually applying dialogue act tags and then leveraging supervised machine learning (Di Eugenio et al., 2010; Keizer et al., 2002; Reithinger and Klesen, 1997; Serafin and Di Eugenio, 2004). This process involves engineering a dialogue act taxonomy (or using an existing one, though domain-specific phenomena can be difficult to capture within multi-purpose dialogue act taxonomies) and manually annotating each utterance in the corpus. Then, the tagged utterances are provided to a supervised machine learner. This supervised approach can achieve strong performance, in excess of 75% accuracy on manual tags, approaching the agreement level that is sometimes observed between human annotators (Sridhar et al., 2009; Serafin and Di Eugenio, 2004; Chen and Di Eugenio, 2013).

However, the supervised approach has several major drawbacks, including the fact that handcrafting dialogue act tagsets and applying them manually tend to be bottlenecks within the research and design process. To overcome these drawbacks, the field has recently seen growing momentum surrounding unsupervised approaches, which do not require any manual labels during model training (Crook et al., 2009; Joty et al., 2011; Lee et al., 2013). A variety of unsupervised machine learning techniques have been investigated for dialogue act classification, and each line of investigation has explored which features best support this goal. However, to date the best performing unsupervised models achieve in the range of 40% (Rus et al., 2012) to 60% (Joty et al., 2011) training set accuracy on manual tags, substantially lower than the mid-70% accuracy (Sridhar et al., 2009) often achieved on testing sets with supervised models.

In order to close this performance gap between unsupervised and supervised techniques, we suggest that it is crucial to enrich the features available to unsupervised models. In particular, when a dialogue is task-oriented and includes a rich source of information within a parallel task stream, these features may substantially boost the ability of an unsupervised model to distinguish dialogue acts. For example, in situated dialogue, features representing the state of the physical world may be highly influential for dialogue act modeling (Grosz and Sidner, 1986).

Human tutorial dialogue, which is the domain being considered in the current work, often exhibits this structure: the task artifact is external to the dialogue utterances themselves (in the case of our work, this artifact is a computer program that the student is constructing). Task features have already been shown beneficial for supervised dialogue act classification in our domain (Ha et al., 2012). We hypothesize that including these task features within an unsupervised model will significantly improve its performance. In addition, we hypothesize that including dialogue history as a prominent feature within an unsupervised model will provide significant improvement.

This paper represents the first investigation into combining task and dialogue features within an unsupervised dialogue act classification model. First, we discuss representation of these task features and dialogue structure features, and compare these representations within both flat and hierarchical clustering approaches. Second, we report on experiments that demonstrate that the inclusion of task features significantly improves dialogue act classification, and that a hierarchical cluster structure which explicitly captures dialogue history performs best. Finally, we break down the model's performance by dialogue act and investigate which features are most beneficial for distinguishing particular acts. These contributions constitute a step toward building high-performing unsupervised dialogue act models that can be used in the next generation of task-oriented dialogue systems.

2 Related Work

There is a rich body of work on dialogue act classification. Supervised approaches for dialogue act classification aimed at improving performance by using several features such as dialogue structure including position of the turn (Ferschke et al., 2012), speaker of an utterance (Tavafi et al., 2013), previous dialogue acts (Kim et al., 2010), lexical features such as words (Stolcke et al., 2000), syntactic features including part-of-speech tags (Bangalore et al., 2008; Marineau et al., 2000), task-subtask structure (Boyer et al., 2010) acoustic and prosodic cues (Sridhar et al., 2009; Jurafsky et al., 1998), and body posture (Ha et al., 2012).

For the growing body of work in unsupervised dialogue act classification a subset of these features have been utilized. The words (Crook et al., 2009), topic words (Ritter et al., 2010), function words (Ezen-Can and Boyer, 2013b), beginning portions of utterances (Rus et al., 2012), part-of-speech tags and dependency trees (Joty et al., 2011), and state transition probabilities in Markov models (Lee et al., 2013) are among the list of features investigated for unsupervised modeling of dialogue acts. However, the accuracies achieved by the best of these models are well below the accuracies achieved by supervised techniques. To improve performance of unsupervised models for task-oriented dialogue, utilizing a combination of task and dialogue features is a promising direction.

3 Corpus

The task-oriented dialogue corpus used in this work was collected in a computer-mediated human tutorial dialogue study. Students (n = 42) and tutors interacted through textual dialogue within an online learning environment for introductory Java programming (Ha et al., 2012). The students were novices, never having programmed in Java previously. The tutorial dialogue interface consisted of four windows, one describing the learning task, another where students wrote programming code, beneath that the output of either compiling or executing the program, and finally the textual dialogue window (Figure 1).

As students and tutors interacted through this interface, all dialogue messages and keystroke-level task events were logged to a database. Only students could compose, compile, and execute the code, so task actions represent student actions while dialogue messages were composed by both participants. The corpus contains six lessons for each student-tutor pair, of which only the first lesson was annotated with dialogue act tags (κ=0.80).

This annotated set contains 5,705 utterances (4,065 tutor and 1,640 student). The average num-

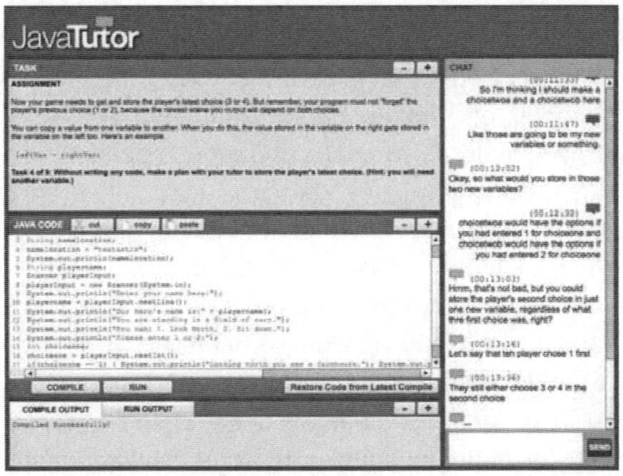

Figure 1: The tutorial dialogue interface with four windows.

ber of utterances (both tutor and student) per tutoring session was 116 (min = 70, max = 211). The average number of tutor utterances per session is 96 (min=44, max=156) whereas for students it is 39 (min=18, max=69) for the annotated set. The average number of words per utterance for students is 4.4 and for tutors it is 5.4. This annotated set is used in the current analysis for both training and testing where cross-validation is applied. As described later, a separate set containing 462 unannotated utterances is used as a development set for determining the number of clusters.

The dialogue stream of this corpus was manually annotated as part of previous work on supervised dialogue act modeling which achieved 69% accuracy with Conditional Random Fields (Ha et al., 2012). A brief description of the student dialogue act tags, which are the focus of the models reported in this paper, is shown in Table 1. The most frequent dialogue act (A) constitutes the baseline chance (39.85%). In the current work, the manually applied dialogue act labels are not utilized during model training, but are only used for evaluation purposes as our models' accuracies are reported for manual tags on a held-out test set.

An excerpt from the corpus is shown in Table 2. Note that the current work focuses on classifying student dialogue act tags, since in an automated dialogue system the tutor moves would be generated by the system and their dialogue acts tags would therefore be known.

4 Features

A key issue for dialogue act classification in task-oriented dialogue involves how to represent dialogue and task events. This section describes how features were extracted from the corpus of human tutorial dialogue.

Student Dialogue Act	Distribution
Answer (A)	39.85
Acknowledgement (ACK)	21.31
Statement (S)	21.20
Question (Q)	15.15
Request for Feedback (RF)	0.98
Clarification (C)	0.79
Other (O)	0.61

Table 1: Student dialogue act tags and their frequencies.

Tutor: ready? [*Q*]
Student: yep [*A*]
Tutor moves on to next task
Student: cool [*S*]
Student compiles and runs the code.
Program output: 'Hello World'
Tutor: excellent [*PF*]
Tutor: add a space to make the output look prettier [*DIR*]
Student: why doesnt it stop on the next line in this case? [*Q*]
Program halts
Tutor: it did [*A*]
Student runs the program successfully.
Tutor: good. [*PF*]

Table 2: Excerpt of dialogue from the corpus and the task action that follows utterances.

We use three sets of features: lexical features, dialogue context features, and task features. The lexical and dialogue context features are extracted from the textual dialogue utterances within the corpus. The task features are extracted from the interaction traces within the computer-mediated learning environment and represent a keystroke-level log of events as students worked toward solving the computer programming problems.

4.1 Lexical Features

Because one of the main goals of our work in the longer term is to perform automatic dialogue act classification in real time, we took as a primary consideration the ability to quickly extract lexical features. The features utilized in the current investigation consist only of word unigrams. In addition to their ease of extraction, our prior work has shown that addition of part-of-speech tags and and syntax features did not significantly improve the accuracy of supervised dialogue act classifiers in this domain (Boyer et al., 2010), and these features can be time-consuming to extract in real time (Ha et al., 2012).

The choice to use word unigrams rather than higher order n-grams is further facilitated by the fact that our clustering technique leverages the ***longest common sub-sequence (LCS)*** metric to measure distances between utterances. This metric counts shared sub-sequences of not-necessarily contiguous words (Hirschberg, 1975). In this way, the LCS metric provides a flexible way for n-grams and skip-n-grams to be treated as important units within the clustering, while the raw features themselves consist only of word unigrams. (We report on a comparison between LCS and bigrams later in the discussion section.) Utilizing LCS, there exists a distance (1-similarity) value from each utterance to every other utterance.

4.2 Dialogue Context Features

Based on previous work on a similar human tutorial dialogue corpus (Ha et al., 2012), we utilize four features that provide information about the dialogue structure. These features are depicted in Table 3. Note that our goal within this work is to classify *student* dialogue moves, not tutor moves, because in a dialogue system the tutor's moves are system-generated with associated known dialogue acts.

Feature	Description
Utterance position	The relative position of an utterance from the beginning of the dialogue.
Utterance length	The number of tokens in the utterance, including words and punctuation.
Previous author	Author of the previous dialogue message (tutor or student) at the time message sent.
Previous tutor dialogue act	Dialogue act of the previous tutor utterance.

Table 3: Dialogue context features and their descriptions.

4.3 Task Features

As described previously, the corpus contains two channels of information: the dialogue utterances, from which the lexical and dialogue context features were extracted, and in addition, the task stream consisting of student problem-solving activities such as authoring code, compiling, and executing the program. The programming activities of students were logged to a database along with all of the dialogue events during tutoring.

A set of task features was found to be important for dialogue act classification in this domain in prior work, including most recent programming action, status of the most recent task activity and task activity flag representing whether the utterance was preceded by a student's task activity (Ha et al., 2012). We expand this set of features as shown in Table 4.

5 Experiments

The goal of this work is to investigate the impact of including task and dialogue context features on unsupervised dialogue act models. We hypothesize that incorporating task features will significantly improve the performance of an unsupervised model, and we also hypothesize that properly incorporating dialogue context features, which are at a different granularity than the lexical features extracted from utterances, will substantially improve model accuracy.

5.1 Dialogue Act Modeling With k-medoids Clustering

The unsupervised models investigated here use k-medoids clustering, which is a well-known clustering technique that takes actual data points as the center of each cluster (Ng and Han, 1994), in contrast to k-means which may have synthetic points as centroids. In k-medoids, the centroids are initially selected and then the algorithm iterates, reassigning data points in each iteration, until the clusters converge. In standard k-medoids clustering the initial seeds are selected randomly and then a correct distribution of data points is identified through the iteration and convergence process. For dialogue act classification, the influence of the initial seeds is substantial because the frequencies across dialogue tags are typically unbalanced. To overcome this challenge, we use a greedy seed selection approach similar to the one used in k-means++ (Arthur and Vassilvitskii,

Feature	Description
prev_action	Most recent action of the student (composing a dialogue utterance, constructing code, compiling or executing code).
task_begin	Whether the student utterance is the first utterance since the beginning of the subtask.
task_stu	Whether the student utterance was preceded by a task event.
task_prev_tut	Task activity flag indicating whether the closest tutor utterance in this subtask was preceded by a task activity.
task_status	The status of the most recent coding action (*begin*, *stop*, *success*, *error* and *input_sent*).
time_elapsed	Time elapsed between the previous tutor message and the current student utterance.
errors	Number of errors in the student's latest code.
delta_errors	Difference in the number of errors in the task between two utterances in the same dialogue.
stu_#_task	Number of student dialogue messages sent within the current task.
stu_#_dial	Number of student dialogue messages sent within the current dialogue.
tut_#_task	Number of tutor dialogue messages sent within the current subtask.
tut_#_dial	Number of tutor dialogue messages sent within the current dialogue.

Table 4: Task features extracted from student computer programming activities.

2007) which selects the first seed randomly and then greedily chooses seeds that are farthest from the chosen seeds. The goal of using this approach in our application is to choose seeds from different dialogue acts so that the final model achieves good coverage. Our preliminary experiments demonstrated that this greedy seed selection combined with k-medoids outperforms other clustering approaches including those utilized in our prior work (Ezen-Can and Boyer, 2013a).

In order to select the number of clusters k, a subset of the corpus, constituting 25% of the full corpus (that were not tagged) composed of 462 utterances, was separated as a development set. First, we examined the coherence of clusters at different values of k using intra-cluster distances. This technique involves identifying an 'elbow' where the decrease in intra-cluster distance becomes less rapid (since adding more clusters can continue to decrease intra-cluster distance to the point of overfitting) (Figure 2). The graph suggests an elbow at k=5. Because there may be multiple elbows in the intra-cluster distance, a second method utilizing Bayesian Information Criterion (BIC) was used which penalizes models as the number of parameters increases. The lower the BIC value, the better the model is, achieved at k=5 as well.

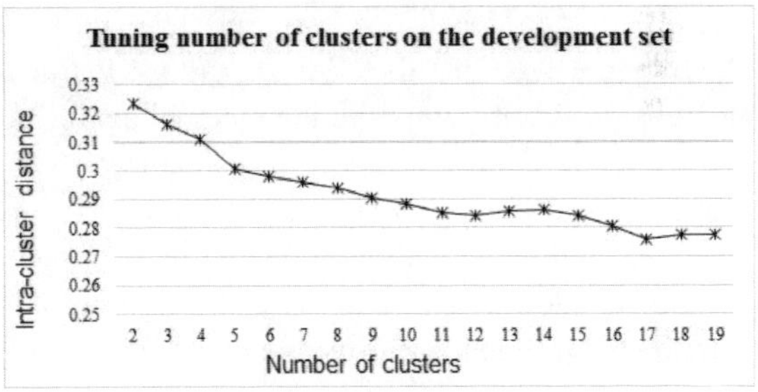

Figure 2: Intra-cluster distances with varying number of clusters.

Unlike many other investigations into unsupervised dialogue act classification, the current approach reports accuracy on held-out test data, not on the data on which the model was trained. Even though the model training process does not utilize available manual tags, requiring the learned unsupervised model to perform well on held-out test data more closely mimics the broader goal of our work which is to utilize these unsupervised models within deployed dialogue systems, where most utterances to be classified have never been encountered by the model before.

The procedure for model training and testing uses leave-one-student-out cross-validation. Rather than other forms of leave-one-out or stratified cross-validation, leave-one-student-out ensures that each student's set of dialogue utterances are treated as the testing set while the model is trained on all other students' utterances. This process is repeated until each student's utterances have served as a held-out test set (in our case, this results in n=42 folds). Within each fold, the clusters are learned during training and then for each utterance in the test set, its closest cluster is computed by taking the average distance of the test utterance to the elements in the cluster. The majority label of the closest cluster is assigned as the dialogue act tag for the test utterance. If the assigned dialogue act tag matches the manual label of the test utterance, the utterance is counted as correct classification. The average accuracy is computed as the number of correct classifications divided by the total number of classifications.

5.2 Experimental Results

We conducted experiments with seven different feature combinations: L, lexical features only, T, task features only, D, dialogue context features only, and then the combinations of these features, $T + D$, $T + L$, $D + L$, and $T + D + L$. We hypothesized that the addition of task features would significantly improve the models' accuracy. As shown in Table 5, adding task features to dialogue context features significantly outperforms dialogue context features alone ($T + D > D$). Similarly, adding task features to lexical features provides significant improvement ($T + L > L$). However, adding task features to the dialogue context plus lexical features model does not provide benefit, and in fact slightly (not significantly) degrades performance ($T + D + L \ngtr D + L$). As reflected by the Kappa scores, the test set performance attained by these models is hardly better than would be expected by chance.

	Features	Accuracy (%)	Kappa
Flat Clustering	L	33	0.02
	T	37.7	0.07
	D	37.6	0.07
	T+D	39.1*	0.07
	T+L	38*	0.06
	D+L	38.3	0.07
	T+D+L	37.3	0.05

Table 5: Test set accuracies and Kappa for the flat clustering model (L: Lexical features, D: Dialogue context features, T: Task features) *indicates statistically significant compared to the similar model without task features ($p < 0.05$).

5.3 Utilizing Dialogue History

The importance of dialogue history, particularly the influence of the most recent turn on an upcoming turn, is widely recognized within dialogue research, notably by work on adjacency pairs (Schegloff and Sacks, 1973; Forbes-Riley et al., 2007; Midgley et al., 2009). Based on these findings, we hypothesized that dialogue history would be substantially beneficial for unsupervised dialogue act models as it has been observed to be in numerous studies on supervised classification. However, as seen in the previous section, adding these dialogue context features with equal weight to the model using Cosine distance only improved its performance slightly though statistically significantly (for example, $T+D > T$), while the overall performance is still barely above random chance.

In an attempt to substantially boost the performance of the unsupervised dialogue act classifier, we experimented with a hierarchical clustering structure in which the model first branches on the previous tutor move, and then the clustering models are learned as described previously at the leaves of the tree (Figure 3).

This branching approach results in some branches with too few utterances to train a multi-cluster model. To deal with this situation we set a threshold of n=10 utterances. For those subgroups with fewer than 10 utterances, we take a simple majority vote to classify test cases, and for those subgroups with 10 or larger utterances we train a cluster model and use it to classify test cases. For the entire corpus, the number of utterances in each branch is presented in Table 6.

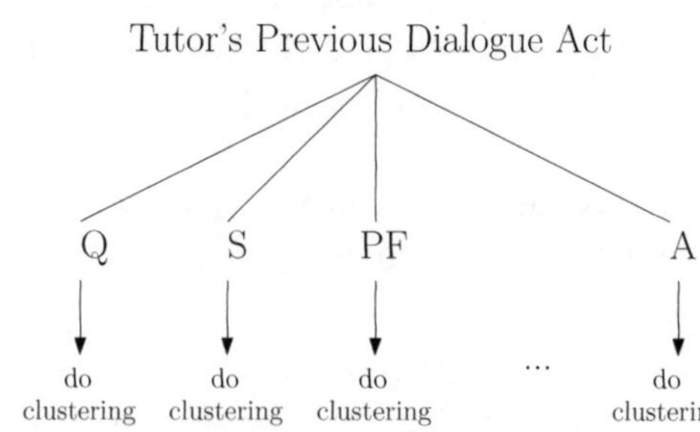

Figure 3: Branching student utterances according to previous tutor dialogue act.

As the results in Table 7 show, the performance of the model with hierarchical structure is significantly better than the flat clustering model. Note that each feature in this table leverages previous

Tutor Dialogue Act	# of student utterances
Q	818
S	464
H	125
PF	91
A	61
ACK	11
C	8
O	8
RACK	6

Table 6: The number of student utterances after branching on the previous tutor dialogue act.

tutor dialogue act while branching. Branching on previous tutor move boosted the model's accuracy for student move dialogue act classification by approximately 30% accuracy across all feature sets, a difference that is statistically significant in every case. With the hierarchical model structure, the best performance is achieved by including all three types of features: lexical, dialogue context and task. However, our hypothesis that task features would significantly improve the accuracy does not hold within the hierarchical clustering model ($T + D \not> D$ and $T + L \not> L$).

	Features	Accuracy (%)	Kappa
Hierarchical	T	64.2†	0.45
	D	63.2†	0.46
	L	60.7†	0.41
	T+D	62.1†	0.44
	T+L	63.3*†	0.45
	D+L	63.6†	0.46
	T+D+L	**65*†**	0.48

Table 7: Test set accuracies and Kappa for branching on previous tutor dialogue act (L: Lexical features, D: Dialogue context features, T: Task features) *indicates statistically significant compared to the similar model without task features and † indicates hierarchical clustering performing significantly better than flat with same features. ($p < 0.05$).

6 Discussion

The experimental results provide compelling evidence that an inclusive approach to features for unsupervised dialogue act modeling holds great promise. However, we observed a stark difference in model performance when the tutor's previous move was simply included as one of many features within a flat clustering model compared to when the previous tutor move was treated as a branching feature. In this section we take a closer look and discuss the features that help distinguish particular dialogue acts from each other.

Using the hierarchical $T + D + L$ model which performed best within the experiments, we examine the confusion matrix (Figure 4). Statements and acknowledgments prove challenging for the model, 51.3% and 61.5% accuracy overall. Moreover, these two tags are easily confused with each other: 29.7% of statements were misclassified as acknowledgments, while 21.2% of acknowledgments were misclassified as statements. The worst overall classification accuracy was for questions (6%) and the best was achieved for answers (95.3%).

Predicted

True	S	A	Q	ACK	C	RF	O
S	181	48	17	105	2	0	0
A	15	645	6	11	0	0	0
Q	83	78	14	58	0	0	0
ACK	74	44	14	206	0	0	0
C	8	4	1	1	0	0	0
RF	6	5	2	2	0	0	0
O	5	5	0	0	0	0	0

Figure 4: Confusion matrix for hierarchical model utilizing all features: T+D+L.

When we analyze the performance of different sets of features with respect to individual dialogue acts, some interesting results emerge. The analysis shows that task features are especially good for classifying statements. Using only task features, the model correctly classified 61.8% statements, compared to the lower 51.3% accuracy that the overall best model ($T + D + L$) achieved on statements. When we consider the nature of the statement dialogue act within this corpus, we note that it is a large category that encompasses a variety of utterances, some of which have lexical features in common with acknowledgments. In this case, task features are particularly helpful.

For acknowledgments, a combination of task and lexical features performed best (63.6% accuracy) compared to the overall best performing model which achieved a slightly lower 61.5% accuracy on acknowledgments. Acknowledgments are another example of an act that may take ambiguous surface form; for example, in our corpus an utterance 'yes' appears as both an answer and an acknowledgment depending on its context. Therefore, higher level features such as the ones provided by task may be more helpful.

For questions, the highest performing feature set is L. However, as shown in Table 8, the model performed poorly on questions. Inspection of the models reveals that questions are varied in terms of structure throughout the corpus and it is hard to distinguish them from other dialogue acts. For instance there are two consequent utterances "i need a write statement" and "don't i", both of which are manually labeled as questions. However, in terms of the structure, the first utterance looks very similar to a statement and therefore the model has difficulty grouping it with questions. Due to the large variety of question forms in the corpus, it is possible that the clustering performed poorly on this dialogue act. In future work it will be promising to investigate the dialogue structures which produce questions and to weight them more in the feature set in order to increase performance of clustering for questions.

We performed one additional experiment to compare the performance of the LCS metric with bigrams. For bigrams, the average leave-one-student-out test accuracy was 25% with flat clustering compared to the lexical-only case using LCS (L) which reached 33%.

Features	S	A	Q	ACK
L	21.5	41.3	**14.2**	20.4
T	**61.76**	95.27	7.30	40.90
D	48.16	95.27	3.00	60.30
T+D	52.69	94.68	3.43	51.64
T+L	42.78	95.13	6.01	**63.58**
D+L	43.63	94.98	8.58	62.09
T+D+L	51.27	95.27	6.01	61.49

Table 8: Accuracies for individual dialogue acts. Acts with fewer than 10 utterances after branching are omitted from the table.

7 Conclusion and Future Work

Dialogue act classification is crucial for dialogue management, and unsupervised modeling approaches hold great promise for automatically extracting classification models from corpora. This paper has focused on unsupervised dialogue act classification for task-oriented dialogue, investigating the impact of task features and dialogue context features on model accuracy within both flat and hierarchical clusterings. Experimental results confirm that utilizing a combination of task and dialogue features improves accuracy and that incorporating one previous tutor move as a high-level branching feature a provides particularly marked benefit. Moreover, it was found that task features are particularly important for identifying particular dialogue moves such as statements, for which the model with task features only outperformed the model with all features.

In addition to the task stream, future work should consider other sources of nonverbal cues such as posture, gesture and facial expressions to investigate the extent to which these can be successfully incorporated in unsupervised dialogue act models. Second, models that are built in specialized ways to different user groups (e.g., by gender or by incoming skill level) should be investigated. Finally, the performance of unsupervised dialogue act classification models must ultimately move toward evaluation within implemented dialogue systems (Ezen-Can and Boyer, 2013a). The overarching goal of these investigations is to create unsupervised dialogue act models that perform well enough to be used within deployed dialogue systems and enable the system to respond successfully. It is hoped that in the future, dialogue act classification models for many domains can be extracted automatically from corpora of human dialogue in those domains without the need for any manual annotation.

Acknowledgments

Thanks to the members of the LearnDialogue group at North Carolina State University for their helpful input. This work is supported in part by the National Science Foundation through Grant DRL-1007962 and the STARS Alliance, CNS-1042468. Any opinions, findings, conclusions, or recommendations expressed in this report are those of the participants, and do not necessarily represent the official views, opinions, or policy of the National Science Foundation.

References

James F. Allen, Lenhart K. Schubert, George Ferguson, Peter Heeman, Chung Hee Hwang, Tsuneaki Kato, Marc Light, Nathaniel Martin, Bradford Miller, Massimo Poesio, et al. 1995. The TRAINS project: A case study in building a conversational planning agent. *Journal of Experimental & Theoretical Artificial Intelligence*, 7(1):7–48.

David Arthur and Sergei Vassilvitskii. 2007. k-means++: The advantages of careful seeding. In *Proceedings of the 18th ACM-SIAM Symposium on Discrete Algorithms*, pages 1027–1035. Society for Industrial and Applied Mathematics.

John Langshaw Austin. 1975. *How To Do Things with Words*, volume 1955. Oxford University Press.

Srinivas Bangalore, Giuseppe Di Fabbrizio, and Amanda Stent. 2008. Learning the structure of task-driven human–human dialogs. *IEEE Transactions on Audio, Speech, and Language Processing*, 16(7):1249–1259.

Kristy Elizabeth Boyer, Eun Young Ha, Robert Phillips, Michael D. Wallis, Mladen A. Vouk, and James C. Lester. 2010. Dialogue act modeling in a complex task-oriented domain. In *Proceedings of SIGDIAL*, pages 297–305. Association for Computational Linguistics.

Kristy Elizabeth Boyer, Eun Young Ha, Robert Phillips, and James Lester. 2011. The impact of task-oriented feature sets on HMMs for dialogue modeling. In *Proceedings of SIGDIAL*, pages 49–58. Association for Computational Linguistics.

Lin Chen and Barbara Di Eugenio. 2013. Multimodality and dialogue act classification in the RoboHelper project. In *Proceedings of SIGDIAL*, pages 183–192.

Mark G. Core and James Allen. 1997. Coding dialogs with the DAMSL annotation scheme. In *Proceedings of the AAAI Fall Symposium on Communicative Action in Humans and Machines*, pages 28–35.

Nigel Crook, Ramon Granell, and Stephen Pulman. 2009. Unsupervised classification of dialogue acts using a Dirichlet process mixture model. In *Proceedings of SIGDIAL*, pages 341–348. Association for Computational Linguistics.

Barbara Di Eugenio, Zhuli Xie, and Riccardo Serafin. 2010. Dialogue act classification, higher order dialogue structure, and instance-based learning. *Dialogue & Discourse*, 1(2):1–24.

Myroslava O. Dzikovska, Elaine Farrow, and Johanna D. Moore. 2013. Combining semantic interpretation and statistical classification for improved explanation processing in a tutorial dialogue system. In *Artificial Intelligence in Education*, pages 279–288.

Aysu Ezen-Can and Kristy Elizabeth Boyer. 2013a. In-context evaluation of unsupervised dialogue act models for tutorial dialogue. In *Proceedings of SIGDIAL*, pages 324–328.

Aysu Ezen-Can and Kristy Elizabeth Boyer. 2013b. Unsupervised classification of student dialogue acts with query-likelihood clustering. In *International Conference on Educational Data Mining*, pages 20–27.

Oliver Ferschke, Iryna Gurevych, and Yevgen Chebotar. 2012. Behind the article: Recognizing dialog acts in Wikipedia talk pages. In *Proceedings of the 13th Conference of the European Chapter of the Association for Computational Linguistics*, pages 777–786.

Kate Forbes-Riley and Diane J. Litman. 2005. Using bigrams to identify relationships between student certainness states and tutor responses in a spoken dialogue corpus. In *Proceedings of the SIGDIAL Workshop*, pages 87–96.

Kate Forbes-Riley, Mihai Rotaru, Diane J. Litman, and Joel Tetreault. 2007. Exploring affect-context dependencies for adaptive system development. In *Human Language Technologies 2007: The Conference of the North American Chapter of the Association for Computational Linguistics*, pages 41–44.

Barbara J. Grosz and Candace L. Sidner. 1986. Attention, intentions, and the structure of discourse. *Computational Linguistics*, 12(3):175–204.

Eun Young Ha, Joseph F. Grafsgaard, Christopher M. Mitchell, Kristy Elizabeth Boyer, and James C. Lester. 2012. Combining verbal and nonverbal features to overcome the 'information gap' in task-oriented dialogue. In *Proceedings of SIGDIAL*, pages 247–256.

Daniel S. Hirschberg. 1975. A linear space algorithm for computing maximal common subsequences. *Communications of the ACM*, 18(6):341–343.

Shafiq Joty, Giuseppe Carenini, and Chin-Yew Lin. 2011. Unsupervised modeling of dialog acts in asynchronous conversations. In *Proceedings of the 22nd International Joint Conference on Artificial Intelligence*, pages 1807–1813.

Daniel Jurafsky, Elizabeth Shriberg, Barbara Fox, and Traci Curl. 1998. Lexical, prosodic, and syntactic cues for dialog acts. In *Proceedings of the ACL/COLING-98 Workshop on Discourse Relations and Discourse Markers*, pages 114–120.

Simon Keizer, Rieks op den Akker, and Anton Nijholt. 2002. Dialogue act recognition with Bayesian networks for Dutch dialogues. In *Proceedings of the SIGDIAL Workshop*, pages 88–94.

Su Nam Kim, Lawrence Cavedon, and Timothy Baldwin. 2010. Classifying dialogue acts in one-on-one live chats. In *Proceedings of the 2010 Conference on Empirical Methods in Natural Language Processing*, pages 862–871.

Donghyeon Lee, Minwoo Jeong, Kyungduk Kim, and Seonghan Ryu. 2013. Unsupervised spoken language understanding for a multi-domain dialog system. *IEEE Transactions On Audio, Speech, and Language Processing*, 21(11):2451–2464.

Johanna Marineau, Peter Wiemer-Hastings, Derek Harter, Brent Olde, Patrick Chipman, Ashish Karnavat, Victoria Pomeroy, Sonya Rajan, Art Graesser, Tutoring Research Group, et al. 2000. Classification of speech acts in tutorial dialog. In *Proceedings of the Workshop on Modeling Human Teaching Tactics and Strategies at the Intelligent Tutoring Systems Conference*, pages 65–71.

T. Daniel Midgley, Shelly Harrison, and Cara MacNish. 2009. Empirical verification of adjacency pairs using dialogue segmentation. In *Proceedings of SIGDIAL*, pages 104–108.

Raymond Ng and Jiawei Han. 1994. Efficient and effective clustering methods for spatial data mining. In *Proceedings of the 20th International Conference on Very Large Data Bases*, pages 144–155.

Norbert Reithinger and Martin Klesen. 1997. Dialogue act classification using language models. In *Proceedings of EuroSpeech*, pages 2235–2238.

Alan Ritter, Colin Cherry, and Bill Dolan. 2010. Unsupervised modeling of twitter conversations. In *Proceedings of the Association for Computational Linguistics*, pages 172–180.

Vasile Rus, Cristian Moldovan, Nobal Niraula, and Arthur C. Graesser. 2012. Automated discovery of speech act categories in educational games. In *International Conference on Educational Data Mining*, pages 25–32.

Emanuel A. Schegloff and Harvey Sacks. 1973. Opening up closings. *Semiotica*, 8(4):289–327.

John R. Searle. 1969. *Speech Acts: An Essay in the Philosophy of Language*. Cambridge University Press.

Riccardo Serafin and Barbara Di Eugenio. 2004. FLSA: Extending latent semantic analysis with features for dialogue act classification. In *Proceedings of the 42nd Annual Meeting on Association for Computational Linguistics*, pages 692–699. Association for Computational Linguistics.

Rangarajan Sridhar, Vivek Kumar, Srinivas Bangalore, and Shrikanth Narayanan. 2009. Combining lexical, syntactic and prosodic cues for improved online dialog act tagging. *Computer Speech & Language*, 23(4):407–422.

Andreas Stolcke, Klaus Ries, Noah Coccaro, Elizabeth Shriberg, Rebecca Bates, Daniel Jurafsky, Paul Taylor, Rachel Martin, Carol Van Ess-Dykema, and Marie Meteer. 2000. Dialogue act modeling for automatic tagging and recognition of conversational speech. *Computational Linguistics*, 26(3):339–373.

Maryam Tavafi, Yashar Mehdad, Shafiq Joty, Giuseppe Carenini, and Raymond Ng. 2013. Dialogue act recognition in synchronous and asynchronous conversations. In *Proceedings of SIGDIAL*, pages 117–121.

David R. Traum. 1999. Speech acts for dialogue agents. In *Foundations of Rational Agency*, pages 169–201. Springer.

Dialogue Act Modeling for Non-Visual Web Access

Vikas Ashok
Dept of Computer Science
Stony Brook University
Stony Brook , New York

Yevgen Borodin
Charmtech Labs LLC
CEWIT SBU R & D Park
Stony Brook , New York

Svetlana Stoyanchev
AT&T Labs Research
New York City, New York
(While at Columbia University)

I V Ramakrishnan
Charmtech Labs LLC
CEWIT SBU R & D Park
Stony Brook , New York

vganjiguntea@cs.sunysb.edu, borodin@charmtechlabs.com,
sstoyanchev@cs.columbia.edu, ram@charmtechlabs.com

Abstract

Speech-enabled dialogue systems have the potential to enhance the ease with which blind individuals can interact with the Web beyond what is possible with screen readers - the currently available assistive technology which narrates the textual content on the screen and provides shortcuts to navigate the content. In this paper, we present a dialogue act model towards developing a speech enabled browsing system. The model is based on the corpus data that was collected in a wizard-of-oz study with 24 blind individuals who were assigned a gamut of browsing tasks. The development of the model included extensive experiments with assorted feature sets and classifiers; the outcomes of the experiments and the analysis of the results are presented.

1 Introduction

The Web is the "go-to" computing infrastructure for participating in our fast-paced digital society. It has the potential to provide an even greater benefit to blind people who once required human assistance with many of their activities. According to the American Federation for the Blind, there are 21.5 million Americans who have vision loss, of whom 1.5 million are computer users (AFB, 2013).

Blind users employ screen readers as the assistive technology to interact with digital content (e.g.., JAWS (Freedom-Scientific, 2014) and VoiceOver (Apple-Inc., 2013)). Screen readers serially narrate the content of the screen using text-to-speech engines and enable users to navigate in the content using keyboard shortcuts and touch-screen gestures.

Navigating content-rich web pages and conducting online transactions spanning multiple pages requires using shortcuts and this can get quite cumbersome and tedious. Specifically, in online shopping a user typically browses through product categories, searches for products, adds products to cart, logs into his/her account, and finally makes a payment. All these steps require screen-reader users listen through a lot of content, fill forms, and find links and buttons that have to be selected to get through these steps. If users do not want to go through all content on the page, they have to remember and use a number of different shortcuts. Beginner users often use the "Down" key to go through the page line by line, listening to all content on the way (Borodin et al., 2010).

Now suppose that blind users were to tell the web browser what they wanted to accomplish and let the browsing application automatically determine what has to be clicked, fill out forms, help find products, answer questions, breeze through checkout, and wherever possible, relieve the user from doing all the mundane and tedious low-level operations such as clicking, typing, etc. The ability to carry out a dialogue with the web browser at a higher level has the potential to overcome the limitations of shortcut-based screen reading and thus offers a richer and more productive user experience for blind people.

The first step toward building a dialogue-based system is the understanding of what users could say and dialogue act modeling. Although dialogue act modeling is a well-researched topic (with details provided in related work - Section 2), it has remained unexplored in the context of web accessibility for blind people. The commercial speech-based applications have been around for a while and new ones continue to emerge at a rapid pace; however, these are mainly stand-alone (e.g.., Apple's Siri) domain specific systems that are not connected to web browsers, which precludes dialogue-based interaction with the Web. Current spoken input modules integrated with web browsers are limited to certain specific functionalities such as search (e.g.., Google's voice search) or are used as a measure of last resort (e.g.., Siri searching for terms online).

In this paper, we made a principal step towards building a dialogue-based assistive web browsing system for blind people; specifically, we built a dialogue act model for non-visual access to the Web. The contributions of this paper include: 1) a unique dialogue corpus for non-visual web access, collected during the wizard-of-oz user study conducted with 24 blind participants (Section 3); 2) the design of a suitable dialogue act scheme (Section 3); 3) experimentation with classifiers capable of identifying the dialogue acts associated with utterances based on combinations of lexical/syntactic, contextual, and task-related feature sets (Section 4); 4) investigation of the importance of each feature set with respect to classification performance to assess whether simple lexical/syntactic features are sufficient for obtaining an acceptable performance (Section 5).

2 Related Work

While previous research addressed spoken dialogue interfaces for a domain-specific websites, such as news or movie search (Ferreras and Cardeñoso-Payo, 2005; Wang et al., 2014), dialogue interface to generic web sites is a novel task. Spoken dialogue systems (SDS) can be classified by the type of initiative: system, user, or mixed initiative (Lee et al., 2010). In a system-initiative SDS, a system guides a user through a series of information gathering and information presenting prompts. In a user-initiative system, a user can initiate and steer the interaction. Mixed-initiative systems allow both system and user-initiated actions.

Dialogue systems also differ in the types of dialogue manager: finite state based, form based, or agent based (Lee et al., 2010), (Chotimongkol, 2008). Finite state and form filling systems are usually system-initiative. These systems have a fixed set of dialogue states and finite set of possible user commands that map to system actions. In contrast, a speech-enabled browsing system proposed in this work is an agent-based system. The set of actions of this system correspond to user actions during web browsing. The domain of possible user commands at each point of the dialogue depends on the current web page that is viewed by a user. The dialogue state in a voice browsing system is compiled at run-time as the user can visit any web page.

While a users dialogue acts in a form-based or finite state system depends primarily on a dialogue state, in an agent-based system with user-initiative, the space of users dialogue acts at each dialogue state is open. To determine dialogue manager action, it is essential for the system to identify users intent or dialogue act. In this work, we address dialogue act modelling for open-domain voice web browsing as a proof of concept for the system.

Dialogue act (DA) annotation schemes for spoken dialogue systems follow theories on speech acts originally developed by Searle (1975). A number of DA annotation schemes have been developed previously (Core and Allen, 1997), (Carletta et al., 1997). Several of dialogue tagging schemes strive to provide domain-independence (Core and Allen, 1997), (Bunt, 2011).

Bunt (2011) developed a NIST standardized domain-independent annotation scheme which incorporates elements from the previously developed annotation schemes. It is a hierarchical multi-dimensional annotation scheme. Each functional segment (part of an utterance corresponding to a DA) can have a general purpose function, such as Inform, Propositional Question, Yes/No Question, and a dimension-specific function in any number of 10 defined dimensions, such as Task, Feedback, or Time management.

In the analysis of human-computer dialogues, it is common to adopt DA annotation schemes to suit specific domains. Generic domain-independent schemes are geared towards the analysis of natural human-human dialogue and provide rich annotation structure that can cover complexity of natural dialogue. Domain-specific dialogues use a subset of the generic dialogue structure. For example, Ohtake et al. (2009) developed a DA scheme for tourist-guide domain motivated by a generic annotation scheme (Ohtake et al., 2010), and Bangalore and Stent (2009) created a dialogue scheme for a catalogue product ordering dialogue system. In our work we design DA scheme for Web-Browsing domain motivated by the DAMSL (Core and Allen, 1997) schema for task-oriented dialogue.

We used a Wizard-of-Oz (WOZ) approach to collect an initial dataset of spoken voice com-

Task	τ_u	τ_d
Shopping	121	16
Email	92	16
Flight	180	16
Hotel	179	16
Job	76	16
Admission	144	16
Overall	792	96

Table 1: Corpus details. τ_u - number of utterances, τ_d - number of dialogs.

mands by both blind and sighted users. WOZ is commonly used before building a dialogue system (Chotimongkol, 2008), (Ohtake et al., 2009), (Eskenazi et al., 1999).

In previous work on dialogue modelling, Stolcke et al. (2000) used HMM approach to predict dialogue acts in a switchboard human-human dialogue corpus achieving 65% accuracy. Rangarajan Sridhar et al. (2009) applied a maximum entropy classifier on the Switchbord corpus. Using a combination of lexical, syntactic, and prosodic features, the authors achieve accuracy of 72% on that corpus. Following the work of Rangarajan Sridhar et al. (2009), we use supervised classification approach to determine dialogue act on the annotated corpus of human-wizard web-browsing dialogues.

3 Corpus and Annotation

In this section, we describe the corpus and the associated dialogue act scheme. The corpus was collected using a WOZ user study with 24 blind participants. Exactly 50% of the participants indicated that they were very comfortable with screen readers, while the remaining 50% said they were not comfortable with computers. We will refer to them as "experts" and "beginners" respectively.

The study required each participant to complete a set of typical web browsing tasks (shopping, sending an email, booking a flight, reserving a hotel room, searching for a job and applying for university admission) using unrestricted speech commands ranging from simple commands such as "click the search button", to complex commands such as "buy this product". Unknown to the participants, these commands were executed by a wizard and appropriate responses were narrated using a screen reader. The dialogs were effective; almost every participant was able to complete each assigned task by engaging in a dialogue with the wizarded interface.

As shown in Table 1, the corpus consists of a total of 96 dialogs collected during the execution of 6 tasks and captures approximately 22 hours of speech with a total of 792 user utterances and 774 system utterances. There is exactly 1 dialogue per task for any given participant. Each user turn consists of a single command that is usually a simple sentence or phrase. Each system turn is either narration of webpage content or information request for the purpose of either form filling or disambiguation. Therefore, each dialogue turn was treated as a single utterance and every utterance was identified with a single associated dialogue act.

The corpus was manually annotated with dialogue act labels and the labeling scheme was verified by measuring the inter-annotator agreement. The rest of this section describes the annotation scheme.

3.1 Dialogue Act Annotation

The dialogue act annotation scheme was inspired by the DAMSL scheme (Core and Allen, 1997) for task oriented dialogue. The proposed scheme was also influenced by extended DAMSL tagset (Stolcke et al., 2000) and the DIT++ annotation scheme (Bunt, 2011). We customized the annotation scheme to suit the non-visual web access domain, thereby making it more relevant to our corpus and tasks.

Table 2 lists the dialogue acts for both user and system utterances. The user dialogue act tagset consists of labels representing task related requests (Command-Intention, Command-Task, Command-Multiple, Command-Navigation), inquiries (Question-Task, Help-Task) and information input (Information-Task), whereas the system DA tagset contains labels representing information requests (Prompt), answers to user inquiries (Question-Answer, Help-Response) and other system responses (Short-Response, Long-Response, etc.) to user commands.

Inter-rater agreement values for different tasks in the corpus are presented in Table 3. The κ values for all tasks are above 0.80, which according to Fleiss' guidelines (Fleiss, 1973), indicates excellent inter-rater reliability on the DA annotation. Therefore, the DA tagset is generic enough to be applicable for a wide varity of tasks that can be performed on the web. Note that the dialogue act scheme was specially designed for non-visual web

User dialogue Acts		
Dialogue Act	**Description**	**Frequency**
Command-Intention	Indication of user's intention or end goal, e.g. *I wish to buy a Bluetooth speaker*	0.117
Command-Task	Basic action commands like *click, select, enter*, etc.	0.072
Command-Multiple	Complex commands requiring an execution plan comprising a sequence of basic commands, e.g. *buy this product, book this room*, etc.	0.162
Command-Navigation	Commands directing the movement of cursor like *go to, stop, next* etc.	0.136
Information-Task	Information required for completing a task, e.g. *departure date/return date* information for flight booking task, *first name, phone number*, etc.	0.442
Question-Task	Task specific questions like *What is the cheapest flight?, What is the basic salary?*, etc.	0.041
Self-Talk	Utterances not directed towards the system, e.g. *hmmm, what should I do next?*	0.002
Help-Task	Request for help when the user wishes to speak with the experimenter, e.g. *Help, what does that mean?*	0.024
System dialogue Acts		
dialogue Act	**Description**	**Frequency**
Prompt	Request for information from user to complete a task, e.g. *First Name, text box blank*	0.460
Short-Response	A short response to a user command, e.g. *description of product, brief details of flight, acknowledgements*, etc.	0.198
Long-Response	A lengthy response to a user command, e.g. *Narration of entire page, list of search results*, etc.	0.120
Keyboard-Response	Response to user keyboard actions	0.072
Article-Response	Narration of an article	0.034
Question-Answer	Response to a user question regarding task (non-help)	0.044
No-Response	No response for some navigation commands like *Stop*	0.041
Help-Response	Response to a help request from the user	0.026

Table 2: dialogue acts for non-visual Web access

access. Insofar as sighted people are concerned, a more elaborate scheme would be required since their utterances are dominated by visual cues, a fact that was confirmed by a parallel user study with sighted participants on the same set of web tasks that were used in the wizard-of-oz study.

4 Features

This section describes the different feature sets that we experimented with for our classification tasks. The vector representation for training the DA classifiers integrates several types of features (Table 4): unigrams ($\mathcal{U}$) and syntactic features ($\mathcal{S}$), context related features ($\mathcal{C}$), task related features ($\mathcal{T}$), presence of words anywhere in an utterance($\mathcal{P}$) and presence of words at the beginning of an utterance($\mathcal{B}$). The last two feature sets are similar to the ones used in Boyer et al. (2010).

Task	κ
Shopping	0.865
Email	0.829
Flight	0.894
Hotel	0.848
Job	0.824
Admission	0.800

Table 3: Inter-rater agreement measured in terms of Cohen's κ for all tasks in the corpus.

The feature sets $\mathcal{C}$, $\mathcal{P}$, $\mathcal{B}$ and $\mathcal{S}$ are specific to the domain of non-visual web access and were hand-crafted based on the following three factors: knowledge of the browsing behavior of blind users reported in previous studies, e.g. (Borodin et al., 2010); manual analysis of the corpus; mitigate the effect of noise that is usually present in standard lexical/syntactic feature sets such as n-grams and parse tree rules. Each of the features in $\mathcal{C}$, $\mathcal{P}$, $\mathcal{B}$ and $\mathcal{S}$ were crafted to have a close correspondence to some dialogue act. For example, p_{nav} is closely tied to the *Command-Navigation* dialogue act.

4.1 Unigrams

Unigrams ($\mathcal{U}$ in Table 4) are one of the commonly used lexical features for training dialogue act classifiers (e.g. (Boyer et al., 2010), (Stolcke et al., 2000), (Rangarajan Sridhar et al., 2009)). Encoding unigrams as features is based on the observation that some words appear more frequently in certain dialogue acts compared to other dialogue acts. For example, approximately 73% of "*want*" occur in the *Command-Intention* DA, 100% of "*skip*" occur in the *Command-Navigation* DA and approximately 92% of "*select*" occur in the *Command-Task* DA. Word-DA corrections can also be automatically identified using SVM classifers trained on unigram features. Table 5

Feature	Description	Binary
Overall Feature Set		
UNIGRAMS ($\mathcal{U}$)		
Feature	**Description**	**Binary**
u	Unigrams	N
PRESENCE OF WORDS IN COMMANDS ($\mathcal{P}$)		
p_{iyou}	The utterance contains either *I* or *you*	Y
p_{help}	The utterance contains the word *help*	Y
p_{helpq}	The utterance contains words usually associated with help requests. E.g., *how, am I*, etc.	Y
p_{prev}	The immediately preceding system DA is *Prompt* and the utterance contains words also present in this immediately preceding system utterance	Y
p_{intent}	The utterance contains words , *need, desire, prefer, like* and their synonyms	Y
$p_{browser}$	The utterance contains words also present in the web browser tab title. E.g., *email, job*	Y
p_{html}	The utterance contains references to HTML elements. E.g., *form, box, link, page*, etc.	Y
p_{basic}	The utterance contains a verb representing basic operations on a web page. E.g., *click, edit.*	Y
p_{nbasic}	The utterance contains a verb not related to basic web page operations; a verb usually associated with task or domain related actions. E.g. *send, open, compose*, etc.	Y
p_{nav}	The utterance contains words related to cursor movement. E.g., *go to, continue, next*, etc.	Y
$p_{question}$	The utterance contains words usually associated with questions. E.g., *what, when, why*	Y
SYNTACTIC STRUCTURE OF COMMANDS ($\mathcal{S}$)		
s_{np}	The utterance is a noun phrase with atleast two words	Y
s_{noun}	The utterance consists of a single noun	Y
s_{basic}	The utterance consists of a single verb representing basic web page operations. E.g., *click, edit, erase, select*, etc.	Y
s_{nbasic}	The utterance consists of a single verb representing task or domain related actions. e.g. *send, open, compose, order*, etc.	Y
CONTEXT RELATED FEATURES ($\mathcal{C}$)		
c_{first}	The utterance is the first command to be issued when a new website is loaded in the browser	Y
$c_{previous}$	dialogue act of the immediately preceding system utterance	N
POSITION OF WORDS IN COMMANDS ($\mathcal{B}$)		
b_{nav}	The utterance begins with word(s) related to cursor movement. e.g. *go to, continue*, etc.	Y
$b_{question}$	The utterance begins with a word that is usually associated with a question. E.g., *what, when, where, why*, etc.	Y
b_i	The utterance begins with the personal pronoun *I*.	Y
b_{helpq}	The utterance begins with word(s) usually associated with help requests. E.g., *how, am I*	Y
TASK RELATED FEATURES ($\mathcal{T}$)		
t_{name}	Name of the task associated with the utterance	N

Table 4: Feature set for user dialogue act classification. The complete list of words associated with each feature in $\mathcal{P}$ and $\mathcal{B}$ is provided in Appendix A.

presents few such correlations. Note that some of the words in Table 5 are task-specific (noise); a consequence of using a small dataset.

4.2 Presence of Words in Commands

In constract to unigram features that take into account all possible word-DA correlations, the presence-of-word features ($\mathcal{P}$ in Table 4) are limited to certain specific words that have strong correlations with the DA types. For each feature $p \in \mathcal{P}$, if the presence of certain specific words associated with p occur in an utterance, then p is set to *true*. The set of words for every p that corresponds to some dialogue act d was contructed by determining the discriminatory words for d using simple statistical analysis of the corpus (e.g. relative frequencies of words) as well as by an examination of the weights of different words learnt by the SVM classifier trained on a development dataset using unigram features alone. e.g.., the words *continue* and *skip* occur much more frequently in Command-Navigation than in other dialogue acts (see Table 5) and hence are included in p_{nav}. Note however that not all discriminatory words in Table 5 were used. Only generic words, independent of any specific task, were selected (see Appendix A for details).

4.3 Syntactic Structure of Commands

The binary syntactic features ($\mathcal{S}$ in Table 4) were automatically extracted using the Stanford parser (Klein and Manning, 2003). As in word-DA correlations, some of the syntactic structure-DA correlations were also identified by a manual in-

Dialogue Act	Discriminatory Words
Command-Intention	want, compose, book, for, look, email, find, an, accounting, Stanford, a, airplane, message, I, music, get, ticket, positions, need, bluetooth, jobs, new
Command-Task	repeat, choose, delete, select, link, edit, enter, erase, clear, fill, in, click, third, at, body, box, again, blue, that
Command-Multiple	play, read, senior, send, reviews, Harlem, artists, study, submit, details, law, description, Kitaro, mornings, availability, apply, construction, pay, reservations, proceed, it, this, available
Comand-Navigation	skip, next, previous, go, page, finish, stop, item, continue, back, line, before, box, first, second, to, top, home, part, would
Information-Task	JFK, customer, no, August, July, USA, October, Kahalui, October30th, anytime, coach, today, nonstop, movies, York
Question-Task	price, time, fare, layover, times, is, what's, anything, cheaper, best, flight, airline, complete, onestop, departure, cards, price, much, cost, weekly.
Help-Task	help, do, mean, does, say, can, supposed, something, how, use, voice, have, apply, reservation, by, address, give, get

Table 5: Top discriminative unigrams based on weights from SVM classifier.

vestigation of the corpus. For example, 82.1% of single noun-only utterances (s_{noun}) have the DA *Information-Task*, 76.2% of "*basic*" verb-only utterances (s_{basic}) have the DA *Command-Task* and 83.3% of "*non-basic*" verb-only utterances (s_{nbasic}) have the DA *Command-Multiple*.

4.4 Context Related Features

The local context ($\mathcal{C}$ in Table 4) provides valuable cues to identify the dialogue act associated with a user utterance. It was observed during the study that user utterance is influenced to a large extent by the immediately preceding system utterance. For example, 89.95% of all user utterances immediately following the system *Prompt* were observed to be *Information-Task*. In addition, most of the time (probability 87.5%), the first utterance issued for a task was *Command-Intention*.

4.5 Position-of-Word in Commands

Design of feature set $\mathcal{B}$ in Table 4 was inspired by an analysis of the corpus which revealed that certain dialogue acts are characterized by the presence of certain words at the beginning of the corresponding utterances. For example, 93.4% of all *Command-Navigation* utterances begin with a cursor-movement related word (e.g. next, previous, etc. see Appendix A for the complete list).

4.6 Task Related Features

Since it is possible for different tasks to exhibit different feature vector patterns for the same dialogue act, incorporating task name ($\mathcal{T}$ in Table 4) as an additional feature may therefore improve classification performance by exploiting these variations (if any) between tasks.

Group	Composition
$\mathcal{G}1$	$\mathcal{U}$
$\mathcal{G}2$	$\mathcal{P} \cup \mathcal{B} \cup \mathcal{S}$
$\mathcal{G}3$	$\mathcal{C} \cup \mathcal{B} \cup \mathcal{S}$
$\mathcal{G}4$	$\mathcal{C} \cup \mathcal{P} \cup \mathcal{S}$
$\mathcal{G}5$	$\mathcal{C} \cup \mathcal{P} \cup \mathcal{B}$
$\mathcal{G}6$	$\mathcal{C} \cup \mathcal{P} \cup \mathcal{B} \cup \mathcal{S}$
$\mathcal{G}7$	$\mathcal{C} \cup \mathcal{P} \cup \mathcal{B} \cup \mathcal{S} \cup \mathcal{T}$
$\mathcal{G}8$	$\mathcal{C} \cup \mathcal{P} \cup \mathcal{B} \cup \mathcal{S} \cup \mathcal{U}$

Table 6: Feature groups.

5 Classification Results

All classification tasks were performed using the WEKA toolkit (Hall et al., 2009). The classification experiments were done using Support Vector Machine (frequently used for benchmarking), J48 Decision Tree (appropriate for a small size mostly binary feature set) and Random Forest classifiers. The model parameters for all classifiers were optimized for maximum performance.

In addition, experiments were also performed to assess the utility of each feature set (Table 4). Specifically, the performance of classifiers with different combinations (Groups 1-8 in Table 6) of feature sets was evaluated to assess the importance of each individual feature set. We primarily focussed on domain-specific feature sets ($\mathcal{P}$, $\mathcal{B}$, $\mathcal{C}$ and $\mathcal{S}$). Observe that group $\mathcal{G}6$ differs from any of $\mathcal{G}2 - \mathcal{G}5$ by exactly one feature set. This lets us to assess the individual utility of $\mathcal{P}$, $\mathcal{B}$, $\mathcal{C}$ and $\mathcal{S}$. In addition, we also extended $\mathcal{G}6$ by including $\mathcal{U}$ ($\mathcal{G}7$) and $\mathcal{T}$ ($\mathcal{G}8$) to determine if there was any noticeable improvement in performance. $\mathcal{G}1$ with only unigram features serves as a baseline. All reported results (Table 7) are based on 5-fold cross validation: 632 instances for training and 158 instances for testing. Table 7 presents the classification results for different feature groups. The DA *Self-Talk* was excluded from classification due to insufficient number (2) of data points.

5.1 Classification Performance

Overall Performance: As seen in Table 7, the tree-based classifiers (J48 and RF) performed better than SVM in a majority of the feature groups (6 out of 8). The random forest classifier yielded the best performance (91% Precision, 90% Recall) for feature group $\mathcal{G}6$, whereas the $\mathcal{G}3$-SVM combination had the lowest performance (69% Precision, 67% Recall). However, all groups includ-

		Performance of Feature Groups															
		$\mathcal{G}1$		$\mathcal{G}2$		$\mathcal{G}3$		$\mathcal{G}4$		$\mathcal{G}5$		$\mathcal{G}6$		$\mathcal{G}7$		$\mathcal{G}8$	
DA	**MODEL**	**P**	**R**	**P**	**R**	**P**	**R**	**P**	**R**	**P**	**R**	**P**	**R**	**P**	**R**	**P**	**R**
CI	SVM	.83	.80	.84	.95	.71	.95	**.91**	**.96**	.82	.90	**.91**	.95	.89	**.96**	.89	.94
	J48	.74	.74	.83	.90	.80	.93	.84	.95	.81	.93	.83	.95	.85	.93	**.91**	.95
	RF	.76	.74	.81	.90	.85	.94	.88	.90	.80	.87	.84	.93	.88	.89	.87	.95
CT	SVM	.87	.73	.86	.81	.93	.30	.89	.87	.84	.81	.89	.83	.89	.81	.92	.88
	J48	.80	.64	.80	.70	**1.0**	.28	.88	.79	.80	.70	.85	.75	.83	.87	.86	.67
	RF	.72	.58	.84	.89	.81	.26	.88	.89	.85	.85	.79	**.93**	.77	.78	.88	.80
CM	SVM	.73	.65	.77	.58	.36	.30	.78	.64	.78	.59	.78	.64	.80	.62	.79	.78
	J48	.74	.36	.78	.79	.68	.87	**.83**	.59	.81	.78	.76	.83	.81	.80	.76	.87
	RF	.79	.56	.80	.81	.68	.83	.80	.59	.82	.79	.81	.83	.80	.82	.76	**.89**
CN	SVM	.89	.84	.93	.87	**.96**	.82	.67	**.96**	.94	.87	**.96**	.89	.94	.87	.90	.92
	J48	.89	.65	.95	.95	**.96**	.92	.65	.93	.95	.95	.95	.92	.92	.93	.87	.90
	RF	.82	.86	.94	.94	.95	.92	.66	.95	.95	.95	.95	.95	.94	.93	.91	.88
IT	SVM	.70	.89	.82	.93	.70	.81	.81	.79	.82	.93	.82	.93	.82	.94	.85	.90
	J48	.54	.93	.96	.97	.94	.97	.80	.82	.96	.97	.97	.96	.96	.97	.94	.94
	RF	.65	.93	**.98**	**.98**	.95	.97	.81	.82	.97	**.98**	**.98**	.97	**.98**	**.98**	.97	.92
QT	SVM	.66	.46	.87	.27	.90	.30	.80	.30	.62	.31	.80	.31	.70	.33	.85	.49
	J48	.44	.36	.62	.33	.80	.23	.90	.30	.53	.34	.62	.31	.56	.47	**.93**	.32
	RF	.63	.36	.65	.31	.61	.39	.78	.27	.54	.35	.83	.39	.68	**.51**	.87	.33
HT	SVM	.77	.71	.73	.65	.80	.45	.79	.63	.63	.67	.78	.63	.72	.64	.92	.76
	J48	.86	.79	.80	.57	.80	.33	.81	.60	.70	.50	.81	.55	.55	.52	**.93**	**.91**
	RF	.85	.70	.79	.65	.78	.33	.75	.60	.74	.67	.90	.48	.67	.67	.90	.80
Overall	SVM	.77	.76	.83	.82	.69	.67	.80	.79	.82	.82	.84	.83	.84	.83	.85	.85
	J48	.70	.66	.88	.88	.87	.85	.80	.78	.88	.88	.89	.88	.88	.89	.87	.86
	RF	.74	.73	.90	**.90**	.86	.85	.80	.79	.89	.89	**.91**	**.90**	.90	.89	.88	.87

Table 7: Classification Results. The overall performance is the weighted average over all dialogue acts. Notation: J48-Decision Tree, RF-Random Forest, SVM-Support Vector Machine, P-Precision, R-Recall, CI-Command-Intention, CT-Command-Task, CM-Command-Multiple, CN-Command-Navigation, IT-Information-Task, QT-Question-Task, HT-Help-Task. The best performances for each DA are highlighted in bold.

ing $\mathcal{G}3$ did better than $\mathcal{G}1$ with tree-based classifiers. $\mathcal{G}1$ was consistently outperformed by the other groups.

Performance on dialogue acts: In $6/8$ feature groups, the performance of SVM with respect to IT dialogue act was significantly worse than that of tree-based classifiers. However, SVM produced consistently good results ($> 80\%$ in most cases) for the CI and CT dialogue acts. All classifiers performed very well in case of CN dialogue act ($> 80\%$ for $7/8$ groups). However, none of the classifiers performed well in case of QT.

5.2 Importance of feature sets

From Table 7, it can be inferred that contextual features ($\mathcal{C}$) do not contribute to improving overall classification performance. In particular, for each classifier, the difference in overall performance between groups $\mathcal{G}2$ (excluding $\mathcal{C}$) and $\mathcal{G}6$ (including $\mathcal{C}$) is very small (worst case: 1% difference in both P and R). However, inclusion of $\mathcal{C}$ significantly improved the classification performance of RF for QT and CI dialogue acts (18% improvement in P, 8% improvement in R for QT, 3% improvement in both P and R for CI). Even in case of J48, where group $\mathcal{G}6$ yields the best performance,

Dialogue Act	Discriminatory Rules
Command-Intention	• $c_{first} \wedge \neg b_{nav} \wedge \neg p_{html} \wedge \neg s_{noun}$ • $c_{first} \wedge \neg b_{nav} \wedge p_{html} \wedge p_{iyou}$ • $\neg c_{first} \wedge \neg b_{nav} \wedge p_{intent} \wedge \neg p_{nav} \wedge \neg p_{question}$
Command-Task	• $\neg c_{first} \wedge \neg b_{nav} \wedge \neg p_{intent} \wedge \neg p_{helpq} \wedge p_{basic} \wedge \neg p_{nbasic}$ • $\neg c_{first} \wedge \neg b_{nav} \wedge \neg p_{intent} \wedge \neg p_{helpq} \wedge p_{basic} \wedge p_{nbasic} \wedge p_{html}$
Command-Multiple	• $\neg c_{first} \wedge \neg b_{nav} \wedge \neg p_{intent} \wedge \neg p_{helpq} \wedge \neg p_{basic} \wedge \neg p_{nbasic} \wedge c_{previous} = [h\|k\|l\|n] \wedge \neg p_{html} \wedge \neg p_{question}$ • $\neg c_{first} \wedge \neg b_{nav} \wedge \neg p_{intent} \wedge \neg p_{helpq} \wedge \neg p_{basic} \wedge p_{nbasic} \wedge c_{previous} = [\hat{}p]$
Comand-Navigation	• $c_{first} \wedge b_{nav}$ • $c_{first} \wedge \neg b_{nav} \wedge p_{html} \wedge \neg p_{iyou}$ • $\neg c_{first} \wedge b_{nav} \wedge \neg s_{np}$ • $\neg c_{first} \wedge b_{nav} \wedge s_{np} \wedge c_{previous} = [s\|a]$
Information-Task	• $\neg c_{first} \wedge \neg b_{nav} \wedge \neg p_{intent} \wedge \neg p_{helpq} \wedge \neg p_{basic} \wedge \neg p_{nbasic} \wedge c_{previous} = [p]$ • $\neg c_{first} \wedge \neg b_{nav} \wedge \neg p_{intent} \wedge \neg p_{helpq} \wedge \neg p_{basic} \wedge p_{nbasic} \wedge c_{previous} = [p] \wedge \neg p_{iyou}$
Question-Task	• $\neg c_{first} \wedge \neg b_{nav} \wedge \neg p_{intent} \wedge \neg p_{helpq} \wedge \neg p_{basic} \wedge \neg p_{nbasic} \wedge c_{previous} = [h\|k\|l\|n] \wedge \neg p_{html} \wedge p_{question}$ • $\neg c_{first} \wedge \neg b_{nav} \wedge \neg p_{intent} \wedge \neg p_{helpq} \wedge \neg p_{basic} \wedge \neg p_{nbasic} \wedge c_{previous} = [q\|s\|a] \wedge \neg p_{nav} \wedge \neg p_{html} \wedge \neg s_{noun}$
Help-Task	• $\neg c_{first} \wedge \neg b_{nav} \wedge \neg p_{intent} \wedge p_{helpq} \wedge p_{iyou} \wedge \neg b_i$

Table 8: A select sample of J48 rules ($conf \geq 0.75$ and descending order of support) for group $\mathcal{G}6$. Notation: $\neg c_{first}$ stands for $c_{first} = false$ and c_{first} stands for $c_{first} = true$.

Utterance	Actual DA	Predicted DA	Comments
"*Continue to booking it*"	Command-Multiple	Command-Navigation	This utterance was issued while performing the *book a hotel room* task. This command essentially is the same as "book it". The presence of a navigation related verb *continue* at the beginning caused the classifiers to incorrectly classify it as *Command-Navigation*.
"*I am looking to check in on July 23rd*"	Information-Task	Command-Intention	This utterance was in response to a system prompt for check-in date while performing the *book a hotel room* task. The presence of first person nominative pronoun "I" caused the classifiers to categorize it as *Command-Intention*.
"What does that mean?"	Help-Task	Question-Task	This utterance was directed towards the experimenter and therefore it was annotated as *Help-Task*. However, the absence of the keyword *help* and the presence of a Wh-word *what* at the beginning of the command caused the classifiers to incorrectly classify this command as *Question-Task*.
"*Best available price?*" "*Ok, return time?*" "*Price?*" "*Layover?*"	Question-Task	Command-Multiple Information	The absence of Question related words like *Wh-words*, *is*, etc. at the beginning coupled with the fact that these commands are *noun phrases* caused the classifiers to incorrectly classify them as either *Command-Multiple* or *Information*.

Table 9: A few incorrectly classified utterances.

contextual features were found to be a component of some of the high-confidence, high-support J48 rules (Table 8) for CI and QT. Similar claims can also be made for syntactic features($\mathcal{S}$), where although there is not much difference in overall performance between groups $\mathcal{G}5$ and $\mathcal{G}6$ (Worst Case: 2% drop in P, 1% drop in R), improvements were observed in case of RF for QT and CI dialogue acts (29% improvement in P, 4% improvement in R for QT, 4% improvement in P, 6% improvement in R for CI).

Excluding either word-existential features ($\mathcal{P}$) or word-position related features ($\mathcal{B}$), however, caused a significant drop in overall performance (Worst case: 15% drop in P, 16% drop in R without $\mathcal{P}$, 11% drop in both P and R without $\mathcal{B}$). Table 8 further highlights the importance of feature set $\mathcal{P}$, since over 50% of the high performing J48 rules (Table 8) have at least one feature of type $\mathcal{P}$ with *true* as their truth values.

It can be seen in Table 7 that adding either unigrams or task-name to the existing feature set of $\mathcal{G}6$ does not affect the overall performance. However, the use of unigram features improved results of all the classifiers for the HT DA. No such DA specific improvements were seen with task-name as an added feature to $\mathcal{G}6$. This suggests that the feature values of $\mathcal{G}6$ for all DAs are *task-independent*.

5.3 Prediction Errors

It is clear from Table 7 that the prediction accuracies of CM, QT and HT are not nearly as good as those of other dialogue acts. Table 9 provides some insights into this issue via illustrative examples from the corpus.

Notice that the errors in case of CI, CM and HT are mostly related to choice of words used in the utterances, whereas mistakes in the prediction of QT are mainly due to inadequate information or the incompleteness of the utterances. Therefore, it is recommended that the speech enabled web dialogue systems enforce a constraint requiring users to express their complete thoughts in each of their corresponding utterances.

6 Conclusion

Experiments with the dialogue act model described in the paper indicate that with a small set of simple lexical/syntactic features it is possible to achieve a high overall dialogue act recognition accuracy (over 90% precision and recall) using simple and well-known tree-based classifiers such as decision trees and random forests. It is hence possible to build speech-enabled dialogue-based assistive web browsing systems with low computational overhead that, inturn, can result in low latency response times - a critical requirement from a usability perspective for blind users. Finally, a dialogue model for non-visual web access, such as the one described in this paper, can be the key driver of goal-oriented web browsing - a next generation assistive technology that will empower blind users to stay focused on high-level browsing tasks, while the system does all of the low-level operations such as clicking on links, filling forms, etc., necessary to accomplish the tasks.

Acknowledgements

Research reported in this publication was supported by the National Eye Institute of the National Institutes of Health under award number 1R43EY21962-1A1. We would like to thank Lighthouse Guild International and Dr. William Seiple in particular for helping conduct user studies.

References

AFB. 2013. Facts and figures on american adults with vision loss. http://www.afb.org/info/blindness-statistics/adults/facts-and-figures/235, January.

Apple-Inc. 2013. Voiceover for os x. http://www.apple.com/accessibility/osx/voiceover/.

Srinivas Bangalore and Amanda J Stent. 2009. Incremental parsing models for dialog task structure. In *Proceedings of the 12th Conference of the European Chapter of the Association for Computational Linguistics*, pages 94–102. Association for Computational Linguistics.

Yevgen Borodin, Jeffrey P Bigham, Glenn Dausch, and IV Ramakrishnan. 2010. More than meets the eye: a survey of screen-reader browsing strategies. In *Proceedings of the 2010 International Cross Disciplinary Conference on Web Accessibility (W4A)*, page 13. ACM.

Kristy Elizabeth Boyer, Eun Young Ha, Robert Phillips, Michael D Wallis, Mladen A Vouk, and James C Lester. 2010. Dialogue act modeling in a complex task-oriented domain. In *Proceedings of the 11th Annual Meeting of the Special Interest Group on Discourse and Dialogue*, pages 297–305. Association for Computational Linguistics.

Harry Bunt. 2011. Multifunctionality in dialogue. *Computer Speech & Language*, 25(2):222–245.

Jean Carletta, Stephen Isard, Gwyneth Doherty-Sneddon, Amy Isard, Jacqueline C Kowtko, and Anne H Anderson. 1997. The reliability of a dialogue structure coding scheme. *Computational linguistics*, 23(1):13–31.

Ananlada Chotimongkol. 2008. *Learning the structure of task-oriented conversations from the corpus of in-domain dialogs*. Ph.D. thesis, SRI International.

Mark G Core and James Allen. 1997. Coding dialogs with the damsl annotation scheme. In *AAAI fall symposium on communicative action in humans and machines*, pages 28–35. Boston, MA.

Maxine Eskenazi, Alexander I Rudnicky, Karin Gregory, Paul C Constantinides, Robert Brennan, Christina L Bennett, and Jwan Allen. 1999. Data collection and processing in the carnegie mellon communicator. In *EUROSPEECH*.

César González Ferreras and Valentín Cardeñoso-Payo. 2005. Development and evaluation of a spoken dialog system to access a newspaper web site. In *INTERSPEECH*, pages 857–860.

J.L. Fleiss. 1973. *Statistical methods for rates and proportions Rates and proportions*. Wiley.

Freedom-Scientific. 2014. Screen reading software from freedom scientific. http://www.freedomscientific.com/products/fs/jaws-product-page.asp.

Mark Hall, Eibe Frank, Geoffrey Holmes, Bernhard Pfahringer, Peter Reutemann, and Ian H Witten. 2009. The weka data mining software: an update. *ACM SIGKDD explorations newsletter*, 11(1):10–18.

Dan Klein and Christopher D Manning. 2003. Accurate unlexicalized parsing. In *Proceedings of the 41st Annual Meeting on Association for Computational Linguistics-Volume 1*, pages 423–430. Association for Computational Linguistics.

Cheongjae Lee, Sangkeun Jung, Kyungduk Kim, Donghyeon Lee, and Gary Geunbae Lee. 2010. Recent approaches to dialog management for spoken dialog systems. *JCSE*, 4(1):1–22.

George A Miller. 1995. Wordnet: a lexical database for english. *Communications of the ACM*, 38(11):39–41.

Kiyonori Ohtake, Teruhisa Misu, Chiori Hori, Hideki Kashioka, and Satoshi Nakamura. 2009. Annotating dialogue acts to construct dialogue systems for consulting. In *Proceedings of the 7th Workshop on Asian Language Resources*, pages 32–39. Association for Computational Linguistics.

Kiyonori Ohtake, Teruhisa Misu, Chiori Hori, Hideki Kashioka, and Satoshi Nakamura. 2010. Dialogue acts annotation for nict kyoto tour dialogue corpus to construct statistical dialogue systems. In *LREC*.

Yury Puzis, Yevgen Borodin, Rami Puzis, and IV Ramakrishnan. 2013. Predictive web automation assistant for people with vision impairments. In *Proceedings of the 22nd international conference on World Wide Web*, pages 1031–1040. International World Wide Web Conferences Steering Committee.

Vivek Kumar Rangarajan Sridhar, Srinivas Bangalore, and Shrikanth Narayanan. 2009. Combining lexical, syntactic and prosodic cues for improved online dialog act tagging. *Computer Speech & Language*, 23(4):407–422.

John R Searle. 1975. Indirect speech acts. *Syntax and semantics*, 3:59–82.

Andreas Stolcke, Klaus Ries, Noah Coccaro, Elizabeth Shriberg, Rebecca Bates, Daniel Jurafsky, Paul Taylor, Rachel Martin, Carol Van Ess-Dykema, and Marie Meteer. 2000. Dialogue act modeling for automatic tagging and recognition of conversational speech. *Computational linguistics*, 26(3):339–373.

Lu Wang, Larry Heck, and Dilek Hakkani-Tur. 2014. Leveraging semantic web search and browse sessions for multi-turn spoken dialog systems.

A List of Words Predictive of Dialogue Acts

Table 10 lists all the words associated with presence-of-word ($\mathcal{P}$) and position-of-word ($\mathcal{B}$) related features (Table 4) used in this work. Notice that all words specified in Table 10 are task-independent. This ensures that the proposed feature set is generic enough to be applicable for a wide variety of tasks on the web. The proposed list of words can be easily extended by adding synonyms, which can be obtained automatically from publicly available sources like WordNet (Miller, 1995).

Features	Predictive Words
p_{iyou}	*I, you*
p_{help}	*help*
p_{helpq}, b_{helpq}	*how, can, do, am I*
p_{prev}	dynamically determined at runtime
p_{intent}	*want, like, would, need, prefer*
$p_{browser}$	dynamically determined at runtime
p_{html}	*body, page, form, box, field, search, link, button, list, dropdown*
p_{basic}	*clear, select, fill, delete, click, edit, erase, submit, repeat, choose, enter, check*
p_{nbasic}	any verb not in the p_{basic} list above
p_{nav}, b_{nav}	*skip, go to, next, first, last, back, continue, previous, stop, go back, finish, home page*
$p_{question}$, $b_{question}$	*what, where, why, when, how*

Table 10: Complete list of predictive words for features in $\mathcal{P}$ and $\mathcal{B}$ of Table 4.

As explained earlier, the words in Table 10 were selected by performing simple statistical analysis of corpus and also by examining the word-weights produced by the SVM classifier trained on unigram features alone. In other words, some of the words in Table 10 were borrowed from Table 5 that lists discriminatory unigrams for different dialogue acts. Note that the task-dependent words (e.g. "Stanford", "airplane", etc.) in Table 5 were ignored while constructing Table 10.

B Sample Dialogue in the Corpus

Table 11 presents an example of a dialogue that was collected during the execution of the *Shopping* task by a participant in the Wizard-Of-Oz study. For deeper understanding, the wizard actions for every user utterance are also listed.

Subject:	"I want to buy CD"
Wizard:	[enter 'CDs' in the search box, clicks 'Go', and narrate search results one by one]
Screen reader:	Verbatim 97458 700 MB 80 Minute ... Disc CD-R by Verbatim link ...
Subject:	"Search for new age items"
Wizard:	[searches for 'new age items', clicks on results]
Screen reader:	Age of Wushu - Free Amazon ... Game Connect link by Snail Games USA ...
Subject:	"stop"
Wizard:	[presses pause shortcut]
Subject:	"new age music CDs"
Wizard:	[searches for 'new music CDs']
Screen reader:	The ultimate Most Relaxing New Age ....
Subject:	"new age music CDs by Kitaro"
Wizard:	[Searches for 'new music cds by Kitaro']
Screen reader:	Most Relaxing New Age Music link by Kitaro, List 8 items, $10.87 link, order in the next 3 hours ... Tenku link by Kitaro ...
Subject:	"sample recordings"
Wizard:	[follows the current link]
Screen reader:	Page loading
Wizard:	[plays the first sample track]
Screen reader:	[audio sample]
Subject:	"next"
Wizard:	[plays the next sample track]
Screen reader:	[audio sample]
Subject:	"next"
Wizard:	[plays the next sample track]
Screen reader:	[audio sample]
Subject:	"go back"
Wizard:	[presses back button]
Screen reader:	page loading, [repeats the visited link]
Subject:	"next CD"
Wizard:	[clicks the title of the next item in search result]
Screen Reader:	Ancient link by Kitaro ... $14.98 link ...
Subject:	"listen to audio"
Wizard:	[follows link]
Screen Reader:	Page loading
Wizard:	[plays the next sample track]
Screen reader:	[audio sample]
Subject:	"next"
Wizard:	[plays the next sample track]
Screen reader:	[audio sample]
Subject:	"buy this cd"
Wizard:	[clicks 'Add to cart' button, then clicks 'Proceed to Checkout' button]
Screen reader:	[reads out all captions]

Table 11: An example dialogue from corpus along with associated wizard actions.

Extractive Summarization and Dialogue Act Modeling on Email Threads: An Integrated Probabilistic Approach

Tatsuro Oya and **Giuseppe Carenini**
Department of Computer Science
University of British Columbia
Vancouver, B.C. Canada
{toya, carenini}@cs.ubc.ca

Abstract

In this paper, we present a novel supervised approach to the problem of summarizing email conversations and modeling dialogue acts. We assume that there is a relationship between dialogue acts and important sentences. Based on this assumption, we introduce a sequential graphical model approach which simultaneously summarizes email conversation and models dialogue acts. We compare our model with sequential and non-sequential models, which independently conduct the tasks of extractive summarization and dialogue act modeling. An empirical evaluation shows that our approach significantly outperforms all baselines in classifying correct summary sentences without losing performance on dialogue act modeling task.

1 Introduction

Nowadays, an overwhelming amount of text information can be found on the web. Most of this information is redundant and thus the task of document summarization has attracted much attention. Since emails in particular are used for a wide variety of purposes, the process of automatically summarizing emails might be of great benefit in dealing with this excessive amount of information. Much work has already been conducted on email summarization. The first research on this topic was conducted by Rambow *et al.* (2004), who took a supervised learning approach to extracting important sentences. A study on the supervised summarization of email threads was also performed by Ulrich *et al.* (2009). This study used the regression-based method for classification. There have been studies on unsupervised summarization of email threads as well. Zhou *et al.* (2007, 2008) proposed a graph-based unsupervised approach to email conversation summarization using clue words, i.e., recurring words contained in replies.

In addition, the task of labeling sentences with dialogue acts has become important and has been employed in many conversation analysis systems. For example, applications such as meeting summarization and collaborative task learning agents use dialogue acts as their underlying structure (Allen *et al.*, 2007; Murray *et al.*, 2010). In a previous work, Cohen *et al.* (2004) defined a set of "email acts" and employed text classification methods to detect these acts in emails. Later, Carvalho *et al.* (2006) employed a combination of n-gram sequences as features and then used a supervised machine learning method to improve the accuracy of this email act classification. In addition, Shafiq *et al.* (2011) presented unsupervised dialogue act labeling methods. In their work, they introduced a graph-based method and two probabilistic sequence-labeling methods for modeling dialogue acts.

However, little work has been done on discovering the relationship between dialogue acts and extractive summaries. If there is a relationship between them, combining these approaches so as to model both simultaneously will yield better results. In this paper, we investigate this hypothesis by introducing a new sequential graphical model approach that performs dialogue act modeling and extractive summarization jointly on email threads.

2 Related Work

While email summarization and dialogue act modeling have been effectively studied, in most previous work, these tasks were studied independently. This section provides related work for each task separately.

2.1 Extractive Summarization

Rambow *et al.* (2004) introduced sentence extraction techniques that work for email threads. In their work, they introduced email-specific features and used a machine learning method to classify whether or not a sentence should be incorporated into a summary. Their experiments demonstrated that their features were highly effective for email summarization.

Ulrich *et al.* (2009) proposed a regression-based machine learning approaches to email thread summarization. They compared regression-based classifiers to binary classifiers and showed that their approach significantly improves the summarization accuracy. They employed the feature set introduced by Rambow *et al.* (2004) as their baseline and introduced new features that are also effective for email summarization. Some of their features refer to dialogue acts but the assumption is that they are computed before the summarization task is performed. Our work is aimed at a much closer integration of the two tasks by modeling them simultaneously.

Carenini *et al.* (2007) developed a fragment quotation graph that can capture a fine-grain conversation structure in email threads, which we will describe in detail in Section 3. They then introduced a ClueWordSummarizer (CWS), a graph-based unsupervised summarization approach based on the concept of clue words, which are recurring words found in email replies. Their experiment showed that the CWS performs better than the email summarization approach in Rambow *et al.* (2004).

Extractive summarization using a sequential labeling technique has also been studied. While this is not an email summarization, Shen *et al.* (2007) proposed a linear-chain Conditional Random Field (CRF) based approach for extractive document summarization. In their work, they treated the summarization task as a sequence labeling problem to take advantage of interaction relationships between sentences; their approach showed significant improvement when compared with non-sequential classifiers.

2.2 Dialogue Act Modeling

The first studies on the dialogue act modeling in emails were performed by Cohen *et al.* (2004). They defined "email speech acts" (e.g., Request, Deliver, Propose, and Commit) and used machine learning methods to classify emails according to the intent of the sender.

Carvalho *et al.* (2006) further developed this initial proposal by using contextual information such as combinations of n-gram sequences in emails as their features for a supervised learning approach. The experiment showed that their approach reduced classification error rates by 26.4%. Shafiq *et al.* (2011) proposed unsupervised dialogue act modeling in email threads and on forums. They introduced a graph-based and two probabilistic unsupervised approaches for modeling dialogue acts. By comparing those approaches, they demonstrated that the probabilistic approaches were quite effective and performed better than the graph-based one.

While the following work is not done on the email domain, Kim *et al.* (2010) introduced a dialogue act classification on one-on-one online chat forums. To be able to capture sequential dialogue act dependency on chats, they applied a CRF model. They demonstrated that, compared with other classifiers, their CRF model performed the best. In their later work (Kim *et al.*, 2012), they extended the domain to multi-party live chats and proposed new features for that domain.

3 Capturing Conversation Structure in Email Threads

In this section, we describe how to build a fragment quotation graph which captures the conversation structure of any email thread at finer granularity. This graph was developed and shown to be effective by Carenini *et al.* (2011). A key assumption of this approach is that in order to effectively perform summarization and dialogue act modeling, a fine graph representation of the underlying conversation structure is needed.

Here, we start with the sample email conversation shown in Figure 1 (a). For convenience, the content of the emails is represented as a sequence of fragments.

First, we identify all new and quoted fragments. For example, email E1 is composed of one new fragment, 'b', and one quoted fragment, 'a'. As for email E3, since we do not yet know whether or not 'd' and 'e' are different fragments, we consider E3 as being composed of one new fragment, 'de' and one quoted fragment, 'b'.

Second, we identify distinct fragments. To do this, we first identify overlaps by comparing fragments with each other. If necessary, we split the fragments and remove any duplicates from them. For example, a fragment, 'de', in E3 is split into 'd' and 'e' after being compared with fragments in E4 and the duplicates are removed. By applying this process to all of the emails, seven distinct fragments, a, b ..., and, g remain in this example.

In the third step, edges which represent the replying relationships among the fragments are created. These edges are determined based on the assumption that any fragment is a reply to neighboring quotations (the quoted fragments immediately preceding or following the current one). For example, the neighboring nodes of 'f' in E4 are 'd' and 'e'. Thus, we create two edges from node 'f' in E4 to node 'd' and 'e' in E3. In the same way, we see that the neighboring node of 'g' in E4 is 'e'. Hence, there is one edge from node 'g' to 'e'. If no quotation is contained in a reply email, we connect the fragments in the email to fragments in emails to which it reply.

In email threads, there are cases in which the original email with its quotations is missing from the user's folder, as in the case of 'a' in Figure 1 (a). These types of emails are called hidden emails. Carenini *et al.* (2005) studied in detail how these email types might be treated and their influence on email summarization.

Figure 1 (b) shows the completed fragment quotation graph of the email thread shown in Figure 1 (a). In the fragment quotation graph structure, all paths (e.g., a-b-c, a-b-d-f, a-b-e-f, and a-b-e-g in Figure 1 (b)) capture the adjacent relationships between email fragments. Hence, we use every path that can be derived from the graph as our dataset. However, in this case, when we run the labeling task on these paths, we obtain multiple labels for some of the sentences because the sentences in fragments such as 'a', 'b', and 'f' in Figure 1 (b) are shared among multiple paths. Therefore, to assign a label to one of these sentences, we take the label more frequently assigned to that sentence when all its paths are considered (i.e., the majority vote).

4 Features

For both dialogue act modeling and extractive summarization, many effective sentence features have been discovered so far. Interestingly, some common features are shown to be effective in both tasks. This section explains the features used in our model. We begin with the features for extractive summarization and then describe how we derive the features for dialogue act modeling. All the features explained in this section, whether they belong to extractive summarization or dialogue act modeling, are included in our model.

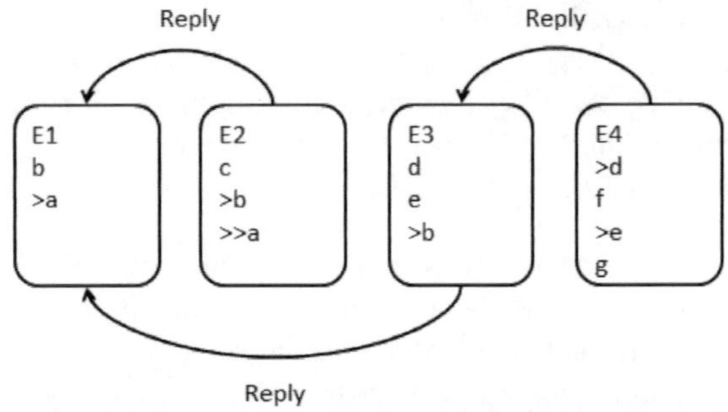

(a) A possible configuration of an email conversation (E2 and E3 reply to E1, and E4 replies to E3)

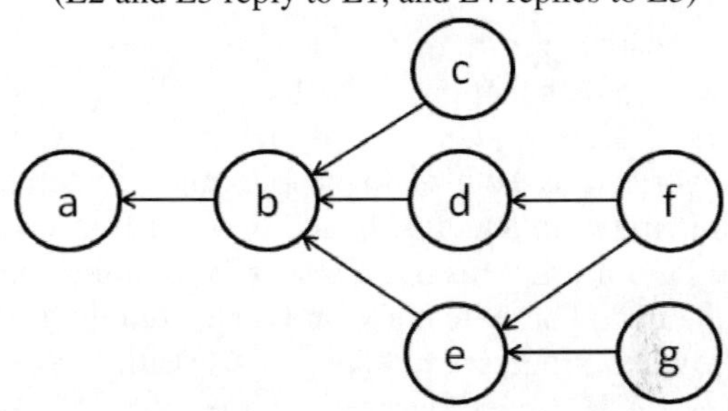

(b) An example of a fragment quotation graph

Figure 1: A fragment quotation graph derived from a possible configuration of an email conversation

4.1 Extractive Summarization Features

The features we use for extractive summarization are mostly from Carenini *et al.* (2008) and Rambow *et al.* (2004) and have proven to be effective on conversational data. Details of these features are described below. Note that all sentences in an email thread are ordered based on paths derived from a fragment quotation graph.

Length Feature: The number of words in each sentence.
Relative Position Feature: The number of sentences preceding the current divided by the total number of sentences in one path.
Thread Name Overlaps Feature: The number of overlaps of the content words between the email thread title and a sentence.
Subject Name Overlaps Feature: The number of overlaps of the content words between the subject of the email and a sentence.
Question Feature: A binary feature that indicates whether or not a sentence has a question mark.
CC Feature: A binary feature that indicates whether or not an email contains CC.

Participation Dominance Feature: The number of utterances each person makes in one path.

Finally, we also include a simplified version of the ClueWordScore (CWS) developed by Carenini *et al.* (2007), which is listed below.

Simplified CWS Feature: The number of overlaps of the content words that occur in both the current and adjacent sentences in the path, ignoring stopwords.

4.2 Dialogue Act Features

The relative positions and length features have proven to be beneficial to both tasks (Jeong et al., 2009; Carenini *et al.*, 2008). Hence, these are categorized as both dialogue acts and extractive summarization features. In addition, we use word and POS n-grams as our features for dialogue act modeling. These features are extracted by the following process explained in Carvalho *et al.* (2006). However, we extend the original approach in order to further abstract n-gram features to avoid making them too sparse to be effective. In this section, we describe the derivation process in detail.

A multi-step approach is used to generate word n-gram features. First, all words are tagged with the named entity using the Stanford Named Entity Recognizer (Finkel *et al.*, 2005), and are then replaced with these tags. Second, a sequence of word-replacement tasks is applied to all email messages. Initially, some types of punctuation marks (e.g., <>()[];:. and ,) and extra spaces are removed. Then, shortened phrases such as "I'm" and "We'll" are substituted for more formal versions such as "I am" and "We will". Next, other replacement tasks are performed. Some of them are described in Table1. In the third step, unigrams and bigrams are extracted. In this paper, unigrams and bigrams refer to all possible sequences of length one and two terms. After extracting all unigrams and bigrams for each dialogue act, we then compute Information Gain Score (Forman, 2003) and select the n-grams whose scores are in the top five greatest on the training set. In this way, we can automatically detect features that represent the characteristics of each dialogue act. In addition to word n-grams, we also include POS n-grams in our features. In a similar way, we first tag each word in sentences with POS using the Stanford POS tagger (Toutanova *et al.*, 2003). Then, for each dialogue act, we extract bigrams and trigrams, all of which are scored by the Information Gain. Based on their scores, we select the POS bigram and trigram features whose scores are within the top five greatest. One example of word n-gram features for a Question dialogue act selected by this derivation method is shown in Table 2.

Pattern	**Replacement**
'why', 'where', 'who', 'what' 'when'	[WWHH]
nominative pronouns	[I]
objective pronouns	[ME]
'it', 'those', 'these', 'this', 'that'	[IT]
'will', 'would', 'shall', 'should', 'must'	[MODAL_STRONG]
'can', 'could', 'may', 'might'	[MODAL_WEAK]
'do', 'does', 'did', 'done'	[DO]
'is', 'was', 'were', 'are', 'been' 'be', 'am'	[BE]
'after' , 'before', 'during'	[AAAFTER]
'Jack", "Wendy"	[Personal_PRONOUN]
"New York"	[LOCATION]
"Acme Corp."	[ORGANIZATION]

Table 1: Some Preprocessing Replacement Pattern

Word Unigram	**Word Bigram**
?	[MODAL_STRONG] [I]
anyone	[IT] ?
WWHH	[DO] anyone
deny	[WWHH] [BE]
[Personal _PRONOUN]	[BE] [IT]

Table 2: Sample word n-grams selected as the features for Question dialogue act

5 The Sequential Labeling Task

We use a Dynamic Conditional Random Field (DCRF) (Sutton *et al.*, 2004) for labeling tasks. A DCRF is a generalization of a linear-chain CRF which allows us to represent complex interaction between labels. To be more precise, it is a conditionally-trained undirected graphical model whose structure and parameters are repeated over a sequence. Hence, it is the most appropriate method for performing multiple labeling tasks on the same sequence.

Our DCRF uses the graph structure shown in Figure 2 with one chain (the top X nodes) modeling extractive summary and the other (the middle Y nodes) modeling dialogue acts. Each node in the observation sequence (the bottom Z nodes) corresponds to each sentence in a path of the fragment quotation graph of the email thread. As shown in Figure 2, the graph structure captures the relationship between extractive summaries and dialogue acts by connecting their nodes.
We use Mallet[1] (McCallum, 2002) to implement our DCRF model. It uses l2-based regularization to avoid overfitting, and a limited BFGS fitting algorithm to learn the DCRF model parameters. Also, it uses tree-based reparameterization (Wainwright *et al.*, 2002) to compute the posterior marginal, or inference.

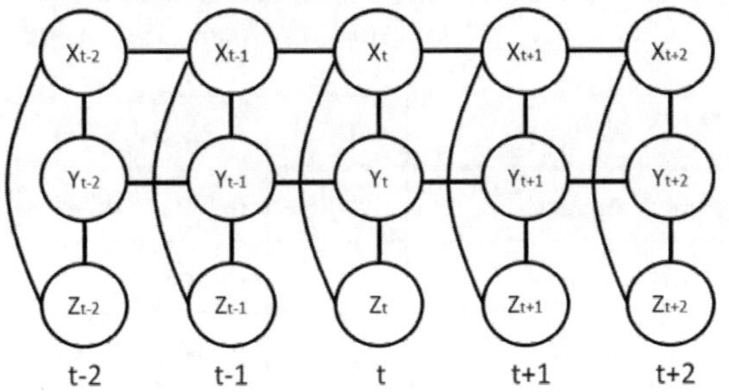

Figure 2: The DCRF model used to create extractive summaries and model dialogue acts

6 Empirical Evaluations

6.1 Dataset Setup

In our experiment, the publically available BC3 corpus[2] (Ulrich *et al.*, 2008) is used for training and evaluation purposes. The corpus contains email threads from the World Wide Web Consortium (W3C) mailing list. It consists of 40 threads with an average of five emails per thread. The corpus provides extractive summaries of each email thread, all of which were annotated by three annotators. Hence, we use sentences that are selected by more than one annotator as the gold standard summary for each conversation.

In addition, all sentences in the 39 out of 40 threads are annotated for dialogue act tags. The tagset consists of five general and 12 specific tags. All of these tags are based on Jeong *et al.* (2009). For our experiment, considering that our data is relatively small, we decide to use the coarser five tag set. The details are shown in Table 3.

[1] http://mallet.cs.umass.edu
[2] http://www.cs.ubc.ca/nest/lci/bc3.html

Tag	Description	Relative Frequency (%)
S	Statement	73.8
Q	Question	7.92
R	Reply	5.23
Su	Suggestion	5.62
M	Miscellaneous	7.46

Table 3: Dialogue act tag categories and their relative frequency in the BC3 corpus

After removing quoted sentences and redundant information such as senders and addresses, 1300 distinct sentences remain in the 39 email threads. The detailed content of the corpus is summarized in Table 4.

	Total Dataset
No. of Threads	39
No. of Sentences	1300
No. of Extractive Summary Sentences	521
No. of S Sentences	959
No. of Q Sentences	103
No. of R Sentences	68
No. of Su Sentences	73
No. of M Sentences	97

Table 4: Detailed content of the BC3 corpus

6.2 Evaluation Metrics

Here, we introduce evaluation metrics for our joint model of extractive summarization and dialogue act recognition.

The CRF model has been shown to be the effective one in both dialogue act modeling and extractive summarization (Shen *et al.*, 2007; Kim *et al.*, 2010; Kim *et al.*, 2012). Hence, for comparison, we implement two different CRFs, one for extractive summarization and the other for dialogue act modeling. When classifying extractive summaries using the CRF, we only use its extractive summarization features. Similarly, when modeling dialogue acts, we only use its dialogue act features. In addition, we also compare our system with a non-sequential classifier, a support vector machine (SVM), with the same settings as those described above. For these implementations, we use Mallet and SVM-light package[3] (Joachims, 1999).

In our experiment, we first measure separately the performance of extractive summarization and dialogue act modeling. The performance of extractive summarization is measured by its averaged precision, recall, and F-measure. For dialogue acts, we report the averaged-micro and macro accuracies as well as the averaged accuracies of each dialogue act.

Second, we evaluate the combined performance of extractive summarization and dialogue act modeling tasks. In general, we are interested in the dialogue acts in summary sentences because they can be later used as input for other natural language processing applications such as automatic abstractive summarization (Murray *et al.*, 2010). Therefore, we measure the performance of our model with the following modified precision (*Pre'*), recall (*Rec'*), and F-measure (*F'*):

$$Pre' = \frac{\{No.\ of\ correctly\ classified\ sentences\}}{\{No.of\ sentences\ classified\ as\ summary\ setences\}} \quad (1)$$

$$Rec' = \frac{\{No.\ of\ correctly\ classified\ sentences\}}{\{No.of\ true\ summary\ sentences\}} \quad (2)$$

$$F' = \frac{2 \times Pre' \times Rec'}{Pre' + Rec'} \quad (3)$$

where a *correctly classified sentence* refers to a true summary sentence that is classified as such and whose dialogue acts are also correctly classified.

6.3 Experiment Procedure

For all cases, we run five sets of 10-fold cross validation to train and test the classifiers on a shuffled dataset and calculate the average of the results. For each cross validation run, we extract all features following the process described in Section 4 on the training set. When comparing these two baselines with our model, we report p-values obtained from a student paired t-test on the results to determine their significance.

[3] http://www.cs.cornell.edu/people/tj/svm_light

6.4 Results

The performances of extractive summarization and dialogue act modeling using the three methods are summarized in Table 5 and 6, respectively.

	DCRF	CRF	SVM
F-measure	**0.485**	0.428	0.397
t-test's p-value		0.00046	2.5E-07
Precision	0.562	0.591	**0.675**
Recall	**0.457**	0.370	0.308

Table 5: A comparison of the extractive summarization performance of our DCRF model and the two baselines based on precision, recall, and F-measure

	DCRF	CRF	SVM
Micro Accuracy	**0.785**	0.779	0.775
t-test's p-value		0.116	0.036
Macro Accuracy	**0.516**	**0.516**	0.304
t-test's p-value		0.950	5.2E-32
S Accuracy	0.901	0.892	**0.999**
Q Accuracy	**0.832**	0.809	0.465
R Accuracy	**0.580**	0.575	0.05
Su Accuracy	**0.139**	0.108	0.00
M Accuracy	0.126	**0.198**	0.00

Table 6: A comparison of the dialogue act modeling performance of our DCRF model and the two baselines based on averaged accuracies

From Table 5, we observe that, in terms of extractive summarization results, our DCRF model significantly outperforms the two baselines. Noticeable improvements can be seen for the recall and F-measure. In terms of F-measure, compared with the CRF and SVM, our model improves by 5.7% and 8.8% respectively. The p-values obtained from the t-test indicate that our results are statistically significantly different ($p <$ 0.05) from those of the two baselines.

Regarding dialogue act modeling, the results are summarized in Table 6. While no improvement is shown for the micro-averaged accuracy, our model and the CRF significantly outperform the SVM in terms of the macro-averaged accuracy. Both our model and the CRF consider the sequential structure of the conversation, which is not captured in the SVM model. Clearly, this indicates that the sequential models are effective in modeling dialogue acts due to their ability to capture the inter-utterance relations of conversations.

Compared with the CRF, our DCRF model outperforms it in most cases except in classifying the 'M' dialogue act. However these improvements are not significant as t-test of both macro and micro-averaged accuracies indicate that the differences are not statistically significant ($p > 0.05$).

Another item to be mentioned here is that the accuracies of classifying 'R', 'Su' and 'M' dialogue acts are relatively low. This issue applies to all classifiers and is plausibly due to the small dataset. There are only 68, 73 and 97 sentences, respectively, out of 1300 that are labeled as 'R', 'Su' and 'M' in the BC3 corpus. Since our dialogue act classifiers rely heavily on n-gram features, were the data small, these features would be too sparse to effectively represent the characteristics of the dialogue acts. However, compared with the SVM results, our joint model and the CRF perform significantly better in classifying these dialogue acts. This also explains why the sequential model is preferable in dialogue act modeling.

Note that despite the small dataset, all the classifiers are relatively accurate in classifying 'Q'. This is because n-gram features selected for 'Q' such as '?' and 'WWHH' are very specific to this dialogue act, which makes the task of 'Q' classification easier compared to those of others.

Next, we discuss the result of the combined performance. The performances of our model and the two baselines are summarized in Table 7.

	DCRF	CRF	SVM
F-measure'	**0.352**	0.324	0.292
t-test's p-value		0.015	3.3E-05
Precision'	0.407	0.450	**0.501**
Recall'	**0.335**	0.280	0.227

Table 7: A comparison of the overall performance of our DCRF model and the two baselines based on modified precision, recall and F-measure

We see that our DCRF model significantly outperforms the two baselines. While our model yields the lowest *Pre'* of all, its *Rec'* is much greater than the other two baselines and this leads to its achieving the highest *F'*. Compared with the CRF and SVM, the *F'* obtained from our system improves by 2.8% and 6% respectively. In addition, the p-values show that the results of our model are statistically significant ($p < 0.05$) compared with those of the two baselines.

Overall, these experiments clearly indicate that our model is effective in classifying both dialogue acts and summary sentences.

7 Conclusions and Future Work

In this work, we have explored a new automated approach for extractive summarization and dialogue act modeling on email threads. In particular, we have presented a statistical approach for jointly modeling dialogue acts and extractive summarization in a single DCRF. The empirical results demonstrate that our approach outperforms the two baselines on the summarization task without loss of performance on the dialogue act modeling one. In the future, we would like to extend our approach by exploiting more effective features. We also plan to apply our approach to different domains possessing large dataset.

Acknowledgements

We are grateful to Yashar Mehdad, Raimond Ng, Maryam Tavafi and Shafiq Joty for their comments and UBC LCI group and ICICS for financial support.

References

J. Allen, N. Chambers, G. Ferguson, L. Galescu, H. Jung, and W. Taysom. Plow: A collaborative task learning agent. In AAAI-07, pages 22–26, 2007.

Giuseppe Carenini, Gabriel Murray, and Raymond Ng. 2011. Methods for Mining and Summarizing Text Conversations. *Morgan Claypool*.

Giuseppe Carenini, Raymond Ng, and Xiaodong Zhou. 2005. Scalable discovery of hidden emails from large folders. In *ACM SIGKDD'05*, pages 544–549.

Giuseppe Carenini, Raymond Ng, and Xiaodong Zhou. 2008. Summarizing Emails with Conversational Cohesion and Subjectivity In *proceeding 46th Annual Meetint Assoc.for Computational Linguistics,* page 353-361.

Giuseppe Carenini, Raymond Ng, and Xiaodong Zhou. 2007. Summarizing email conversations with clue words. *16th International World Wide Web Conference (ACM WWW'07).*

Vitor R. Carvalho and William W. Cohen. 2006. Improving "email speech acts" analysis via n-gram selection. In *Proceedings of the HLT-NAACL 2006 Workshop on Analyzing Conversations in Text and Speech, ACTS '09*, pages 35–41, Stroudsburg, PA, USA. Association for Computational Linguistics.

William W. Cohen, Vitor R. Carvalho, and Tom M. Mitchell. 2004. Learning to classify email into "speech acts". In *Proceedings of Empirical Methods in Natural Language Processing*, pages 309–316, Barcelona, Spain, July.

Jenny Rose Finkel, Trond Grenager, and Christopher Manning. 2005. Incorporating Non-local Information into Information Extraction Systems by Gibbs Sampling. In *Proceedings of the 43nd Annual Meeting of the Association for Computational Linguistics (ACL 2005)*, pp. 363-370.

George Forman. 2003. An extensive empirical study of feature selection metrics for text classification. The Journal of Machine Learning Research, 3:1289–1305.

Minwoo Jeong, Chin-Yew Lin, and Gary Geunbae Lee. 2009. Semi-supervised speech act recognition in emails and forums. In *Proceedings of the 2009 Conference on Empirical Methods in Natural Language Processing*.

Thorsten Joachims. 1999 Making large-Scale SVM Learning Practical. Advances in Kernel Methods - Support Vector Learning, B. Schölkopf and C. Burges and A. Smola (ed.), *MIT-Press, 1999.*

Shafiq Joty, Giuseppe Carenini, and Lin, Chin-Yew Lin. 2011. Unsupervised Modeling of Dialog Acts in Asynchronous Conversations. In *Proceedings of the twenty second International Joint Conference on Artificial Intelligence (IJCAI) 2011*. Barcelona, Spain.

Shafiq Joty, Giuseppe Carenini, Gabriel Murray, and Raymond Ng. 2009 Finding Topics in Emails: Is LDA enough? *NIPS-2009 workshop on applications for topic models: text and beyond.* Whistler, Canada.

McCallum, A. Kachites, 2002. MALLET: A Machine Learning for Language Toolkit. http://mallet.cs.umass.edu.

Su Nam Kim, Lawrence Cavedon, and Timothy Baldwin. 2010a. Classifying dialogue acts in 1-to-1 live chats. In *Proceedings of the 2010 Conference on Empirical Methods in Natural Language Processing* (EMNLP 2010), pages 862–871, Boston, USA.

Su Nam Kim, Lawrence Cavedon and Timothy Baldwin (2012) Classifying Dialogue Acts in Multiparty Live Chats, In *Proceedings of the 26th Pacific Asia Conference on Language, Information and Computation (PACLIC 26)*, Bali, Indonesia, pp. 463—472.

Gabriel Murray and Giuseppe Carenini. 2008. Summarizing Spoken and Written Conversations. *Empirical Methods in NLP (EMNLP 2008)*, Waikiki, Hawaii, 2008.

Gabriel Murray and Giuseppe Carenini. 2010. Summarizing Spoken and Written Conversations. *Generating and Validating Abstracts of Meeting Conversations: a User study (INLG 2010)*, Dublin, Ireland, 2010.

Gabriel Murray, Renals Steve, and Carletta Jean. 2005a. Extrative summarization of meeting recordings. In *Proceeding of Interspeech 2005*, Lisbon, Portugal, pages 593-596.

Owen Rambow, Lokesh Shrestha, John Chen, and Chirsty Lauridsen. 2004. Summarizing email threads. In *Proceedings of HLTNAACL 2004*.

Dou Shen, Jian-Tao Sun, Hua Li, Qiang Yang, and Zheng Chen. 2007. Document summarization using conditional random fields. In Proc. of IJCAI, volume 7, 2862–2867.

Charles Sutton, Khashayar Rohanimanesh, and Andrew McCallum. 2004. Dynamic conditional random fields: Factorized probabilistic models for labeling and segmenting sequence data. In *Proc. ICML.*

Maryam Tavafi, Yashar Mehdad, Shafiq Joty, Giuseppe Carenini and Raymond Ng. 2013. Dialogue Act Recognition in Synchronous and Asynchronous Conversations. *In Proceedings of the SIGDIAL 2013 Conference,* pages 117–121, Metz, France. Association for Computational Linguistics.

Kristina Toutanova, Dan Klein, Christopher Manning, and Yoram Singer. 2003. Feature-Rich Part-of-Speech Tagging with a Cyclic Dependency Network. In *Proceedings of HLT-NAACL 2003*, pp. 252-259.

Jan Ulrich, Giuseppe Carenini, Gabriel Murray, and Raymond T. Ng: Regression-Based Summarization of Email Conversations. ICWSM 2009

Jan Ulrich, Gabriel Murray, and Giuseppe Carenini. 2008. A publicly available annotated corpus for supervised email summarization. *AAAI-2008 EMAIL Workshop.*

Martin J. Wainwright, Tommi Jaakkola, and Alan S. Willsky. 2002. Treebased Reparameterization for Approximate Inference on Loopy Graphs. In *Advances in Neural Information Processing Systems 14*, pages 1001 1008. MIT Press.

Keynote: Language Adaptation

Lillian Lee
Cornell University, U.S.A.
llee@cs.cornell.edu

As we all know, more and more of life is now manifested online, and many of the digital traces that are left by human activity are increasingly recorded in natural-language format. This availability offers us the opportunity to glean user-modeling information from individual users' linguistic behaviors. This talk will discuss the particular phenomenon of individual language adaptation, both in the short term and in the longer term. We'll look at connections between how people adapt their language to particular conversational partners or groups, on the one hand, and on the other hand, those people's relative power relationships, quality of relationship with the conversational partner, and propensity to remain a part of the group.

Addressing Class Imbalance for Improved Recognition of Implicit Discourse Relations

Junyi Jessy Li
University of Pennsylvania
ljunyi@seas.upenn.edu

Ani Nenkova
University of Pennsylvania
nenkova@seas.upenn.edu

Abstract

In this paper we address the problem of skewed class distribution in implicit discourse relation recognition. We examine the performance of classifiers for both binary classification predicting if a particular relation holds or not and for multi-class prediction. We review prior work to point out that the problem has been addressed differently for the binary and multi-class problems. We demonstrate that adopting a unified approach can significantly improve the performance of multi-class prediction. We also propose an approach that makes better use of the full annotations in the training set when downsampling is used. We report significant absolute improvements in performance in multi-class prediction, as well as significant improvement of binary classifiers for detecting the presence of implicit Temporal, Comparison and Contingency relations.

1 Introduction

Discourse relations holding between adjacent sentences in text play an essential role in establishing local coherence and contribute to the semantic interpretation of the text. For example, the causal relationship is helpful for textual entailment or question answering while restatement and exemplification are important for automatic summarization.

Predicting the type of implicit relations, which are not signaled by any of the common explicit discourse connectives such as *because*, *however*, has proven to be a most challenging task in discourse analysis. The Penn Discourse Treebank (PDTB) (Prasad et al., 2008) provided valuable annotations of implicit relations. Most research to date has focused on developing and refining lexical and linguistically rich features for the task (Pitler et al., 2009; Lin et al., 2009; Park and Cardie, 2012). Mostly ignored remains the problem of addressing the highly skewed distribution of implicit discourse relations. Only about 35% of pairs of adjacent sentences in the PDTB are connected by three of the four top level discourse relation: 5% participate in *Temporal* relation, 10% in *Comparison* (contrast) and 20% in *Contingency* (causal) relations. The remaining pairs are connected by the catch-all *Expansion* relation (40%) or by some other linguistic devices (24%). Finer grained relations of interest to particular applications account for increasingly smaller percentage of the PDTB data.

Class imbalance is particularly problematic for training a binary classifier to distinguish one relation from the rest. As we will show later, it also impacts the performance of multi-class prediction in which each pair of sentences is labeled with one of the five possible relations.

All prior work has resorted to downsampling the training data for binary classifiers to distinguish a particular relation and use the full training set for multi-class prediction. In this paper we compare several methods for addressing the skewed class distribution during training: downsampling, upsampling and computing feature weights and performing feature selection on the unaltered full training data. A major motivation for our work is to establish if any of the alternatives to downsampling would prove beneficial, because in downsampling most of the expensively annotated data is not used in the model. In addition, we seek to align the treatment of data imbalance for the binary and multi-class tasks. We show that downsampling in general leads to the best prediction accuracy but that the alternative models provide complementary information and significant improvement can be obtained by combining both types of models. We also report significant improvement of multi-class prediction accuracy, achieved by using the alternative binary classifiers to perform the task.

2 The Penn Discourse Treebank

In the PDTB, discourse relations are viewed as a predicate with two arguments. The predicate is the relation, the arguments correspond to the minimum spans of text whose interpretations are the abstract objects between which the relation holds. Consider the following example of a contrast relation. The italic and bold fonts mark the arguments of the relation.

Commonwealth Edison said *the ruling could force it to slash its 1989 earnings by $1.55 a share.* [Implicit = BY COMPARISON] **For 1988, Commonwealth Edison reported earnings of $737.5 million, or $3.01 a share.**

For explicit relations, the predicate is marked by a discourse connective that occurs in the text, i.e. *because, however, for example.*

Implicit relations are marked between adjacent sentences in the same paragraph. They are inferred by the reader but are not lexically marked. Alternative lexicalizations (*AltLex*) are the ones where there is a phrase in the sentence implying the relation but the phrase itself was not one of the explicit discourse connectives. There are 16,224 and 624 examples of implicit and *AltLex* relations, respectively, in the PDTB.

The sense of discourse relations in the PDTB is organized in a three-tiered hierarchy. The four top level relations are: *Temporal* (the two arguments are related temporally), *Comparison* (contrast), *Contingency* (causal) and *Expansion* (one argument is the expansion of the other and continues the context) (Miltsakaki et al., 2008). These are the classes we focus on in our work.

Finally, 5,210 pairs of adjacent sentences were marked as related by an entity relation (*EntRel*), by virtue of the repetition of the same entity or topic. *EntRel*s were marked only if no other relation could be identified and they are not considered a discourse relation, rather an alternative discourse phenomena related to entity coherence (Grosz et al., 1995). There are 254 pairs of sentences where no discourse relation was identified (*NoRel*).

Pitler et al. (2008) has shown that performance as high as 93% in accuracy can be easily achieved for the explicit relations, because the connective itself is a highly informative feature. Efforts in identifying the argument spans have also yielded high accuracies (Lin et al., 2014; Elwell and Baldridge, 2008; Ghosh et al., 2011).

However, in the absence of a connective, recognizing non-explicit relations, which includes implicit relations, alternative lexicalizations, entity relation and no relation present, has proven to be a real challenge. Prior work on supervised implicit discourse recognition studied a wide range of features including lexical, syntactic, verb classes, semantic groups via General Inquirer and polarity (Pitler et al., 2009; Lin et al., 2009). Park and Cardie (2012) studied the combination of features and achieved better performance with a different combination for each individual relation. Methods for improving the sparsity of lexical representations have been proposed (Hernault et al., 2010; Biran and McKeown, 2013), as well as web-driven approaches which reduce the problem to explicit relation recognition (Hong et al., 2012).

Remarkably, no prior work has discussed the highly skewed class distribution of discourse relation types. The tacitly adopted solution has been to downsample the negative examples for one-vs-all binary classification aimed at discovering if a particular relation holds and keeping the full training set for multi-class prediction.

To highlight the problem, in Table 1 we show the distribution of implicit relation classes in the entire PDTB. In our work, we aim to develop classifiers to identify the four top-level relations listed in the table[1].

	# of samples	Percentage
Temporal	1038	4.3%
Comparison	2550	11.3%
Contingency	4532	20%
Expansion	9082	40%

Table 1: Distribution of implicit relations in the PDTB.

3 Experimental settings

In our experiments, we used all non-explicit instances in the PDTB sections 2-19 for training and those in sections 20-24 for testing. Like most studies, we kept sections 0-1 as development set. In order to ensure we have a large enough test set to properly perform tests for statistical significance over F scores and balanced accuracies, we did not follow previous work (Lin et al., 2014; Park and Cardie, 2012) that used only section 23 or sections 23-24 for testing. Also, the traditional rule of thumb is to split the available data into training

[1]The rest of the data are EntRel/NoRel.

and testing sets with 80%/20% ratio. Our choice ensures that this is the case for all of the relations.

The only features that we use in our experiments are production rules. We exclude features that occur fewer than five times in the training set. Production rules are the state-of-the-art representation for discourse relation recognition. This representation leads to only slightly lower results than a system including a much larger variety of features in the first end-to-end PDTB style discourse parser (Lin et al., 2014) .

The production rule representation is based on the constituency parse of the arguments and includes both syntactic and lexical information. A production rule is the parent with an left-to-right ordered list of all of its children in the parse tree (for example, S→NP VP). All non-terminal nodes are included as a parent, from the sentence head to the part-of-speech of a terminal. Thus words that occur in each sentence augmented with their part of speech are part of the representation (for example, NN→company), along with more general structures of the sentence corresponding to production rules with only non-terminals on the right-hand side.

There are three features corresponding to a production rule, tracking if the rule occurs in the parse of first argument of the relation, in the second, or in both.

Adopting this representation allows us to focus on the issue of class imbalance and how the choices of tackling this problem affect eventual prediction performance. Our findings are representation-independent and will most likely extend to other representations.

We train and evaluate a binary classifier with linear kernel using SVMLight[2] (Joachims, 1999) for each of the four top level classes of relations: *Temporal*, *Comparison*, *Contingency* and *Expansion*. We used SVM-Multiclass[3] for standard multiway classification. We also develop and evaluate two approaches for multiway classification for the four classes plus the additional class of entity relation and no relation.

Due to the uneven distribution of classes, we use precision, recall and f-measure to measure binary prediction performance. For multiway classification, we use the balanced accuracy (BAC):

$$BAC = \frac{1}{k}\sum_{i=1}^{k}\frac{c_i}{n_i}, \quad (1)$$

where k is the number of relations to predict, c_i is the number of instances of relation i that are correctly predicted, n_i is the total number of instances of relation i.

Balanced accuracy (or averaged accuracy) has a more intuitive interpretation than F-measure. It is not dominated by the majority class as much as standard accuracy is. For example for two classes, in a dataset where one class makes up 90% of the data, predicting the majority class has accuracy of 90% but balanced accuracy of 45%.

In testing, we keep the original distribution intact and make predictions for all pairs of adjacent sentences in the same paragraph that do not have an explicit discourse relation [4]. In order to perform tests for statistical significance over F scores, precision, recall and balanced accuracies, we randomly partitioned the testing data into 10 groups. We kept the data distribution in each group as close as possible to the overall testing set. To compare the performance of two different systems, a paired t-test is performed over these 10 groups.

4 Why downsampling?

Binary classification As mentioned in the previous sections, in all prior work of supervised implicit relation classification, the technique to cope with highly skewed distribution for binary classification is to downsample the negative training instances so that the sizes of positive and negative classes are equal. The reason for doing so is that the classifier can achieve high accuracy just by ignoring the small class, learning nothing and aways predicting the larger class. We illustrate this effect in Table 2. Without downsampling, the only reasonable F measure is achieved for *Expansion* where the smaller class accounts for 40% of the data. Note that with downsampling, the recognition of *Expansion* is also improved considerably.

Multiway classification In prior work multiway classifiers are trained on all available training data. As we just saw, however, this approach leads

[2]http://svmlight.joachims.org/

[3]http://svmlight.joachims.org/svm_multiclass.html

[4]Note the contrast with prior work where in some cases *EntRels* are part of *Expansion*, or in some cases the performance of methods is evaluated only on pairs of sentences where a discourse relation holds, excluding *EntRels*, *NoRels* or *AltLexs*.

	All data	Downsample
Temp.	0 (nan/0.0)	15.52 (8.8/65.4)
Comp.	2.17 (71.4/1.1)	27.65 (17.3/69.2)
Cont.	0.96 (100.0/0.5)	47.14 (34.5/74.5)
Exp.	44.27 (54.9/37.1)	55.42 (49.3/63.3)

Table 2: F measure (precision/recall) of binary classification: including all of the data vs downsampling.

to poor results in identifying the core *Temporal*, *Comparison* and *Contingency* discourse relations. We propose an alternative approach to multi-class prediction, based on binary one-against-all classifiers for each of the four discourse relations, including *Expansion*, trained using downsampling.

The intuition is that an instance of adjacent sentences S_i is assigned to a discourse relation R_j if the binary classifier for R_j recognizes S_i as a positive instance with confidence higher than that of the classifiers for other relations. If none of the binary classifiers recognizes the instance as a positive example, the instance is assigned to class *EntRel/NoRel*. This approach modifies the way multi-class classifiers are normally constructed by including downsampling and having special treatment of the *EntRel/NoRel* class.

Specifically, we first use the four binary classifiers C_j for each relation j to get the confidence p_j of instance i belonging to class j. We approximate the confidence by the distance to the hyperplane separating the two classes, which SVMLight provides. If at least one p_j is greater than zero, assign instance i the class k where the classifier confidence is the highest. If none of the p_j's is greater than zero, assign i to be the *EntRel/NoRel* class.

We show balanced accuracies of these two multiway classification methods in Table 3.

	Multiway SVM	One-Against-All
5-way	32.58	37.15

Table 3: Balanced accuracies for SVM-Multiclass and one-against-all 5-way classification.

The one-against-all approach leads to 5% absolute improvement in performance. A t-test analysis confirms that the difference is significant at $p < 0.05$. Note that the improvement comes entirely from acknowledging that skewed class distribution poses a problem for the task and by addressing the problem in the same way for binary and multi-class prediction.

5 Using more data

Although downsampling gives much better performance than simply including all of the original data, it still appears to be an undesirable solution because in essence it throws away much of the annotated data. This means that for the smallest relations, as much as 90% of the data will not be used. Feature selection and feature values are computed only based on this much smaller dataset and do not properly reflect the information about discourse relations encoded in the PDTB. In this section we first discuss some of the widely used methods for handling skewed data distribution, that is, weighted cost and upsampling. First, we show that with highly skewed distributions, the two methods result in almost identical classifiers. Then we introduce a method for feature selection and shaping which computes feature weights on the full dataset and thus captures much of the information lost in downsampling.

5.1 Weighted cost and upsampling

A number of methods have been developed for the skewed distribution problem (Morik et al., 1999; Veropoulos et al., 1999; Akbani et al., 2004; Batista et al., 2004; Chawla et al., 2002). Here we highlight weighted cost and random upsampling, which are known to work well and widely used.

The idea behind weighted cost (Morik et al., 1999; Veropoulos et al., 1999) is to use weights to adjust the penalties for false positives and false negatives in the objective function. As in Morik et al. (1999), we specify the cost factor to be the ratio of the size of the negative class vs. that of the positive class.

In the case of upsampling, instead of randomly downsampling negative instances, positive instances are randomly upsampled. In our experiments we randomly replicate positive instances with replacement until the numbers of positive and negative instances are equal to each other.

The binary and multiway classification results for these two methods are shown in Table 4 and Table 5. For binary classification, we can see significantly higher F score for the smallest *Temporal* class. Weighted cost is also able to achieve significantly better F-score for *Expansion*. For *Comparison* and *Contingency*, the F-scores are similar to that of plain downsampling. The balanced accuracies of multi-class classification with either methods are lower, or significantly lower in the case of weighted cost, than using downsampling in one-against-all manner.

	Upsample	WeightCost
Temp.	20.35* (16.8/25.9)	20.61* (16.9/26.3)
Comp.	28.11 (20.6/44.5)	28.38 (19.9/49.6)
Cont.	46.46 (37.4/61.3)	46.36 (34.6/70.1)
Exp.	54.93 (50.3/60.5)	57.43* (43.9/83.1)

Table 4: F-measure (precision/recall) of binary classification: upsampling vs. weighted cost.

For *Temporal* and *Comparison* relations listed in Table 4, we noticed an interesting similarity between the F and precision values of upsampling and weighted cost. To quantify this similarity, we calculated the Q-statistic (Kuncheva and Whitaker, 2003) between the two classifiers. The Q-statistic is a measurement of classifier agreement raging between -1 and 1, defined as:

$$Q_{w,u} = \frac{N_{11}N_{00} - N_{01}N_{10}}{N_{11}N_{00} + N_{01}N_{10}} \quad (2)$$

Where w denotes the system using weighted cost, u denotes the upsampling system. N_{11} means both systems make a correct prediction, N_{00} means both systems are incorrect, N_{10} means w is incorrect but u is correct, and N_{01} means w is correct but u is incorrect.

We have the following Q statistics: *Temporal*: 0.999, *Comparison*: 0.9938, *Contingency*: 0.9746, *Expansion*: 0.7762. These are good indicators that for highly skewed relations, the two methods give classifiers that behave almost identically on the test data. In the discussions that follow, we discuss only weighted cost to avoid redundancy.

5.2 Feature selection and shaping

While weighted cost or upsampling can give better performance over downsampling for some relations, their disadvantages towards multi-class classification and the obvious favor towards the majority class give rise to the following question: is it possible to inform the classifier of the information encoded in the annotation of *all* of the data while still using downsampling to handle the skewed class distribution? Our proposal is feature value augmentation. Here we introduce a relational matrix in which we calculate augmented feature values via feature shaping. We first compute the values of features on the entire training set, then use the downsampled set for training with these values. In this way we pass on to the classifiers information about the relative importance of features gleaned from the entire training data.

5.2.1 Feature shaping

The idea of feature shaping was introduced in the context of improving the performance of linear SVMs (Forman et al., 2009). In linear SVMs the prediction is based on a linear combination of *weight×feature values*. The sign of *weight* indicates the preference for a class (positive or negative), the value of the feature should correspond to how strongly it indicates that class. Thus, features that are strongly discriminative should have high values so that they can contribute more to the final class decision. Here we augment feature values for a relation according to the following criteria: 1. Features are considered "good" if they strongly indicate the *presence* of the relation; 2. Features are considered "good" if they strongly indicate the *absence* of the relation; 3. features are considered "bad" if their presence give no information about *either the presence or the absence* of the relation.

To capture this information, we first construct a relation matrix M with each entry M_{ij} defined as the conditional probability of relation R_j given the feature F_i computed as the maximum likelihood estimate from the full training set:

$$M_{ij} = P(R_j|F_i)$$

Each column of the relation matrix captures the predictive power of each feature to a certain relation. A feature with value M_{ij} higher than the column mean indicates that it is predictive for the presence of relation j, while a feature with M_{ij} lower than the mean is predictive for its absence; the strength of such indication depends on how far away M_{ij} is from the mean: the further away it is, the more valuable this feature should be for relation j. With this idea we give the following augmented value for each feature:

$$M'_{ij} = \begin{cases} M_{ij}, & \text{if } M_{ij} \geq \mu_j. \\ \mu_j + (\mu_j - M_{ij}), & \text{if } M_{ij} < \mu_j. \end{cases} \quad (3)$$

where μ_j is the mean of the jth column corresponding to the jth relation.

Given a feature F_i, very small and very high probabilities of a certain relation j, i.e., $P(R_j|F_i)$, are both useful information. However, in linear SVMs, lower values of a feature would mean that it contributes less to the decision of the class. By feature shaping, we allow features that strongly indicate the absence of a class to influence the decision and rely on the classifier to identify the negative association and reflect it by assigning a negative weight to these features.

When constructing the relation matrix, we used the top four relation classes along with an *EntRel/NoRel* class. We computed the matrix before downsampling to preserve the natural data distribution and features that strongly indicate the absence of a class, then downsample the negative data just like the previous downsampling setting.

5.2.2 Feature selection

The relation matrix also provides information for feature selection using a binomial test for significance, $B(n, N, p)$, which gives the probability of observing a feature n times in N instances of a relation if the probability of any feature occurring with the relation is p. For each relation, we use the binomial test to pick the features that occur significantly more or less often than expected with the relation. In the binomial test, p is set to be equal to the probability of that relation in the PDTB training set. We select only the features which result in a low p-value for the binomial test for at least some relation. We used 9-fold cross validation on the training data to pick the best p-values for each relation individually; all best p-values were between 0.1 and 0.2.

Result listing Table 5 and Table 6 show the multiway and binary classification performance using feature shaping and feature selection. We also show the precision and recall for binary classifiers.

	Multiway SVM	One-Against-All
AllData	32.58	NA
Downsample	NA	37.15
Upsample	NA	36.63
Weighted Cost	NA	34.23
Selection	32.52	38.42*
Shaping	NA	38.81**
Shape+Sel	NA	39.13**

Table 5: Balanced accuracy for multiway SVM and one-against-all for 5-way classification. One asterisk (*) means significantly better than weighted cost and upsampling, and two means significantly better than downsampling, at $p < 0.05$.

For multi-way classification, performing feature shaping leads to significant improvements over downsampling, upsampling and weighted cost. The binomial method for feature selection that relies on the full training data distribution has a similar effect. Combined feature shaping and selection leads to 2% absolute improvement in discourse relation recognition. For binary classification, though, the improvement is significant only for *Temporal*.

6 Classifier analysis and combination

6.1 Discussion of precision and recall

A careful examination of Tables 5 and 6 leads to some intriguing observations. For the most skewed relations, if we consider not only the F measure, but also the precision and recall, there is an interesting difference between the systems. While downsampling has the lowest precision, it gives the highest recall. The case for weighted cost is another story. For highly skewed relations such as *Temporal* and *Comparison*, it gives the highest precision and the lowest recall; but as the data set balances out in downsampling, the classifier shifts towards high recall and low precision.

We can also rank the three feature augmentation techniques in terms of how much they reflect distributional information in the training data. Feature selection reflects the training data least among the three, because it uses information from all of the data to select the features, but the feature values are still either 1 or 0. Feature shaping engages more data because the value of a feature encodes its relative "effectiveness" for a relation. We can see that feature selection gives slightly higher precision than just downsampling; feature shaping, on the other hand, gives precision and recall values between these two. This is most obvious in smaller relations, i.e. *Temporal* and *Comparison*.

To see if this trend is statistically significant, we did a paired t-test over the precision and recall for each system and each relation. For the *Temporal* relation, all systems that use more data have significantly higher ($p < 0.05$) precision than that for downsampling. For *Comparison*, the changes in precision are either significant or tend towards significance for three methods: feature shaping ($p < 0.1$), feature shaping+election ($p < 0.1$) and weighted cost ($p < 0.05$). For *Contingency*, feature shaping gives an improvement in precision that tends toward significance ($p < 0.1$). The drops in recall using feature shaping or weighted cost for the above three relations are significant ($p < 0.05$). For the *Expansion* relation, being the largest class with 40% positive data, changes in

	Downsample	WeightCost	Selection	Shaping	Shape+Sel
Temp.	15.52 (8.8/65.4)	20.61* (16.9/26.3)	18.47* (10.7/65.9)	20.37* (12.6/53.2)	21.30* (13.7/47.8)
Comp.	27.65 (17.3/69.2)	28.38 (19.9/49.6)	26.98 (17.4/60.1)	27.79 (18.3/58.2)	26.92 (18.7/48.2)
Cont.	47.14 (34.5/74.5)	46.36 (34.6/70.1)	47.45 (34.7/75.2)	47.62 (35.4/72.9)	46.93 (35.2/70.5)
Exp.	55.42 (49.3/63.3)	57.43* (43.9/83.1)	55.52 (49.3/63.5)	55.13 (49.3/62.5)	54.90 (49.2/62.1)

Table 6: F score (precision/recall) of classifiers with feature augmentation. Asterisk(*) means F score or BAC is significantly greater than plain downsampling at $p < 0.05$.

precision and recall with downsampling systems are not significant; yet weighted cost shifted towards predicting more of the positive instances, i.e., giving a significantly higher recall by trading with a significantly lower precision ($p < 0.05$).

6.2 Discussion of classifier similarity

To better understand the differences of classifier behaviors under the weighted cost and each downsampling technique (plain downsampling, feature selection, feature shaping, feature shaping+selection), in Table 7 we show the percentage of test instances that the weighted cost system and each downsample system agree or do not agree. In particular, we study the following situations:

1. The downsample system predicts correctly but the weighted cost system does not ("D+C-");
2. The weighted cost system predicts correctly but the downsample system does not ("D-C+");
3. Both systems are correct ("D+C+").

At a glance of the Q statistic, it seems that the systems are not behaving very differently. However, as only the sum of disagreements is reflected in the Q statistic, we look more closely at where the systems do not agree in each situation. If we focus on the rarer *Temporal* and *Comparison* relations, first note that in the plain downsampling vs. weighted cost, the percentage of test instances in the "D+C-" column is much smaller than that in the "D-C+" column. This aligns with the above observation that plain downsampling gives much lower precision for these relations than weighted cost. Now, as more data is engaged from first using feature selection, then using feature shaping, then using both, the percentage of instances where both systems predict correctly increase. At the same time, there is a drop in the percentage of test instances in the "D-C+" column. This trend is also a reflection of the observation that as more data is engaged, the precision got higher as the recall drops lower. As the data gets more evenly distributed, this phenomenon fades away. The table also reveals a subtle difference between feature shaping and feature selection. Compared to

	D+C- (%)	D-C+ (%)	D+C+ (%)	Q Stat
Temporal				
Downsamp	2.56	28.27	61.47	0.73
Selection	2.91	22.04	67.71	0.77
Shaping	2.61	13.36	76.39	0.89
Sel+Shape	2.83	10.42	79.32	0.90
Comparison				
Downsamp	5.74	18.24	53.76	0.84
Selection	7.72	16.14	55.85	0.80
Shaping	6.14	11.95	60.04	0.89
Sel+Shape	9.69	10.99	61.01	0.83
Contingency				
Downsamp	6.88	7.89	58.74	0.93
Selection	8.01	8.92	57.70	0.91
Shaping	7.07	6.73	59.90	0.94
Sel+Shape	8.68	8.13	58.49	0.91
Expansion				
Downsamp	16.39	8.23	44.66	0.82
Selection	17.87	9.71	43.18	0.76
Shaping	16.64	8.45	44.44	0.81
Sel+Shape	18.36	10.30	42.59	0.73

Table 7: Q statistics and agreements (in percentages) of each downsampling system vs. weighted cost. "D" denotes the respective downsample system in the left most column; "C" denotes the weighted cost system. A "+" means that a system makes a correct prediction; a "-" means a system makes an incorrect prediction.

downsampling, feature selection introduces an increase in the column "D+C-" (i.e. the weighted cost system makes a mistake but the downsample system is correct). Feature shaping, on the other hand, do not necessarily increase this new kind of difference between classifiers.

6.3 Classifier combination

Our classifier comparisons revealed that for highly skewed distributions, there are consistent differences in the performance of classifiers obtained by using the training data in different ways. It stands to reason that a combination of these classifiers with different strengths will result in an overall improved classifier. This idea is explored here.

Suppose on a sample i, the downsampling classifier predicts the target class with confidence p_{id}, and the weighted cost classifier predicts the target class with confidence p_{ic}. Here again we approximate the confidence of the class by the distance from the hyperplane dividing the two classes. We weight the two predictions and get a new prediction confidence by:

$$p'_i = \frac{\alpha_d p_{id} + \alpha_u p_{ic}}{\alpha_d + \alpha_c}. \quad (4)$$

where the αs are parameters we want to encode how much we trust each classifier. To get these values, we train the classifiers and get the accuracies from each of them on the development set. Since we are using linear SVMs in our experiments, we mark the sample as positive if $p_i > 0$, and negative otherwise.

The results for the combination are shown in Table 8. We include the original performances of the classifiers by themselves for reference.

	Original Classifier	Combined Classifier
Temporal		
WeightCost	20.61 (16.9/26.3)	
Downsamp	15.52 (8.8/65.4)	21.78* (14.9/40.5)
Selection	18.47 (10.7/65.9)	22.99* (15.8/42.0)
Shaping	20.37 (12.6/53.2)	23.88* (17.5/37.6)
Sel+Shape	21.30 (13.7/47.8)	23.72* (17.7/36.1)
Comparison		
WeightCost	28.38 (19.9/49.6)	
Downsamp	27.65 (17.3/69.2)	28.72 (19.3/56.4)
Selection	26.98 (17.4/60.1)	29.25* (20.1/54.0)
Shaping	27.79 (18.3/58.2)	29.89^{*+} (20.5/54.9)
Sel+Shape	26.92 (18.7/48.2)	29.83* (21.3/50.0)
Contingency		
WeightCost	46.36 (34.6/70.1)	
Downsamp	47.14 (34.5/74.5)	48.38^{+} (35.9/74.4)
Selection	47.45 (34.7/75.2)	47.76^{+} (35.5/72.9)
Shaping	47.62 (35.4/72.9)	48.16^{+} (36.0/72.9)
Sel+Shape	46.93 (35.2/70.5)	47.37 (35.6/70.7)
Expansion		
WeightCost	57.43 (43.9/83.1)	
Downsamp	55.42 (49.3/63.3)	56.61* (46.4/72.7)
Selection	55.52 (49.3/63.5)	57.10* (46.5/73.0)
Shaping	55.13 (49.3/62.5)	56.74* (46.4/73.0)
Sel+Shape	54.90 (49.2/62.1)	57.06* (46.4/74.0)

Table 8: Classifier combination results for binary classification. An asterisk(*) means significantly better than the corresponding downsampling system at, and a plus(+) means significantly better than weighted cost, at $p < 0.05$. Improvements that tend toward significance ($p < 0.1$) are not shown here but are discussed in the text.

F measure For *Temporal*, the combined classifier performs better than the original classifiers. We see significant ($p < 0.05$) improvements over the corresponding downsampling system and the weighted cost system. If feature shaping is involved in the combination, it is also having better performance that tend toward significance ($p < 0.1$) over the weighted cost classifier. For *Comparison*, the benefits of a combined system is also obvious for feature shaping and/or selection. Feature shaping combined with weighted cost gives significantly ($p < 0.05$) better performance than either of them individually, and feature selection and shaping+selection combined with weighted cost is better than themselves alone. For *Contingency*, though weighted cost do not give better results, the improvement tends toward significance ($p < 0.1$) when combined with plain downsampling. For *Expansion* where weighted cost gives the lowest precision, combination with other classifiers do not give significant improvements over F scores.

Precision and recall We can also compare the precision and recall for each system before and after combination. In all but one cases for *Temporal* and *Comparison*, we observe significantly higher precision and much lower recall after the combination. The case for *Expansion* is just the opposite as expected.

7 Conclusion

In this paper, we studied the effect of the use of annotated data for binary and multiway classification in supervised implicit discourse relation recognition. The starting point of our work was to establish the effectiveness of downsampling negative examples, which was practiced but not experimentally investigated in prior work. We also evaluated alternative solutions to the skewed data problem, as downsampling throws away most of the data. We examined the effect of upsampling and weighted cost. In addition, we introduced the relation matrix to give more emphasis on informative features through augmenting the feature value via feature shaping. We found that as we summarize more detailed information about the data in the full training set, performance for multiway classification gets better. We also observed through precision and recall that there are fundamental differences between downsampling and weighted cost, and this difference can be beneficially exploited by combining the two classifiers. We showed that our way of doing such combination gives significantly higher performance results for binary classification in the case of rarer relations.

References

Rehan Akbani, Stephen Kwek, and Nathalie Japkowicz. 2004. Applying support vector machines to imbalanced datasets. In *Machine Learning: ECML 2004*, pages 39–50.

Gustavo E. A. P. A. Batista, Ronaldo C. Prati, and Maria Carolina Monard. 2004. A study of the behavior of several methods for balancing machine learning training data. *ACM SIGKDD Explorations Newsletter - Special issue on learning from imbalanced datasets*, 6(1):20–29, June.

Or Biran and Kathleen McKeown. 2013. Aggregated word pair features for implicit discourse relation disambiguation. In *Proceedings of the 51st Annual Meeting of the Association for Computational Linguistics (ACL): Short Papers*, pages 69–73.

Nitesh V. Chawla, Kevin W. Bowyer, Lawrence O. Hall, and W. Philip Kegelmeyer. 2002. SMOTE: Synthetic minority over-sampling technique. *Journal of Artificial Intelligence Research*, 16(1):321–357, June.

R. Elwell and J. Baldridge. 2008. Discourse connective argument identification with connective specific rankers. In *IEEE International Conference on Semantic Computing (IEEE-ICSC)*, pages 198 –205.

George Forman, Martin Scholz, and Shyamsundar Rajaram. 2009. Feature shaping for linear SVM classifiers. In *Proceedings of the 15th ACM International Conference on Knowledge Discovery and Data Mining (KDD)*, pages 299–308.

Sucheta Ghosh, Richard Johansson, Giuseppe Riccardi, and Sara Tonelli. 2011. Shallow discourse parsing with conditional random fields. In *Proceedings of the 5th International Joint Conference on Natural Language Processing (IJCNLP)*, pages 1071–1079.

Barbara J. Grosz, Scott Weinstein, and Aravind K. Joshi. 1995. Centering: A framework for modeling the local coherence of discourse. *Computational Linguistics*, 21:203–225.

Hugo Hernault, Danushka Bollegala, and Mitsuru Ishizuka. 2010. A semi-supervised approach to improve classification of infrequent discourse relations using feature vector extension. In *Proceedings of the 2010 Conference on Empirical Methods in Natural Language Processing (EMNLP)*, pages 399–409.

Yu Hong, Xiaopei Zhou, Tingting Che, Jianmin Yao, Qiaoming Zhu, and Guodong Zhou. 2012. Cross-argument inference for implicit discourse relation recognition. In *Proceedings of the 21st ACM International Conference on Information and Knowledge Management (CIKM)*, pages 295–304.

Thorsten Joachims. 1999. Making large-scale support vector machine learning practical. In *Advances in kernel methods*, pages 169–184.

Ludmila I. Kuncheva and Christopher J. Whitaker. 2003. Measures of diversity in classifier ensembles and their relationship with the ensemble accuracy. *Machine Learning*, 51(2):181–207, May.

Ziheng Lin, Min-Yen Kan, and Hwee Tou Ng. 2009. Recognizing implicit discourse relations in the Penn Discourse Treebank. In *Proceedings of the 2009 Conference on Empirical Methods in Natural Language Processing (EMNLP)*, pages 343–351.

Ziheng Lin, Hwee Tou Ng, and Min-Yen Kan. 2014. A PDTB-styled end-to-end discourse parser. *Natural Language Engineering*, 20:151–184, 4.

Eleni Miltsakaki, Livio Robaldo, Alan Lee, and Aravind Joshi. 2008. Sense annotation in the Penn Discourse Treebank. In *Proceedings of the 9th International Conference on Computational Linguistics and Intelligent Text Processing (CICLing)*, pages 275–286.

Katharina Morik, Peter Brockhausen, and Thorsten Joachims. 1999. Combining statistical learning with a knowledge-based approach - a case study in intensive care monitoring. In *Proceedings of the Sixteenth International Conference on Machine Learning (ICML)*, pages 268–277.

Joonsuk Park and Claire Cardie. 2012. Improving implicit discourse relation recognition through feature set optimization. In *Proceedings of the 13th Annual Meeting of the Special Interest Group on Discourse and Dialogue (SIGDIAL)*, pages 108–112.

Emily Pitler, Mridhula Raghupathy, Hena Mehta, Ani Nenkova, Alan Lee, and Aravind Joshi. 2008. Easily identifiable discourse relations. In *Proceedings of the International Conference on Computational Linguistics (COLING): Companion volume: Posters*, pages 87–90.

Emily Pitler, Annie Louis, and Ani Nenkova. 2009. Automatic sense prediction for implicit discourse relations in text. In *Proceedings of the Joint Conference of the 47th Annual Meeting of the ACL and the 4th International Joint Conference on Natural Language Processing of the AFNLP (ACL-IJCNLP)*, pages 683–691.

Rashmi Prasad, Nikhil Dinesh, Alan Lee, Eleni Miltsakaki, Livio Robaldo, Aravind Joshi, and Bonnie Webber. 2008. The Penn Discourse TreeBank 2.0. In *Proceedings of the Sixth International Conference on Language Resources and Evaluation (LREC)*.

Konstantinos Veropoulos, Colin Campbell, and Nello Cristianini. 1999. Controlling the sensitivity of support vector machines. In *Proceedings of the International Joint Conference on Artificial Intelligence (IJCAI)*, volume 1999, pages 55–60.

The Role of Polarity in Inferring Acceptance and Rejection in Dialogue

Julian J. Schlöder and **Raquel Fernández**
Institute for Logic, Language & Computation
University of Amsterdam
julian.schloeder@gmail.com, raquel.fernandez@uva.nl

Abstract

We study the role that logical polarity plays in determining the rejection or acceptance function of an utterance in dialogue. We develop a model inspired by recent work on the semantics of negation and polarity particles and test it on annotated data from two spoken dialogue corpora: the Switchboard Corpus and the AMI Meeting Corpus. Our experiments show that taking into account the relative polarity of a proposal under discussion and of its response greatly helps to distinguish rejections from acceptances in both corpora.

1 Introduction

In order to establish and maintain coherence, dialogue participants need to keep track of the information they jointly take for granted—their *common ground* (Stalnaker, 1978). As a dialogue progresses, the common ground typically evolves. New information becomes shared as the interlocutors exchange moves (such as assertions, questions, acceptances, and rejections) through the collaborative process of *grounding* (Clark and Schaefer, 1989; Clark, 1996). To keep track of the common ground, speakers must identify which information is accepted or rejected by their addressees. The basic idea is simple: If a proposal is rejected, its content does not enter the common ground, while if it is accepted, its content does become common belief.

Yet, determining whether a response to a move counts as an acceptance or a rejection is far from trivial. In many cases, the surface form of an utterance is not explicit enough to determine its acceptance or rejection force and inference is required (Horn, 1989; Lascarides and Asher, 2009; Walker, 1996). For instance, B's utterance in (1), extracted from the AMI Meeting Corpus (Carletta, 2007), exemplifies what Walker (1996) calls *implicature rejection* (the rejection arises from an inferred scalar implicature: *"normal"* implicates *"not interesting"*; see also Hirschberg (1985)).

(1) A: This is a very interesting design.
B: It's just the same as normal.

The goal of this paper is to investigate the role of *logical polarity* in distinguishing rejections from acceptances. Consider the following dialogue excerpts, again from AMI, where the same utterance form (*"Yes it is"*) acts as an acceptance in (2) and as a rejection in (3):

(2) A: But it's uh yeah it's uh original idea.
B: Yes it is.

(3) A: the shape of a banana is not it's not really handy .
B: Yes it is.

To determine whether B's utterance in either case above functions as an acceptance or a rejection, it is critical to not only look beyond the utterance itself and take into account the proposal under discussion (A's utterance), but also to specify (a) the polarity (positive *vs.* negative) of both the proposal and the response, and (b) how these polarities interact to give rise to a particular interpretation. Our aim in this paper is to develop a model of how logical polarity influences acceptance/rejection interpretation, inspired by recent work on the semantics of negation and polarity particles (Cooper and Ginzburg, 2011; Cooper and Ginzburg, 2012; Farkas and Roelofsen, 2013), and to test it on annotated data from two spoken dialogue corpora: the Switchboard Corpus (Godfrey et al., 1992) and the AMI Meeting Corpus (Carletta, 2007).

In the next section, we give an overview of related computational work on acceptance/rejection detection. In Section 3, we first briefly review recent formal semantics approaches to polarity and then present our model of logical polarity in acceptance and rejection moves. Section 4 describes our experiments: We derive machine learning features from our polarity theory and test them in Switchboard and AMI datasets, achieving competitive F-scores of around 60 on the task of retrieving rejections. We conclude in Section 5 with a discussion of our results.

2 Related Computational Work

The first attempts to automatically identify acceptances and rejections (often referred to as agreements and disagreements) were carried out in the context of multiparty meetings for the purpose of dialogue summarisation tasks. Hillard et al. (2003) and Hahn et al. (2006) used the ICSI Meeting Corpus (Janin et al., 2003) to develop systems that would classify utterances into agreements, disagreements, backchannels, and 'other'. While these authors only leveraged lexical and prosodic features of the utterance to be classified (i.e., *local* features), Galley et al. (2004) showed that accuracy could be improved by taking into account contextual dependencies, in particular previous (dis)agreements between the dialogue participants, achieving an overall accuracy of 86.9%. Subsequent work built on Galley et al.'s approach showed that detecting agreement acts helped to identify public commitments to tasks (Purver et al., 2007) and other decisions made in a meeting (Fernández et al., 2008).

A difficulty shared by all approaches mentioned above is the skewness of the data, not only regarding (dis)agreement *vs.* other types of acts, but also agreement *vs.* disagreement. In the dialogue settings considered, acceptance/agreement is much more common than rejection/disagreement (e.g., 11.9% *vs.* 6.7% in the portion of the ICSI Meeting Corpus used by Galley et al. (2004) and 3.6% *vs.* 0.4% in the section of the AMI Meeting Corpus used by Germesin and Wilson (2009)). This can lead to reasonable overall accuracy but poor results on recognising rejections. Indeed, Germesin and Wilson (2009), who apply an approach based on Galley et al. (2004) to the AMI Meeting Corpus, achieve 98.1% accuracy, but report 0% recall for rejections/disagreements. Wang et al. (2011), who also work with AMI data, use different resampling methods to balance their dataset and then apply Conditional Random Fields (using therefore contextual information from sequences of utterances), achieving 56.9% recall and 55.9 F1 for disagreement detection.

Some recent work has moved away from spoken dialogue to address similar tasks in online discussion forums. An advantage of this kind of scenarios is that they seem to offer more opportunity for disagreement/rejection, thereby yielding more inherently balanced datasets. Abbott et al. (2011) and Misra and Walker (2013) use the Internet Argument Corpus (Walker et al., 2012), an annotated collection of posts in discussion forums with a balanced distribution of agreeing and disagreeing posts. They address a 2-way classification task—determining whether each response to a post (or to a quoted portion of a post in the case of Abbott et al. (2011)) is either an agreement or a disagreement—using a collection of features inspired by previous computational and theoretical approaches. The system developed by Misra and Walker (2013) uses only local features of the to-be-classified post, achieving an accuracy of 66% (over a 50% baseline). Abbott et al. (2011)'s best system uses features from both the quoted post and the response post, achieving an accuracy of 68.2%. However adding this contextual information does not significantly outperform a system based only on local features of the response, which yields 66.6% accuracy. Using both features from the post and the post response, Yin et al. (2012) obtain similar results: 68% accuracy on a different online corpus (the Political Forum), where the datasets are not balanced (they report a ratio of about 2 to 1 for agreement *vs.* disagreement).

All in all, this body of work has identified several linguistic features that are useful for inferring acceptances and rejections, often building on observations made by conversational analysts (Pomerantz, 1984; Brown and Levinson, 1987). Furthermore, recent work by Bousmalis et al. (2013) suggests that there are specific non-verbal behaviours associated with agreement and disagreement, such as different types of head, lip, and hand movements. However, to our knowledge, the role of logical polarity has not been investigated in any detail by computational approaches. Several systems make use of *subjective* polarity, i.e., sentiment. For instance, Galley et al. (2004) use the list of subjective adjectives compiled by Hatzivassiloglou and McKeown (1997) to assign a positive and a negative polarity value to an utterance given the number of subjective positive/negative adjectives it contains. Similarly, Misra and Walker (2013) use the MPQA Subjectivity Lexicon (Wilson et al., 2005) to capture the local sentiment of an online post response given the number of words in the response with strongly subjective positive/negative polarity according to the subjectivity lexicon. Yin et al. (2012) assign a positive and a negative score to a post by aggregating the sentiment scores of those words that can be found in SentiWordNet (Baccianella et al., 2010).

Although subjective polarity may be helpful (e.g., utterances with a high positive sentiment score may be more likely to be acceptances), this is not the kind of polarity that concerns us in this paper. Note, furthermore, that local sentiment information may be superseded by logical polarity.

(4) A: But then it wouldn't sit as comfortably in your hand.
B: It would still be comfortable.

Despite the fact that B's utterance in (4)—extracted from the AMI corpus—would be assigned a positive sentiment score (given the presence of the word *"comfortable"*, classified as positive in the MPQA Subjectivity Lexicon, and the absence of negative subjective words), the utterance acts as a rejection due to logical polarity constraints, as we shall make clear in the next section.

3 Polarity in Acceptances and Rejections

In this section, we first give a brief overview of some of the main ideas put forward in recent theoretical approaches to polarity. Afterwards, we introduce our approach to logical polarity in the context of acceptance and rejection moves.

3.1 Formal Semantics Approaches

Polarity and in particular negation are central concepts in formal semantics and pragmatics (Horn, 1989). Recent work independently put forward within the frameworks of Type Theory with Records (Cooper and Ginzburg, 2011; 2012) and of Inquisitive Semantics (Farkas and Roelofsen, 2013) has proposed to semantically distinguish between *positive* and *negative* propositions. Such a proposal departs from the traditional view in formal semantics where propositions are taken to denote sets of possible worlds (see Partee (1989) for a survey). According to this traditional view, the meaning of (5a) would be indistinguishable from that of (5b), given that the two propositions are true in exactly the same possible worlds:

(5) a. Sue failed the exam.
b. Sue didn't pass the exam.

These utterances, however, license different types of responses. For instance, responding *"no"* to (5a) would assert that Sue did pass the exam, while the same response to (5b) would typically be understood as asserting the opposite. Leaving aside many details that distinguish the two theories, Cooper/Ginzburg and Farkas/Roelofsen propose that polarity particles—words like *"yes"* and *"no"*—are sensitive to the polarity of their antecedent: *"yes"* presupposes that a positive proposition is under discussion, while *"no"* presupposes a negative proposition. If the presupposition is met, both *"yes"* and *"no"* assert the proposition under discussion (i.e., in our terms, they act as *acceptances*); if the presupposition fails, they assert the negation of the proposition under discussion (i.e., they act as *rejections*).

This characterises the standard behaviour of polarity particles. However, the picture is slightly more complicated since, when the proposition under discussion is negative, in English *"yes"* and *"no"* can also be used to agree or disagree, respectively (contrary to the standard case):

(6) Sue didn't pass the exam.
a. No (she didn't). $\rightsquigarrow$ *standard acceptance*
Yes, she didn't.
b. Yes, <u>she did</u>. / #Yes. $\rightsquigarrow$ *standard rejection*
No, she did.

According to Farkas and Roelofsen (2013), this ambiguity of use makes bare forms of *"yes"*/*"no"* less likely in the non standard cases exemplified in (6) and favours more explicit sentential forms where the presence of the verb disambiguates the intended interpretation. In this respect, however, the standard rejection in (6b) constitutes a special case: While in standard acceptances the sentential form is not required, in standard rejections it seems needed. According to these authors, in English the positive polarity particle *"yes"* has a strong preference for realising an agreement move and therefore its use as a rejection is *marked*.[1] This makes the explicit sentential form *"Yes, she did"* in (6b) more felicitous than the bare form *"Yes"*. Thus, the two types of rejections to a negative proposition we see in (6b)—with *"yes"* and

[1]The special status of English *"yes"* for rejection seems to be supported by cross-linguistic evidence. For instance, German has a special positive polarity particle *"doch"* for rejecting a negative proposition: in response to the assertion in (6), *"doch"* would be used to disagree (*"yes, she did"*) while *"ja"* would be used to agree (*"yes, she didn't"*).

Polarity of P-R	Type	Example from AMI Meeting Corpus
positive – positive	default relative acceptance	A: *And then you can buy the covers.* B: *Yes*
negative– negative	reverse relative acceptance	A: *It's not very well advertised.* B: *No, it's not.*
positive – negative	default relative rejection	A: *It's a frog.* B: *No, it's a turtle.*
negative– positive	reverse relative rejection	A: *TVs aren't capable of sending.* B: *Yes, they are.*

Table 1: Relative response types.

"no"—are expected to contain an explicit verbal constituent. We refer to this as the *markedness expectation.*

3.2 Our Model

Our aim is to exploit insights from the theories sketched above to develop a model that can be operationalised in a computational setting to test whether information regarding logical polarity can contribute to automatically distinguish acceptances from rejections.

We focus on proposal-response pairs (P-R), where R either accepts or rejects P. We propose to assign both the proposal and the response a logical polarity: either positive or negative. Furthermore, we differentiate *absolute* (polarity independent) from *relative* (polarity independent) responses. A response type R is absolute if its acceptance/rejection function does not depend on the polarity of P, and it is relative if it does. Formally, we say that a proposal P is rejected by a response R if $P \wedge R$ is inconsistent. This gives us the following four possible responses to P:

- $R \equiv \top$: absolute acceptance
- $R \equiv \bot$: absolute rejection
- $R \equiv P$: relative acceptance
- $R \equiv \neg P$: relative rejection

Our focus of attention is on relative responses. Given a P-R pair with a relative response, we infer an acceptance if the polarities of P and R align, and a rejection if the polarities differ. This gives us four possible relative responses, shown in Table 1. In the default cases, where P is positive, positive responses act as acceptances and negative responses as rejections—exactly as absolute response types would act. When P is negative (i.e., $P \equiv \neg P'$), we are faced with what we call *reverse* relative responses: Negative polarity responses act as acceptances and positive polarity responses as rejections. An acceptance can have the form $R \equiv P \equiv \neg P'$ while a rejection can have the form $R \equiv \neg P \equiv P'$ (with R being positive, i.e., with the double negation $\neg\neg P'$ eliminated). We call these cases reverse responses because their polarity signature is precisely the negation of the respective default cases (*cf.* Table 1).

The next obvious question to address is how the polarity of proposals and responses can be determined. Clearly, this will differ across languages. For the case of English, we shall assume that polarity is linked to the presence of particular particles and grammatical indicators. In particular, we consider the words in Table 2 to be positive and negative polarity markers.[2] Amongst negative polarity markers, we distinguish between negative polarity particles and negation indicators.

positive	particles:	*yes, yeah, yep*
negative	particles:	*no, nope, nah*
	negation:	*not, -n't, never, nothing, nobody, nowhere*

Table 2: Polarity markers.

All markers in Table 2 are key cues of polarity. However, they do not straightforwardly determine the polarity of a contribution. Firstly, there are cases where the presence of a marker does not have the expected effect on polarity. For instance, a negative tag question (*"isn't it?"*) at the end of an utterance does not mark that utterance as negative. Also, the polarity effect of a marker can be invalidated if it is followed by the contrast connective *"but"*. For instance, in the following AMI examples, *"but"* cancels out the effect of the negative polarity particle *"no"* in (7), making B's utterance positive, and the effect of the positive polarity particle *"yeah"* in (8), making B's utterance negative (in conjunction with the verbal negation in this case):

(7) *Reverse rejection: negative–positive*
A: Yes, but some televisions don't support it.
B: No, *but* then they would also support that button, because it's the same thing.

(8) *Default rejection: positive–negative*
A: Yeah, uh materials like wood that
B: Yeah, *but* wood is not a not a material you which you build a a remote control of .

[2]We do not claim that this list is exhaustive.

Secondly, it is important to take into account that a large amount of acceptances and rejections do not include any marker of polarity at all. For instance, in our datasets extracted from the AMI and Switchboard (SWB) corpora (which we will describe in detail in Section 4.1), 49% and 70% of acceptances in AMI and SWB, respectively, do not contain any explicit polarity marker; and similarly for 40% (AMI) and 15% (SWB) of rejections. In part this is due to the fact that in English (as in most languages) there is no morphologically-realised positive counterpart of verbal negation.

Given the observations above, we adopt the heuristics in Figure 1 to assign a polarity to P and R. Since this heuristics is intended to be applicable to dialogue corpora, we forgo the use of deep semantic analysis, which is difficult to achieve when dealing with naturally occurring spoken language.[3]

P-**polarity:** A proposal P has negative polarity if it contains a negation indicator (excluding tag questions); otherwise, P has positive polarity.

R-**polarity:** We define a precedence order on polarity markers: negative polarity particles take precedence over positive polarity particles, which in turn take precedence over negation indicators.

- If a response R contains a negative polarity particle (not followed by *"but"*), its polarity is negative.
- Else, if R contains a positive polarity marker (not followed by *"but"*), its polarity is positive.
- Else, if R contains a negation indicator, its polarity is negative.
- Otherwise, R has positive polarity.

Figure 1: Heuristics for polarity determination.

Drawing on the notion of *markedness expectation* we introduced at the end of Section 3.1, we hypothesise that the lack of explicit positive polarity markers will be compensated for by the presence of sentential similarity patterns between proposals and responses. It follows from our description of relative responses (see Table 1) that they will either semantically mirror the proposal (acceptances) or negate it (rejections). In the absence of an explicit positive polarity marker in the proposal or the response, therefore, we expect to find some form of sentential parallelism, potentially in both cases—when P-R polarities align, as in (9), and when they differ, as in (10):[4]

(9) A: It's still it's still working,
B: It is.

(10) A: It's a fat cat.
B: It is not a fat cat.

According to the markedness expectation, this type of parallelism is expected in reverse relative responses even when polarity particles are present as in (11) from Switchboard and in the reverse response examples in Table 1. Hence, we conjecture that parallelism will be present with higher frequency in the reverse cases.

(11) A: They wouldn't be able to own a house.
B: Yes, they would.

4 Experiments

In order to automatically test the extent to which logical polarity plays a role in determining the function of naturally occurring acceptances and rejections, we conduct machine learning experiments on dialogue corpus data. We first explain how we create our dataset, then describe how we devise features that encode polarity information, and finally report the results obtained.

4.1 Datasets

We test our model on two different corpora: The Switchboard Corpus (SWB) (Godfrey et al., 1992) and the AMI Meeting Corpus (Carletta, 2007). SWD is a collection of around 2400 recorded and transcribed telephone conversations between two dialogue participants. The speakers are provided with a topic and then converse freely. In contrast, AMI contains transcriptions from around 100 hours of recorded multiparty conversations amongst four dialogue participants who interact face-to-face in a meeting setting. The speakers converse freely, but they play roles (such as industrial designer or project manager) in a fictitious design team whose goal is to design a remote control. Therefore the dialogue is mildly task-oriented. Both corpora have been annotated with dialogue acts (DAs), albeit with slightly different DA annotation schemes: SWD is annotated with the SWBD-DAMSL tagset (Jurafsky et al., 1997), while AMI uses a coarser-grained tagset but includes relations between some DAs (loosely called *adjacency pair* annotations).[5]

[3] Amongst other things, this means we do not account for the scope of negation.

[4] Both examples are extracted from the AMI corpus.

[5] The AMI DA annotation manual is available at http://mmm.idiap.ch/private/ami/annotation/dialogue_acts_manual_1.0.pdf

	acceptances	rejections	total P-R
SWB	4534 (97%)	145 (3%)	4679
AMI	7405 (91%)	697 (9%)	8102

Table 3: Class distribution in our datasets.

We use the DA annotations to extract a dataset of proposal-response (P-R) pairs for each corpus as follows. To construct the SWB dataset, we extract all utterances u annotated as `Agree/Accept` or `Reject` that are turn-initial and that are immediately preceded by a turn whose last utterance u' is annotated as `Statement-non-opinion`, `Statement-opinion` or `Summarize/Reformulate`. To construct the AMI dataset, we extract all utterances u annotated as `Assessment` that are turn initial and that are linked with the relations `Support/Positive Assessment` or `Objection/Negative Assessment` to an earlier utterance u' that is not annotated as `Elicit Inform` or `Elicit Assessment` (i.e., that is not a question). In both cases, P corresponds to u' and R to the first five words of u. We consider R an acceptance if u is annotated as `Agree/Accept` in SWB or as `Support/Positive Assessment` in AMI, and a rejection if it is annotated as `Reject` in SWB or as `Objection/Negative Assessment` in AMI.

We take the first five words of a turn-initial utterance to be the most relevant ones for conveying acceptance or rejection. This is motivated by the fact that dialogue participants typically provide evidence of understanding—and, by extension, of agreement or disagreement—at the earliest opportunity in order to avoid misunderstandings on what they take to be common ground (Pomerantz, 1984; Clark, 1996). However, when extracting our P-R pairs we retain the entire utterance u (of which R is a prefix) in order to be able to take its length into account in the automatic classification experiment, as explained in the next section.

Finally, we observe that in the two corpora all the P-R pairs where R is just a single *"yeah"* are acceptances. Thus, in the terminology we introduced in Section 3.2, bare *"yeah"* seems to be an *absolute* response type, whose acceptance function is independent of the polarity of P (in contrast to the relative response types in Table 1). Since identification of these acceptances is trivial, we discard them from our datasets. The final distribution of acceptances and rejections in each of the datasets is shown in Table 3. As can be seen, the data is highly skewed, with less than 10% of P-R pairs corresponding to rejections.

4.2 Features

We derive different types of features to test our model. We are not interested in using large amounts of unmotivated features, but rather in exploiting a small set of meaningful domain- and setting-independent features that can help us to investigate the impact of logical polarity. The feature we use are summarised in Figure 2. We consider several local features of the response. Most of these features are inspired by earlier approaches reviewed in Section 2, such as those by Galley et al. (2004) and Misra and Walker (2013). We use several lexical features that act as cues for acceptance or rejection. For instance, the presence of *"yeah"* is a good cue for acceptance, while the presence of *"but"* is a strong cue for rejection. The bigram *"yeah, but"* is in turn a good indicator for rejection—the *"yeah"* in such cases seems to be an attempt at politeness (Brown and Levinson, 1987; Bousfield, 2008). Since rejections are dispreferred moves, they are frequently initiated with a hedging such as *"well"* or with hesitation or stalling (Byron and Heeman, 1997). These utterance-initial cues are aggregated into one feature. Rejections also tend to be longer than acceptances since the speaker feels the need to justify the unexpected move (Pomerantz, 1984). We take into account the length of the entire utterance containing R with three binary features.[6] We also consider less frequent semantic indicators for acceptance and rejection, respectively, which we group into two aggregate features that record the presence of agreement words such as *"okay"* or *"correct"* and contrast words such as *"however"* or *"although"*. Given our observations regarding polarity and polarity particles in Section 3, in contrast to previous approaches we don't include *"yes"* and *"no"* as local lexical cues. Instead, we add a new local feature encoding the polarity of the response as determined by the R-polarity heuristics in Figure 1.[7]

[6]The use of Boolean features here is motivated by our choice of classifier, as we point out in the next subsection. The length thresholds have been set up manually after qualitative examination of several examples.

[7]We have tested other theoretically motivated local features, such as turn-length and number of disfluencies. The local R features in Fig. 2 combined with the local R polarity feature correspond to the best performing local feature set.

Local features cannot capture the most interesting aspects of logical polarity, which originate from the interaction between the polarities of the proposal and the response in relative response types. To account for this, we introduce four relative P-R polarity features corresponding to the response types described in Table 1. Finally, we introduce a feature that records the presence of some form of parallelism between P and R. As we mentioned at the end of Section 3.2, the markedness expectation predicts that sentential parallelism will occur more frequently in reverse relative responses, i.e., responses to negative proposals. The parallelism feature targets such cases. We restrict ourselves to strict identity between P and R of a pronominal subject and a verb (in negative *vs.* positive form).[8] The feature therefore is only able to capture examples such as (12a) but not (12b), where anaphora resolution would be required.[9]

(12) a. A: But it wouldn't be very attractive.
B: No, it would.
b. A: TVs aren't capable of sending.
B: Yes, they are.

4.3 Results

We conducted the machine learning experiment using `BernoulliNB`, the Bernoulli-distributed Naive Bayesian classifier from *scikit-learn* (Pedregosa et al., 2011), which outperformed several other classifiers, including Random Forests and a Support Vector Machine. We chose this classifier because our main features—the relative polarities—are Boolean and our data is highly imbalanced.[10] Given the high relative frequency of acceptances over rejections in our datasets (see Table 3), measuring accuracy or retrieving acceptances would yield very good results. Hence, as discussed in section 2, we believe that the most discerning task is the retrieval of rejections. Precision, recall and F-scores for this task, with the classifier trained on different combinations of feature sets, are shown in Table 4. We developed the classifier on the whole AMI dataset, as the small number of rejections makes splitting up the corpus into a development and a test set infeasible. The SWB corpus was exclusively used for testing. In the AMI dataset we tested the classifier with 10-fold cross-validation and in the SWB dataset with 5-fold cross-validation, due to the more limited amount of rejections in this corpus. Also, due to the lack of training data, the more specific Relative P-R Parallelism feature could not be applied to the SWB corpus.

LOCAL R FEATURES

Length of utterance containing R in number of words:
- Three features: $l>2$, $l>12$, $l>24$

Acceptance Indicators:
- R contains *yeah*
- R contains any of *absolutely, okay, accept, agree, correct, either, true, sure,* not preceded by *not*

Rejection Indicators:
- R contains *but*
- R contains the bigram *'yeah, but'*
- R starts with any of *well, oh, uh, mm*
- R contains any of *actually, however, though, although*

LOCAL R POLARITY FEATURE
- *positive* or *negative*, according to R-polarity in Fig. 1

RELATIVE P-R POLARITY FEATURES (*cf.* Fig. 1)
- *positive–positive*
- *positive–negative*
- *negative–negative*
- *negative–positive*

RELATIVE P-R PARALLELISM FEATURE

One of the following patterns appears in P-R, where a pronoun p, an auxiliary verb aux and a main verb v are identical in P and R:
- *'p aux not' – 'p aux'* not followed by $\{$*n't*$|$ *not*$\}$
- *'p (aux) not v' – 'p v'*
- *'I do*$\{$*n't*$|$ *not*$\}$ $\{$*think*$|$*know*$\}$ $\{$*that*$|$*if*$\}$ *p aux' –* *'p aux'* not followed by $\{$*n't*$|$ *not*$\}$

Figure 2: Feature types (all features are Boolean).

For comparison we report the results of a simple unigram baseline: Each content word that occurs at least 5 times in the dataset is used as a Boolean feature (occurrence *vs.* non-occurrence). This achieves F-scores of 31.66 in AMI and 16.63 in SWB. As a more substantial baseline we consider a system that uses only local features of the response, including local polarity. This feature-set is expected to capture relatively well the accepting/rejecting function of absolute responses and default relative responses, since their function aligns with their local polarity. This yields an F-score of 52.24 in AMI and of 33 in SWB. The Relative Polarity features were conceived to reduce classification confusion grounded in reverse polarity: If only local features are considered, a reverse polarity acceptance would appear to be a rejection,

[8] We use the NLTK POS tagger to implement this feature (Bird et al., 2009).

[9] Given the high frequency of pronominal forms in spoken dialogue, pronoun identity turns out to be reasonably useful.

[10] The scikit-learn documentation indicates that this classifier is particularly suited for sparse data and Boolean features.

Feature sets	AMI Precision	AMI Recall	AMI F1	SWB Precision	SWB Recall	SWB F1
Unigrams	35.61%	28.97%	31.66	24.20%	12.93%	16.63
Local + Local Polarity	44.13%	64.12%	52.24	20.80%	82.46%	33.00
Local + Relative Polarity	58.08%	61.63%	59.75	49.12%	72.93%	58.49
Local + Relative Pol. + Parallelism	58.23%	64.04%	60.96	n/a	n/a	n/a

Table 4: Precision, Recall, and F-scores for rejection identification.

while a reverse polarity rejection would seem to be an acceptance. Moving from local to relative polarity features should therefore reduce this confusion. Indeed, in both corpora the precision is increased substantially (from 44.13% to 58.08% in AMI and from 20.8% to 49.12% in SWB), causing a great increase in F-scores: 59.75 in AMI and 58.49 in SWB (paired t-tests show all these increases are significant, with $p < 0.001$).

However, in both datasets we observe a reduction in recall when moving from local to relative polarity. We believe that this is in part due to the relative polarity features ignoring some absolute uses of polarity particles, which may have been captured by Local Polarity.[11] The Relative Parallelism feature should be able to help in such cases. For instance, in example (12a) B's utterance would be assigned negative polarity and therefore the relative polarity features would contribute to classify it as an acceptance (since in the large majority of cases negative-negative P-R pairs do correspond to acceptances). In this case, however, *"no"* is used absolutely, i.e., as a rejection. Due to the markedness expectation, this is likely to show up in the form of contrastive parallelism, which we can—at least in part—capture with our simple feature. Indeed, adding this feature to the AMI dataset raises recall back to baseline level: 64.04% *vs.* 61.63% ($p < 0.005$). This, in turn, increase the AMI F-score from 59.75 to 60.96 ($p < 0.05$).

5 Conclusions

The overall aim of this paper has been to investigate the influence of logical polarity in interpreting utterances as acceptance or rejection moves in dialogue. We have built on recent work on the semantics of negation and polarity particles by Cooper and Ginzburg (2011; 2012) and Farkas and Roelofsen (2013) to develop an approach to polarity that is theoretically motivated and that can be computationally tested on corpus data. Although there is a substantial amount of previous work on automatically detecting agreement and disagreement in dialogue corpora, to our knowledge the role of logical polarity had not been explicitly investigated before.

Our focus has been on relative responses, i.e., responses where simply taking into account clues from the utterance to be classified is insufficient—or can even be misleading—to infer acceptance or rejection. We have argued that relative responses require taking into account how the polarities of the response and of the current proposal under discussion interact, and have put forward a model that captures such interaction. Our experiments show that the use of information on relative polarity substantially helps to distinguish acceptances from rejections. This indicates, on the one hand, that our model does a reasonably good job at capturing this phenomenon, and on the other hand, that relative polarity responses are not merely a theoretically interesting phenomenon but are in fact widespread in actual dialogue.

There is certainly room for improving the implementation of our heuristics, for instance by using finer-grained semantic and syntactic information: e.g., we cannot currently capture acceptance/rejection of a subclause, implicature rejections, rhetorical questions, nor sarcasm—all of which affect the recall of our system. Interestingly, the classification experiments yield very similar results in the two corpora with the Local + Relative Polarity feature set—F-scores of 59.75 in AMI and 58.49 in SWB. This indicates that our theoretical observations are applicable independently of setting, domain and number of speakers. There seem to be some differences across the two corpora, however, since the impact of relative polarity information is much higher in SWB than in AMI (the F-score goes up around 7 in AMI when moving from local to relative polarity, while in SWB it increases by 25). A deeper investigation into the shortcomings of our implemented model and of where these shortcomings affect AMI differently than SWB are issues we leave for future work.

[11] We note that the featureset Local + Local Polarity + Relative Polarity does not outperform Local + Local Polarity in the classification experiments. We believe this indicates that polarity is indeed mostly a contextual phenomenon.

References

Rob Abbott, Marilyn Walker, Pranav Anand, Jean E. Fox Tree, Robeson Bowmani, and Joseph King. 2011. How Can You Say Such Things?!?: Recognizing Disagreement in Informal Political Argument. In *Proceedings of the Workshop on Languages in Social Media*, pages 2–11.

Stefano Baccianella, Andrea Esuli, and Fabrizio Sebastiani. 2010. SentiWordNet 3.0: An Enhanced Lexical Resource for Sentiment Analysis and Opinion Mining. In *Proceedings of LREC*, pages 2200–2204.

Steven Bird, Edward Loper, and Ewan Klein. 2009. *Natural Language Processing with Python*. O'Reilly Media Inc.

Derek Bousfield. 2008. *Impoliteness in Interaction*. John Benjamins.

Konstantinos Bousmalis, Marc Mehu, and Maja Pantic. 2013. Towards the Automatic Detection of Spontaneous Agreement and Disagreement Based on Nonverbal Behaviour: A Survey of Related Cues, Databases, and Tools. *Image Vision Computing*, 31(2):203–221.

Penelope Brown and Stephen Levinson. 1987. *Politeness: Some universals in language usage*. Cambridge University Press.

Donna K. Byron and Peter A. Heeman. 1997. Discourse marker use in task-oriented spoken dialog. In *Proceedings of Eurospeech*, pages 2223–2226.

Jean Carletta. 2007. Unleashing the killer corpus: experiences in creating the multi-everything AMI Meeting Corpus. *Language Resources and Evaluation*, 41(2):181–190.

Herbert H. Clark and Edward F. Schaefer. 1989. Contributing to discourse. *Cognitive Science*, 13(2):259–294.

Herbert H. Clark. 1996. *Using language*. Cambridge University Press.

Robin Cooper and Jonathan Ginzburg. 2011. Negation in dialogue. In *Proceedings of the 15th SemDial Workshop (Los Angelogue)*, pages 130–139.

Robin Cooper and Jonathan Ginzburg. 2012. Negative inquisitiveness and alternatives-based negation. In *Logic, Language and Meaning: Proceedings of the 18th Amsterdam Colloquium*, Lecture Notes in Computer Science, pages 32–41. Springer.

Donka Farkas and Floris Roelofsen. 2013. Polar initiatives and polar particle responses in an inquisitive discourse model. Available from `http://www.illc.uva.nl/inquisitivesemantics/`.

Raquel Fernández, Matthew Frampton, Patrick Ehlen, Matthew Purver, and Stanley Peters. 2008. Modelling and Detecting Decisions in Multi-Party Dialogue. In *Proceedings of the 9th SIGdial Workshop on Discourse and Dialogue*, pages 156–163.

Michel Galley, Kathleen McKeown, Julia Hirschberg, and Elizabeth Shriberg. 2004. Identifying agreement and disagreement in conversational speech: Use of bayesian networks to model pragmatic dependencies. In *Proceedings of the 42nd Meeting of the Association for Computational Linguistics (ACL'04)*, pages 669–676.

Sebastian Germesin and Theresa Wilson. 2009. Agreement detection in multiparty conversation. In *Proceedings of the 2009 international conference on Multimodal interfaces*, pages 7–14. ACM.

John J. Godfrey, E. C. Holliman, and J. McDaniel. 1992. SWITCHBOARD: Telephone Speech Corpus for Research and Development. *IEEE Conference on Acoustics, Speech, and Signal Processing*, 1:517–520.

Sangyun Hahn, Richard Ladner, and Mari Ostendorf. 2006. Agreement/disagreement classification: Exploiting unlabeled data using contrast classifiers. In *Proceedings of the HLT-NAACL*, pages 53–56.

Vasileios Hatzivassiloglou and Kathleen R McKeown. 1997. Predicting the semantic orientation of adjectives. In *Proceedings of the 35th Annual Meeting of the Association for Computational Linguistics and Eighth Conference of the European Chapter of the Association for Computational Linguistics*, pages 174–181.

Dustin Hillard, Mari Ostendorf, and Elizabeth Shriberg. 2003. Detection of agreement vs. disagreement in meetings: training with unlabeled data. In *Proceedings of the HLT-NAACL 2003*, pages 34–36.

Julia L. B. Hirschberg. 1985. *A theory of scalar implicature*. Ph.D. thesis, University of Pennsylvania.

Laurence R. Horn. 1989. *A Natural History of Negation*. University of Chicago Press.

Adam Janin, Don Baron, Jane Edwards, Dan Ellis, David Gelbart, Nelson Morgan, Barbara Peskin, Thilo Pfau, Elisabeth Shriberg, Andreas Stolcke, and Chuck Wooters. 2003. The ICSI Meeting Corpus. In *Proceedings of ICASSP'03*, pages 364–367.

Dan Jurafsky, Elizabeth Shriberg, and Debra Biasca. 1997. Switchboard SWBD-DAMSL shallow-discourse-function-annotation coder's manual, draft 13. Technical Report TR 97-02, Institute for Cognitive Science, University of Colorado at Boulder.

Alex Lascarides and Nicholas Asher. 2009. Agreement, disputes and commitments in dialogue. *Journal of Semantics*, 26(2):109–158.

Amita Misra and Marilyn Walker. 2013. Topic independent identification of agreement and disagreement in social media dialogue. In *Proceedings of the SIGDIAL 2013 Conference*, pages 41–50, Metz, France. Association for Computational Linguistics.

Barbara Partee. 1989. Possible worlds in model-theoretic semantics: A linguistic perspective. In S. Allen, editor, *Possible Worlds in Humanities, Arts and Sciences*, pages 93–123. Walter de Gruyter.

F. Pedregosa, G. Varoquaux, A. Gramfort, V. Michel, B. Thirion, O. Grisel, M. Blondel, P. Prettenhofer, R. Weiss, V. Dubourg, J. Vanderplas, A. Passos, D. Cournapeau, M. Brucher, M. Perrot, and E. Duchesnay. 2011. Scikit-learn: Machine learning in Python. *Journal of Machine Learning Research*, 12:2825–2830.

Anita Pomerantz. 1984. Agreeing and disagreeing with assessments: Some features of preferred/dispreferred turn shapes. In *Structures of Social Action*. Cambridge University Press.

Matthew Purver, John Dowding, John Niekrasz, Patrick Ehlen, Sharareh Noorbaloochi, and Stanley Peters. 2007. Detecting and summarizing action items in multi-party dialogue. In *Proceedings of the 8th SIGdial Workshop on Discourse and Dialogue*, pages 18–25.

Robert Stalnaker. 1978. Assertion. In P. Cole, editor, *Pragmatics*, volume 9 of *Syntax and Semantics*, pages 315–332. New York Academic Press.

Marilyn A Walker, Jean E Fox Tree, Pranav Anand, Rob Abbott, and Joseph King. 2012. A corpus for research on deliberation and debate. In *LREC*, pages 812–817.

Marilyn A. Walker. 1996. Inferring acceptance and rejection in dialog by default rules of inference. *Language and Speech*, 39(2-3):265–304.

Wen Wang, Sibel Yaman, Kristin Precoda, Colleen Richey, and Geoffrey Raymond. 2011. Detection of agreement and disagreement in broadcast conversations. In *Proceedings of ACL*, pages 374–378.

Theresa Wilson, Janyce Wiebe, and Paul Hoffmann. 2005. Recognizing contextual polarity in phrase-level sentiment analysis. In *Proceedings of HLT-EMNLP*, pages 347–354.

Jie Yin, Paul Thomas, Nalin Narang, and Cecile Paris. 2012. Unifying Local and Global Agreement and Disagreement Classification in Online Debates. In *Proceedings of the 3rd Workshop in Computational Approaches to Subjectivity and Sentiment Analysis*, pages 61–69.

In-depth Exploitation of Noun and Verb Semantics to Identify Causation in Verb-Noun Pairs

Mehwish Riaz and Roxana Girju
Department of Computer Science and Beckman Institute
University of Illinois at Urbana-Champaign
Urbana, IL 61801, USA
{mriaz2,girju}@illinois.edu

Abstract

Recognition of causality is important to achieve natural language discourse understanding. Previous approaches rely on shallow linguistic features. In this work, we propose to identify causality in verb-noun pairs by exploiting deeper semantics of nouns and verbs. Particularly, we acquire and employ three novel types of knowledge: (1) semantic classes of nouns with a high and low tendency to encode causality along with information regarding metonymies, (2) data-driven semantic classes of verbal events with the least tendency to encode causality, and (3) tendencies of verb frames to encode causality. Using these knowledge sources, we achieve around 15% improvement in F-score over a supervised classifier trained using linguistic features.

1 Introduction

The identification of cause-effect relations is critical to achieve natural language discourse understanding. Causal relations are encoded in text using various linguistic constructions e.g., between two verbs, a verb and a noun, two discourse segments, etc. In this research, we focus on identifying causality encoded between a verb and a noun (or noun_phrase). For example, consider the following example:

1. At least 1,833 people **died** in **the hurricane**.

In example (1), the verb-noun_phrase pair "died"-"the hurricane" encodes causality where event "died" is the effect of "hurricane" event.

Previously several approaches have been proposed to identify causality between two verbs (Bethard and Martin, 2008; Riaz and Girju, 2010; Do et al., 2011; Riaz and Girju, 2013) and discourse segments (Sporleder and Lascarides, 2008; Pitler and Nenkova, 2009; Pitler et al., 2009). However, the problem of identifying causality in verb-noun pairs has not received a considerable attention. For example, Do et al. (2011) have studied this task but they worked only with a list of predefined nouns representing events. In this work, we focus on the linguistic construction of verb-noun (or noun_phrase) pairs where noun can be of any semantic type.

Traditional approaches for identifying causality mainly employ linguistic features (e.g., lexical items, part-of-speech tags of words, etc.) in the framework of supervised learning (Girju, 2003; Sporleder and Lascarides, 2008; Bethard and Martin, 2008; Pitler and Nenkova, 2009; Pitler et al., 2009) and do not involve deeper semantics of language. Analysis of such approaches by Sporleder and Lascarides (2008) have revealed that the linguistic features are not always sufficient to achieve a good performance on the task of identifying semantic relations including causality. In this work, we propose a model that deeply processes and acquires the specific semantic information about the participants of a verb-noun_phrase (v-np) pair (i.e., noun and verb semantics) to identify causality with a better performance over the baseline model depending merely on shallow linguistic features.

The work in this paper builds on our recent work reported in Riaz and Girju (2014). In that previous model, we identified the semantic classes of nouns and verbs with a high and low tendency to encode causation. For example, a named entity such as LOCATION may have the least tendency to encode causation. We leveraged such information about nouns to filter false positives. Similarly, we utilized the TimeBank's (Pustejovsky et al., 2006) classification of verbal events (i.e., Occurrence, Perception, Aspectual, State, I_State, I_Action and Reporting) and their definitions to claim that the reporting events (e.g., say, tell, etc.)

just describe and narrate other events instead of encoding causality with them. We proposed an Integer Linear Programming (ILP) model (Roth and Yih, 2004; Do et al., 2011) to combine noun and verb semantics with the decisions of a supervised classifier which only relies on linguistic features.

In this paper, we extend our previous model by acquiring and exploiting the following three novel types of knowledge:

1. We learn the information about tendencies of various verb frames to encode causation. For example, our model identifies if the subject of verb "destroy" ("occur") has a high (low) tendency to encode causation. Such information helps gain performance by exploiting causal semantics of each verb frame separately. We also learn and incorporate information about the verb frames in general e.g., how likely it is for the subject of any verb to encode causation with its verb.
2. In Riaz and Girju (2014), we utilized the TimeBank's definition of reporting events to argue that such events have the least tendency to encode causation. Instead of relying on human judgment we now introduce a data intensive approach to identify the TimeBank's classes of events with the least tendency to encode causation.
3. Although, information about the nouns with the least tendency to encode causation helps to filter false positives it can lead to false negatives when metonymic readings are associated with such nouns. Therefore, we introduce a metonymy resolver on top of our current model to avoid false negatives.

We provide details of our previously proposed model in section 3. We introduce new model and discuss its performance in sections 4 and 5. Section 6 concludes the current research.

2 Relevant Work

In Natural Language Processing (NLP), researchers are showing lots of interest in the task of identifying causality due to its various applications e.g., question answering (Girju, 2003), summarization (Chklovski and Pantel, 2004), future prediction (Radinsky and Horvitz, 2013), etc.

Several approaches have been proposed to identify causality in pairs of verbal events (Bethard and Martin, 2008; Riaz and Girju, 2010; Do et al., 2011; Riaz and Girju, 2013) and discourse segments (Sporleder and Lascarides, 2008; Pitler and Nenkova, 2009; Pitler et al., 2009). However causality a pervasive relation of language can be encoded via various linguistic constructions. For example, verbs and nouns are the key components of language to represent events. Therefore in this work we focus on identifying causality in verb-noun pairs.

Previously researchers have followed the path of utilizing linguistic features in the framework of supervised learning (Girju, 2003; Bethard and Martin, 2008; Sporleder and Lascarides, 2008; Pitler and Nenkova, 2009; Pitler et al., 2009). Though linguistic features are important but other sources of knowledge are also critically required to achieve progress on the current task.

In recent years, researchers have proposed unsupervised metrics to identify causality between events (Riaz and Girju, 2010; Do et al., 2011). For example, Riaz and Girju (2010) and Do et al. (2011) introduced unsupervised metrics to learn causal dependencies between events. These metrics mainly depend on probabilities of co-occurrences of events and do not distinguish well causality from any other types of correlation (Riaz and Girju, 2013). In order to overcome this problem Riaz and Girju (2013) proposed some advanced metrics which combine probabilities of co-occurrences of events with the supervised estimates of cause and non-cause relations.

Considering the importance of employing rich sources of knowledge other than linguistic features for the current task, we have recently proposed a model that incorporates semantic classes of nouns and verbs with a high and low tendency to encode causation (Riaz and Girju, 2014). In this work, we exploit information about verb frames, data-driven verb semantics and metonymies to achieve more progress on our recent work.

3 Model for Recognizing Causality

In this section we provide an overview of our previous model (Riaz and Girju, 2014) for identifying causality in v-np pairs where v (np) stands for verb (noun_phrase). This model works in the following two stages: (1) A supervised classifier is used to make binary predictions (i.e., the label cause (C) or non-cause ($\neg$C)) employing linguistic features, and (2) noun and verb semantics are then combined with the predictions of supervised classifier in the ILP framework to identify causality.

3.1 Supervised Classifier

To the best of our knowledge, there is no data set of v-np pairs with the labels C and ¬C available to us. For the current task we employ some heuristics to extract a training corpus of v-np pairs using FrameNet (Baker et al., 1998). FrameNet provides frame elements for the verbs and hand annotated examples (aka annotations) of these frame elements. Consider the following annotation from FrameNet "They **died** [$_{Cause}$from **shotgun wounds**]" where the frame element "Cause" is given for the verb "died". We remove the preposition "from" from the above annotation of frame element to acquire an instance of v-np (i.e., died-shotgun wounds) pair. We extract all annotations for verbs from FrameNet in which a frame element must contain at least one noun and no verb in it. We found such annotations for 729 distinct frame elements. We manually assigned the labels C and ¬C to these frame elements. Cause, Purpose, Reason, Result, Explanation are some examples of the frame elements to which we assigned the label C. Using the above mentioned assignments of labels C and ¬C to frame elements, we have acquired a training corpus of $4,141$ $(77,119)$ C (¬C) instances from FrameNet. In order to avoid class imbalance while training we employ an equal number of instances of both labels.

Due to space constraints, we refer the reader to Appendix A for the details of linguistic features to build the supervised classifier. We employ both Naive Bayes (NB) and Maximum Entropy (MaxEnt) algorithms to acquire predictions and probabilities of assignments of labels. We set up the following ILP using these probabilities:

$$Z_1 = \max \sum_{\text{v-np} \in I} \sum_{l \in L_1} x_1(\text{v-np}, l) P(\text{v-np}, l) \quad (1)$$

$$\sum_{l \in L_1} x_1(\text{v-np}, l) = 1 \quad \forall \text{v-np} \in I \quad (2)$$

$$x_1(\text{v-np}, l) \in \{0, 1\} \quad \forall \text{v-np} \in I \quad \forall l \in L_1 \quad (3)$$

Here, $L_1 = \{\text{C}, \neg\text{C}\}$, I is the set of all v-np pairs. $x_1(\text{v-np}, l)$ is a binary decision variable set to 1 only if the label $l \in L_1$ is assigned to a v-np pair and only one label out of $|L_1|$ choices can be assigned to a v-np pair (see constraints 2 and 3). In particular, we maximize the objective function Z_1 (1) assigning the labels $l \in \{L_1\}$ to v-np pairs depending on the probabilities of assignments (i.e., $P(\text{v-np}, l)$) obtained through the supervised classifier.

3.2 Noun and Verb Semantics

We automatically acquire and employ semantic classes of nouns and verbs with a high and low tendency to encode causation. Such information helps to reduce errors in predictions of the supervised classifier.

We derive two semantic classes of nouns for our purpose i.e., C_{np} and $\neg\text{C}_{\text{np}}$ where the class C_{np} ($\neg\text{C}_{\text{np}}$) represents the noun_phrases with a high (low) tendency to encode causation. For example, a noun_phrase expression for a location has the least tendency to encode causation unless a metonymic reading is associated with it. In order to acquire these classes, we extract annotations of 936 distinct frame elements from FrameNet in which a frame element must contain at least one noun and no verb in it. These annotations of frame elements roughly represent instances of noun_phrases (np). We manually assigned the labels C_{np} and $\neg\text{C}_{\text{np}}$ to the frame elements. For example, we assign the label $\neg\text{C}_{\text{np}}$ to the frame element "Place" which represents a location (see Appendix B for some examples of the frame elements with labels C_{np} and $\neg\text{C}_{\text{np}}$). We also follow the approach similar to Girju and Moldovan (2002) to employ WordNet senses of nouns to acquire more instances of the classes C_{np} and $\neg\text{C}_{\text{np}}$ (see Appendix B for the details). We have acquired a total of $280,212$ instances of np (50% for each of the two classes i.e., C_{np} and $\neg\text{C}_{\text{np}}$) using both FrameNet and WordNet. Using these instances, we build a supervised classifier to identify the semantic class of np (see Appendix B for the details of features to build the classifier). We incorporate the knowledge of semantic classes of nouns by making the following additions to ILP:

$$Z_2 = Z_1 + \sum_{\text{v-np} \in I - M} \sum_{l \in L_2} x_2(\text{f}_{\text{np}}(\text{v-np}), l) P(\text{f}_{\text{np}}(\text{v-np}), l) \quad (4)$$

$$\sum_{l \in L_2} x_2(\text{f}_{\text{np}}(\text{v-np}), l) = 1 \quad \forall \text{v-np} \in I - M \quad (5)$$

$$x_2(\text{f}_{\text{np}}(\text{v-np}), l) \in \{0, 1\} \quad \forall \text{v-np} \in I - M \quad \forall l \in L_2 \quad (6)$$

$$x_1(\text{v-np}, \neg\text{C}) - x_2(\text{f}_{\text{np}}(\text{v-np}), \neg\text{C}_{\text{np}}) \geq 0 \quad \forall \text{v-np} \in I - M \quad (7)$$

Here $L_2 = \{\text{C}_{\text{np}}, \neg\text{C}_{\text{np}}\}$. $\text{f}_{\text{np}}(\text{v-np})$ is a function which returns np of a v-np pair. M is the set of v-np pairs with metonymic readings associated with np. Currently, this set is empty and in section 4.3 we introduce a metonymy resolver to populate this set. $x_2(\mathrm{f_{np}}(\text{v-np}), l)$ is a binary decision variable set to 1 only if the label $l \in L_2$ is assigned to np and only one label out of $|L_2|$ choices can be assigned to np (see constraints 5 and 6). Constraint 7 enforces that if an np belongs to the class $\neg \mathrm{C_{np}}$ then its corresponding v-np pair is assigned the label $\neg$C. In particular, we maximize the objective function Z_2 (4) subject to the constraints introduced till now. For each v-np pair, we predict the semantic class of np using our supervised classifier for the labels $l \in L_2$ and set the probabilities – i.e., $P(\mathrm{f_{np}}(\text{v-np}), l) = 1, P(\mathrm{f_{np}}(\text{v-np}), \{L_2\} - \{l\}) = 0$ if the label $l \in L_2$ is assigned to np. Also before running our supervised classifier, we run a named entity recognizer (Finkel et al., 2005) and assign the label $\neg \mathrm{C_{np}}$ to all noun_phrases identified as named entities. We also determine association of metonymies with the noun_phrases identified as named entities.

For the current task we also acquire two semantic classes of verbs i.e., $\mathrm{C_{e_v}}$ and $\neg\mathrm{C_{e_v}}$ where the class $\mathrm{C_{e_v}}$ ($\neg\mathrm{C_{e_v}}$) contains the verbal events with a high (low) tendency to encode causation. In order to derive these two classes we exploit the TimeBank corpus (Pustejovsky et al., 2003) which provides seven semantic classes of verbal events – i.e., Occurrence, Perception, Aspectual, State, I_State, I_Action and Reporting. According to the definitions of these classes, we claim that the reporting events (e.g., say, tell, etc.) just describe and narrate other events instead of encoding causality with them. Using this claim, we consider that all instances of reporting verbal events of TimeBank belong to the class $\neg\mathrm{C_{e_v}}$ and the rest of instances of verbal events lie in the class $\mathrm{C_{e_v}}$. After acquiring instances of the classes $\mathrm{C_{e_v}}$ and $\neg\mathrm{C_{e_v}}$, we build a supervised classifier for these two classes. We use the features introduced by Bethard and Martin (2006) to build this classifier (see Bethard and Martin (2006) for the details). Employing predictions and probabilities of assignments of the labels $\mathrm{C_{e_v}}$ and $\neg\mathrm{C_{e_v}}$ we add the following two constraints to ILP: (1) if the event represented by v belongs to $\neg\mathrm{C_{e_v}}$ then the corresponding v-np pair must be labeled with $\neg$C and (2) if a v-np pair is a causal pair then the event represented by v must be labeled with $\mathrm{C_{e_v}}$.

4 Enriched Verb and Noun Semantics

This section describes the novel contributions of this work i.e., identification of semantics of verb frames, semantic classes of verbal events via a data intensive approach and association of metonymic readings with noun_phrases to identify causality with a better performance.

4.1 Verb Frames

We introduce a method to acquire tendencies of various verb frames to encode causation. Consider the following two examples to understand the tendencies of verb frames of form $\{\text{v}, \text{gr}\}$ to encode causation where v is the verb and gr is the grammatical relation of np with the verb v.

1. **The Great Storm of October 1987** almost totally **destroyed** the eighty year old pinetum at Nymans Garden in Sussex. (Cause (C))
2. **The explosion occurred** in the city's main business area. (Non-Cause ($\neg$C))

In above two examples the nps "The Great Storm of October 1987" and "The explosion" have the grammatical relations of subject with the verbs "destroyed" and "died". In examples (1) and (2) the verb frames $\{$destroy, subject$\}$ and $\{$occur, subject$\}$ encode cause and non-cause relations. These examples reveal that each verb frame has its own tendency to encode causation. This type of knowledge helps gain performance by exploiting the semantics of each verb frame separately.

We leverage FrameNet annotations to acquire such type of knowledge. We collect all annotations of verbs from FrameNet and assign the labels C and $\neg$C to the frame elements as discussed in section 3.1. In FrameNet, example (1) is given as follows:

3. [$_{Cause}$ The Great Storm of October 1987] [$_{Degree}$ almost totally] **destroyed** [$_{Undergoer}$ the eighty year old pinetum at Nymans Garden in Sussex].

According to our assignments of labels C and $\neg$C to the frame elements, example (1) is given as "[$_{\mathrm{C}}$ The Great Storm of October 1987] [$_{\neg\mathrm{C}}$ almost totally] **destroyed** [$_{\neg\mathrm{C}}$ the eighty year old pinetum at Nymans Garden in Sussex].". After acquiring instances of the labels C and $\neg$C from example (1), we populate the fields of a knowledge base of verb frames (see Table 1). Fields of this knowledge base are $\{\text{v}, \text{gr}\}$, count($\{\text{v}, \text{gr}\}$, C) and count($\{\text{v}, \text{gr}\}, \neg$C). gr is the dependency relation of the frame element with the verb v. We use Stanford's dependency parser (Marneffe et al., 2006) to collect dependency relations. count($\{\text{v}, \text{gr}\}$, C) (count($\{\text{v}, \text{gr}\}, \neg$C)) is the count of the label C ($\neg$C) of the frame $\{$v, gr$\}$. As shown in Table 1, for the frame element "The Great Storm of October 1987", the word "Storm" has the dependency relation of "nsubj" with the verb "destroy". If there exists more than one dependency relations between the frame element and its verb then we choose the very first relation in the text order. According to the counts given in Table 1, {destroy, nsubj} has more tendency to encode a cause relation than the non-cause one. We have acquired 7,156 and 114,898 instances of the labels C and ¬C from FrameNet for populating the knowledge base of verb frames. We compute tendencies of verb frames to encode causality using the following scores:

$$S(\{\mathrm{v},\mathrm{gr}\},l) = S_1(\{\mathrm{v},\mathrm{gr}\},l) \times S_2(\{*,\mathrm{gr}\},l) \quad (8)$$

$$S_1(\{\mathrm{v},\mathrm{gr}\},l) = \frac{count(\{\mathrm{v},\mathrm{gr}\},l)}{count(\{\mathrm{v},\mathrm{gr}\},l)+count(\{\mathrm{v},\mathrm{gr}\},L_1-\{l\})}$$

$$S_2(\{*,\mathrm{gr}\},l) = \frac{count(\{*,\mathrm{gr}\},l)}{count(\{*,\mathrm{gr}\},l)+count(\{*,\mathrm{gr}\},L_1-\{l\})}$$

Counts of first component (S_1) can be taken from the knowledge base of verb frames of form $\{\mathrm{v},\mathrm{gr}\}$. The second component ($S_2$) with counts $count(\{*,\mathrm{gr}\},l)$ and $count(\{*,\mathrm{gr}\},L_1 - \{l\})$ captures tendencies of verb frames in general. For example, what is the tendency of any subject to encode causality with its verb i.e., the score $S_2(\{*, nsubj\},\mathrm{C})$. We populate the knowledge base of Table 1 with equal number of C and ¬C instances to calculate counts for S_2. We make the following additions to ILP to incorporate information about verb frames:

$$Z_3 = Z_2 + \sum_{\substack{\text{v-np}\in I\wedge\\ g(\text{v-np})\in KB\wedge\\ f_{\text{np}}(\text{v-np})\in \mathrm{C}_{\text{np}}}} \sum_{l\in L_1} x_3(g(\text{v-np}),l)S(g(\text{v-np}),l) \quad (9)$$

$$\sum_{l\in L_1} x_3(g(\text{v-np}),l) = 1 \quad \forall \substack{\text{v-np}\in I\wedge\\ g(\text{v-np})\in KB\wedge\\ f_{\text{np}}(\text{v-np})\in \mathrm{C}_{\text{np}}} \quad (10)$$

$$x_3(g(\text{v-np}),l) \in \{0,1\} \quad \forall l \in L_1, \forall \substack{\text{v-np}\in I\wedge\\ g(\text{v-np})\in KB\wedge\\ f_{\text{np}}(\text{v-np})\in \mathrm{C}_{\text{np}}} \quad (11)$$

$$x_3(g(\text{v-np}),l) \le x_1(\text{v-np},l) \quad \forall l \in L_1, \quad \forall \substack{\text{v-np}\in I\\ \wedge g(\text{v-np})\in KB\\ \wedge f_{\text{np}}(\text{v-np})\in \mathrm{C}_{\text{np}}} \quad (12)$$

$$x_1(\text{v-np},l) \le x_3(g(\text{v-np}),l) \quad \forall l \in L_1, \quad \forall \substack{\text{v-np}\in I\wedge\\ g(\text{v-np})\in KB\wedge\\ f_{\text{np}}(\text{v-np})\in \mathrm{C}_{\text{np}}} \quad (13)$$

Here, KB is the knowledge base of verb frames and $g(\text{v-np})$ is the function which returns the verb frame i.e., $\{\mathrm{v},\mathrm{gr}\}$. This function returns NULL value if there is no grammatical relation between v and np in an instance. The above changes in ILP are only applicable for the v-np pairs with

{v, gr}	count({v, gr}, C)	count({v, gr}, ¬C)
{destroy,nsubj}	1	0
{destroy,advmod}	0	1
{destroy,dobj}	0	1
[$_{\mathrm{C}}$ The Great Storm of October 1987] [$_{\neg\mathrm{C}}$ almost totally] **destroyed** [$_{\neg\mathrm{C}}$ the eighty year old pinetum at Nymans Garden in Sussex].		

Table 1: A knowledge base of verb frames. This knowledge base is populated using the instances of C and ¬C labels given in this table.

$g(\text{v-np}) \in KB$ and np identified as of class C_{np} because we have already filtered the cases of $np \in \neg\mathrm{C}_{\text{np}}$ in section 3.2. $x_3(g(\text{v-np}),l)$ is a binary decision variable set to 1 only if the label $l \in L_1$ is assigned to $g(\text{v-np})$ and only one label out of $|L_1|$ choices can be assigned to $g(\text{v-np})$ (see constraints 10 and 11). We add information about verb frames using constraints 12 and 13. These constraints enforce the predictions of the supervised classifier of causality (section 3.1) to be consistent with the predictions using tendencies of verb frames (i.e., score $S(\{\mathrm{v},\mathrm{gr}\},l)$). We maximize objective function (9) subject to the above constraints. We remove those $\{\mathrm{v},\mathrm{gr}\}$ from KB which have $count(\{\mathrm{v},\mathrm{gr}\},\mathrm{C})+count(\{\mathrm{v},\mathrm{gr}\},\neg\mathrm{C}) < 5$ to avoid wrong predictions based on the small counts of verb frames.

4.2 Data-driven Verb Semantics

In section 3.2 we considered that reporting events belong to the class $\neg\mathrm{C}_{e_v}$ with the least tendency to encode causation using the definition of these events in the TimeBank corpus. Instead of relying on definitions of events we now introduce a data intensive approach to automatically identify the class $\neg\mathrm{C}_{e_v}$ of verbal events. In order to identify this class we extract training instances of verbal events encoding C and ¬C relations. Verbal events encode cause-effect relations using verb-verb (e.g., Five shoppers were **killed** when a car **blew up**.) and verb-noun linguistic constructions. Therefore for the current purpose we use the following two types of training instances: (A) a training corpus of 240K instances of verb-verb ($\mathrm{v_i}$-$\mathrm{v_j}$) pairs encoding C and ¬C relations (named as $\mathrm{Training}_{\mathrm{v_i\ v_j}}$) (we refer the reader to Riaz and Girju (2013) for the details of this training corpus) and (B) the training corpus v-np instances introduced in section 3.1 (named as $\mathrm{Training}_{\text{v-np}}$).

Following is the procedure to derive $\mathrm{V}_{\neg\mathrm{C}} \subseteq \mathrm{V}$ where V={Occurrence, Perception, Aspectual, State, I_State, I_Action, Reporting} and the set $\mathrm{V}_{\neg\mathrm{C}}$ contains the TimeBank's semantic classes with the least tendency to encode a cause relation.

1. **Input:** Training corpus, V
2. **Output:** Set $V_{\neg C}$
3. For each training instance k employ the supervised classifier of Bethard and Martin (2006) to do the following:
   (a) if $k \in \text{Training}_{v_i\text{-}v_j}$ then identify the semantic class (sc) of both events represented by both verbs v_i and v_j and add this information to a set i.e., $T = T \cup (k_{v_i}, sc_{v_i}, l) \cup (k_{v_j}, sc_{v_j}, l)$ where sc_{v_i} is the semantic class of event of the verb v_i of instance k and $l \in \{C, \neg C\}$.
   (b) Else if $k \in \text{Training}_{v\text{-}np}$ then identify the semantic class (sc) of event represented by the verb v and set $T = T \cup (k_v, sc_v, l)$.
4. Using results of step 3, calculate tendency of each semantic class sc $\in$ V to encode non-causality (i.e., $score(\text{sc}, \neg C)$) as follows:

$$score(\text{sc}, \neg C) = score_1(\text{sc}, \neg C) \times score_2(\text{sc}, \neg C)$$

$$score_1(\text{sc}, \neg C) = (\frac{count(\text{sc}, \neg C)}{count(\text{sc})} - \frac{count(\text{sc}, C)}{count(\text{sc})})$$

$$score_2(\text{sc}, \neg C) = (\frac{count(\text{sc}, \neg C)}{count(\neg C)} - \frac{count(\text{sc}, C)}{count(C)})$$

   where count(m, n) is the number of instances of verbal events with the labels m and n and count(m) is the number of instances of verbal events with the label m.

5. Acquire a ranked list of semantic classes $\text{list}_{sc} = [sc_1, sc_2, \ldots sc_m]$ s.t. $score(sc_i, \neg C) \geq score(sc_{i+1}, \neg C)$. From this list we remove the class sc_i if either $score_1(sc_i, \neg c) < 0$ or $score_2(sc_i, \neg c) < 0$.

   ▷ The following steps are used to determine the cutoff class $sc_i \in \text{list}_{sc}$ s.t. the semantic classes $\{sc_1, sc_2, \ldots, sc_{i-1}\}$ have the least tendency to encode causation.

6. $\text{result}_{sc_{-1}} = 0$ and $\text{result}_{sc_0} = 0$.
7. Remove sc_i from the front of list_{sc} and do the following:
   (c) Predict the label (l) $\neg C$ for all tuples of form $(m, \text{sc}, l) \in T$ if $\text{sc} \in \{sc_1, sc_2, \ldots, sc_i\}$ and predict C for the rest of the tuples.
   (d) Using predictions from step (c), calculate the $\text{result}_{sc_i} = \text{F1-score} \times \text{accuracy}$ for the label $l \in \{C, \neg C\}$.
   (e) If $\text{result}_{sc_i} - \text{result}_{sc_{i-1}} < \text{result}_{sc_{i-1}} - \text{result}_{sc_{i-2}}$ then output $\{sc_1, sc_2, \ldots, sc_{i-1}\}$
   (f) Else go to step 7.

Using the above procedure, we obtain the sets {Aspectual} and {Reporting, I_State} with $\text{Training}_{v_i\text{-}v_j}$ and $\text{Training}_{v\text{-}np}$ corpora. We consider that the Aspectual, Reporting and I_State events of the TimeBank corpus belong to the class $\neg C_{e_v}$ and rest of the events lie in C_{e_v}. Using these semantic classes we apply the constraints introduced in section 3.2.

4.3 Metonymy Resolution:

Metonymy resolution is the task to determine if a literal or non-literal reading is associated with a natural language expression (Markert and Nissim, 2009). Consider the following example:

{v, gr}	count({v, gr}, C_{np})	count({v, gr}, $\neg C_{np}$)
{kill,nsubj}	1	0
{kill,dobj}	0	1
[$_{C_{np}}$ Pissed off Angelus] just kills [$_{\neg C_{np}}$ me]		

Table 2: A knowledge base of verb frames. This knowledge base is populated using the instances of C_{np} and $\neg C_{np}$ labels given in this table.

4. **The United States** has **killed** Osama bin Laden and has custody of his body. (Cause (C))

In example (4) "The United States" refers to a non-literal reading i.e., the event of "raid in Abbottabad on May 2, 2011 by the United States" rather than merely referring to a literal sense i.e., a country. The association of non-literal reading with "The United States" results in killing event. Previously, researchers have worked with hand-annotated selectional restrictions violation for this task (Markert and Nissim, 2009). In the example (4) a country cannot "kill" someone and thus a metonymic reading is associated with it. In this work we identify association of metonymies with noun_phrases via verb frames and prepositions as explained below in this section.

In the first part of our approach we employ violations of tendencies of verb frames to identify if a non-literal reading is associated with a noun_phrases. Particularly, we build a knowledge base of verb frames using C_{np} and $\neg C_{np}$ classes as discussed in section 4.1. Consider the knowledge base given in Table 2 populated using the following FrameNet annotations "[$_{Stimulus}$Pissed off Angelus] just kills [$_{Experiencer}$me]." with assignments of labels C_{np} and $\neg C_{np}$ to the frame elements. We populate the knowledge base using only those FrameNet annotations in which a frame element does not contain a verb.

Now we introduce our method to identify the association of non-literal reading with the "The United States" in example (4). The supervised classifier predicts the class $\neg C_{np}$ for the np "The United States". However, in the current state of knowledge base (Table 2) P({destroy, nsubj}, C_{np}) > P({destroy, nsubj}, $\neg C_{np}$) where P is the probability. The prediction of $\neg C_{np}$ for "The United States" violates the above probabilities. Considering this violation, we predict the association of metonymy with np.

In the second part of our approach we identify tendencies of prepositions to encode causation and use violation of these tendencies to identify metonymies. For this purpose, we use the training corpus of v-np pairs with $4,141$ C and $77,119$ $\neg$C training instances (see section 3.1). We employ only those training instances in which a preposition appears between v and np and there appears no verb between them. From these instances, we acquire a set of prepositions that appear between v and np. Using this set of prepositions (PR) as input to the following procedure, we acquire a set of prepositions ($\mathrm{PR_C}$) with the highest tendency to encode causation:

1. **Input:** Training Corpus of v-np pairs, PR
2. **Output:** $\mathrm{PR_C}$
3. Calculate tendency of each preposition pr $\in$ PR to encode causality (i.e., $score(\mathrm{pr}, \mathrm{C})$) as follows:

$$score(\mathrm{pr}, \mathrm{C}) = score_1(\mathrm{pr}, \mathrm{C}) \times score_2(\mathrm{pr}, \mathrm{C})$$

$$score_1(\mathrm{pr}, \mathrm{C}) = (\frac{count(\mathrm{pr}, \mathrm{C})}{count(\mathrm{pr})} - \frac{count(\mathrm{pr}, \neg\mathrm{C})}{count(\mathrm{pr})})$$

$$score_2(\mathrm{pr}, \mathrm{C}) = (\frac{count(\mathrm{pr}, \mathrm{C})}{count(\mathrm{C})} - \frac{count(\mathrm{pr}, \neg\mathrm{C})}{count(\neg\mathrm{C})})$$

4. Acquire a ranked list of prepositions $\mathrm{list_{pr}} = [\mathrm{pr}_1, \mathrm{pr}_2, \ldots \mathrm{pr}_m]$ s.t. $score(\mathrm{pr}_i, \mathrm{C}) \geq score(\mathrm{pr}_{i+1}, \mathrm{C})$. From this list we remove pr_i if either $score_1(\mathrm{pr}_i, \mathrm{C})$ or $score_2(\mathrm{pr}_i, \mathrm{C}) < 0$.
5. $\mathrm{result_{pr_{-1}}} = 0$, $\mathrm{result_{pr_0}} = 0$
6. Remove pr_i from the front of the $\mathrm{list_{pr}}$ and do the following:
   (a) Predict the label C for all v-np training instances with pr $\in \{\mathrm{pr}_1, \mathrm{pr}_2, \ldots, \mathrm{pr}_i\}$ and assign the label $\neg$C to the rest of the instances.
   (b) Using predictions from step (a) calculate the $\mathrm{result_{pr_i}}$ = F1-score $\times$ accuracy.
   (c) If $\mathrm{result_{pr_i}}$-$\mathrm{result_{pr_{i-1}}} < \mathrm{result_{pr_{i-1}}}$ $\mathrm{result_{pr_{i-2}}}$ then output $\{\mathrm{pr}_1, \mathrm{pr}_2, \ldots, \mathrm{pr}_{i-1}\}$.
   (d) Else go to step 6.

The above procedure outputs the set $\mathrm{PR_C} = \{$for, by$\}$. Now we introduce method to identify association of non-literal reading for the example "All weapon sites in Iraq were **destroyed** by **the United States**" where "the United States" $\in \neg\mathrm{C_{np}}$ as identified by the supervised classifier. However, the preposition "by" has a high tendency to encode causation and thus "the United States" may encode causation. Therefore, there is a possibility that this noun_phrase has a non-literal sense attached to it which results in encoding causality. Using this method, we predict metonymies only for the v-np instances where preposition appears between v and np and there appears no verb between them. If any of two methods of metonymy resolution predicts the association of metonymy with np then we add v-np to the set M used in ILP (see section 3.2).

5 Evaluation and Discussion

In this section we present experiments and discussion on the performance achieved for the current task. In order to evaluate our model, we generated a test set of instances of v-np pairs. For this purpose, we collected three wiki articles on the topics of Hurricane Katrina, Iraq War and Egyptian Revolution of 2011. We apply a part-of-speech tagger and a dependency parser on all sentences of these three articles (Toutanova et al., 2003; Marneffe et al., 2006). We extracted all v-np pairs from each sentence of these articles. For each of the these three articles, we selected first 500 instances of v-np pairs. Two annotators were asked to provide the labels C and $\neg$C to the instances of v-np pairs using the annotation guidelines from Riaz and Girju (2010). We have achieved a 0.64 kappa score for the human inter-annotator agreement on a total of 1,500 v-np instances. This results in a total of 1,365 instances of v-np pairs with 11.86% C pairs.

In this section, we present performance of the following models (see Table 3):

1. **Baseline**: NB and MaxEnt (McCallum, 2002) supervised classifiers using only the shallow linguistic features (see section 3.1).
2. **Basic noun and verb semantics**: ILP with the addition of semantic classes of nouns without metonymy (denoted by $+\mathrm{N_{!M}}$) and the addition of semantic classes of verbs where $\neg\mathrm{C_{e_v}}$=$\{$(R)eporting events$\}$ (denoted by $+\mathrm{N_{!M}}+\mathrm{V_{\{R\}}}$). These models represent the work proposed in Riaz and Girju (2014) (section 3).
3. **Noun semantics with metonymies**: ILP with the addition of noun semantics involving metonymies resolved via verb frames (denoted by $+\mathrm{N_{M_1}}$), metonymies resolved via verb frames $\{$v, gr$\}$ where gr $\in$ GR = $\{$csubj, csubjpass, nsubj, nsubjpass, xsubj, dobj, iobj, pobj, agent$\}$ a set of core dependency relations of subjects and objects (denoted by $+\mathrm{N_{M_{1_{GR}}}}$) and metonymies resolved via both verb frames and prepositions (denoted by $+\mathrm{N_{M_{1_{GR}}+M_2}}$).
4. **Verb frames and data-driven verb semantics**: ILP with the addition of information about verb frames (denoted by $+\mathrm{N_M}$+VF where $\mathrm{M} = \mathrm{M_{1_{GR}}} + \mathrm{M_2}$), data-driven verb semantics i.e., $\neg\mathrm{C_{e_v}}$ =$\{$(A)spectual, (R)eporting, (I)_(S)tate events$\}$ (denoted by $+\mathrm{N_M}+\mathrm{V_{\{A,R,IS\}}}$) and both verb frames and data-driven verb semantics (denoted by $+\mathrm{N_M}$+VF+$\mathrm{V_{\{A,R,IS\}}}$)

S	B	$+N_{!M}$	$+N_{!M}+V_{\{R\}}$	$+N_{M_1}$	$+N_{M_{1GR}}$	$+N_{M_{1GR}+M_2}$	$+N_M+VF$	$+N_M+V_{\{A,R,IS\}}$	$+N_M+VF+V_{\{A,R,IS\}}$
A	28.86	71.86	73.40	71.35	71.42	71.64	72.96	75.16	76.19
P	13.52	26.18	27.21	26.29	26.34	27.54	28.39	29.93	30.82
R	92.59	75.30	74.07	78.39	78.39	85.18	83.95	81.48	80.86
F	23.60	38.85	39.80	39.37	39.44	41.62	42.43	43.78	44.63
A	61.46	80.73	81.17	80.65	80.73	81.02	81.39	81.75	82.05
P	19.46	32.02	32.72	32.41	32.52	34.09	34.66	35.25	35.64
R	71.60	55.55	55.55	58.02	58.24	64.19	64.19	64.19	63.58
F	30.60	40.63	41.18	41.59	41.68	44.53	45.02	45.51	45.67

Table 3: Performance of (B)aseline, $+N_{!M}$, $+N_{!M}+V_{\{R\}}$, $+N_{M_1}$, $+N_{M_{1GR}}$, $+N_{M_{1GR}+M_2}$, $+N_M+VF$, $+N_M+V_{\{A,R,IS\}}$ and $+N_M+VF+V_{\{A,R,IS\}}$ (see text for details) in terms of (S)cores of (A)ccuracy, (P)recision, (R)ecall, (F)-score. The row 1 (2) of this table presents results over NB (MaxEnt) baseline supervised classifier, respectively.

Table 3 shows that MaxEnt gives a very high accuracy and F-score as compared with NB. Model $+N_{!M}+V_{\{R\}}$ with basic noun and verb semantics introduced in section 3.2 results in more than 10% improvement in F-score over NB and MaxEnt classifiers relying only on shallow linguistic features. Model $+N_M+VF+V_{\{A,R,IS\}}$ with enriched verb and noun semantics brings more than 4% improvement in F-score over $+N_{!M}+V_{\{R\}}$ with MaxEnt as baseline. We perform statistical significance test using bootstrap sampling method given in Berg-Kirkpatrick et al. (2012) (see Berg-Kirkpatrick et al. (2012) for the details). $+N_M+VF+V_{\{A,R,IS\}}$ brings significant improvement in F-score over $+N_{!M}+V_{\{R\}}$ with p-value 0.0.

Though $+N_{!M}$ gives significantly better F-score over baseline, it drops recall by more than 16%. Metonymy resolution helps perform quite better by recovering more than 8% recall with $+N_{M_{1GR}+M_2}$ over $+N_{!M}$. $+N_{M_{1GR}+M_2}$ also results in 3.9% improvement in F-score over $+N_{!M}$ with MaxEnt as baseline model (significant improvement with p-value 0.0). Metonymies resolved via verb frames with all and core grammatical relations (i.e., set GR) recover more than 2% recall and slightly improve F-score.

Model with the addition of information of verb frames (i.e.,$+N_M+VF$) brings 0.49% improvement in F-score over $+N_{M_{1GR}+M_2}$ using MaxEnt as baseline model (significant improvement with p-value 0.027). Model with the addition of data-driven verb semantics (i.e., $+N_M+V_{\{A,R,IS\}}$) results in 0.98% improvement in F-score over $+N_{M_{1GR}+M_2}$ using MaxEnt as baseline model (significant improvement with p-value 0.0021). Overall the model $+N_M+VF+V\{A,R,IS\}$ yields more than 16% (20%) F-score (accuracy) over the baseline models build via NB and MaxEnt.

5.1 Error Analysis

We performed error analysis for the model $+N_M+VF+V_{\{A,R,IS\}}$ by randomly selecting 50 False Positives (FP) and 50 False Negatives (FN).

For 32% FP instances information about verb frames is not available in the knowledge base of verb frames. To avoid this problem researchers should exploit some abstractions e.g., {semantic sense of v, gr} frames. Our model fails to identify the class $\neg C_{np}$ for noun_phrases of 29% FP instances due to the lack of enough training data for the semantic classes of nouns. In 21% FP instances v and np are not even relevant to each other. Our model first needs to determine relevance between v and np before identifying causality. Remaining 18% instances have v and np in temporal only sense, comparison relation or both represent parts of same event. There is need to extract more knowledge sources to better distinguish causality from any other type of relation.

77% FN instances are classified as non-causal due to the lack of enough v-np training data and require more sources of knowledge e.g., background knowledge. On remaining 23% FN instances our model fails to identify C_{np} class due to the lack of enough training data for the semantic classes of nouns.

6 Conclusion

This work has revealed that enriched semantics of nouns and verbs help gain significant improvement in performance over a baseline relying only on shallow linguistic features. Through empirical evaluation and error analysis of our model we have highlighted strengths and weaknesses of our model for the current task. Our work has provided a novel direction to exploit semantics of participants of causal relations to solve the challenge of identifying causality.

References

Collin F. Baker, Charles J. Fillmore and John B. Lowe. 1998. The Berkeley FrameNet project. *In proceedings of COLING-ACL. Montreal, Canada.*

Taylor Berg-Kirkpatrick, David Burkett, and Dan Klein. 2012. An empirical investigation of statistical significance in NLP. *In Proceedings of the Joint Conference on Empirical Methods in Natural Language Processing and Computational Natural Language Learning (EMNLP-CoNLL)..*

Steven Bethard and James H. Martin. 2006. Identification of Event Mentions and their Semantic Class. *In Proceedings of the Conference on Empirical Methods in Natural Language Processing (EMNLP).*

Steven Bethard and James H. Martin. 2008. Learning Semantic Links from a Corpus of Parallel Temporal and Causal Relations. *In proceedings of ACL-08: HLT.*

Timothy Chklovski and Patrick Pantel. 2004. VerbOcean: Mining the Web for Fine-Grained Semantic Verb Relations. *In proceedings of Conference on Empirical Methods in Natural Language Processing (EMNLP-04). Barcelona, Spain.*

Quang X. Do, Yee S. Chen and Dan Roth. 2011. Minimally Supervised Event Causality Identication. *In proceedings of EMNLP-2011.*

Jenny R. Finkel, Trond Grenager, and Christopher Manning. 2005. Incorporating Non-local Information into Information Extraction Systems by Gibbs Sampling. *In Proceedings of the Association for Computational Linguistics (ACL).*

Roxana Girju and Dan Moldovan. 2002. Mining Answers for Causation Questions. *In American Associations of Artificial Intelligence (AAAI), 2002 Symposium.*

Roxana Girju. 2003. Automatic detection of causal relations for Question Answering. *Association for Computational Linguistics ACL, Workshop on Multilingual Summarization and Question Answering Machine Learning and Beyond 2003.*

Katja Markert and Malvina Nissim 2009. Data and models for metonymy resolution. *Language Resources and Evaluation Volume 43 Issue 2, Pages 123–138.*

Marie-Catherine de Marneffe, Bill MacCartney and Christopher D. Manning. 2006. Generating typed dependency parses from phrase structure parses. *In Proceedings of the International Conference on Language Resources and Evaluation (LREC).*

Andrew K. McCallum. 2002. MALLET: A Machine Learning for Language Toolkit. http://mallet.cs.umass.edu.

Emily Pitler, Annie Louis and Ani Nenkova. 2009. Automatic Sense Prediction for Implicit Discourse Relations in Text. *In proceedings of ACL-IJCNLP, 2009.*

Emily Pitler and Ani Nenkova. 2009. Using Syntax to Disambiguate Explicit Discourse Connectives in Text. *In proceedings of ACL-IJCNLP, 2009.*

James Pustejovsky, Patrick Hanks, Roser Saur, Andrew See, Robert Gaizauskas, Andrea Setzer, Dragomir Radev, Beth Sundheim, David Day, Lisa Ferro and Marcia Lazo. 2003. The TIMEBANK Corpus. *In Proceedings of Corpus Linguistics.*

Kira Radinsky and Eric Horvitz. 2013. Mining the Web to Predict Future Events. *In proceedings of sixth ACM international conference on Web search and data mining, WSDM '13.*

Mehwish Riaz and Roxana Girju. 2010. Another Look at Causality: Discovering Scenario-Specific Contingency Relationships with No Supervision. *In proceedings of the IEEE 4th International Conference on Semantic Computing (ICSC).*

Mehwish Riaz and Roxana Girju 2013. Toward a Better Understanding of Causality between Verbal Events: Extraction and Analysis of the Causal Power of Verb-Verb Associations. *Proceedings of the annual SIGdial Meeting on Discourse and Dialogue (SIGDIAL).*

Mehwish Riaz and Roxana Girju 2014. Recognizing Causality in Verb-Noun Pairs via Noun and Verb Semantics. *Proceedings of the Workshop on Computational Approaches to Causality in Language EACL, 2014.*

Dan Roth and Wen-tau Yih 2004. A Linear Programming Formulation for Global Inference in Natural Language Tasks. *In Proceedings of the Annual Conference on Computational Natural Language Learning (CoNLL).*

Caroline Sporleder and Alex Lascarides. 2008. Using automatically labelled examples to classify rhetorical relations: An assessment. *Journal of Natural Language Engineering Volume 14 Issue 3, July 2008 Pages 369–416.*

Kristina Toutanova, Dan Klein, Christopher Manning, and Yoram Singer. 2003. Feature-Rich Part-of-Speech Tagging with a Cyclic Dependency Network. *In Proceedings of Human Language Technology and North American Chapter of the Association for Computational Linguistics (HLT-NAACL).*

Appendix A. Supervised Classifier

In this appendix, we provide a set of linguistic features taken from Riaz and Girju (2014) to identify causality in v-np pairs employing a supervised classifier (see section 3.1 for the details).

- **Lexical Features:** verb, lemma of verb, noun_phrase, lemmas of all words of noun_phrase, head noun of noun_phrase, lemmas of all words between verb and noun_phrase.
- **Syntatic Features:** part-of-speech tags of verb and head noun of noun_phrase.
- **Semantic Features:** We adopted this feature from Girju (2003) to capture semantics of nouns. The 9 noun hierarchies of WordNet i.e., entity, psychological feature, abstraction, state, event, act, group, possession, phenomenon are used as this feature. Each of these hierarchies is set to 1 if any sense of head noun of noun_phrase lies in that hierarchy, otherwise set to 0.
- **Structural Features:** This feature is applied by considering both subject (i.e., sub_in_np) and object (i.e., obj_in_np) of verb (v). For example, for the pair v-np the variable sub_in_np is set to 1 if the subject $\in$ np, set to 0 if the subject $\notin$ np and set to -1 if the subject is not available in an instance. The subject and object of a verb are its core arguments and may sometime be part of an event represented by a verb. Therefore, these arguments may have high tendency to encode non-causation with their verb.
- **Pairs:** The following pairs (verb, head noun of noun_phrase), (subject$_{verb}$, head noun of noun_phrase) and (object$_{verb}$, head noun of noun_phrase) are used to capture relations.

Appendix B. Noun Semantics

In this appendix, some examples of the frame elements of FrameNet and the WordNet senses belonging to the classes C_{np} and $\neg C_{np}$ are given in Tables 4 and 5 (see section 3.2 for the details). We employ training instances acquired using the FrameNet annotations and WordNet senses for building a supervised classifier for the classes C_{np} and $\neg C_{np}$. Following is the list of features we use for this supervised classifier:

- **Lexical Features:** All words of noun_phrase, lemmas of all words of noun_phrase, head noun of noun_phrase, first two (three) (four) letters of head noun of noun_phrase, last two, (three) (four) letters of head noun of noun_phrase.
- **Word Class Features:** part-of-speech tags of all words of noun_phrase and head noun of noun_phrase.
- **Semantic Features:** Frequent sense of head noun of noun_phrase.

SC	FrameNet Labels
c_{np}	Event, Goal, Purpose, Cause, Internal cause, External cause, Result, Means, Reason, Phenomena, Coordinated event, Action, Activity, Circumstances, Desired goal, Explanation
$\neg c_{np}$	Artist, Performer, Duration, Time, Place, Distributor, Area, Path, Direction, Sub-region Frequency, Body part, Area, Degree, Angle, Fixed location, Path shape, Addressee, Interval

Table 4: Some examples of the frame elements of FrameNet to which we assign the semantic classes C_{np} and $\neg C_{np}$.

SC	WordNet Senses
c_{np}	{act, deed, human action, human activity}, {phenomenon}, {state}, {psychological feature}, {event}, {causal agent, cause, causal agency}
$\neg c_{np}$	{time period, period of time, period}, {measure, quantity, amount}, {group, grouping}, {organization, organisation}, {time unit, unit of time}, {clock time, time}

Table 5: This table shows our selected WordNet senses of nouns belonging to classes C_{np} and $\neg C_{np}$. For example, using the information provided in this table we assume that any noun concept whose all senses of WordNet lie in the semantic hierarchy of the sense {time period, period of time, period} is of class $\neg C_{np}$. We use English Gigaword corpus to collect instances of noun (or noun_phrases) and label them with C_{np} and $\neg C_{np}$ according to their senses in WordNet.

Identifying Narrative Clause Types in Personal Stories

Reid Swanson, Elahe Rahimtoroghi, Thomas Corcoran and Marilyn A. Walker
Natural Language and Dialog Systems Lab
University of California Santa Cruz
Santa Cruz, CA 95064, USA
{reid,elahe,maw}@soe.ucsc.edu, tcorcora@ucsc.edu

Abstract

This paper describes work on automatically identifying categories of narrative clauses in personal stories written by ordinary people about their daily lives and experiences. We base our approach on Labov & Waletzky's theory of oral narrative which categorizes narrative clauses into subtypes, such as ORIENTATION, ACTION and EVALUATION. We describe an experiment where we annotate 50 personal narratives from weblogs and experiment with methods for achieving higher annotation reliability. We use the resulting annotated corpus to train a classifier to automatically identify narrative categories, achieving a best average F-score of .658, which rises to an F-score of .767 on the cases with the highest annotator agreement. We believe the identified narrative structure will enable new types of computational analysis of narrative discourse.

1 Introduction

Sharing personal experiences by storytelling is a fundamental aspect of human social behavior (Fivush et al., 2005; Fivush and Nelson, 2004; Habermas and Bluck, 2000; Bamberg, 2006; Thorne, 2004; Bohanek et al., 2008; Thorne and Nam, 2009; McLean and Thorne, 2003; Pratt and Fiese, 2004). Humans appear to be wired to engage with information that is narratively structured (Gerrig, 1993; Bamberg, 2006; Bruner, 1991), and telling stories provides a critical developmental and societal function, by serving as a means to reinforce community value systems and to define individual identity (Thorne and Shapiro, 2011; Thorne et al., 2007). This has led some theorists to claim that "the stories they tell" is the defining aspect of both individuals and cultures.

Unlike any prior time in human history, personal narratives about many life experiences are being told online, and are widely available in social media sources such as weblogs. A personal narrative about an arrest is shown in Fig. 1, and one about a protest is in Fig. 4. Narratives such as these provide a valuable resource for learning a wealth of commonsense knowledge about people, the types of activities they engage in, and the attitudes they hold. They are also well suited to learning about causal and temporal relationships between events because narrative interpretation explicitly depends on the coherence of these relationships (Graesser et al., 1994; Elson, 2012; Gordon et al., 2011; Hu et al., 2013).

This paper applies and tests a narrative clause labeling scheme to personal narratives. Our scheme is derived from Labov & Waletzky's (henceforth **L&W**) theory of oral narrative (Labov, 1997; Labov and Waletzky, 1967). L&W's theory distinguishes (1) clauses that indicate causal relationships (ACTION), from (2) clauses that provide traits or properties of the setting or characters (ORIENTATION), from (3) clauses describing the story characters' emotional reactions to the events (EVALUATION).

We adopt L&W's theory for three reasons. First, we believe that the narrative structure of personal narratives posted on weblogs will be more similar to oral narrative than they are to classical stories. Second, we believe that any narrative discourse typology must at least distinguish ACTION, from ORIENTATION, and EVALUATION. Third, personal stories found on the web are often noisy and difficult to interpret; they do not always clearly follow well defined narrative conventions. A deep analysis

#	Category	Story Clause
1	Orientation	Now, on with this week's story...
2	Orientation	The last month has been hectic.
3	Orientation	Turbo charged.
4	Orientation	Lot's of work because I was learning from Tim, my partner in crime.
5	Orientation	This hasn't been helped by the intense pressure in town due to the political transition coming to an end.
6	Orientation	This week things started alright and on schedule.
7	Action	But I managed to get myself arrested by the traffic police (rouleage) early last Wednesday.
8	Action	After yelling excessively at their outright corrupted methods
9	Action	and asking incessently for what law I actually broke,
10	Action	they managed to bring me in at the police HQ.
11	Action	I was drawing too much of a curious crowd for the authorities.
12	Action	In about half an hour at police HQ I had charmed every one around.
13	Action	I had prepared my "gift" as they wished.
14	Evaluation	Decision witheld, they decided that I neednt to bother,
15	Evaluation	they liked me too much.
16	Evaluation	I should go free.
17	Action	I even managed to meet famous Raus, the big chief.
18	Evaluation	He was too happy to let me go when he realized I was no one.
19	Action	But then, a Major at his side noticed my Visa was expired.
20	Evaluation	Damn!
21	Orientation	My current Visa is being renewed in my other passport at Immigration's.
22	Evaluation	Fuck.
23	Evaluation	In custody, for real.

Figure 1: An excerpt from an example story from our corpus annotated with the L&W categories.

and annotation scheme, such as the one employed by DramaBank (Elson and McKeown, 2010; Elson, 2012) that extends theories of narrative structure and plot units (Stein et al., 2000; Lehnert, 1981), offers many advantages. However, acquiring this level of analysis on user generated content, such as blog stories, is resource intensive.

Research on computational models of narrative structure typically focus on inferring the causal and temporal relationships between events (Goyal et al., 2010; Chambers and Jurafsky, 2009; Riaz and Girju, 2010; Beamer and Girju, 2009; Do et al., 2011; Manshadi et al., 2008; Gordon et al., 2011; Hu et al., 2013). Yet L&W point out that stories are not just about the events that occur. In fact, L&W say that stories that are only about events are boring. Current methods for inferring narrative structure, including our own (Hu et al., 2013), do not distinguish event clauses from other narrative clause types. But note that actions only constitute about one third of the clauses in the narratives in Fig. 1 and Fig. 4.

Sec. 2 provides more detail about L&W's theory. Sec. 3 describes the annotation experiments and efforts to improve annotation reliability. Sec. 4 presents experiments on learning to automatically classify L&W categories, where we examine the the most predictive features, and the effect of annotator agreement on classification accuracy. We achieve a best average F-score of .658, which rises to an F-score of .767 on the cases with the highest annotator agreement. We analyze the types of errors the classifier makes in Sec. 5.1 and conclude in Sec. 6.

2 Labov & Waletzky's Theory of Narrative Discourse

L&W's theory of oral narrative defines a story as a series of ACTION clauses (events), of which at least two must be temporally joined (e.g., clauses 7-13 in Fig. 1 and clauses 7-11 in Fig. 4) (Labov and Waletzky, 1967; Labov, 1997) Stories also contain ORIENTATIONS (setting the scene, describing the characters), e.g. utterances 1-6 in Fig. 1. An orientation clause introduces the time and place of the events of the story, and identifies the participants of the story and their initial behavior. To properly understand narrative structure, orientations need to be identified as a separate type of utterance distinct from events. L&W define two other structural types called ABSTRACT and CODA. The ABSTRACT is an initial narrative clause summarizing the entire sequence of events. A CODA is final clause which returns the narrative to the time of speaking, indicating the end of the narrative. The CODA often provides the "moral" of the story.

The final element of a story according to L&W is EVALUATION, which L&W identify as essential to every story. According to L&W, evaluation gives the reason for telling the story, or the point of the story: without EVALUATION there is no story, merely a boring recitation of events. L&W state that the EVALUATION clauses may also provide information on the consequences of the events as they relate to the goals and desires of the participants, and can be used to describe the events that did not occur, may have occurred, or could occur in the future in the story. Clauses 14-16 and 18 in Fig. 1 provide the narrator's evaluation of the transpiring events as well as introducing possible but unrealized alternative timelines. In theories of narrative identity (McAdams, 2003; Thorne, 2004), evaluation performs two additional functions: (1) it expresses the tellers opinion and in doing so reflects the value system of that person and their community; (2) it constructs and maintains relations between the teller and the listener. Clauses 20 and 22 illustrate these functions where the narrator directly reveals his affective response to the prior events.

3 Dataset

Corpus of Personal Stories. Previous work (Gordon and Swanson, 2009) showed that about 5% of all weblog entries are personal stories describing an event in the author's daily life. They developed an automatic classifier for identifying personal narratives from a random sample of 5,000 posts from a corpus of 44 million entries available as part of the ICWSM 2010 dataset challenge (Burton et al., 2009). 229 of these posts were manually labeled as personal stories. Our experiments are based on 50 of these 229 stories.

Annotation Process. L&W's theory applies to sub-sentence discourse units in a narrative. It is an open question what level of phrasal granularity is appropriate to apply to written narratives. Here, we treat each independent clause as the basic unit of discourse and manually segment each story in our dataset using this definition. This results in a collection of 1,602 independent clauses. We then divided the 50 stories into 4 groups and annotated them in batches among 3 annotators in order to refine our annotation guidelines and process. This dataset is freely available at https://nlds.soe.ucsc.edu/lw.

Previous work has applied L&W's theory to Aesop's fables and achieved high levels of interannotator agreement and extremely high machine learning accuracies (Rahimtoroghi et al., 2013). However personal narratives clearly provide a more challenging context for annotation. There was a high level of disagreement after the initial round of annotation. We found at least 6 primary sources of disagreements:

- Clauses of more than one category are common with rising action and evaluation, e.g. a clause containing elements of orientation, action, and evaluation: *After leaving the apartment at 6:45 AM, flying 2 hours, taking a cab to Seattle, and then driving seven hours up to Whistler including a border crossing, it's safe to say that I felt pretty much like a dick with legs.*
- Actions that are implied but not explicitly stated in the text.
- Stative descriptions of the world as a result of an action that are not intuitively orientation.
- Stative descriptions of the world that are localized to a specific place in the narrative, which is problematic to L&W's definition of orientation.
- Subjective clauses in scene setting are usually orientation, but are lexically similar to evaluation.
- Disambiguating the functional purpose of clauses that describe actions, but may be intended to set the scene as opposed to the rising action.
- Disambiguating the functional purpose of subjective language in the description of an event or state, e.g., *The gigantic tree outside my window, The radiant blue of the sky.*

After several rounds of annotation we stabilized on a labeling scheme that hierarchically extends the original L&W categories, along with annotation guidelines that annotators could use to disambiguate recurring problematic cases. The final set of extended category labels along with two reduced hierarchical mappings are shown in Table 1.

STATIVE-LOCAL CONTEXT is a category for distinguishing stative descriptions of the world, that are not intuitively orientation. For example:

- I saw the sign I expected to turn south on Hwy 138. *The traffic sign pointed to Sutherlin and Roseburg,*

The clause in italics is a stative that describes the sign seen in the previous action. It is clearly not an action or evaluation, but is not intuitively an orientation, because it is so locally dependent.

STATIVE-IMPLIED ACTIONS are clauses, which do not explicitly mention an action or event, but imply one that is necessary to maintain the causal or temporal coherence of the remaining story. For example: *After that, we decided to walk some more.* In the context of the story it is necessary to know that they *actually* did walk some more in order to interpret the other actions described in the narrative. Implied actions are often passive constructions that describe a state of the world that could only be true

Label Set	κ					Labels		
Extended	0.582	¬ Story	Orient	Action	Eval	Local Context	Implied Action	Consequence
Stative	0.597	¬ Story	Orient	Action	Eval	Stative	Stative	Stative
L&W	0.630	¬ Story	Orient	Action	Eval	Orient	Action	Eval

Table 1: The extended L&W label categories and two reduced hierarchical mappings.

if an action had taken place. For example: *We were at the convention center in about 10 minutes.*

STATIVE-CONSEQUENCE is a category that describes the state of the world that has resulted as a consequence of an action, but does not directly evaluate the goals, intentions or desires of the participants. For example, clause 23 in Fig. 1.

Using this extended label set we were able to achieve an inter-annotator agreement between the 3 annotators of 0.582 using Fleiss' κ on assigning categories to clauses. We also mapped the full set of labels to a smaller subsets to see if the finer grained distinctions helped improve reliability on more coarse grained labeling schemes. The extended labels we included were generally different types of stative descriptions of the world, which were all mapped to a single category for the *Stative* label set. Finally, we mapped each extended label to an original L&W category that we thought best fit the original definitions. When mapping back to these reduced label sets we were able to increase the κ to 0.597 for the stative set and 0.630 for the original L&W categories. This result indicates that we can achieve higher reliability by ensuring that the annotators think carefully about particular kinds of distinctions between different stative clauses.

Gold standard labels were selected based on a simple majority of the annotator assignments. When no annotators agreed on a label, one of the selected labels was chosen at random. Once completed there were 424 action clauses, 702 evaluations, 26 not stories, 306 orientation, 17 stative consequences, 12 implied actions and 115 local contexts. Note that EVALUATION and ORIENTATION clauses that would not be distinguished from ACTION by previous work constitute two thirds of the clauses.

4 Experiments

The triply annotated dataset described above was used as training and test data for experiments on learning to automatically label narrative clauses. 40 narratives were randomly selected to be used as training and development data and the remaining 10 narratives for test data. The average story in the training data had 29.3 clauses with the shortest story consisting of 4 and the maximum consisting of 100. The average story in the test data had 43 clauses with the shortest story consisting of 4 and the maximum consisting of 114.

Feature Set	Description
Linguistic	Parts of Speech, Number of Characters in post, Average Word Length, Unigrams, Bigrams
Lexical and Sentiment Categories	LIWC counts and frequencies, negation
Story Position	First Clause, Last Clause, Position in the story binned into ten story regions

Table 2: Feature Sets for L&W Classification.

To derive feature representations of each type of narrative clause we started with the features presented in (Rahimtoroghi et al., 2013). We refined these by examining L&W's descriptions of distinguishing features of each category. Table 2 summarizes the features we automatically extracted from all narrative clauses in the weblogs.

First, we used the Stanford Parser to distinguish independent and dependent clauses and kept track separately of features that occurred in both types of clause. This is because L&W state that the unit of analysis should be an independent clause with its subordinate clauses, but we felt that these were exactly the cases that often caused difficulties during annotation. However distinguishing between the features occurring in the two clause types would allow us to determine if and when the features of the subordinate clause were relevant or more informative for automatic classification. Then, within both dependent and independent clauses, we distinguished the part-of-speech of the main verb (POS), whether the clause contained a negation (Negate), lexical semantic categories from LIWC (Pennebaker et al., 2001), dependency relations (DEP), lexical unigrams (STEM), and whether the verb was one of a class of verbs that are likely to be stative.

We also developed a set of features describing the relative position of the clause in the story (BinPosition, FirstClause, LastClause), because different story regions are often associated with different

Feature	Gain	Act	Ori	Eval	¬
POS:IND-VBD	0.128	**0.084**	0.002	0.031	0.011
BinPosition0	0.076	0.017	**0.042**	0.014	0.003
FirstClause	0.044	0.010	**0.019**	0.011	0.003
POS:IND-VBZ	0.042	**0.029**	0.008	0.002	0.003
IND-Negate	0.040	0.025	0.000	**0.013**	0.002
IND-Copula	0.039	**0.030**	0.004	0.005	0.001
POS:IND-:	0.036	0.001	0.000	0.002	**0.033**
IND-FirstPerson	0.035	**0.017**	0.004	0.002	0.013
IND-LIWC_Motion	0.034	**0.021**	0.003	0.006	0.004
POS:IND-VBP	0.033	**0.023**	0.001	0.007	0.002

Table 3: The 10 most highly correlated features with each label and cumulatively over all the labels using mutual information and information gain.

clause types. For example, in Fig. 1 and Fig. 4, the beginning of the story contains more ORIENTATION clauses, while ACTION clauses are concentrated in the middle of the story. The EVALUATION clauses typically occur part-way through the story where they provide the narrator's reaction to story events. See Table 2.

In total there were 3,510 unique binary valued features extracted from our training dataset. We used mutual information to find the features that had the highest correlation with each category and the information gain over all the labels. The 10 highest valued features are in Table 3, e.g. the top feature is when the part-of-speech (POS) of the main verb in the independent clause (IND) is past tense (VBD).

This feature encoding was used for machine learning experiments with classification algorithms from Mallet (McCallum, 2002): Naive Bayes (NB) (Witten and Frank, 2005), Confidence Weighted Linear Classifier (CWLC) (Dredze et al., 2008), Maximum Entropy (ME)(Witten and Frank, 2005) and a sequential classifier (CRF) (Lafferty et al., 2001).

5 Evaluation and Results

We evaluate the performance of our classifiers with experiments using the 50 annotated stories. Using the 40 stories in the training set we calculated the information gain for each feature (see Table 3). For each subset of the highest valued features (in the range of 2^2-2^{12}), we performed a 10-fold cross-validation on the training data and assessed the performance of each classifier to find the right number of features. Within each fold of the cross-validation we also perform a simple grid search for the optimal hyper-parameters of the model (e.g., the prior in the ME and CRF models) using only the data within the training fold.

The feature selection experimental results are shown in Table 4. We report the optimal number of features and the corresponding macro F-score, weighted by the relative frequency of each category, for each algorithm and label set. For all algorithms, performance increases for label sets with higher levels of abstraction. The Naive Bayes and CRF models perform better with a small subset of the features, while the ME and CWLC algorithms use a much larger subset. Surprisingly the sequential classifier has the lowest F-score and Naive Bayes performs the best. A * indicates a significant improvement over CRF at $p < 0.05$ using a two-sided t-test. No other differences were significant.

	Extended		Stative		L&W	
Classifier	#	F1	#	F1	#	F1
CRF	2^7	0.61	2^9	0.61	2^7	0.65
CWLC	2^{11}	0.67	2^{11}	0.68*	2^{11}	0.73*
ME	2^{11}	0.67	2^{10}	0.68*	2^{10}	0.73*
NB	2^9	0.68*	2^9	0.70*	2^{10}	0.76*

Table 4: The optimal number of features found for each model and the average F-score obtained using a 10-fold cross-validation on the training data.

Using the optimal number of features obtained from this search we trained a model for each algorithm using the entire training dataset and selecting the hyper-parameters as before. We applied these models to the unseen test data and evaluated the performance of each classifier as applied to the entire set of clauses and to individual narratives.

We first computed the precision, recall and F-score aggregated over all the clauses in the test set. Table 5 summarizes the results for each classifier and label set. The left hand side of the table shows the macro precision, recall and F-score weighted by the relative frequency of each label. The right hand side of the table shows the F-score of each individual label separately. On this evaluation, Naive Bayes outperforms all other methods on all label sets. Overall, precision and recall are relatively balanced achieving a maximum F-score of 0.689 when the labels are mapped back to the original L&W categories. The CRF does surprisingly well considering its poor performance during the feature selection search. The classifiers perform the poorest on orientation clauses and the best on evaluation clauses.

As mentioned above, the annotation task is highly subjective, requiring interpreting the narrative and the author's intention, which prevents us from obtaining high levels of inter-rater agreement. Because of the noise in the annotations, the standard evalua-

		Overall				Per Label						
						L&W				Stative		
Label Set	Model	Prec	Rec	F1	κ	Ori	Eva	Act	$\neg$	Imp	Loc	Con
Extended	CRF	0.568	0.626	0.593	0.419	**0.532**	0.727	0.651	0.000	0.000	0.041	0.000
	CWLC	0.567	0.616	0.582	0.398	0.377	0.763	0.612	0.000	0.000	0.087	0.000
	ME	0.597	0.649	0.614	0.450	0.496	0.767	**0.667**	0.000	0.000	0.085	0.000
	NB	**0.625**	**0.656**	**0.623**	**0.459**	0.478	**0.781**	0.650	0.000	0.000	**0.174**	0.000
Stative	CRF	0.563	0.591	0.574	0.370	0.412	0.695	0.628	0.000		**0.235**	
	CWLC	0.572	0.621	0.587	0.403	0.417	0.760	0.614	0.000		0.077	
	ME	0.610	0.644	0.611	0.441	0.464	0.759	0.673	0.000		0.118	
	NB	**0.650**	**0.667**	**0.638**	**0.477**	**0.496**	**0.779**	**0.676**	0.000		0.226	
L&W	CRF	0.650	0.665	0.656	0.468	0.556	0.742	0.640	0.000			
	CWLC	0.624	0.647	0.632	0.424	0.480	0.747	0.609	0.000			
	ME	0.681	0.700	0.688	**0.517**	**0.580**	**0.780**	0.670	0.000			
	NB	**0.687**	**0.705**	**0.689**	0.514	0.565	**0.780**	**0.687**	0.000			

Table 5: The performance of each of classifier on the test set when all clauses are aggregated together.

Agreement	Total #	Prec	Rec	F1	κ	Ori	Eva	Act	$\neg$
1 of 3	15	0.333	0.400	0.339	0.069	0.000	0.625	0.333	0.000
2 of 3	146	0.597	0.610	0.580	0.405	0.472	0.700	0.622	0.000
3 of 3	269	0.770	0.773	**0.767**	0.607	0.667	0.824	0.746	0.000
All	430	0.687	0.705	0.689	0.514	0.565	0.780	0.687	0.000
Adjusted	430	0.646	0.660	0.643	0.447	0.516	0.745	0.623	0.000

Table 6: Performance measures for different levels of agreement among the annotators.

tion metrics may hide information about the ability of the classifiers to learn from our feature set. For example, the best performing classifier (NB) incorrectly labeled 127 clauses out of 430 possible in the test set. However, 44 of these errors agreed with at least one annotator, but were counted as entirely incorrect in the previous evaluations.

To address these concerns we also evaluated the performance of the the best performing classifier based on the level of agreement of each instance using two different approaches. See Table 6. The first approach was inspired by the approach in (Louis and Nenkova, 2011) where the clauses in the test set are binned based on the number of annotators who agreed with the gold standard label. The performance is then calculated for each bin. The first three rows of Table 6 show the performance for the different levels of agreement in the dataset. There were only 15 clauses in the test set where there was no agreement at all. It is unsurprising that when the annotators could not agree on a label the system performed near chance levels. However, **when all three annotators agreed on the gold standard label the F-score improved to 0.767**. As a comparison, the F-score of the entire test set was 0.689 as shown in the row labeled *All*.

Our second approach is based on the proposal of Tetreault et al. (Tetreault et al., 2013). They introduce a modification to the standard precision, recall and F-scores that takes into account the level of agreement of each instance, where the values of true-positives and false-negatives are assigned fractional counts based on the proportion of annotators who assigned that label. The final row of Table 6 provides the results using these adjusted values.

Label Set	Model	Min	Max	Mean $\pm$ CI
Extended	CRF	**0.333**	**0.763**	0.540 $\pm$ 0.080
	CWLC	0.276	**0.763**	**0.582** $\pm$ 0.099
	ME	**0.333**	0.753	0.572 $\pm$ 0.088
	NB	**0.333**	0.741	0.573 $\pm$ 0.093
Stative	CRF	0.298	**0.762**	0.521 $\pm$ 0.099
	CWLC	**0.345**	0.758	**0.591** $\pm$ 0.090
	ME	0.333	0.753	0.562 $\pm$ 0.098
	NB	0.333	0.758	0.582 $\pm$ 0.088
L&W	CRF	0.333	0.837	0.609 $\pm$ 0.097
	CWLC	**0.458**	**0.877**	**0.658** $\pm$ 0.081
	ME	0.333	0.830	0.649 $\pm$ 0.095
	NB	0.333	0.851	0.647 $\pm$ 0.096

Table 7: Summary statistics of the F-score, with 95% confidence intervals, when evaluating stories.

We also investigated the performance of the classifiers when evaluating each story separately. Table 7 summarizes these results. Each classifier was applied to the clauses of the 10 narratives in the test set and the F-score was computed for each narrative individually. The table shows the minimum, maximum and average F-score with 95% confidence in-

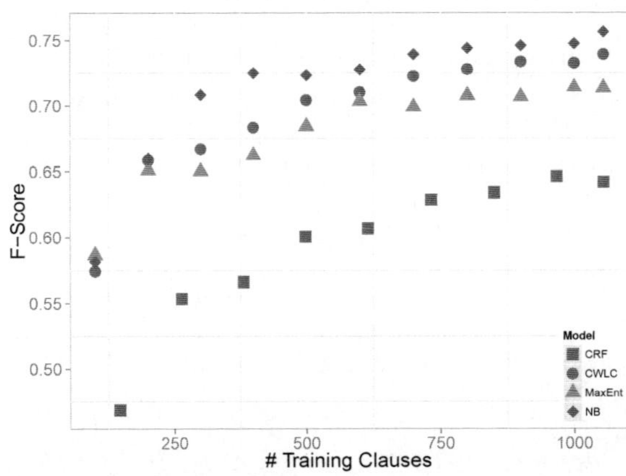

Figure 2: Learning curves of the Naive Bayes classifier using the optimal number of features.

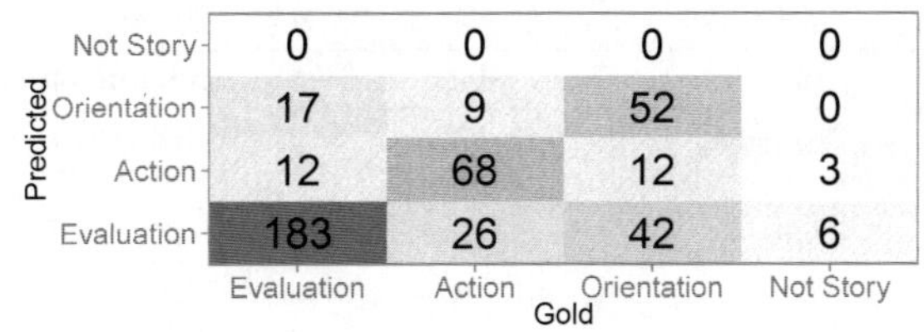

Figure 3: Confusion matrix for the best classifier.

tervals over the 10 narratives.

The CWLC performed the best on this test and the performance of all the algorithms generally improved using the higher-level label sets. The results also show that there is a high variance in performance between stories, with a minimum F-score of 0.458 and a maximum of 0.877 for the CWLC on the L&W label set. This indicates that some clauses are ambiguous and difficult to label, but also that some *stories* are more difficult to classify.

To assess whether more annotated data could improve performance, we ran a series of learning curves in Fig. 2. Only the training data was used for these experiments. The curves were created by randomly sampling 90% of the data for training and 10% for testing. A model was trained, using the same process as above, on successively larger subsets of the data and applied to the 10% held out clauses. This process was repeated 10 times and the mean F-Score is reported. In nearly all cases, the performance of classifiers is still increasing when all of the data is used indicating that we have not exhausted the expressive power of our features and more annotated data would be useful. However, we also see we can reach about 93% of our maximum performance with only a few hundred examples. We plan to increase the size of our annotated data set in future work.

5.1 Error Analysis

Our results to date indicate that we achieve an overall F-score of 0.689, and that our classifiers are most accurate for the *evaluation* and *action* categories. See Table 6. Fig. 3 presents a confusion matrix showing the frequency of predicted labels against the gold standard labels for the Naive Bayes classifier on the L&W label set. With the exception of *not story* there are cases of confusion between all categories. However, in the vast majority of cases both action and orientation are confused with evaluation and the classifier overpredicts evaluation.

We also categorized errors for the Naive Bayes classifier into the the 4 sources of errors in the predictions shown in Table 8. The most common errors involved clauses with lexical INDICATORS that are highly correlated with one category, but in the context and interpretation of the story actually function as a different type. For example, **unfortunately**, **could** and **n't** are all strong indicators of evaluation, but in this case the primary function of the clause is to set the scene for the rest of the story, i.e., orientation. The interpretation of these clauses is clear to a human, despite the lexical items misleading the classifier.

Another source of error is when the function of the clause in the narrative is ambiguous (PURPOSE in Table 8). While there may be some misleading lexical indicators in these clauses, there were often no strongly correlated words, such as the adjectives and modal verbs in EVALUATIONS. The distinction in these cases is that the primary function of the clause within the story is unclear, even to a human reader. Unsurprisingly, most of the examples in this category had low inter-rater agreement.

Some of the clauses contain figurative language or complex constructions that require a significant amount of world knowledge and INFERENCE to interpret. For example, understanding the INFERENCE clause in Table 8 requires recognizing the metaphor about rabbit food in order to identify the subjective evaluation the narrator is making.

There are also cases of clauses that contain MULTIPLE categories, at least partially because of the granularity of our segmentation. In the example in Table 8 a new character, Alejandrio, is introduced and a rising action is described, trekking to the waterfall.

Error Type	Freq	Gold	Pred	Example
Indicators	57	Ori	Eva	So, **unfortunately** I **couldn't** make the Gamesindustry.biz party tonight.
Purpose	20	Ori	Eva	I know it is a remarkable haircut because on the way home a handsome young Moroccan man nearly died to tell me how beautiful I was.
Inference	6	Eva	Ori	That's that rabbit food that all of those Northeastern Kerry voters...
Multiple	4	Act	Ori	We trekked to a waterfall in the park with the help of Alejandrio a 65 year old Honduran guy who not only walked quicker than us but also carried all the water.
Unclear	39	Ori	Eva	We have diners out east,
Not Story	7	Not	Act	scroll down to the Hobbit post,

Table 8: Several common sources of errors with a prototypical example.

Our annotation guidelines instructed us to prefer actions in these types of clauses, however, both ORIENTATION and ACTION are present in this situation.

There were also 39 clauses that were labeled incorrectly that had no clear reason (UNCLEAR) for being mislabelled. We also explicitly excluded the 7 clauses marked not part of the story.

The types of errors described above are not mutually exclusive and in some cases are causally related. For example, the purpose of a clause may be ambiguous because it contains conflicting lexical indicators. Similarly, a clause containing multiple categories will likely have strong lexical indicators from each of these categories so that the classification algorithms cannot disambiguate among possible labels. This might be improved by more data, more sophisticated semantic features, or possibly an analysis focused on discourse relations, such as those in the PDTB (Louis et al., 2010; Prasad et al., 2008), or Elson's STORY INTENTION GRAPH (Rishes et al., 2013; Elson and McKeown, 2010; Elson, 2012).

6 Discussion

This paper describes work on categorization of narrative clauses based on Labov & Waletzky's theory of oral narrative, applied to personal narratives written by ordinary people. We show that we can automatically classify narrative clauses with these categories achieving an overall F-score of 0.689, which is substantially higher than a random (0.250) or majority class (0.437) baseline, which increases to an F-score of .767 on the cases where all three annotators agreed. The learning curves plotted in Fig. 2 clearly suggest that more training data would be beneficial before we investigate more complex features and learning algorithms.

We believe the ability to automatically perform this type of simple narrative analysis will enable and improve many other types of deeper narrative understanding (Rahimtoroghi et al., 2014; Hu et al., 2013). For example, causal and temporal relationship extraction methods that focus only on clauses in the same *action* sequence be more accurate, because they exclude disconnected events from the orientation or evaluation sections. This type of analysis will also enable new methods for learning attitudes and values of societal groups based on the different affective evaluations that are provided in response to action clauses.

Our results also highlight several properties of the data. Performance is different for results by story rather than over all clauses. This indicates that some stories are more difficult to classify than others and that ambiguous clauses are not uniformly distributed but are likely to be correlated with particular authors or writing styles. In other work, we have started to investigate whether we can automatically rate the temporal coherence of personal narratives (Ryan et al., 2014). We can use this to identify stories with utterances that are likely to be difficult to classify because of the poor quality of the narrative input. These cases are unlikely to have usable narrative structure.

Acknowledgments

This research was supported by NSF Grants IIS #1002921 and IIS #123855. The content of this publication does not necessarily reflect the position or policy of the government, and no official endorsement should be inferred.

Appendix A

See Fig. 4 for an additional example labelled with L&W Categories.

#	Category	Story Clause
1	Abstract	Today was a very eventful work day.
2	Orientation	Today was the start of the G20 summit.
3	Orientation	It happens every year
4	Orientation	and it is where 20 of the leaders of the world come together to talk about how to run their governments effectively and what not.
5	Orientation	Since there are so many leaders coming together their are going to be a lot of people who have different views on how to run the government they follow so they protest.
6	Orientation	This week things started alright and on schedule.
7	Action	There was a protest that happened along the street where I work
8	Action	and at first it looked peaceful until a bunch of people started rebelling
9	Action	and creating a riot.
10	Action	Police cars were burned
11	Action	and things were thrown at cops.
12	Orientation	Police were in full riot gear to alleviate the violence.
13	Action	As things got worse tear gas and bean bag bullets were fired at the rioters
14	Action	while they smash windows of stores.
15	Evaluation	And this all happened right in front of my store
16	Evaluation	which was kind of scary
17	Evaluation	but it was kind of interesting
18	Coda	since I've never seen a riot before.

Figure 4: A personal narrative about a protest, with narrative categories of Labov & Waletzky, 1967.

References

Michael Bamberg. 2006. Stories: Big or small: Why do we care? *Narrative inquiry*, 16(1):139–147.

Brandon Beamer and Roxana Girju. 2009. Using a bigram event model to predict causal potential. In *Computational Linguistics and Intelligent Text Processing*, p. 430–441. Springer.

Jennifer G Bohanek, Kelly A Marin, and Robyn Fivush. 2008. Family narratives, self, and gender in early adolescence. *The Journal of Early Adolescence*, 28(1):153–176.

Jerome Bruner. 1991. The narrative construction of reality. *Critical Inquiry*, 18:1–21.

Kevin Burton, Akshay Java, and Ian Soboroff. 2009. The ICWSM 2009 spinn3r dataset. In *Proc. of the Third Annual Conf. on Weblogs and Social Media.*

N. Chambers and D. Jurafsky. 2009. Unsupervised learning of narrative schemas and their participants. In *Proc. of the 47th Annual Meeting of the ACL*, p. 602–610.

Quang Xuan Do, Yee Seng Chan, and Dan Roth. 2011. Minimally supervised event causality identification. In *Proc. of the Conf. on Empirical Methods in Natural Language Processing*, p. 294–303.

Mark Dredze, Koby Crammer, and Fernando Pereira. 2008. Confidence-weighted linear classification. In *Proc. of the 25th international conference on Machine learning*, p. 264–271. ACM.

D.K. Elson and K.R. McKeown. 2010. Building a bank of semantically encoded narratives. In *Proc. of the Seventh International Conf. on Language Resources and Evaluation (LREC 2010).*

David K Elson. 2012. Detecting story analogies from annotations of time, action and agency. In *Proc. of the LREC 2012 Workshop on Computational Models of Narrative, Istanbul, Turkey.*

Robyn Fivush and Katherine Nelson. 2004. Culture and language in the emergence of autobiographical memory. *Psychological Science*, 15(9):573–577.

Robyn Fivush, Jennifer G Bohanek, and Marshall Duke. 2005. The intergenerational self: Subjective perspective and family history. *Individual and collective self-continuity. Mahwah, NJ: Erlbaum.*

R.J. Gerrig. 1993. *Experiencing narrative worlds: On the psychological activities of reading.*

Andrew Gordon and Reid Swanson. 2009. Identifying personal stories in millions of weblog entries. In *Third International Conf. on Weblogs and Social Media, Data Challenge Workshop.*

Andrew Gordon, Cosmin Bejan, and Kenji Sagae. 2011. Commonsense causal reasoning using millions of personal stories. In *Twenty-Fifth Conf. on Artificial Intelligence (AAAI-11).*

Amit Goyal, Ellen Riloff, and Hal Daumé III. 2010. Automatically producing plot unit representations for narrative text. In *Proc. of the 2010 Conf. on Empirical Methods in Natural Language Processing*, p. 77–86.

Arthur C Graesser, Murray Singer, and Tom Trabasso. 1994. Constructing inferences during narrative text comprehension. *Psychological review*, 101(3):371.

T. Habermas and S. Bluck. 2000. Getting a life: the emergence of the life story in adolescence. *Psychol Bull*, 126(5):748–69.

Zhichao Hu, Elahe Rahimtoroghi, Larissa Munishkina, Reid Swanson, and Marilyn A Walker. 2013. Unsupervised induction of contingent event pairs from film scenes. In *Proc. of Conf. on Empirical Methods in Natural Language Processing*, p. 370–379.

W. Labov and J. Waletzky. 1967. Narrative analysis: Oral versions of personal experience. In J. Helm, ed., *Essays on the Verbal and Visual Arts*, p. 12–44.

W. Labov. 1997. Some further steps in narrative analysis. *Journal of narrative and life history*, 7:395–415.

John Lafferty, Andrew McCallum, and Fernando CN Pereira. 2001. Conditional random fields: Probabilistic models for segmenting and labeling sequence data.

Wendy G Lehnert. 1981. Plot units and narrative summarization. *Cognitive Science*, 5(4):293–331.

Annie Louis and Ani Nenkova. 2011. Automatic identification of general and specific sentences by leveraging discourse annotations. In *International Joint Conf. on Natural Language Processing*, p. 605–613.

Annie Louis, Aravind Joshi, Rashmi Prasad, and Ani Nenkova. 2010. Using entity features to classify implicit relations. In *Proc. of the 11th Annual SIGdial Meeting on Discourse and Dialogue*.

Mehdi Manshadi, Reid Swanson, and Andrew S Gordon. 2008. Learning a probabilistic model of event sequences from internet weblog stories. In *Proc. of the 21st FLAIRS Conf.* .

Dan P McAdams. 2003. Identity and the life story. *Autobiographical memory and the construction of a narrative self: Developmental and cultural perspectives*, 9:187–207.

Andrew Kachites McCallum. 2002. MALLET: a machine learning for language toolkit. http://mallet.cs.umass.edu.

K.C. McLean and A. Thorne. 2003. Adolescents' self-defining memories about relationships. *Developmental Psychology*, (39):635–645.

J. W. Pennebaker, M. E. Francis, and R. J. Booth. 2001. *Inquiry and Word Count: LIWC 2001*.

Rashmi Prasad, Nikhil Dinesh, Alan Lee, Eleni Miltsakaki, Livio Robaldo, Aravind Joshi, and Bonnie Webber. 2008. The Penn Discourse TreeBank 2.0. In *Proc. of 6th International Conf. on Language Resources and Evaluation (LREC 2008)*.

Michael W Pratt and Barbara H Fiese. 2004. *Families, Stories, and the Life Course: An Ecological Context.*

Elahe Rahimtoroghi, Reid Swanson, and Marilyn A. Walker. 2013. Evaluation, orientation, and action in interactive storytelling. In *Proc. of Intelligent Narrative Technologies 6*.

Elahe Rahimtoroghi, Thomas Corcoran, Reid Swanson, Marilyn A. Walker, Kenji Sagae, and Andrew S. Gordon. 2014. Minimal narrative annotation schemes and their applications. In *Proc. of Intelligent Narrative Technologies 7*.

Mehwish Riaz and Roxana Girju. 2010. Another look at causality: Discovering scenario-specific contingency relationships with no supervision. In *Semantic Computing (ICSC)*, p. 361–368. IEEE.

Elena Rishes, Stephanie Lukin, David K. Elson, and Marilyn A. Walker. 2013. Generating dierent story tellings from semantic representations of narrative. In *Int. Conf. on Interactive Digital Storytelling, ICIDS'13*.

James Owen Ryan, Marilyn A. Walker, and Noah Wardrip-Fruin. 2014. Toward recombinant dialogue in interactive narrative. In *7th Workshop on Intelligent Narrative Technologies*.

Nancy L. Stein, Tom Trabasso, and Maria D. Liwag. 2000. A goal appraisal theory of emotional understanding: Implications for development and learning. In M. Lewis and J. M. Haviland-Jones, ed, *Handbook of emotions (2nd ed.)*, p. 436–457.

Joel Tetreault, Martin Chodorow, and Nitin Madnani. 2013. Bucking the trend: improved evaluation and annotation practices for esl error detection systems. *Language Resources and Evaluation*, p. 1–27.

A. Thorne and V. Nam. 2009. The storied construction of personality. In Kitayama S. and Cohen D., ed, *Handbook of Cultural Psychology*, p. 491–505.

A. Thorne and L. A. Shapiro. 2011. Testing, testing: Everyday storytelling and the construction of adolescent identity. *Adolescent Vulnerabilities and Opportunities: Developmental and Constructivist Perspectives*, 38:117.

A. Thorne, N. Korobov, and E. M. Morgan. 2007. Channeling identity: A study of storytelling in conversations between introverted and extraverted friends. *Journal of research in personality*, 41(5):1008–1031.

Avril Thorne. 2004. Putting the person into social identity. *Human Development*, 47(6):361–365.

Ian H. Witten and Eibe Frank. 2005. *Data Mining: Practical machine learning tools and techniques*. Morgan Kaufmann, San Francisco, CA.

Evaluating a Spoken Dialogue System that Detects and Adapts to User Affective States

Diane Litman
Computer Science Dept. & LRDC
University of Pittsburgh
Pittsburgh, PA 15260 USA
dlitman@pitt.edu

Kate Forbes-Riley
Learning Research & Development Center
University of Pittsburgh
Pittsburgh, PA 15260 USA
forbesk@pitt.edu

Abstract

We present an evaluation of a spoken dialogue system that detects and adapts to user disengagement and uncertainty in real-time. We compare this version of our system to a version that adapts to only user disengagement, and to a version that ignores user disengagement and uncertainty entirely. We find a significant increase in task success when comparing both affect-adaptive versions of our system to our non-adaptive baseline, but only for male users.

1 Introduction

There is increasing interest in building dialogue systems that can detect and adapt to user affective states.[1] However, while this line of research is promising, there is still much work to be done. For example, most research has focused on detecting user affective states, rather than on developing dialogue strategies that adapt to such states once detected. In addition, when affect-adaptive dialogue systems have been developed, most systems detect and adapt to only a single user state, and typically assume that the same affect-adaptive strategy will be equally effective for all users.

In this paper we take a step towards examining these issues, by presenting an evaluation of three versions of an affect-adaptive spoken tutorial dialogue system: one that detects and adapts to both user disengagement and uncertainty, one that adapts to only disengagement, and one that doesn't adapt to affect at all. Our evaluation examines the impact of adapting to differing numbers of affective states on task success, and also examines interactions with user gender. We target disengagement and uncertainty because these were the most frequent affective states in prior studies with our system and their presence was negatively correlated with task success[2] (Forbes-Riley and Litman, 2011; Forbes-Riley and Litman, 2012). The detection of these and similar states is also of interest to the larger speech and language processing communities, e.g. (Wang and Hirschberg, 2011; Bohus and Horvitz, 2009; Pon-Barry and Shieber, 2011). Our results suggest that while adapting to affect increases task success compared to not adapting at all, the utility of our current methods varies with user gender. Also, we find no difference between adapting to one or two states.

2 Related Work

2.1 Adapting to Multiple Affective States

While prior research has shown that users display a range of affective states during spoken dialogue (e.g. (Schuller et al., 2009)), only a few dialogue systems have been developed that can adapt to more than one user affective state (e.g., (D'Mello et al., 2010; Acosta and Ward, 2011)). Furthermore, prior evaluations have compared adapting to at least one affective state to not adapting to affect at all, but have not examined the benefits of adapting to one versus multiple affective states.

In a first evaluation comparing singly and multiply affect-adaptive dialogue systems, we compared an existing system that adapted to uncertainty to a new version that also adapted to disengagement (Forbes-Riley and Litman, 2012). The multiply-adaptive system increased motivation for users with high disengagement, and reduced both uncertainty and the likelihood of continued disengagement. However, this evaluation was only conducted in a "Wizard-of-Oz" scenario, where a hidden human replaced the speech recognition, semantic analysis, and affect detection components of our dialogue system. We also conducted a post-

[1] We use the term *affect* to describe emotions and attitudes that impact how people communicate. Other researchers also combine concepts of emotion, arousal, and attitudes where emotion is not full-blown (Cowie and Cornelius, 2003).

[2] Our success measure is learning gain (Section 4).

hoc correlational (rather than causal) study, using data from an earlier fully-automated version of the uncertainty-adaptive system. Regressions demonstrated that using both automatically labeled disengagement and uncertainty to predict task success significantly outperformed using only disengagement (Forbes-Riley et al., 2012). However, if manual labels were instead used, only disengagement was predictive of learning, and adding uncertainty didn't help. This suggests that detecting multiple affective states might compensate for the noise that is introduced in a fully-automated system. In this paper we further investigate this hypothesis, by evaluating the utility of adapting to zero, one, or two affective states in a controlled experiment involving fully-automated systems.

2.2 Gender Effects in Dialogue

Differences in dialogue structure have been found between male and female students talking to a human tutor (Boyer et al., 2007). Studies have also shown gender differences in conversational entrainment patterns, for acoustic-prosodic features in human-human dialogues (Levitan et al., 2012) and articles in movie conversations (Danescu-Niculescu-Mizil and Lee, 2011). For dialogue systems involving embodied conversational agents, gender effects have been found for facial displays, with females preferring more expressive agents (Foster and Oberlander, 2006). When used for tutoring, females report more positive affect when a learning companion is used, while males are more negative (Woolf et al., 2010).

In our own prior work, we compared two uncertainty-adaptive and one non-adaptive versions of a wizarded dialogue system. Our results demonstrated that only one method of adapting to user uncertainty increased task success, and only for female users (Forbes-Riley and Litman, 2009). In this paper we extend this line of research, by adding an affective dialogue system that adapts to two rather than just one user state to our evaluation, and by moving from wizarded to fully-automated systems.

3 System, Experiment and Corpus

Our corpus consists of dialogues between users and three different versions of ITSPOKE (**I**ntelligent **T**utoring **SPOKE**n dialog system) (Forbes-Riley and Litman, 2011; Forbes-Riley and Litman, 2012). ITSPOKE is a speech-enhanced and otherwise modified version of the Why2-Atlas text-based qualitative physics tutor (VanLehn et al., 2002) that interacts with users using a system initiative dialogue strategy. User speech is first digitized from head-mounted microphone input and sent to the PocketSphinx recognizer.[3] The recognition output is then classified as (in)correct with respect to the anticipated physics content via semantic analysis (Jordan et al., 2007). Simultaneously, user uncertainty (UNC) and disengagement (DISE) are classified from prosodic, lexical and contextual features using two binary classification models (Forbes-Riley et al., 2012). All statistical components of the speech recognizer, the semantic analyzer, and the uncertainty and disengagement detectors were trained using prior ITSPOKE corpora.[4] Finally, ITSPOKE's response is determined based on the answer's automatically labeled (in)correctness, (un)certainty, and (dis)engagement and then sent to the Cepstral text-to-speech system,[5] as well as displayed on a web-based interface.

Our corpus was collected in an experiment consisting of three conditions (CONTROL, DISE, DISE+UNC), where ITSPOKE used a different method of affect-adaptation in each condition. The experiment was designed to compare the effectiveness of not adapting to user affect in ITSPOKE (CONTROL), adapting to user disengagement (DISE), and adapting to user disengagement as well as user uncertainty (DISE+UNC).[6]

In CONTROL, ITSPOKE's responses to user utterances were based on only the correctness of user answers. This version of the system thus ignored any automatically detected user disengagement or uncertainty. In particular, after each correct answer, ITSPOKE provided positive feedback then moved on to the next topic. After incorrect answers, ITSPOKE instead provided negative

[3]http://www.speech.cs.cmu.edu/pocketsphinx

[4]We have not yet performed the manual annotations needed to evaluate our current versions of these components in isolation. However, earlier versions of our affect detectors yielded FMeasures of 69% and 68% for disengagement and uncertainty, respectively, on par with the best performing affect detectors in the wider literature (Forbes-Riley and Litman, 2011; Forbes-Riley et al., 2012).

[5]http://www.cepstral.com

[6]We did not include an uncertainty-only condition (UNC) because in previous work we compared UNC versus CONTROL (Forbes-Riley and Litman, 2011) and DISE+UNC versus UNC (Forbes-Riley and Litman, 2012). Further details and motivation for all experimental conditions can be found in the description of our earlier Wizard-of-Oz experiment (Forbes-Riley and Litman, 2012).

feedback, then provided remediation tutoring before moving on to the next topic.

In DISE, two adaptive responses were developed to allow ITSPOKE's responses to consider user disengagement as well as the correctness of the user's answer;[7] however, this system version still ignored user uncertainty. In particular, after each disengaged+correct answer, ITSPOKE provided correctness feedback, a progress chart showing user correctness on prior problems and the current problem, and a brief re-engagement tip. After each disengaged+incorrect answer, ITSPOKE provided incorrectness feedback, a brief re-engagement tip, and an easier supplemental exercise, which consisted of an easy fill-in-the-blank type question to reengage the user, followed by remediation targeting the material on which the user disengaged and answered incorrectly. Examples of both types of adaptive responses are shown in A.1 and A.2 of Appendix A, respectively.

In DISE+UNC, ITSPOKE responded to disengagement as just described, but also adapted to uncertainty. In particular, after each uncertain+correct answer, ITSPOKE provided positive correctness feedback, but then added the remediation designed for incorrect answers with the goal of reducing the user's uncertainty. A dialogue excerpt illustrating this strategy is shown in A.3 of Appendix A. Note that when a single utterance is predicted to be both disengaged and uncertain, the DISE and UNC adaptations are combined.

Finally, our experimental procedure was as follows. College students who were native English speakers and who had no college-level physics read a short physics text, took a pretest, worked 5 physics problems (one problem per dialogue) with the version of ITSPOKE from their experimental condition, and took a posttest isomorphic to the pretest. The pretest and posttest were taken from our Wizard-of-Oz experiment and each contained 26 multiple choice physics questions. Our experiment yielded a corpus of 335 dialogues (5 per user) from 67 users (39 female and 28 male). Average pretest[8] and posttest scores were 50.4% and 74.7% (out of 100%), respectively.

4 Performance Analysis

Based on the prior research discussed in Section 2, we had two experimental hypotheses:

[7] Engaged answers were treated as in CONTROL.

[8] Pretest did not differ across conditions (p = .92).

Condition	Learning Gain		N
	Mean (%)	*Std Err*	
DISE+UNC	53.2	5.0	23
DISE	51.4	4.8	22
CONTROL	46.6	4.7	22
Gender	**Learning Gain**		**N**
Male	53.2	4.3	28
Female	47.6	3.6	39

Table 1: No effect of experimental condition (p=.62) or gender (p=.32) on learning gain.

Gender	Condition	Learning Gain		N
		Mn (%)	*Std Err*	
Male	DISE+UNC	58.8	8.4	7
	DISE	62.2	7.0	10
	CONTROL	38.7	6.7	11
Female	DISE+UNC	47.5	5.6	16
	DISE	40.6	6.4	12
	CONTROL	54.6	6.7	11

Table 2: Significant interaction between the effects of gender and condition on learning (p=.02).

H1: Responding to multiple affective states will yield greater task success than responding to only a single state (DISE+UNC > DISE), which in turn will outperform not responding to affect at all (DISE > CONTROL).

H2: The effects of ITSPOKE's affect-adaptation method and of gender will interact.

A two-way analysis of variance (ANOVA) was thus conducted to examine the effect of experimental condition (DISE+UNC, DISE, CONTROL) and user gender (Male, Female) on task success. As is typical in the tutoring domain, task success was computed as (normalized) learning gain: $\frac{posttest-pretest}{100-pretest}$.

Table 1 shows that although our results patterned as hypothesized when considering all users, the differences in learning gains were not statistically different across experimental conditions, F (2, 61) = .487, p = .617. There were also no main effects of gender, F (1, 61) = 1.014, p = .318.

In contrast, as shown in Table 2, there was a statistically significant interaction between the effects of user gender and experimental condition on learning gains, F (2, 61) = 4.141, p = .021. We thus tested the simple effects of condition within each level of gender to yield further insights.

For males, simple main effects analysis showed

that there were statistically significant differences in learning gains between experimental conditions (p = .042). In particular, males in the DISE condition had significantly higher learning gains than males in the CONTROL condition (p = .019). Males in the DISE+UNC condition also showed a trend for higher learning gains than males in the CONTROL condition (p = .066). However, males in the DISE and DISE+UNC conditions showed no difference in learning gains (p= .760).

For females, in contrast, simple main effects analysis showed no statistically significant differences in learning gains between any experimental conditions (p = .327).

In sum, hypothesis H1 regarding the utility of affect adaptations was only partially supported by our results, where (DISE+UNC = DISE) > CONTROL, and only for males. That is, adapting to affect was indeed better than not adapting at all, but only for males (supporting hypothesis H2). Contrary to H1, adapting to uncertainty over and above disengagement did not provide any benefit compared to adapting to disengagement alone (DISE+UNC = DISE), for both genders.

5 Discussion and Future Directions

Our results contribute to the increasing body of literature demonstrating the utility of adding fully-automated affect-adaptation to existing spoken dialogue systems. In particular, males in our two affect-adaptive conditions (DISE+UNC and DISE) learned more than males in the non-adaptive CONTROL. While our prior work demonstrated the benefits of adapting to uncertainty, the current results demonstrate the importance of adapting to disengagement either alone or in conjunction with uncertainty. However, we also predicted that DISE+UNC should outperform DISE, which was not the case. In future work we will examine other performance measures besides learning, and will manually annotate true disengagement and uncertainty in order to group students by amount of disengagement. Furthermore, since the motivating prior studies discussed in Section 2 were based on older versions of our system, annotation could identify problematic differences in training and testing data. A final potential issue is that the re-engagement tips do not convey exactly the same information.

Second, our results contribute to the literature suggesting that gender effects should be considered when designing dialogue systems. We see similar results as in our prior work; namely our current results continue to suggest that males don't benefit from adapting to their uncertainty as compared to ignoring it, but our current results also suggest that males do benefit from adapting to their disengagement. On the other hand, our current results suggest that females do not benefit from our disengagement adaptation and moreover, combining it with our uncertainty adaptation reduces the benefit of the uncertainty adaptation for them. This suggests the possibility of a differing affective hierarchy, in terms of how affective states may impact the learning process of the two genders differently. Our results yield an empirical basis for future investigations into whether adaptive system performance can improve by adapting to affect differently based on gender. However, further research is needed to determine more effective combinations of disengagement and uncertainty adaptations for both males and females, and to investigate whether gender differences might be related to other types of measurable user factors.

Acknowledgments

This work is funded by NSF 0914615. We thank S. Silliman for experimental support, and H. Nguyen, W. Xiong, and the reviewers for feedback.

References

J. C. Acosta and N. G. Ward. 2011. Achieving rapport with turn-by-turn, user-responsive emotional coloring. *Speech Communication*, 53(9-10):1137–1148.

D. Bohus and E. Horvitz. 2009. Models for multiparty engagement in open-world dialog. In *Proceedings of SIGdial*, pages 225–234, London, UK.

K. Boyer, M. Vouk, and J. Lester. 2007. The influence of learner characteristics on task-oriented tutorial dialogue. *Frontiers in Artificial Intelligence and Applications*, 158:365.

R. Cowie and R. R. Cornelius. 2003. Describing the emotional states that are expressed in speech. *Speech Communication*, 40(1-2):5–32.

C. Danescu-Niculescu-Mizil and L. Lee. 2011. Chameleons in imagined conversations: A new approach to understanding coordination of linguistic style in dialogs. In *Proceedings of the 2nd Workshop on Cognitive Modeling and Computational Linguistics*, pages 76–87.

S. D'Mello, B. Lehman, J. Sullins, R. Daigle, R. Combs, K. Vogt, L. Perkins, and A. Graesser.

2010. A time for emoting: When affect-sensitivity is and isn't effective at promoting deep learning. In *Intelligent Tutoring Systems Conference*, pages 245–254, Pittsburgh, PA, USA.

K. Forbes-Riley and D. Litman. 2009. A user modeling-based performance analysis of a wizarded uncertainty-adaptive dialogue system corpus. In *Proceedings Interspeech*, pages 2467–2470.

K. Forbes-Riley and D. Litman. 2011. Benefits and challenges of real-time uncertainty detection and adaptation in a spoken dialogue computer tutor. *Speech Communication*, 53(9–10):1115–1136.

K. Forbes-Riley and D. Litman. 2012. Adapting to multiple affective states in spoken dialogue. In *Proceedings of the 13th Annual Meeting of the Special Interest Group on Discourse and Dialogue*, SIGDIAL '12, pages 217–226.

K. Forbes-Riley, D. Litman, H. Friedberg, and J. Drummond. 2012. Intrinsic and extrinsic evaluation of an automatic user disengagement detector for an uncertainty-adaptive spoken dialogue system. In *Proceedings of the North American Chapter of the Association for Computational Linguistics: Human Language Technologies*, pages 91–102.

M. Foster and J. Oberlander. 2006. Data-driven generation of emphatic facial displays. *Proceedings of EACL*, 2006:353–363.

P. Jordan, B. Hall, M. Ringenberg, Y. Cui, and C.P. Rose. 2007. Tools for authoring a dialogue agent that participates in learning studies. In *Proc. Artificial Intelligence in Education (AIED)*, pages 43–50.

R. Levitan, A. Gravano, L. Willson, S. Benus, J. Hirschberg, and A. Nenkova. 2012. Acoustic-prosodic entrainment and social behavior. In *Proceedings of the North American Chapter of the Association for Computational Linguistics: Human Language Technologies*, pages 11–19.

H. Pon-Barry and S. Shieber. 2011. Recognizing uncertainty in speech. *EURASIP Journal on Advances in Signal Processing*.

B. Schuller, S. Steidl, and A. Batliner. 2009. The Interspeech 2009 emotion challenge. In *Proc. Interspeech*, pages 312–315, ISCA, Brighton, UK.

K. VanLehn, P. W. Jordan, C. Rosé, D. Bhembe, M. Böttner, A. Gaydos, M. Makatchev, U. Pappuswamy, M. Ringenberg, A. Roque, S. Siler, R. Srivastava, and R. Wilson. 2002. The architecture of Why2-Atlas: A coach for qualitative physics essay writing. In *Proc. Intl. Conf. on Intelligent Tutoring Systems*.

W. Wang and J. Hirschberg. 2011. Detecting levels of interest from spoken dialog with multistream prediction feedback and similarity based hierarchical fusion learning. In *Proc. SIGDIAL*, pages 152–161, Portland, Oregon.

B. Woolf, I. Arroyo, D. Cooper, W. Burleson, and K. Muldner. 2010. Affective tutors: Automatic detection of and response to student emotion. In *Advances in Intelligent Tutoring Systems*, pages 207–227. Springer.

Appendix A. Affect-Adaptive Examples.

A.1 After a Predicted Disengaged+Correct Turn

ITSPOKE: How does his velocity compare to that of his keys?

USER: same same same

ITSPOKE: Right. *[Feedback]* Here's a quick progress update. *[See Screenshot]* It might help to remember we will build on the topics we're discussing now. *[Re-engagement Tip]* Now let's see what happens after the man releases his keys. *[Next Topic]*

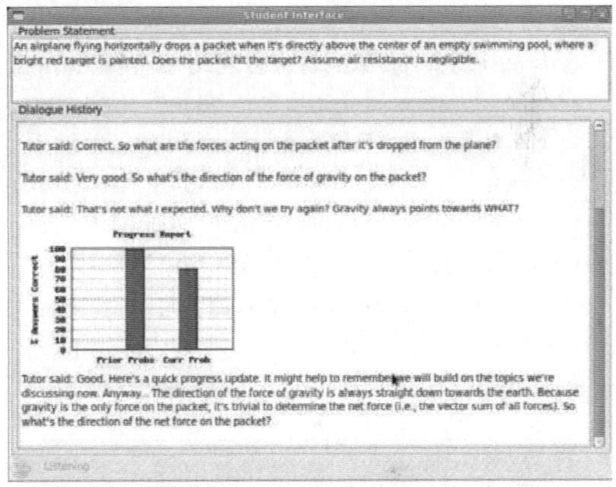

A.2 After Predicting Disengaged+Incorrect

ITSPOKE: How does his velocity compare to that of his keys?

USER: vertical

ITSPOKE: That doesn't sound right. *[Feedback]* Let's think about this a little more. *[Re-engagement Tip]* Since the man is holding his keys, they aren't moving relative to each other. So their velocities must be WHAT? *[Supplemental Exercise]*.

A.3 After a Predicted Uncertain+Correct Turn

ITSPOKE: What are the forces exerted on the man after he releases his keys?

USER: gravity???

ITSPOKE: Right. *[Feedback]* Gravity is the only force acting on the man. This force is also called the weight of the man. It's always present when an object is in earth's gravitational field. *[Remediation]*. So what's the direction of the force of gravity on the man ? *[Next Topic]*

Initiative Taking in Negotiation

Elnaz Nouri
University of Southern California
Los Angeles, CA, USA
nouri@ict.usc.edu

David Traum
USC Institute for Creative Technologies
12015 Waterfront Dr
Playa Vista, CA 90094, USA
traum@ict.usc.edu

Abstract

We examine the relationship between initiative behavior in negotiation dialogues and the goals and outcomes of the negotiation. We propose a novel annotation scheme for dialogue initiative, including four labels for initiative and response behavior in a dialogue turn. We annotate an existing human-human negotiation dataset, and use initiative-based features to try to predict both negotiation goal and outcome, comparing our results to prior work using other (non-initiative) features sets. Results show that combining initiative features with other features leads to improvements over either set and a majority class baseline.

1 Introduction

Negotiation is a complex interaction in which two or more parties confer with one another to arrive at the settlement of some matter, for example resolving a conflict or to share common resources. The parties involved in the negotiation often have non-identical preferences and goals that they try to reach. Sometimes the parties simply try to change a situation to their favor by haggling over price. In other cases, there can be a more complex trade-off between issues. Investigating these rich and complex interactions in a scientific manner has been important to researchers in different fields due to the significant implications and potential applications for business and profit making. Being a good negotiator is not a skill that all humans naturally have; therefore, this line of research can potentially be used to help humans become better negotiators. Computer agents will also benefit from the ability to understand human negotiators. There has been a fair amount of previous work in understanding negotiation dialogs, e.g., (Walton and McKersie, 1991; Baker, 1994); as well as agents who can engage in negotiation, e.g. (Jameson et al., 1994; Sidner, 1994; Kraus et al., 2008; Traum et al., 2008). In this paper we investigate the role that dialogue initiative plays in negotiation.

Negotiations can be characterized by both the goals that each negotiator is trying to achieve, as well as the outcomes. Even for negotiations that attempt to partition a set of goods, the participants may have differences in their valuation of items, and the negotiations can be very different if people are trying to maximize the total gain or their individual gain, or gain a competitive advantage over the other.

Negotiations between two people are usually mixed-initiative (Walker and Whittaker, 1990), with control of conversation being transferred from one person to another. To our knowledge, no previous studies have investigated the relationship between verbal initiative taking patterns and the goal or the outcome of the negotiation. We suspected that both of the mentioned characteristics of the negotiation (goal and outcome) might be correlated with different initiative-taking patterns. We used an existing negotiation dataset in order to study the mixed initiative patterns between the two parties in the negotiation. We describe this data set in Section 2, as well as previous work that attempted to predict outcome and goal, using other features (Nouri et al., 2013).

This paper makes the following contributions: a new annotation scheme for dialogue initiative is introduced in Section 3 and used to annotate the negotiation dataset. We then study the relationship between initiative taking patterns and the goal and outcome of the negotiation for the participants (Section 4).

2 Data

We make use of a previously collected and analyzed dataset in order to examine the relative contribution of initiative to problems of goal and outcome detection. We briefly describe the dataset and relevant prior work on this dataset.

The Farmers Market dataset (Carnevale, 2013) contains audio, video and transcription of 41 dyadic negotiation sessions. Participants were undergraduate students majoring in business. Each participant only took part in one negotiation session.

Before each negotiation session, the experimenter told participants that they were randomly assigned to represent one of two restaurants in the task. The owners of the two restaurants had asked the participants to go to the market and get some apples, bananas, lemons, peppers and strawberries. The payoff matrix for each restaurant and type of item is shown in Table 1. There were multiple items of each type available. Each participant was only given the pay-off matrix of his assigned restaurant and the total score of the negotiation for each participant was calculated by adding up the points for each item they received in the negotiation. The participants were told that they had 10 minutes to negotiate how to distribute the items on the table and reach an agreement. As an incentive, each participant could receive up to 50 dollars depending on the final points earned by each participant for his/her restaurant.

	R1	R2
Apples	1	3
Bananas	3	3
Lemons	0	0
Peppers	3	1
Strawberries	1	1

Table 1: The Payoff Matrix for each Restaurant

2.1 Goals

The study was originally designed to investigate negotiators' behavior when they have different goals in the negotiation. There were three types of instructions given to the participants. All the details were the same except for their goal in the negotiation.

- In "individualistic" instructions participants were told that their goal was to get at as many points as they could for themselves. An excerpt from an individualistic negotiation is shown in Table 13 in the Appendix.
- in "cooperative" instructions they were told that they should try to maximize the joint gain with the other side of the negotiation. An excerpt from a cooperative negotiation is shown in Table 11 in the Appendix.
- in "competitive" instructions they were told to try to get more points than the other party. An excerpt from a competitive negotiation is shown in Table 12 in the Appendix.

Out of the 41 interactions in the dataset 15 were competitive, 13 were individualistic and 13 were cooperative sessions.

2.2 Outcomes

The outcome of the negotiation in this case is measured based on the calculation of the scores corresponding to the items that each negotiator has received by the end of the negotiation. In order to make the prediction of outcome possible based on our small dataset, we labeled the calculated score for each participant with one of the three labels: H,E or L, showing whether the participant had received more, equal or fewer points than the other person.

The goal of the "competitive" instructions was to get a higher score. For cooperative negotiations, the relative score did not matter. For the individualistic goal, higher score is somewhat correlated with the goal, but not absolutely (what matters is only an individual high score, not the relation to the other partner). 17 negotiations resulted in equal final scores for the two parties and 24 with one side scoring more than the other side. Table 2 shows the average scores for each restaurant, across the three types of goals. The scores are on average higher in the cooperative negotiations than in the other two conditions.

Average score	**R1**	**R2**	**Joint Gain**
Cooperative	24.9	25.1	50
Competitive	23.7	23.6	47.3
Individualistic	25.5	22.5	48

Table 2: Average Score by Restaurant and Goal

The average score for individuals who score higher (labeled as H) than the other side of the negotiation was 26.46 whereas the average score for their counterparts (labeled as L) was 21.65. The average score for individuals who ended up in a tie (labeled as E) was 24.16.

2.3 Previous Work and Baseline System

This data set was previously used for various purposes but (Nouri et al., 2013) was most similar to our current work in that it also tried to predict the goal and outcome in the negotiation, using a different set of features, and a slightly different formulation of the problem. (Nouri et al., 2013) used multimodal features (such as acoustic features and sentiments of the turns) for this purpose. We use initiative-features to build our prediction models. In order to make a baseline classifier, we used the following automatically derivable features from (Nouri et al., 2013):

- The mean and standard deviation of acoustic features automatically extracted;
- The amount of silence and speaking time for each speaker;
- Sentiment (positive, negative) and subjectivity scores calculated for words and turns
- number of words, turns, words per turn and words related to the negotiation objects

We used only features that were easily and automatically derivable, excluding features from (Nouri et al., 2013) such as the number of offers and the number of rejections or acceptances.

3 Initiative Labeling

A common way of structuring dialogue is with Initiative-Response pairs, or IR units (Dahlbäck and Jönsson, 1998), which are also similar to adjacency pairs (Levinson, 1983), or simple exchange units (Sinclair and Coulthard, 1975). Several researchers have also proposed multiple levels of initiative. For example, (Whittaker and Stenton, 1988) had levels based on the type of utterance (commands, questions, assertions, and prompts). (Chu-Carroll and Brown, 1997) posit two levels of initiative: discourse initiative, attained by providing reasons for responses, and critiques of proposed plans, and task initiative, obtained by suggesting new tasks or plans. Linell et al. examine several factors, such as initiative vs response, strength of initiative, adequacy of response, scope and focality of response (Linell et al., 1988). They end up with an ordered set of six possible strengths of initiative. Each of these schemes is somewhat complicated by the fact that turns can consist of multiple basic elements.

Analyzing previous work, we can see that *initiative* breaks down into two distinct concepts. First there is providing unsolicited, or optional, or extra material, that is not a required response to a previous initiative. Second, there is the sense of putting a new discourse obligation (Traum and Allen, 1994) on a dialogue partner to respond. These two concepts often come together, such as for new questions or proposals that require some sort of response: they are both unsolicited and impose an obligation, which is why (Whittaker and Stenton, 1988) indicate that control should belong to the speaker of these utterances. However, it is also possible to have each one without the other. Statements can include new unsolicited material, without imposing an obligation to respond (other than the weak obligation to ground understanding of any contribution). Likewise, clarification questions impose new obligations on the other, but often do not contribute new material or are not optional, in that the responder can not reply appropriately without the clarification. For (Whittaker and Stenton, 1988), the issue of whether a question or assertion was a "response" would determine whether control went to the speaker or remained with a previous speaker. On the other hand, (Narayanan et al., 2000) call a response that includes unsolicited material "mixed-initiative" rather than "system initiative" for user responses that contain only prompted material.

Likewise, *response* can also be broken down into two related concepts. One concerns fulfilling obligations imposed by prior initiatives. To not do so could be considered rude and a violation of conversational norms in some cases. This is only relevant, if there is an existing initiative-related obligation as part of the conversational state. Another concept generalizes the notion of response to anything that contributes to the same topic and makes an effort to relate to prior utterances by the other party, whether or not it fulfills an obligation or whether there even is a pending obligation. This is like *relevance* in the sense of Sperber and Wilson (Sperber and Wilson, 1986) and Lascarides and Asher (Asher and Lascarides, 2003).

Our annotation scheme thus includes four labels, as indicated in Table 4. Each of the labels can either be present or absent from a dialogue

Time/Speaker	**Example Utterance**	**Labels (R,F,I,N)**
[1 : 58] Person 1:	Do you want to do just like one grab at a time? Or do you know how you want to divvy it up?	(-,-,I,N)
[2 : 13] Person 2:	Um, I'm just thinking.	(R,F,-,-)
[3 : 38] Person 1:	Do you want it? I'll take it. Um, do you want to do any trading?	(R,-,I,-)
[4 : 15] Person 2:	Um, how much is a banana for you?	(-,-,I,N)
[4 : 15] Person 1:	For me? A point, or two points. How much is the pepper worth?	(R,F,I,N)

Table 3: Sample Annotated Utterances

Label	**Description**
R	directly relates to prior utterance
F	fulfills a pending discourse obligation
I	imposes a discourse obligation
N	provides new material that is optional and not just fulfilling an obligation.

Table 4: Initiative Labels

segment. The annotation is done on each turn on the conversation. In general, a turn can consist of almost any combination of these four initiative labels (I,R,F,N). We thus treat each of these as an independent binary dimension, and code each turn as to which set of these labels it contains. Table 3 shows an example from the corpus with initiative annotations. More examples can be found in the Appendix, Tables 11, 12, and 13.

3.1 Inter Annotator Reliability

To assess the reliability of our annotations, approximately 10% of the dialogs (4 dialogs) were annotated by two annotators. The level of the agreement was then assessed using the Kappa statistic (Carletta, 1996; Siegel and Castellan, 1988). Table 5 shows the result of the assessment of the reliability of the annotations for the four annotation labels.[1] Based on this metric our results indicate that the annotators have reasonable level of agreement in labeling utterances with the I, F ,N labels, though there is less reliability for the "related" label. Further work is needed to clarify the degree of relation that should count and also whether relation refers just to the immediately prior turn or something further back. The remainder of the dialogues were annotated by one annotator.

[1]Chance agreement is the probability of agreement using the frequencies of each label, but applied randomly.

	R	**F**	**I**	**N**
kappa	0.36	0.64	0.66	0.73
actual agreement	0.76	0.83	0.83	0.86
chance agreement	0.62	0.52	0.49	0.50

Table 5: Inter-Annotator Reliability Assessment

3.2 Initiative Taking Patterns

Table 6 shows the average frequency of each initiative label for each negotiation goal. We can see that competitive dialogues have more turns that impose and fulfill obligations than the other conditions, while individualistic dialogues include a higher percentage of turns introducing new material.

Label	**R**	**F**	**I**	**N**
Cooperative	0.79	0.35	0.40	0.33
Competitive	0.82	0.38	0.47	0.34
Individualistic	0.82	0.34	0.39	0.40

Table 6: Comparison of the Relative Frequency of the Initiative Labels for Each Goal

Table 7 shows the relative frequency of initiative labels for the different outcome conditions. The higher scoring participants had a higher frequency of initiative-related turns (labels I and N), while their lower scoring partners had a higher frequency of responsive turns (R,F). Equal scoring participants tended to pattern closer to higher scoring participants, concerning responses, but closer to lower scoring participants, considering initiative.

3.3 Initiative Features

After the Initiative annotation was done, the following features were automatically extracted:

- the count of each label (I,F,R,N) per negotiation and per person

Label	R	F	I	N
H	0.80	0.35	0.47	0.38
E	0.81	0.35	0.40	0.34
L	0.84	0.38	0.43	0.36

Table 7: Comparison of the Relative Frequency of the Initiative Labels for Each Score Label

- the ratio, difference and absolute difference of the number of labels for each person against the number of labels for their negotiation counterpart
- the above measures normalized by the number of turns in dialog
- **Within-turn patterns** the number of all possible combinations of labels for each utterance. There are 16 possible combinations for the 4 types of labels that can be shown as tuples (R,F,I,N). Refer to Table 5 for examples.
- **Across-turn Patterns** the number of all possible sequences of labels across two adjacent turns. There are also 16 possible combinations capturing how often each label is followed by labels. For example, the feature (I,F) applies to all two-turn sequences where the first turn contains label I and the second contains label F, such as in the last two lines of Figure 3. We count the these features for the dialogue and for each speaker.

All of the above features were automatically extracted from the annotated dialogues. We examined four different spans of the dialogues, to investigate whether the most salient initiative information comes early in the dialogue or requires the full dialogue. We calculated features for the first quarter (q1), first half (q2), first three quarters (q3), and the whole negotiation (q4).

4 Prediction Models

We conducted experiments to recognize negotiation goal and score for each of the 82 negotiators. We made prediction models for recognizing the goal and outcome for each individual.For the prediction models, we compared the result of support vector machine (SVM- with the polynomial kernel function) classifier, Naive Bayes and Decision Tree. None of the classifiers outperformed the others on all cases, we are reporting the result of SVM classifier here. Considering the size of our dataset which consists of 82 samples (41 pairs of individuals) and the distribution of the samples in different classes, we decided to use the 10-fold cross validation paradigm for our prediction tasks. In splitting the dataset into the folds we controlled so that the participants from the same negotiation were not split across training and test sets. We trained and tested at the end of the each quarter of the negotiation.

We used three sets of features to make three prediction models for each task:

1. Non-initiative features from (Nouri et al., 2013), described in section 2.3. We refer to these non-initiative features as IS2013' from this point on.
2. Initiative features
3. All features combined.

We compare the performance of these models with two baseline prediction models: one that chooses one of the outcomes at random, and one that predicts the majority class for all instances. In the upcoming sections, we use q1, q2, q3 and q4 to refer to the ends of the first, second, third and the forth quarters of the negotiation (e.g. q3 includes all data from the first three quarters, but not the last).

4.1 Automatic Prediction of Goal

This task predicts whether the negotiators are following the cooperative, competitive or individualistic instructions. It is important to note that none of the features used require understanding of the content or a semantic analysis of the conversation. However, using these basic features it's possible to make the classification into the mentioned three classes with accuracy that is significantly higher than chance. The average accuracy of prediction at the four different points in the negotiation are shown in Table 8.

	q1	q2	q3	q4
Random	0.33	0.33	0.33 ♣	0.33 ♣
Majority	0.37	0.37	0.37 ♣	0.37
IS2013	0.41	0.34	0.40 ♣	0.48 $*\dagger$
Initiative	0.29 ♣	0.52 $*\dagger$♣	0.48 $*\dagger$	0.29 ♣
Combined	0.41	0.40	0.57 $*\dagger$	0.44 $*$

Table 8: Accuracy of the Prediction of Goal

We use the two-sided binomial test to measure the significance of the differences of the prediction models' performances. Table 8 and the upcoming Tables 9 and 10 use symbols to indicate the results of these significance tests. Symbols (∗),(†) and (♣) show which models' performances are significantly different from the random baseline, majority baseline or the "Combined" classifier respectively ($p < 0.05$).

The combined classifier is always better than both baselines, as well as the lower of classifiers for the IS2013 and Initiative features. In q3, where the two are close in performance, the combined classifier significantly outperforms both baselines and the IS2013 model. Note that except for q3, these numbers are lower than those reported by (Nouri et al., 2013). However the prior work did not ensure that both individuals in a negotiation were in the same training/test partition, and some features are the same for both participants. That work also made use of higher-level features, such as the offers, and final distributions of items.

4.2 Automatic Prediction of Outcome

In this task the goal is to predict how a participant in the negotiation is going to do in terms of the scores at the end of the negotiation. The model predicts whether the negotiator would score higher, lower or equal to the other player at the end of the different quarters of the negotiation. Results are shown in Table 9.

	q1	q2	q3	q4
Random	0.33	0.33	0.33	0.33 ♣
Majority	0.41	0.41	0.41	0.41
IS2013	0.43 ∗	0.34	0.23 ∗†♣	0.39
Initiative	0.37	0.35	0.32	0.39
Combined	0.38	0.40	0.41	0.4 6∗

Table 9: Accuracy of the Prediction of Outcome

Except for the combined model in q4, these models are not able to significantly outperform the baseline of selecting the random class (with equal likelihood). Results were also presented for outcome in (Nouri et al., 2013), however only the final quarter results are comparable, since that paper predicted interim quarter-end results rather than final results. Also, that work did not make sure that both participants in a negotiation were in the same training-test partitions, and used features related to the final deal, that are directly related to outcome.

Because the relative score was not important for cooperative negotiations, where both sides are just trying to maximize their combined points, we next examined outcome for the 28 pairs in individualistic and competitive conditions. Results are shown in table 10. The combined classifier outperforms all the other classifiers, starting from quarter 2. At the end of the negotiation(q4) the performance of this classifier is significantly better than all other models.

	q1	q2	q3	q4
Random	0.33	0.33 ♣	0.33 ♣	0.33 ♣
Majority	0.38	0.38	0.38	0.38 ♣
IS2013	0.39	0.36 ♣	0.36 ♣	0.34 ♣
Initiative	0.27	0.41	0.36 ♣	0.38 ♣
Combined	0.35	0.50 ∗	0.50 ∗	0.55 ∗†

Table 10: Accuracy of the Prediction of Outcome for Negotiations that are not Cooperative

5 Conclusion

We demonstrated how discourse initiatives in negotiation dialog can be used for automatically making predictions about other aspects of the negotiation such as the goals of the negotiators. Previous work has mostly focused on using nonverbal cues for accomplishing similar tasks but they have not used discourse features like initiatives. We also show that initiative features can give clues about the final outcome for the negotiators. Making such predictions are generally challenging tasks even for humans and require understanding of the content of the negotiations. From a dialog system's perspective our results show how more information can be derived about the users intentions and performance by analyzing their discourse behavior.

6 Future Work

The annotations of the initiative taking patterns are done manually at this point. Automatic labeling of the utterances with the initiative tags is our next step. We will use the labels in our dataset for learning how to automatically label new negotiation datasets. We think that HMM and HCRF methods due to their ability to capture the sequential and temporal aspect of the negotiation might be better methods for building the prediction models. We are interested in further analysis of the relationship between initiatives and other aspects of negotiation such as intentions and the use of language. We also want to measure the suitability of our annotation scheme for initiatives for other dialogue genres.

Acknowledgments

We like to thank Kristina Striegnitz, Christopher Wienberg, Angela Nazarian and David DeVault for their help with this work. The effort described here has been sponsored by the US Army. Any opinions, content or information presented does not necessarily reflect the position or the policy of the United States Government, and no official endorsement should be inferred.

References

Nicholas Asher and Alex Lascarides. 2003. *Logics of Conversation*. Cambridge University Press.

Michael Baker. 1994. A model for negotiation in teaching-learning dialogues. *Journal of artificial intelligence in education*.

Jean Carletta. 1996. Assessing agreement on classification tasks: the kappa statistic. *Computational linguistics*, 22(2):249–254.

Peter J Carnevale. 2013. *Audio/video recordings of bilateral negotiations over synthetic objects on a table that vary in monetary value*. Unpublished raw data.

Jennifer Chu-Carroll and Michael K. Brown. 1997. Tracking initiative in collaborative dialogue interactions. In *Proceedings of the Thirty-Fifth Meeting of the Association for Computational Linguistics*, pages 262–270. Association for Computational Linguistics.

Nils Dahlbäck and Arne Jönsson. 1998. A coding manual for the linköping dialogue model. unpublished manuscript.

Anthony Jameson, Bernhard Kipper, Alassane Ndiaye, Ralph Schäfer, Joep Simons, Thomas Weis, and Detlev Zimmermann. 1994. *Cooperating to be noncooperative: The dialog system PRACMA*. Springer.

Sarit Kraus, Penina Hoz-Weiss, Jonathan Wilkenfeld, David R Andersen, and Amy Pate. 2008. Resolving crises through automated bilateral negotiations. *Artificial Intelligence*, 172(1):1–18.

Stephen C. Levinson. 1983. *Pragmatics*. Cambridge University Press.

Per Linell, Lennart Gustavsson, and Päivi Juvonen. 1988. Interactional dominance in dyadic communication: a presentation of initiative-response analysis. *Linguistics*, 26(3):415–442.

Shrikanth Narayanan, Giuseppe Di Fabbrizio, Candace A. Kamm, James Hubbell, Bruce Buntschuh, P. Ruscitti, and Jerry H. Wright. 2000. Effects of dialog initiative and multi-modal presentation strategies on large directory information access. In *INTERSPEECH*, pages 636–639. ISCA.

Elnaz Nouri, Sunghyun Park, Stefan Scherer, Jonathan Gratch, Peter Carnevale, Louie Philippe Morency, and David Traum. 2013. Prediction of strategy and outcome as negotiation unfolds by using basic verbal and behavioral features. In *proceedings of the Interspeech conference*.

Candace L. Sidner. 1994. An artificial discourse language for collaborative negotiation. In *Proceedings of the Fourteenth National Conference of the American Association for Artificial Intelligence (AAAI-94)*, pages 814–819.

S. Siegel and N. J. Castellan. 1988. *Nonparametric statistics for the Behavioral Sciences*. McGraw-Hill, 2nd edition.

J. M. Sinclair and R. M. Coulthard. 1975. *Towards an analysis of Discourse: The English used by teachers and pupils*. Oxford University Press.

Dan Sperber and Deirdre Wilson. 1986. *Relevence: Communication and Cognition*. Harvard University Press.

David R. Traum and James F. Allen. 1994. Discourse obligations in dialogue processing. In *Proceedings of the 32nd Annual Meeting of the Association for Computational Linguistics*, pages 1–8.

David Traum, Stacy C Marsella, Jonathan Gratch, Jina Lee, and Arno Hartholt. 2008. Multi-party, multi-issue, multi-strategy negotiation for multi-modal virtual agents. In *Intelligent Virtual Agents*, pages 117–130. Springer.

Marilyn Walker and Steve Whittaker. 1990. Mixed initiative in dialogue: An investigation into discourse segmentation. In *Proceedings of the 28th annual meeting on Association for Computational Linguistics*, pages 70–78. Association for Computational Linguistics.

Richard E Walton and Robert B McKersie. 1991. *A behavioral theory of labor negotiations: An analysis of a social interaction system*. Cornell University Press.

Steve Whittaker and Phil Stenton. 1988. Cues and control in expert-client dialogues. In *Proceedings ACL-88*, pages 123–130.

Appendix: Sample Annotated Negotiations

The following tables show examples of each of the goal conditions with initiative labeling, using the scheme in Table 4.

Time	Speaker: Utterance		Labels (R,F,I,N)
[2 : 18]	2:	So what's, so what's everything worth to you?	(-,-,I,N)
[2 : 20]	1:	Um, so apples are three, bananas are three, strawberries are one, peppers are one, and lemons are nothing.	(R,F,-,-)
[2 : 33]	2:	Okay so for me peppers are three, bananas are three, and apples and strawberries are one.	(R,-,-,-)
[2 : 39]	1:	Lemons are zero.	(R,-,-,-)
[2 : 40]	2:	Yeah.	(R,-,-,)

Table 11: Sample Annotated Cooperative Negotiation

Time	Speaker: Utterance		Labels
[1 : 40]	2:	So, I think I need peppers and bananas for my restaurant.	(-,-,-,N)
[1 : 46]	1:	Okay. Um, well I really need. I want five apples and um, five bananas. Five apples and five bananas.	(R,-,I,N)
[2 : 05]	2:	Um, how about this: You take five apples, and I take five peppers and we can share the bananas.	(R,F,I,N)
[2 : 13]	1:	Okay. If I give you, if I give you five or if I give you, if we were to share the bananas, if I take three bananas, I'll give you three lemons.	(R,F,I,N)
[2 : 23]	2:	But we don't need lemons in our restaurant. We only use lemons for our store.	(R,F,-,N)
[2 : 27]	1:	Okay. So, um, I need bananas, like that's gonna be my top.	(R,-,-,N)

Table 12: Sample Annotated Competitive Negotiation

Time	Speaker: Utterance		Labels
[3 : 22]	2:	How about we do this. You take two of these, I take one, and since we have five here, I take three, you take two.	(-,F,I,N)
[3 : 37]	1:	I'm not interested in lemons at all. But I can give you...	(R,F,-,N)
[3 : 52]	2:	At my restaurant, one of our dessert dishes is with strawberries, so strawberries are very important to me.	(-,-,-,N)
[4 : 00]	1:	Okay. I'm willing to give you all the strawberries if you give me a banana and two apples. I'm also willing to give you these two.	(R,-,-,N)
[4 : 23]	2:	So you're going to give me those two?	(R,-,I,-)
[4 : 24]	1:	You can have everything on this side, I just want two apples and a banana.	(R,F,-,-)
[4 : 30]	2:	Two apples and a banana? Yeah, let's go.	(R,-,-,-)
[4 : 39]	1:	We have a deal.	(R,F,-,N)

Table 13: Sample Annotated Individualistic Negotiation

Knowledge Acquisition Strategies for Goal-Oriented Dialog Systems

Aasish Pappu **Alexander I. Rudnicky**
School of Computer Science
Carnegie Mellon University
{aasish, air}@cs.cmu.edu

Abstract

Many goal-oriented dialog agents are expected to identify slot-value pairs in a spoken query, then perform lookup in a knowledge base to complete the task. When the agent encounters unknown slot-values, it may ask the user to repeat or reformulate the query. But a robust agent can proactively seek new knowledge from a user, to help reduce subsequent task failures. In this paper, we propose knowledge acquisition strategies for a dialog agent and show their effectiveness. The acquired knowledge can be shown to subsequently contribute to task completion.

1 Introduction

Many spoken dialog agents are designed to perform specific tasks in a specified domain e.g., information about public events in a city. To carry out its task, an agent parses an input utterance, fills in slot-value pairs, then completes the task. Sometimes, information on these slot-value pairs may not be available in its knowledge base. In such cases, typically the agent categorizes utterances as non-understanding errors. Ideally the incident is recorded and the missing knowledge is incorporated into the system with a developer's assistance — a slow offline process.

There are other sources of knowledge: automatically crawling the web, as done by NELL [Carlson et al., 2010], and community knowledge bases such as Freebase [Bollacker et al., 2008]. These approaches provide globally popular slot-values [Araki, 2012] and high-level semantic contexts [Pappu and Rudnicky, 2013]. Despite their size, these knowledge bases may not contain information about the entities in a specific target domain. However, users in the agent's domain can potentially provide specific information on slot/values that are unavailable on the web, e.g., regarding a recent interest/hobby of the user's friend. Lasecki et al. [2013] have elicited natural language dialogs from humans to build NLU models for the agent and Bigham et al. [2010] have elicited answers to visual questions by integrating users into the system. One observation from this work is that both users and non-users can impart useful knowledge to system. In this paper we propose spoken language strategies that allow an agent to elicit new slot-value pairs from its own user population to extend its knowledge base. Open-domain knowledge may be elicited through text-based questionnaires from non-users of the system, but in a situated interaction scenario spoken strategies may be more effective. We address the following research questions:

1. *Can an agent elicit reliable knowledge about its domain from users?* Particularly knowledge it cannot locate elsewhere (e.g., on-line knowledge bases). Is the collective knowledge of the users sufficient to allow the agent to augment its knowledge through interactive means?

2. *What strategies elicit useful knowledge from users?* Based on previous work in common sense knowledge acquisition [Von Ahn, 2006, Singh et al., 2002, Witbrock et al., 2003], we devise spoken language strategies that allow the system to solicit information by presenting concrete situations and by asking user-centric questions.

We address these questions in the context of the EventSpeak dialog system, an agent that provides information about seminars and talks in an academic environment. This paper is organized as follows. In Section 2, we discuss knowledge acquisition strategies. In Section 3, we describe a user study on these strategies. Then, we present an evaluation on system acquired knowledge and finally we make concluding remarks.

Table 1: System initiated strategies used by the agent for knowledge acquisition in the EVENTSPEAK system.

StrategyType	Strategy	Example Prompt
QUERYDRIVEN	QUERYEVENT	I know events on campus. What do you want to know?
	QUERYPERSON	I know some of the researchers on campus.Whom do you want to know about?
PERSONAL	BUZZWORDS	What are some of the popular phrases in *your* research?
	FAMOUSPEOPLE	Tell me some well-known people in *your* research area
SHOW&ASK	TWEET	How would you describe this talk in a sentence, say a tweet.
	KEYWORDS	Give keywords for this talk in your own words.
	PEOPLE	Do you know anyone who might be interested in this talk?

2 Knowledge Acquisition Strategies

We posit three different circumstances that can trigger knowledge acquisition behavior: (1) initiated by expert users of the system [Holzapfel et al., 2008, Spexard et al., 2006, Lütkebohle et al., 2009, Rudnicky et al., 2010], (2) triggered by "misunderstanding" of the user's input [Chung et al., 2003, Filisko and Seneff, 2005, Prasad et al., 2012, Pappu et al., 2014], or (3) triggered by the system. They are described below:

QUERYDRIVEN. The system prompts a user with an open-ended question akin to "how-may-I-help-you" to learn what "values" of a slot are of interest to the user. This strategy does not ground user about system's knowledge limitations. However, it allows the system to acquire information (slot-value pairs) from user's input. The system can choose to respond to the input or ignore the input depending on its knowledge about the slot-value pairs in the input. Table 1 shows strategies of this kind i.e., QUERYEVENT and QUERYPERSON.

PERSONAL. The system asks a user about their own interests and people who may share those interests. This is an open-ended request as well, but the system expects the response to be confined to the user's knowledge about specific entities in the environment. BUZZWORDS and FAMOUSPEOPLE expects the user to provide values for the slots.

SHOW&ASK. The system provides a description of an event and asks questions to ground user's responses in relation to that event. E.g., given the title and abstract of a technical talk, the system asks the user questions about the talk. TWEET strategy is expected to elicit a concise description of the event, which eventually may help the agent to both summarize events for other users and identify keywords for an event. KEYWORDS strategy expects the user to explicitly supply keywords for an event. PEOPLE strategy expects the user to provide names of likely event participants.

We hypothesized that these strategies may allow the agent to learn new slot-value pairs that may help towards better task performance.

3 Knowledge Acquisition Study

We conducted a user study to determine reliability of the information acquired by the system. We performed this study using the EVENTSPEAK[1] dialog system, which provides information about upcoming talks and other events that might be of interest, and about ongoing research on campus. The system presents material on a screen and accepts spoken input, in a context similar to a kiosk.

The study evaluated performance of the seven strategies described above. For SHOW&ASK strategies, we had users respond regarding a specific event. We used descriptions of research talks collected from the university's website. We used a web-based interface for data collection; the interface presented the prompt material and recorded the subject's voice response. Testvox[2] was used to setup the experiments and Wami[3] for audio recording.

3.1 User Study Design

We recruited 40 researchers (graduate students) from the School of Computer Science, at Carnegie Mellon, representative of the user population for the EVENTSPEAK dialog system. Each subject responded to prompts from the QUERYDRIVEN, PERSONAL and SHOW&ASK strategies.

In the QUERYDRIVEN tasks, the QUERYEVENT strategy, the system responds to the user's query with a list of talks. The user's response is recorded, then sent to an open-vocabulary speech recognizer; the result is used as a query to a database of talks. The results are then displayed on the screen. The system applies the QUERYPERSON strategy in a similar way. In the PERSONAL tasks, the system applies the BUZZWORDS strategy to ask the user about popular keyphrases in their research

[1] http://www.speech.cs.cmu.edu/apappu/kacq
[2] https://bitbucket.org/happyalu/testvox/wiki/Home
[3] https://code.google.com/p/wami-recorder/

Figure 1: Time per Task for all strategies

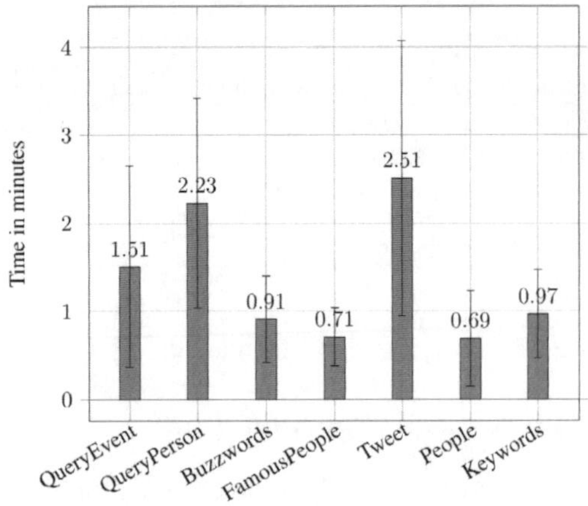

Figure 2: Time per Task vs Expertise

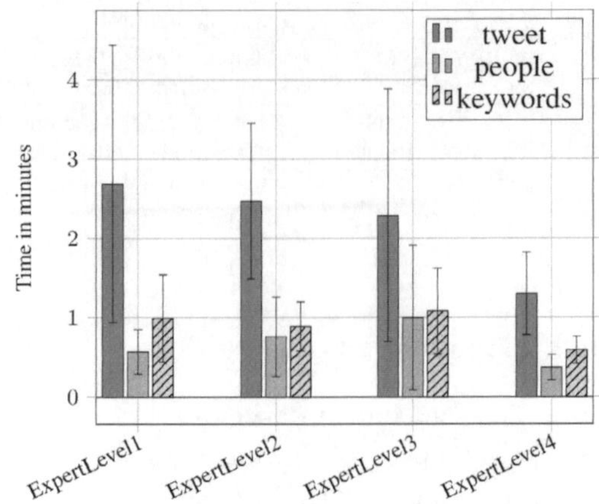

area. The system then asks about well-known researchers (FAMOUSPEOPLE) in the user's area.

In the SHOW&ASK tasks, we use two seminar descriptions per subject (in our pilot study, we found that people provide more diverse responses (in term of entities) in the SHOW&ASK based on the event abstract, compared to PERSONAL, QUERY-DRIVEN). We used a set of 80 research talk announcements (consisting of a title, abstract and other information). For each talk, the system used all three strategies viz., TWEET, KEYWORDS and PEOPLE. For the TWEET tasks, subjects were asked to provide a one sentence description. They were allowed to give a non-technical/high-level description if they were unfamiliar with the topic. For the PEOPLE task, subjects had to give names of colleagues who might be interested in the talk. For the KEYWORDS task, subjects provided keywords, either their own words or ones selected from the abstract.

Since the material is highly technical, we were interested whether the tasks are cognitively demanding for people who are less familiar with the subject of a talk. Therefore, users were asked to indicate their familiarity with a particular talk (research area in general) using a scale of 1–4: 4 being more familiar and 1 being less familiar.

3.2 Corpus Description

This user study produced 64 minutes of audio data, on average 1.6 minutes per subject. We transcribed the speech then annotated the corpus for people names, and for research interests. Table 2 shows the number of unique slot-values found in the corpus. We observe that the number of unique research interests produced during SHOW&ASK is higher than for other strategies. This confirms our initial observations that this strategy elicits diverse responses. The PERSONAL task produced a relatively higher number of researcher names (FAMOUSPEOPLE strategy) than other tasks. One explanation might be that people may find it easier to recall names in their own research area, as compared to other areas. Overall, we identified 139 unique researcher names and 485 interests.

Table 2: Corpus Statistics

StrategyType	Unique Researcher Names	Unique Research Interests
QUERYDRIVEN	21	30
PERSONAL	77	107
SHOW&ASK	76	390
Overall	139	485

3.3 Corpus Analysis

One of the objectives of this work is to determine *What strategies can the agent use to elicit knowledge from users?* Although, time-cost will vary with task and domain, a usable strategy should, in general, be less demanding. We analyzed the time-per-task for each strategy, shown in Figure 1. We found that the TWEET strategy is not only more demanding, it has higher variance than other tasks. One explanation is that people would attempt to summarize the entire abstract including technical details, despite the instructions indicated that a non-technical description was acceptable. We can see a similar trend in Figure 2 that irrespective of expertise-level, subjects take more time to give one sentence descriptions. We also observe high variance and higher time-per-task for QUERYPERSON; this is due to the system deliberately not returning any results for this task. This was done to

Table 3: Mean Precision for 200 researchers, broken down by the "source" strategy used to acquire their name
Note: Only 85 of 200 researchers had Google Scholar pages, GScholar Accuracy is computed for only those 85.

Metric	*Description Text*	SHOW&ASK	PERSONAL	QUERYDRIVEN	*mean*
Mean Precision	89.5%	86.9%	93.6%	86.2%	90.5%
GScholar Acc.	78.3%	82.3%	86.1%	100%	80.0%

find out whether subjects would repeat the task on failure. Ideally the system needs to only rarely use this strategy to not lose user's trust and solicit multiple values for a given slot (e.g., person name) as opposed to requesting list of values as in FAMOUSPEOPLE and PEOPLE strategies. We find that PEOPLE, KEYWORDS, FAMOUSPEOPLE and BUZZWORDS strategies are efficient with a time-per-task of less than one minute. As shown in Figure 2, subjects do not take much time to speak a list of names or keywords.

4 Evaluation of Acquired Knowledge

To answer *Can an agent elicit reliable knowledge about its domain from users?* we analyzed the relevance of acquired knowledge. We have two disjoint list of entities, (a) researchers and (b) research interests; in addition we have speaker names from the talk descriptions. Our goal is to implicitly infer a list of interests for each researcher without soliciting the user for the interests of every researcher exhaustively. To each researcher in the list, we attribute list of interests that were mentioned in the same context as researcher was mentioned. We tag list of names acquired from the FAMOUSPEOPLE strategy with list of keywords acquired from the BUZZWORDS strategy — both lists acquired from same user. We repeat this process for each name mentioned in relation to a talk in the SHOW&ASK strategy. We tag keywords mentioned in the KEYWORDS strategy to researchers mentioned in the PEOPLE strategy.

4.1 Analysis

We produced 200 entries for researchers and their set of interests. We then had two annotators (senior graduate students) mark whether the system-predicted interests were relevant/accurate. The annotators were allowed to use information found on researchers' home pages and Google Scholar[4] to evaluate the system-predicted interests.

This can be seen as an information retrieval (IR) problem, where researcher is "query" and interests are "documents". So, we use *Mean Precision*, a common metric in IR, to evaluate retrieval. In our case, the ground truth for relevant interests comes from the annotators. The results are shown in Table 3. Our approach has high precision, 90.5%, for all 200 researchers. We see that irrespective of the strategy used to acquire entities, precision is good. We also compared our predicted interests with interests listed by researchers themselves on Google Scholar. There are only 85 researchers from our list with a Google Scholar page; for these our accuracy is 80%, again good. Moreover, significant knowledge is absent from the web (at least in our domain) yet can be elicited from users familiar with the domain.

5 Conclusion

We describe a set of knowledge acquisition strategies that allow a system to solicit novel information from users in a situated environment. To investigate the usability of these strategies, we conducted a user study in the domain of research talks. We analyzed a corpus of system-acquired knowledge and have made the material available[5]. Our data show that users on average take less than a minute to provide new information using the proposed elicitation strategies. The reliability of acquired knowledge in predicting relationships between researchers and interests is quite good, with a mean precision of 90.5%. We note that the PERSONAL strategy, which tries to tap personal knowledge, appears to be particularly effective. More generally, automated elicitation appears to be a promising technique for continuous learning in spoken dialog systems.

6 Appendix

System Predicted Researcher-Interests 1

rich stern deep neural networks, speech recognition, signal processing, neural networks, machine learning, speech synthesis

[4]scholar.google.com

[5]www.speech.cs.cmu.edu/apappu/pubdl/eventspeak_corpus.zip

System Predicted Researcher-Interests 2
kishore prahallad dialogue systems, prosody, speech synthesis, text to speech, pronunciation modeling, low resource languages

System Predicted Researcher-Interests 3
carolyn rose crowdsourcing, meta discourse classification, statistical analysis, presentation skills instruction, man made system, education models, human learning

System Predicted Researcher-Interests 4
florian metze dialogue systems, speech recognition, nlp, prosody, speech synthesis, text to speech, pronunciation modeling, low resource languages, automatic accent identification

System Predicted Researcher-Interests 5
madhavi ganapathiraju protein structure, continuous graphical models, generative models, structural biology, protein structure dynamics, molecular dynamics

System Predicted Researcher-Interests 6
alexander hauptmann discriminatively trained models, deep learning, computer vision, big data

System Predicted Researcher-Interests 7
jamie callan learning to rank, search, large scale search, web search, click prediction, information retrieval, web mining, user activity, recommendation, relevance, machine learning, web crawling, distributed systems, structural similarity

System Predicted Researcher-Interests 8
lori levin natural language understanding, knowledge reasoning, construction grammar, knowledge bases, natural language processing

References

Masahiro Araki. Rapid development process of spoken dialogue systems using collaboratively constructed semantic resources. In *Proceedings of the SIGDIAL 2012 Conference*, pages 70–73. ACL, 2012.

Jeffrey P Bigham, Chandrika Jayant, Hanjie Ji, Greg Little, Andrew Miller, Robert C Miller, Robin Miller, Aubrey Tatarowicz, Brandyn White, Samual White, et al. Vizwiz: nearly real-time answers to visual questions. In *Proceedings of the 23rd ACM Symposium on User Interface software and technology*, pages 333–342. ACM, 2010.

Kurt Bollacker, Colin Evans, Praveen Paritosh, Tim Sturge, and Jamie Taylor. Freebase: a collaboratively created graph database for structuring human knowledge. *Proceedings of the SIGMOD*, pages 1247–1249, 2008.

Andrew Carlson, Justin Betteridge, Bryan Kisiel, Burr Settles, Estevam R Hruschka Jr., and Tom M Mitchell. Toward an Architecture for Never-Ending Language Learning. *Artificial Intelligence*, 2(4):1306–1313, 2010.

Grace Chung, Stephanie Seneff, and Chao Wang. Automatic acquisition of names using speak and spell mode in spoken dialogue systems. In *Proceedings of the NAACL-HLT*, pages 32–39. ACL, 2003.

Edward Filisko and Stephanie Seneff. Developing city name acquisition strategies in spoken dialogue systems via user simulation. In *6th SIGdial Workshop on Discourse and Dialogue*, 2005.

Hartwig Holzapfel, Daniel Neubig, and Alex Waibel. A dialogue approach to learning object descriptions and semantic categories. *Robotics and Autonomous Systems*, 56(11): 1004–1013, November 2008.

Walter Stephen Lasecki, Ece Kamar, and Dan Bohus. Conversations in the crowd: Collecting data for task-oriented dialog learning. In *First AAAI Conference on Human Computation and Crowdsourcing*, 2013.

Ingo Lütkebohle, Julia Peltason, Lars Schillingmann, Christof Elbrechter, Britta Wrede, Sven Wachsmuth, and Robert Haschke. The Curious Robot: Structuring Interactive Robot Learning. In *ICRA'09*, pages 4156–4162. IEEE, 2009.

Aasish Pappu and Alexander Rudnicky. Predicting tasks in goal-oriented spoken dialog systems using semantic knowledge bases. In *Proceedings of the SIGDIAL*, pages 242–250. ACL, 2013.

Aasish Pappu, Teruhisa Misu, and Rakesh Gupta. Investigating critical speech recognition errors in spoken short messages. In *Proceedings of IWSDS*, pages 39–49, 2014.

Rohit Prasad, Rohit Kumar, Sankaranarayanan Ananthakrishnan, Wei Chen, Sanjika Hewavitharana, Matthew Roy, Frederick Choi, Aaron Challenner, Enoch Kan, Arvind Neelakantan, et al. Active error detection and resolution for speech-to-speech translation. In *Proceedings of IWSLT*, 2012.

Alexander I Rudnicky, Aasish Pappu, Peng Li, and Matthew Marge. Instruction Taking in the TeamTalk System. In *Proceedings of the AAAI Fall Symposium on Dialog with Robots*, pages 173–174, 2010.

Push Singh, Thomas Lin, Erik T Mueller, Grace Lim, Travell Perkins, and Wan Li Zhu. Open mind common sense: Knowledge acquisition from the general public. In *CoopIS, DOA, and ODBASE*, pages 1223–1237. Springer, 2002.

Thorsten Spexard, Shuyin Li, Britta Wrede, Jannik Fritsch, Gerhard Sagerer, Olaf Booij, Zoran Zivkovic, Bas Terwijn, and Ben Krose. BIRON, where are you? Enabling a robot to learn new places in a real home environment by integrating spoken dialog and visual localization. *Integration The VLSI Journal*, (section II):934–940, 2006.

Luis Von Ahn. Games with a purpose. *Computer*, 39(6): 92–94, 2006.

Michael Witbrock, David Baxter, Jon Curtis, Dave Schneider, Robert Kahlert, Pierluigi Miraglia, Peter Wagner, Kathy Panton, Gavin Matthews, and Amanda Vizedom. An interactive dialogue system for knowledge acquisition in cyc. In *Proceedings of the 18th IJCAI*, pages 138–145, 2003.

Reducing Sparsity Improves the Recognition of Implicit Discourse Relations

Junyi Jessy Li
University of Pennsylvania
ljunyi@seas.upenn.edu

Ani Nenkova
University of Pennsylvania
nenkova@seas.upenn.edu

Abstract

The earliest work on automatic detection of implicit discourse relations relied on lexical features. More recently, researchers have demonstrated that syntactic features are superior to lexical features for the task. In this paper we re-examine the two classes of state of the art representations: syntactic production rules and word pair features. In particular, we focus on the need to reduce sparsity in instance representation, demonstrating that different representation choices even for the same class of features may exacerbate sparsity issues and reduce performance. We present results that clearly reveal that lexicalization of the syntactic features is necessary for good performance. We introduce a novel, less sparse, syntactic representation which leads to improvement in discourse relation recognition. Finally, we demonstrate that classifiers trained on different representations, especially lexical ones, behave rather differently and thus could likely be combined in future systems.

1 Introduction

Implicit discourse relations hold between adjacent sentences in the same paragraph, and are not signaled by any of the common explicit discourse connectives such as *because*, *however*, *meanwhile*, etc. Consider the two examples below, drawn from the Penn Discourse Treebank (PDTB) (Prasad et al., 2008), of a causal and a contrast relation, respectively. The italic and bold fonts mark the arguments of the relation, i.e the portions of the text connected by the discourse relation.

Ex1: *Mrs Yeargin is lying.* [Implicit = BECAUSE] **They found students in an advanced class a year earlier who said she gave them similar help.**

Ex2: *Back downtown, the execs squeezed in a few meetings at the hotel before boarding the buses again.* [Implicit = BUT] **This time, it was for dinner and dancing - a block away.**

The task is undisputedly hard, partly because it is hard to come up with intuitive feature representations for the problem. Lexical and syntactic features form the basis of the most successful studies on supervised prediction of implicit discourse relations in the PDTB. Lexical features were the focus of the earliest work in discourse recognition, when cross product of words (word pairs) in the two spans connected via a discourse relation was studied. Later, grammatical productions were found to be more effective. Features of other classes such as verbs, inquirer tags, positions were also studied, but they only marginally improve upon syntactic features.

In this study, we compare the most commonly used lexical and syntactic features. We show that representations that minimize sparsity issues are superior to their sparse counterparts, i.e. the better representations are those for which informative features occur in larger portions of the data. Not surprisingly, lexical features are more sparse (occurring in fewer instances in the dataset) than syntactic features; the superiority of syntactic representations may thus be partially explained by this property.

More surprising findings come from a closer examination of instance representation approaches in prior work. We first discuss how choices in prior work have in fact exacerbated the sparsity problem of lexical features. Then, we introduce a new syntactically informed feature class, which is less sparse than prior lexical and syntactic features, and improves significantly the classification of implicit discourse relations.

Given these findings, we address the question if any lexical information at all should be preserved in discourse parsers. We find that purely syntactic representations show lower recognition for most relations, indicating that lexical features, albeit sparse, are necessary for the task. Lexical features also account for a high percentage of the most predictive features.

We further quantify the agreement of predictions produced from classifiers using different instance representations. We find that our novel syntactic representation is better for implicit discourse relation prediction than prior syntactic feature because it has higher overall accuracy and makes correct predictions for instances for which the alternative representations are also correct. Different representation of lexical features however appear complementary to each other, with markedly higher fraction of instances recognized correctly by only one of the models.

Our work advances the state of the art in implicit discourse recognition by clarifying the extent to which sparsity issues influence predictions, by introducing a strong syntactic representation and by documenting the need for further more complex integration of lexical information.

2 The Penn Discourse Treebank

The Penn Discourse Treebank (PDTB) (Prasad et al., 2008) contains annotations for five types of discourse relations over the Penn Treebank corpus (Marcus et al., 1993). *Explicit* relations are those signaled by a discourse connective that occurs in the text, such as "because", "however", "for example". *Implicit* relations are annotated between adjacent sentences in the same paragraph. There are no discourse connectives between the two sentences, and the annotators were asked to insert a connective while marking their senses. Some pairs of sentences do not contain one of the explicit discourse connectives, but the insertion of a connective provides redundant information into the text. For example, they may contain phrases such as "the consequence of the act". These are marked *Alternative Lexicalizations* (AltLex). *Entity relations* (EntRel) are adjacent sentences that are only related via the same entity or topic. Finally, sentences where no discourse relations were identified were marked *NoRel*. In this work, we consider *AltLex* to be part of the *Implicit* relations, and *EntRel* to be part of *NoRel*.

All connectives, either explicit or implicitly inserted, are associated with two arguments of the minimal span of text conveying the semantic content between which the relation holds. This is illustrated in the following example where the two arguments are marked in bold and italic:

Ex: *They stopped delivering junk mail.* [Implicit = SO] **Now thousands of mailers go straight into the trash.**

Relation senses in the PDTB are drawn from a 3-level hierarchy. The top level relations are *Comparison* (arg1 and arg2 holds a contrast relation), *Contingency* (arg1 and arg2 are causally related), *Expansion* (arg2 further describes arg1) and *Temporal* (arg1 and arg2 are temporally related). Some of the largest second-tier relations are under *Expansion*, which include *Conjunction* (arg2 provides new information to arg1), *Instantiation* (arg2 exemplifies arg1) and *Restatement* (arg2 semantically repeats arg1).

In our experiments we use the four top level relations as well as the above three subclasses of *Expansion*. All of these subclasses occur with frequencies similar to those of the Contingency and Comparison classes, with thousands of examples in the PDTB.[1] We show the distribution of the classes below:

Temporal	1038	Comparison	2550
Contingency	4532	Instantiation	1483
Restatement	3271	Conjunction	3646
EntRel/NoRel	5464		

3 Experimental settings

In our experiments we use only lexical and syntactic features. This choice is motivated by the fact that lexical features have been used most widely for the task and that recent work has demonstrated that syntactic features are the single best type of representation. Adding additional features only minimally improves performance (Lin et al., 2009). By zeroing in only on these classes of features we are able to discuss more clearly the impact that different instance representation have on sparsity and classifier performance.

We use gold-standard parses from the original Penn Treebank for syntax features.

To ensure that our conclusions are based on analysis of the most common relations, we train binary SVM classifiers[2] for the seven relations described above. We adopt the standard practice in

[1] All other sub-classes of implicit relations are too small for general practical applications. For example the *Alternative* class and *Concession* class have only 185 and 228 occurrences, respectively, in the 16,224 implicit relation annotations of the PDTB.

[2] We use SVMLight (Joachims, 1999) with linear kernel.

prior work and downsampled the negative class so the number of positive and negative samples are equal in the training set.[3]

Our training set consists of PDTB sections 2-19. The testing set consists of sections 20-24. Like most studies, we do not include sections 0-1 in the training set. We expanded the test set (sections 23 or 23-24) used in previous work (Lin et al., 2014; Park and Cardie, 2012) to ensure the number of examples of the smaller relations, particularly of *Temporal* or *Instantiation*, are suitable for carrying out reliable tests for statistical significance.

Some of the discourse relations are much larger than others, so we report our results in term of F-measure for each relation and average unweighted accuracy. Significance tests over F scores were carried out using a paired t-test. To do this, the test set is randomly partitioned into ten groups. In each group, the relation distribution was kept as close as possible to the overall test set.

4 Sparsity and pure lexical representations

By far the most common features used for representing implicit discourse relations are lexical (Sporleder and Lascarides, 2008; Pitler et al., 2009; Lin et al., 2009; Hernault et al., 2010; Park and Cardie, 2012). Early studies have suggested that lexical features, word pairs (cross-product of the words in the first and second argument) in particular, will be powerful predictors of discourse relations (Marcu and Echihabi, 2002; Blair-Goldensohn et al., 2007). The intuition behind word pairs was that semantic relations between the lexical items, such as *drought–famine*, *child–adult*, may in turn signal causal or contrast discourse relations. Later it has been shown that word pair features do not appear to capture such semantic relationship between words (Pitler et al., 2009) and that syntactic features lead to higher accuracies (Lin et al., 2009; Zhou et al., 2010; Park and Cardie, 2012). Recently, Biran and McKeown (2013) aggregated word pair features with explicit connectives and reported improvements over the original word pairs as features.

In this section, we show that the representation of lexical features play a direct role in feature sparsity and ultimately affects prediction performance.

The first two studies that specifically addressed the problem of predicting implicit discourse relations in the PDTB made use of very different instance representations. Pitler et al. (2009) represent instances of discourse relations in a vector space defined by word pairs, i.e. the cross-product of the words that appear in the two arguments of the relation. There, features are of the form (w_1, w_2) where $w_1 \in arg1$ and $w_2 \in arg2$. If there are N words in the entire vocabulary, the size of each instance would be $N \times N$.

In contrast, Lin et al. (2009) represent instances by tracking the occurrences of grammatical productions in the syntactic parse of argument spans. There are three indicator features associated with each production: whether the production appears in $arg1$, in $arg2$, and in both arguments. For a grammar with N production rules, the size of the vector representing an instance will be $3N$. For convenience we call this "binary representation", in contrast to the word-pair features in which the cross product of words constitute the representation. Note that the cross-product approach has been extended to a wide variety of features (Pitler et al., 2009; Park and Cardie, 2012). In the experiments that follow we will demonstrate that binary representations lead to less sparse features and higher prediction accuracy.

	# Features	Avg. F	Avg. Accuracy
word-pairs	92128	29.46	57.22
binary-lexical	12116	31.79	60.42

Table 1: F-scores and average accuracies of paired and binary representations of words.

Lin et al. (2009) found that their syntactic features are more powerful than the word pair features. Here we show that the advantage comes not only from the inclusion of syntactic information but also from the less sparse instance representation they used for syntactic features. In Table 1 we show the number of features for each representation and the average F score and accuracy for word pairs and words with binary representation (*binary-lexical*). The results for each relation are shown in Table 8 and discussed in Section 7.

Using binary representation for lexical information outperforms word pairs. Thus, the difference in how lexical information is represented accounts for a considerable portion of the improvement reported in Lin et al. (2009). Most notably, for the *Instantiation* class, we see a 7.7% increase in F-score. On average, the less sparse representation

[3]We also did not include features that occurred less than 5 times in the training set.

translates into 2.34% absolute improvement in F-score and 3.2% absolute improvement in accuracy. From this point on we adopt the binary representation for the features discussed.

5 Sparsity and syntactic features

Grammatical production rules were first used for discourse relation representation in Lin et al. (2009). They were identified as the most suitable representation, that lead to highest performance in a couple of independent studies (Lin et al., 2009; Park and Cardie, 2012). The comparison representations covered a number of semantic classes related to sentiment, polarity and verb information and dependency representations of syntax.

Production rules correspond to tree chunks in the constituency parse of a sentence, i.e. a node in the syntactic parse tree with all of its children, which in turn correspond to grammar rules applied in the derivation of the tree, such as S→NP VP. This syntactic representation subsumes lexical representations because of the production rules with part-of-speech on the left-hand side and a lexical item on the right-hand side.

We propose that the sparsity of production rules can be reduced even further by introducing a new representation of the parse tree. Specifically, instead of having full production rules where a single feature records the parent and all its children, all (parent,child) pairs in the constituency parse tree are used. For example, the rule S→NP VP will now become two features, S→NP and S→VP. Note that the leaves of the tree, i.e. the part-of-speech→word features are not changed. For ease of reference we call this new representation "production sticks". In this section we show that F scores and accuracies for implicit discourse relation prediction based on production sticks is significantly higher than using full production rules.

First, Table 2 illustrates the contrast in sparsity among the lexical, production rule and stick representations. The table gives the rate of occurrence of each feature class, which is defined as the average fraction of features with non-zero values in the representation of instances in the entire training set. Specifically, let N be the total number of features, m_i be the number of features triggered in instance i, then the rate of occurrence is $\frac{m_i}{N}$.

The table clearly shows that the number of features in the three representations is comparable, but they vary notably in their rate of occurrence.

	# Features	Rate of Occurrence
sticks	14,165	0.00623
prodrules	16,173	0.00374
binary-lexical	12,116	0.00276
word-pairs	92,128	0.00113

Table 2: Number of features and rate of occurrence for binary lexical representation, production rules and sticks.

	Avg. F	Avg. Accuracy
sticks	34.73	64.89
prodrules	33.69	63.55
binary-lexical	31.79	60.42
word-pairs	29.46	57.22

Table 3: F-scores and average accuracies of production rules and production sticks.

Sticks have almost twice the rate of occurrence of that of full production rules. Both syntactic representations have much larger rate of occurrence than lexical features, and the rate of occurrence of word pairs is more than twice smaller than that of the binary lexical representation.

Next, in Table 3, we give binary classification prediction results based on both full rules and sticks. The first two rows of Table 3 compare full production rules (*prodrules*) with production sticks (*sticks*) using the binary representation. They both outperform the binary lexical representation. Again our results confirm that the better performance of production rule features is partly because they are less sparse than lexical representations, with an average of 1.04% F-score increase. Individually the F scores of 6 of the 7 relations are improved as shown in Table 8.

6 How important are lexical features?

Production rules or sticks include lexical items with their part-of-speech tags. These are the subset of features that contribute most to sparsity issues. In this section we test if these lexical features contribute to the performance or if they can be removed without noticeable degradation due to its intrinsic sparsity. It turns out that it is not advisable to remove the lexical features entirely, as performance decreases substantially if we do so.

6.1 Classification without lexical items

We start our exploration of the influence of lexical items on the accuracy of prediction by inspecting the performances of the classifiers with production rules and sticks, but without the lexical items and their parts of speech. Table 4 lists the average F

	Avg. F	Avg. Accuracy
prodrules	33.69	63.55
sticks	34.73	64.89
prodrules-nolex	32.30	62.03
sticks-nolex	33.86	63.99

Table 4: F-scores and average accuracies of production rules and sticks, with (rows 1-2) and without (rows 3-4) lexical items.

	# Features	Rate of Occurrence
prodrules	16,173	0.00374
sticks	14,165	0.00623
prodrules-nolex	3470	0.00902
sticks-nolex	922	0.0619

Table 5: Number of features and rate of occurrence for production rules and sticks, with (rows 1-2) and without (rows 3-4) lexical items.

scores and accuracies. Table 8 provides detailed results for individual relations. Here *prodrules-nolex* and *sticks-nolex* denote full production rules without lexical items, and production sticks without lexical items, respectively. In all but two relations, lexical items contribute to better classifier performance.

When lexical items are not included in the representation, the number of features is reduced to fewer than 30% of that in the original full production rules. At the same time however, including the lexical items in the representation improves performance even more than introducing the less sparse production stick representation. Production sticks with lexical information also perform better than the same representation without the POS-word sticks.

The number of features and their rates of occurrences are listed in Table 5. It again confirms that the less sparse stick representation leads to better classifier performance. Not surprisingly, purely syntactic features (without the lexical items) are much less sparse than syntax features with lexical items present. However the classifier performance is worse without the lexical features. This contrast highlights the importance of a reasonable tradeoff between attempts to reduce sparsity and the need to preserve lexical features.

6.2 Feature selection

So far our discussion was based on the behavior of models trained on a complete set of relatively frequent syntactic and lexical features (occurring more than five times in the training data). Feature selection is a way to reasonably prune out the set

Relation	%-nonlex	%-allfeats
Temporal	25.56	10.95
Comparison	25.40	15.51
Contingency	20.12	25.05
Conjunction	21.15	19.20
Instantiation	25.08	16.16
Restatement	22.16	17.35
Expansion	18.36	18.66

Table 6: Non-lexical features selected using feature selection. %-nonlex records the percentage of non-lexical features among all features selected; %-allfeats records the percentage of selected non-lexical features among all non-lexical features.

and reduce sparsity issues in the model. In fact feature selection has been used in the majority of prior work (Pitler et al., 2009; Lin et al., 2009; Park and Cardie, 2012).

Here we perform feature selection and examine the proportion of syntactic and lexical features among the most informative features. We use the χ^2 test of independence, computed on the following contingency table for each feature F_i and for each relation R_j:

$$\frac{F_i \wedge R_j \; | F_i \wedge \neg R_j}{\neg F_i \wedge R_j \; | \neg F_i \wedge \neg R_j}$$

Each cell in the above table records the number of training instances in which F_i and R_j are present or absent. We set our level of confidence to $p < 0.1$.

Table 6 lists the proportions of non-lexical items among the most informative features selected (column 2). It also lists the percentage of selected non-lexical items among all the 922 purely syntactic features from production rule and production stick representations (column 3). For all relations, at most about a quarter of the most informative features are non-lexical and they only take up 10%-25% of all possible non-lexical features. The prediction results using only these features are either higher than or comparable to that without feature selection (sticks-χ^2 in Table 8). These numbers suggest that lexical terms play a significant role as part of the syntactic representations.

In Table 8 we record the F scores and accuracies for each relation under each feature representation. The representations are sorted according to descending F scores for each relation. Notice that χ^2 feature selection on sticks is the best representation for the three smallest relations: *Comparison*, *Instantiation* and *Temporal*.

This finding led us to look into the selected lexical features for these three classes. We found that these most prominent features in fact capture some semantic information. We list the top ten most predictive lexical features for these three relations below, with examples. Somewhat disturbingly, many of them are style or domain specific to the Wall Street Journal that PDTB was built on.

Comparison a1a2_NN_share a1a2_NNS_cents a1a2_CC_or a1a2_CD_million a1a2_QP_$ a1a2_NP_$ a2_RB_n't a1a2_NN_% a2_JJ_year a2_IN_of

For *Comparison* (contrast), the top lexical features are words that occur in both argument 1 and argument 2. Contrast within the financial domain, such as "share", "cents" and numbers between arguments are captured by these features. Consider the following example:

Ex. *Analyst estimate the value of the BellSouth proposal at about $115 to $125 a share.* [Implicit=AND] **They value McCaw's bid at $112 to $118 a share .**

Here the contrast clearly happens with the value estimation for two different parties.

Instantiation a2_SINV_" a2_SINV_, a2_SINV_" a2_SINV_. a1_DT_some a2_S_ a2_VBZ_says a1_NP_, a2_NP_, a1_DT_a

For *Instantiation* (arg2 gives an example of arg1), besides words such as "some" or "a" that sometimes mark a set of events, many attribution features are selected. it turns out many *Instantiation* instances in the PDTB involve argument 2 being an inverted declarative sentence that signals a quote as illustrate by the following example:

Ex. *Unease is widespread among exchange members.* [Implicit=FOR EXAMPLE] **" I can't think of any reason to join Lloyd's now, "** says Keith Whitten, a British businessman and a Lloyd's member since 1979.

Temporal a1_VBD_plunged a2_VBZ_is a2_RB_later a1_VBD_was a2_VBD_responded a1a2_PRP_he a1_WRB_when a1_PRP_he a1_VBZ_is a2_VBP_are

For *Temporal*, verbs like *plunge* and *responded* are selected. Words such as *plunged* are quite domain specific to stock markets, but words such as *later* and *responded* are likely more general indicators of the relation.

The presence of pronouns was also a predictive feature. Consider the following example:

Ex. *A Yale law school graduate , he began his career in corporate law and then put in years at Metromedia Inc. and the William Morris talent agency.* [Implicit=THEN] **In 1976, he joined CBS Sports to head business affairs and, five years later, became its president.**

Overall, it is fairly easy to see that certain semantic information was captured by these features, such as similar structures in a pair of sentences holding a contrast relation, the use of verbs in a *Temporal* relation. However, it is rather unsettling to also see that some of these characteristics are largely style or domain specific. For example, for an *Instantiation* in an educational scenario where the tutor provides an example for a concept, it is highly unlikely that attribution features will be helpful. Therefore, part of the question of finding a general class of features that carry over to other styles or domains of text still remain unanswered.

7 Per-relation evaluation

Table 8 lists the F-scores and accuracies of each representation mentioned in this work for predicting individual relation classes. For each relation, the representations are ordered by decreasing F-score. We tested the results for statistical significance of the change in F-score. We compare all the representations with the best and the worse representations for the relation. A "Y" marks a significance level of $p \leq 0.05$ for the comparison with the best or worst representation, a "T" marks a significance level of $p \leq 0.1$, which means a tendency towards significance.

For all relations, production sticks, either with or without feature selection, is the top representation. Sticks without lexical items also underperform those including the lexical items for 6 of the 7 relations. Notably, production rules without lexical items are among the three worst representations, outperforming only the pure lexical features in some cases. This is a strong indication that being both a sparse syntactic representation and lacking lexical information, these features are not favored in this task. Pure lexical features give the worst or second to worst F scores, significantly worse than the alternatives in most of the cases.

In Table 7 we list the binary classification results from prior work: feature selected word pairs (Pitler et al., 2009), aggregated word pairs (Biran and McKeown, 2013), production rules only (Park and Cardie, 2012), and the best combination possible from a variety of features (Park and Cardie, 2012), all of which include production rules. We aim to compare the relative gains in performance with different representations. Note that the absolute results from prior work are not exactly comparable to ours for two reasons — the training

Sys.	Pitler et al.	Biran-McKeown
Feat.	wordpair-implicit	aggregated wp
Comp.	20.96 (42.55)	24.38 (61.72)
Cont.	43.79 (61.92)	44.03 (66.78)
Expa.	63.84 (60.28)	66.48 (60.93)
Temp.	16.21 (61.98)	19.54 (68.09)
Sys.	Park-Cardie	Park-Cardie
Feat.	prodrules	best combination
Comp.	30.04 (75.84)	31.32 (74.66)
Cont.	47.80 (71.90)	49.82 (72.09)
Expa.	77.64 (69.60)	79.22 (69.14)
Temp.	20.96 (63.36)	26.57 (79.32)

Table 7: F-score (accuracy) of prior systems. Note that the absolute numbers are not exactly comparable with ours because of the important reasons explained in this section.

and testing sets are different; how *Expansion*, *EntRel/NoRel* and *AltLex* relations are treated differently in each work. The only meaningful indicator here is the absolute size of improvement. The table shows that our introduction of production sticks led to improvements comparable to those reported in prior work.

The aggregated word pair is a less sparse version of the word pair features, where each pair is converted into weights associated with an explicit connective. Just as the less sparse binary lexical representation presented previously, the aggregated word pairs also gave better performance. None of the three lexical features, however, surpasses raw production rules, which again echoes our finding that binary lexical features are not better than the full production rules. Finally, we note that a combination of features gives better F-scores.

8 Discussion: are the features complementary?

So far we have discussed how different representations for lexical and syntactic features can affect the classifier performances. We focused on the dilemma of how to reduce sparsity while still preserving the useful lexical features. An important question remains as whether these representations are complementary, that is, how different is the classifier behaving under different feature sets and if it makes sense to combine the features.

We compare the classifier output on the test data with two methods in Table 9: the Q-statistic and the percentage of data which the two classifiers disagree (Kuncheva and Whitaker, 2003).

Representation	F (A)	sig-best	sig-worst
	Comparison		
sticks-χ^2	27.78 (62.83)	N/A	Y
prodrules	27.65 (59.5)	-	Y
sticks	27.50 (60.73)	-	Y
sticks-nolex	27.01 (59.63)	-	Y
prodrules-nolex	26.40 (58.47)	T	Y
binary-lexical	24.73 (58.32)	Y	-
word-pairs	22.68 (45.03)	Y	N/A
	Conjunction		
sticks	27.55 (63.82)	N/A	T
sticks-χ^2	27.53 (64.06)	-	T
prodrules	27.02 (63.91)	-	-
sticks-nolex	26.56 (61.03)	T	-
binary-lexical	25.90 (61.77)	Y	-
prodrules-nolex	25.20 (62.83)	T	N/A
word-pairs	25.18 (74.51)	T	-
	Contingency		
sticks	48.90 (67.49)	N/A	Y
sticks-χ^2	48.55 (67.76)	-	Y
sticks-nolex	48.08 (67.69)	-	Y
prodrules	47.14 (65.61)	T	Y
prodrules-nolex	45.79 (63.99)	Y	Y
binary-lexical	44.17 (62.68)	Y	Y
word-pairs	40.57 (50.53)	Y	N/A
	Expansion		
sticks	56.48 (61.75)	N/A	Y
sticks-χ^2	56.30 (62.26)	-	Y
sticks-nolex	55.43 (60.56)	-	Y
prodrules	55.42 (61.05)	-	Y
binary-lexical	54.20 (59.26)	Y	-
word-pairs	53.65 (56.64)	Y	-
prodrules-nolex	53.53 (58.79)	Y	N/A
	Instantiation		
sticks-χ^2	30.34 (74.54)	N/A	Y
sticks	29.93 (73.80)	-	Y
prodrules	29.59 (72.20)	-	Y
sticks-nolex	28.22 (72.66)	Y	Y
prodrules-nolex	27.83 (70.72)	Y	Y
binary-lexical	27.29 (70.05)	Y	Y
word-pairs	20.22 (51.00)	Y	N/A
	Restatement		
sticks	35.74 (61.45)	N/A	Y
sticks-χ^2	34.93 (61.42)	-	Y
sticks-nolex	34.62 (61.08)	T	Y
prodrules	33.52 (58.54)	T	Y
prodrules-nolex	32.05 (56.84)	Y	-
binary-lexical	31.27 (57.41)	Y	T
word-pairs	29.81 (47.42)	Y	N/A
	Temporal		
sticks-χ^2	17.97 (66.67)	N/A	Y
sticks-nolex	17.08 (65.27)	T	Y
sticks	17.04 (65.22)	T	Y
prodrules	15.51 (64.04)	Y	-
prodrules-nolex	15.29 (62.56)	Y	-
binary-lexical	14.97 (61.92)	Y	-
word-pairs	14.10 (75.38)	Y	N/A

Table 8: F-score (accuracy) of each relation for each feature representation. The representations in each relation are sorted in descending order. The column "sig-best" marks the significance test result against the best representation, the column "sig-worst" marks the significance test result against the worst representation. "Y" denotes $p \leq 0.05$, "T" denotes $p \leq 0.1$.

Q-statistic is a measure of agreement between two systems s_1 and s_2 formulated as follows:

$$Q_{s_1,s_2} = \frac{N_{11}N_{00} - N_{01}N_{10}}{N_{11}N_{00} + N_{01}N_{10}}$$

Where N denotes the number of instances, a subscript 1 on the left means s_1 is correct, and a subscript 1 on the right means s_2 is correct.

There are several rather surprising findings. Most notably, word pairs and binary lexical representations give very different classification results in each relation. Their predictions disagree on at least 25% of the data. This finding drastically contrast the fact that they are both lexical features and that they both make use of the argument annotations in the PDTB. A comparison of the percentages and their differences in F scores or accuracies easily shows that it is not the case that binary lexical models correctly predict instances word pairs made mistakes on, but that they are disagreeing in both ways. Thus, given the previous discussion that lexical items are useful, it is possible the most suitable representation would combine both views of lexical distribution.

Even more surprisingly, the difference in classifier behavior is not as big when we compare lexical and syntactic representations. The disagreement of production sticks with and without lexical features are the smallest, even though, as we have shown previously, the majority of production sticks are lexical features with part-of-speech tags. If we compare binary lexical features with production sticks, the disagreement becomes bigger, but still not as big as word pairs vs. binary lexical.

Besides the differences in classification, the bigger picture of improving implicit discourse relation classification is finding a set of feature representations that are able to complement each other to improve the classification. A direct conclusion here is that one should not limit the focus on features in different categories (for example, lexical or syntax), but also features in the same category represented differently (for example, word pairs or binary lexical).

Rel.	Q-stat	Disagreement
word-pairs vs. binary-lexical		
Comparison	0.65	33.55
Conjunction	0.71	28.47
Contingency	0.81	26.35
Expansion	0.69	29.38
Instantiation	0.75	31.33
Restatement	0.76	28.42
Temporal	0.25	25.34
binary-lexical vs. sticks		
Comparison	0.78	25.49
Conjunction	0.78	24.67
Contingency	0.86	20.68
Expansion	0.80	24.28
Instantiation	0.83	20.75
Restatement	0.76	26.72
Temporal	0.86	20.61
sticks vs. prodrules		
Comparison	0.88	19.77
Conjunction	0.89	18.43
Contingency	0.94	14.00
Expansion	0.88	19.18
Instantiation	0.90	16.34
Restatement	0.89	18.88
Temporal	0.90	17.94
sticks vs. sticks-nolex		
Comparison	0.94	14.61
Conjunction	0.92	16.63
Contingency	0.97	10.16
Expansion	0.91	17.35
Instantiation	0.97	9.51
Restatement	0.97	11.26
Temporal	0.98	8.42

Table 9: Q statistic and disagreement of different classes of representations

9 Conclusion

In this work we study implicit discourse relation classification from the perspective of the interplay between lexical and syntactic feature representation. We are particularly interested in the tradeoff between reducing sparsity and preserving lexical features. We first emphasize the important role of sparsity for traditional word-pair representations and how a less sparse representation could improve performance. Then we proposed a less sparse feature representation for production rules, the best feature category so far, that further improves classification. We study the role of lexical features and show the contrast between the sparsity problem they brought along and their dominant presence in the highly ranked features. Also, lexical features included in syntactic features that are most informative to the classifiers are found to be style or domain specific in certain relations. Finally, we compare the representations in terms of classifier disagreement and showed that within the same feature category different feature representation can also be complementary with each other.

References

Or Biran and Kathleen McKeown. 2013. Aggregated word pair features for implicit discourse relation disambiguation. In *Proceedings of the 51st Annual Meeting of the Association for Computational Linguistics (ACL): Short Papers*, pages 69–73.

Sasha Blair-Goldensohn, Kathleen McKeown, and Owen Rambow. 2007. Building and refining rhetorical-semantic relation models. In *Human Language Technologies: The Conference of the North American Chapter of the Association for Computational Linguistics (NAACL)*, pages 428–435.

Hugo Hernault, Danushka Bollegala, and Mitsuru Ishizuka. 2010. A semi-supervised approach to improve classification of infrequent discourse relations using feature vector extension. In *Proceedings of the 2010 Conference on Empirical Methods in Natural Language Processing (EMNLP)*, pages 399–409.

Thorsten Joachims. 1999. Making large-scale support vector machine learning practical. In *Advances in kernel methods*, pages 169–184.

Ludmila I. Kuncheva and Christopher J. Whitaker. 2003. Measures of diversity in classifier ensembles and their relationship with the ensemble accuracy. *Machine Learning*, 51(2):181–207, May.

Ziheng Lin, Min-Yen Kan, and Hwee Tou Ng. 2009. Recognizing implicit discourse relations in the Penn Discourse Treebank. In *Proceedings of the 2009 Conference on Empirical Methods in Natural Language Processing (EMNLP)*, pages 343–351.

Ziheng Lin, Hwee Tou Ng, and Min-Yen Kan. 2014. A PDTB-styled end-to-end discourse parser. *Natural Language Engineering*, 20:151–184, 4.

Daniel Marcu and Abdessamad Echihabi. 2002. An unsupervised approach to recognizing discourse relations. In *Proceedings of the 40th Annual Meeting on Association for Computational Linguistics (ACL)*, pages 368–375.

Mitchell P. Marcus, Mary Ann Marcinkiewicz, and Beatrice Santorini. 1993. Building a large annotated corpus of English: The Penn Treebank. *Computational Linguistics - Special issue on using large corpora*, 19(2):313–330.

Joonsuk Park and Claire Cardie. 2012. Improving implicit discourse relation recognition through feature set optimization. In *Proceedings of the 13th Annual Meeting of the Special Interest Group on Discourse and Dialogue (SIGDIAL)*, pages 108–112.

Emily Pitler, Annie Louis, and Ani Nenkova. 2009. Automatic sense prediction for implicit discourse relations in text. In *Proceedings of the Joint Conference of the 47th Annual Meeting of the ACL and the 4th International Joint Conference on Natural Language Processing of the AFNLP (ACL-IJCNLP)*, pages 683–691.

Rashmi Prasad, Nikhil Dinesh, Alan Lee, Eleni Miltsakaki, Livio Robaldo, Aravind Joshi, and Bonnie Webber. 2008. The Penn Discourse TreeBank 2.0. In *Proceedings of the Sixth International Conference on Language Resources and Evaluation (LREC)*.

Caroline Sporleder and Alex Lascarides. 2008. Using automatically labelled examples to classify rhetorical relations: An assessment. *Natural Language Engineering*, 14(3):369–416, July.

Zhi-Min Zhou, Yu Xu, Zheng-Yu Niu, Man Lan, Jian Su, and Chew Lim Tan. 2010. Predicting discourse connectives for implicit discourse relation recognition. In *Proceedings of the 23rd International Conference on Computational Linguistics (COLING)*, pages 1507–1514.

Interaction Quality Estimation in Spoken Dialogue Systems Using Hybrid-HMMs

Stefan Ultes
Ulm University
Albert-Einstein-Allee 43
89081 Ulm, Germany
stefan.ultes@uni-ulm.de

Wolfgang Minker
Ulm University
Albert-Einstein-Allee 43
89081 Ulm, Germany
wolfgang.minker@uni-ulm.de

Abstract

Research trends on SDS evaluation are recently focusing on objective assessment methods. Most existing methods, which derive quality for each system-user-exchange, do not consider temporal dependencies on the quality of previous exchanges. In this work, we investigate an approach for determining Interaction Quality for human-machine dialogue based on methods modeling the sequential characteristics using HMM modeling. Our approach significantly outperforms conventional approaches by up to 4.5% relative improvement based on Unweighted Average Recall metrics.

1 Introduction

Spoken Dialogue Systems (SDSs) play a key role in achieving natural human-machine interaction. One reason is that speech is one major channel of natural human communication. Assessing the quality of such SDSs has been discussed frequently in recent years. The basic principles which all approaches underlie have been analyzed by Möller et al. (2009) creating a taxonomy for quality of human-machine interaction, i.e., Quality of Service (QoS) and Quality of Experience (QoE). Quality of Service describes objective criteria like *total number of turns*. The recent shift of interest in dialogue assessment methods towards subjective criteria is described as Quality of Experience, putting the user in the spotlight of dialogue assessment. For QoE, Möller et al. (2009) identified several aspects contributing to a good user experience, e.g., usability or acceptability. These aspects can be combined under the term user satisfaction, describing the degree by which the user is satisfied with the system's performance. By assessing QoE, the hope of the research community is to better measure the human-like quality of an SDS. While this information may be used during the design process, enabling automatically derived user satisfaction within the dialogue management allows for adaption of the ongoing dialogue (Ultes et al., 2012b).

First work on deriving subjective metrics automatically has been performed by Walker et al. (1997) resulting in the PARADISE framework, which is the current quasi-standard in this field. Briefly explained, a linear dependency is assumed between dialogue parameters and user satisfaction to estimate qualitative performance on the dialogue level.

Measuring the performance of complete dialogues does not allow for adapting to the user *during* the dialogue (Ultes et al., 2012b). Hence, performance measures which provide a measurement for each system-user-exchange[1] are of interest. Approaches based on Hidden Markov Models (HMMs) are widely used for sequence modeling. Therefore, Engelbrecht et al. (2009) used these models for predicting the dialogue quality on the exchange level. Similar to this, we presented work on estimating Interaction Quality using HMMs and Conditioned HMMs (Ultes et al., 2012a). In this contribution, we investigate an approach for recognizing the dialogue quality using a hybrid Markovian model. Here, hybrid means combining statistical approaches such as Support Vector Machines with Hidden Markov Models by modeling the observation probability of the HMMs using classification. While this is the first time hybrid approaches are used for estimating Interaction Quality, they are well-known and have been used before for other classification tasks (e.g. (Valstar and Pantic, 2007; Onaran et al., 2011)).

This paper is outlined as follows: Related work on subjective quality measurement on the ex-

[1] A system-user-exchange consists of a system dialogue turn followed by a user dialogue turn

change level is presented in Section 2. All experiments in this work are based on the Interaction Quality metric of the LEGO corpus described in Section 3. We motivate for introducing time dependency and present our own approach on recognizing Interaction Quality using a Markovian model presented in Section 4 and briefly present the classification algorithms used for the experiments in Section 5. Experiments are presented in Section 6 and their results discussion in Section 7.

2 Significant Related Work

Much research on predicting subjective quality measures on an exchange level has been performed hitherto. However, most of this body of work lacks of either taking account of the sequential structure of the dialogue or resulting in insufficient performance.

Engelbrecht et al. (2009) presented an approach using Hidden Markov Models (HMMs) to model the SDS as a process evolving over time. Performance ratings on a 5 point scale ("bad", "poor", "fair", "good", "excellent") have been applied by the users of the SDS during the dialogue. The interaction was halted while the user rated. A HMM was created consisting of 5 states (one for each rating) and a 6-dimensional input vector. While Engelbrecht et al. (2009) relied on only 6 input variables, we will pursue an approach with 29 input variables. Moreover, we will investigate dialogues of a real world dialogue system annotated with quality labels by expert annotators.

Higashinaka et al. (2010) proposed a model for predicting turn-wise ratings for human-human dialogues. Ratings ranging from 1 to 7 were applied by two expert annotators labeling for smoothness, closeness, and willingness. They achieved an UAR[2] of only 0.2-0.24 which is only slightly above the random baseline of 0.14.

Hara et al. (2010) derived turn level ratings from overall ratings of the dialogue which were applied by the users *after* the interaction on a five point scale within an online questionnaire. Using n-grams to model the dialogue by calculating n-gram occurrence frequencies for each satisfaction value showed that results for distinguishing between six classes at any point in the dialogue to be hardly above chance.

A more robust measure for user satisfaction has been presented by Schmitt et al. (2011) within

[2]Unweighted Average Recall, see Section 6

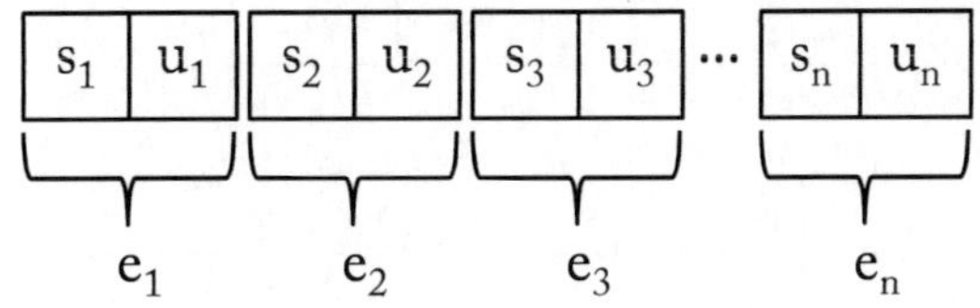

Figure 1: A dialogue may be separated into a sequence of system-user-exchanges where each exchange e_i consists of a system turn s_i followed by a user turn u_i.

their work about Interaction Quality (IQ) for Spoken Dialogue Systems. In contrast to user satisfaction, the labels were applied by expert annotators *after* the dialogue at the exchange level. Automatically derived parameters were used as features for creating a statistical model using static feature vectors. Schmitt et al. (2011) performed IQ recognition on the LEGO corpus (see Section 3) using linear SVMs. They achieved an UAR[2] of 0.58 based on 10-fold cross-validation which is clearly above the random baseline of 0.2. Ultes et al. (2012a) put an emphasis on the sequential character of the IQ measure by applying a Hidden Markov Models (HMMs) and a Conditioned Hidden Markov Models (CHMMs). Both have been applied using 6-fold cross validation and a reduced feature set of the LEGO corpus achieving an UAR[2] of 0.44 for HMMs and 0.39 for CHMMs. While Ultes et al. (2012a) used generic Gaussian Mixture Models to model the observation probabilities, we use confidence distributions of static classification algorithms.

3 The LEGO Corpus

For Interaction Quality (IQ) estimation, we use the LEGO corpus published by Schmitt et al. (2012). Interaction Quality is defined similarly to user satisfaction: While the latter represents the true disposition of the user, IQ is the disposition of the user assumed by an expert annotator. Here, expert annotators are people who listen to recorded dialogues after the interactions and rate them by assuming the point of view of the actual person performing the dialogue. These experts are supposed to have some experience with dialogue systems. In this work, expert annotators were "advanced students of computer science and engineering" (Schmitt et al., 2011), i.e., grad students.

The LEGO corpus is based on 200 calls to

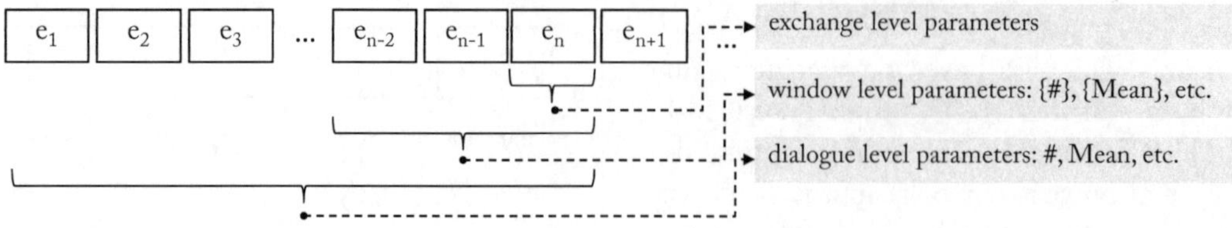

Figure 2: The three different modeling levels representing the interaction at exchange e_n: The most detailed exchange level, comprising parameters of the current exchange; the window level, capturing important parameters from the previous n dialog steps (here $n = 3$); the dialog level, measuring overall performance values from the entire previous interaction.

the "Let's Go Bus Information System" of the Carnegie Mellon University in Pittsburgh (Raux et al., 2006) recorded in 2006. Labels for IQ have been assigned by three expert annotators to 200 calls consisting of 4,885 system-user-exchanges (see Figure 1) in total with an inter-annotator agreement of $\kappa = 0.54$. This may be considered as a moderate agreement (cf. Landis and Koch's Kappa Benchmark Scale (1977)) which is quite good considering the difficulty of the task that required to rate each exchange. For instance, if one annotator reduces the IQ value only one exchange earlier than another annotator, both already disagree on two exchanges. The final label was assigned to each exchange by using the median of all three individual ratings.

IQ was labeled on a scale from 1 (extremely unsatisfied) to 5 (satisfied) considering the complete dialogue up to the current exchange. Thus, each exchange has been rated without regarding any upcoming user utterance. As the users are expected to be satisfied at the beginning, each dialogue's initial rating is 5. In order to ensure consistent labeling, the expert annotators had to follow labeling guidelines (Schmitt et al., 2012).

An example of an annotated dialogue is shown in Table 5. It starts off with a good IQ until the system provides some results and then falls drastically as the user input does not correspond to what the system expects. Thus, the system remains in a loop until the user reacts appropriately.

Parameters used as input variables for the IQ model have been derived from the dialogue system modules automatically for each exchange. Furthermore, parameters on three levels have been created: the *exchange level*, the *dialogue level*, and the *window level* (see Figure 2). As parameters like ASRCONFIDENCE (confidence of speech recognition) or UTTERANCE (word sequence recognized by speech recognition) can directly be acquired from the dialogue modules they constitute the *exchange level*. Counts, sums, means, and frequencies of *exchange level* parameters from multiple exchanges are computed to constitute the *dialogue level* (all exchanges up to the current one) and the *window level* (the three previous exchanges).

4 Hybrid-HMM

As Schmitt et al. (2011) model the sequential character of the data only indirectly by designing special features, our approach applies Markovian modeling to directly model temporal dependencies. Temporal dependencies on previous system-user-exchanges are not taken into account by Schmitt et al.; only parameters derived from the current exchange are used. However, we found out that Interaction Quality is highly dependent on the IQ value of the previous exchange. Adding the parameter IQ_{prev} describing the previous IQ value to the input vector to the IQ model consisting of several parameters results in an extended input vector. Calculating the Information Gain Ratio (IGR) of each parameter of the extended input vector shows that IQ_{prev} achieves the highest IGR value of 1.0. In other words, IQ_{prev} represents the parameter which contains the most information for the classification task.

While performing IQ recognition on the extended features set using the annotated IQ values results in an UAR of 0.82, rather using the estimated IQ value results in an UAR of only 0.43. Consequently, other configurations have to be investigated. Here, Markovian approaches offer a self-contained concept of using these temporal dependencies. However, Ultes et al. (2012a) showed that applying neither a classical HMM nor a conditioned HMM yields results outperforming static approaches.

Therefore, in this Section we present a Hybrid-

HMM approach, which is based on the classical HMM and takes advantage of good performing existing static classification approaches. The classical HMM, specifically used for time-sequential data, consists of a set of states S with transition probability matrix A and initial probability vector π over a set of observations B (also called vocabulary) and an observation function b_{q_t} dependent on the state q_t. For calculating the probability $p(q_t|O_t, \lambda)$ of seeing observation sequence $O_t = (o_1, o_2, \ldots, o_t)$ while being in state q_t at time t given the HMM λ, the Forward Algorithm is used:

$$\begin{aligned} p(q_t = s_j|O_t, \lambda) &= \alpha_t(j) \\ &= \sum_{i=1}^{|S|} \alpha_{t-1}(i) a_{ij} b_j(o_t) \ . \end{aligned} \quad (1)$$

Here, a_{ij} describes the transition probability of transitioning from state s_i to state s_j. To find a suitable model λ, the HMM must be trained, for example, by using the Baum-Welch algorithm. Usually, the observation function b_{q_t} is modeled with Gaussian mixture models (GMMs). For more information on general HMMs, please refer to Rabiner et al. (1989).

For determining the most likely class $\hat{\omega}_t$ at time t, where each state $j \in S$ is associated with one class ω, the following equation is used:

$$\hat{\omega}_t = \arg\max_j \alpha_t(j) \ . \quad (2)$$

For applying an HMM while exploiting existing statistical classification approaches, the observation function $b_j(o_t)$ is modeled by using confidence score distributions of statistical classifiers, e.g., a Support Vector Machine in accordance with Schmitt et al. (2011) (see Section 5). Furthermore, the transition function a_{ij} is computed by taking the frequencies of the state transitions contained in the given corpus. Therefore, an ergodic HMM is used comprising five states with each representing one of the five IQ scores.

Moreover, in SDSs, a system action act is performed at the end of each system turn. This can be utilized by adding an additional dependency on this action to the state transition function a_{ij}. By augmenting Equation 1, this results in

$$\alpha_t(j) = \sum_{i=1}^{|S|} \alpha_{t-1}(i) a_{ij,\text{act}} b_j(o_t) \ . \quad (3)$$

This refinement models differences in state transitions evoked by different system actions, e.g., a different transition probability is expected if a WAIT action is performed compared to a CONFIRMATION. Equation 3 is equal to the belief update equation known from the Partially Observable Markov Decision Process formalism (Kaelbling et al., 1998).

Therefore, two versions of the Hybrid-HMM are evaluated: an action-independent version as in Equation 1 and an action-dependent version as in Equation 3.

5 Classifier Types

For modeling the observation probability $b_j(o_t)$of the hybrid HMM, multiple classification schemes have been applied to investigate the influence of observation distributions with different characteristics on the overall performance.

In general, classification means estimating a class $\hat{\omega}$ to the given observation o by comparing the class-wise probabilities $p(\omega|o)$. In this work, this probability may be used to model the observation probability $b_j(o)$ of the HMM by the posterior probability

$$p(\omega|o) = b_j(o) \quad (4)$$

for $j = \omega$.

As not all classification algorithms provide a posterior probability, it may be replaced by the confidence distribution. A general description of the classification algorithms used in this work are described in the following Section along with a motivation for the feature subset of the LEGO corpus used for estimating the Interaction Quality in this work.

5.1 Support Vector Machine

For a two class problem, a Support Vector Machine (SVM) (Vapnik, 1995) is based on the concept of linear discrimination with maximum margin by defining a hyperplane separating the two classes. The estimated class $\hat{\omega}$ for observation vector $\vec{o}$ is based on the sign of the decision function

$$k(\vec{o}) = \sum_{i=1}^{N} \alpha_i z_i K(\vec{m}_i, \vec{o}) + b \ , \quad (5)$$

where $\vec{m}_i$ represent support vectors defining the hyper plane (together with b), z_i the known class $\vec{m}_i$ belongs to, α_i the weight of $\vec{m}_i$, and $K(\cdot, \cdot)$ a kernel function. The kernel function is defined as

$$K(\vec{m}, \vec{m}') = \langle \varphi(\vec{m}), \varphi(\vec{m}') \rangle \ , \tag{6}$$

where $\varphi(\vec{m})$ represents a transformation function mapping $\vec{m}$ into a space Φ of different dimensionality and $\langle \cdot, \cdot \rangle$ defines a scalar product in Φ. By using the kernel function, the linear discrimination may happen in a space of high dimensionality without explicitly transforming the observation vectors into said space.

The SVM implementation which is used in this contribution is *libSVM* (Chang and Lin, 2011). As this algorithm does not provide class probabilities directly, the respective confidence scores are used.

5.2 Naive Bayes

For deriving the posterior probability, the Naive Bayes classifier may be used. It calculates the posterior probability $P(\omega|o)$ of having class ω when seeing the n-dimensional observation vector $\vec{o}$ by applying Bayes rule (Duda et al., 2001):

$$P(\omega|\vec{o}) = \frac{p(\vec{o}|\omega) \cdot P(\omega)}{p(\vec{o})} \ . \tag{7}$$

In general, observations, i.e., elements of the observation vector, may be correlated with each other and introducing independence assumptions between these elements does usually not reflect the true state of the world. However, correlations are often not very high thus simplifying the Bayes problem has proved to result in reasonable performance. This is utilized by the Naive Bayes classifier by assuming said independence thus calculating

$$p(\vec{o}|\omega) = \prod_{i=1}^{n} p(o_i|\omega) \ . \tag{8}$$

5.3 Rule Induction

The classification algorithm Rule Induction or Rule Learner is based on the idea of defining rules to assign classes $\hat{\omega}$ to observation vectors $\vec{o}$. In this work, the algorithm RIPPER (Repeated Incremental Pruning to Produce Error Reduction) (Cohen, 1995) is used where each rule consists of conjunctions of $A_n = v$, where A_n is a nominal attribute, or $A_c \geq \theta$, $A_c \leq \theta$, where A_c is a continuous attribute. Each part of the observation vector $\vec{o}$ is reflected by one of the attributes. The basic process of the algorithm for generating rules is divided into three steps: First, rules are grown by adding attributes to the rule. Second, the rules are pruned. If the resulting rule set is not of sufficient performance, all training examples which are covered by the generated rules are removed from the example set and a new rule is created.

5.4 Feature selection

As stated previously, all experiments are based on the LEGO corpus presented in Section 3. In order to keep the presented results comparable to previous work based on HMM and CHMM (Ultes et al., 2012a), a reduced parameter set is used. Parameters with constant values for most exchanges have been excluded. These would result in rows of zeros during computation of the covariance matrices of the feature vectors, which are needed for HMM and CHMM classification. A row of zeros in the covariance matrix will make it non-invertible, which will cause errors during the computation of the emission probabilities.

Therefore, a feature set consisting of 29 interaction parameters is used for both defining a baseline and for evaluating the Hybrid-HMM. The set consists of the following parameters (for an explanation of the features, please refer to (Schmitt et al., 2012)):

Exchange Level ASRRECOGNITIONSTATUS, ACTIVITYTYPE, ASRCONFIDENCE, ROLEINDEX, ROLENAME, UTD, REPROMPT?, BARGED-IN?, DD, WPST, WPUT

Dialogue Level MEANASRCONFIDENCE, #ASRREJECTIONS, #TIMEOUTS_ASRREJ, #BARGEINS, %ASRREJECTIONS, %TIMEOUTS_ASRREJ, %BARGEINS, #REPROMPTS, %REPROMPTS, #SYSTEMQUESTIONS

Window Level #TIMEOUTS_ASRREJ, #ASRREJECTIONS, #BARGEINS, %BARGEINS, #SYSTEMQUESTIONS, MEANASRCONFIDENCE, #ASRSUCCESS, #RE-PROMPT

For act in Equation 3, the exchange level parameter ACTIVITYTYPE is used which may take one out of the four values "Announcement", "Confirmation", "Question", or "wait". Their distribution within the LEGO corpus is depicted in Figure 3.

6 Experiments and Results

All experiments are conducted using 6-fold cross-validation[3]. This includes the baseline approach

[3]Six folds have been selected as a reasonable trade-off between validity and computation time.

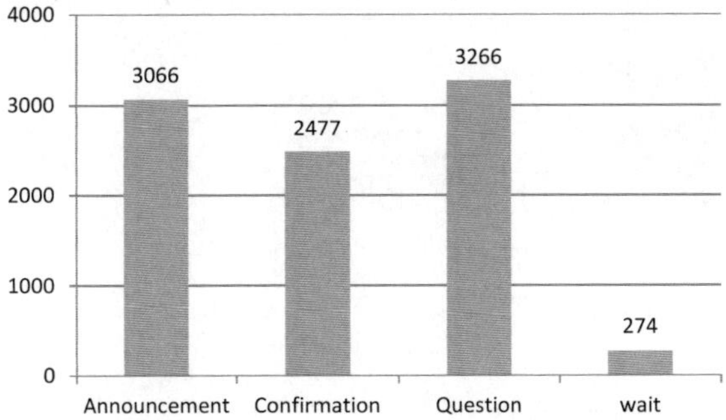

Figure 3: Distribution of the four values for act in Equation 3 in the LEGO corpus. While "wait" occurs rarely, the other three main actions occur at roughly the same frequency.

(also producing the observation probabilities of the Hybrid-HMM approach) and the evaluation of the Hybrid-HMM. For the latter, two phases of cross-validation were applied.

Interaction Quality estimation is done by using three commonly used evaluation metrics: *Unweighted Average Recall (UAR)*, *Cohen's Kappa* (Cohen, 1960) and *Spearman's Rho* (Spearman, 1904). These are also selected as the same metrics have been used in Schmitt et al. (2011) as well.

Recall in general is defined as the rate of correctly classified samples belonging to one class. The recall in UAR for multi-class classification problems with N classes $recall_i$ is computed for each class i and then averaged over all class-wise recalls:

$$UAR = \frac{1}{N} \sum_{i=1}^{N} recall_i \, . \tag{9}$$

Cohen's Kappa measures the relative agreement between two corresponding sets of ratings. In our case, we compute the number of label agreements corrected by the chance level of agreement divided by the maximum proportion of times the labelers could agree. However, Cohen's weighted Kappa is applied as ordinal scores are compared (Cohen, 1968). A weighting factor w is introduced reducing the discount of disagreements the smaller the difference is between two ratings:

$$w = \frac{|r_1 - r_2|}{|r_{max} - r_{min}|} \, . \tag{10}$$

Here, r_1 and r_2 denote the rating pair and r_{max} and r_{min} the maximum and minimum ratings possible.

Table 1: Results for IQ recognition of the statistical classifiers: UAR, κ and ρ for linear SVM, Bayes classification and Rule Induction. σ^2 represents the variances of the confidence scores.

	UAR	κ	ρ	σ^2
SVM (linear)	.495	.611	.774	.020
Bayes	.467	.541	.716	.127
Rule Induction	.596	.678	.790	.131

Correlation between two variables describes the degree by which one variable can be expressed by the other. **Spearman's Rho** is a non-parametric method assuming a monotonic function between the two variables (Spearman, 1904).

6.1 Baseline

As baseline, we adapted the approach of Schmitt et al. (2011). While they focused only on an SVM with linear kernel, we investigate three different static classification approaches. Different classifiers will produce different confidence distributions. These distributions will have different characteristics which is of special interest for evaluating the Hybrid-HMM as will be discussed in Section 7. The confidence characteristics are represented by the variance of the confidence scores σ^2. This variance is used as indicator for how certain the classifier is about its results. If one IQ value has a high confidence while all others have low confidence, the classifier is considered to be very certain. This also results in a high variance. Vice versa, if all IQ values have almost equal confidence indicates high uncertainty. This will result in a low variance.

The classification algorithms, which have been selected arbitrarily, are SVM with linear kernel, Naive Bayes, and Rule Induction (see Section 5). The results in Table 1 show that an SVM with linear kernel (as used by Schmitt et al. (2011)) performs second best with an UAR of 0.495 after Rule Induction with an UAR of 0.596. The results of the SVM differ from the results obtained by Schmitt et al. (UAR of 0.58) as we used a reduced feature set while they used all available features.

6.2 Hybrid-HMM

For evaluating the Hybrid-HMM on Interaction Quality recognition, three aspects are of interest. Most prominent is whether the presented approaches outperform the baseline, i.e., the clas-

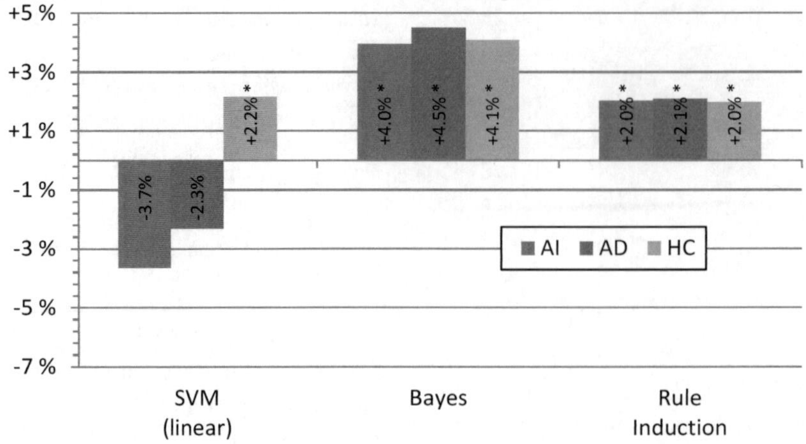

Figure 4: Relative difference of UAR in percent between the baseline performance and the Hybrid-HMM for the action-independent (AI), action-dependent (AD) and handcrafted (HC) transition matrix. Differences marked with an * are significant (Wilcoxon test (Wilcoxon, 1945), $\alpha < 0.05$).

Table 2: Results for the Hybrid-HMM approach: UAR, κ and ρ for the action-independent (AI) and action-dependent (AD) versions.

	UAR		κ		ρ	
	AI	AD	AI	AD	AI	AD
SVM (linear)	.477	.484	.599	.598	.770	.771
Bayes	.486	.489	.563	.564	.737	.741
Rule Induction	.608	.609	.712	.714	.826	.824

sifier which produces the observation probabilities. Moreover, performance values of action-dependent approaches and action-independent approaches are compared. In addition, the results are analyzed with respect to the characteristic of the confidence distribution.

For producing the confidence scores representing the observation probabilities, the statistical classification algorithms presented in Section 6.1 are used. The initial distribution π for each HMM was chosen in accordance with the annotation guidelines of the LEGO corpus starting each dialogue with an IQ score of 5 resulting in

$$\pi_5 = P(IQ = 5) = 1.0$$
$$\pi_4 = \pi_3 = \pi_2 = \pi_1 = P(IQ \neq 5) = 0.0 \,.$$

Results of the experiments with action-dependent (AD) and action-independent (AI) transition function may be seen in Table 2. Again, Rule Induction performed best with Naive Bayes on the second and SVM on the third place.

7 Discussion

While previous work on applying the HMM and CHMM for IQ recognition could not outperform the baseline (Ultes et al., 2012a), Hybrid-HMM experiments show a significant improvement in UAR, Cohen's κ and Spearman's ρ for Naive Bayes and Rule Induction. While performance declines for the linear SVM, this difference has shown to be not significant.

The relative difference of the Hybrid-HMM compared to the respective baseline approaches using an action-dependent and an action-independent transition matrix is depicted in Figure 4. Improvement for the Bayes method was the highest significantly increasing UAR by up to 4.5% relative to the baseline. However, adding action-dependency to the Hybrid-HMM does not show any effect. This may be a result of using ACTIVITYTYPE instead of the actual action. However, using the actual action would result in the need for more data as it contains 45 different values. Significance for all results has been calculated using the Wilcoxon test (Wilcoxon, 1945) by pair-wise comparison of the estimated IQ values of all exchanges. All results except for the decline in SVM performance are significant with $\alpha < 0.05$.

Correlating the confidence variances shown in Table 1 with the improvements of the Hybrid-HMM reveals that for methods with a high variance—and therefore with a greater certainty about the classification result—, an improvement could be accomplished. However, the perfor-

Table 3: Results of Hybrid-HMM with handcrafted transition matrix of the action-independent version.

	UAR	κ	ρ
SVM (linear)	.506	.642	.797
Bayes	.487	.563	.734
Rule Induction	.608	.712	.825

Table 4: Handcrafted transition matrix based on empirical data.

from \ to	1	2	3	4	5
1	0.7	0.3	0	0	0
2	0.25	0.5	0.25	0	0
3	0	0.25	0.5	0.25	0
4	0	0	0.25	0.5	0.25
5	0	0	0	0.3	0.7

mance declined for classification approaches with a low confidence variance, which can be seen as a sign for uncertain classification results.

While the results for Hybrid-HMM are encouraging, creating a simple handcrafted transition matrix for the action-independent version shown in Table 4 achieved even more promising results as performance for all classifier types could be improved significantly compared to the baseline (see Table 3). The handcrafted matrix was created in a way to smooth the resulting estimates as only transitions from one IQ rating to its neighbors have a probability greater than zero. Drastic changes in the estimated IQ value compared to the previous exchange are thus less likely. The exact values have been derived empirically. By applying this handcrafted transition matrix, even SVM performance with linear kernel could be improved significantly by 2.2% in UAR (see Figure 4) compared to the baseline.

For creating the Interaction Quality scores, annotation guidelines were used resulting in certain characteristics of IQ. Therefore, it may be assumed that the effect of exploiting the dependency on previous states is just a reflection of the guidelines. While this might be true, applying a Hybrid HMM for IQ recognition is reasonable as, despite the guidelines, the IQ metric itself is strongly related to user satisfaction, i.e., ratings applied by users (without guidelines), achieving a Spearman's ρ of 0.66 ($\alpha < 0.01$) (Ultes et al., 2013).

8 Conclusions

As previously published, approaches for recognizing the Interaction Quality of Spoken Dialogue Systems are based on static classification without temporal dependency on previous values, a Hybrid Hidden Markov Model approach has been investigated based on three static classifiers. The Hybrid-HMM achieved a relative improvement up to 4.5% and a maximum of 0.61 UAR. Analyzing the experiments revealed that, while an improvement could be achieved with the Hybrid-HMM approach, handcrafting a transition model achieved even better results as performance for all analyzed classifier types could be improved significantly. Furthermore, applying the Hybrid-HMM approach only yields improved performance if the basic classifier itself has a high confidence about its results.

Further research should be conducted investigating the question how the presented approach as well as the Interaction Quality paradigm in general will generalize for different dialogue domains. As IQ is designed to be domain independent, it may be expected that the Hybrid-HMM will be applicable for different dialogue domains as well.

Finally, it is notable that rule induction outperformed SVM approaches in the baseline by 10 percentage points. While this contribution does not focus on this, analyzing the model may help in understanding the problem of estimating Interaction Quality better, especially since rule-based recognition methods allow easy interpretation.

Acknowledgments

This work was supported by the Transregional Collaborative Research Centre SFB/TRR 62 "Companion-Technology for Cognitive Technical Systems" which is funded by the German Research Foundation (DFG).

References

Chih-Chung Chang and Chih-Jen Lin. 2011. LIBSVM: A library for support vector machines. *ACM Transactions on Intelligent Systems and Technology*, 2:27:1–27:27.

Jacob Cohen. 1960. A coefficient of agreement for nominal scales. In *Educational and Psychological Measurement*, volume 20, pages 37–46, April.

Jacob Cohen. 1968. Weighted kappa: Nominal scale agreement provision for scaled disagreement or partial credit. *Psychological bulletin*, 70(4):213.

William W. Cohen. 1995. Fast effective rule induction. In *Proceedings of the 12th International Con-*

ference on Machine Learning, pages 115–123. Morgan Kaufmann, July.

Richard O. Duda, Peter E. Hart, and David G. Stork. 2001. *Pattern Classification (2nd Edition)*. Wiley-Interscience, 2 edition, November.

Klaus-Peter Engelbrecht, Florian Gödde, Felix Hartard, Hamed Ketabdar, and Sebastian Möller. 2009. Modeling user satisfaction with hidden markov model. In *SIGDIAL '09: Proceedings of the SIGDIAL 2009 Conference*, pages 170–177, Morristown, NJ, USA. ACL.

Sunao Hara, Norihide Kitaoka, and Kazuya Takeda. 2010. Estimation method of user satisfaction using n-gram-based dialog history model for spoken dialog system. In *Proceedings of the Seventh conference on International Language Resources and Evaluation (LREC'10)*, Valletta, Malta, May. ELRA.

Ryuichiro Higashinaka, Yasuhiro Minami, Kohji Dohsaka, and Toyomi Meguro. 2010. Issues in predicting user satisfaction transitions in dialogues: Individual differences, evaluation criteria, and prediction models. In *Spoken Dialogue Systems for Ambient Environments*, volume 6392 of *Lecture Notes in Computer Science*, pages 48–60. Springer Berlin / Heidelberg.

L. P. Kaelbling, M. L. Littman, and A. R. Cassandra. 1998. Planning and acting in partially observable stochastic domains. *Artificial Intelligence*, 101(1-2):99–134.

J. R. Landis and G. G. Koch. 1977. The measurement of observer agreement for categorical data. *Biometrics*, 33(1):159–174, March.

Sebastian Möller, Klaus-Peter Engelbrecht, C. Kühnel, I. Wechsung, and B. Weiss. 2009. A taxonomy of quality of service and quality of experience of multimodal human-machine interaction. In *Quality of Multimedia Experience, 2009. QoMEx 2009. International Workshop on*, pages 7–12, July.

Ibrahim Onaran, N Firat Ince, A Enis Cetin, and Aviva Abosch. 2011. A hybrid svm/hmm based system for the state detection of individual finger movements from multichannel ecog signals. In *Neural Engineering (NER), 2011 5th International IEEE/EMBS Conference on*, pages 457–460. IEEE.

Lawrence R. Rabiner. 1989. *A tutorial on hidden Markov models and selected applications in speech recognition*. Morgan Kaufmann Publishers Inc., San Francisco, CA, USA.

Antoine Raux, Dan Bohus, Brian Langner, Alan W. Black, and Maxine Eskenazi. 2006. Doing research on a deployed spoken dialogue system: One year of letâs go! experience. In *Proc. of the International Conference on Speech and Language Processing (ICSLP)*, September.

Alexander Schmitt, Benjamin Schatz, and Wolfgang Minker. 2011. Modeling and predicting quality in spoken human-computer interaction. In *Proceedings of the SIGDIAL 2011 Conference*, Portland, Oregon, USA, June. Association for Computational Linguistics.

Alexander Schmitt, Stefan Ultes, and Wolfgang Minker. 2012. A parameterized and annotated corpus of the cmu let's go bus information system. In *International Conference on Language Resources and Evaluation (LREC)*.

Charles Edward Spearman. 1904. The proof and measurement of association between two things. *American Journal of Psychology*, 15:88–103.

Stefan Ultes, Robert ElChabb, and Wolfgang Minker. 2012a. Application and evaluation of a conditioned hidden markov model for estimating interaction quality of spoken dialogue systems. In *Proceedings of the 4th International Workshop on Spoken Language Dialog System (IWSDS)*, pages 141–150. Springer, November.

Stefan Ultes, Alexander Schmitt, and Wolfgang Minker. 2012b. Towards quality-adaptive spoken dialogue management. In *NAACL-HLT Workshop on Future directions and needs in the Spoken Dialog Community: Tools and Data (SDCTD 2012)*, pages 49–52, Montréal, Canada, June. ACL.

Stefan Ultes, Alexander Schmitt, and Wolfgang Minker. 2013. On quality ratings for spoken dialogue systems – experts vs. users. In *Proceedings of the 2013 Conference of the North American Chapter of the Association for Computational Linguistics: Human Language Technologies*, pages 569–578. ACL, June.

Michel F. Valstar and Maja Pantic. 2007. Combined support vector machines and hidden markov models for modeling facial action temporal dynamics. In *Human-Computer Interaction*, volume 4796 of *Lecture Notes in Computer Science*, pages 118–127. Springer Berlin Heidelberg.

Vladimir N. Vapnik. 1995. *The nature of statistical learning theory*. Springer-Verlag New York, Inc., New York, NY, USA.

Marilyn Walker, Diane Litman, Candace A. Kamm, and Alicia Abella. 1997. Paradise: a framework for evaluating spoken dialogue agents. In *Proceedings of the eighth conference on European chapter of the Association for Computational Linguistics*, pages 271–280, Morristown, NJ, USA. ACL.

Frank Wilcoxon. 1945. Individual comparisons by ranking methods. *Biometrics bulletin*, 1(6):80–83.

Appendix

Table 5: Example of a dialogue annotated with Interaction Quality for each system-user-exchange. As the system fails to interact properly with the user in the end, the IQ value drops down to one. Utterance represents either the system utterance or the recognized user utterance. (CallID 2061123000 of the LEGO corpus.)

	Utterance	IQ
S:	Welcome to the CMU Let's Go bus information system.	
U:		5
S:	To get help at any time, just say Help or press zero.	
U:		5
S:	What can I do for you?	
U:	PENN AT BUTLER TIME IS IT IS THE CENTRE AT HIGHLAND FROM RUNS THE 61A EIGHT THIRTY 61B CAN'T OAKLAND	5
S:	Leaving from OAKLAND . Is this correct?	
U:	OAKLAND	4
S:	Leaving from OAKLAND . Is this correct?	
U:	*YES*	4
S:	Right	
U:	-	4
S:	Where do you want to go?	
U:	*SQUIRREL HILL OF FIFTH AVENUE*	4
S:	Going to FIFTH AVENUE . Is this correct?	
U:	*YES*	5
S:	Alright	
U:	-	5
S:	When do you wanna travel?	
U:	*SUNDAY*	4
S:	At what time do you wanna travel?	
U:	AT FIVE FOUR VERY ABOUT ELEVEN O'CLOCK	4
S:	*Leaving at 11 a.m. . Is this correct?*	
U:	*YES*	5
S:	Right	
U:	-	5
S:	Hold on. Let me check that for you.	
U:	-	5
S:	OAKLAND and FIFTH AVENUE are both the same stop. Please provide a different start or end point.	
U:	-	3
S:	To ask about a different trip, you can say, start a new query. If you are finished, you can say goodbye.	
U:	*61A*	2
S:	You can say start a new query, or goodbye.	
U:	*FIVE DUQUESNE*	1
S:	To ask about a different trip, you can say, start a new query. If you are finished, you can say goodbye.	
U:	*LAST THE NEXT*	1
S:	You can say start a new query, or goodbye.	
U:	*START WH*	1
S:	To ask about a different trip, you can say, start a new query. If you are finished, you can say goodbye.	
U:	*THE*	1
S:	You can say start a new query, or goodbye.	
U:	*THANK YOU QUERY ELEVEN BACK*	1
S:	To ask about a different trip, you can say, start a new query. If you are finished, you can say goodbye.	
U:	*GOODBYE*	1
S:	Thank you for using the cmu Let's Go Bus Information System. Goodbye.	
U:	-	1

Learning to Re-rank for Interactive Problem Resolution and Query Refinement

Rashmi Gangadharaiah
IBM Research,
India Research Lab,
Bangalore, KA, India
rashgang@in.ibm.com

Balakrishnan Narayanaswamy and Charles Elkan
Department of CSE,
University of California, San Diego
La Jolla, CA, USA
{muralib, elkan}@cs.ucsd.edu

Abstract

We study the design of an information retrieval (IR) system that assists customer service agents while they interact with end-users. The type of IR needed is difficult because of the large lexical gap between problems as described by customers, and solutions. We describe an approach that bridges this lexical gap by learning semantic relatedness using tensor representations. Queries that are short and vague, which are common in practice, result in a large number of documents being retrieved, and a high cognitive load for customer service agents. We show how to reduce this burden by providing suggestions that are selected based on the learned measures of semantic relatedness. Experiments show that the approach offers substantial benefit compared to the use of standard lexical similarity.

1 Introduction

Information retrieval systems help businesses and individuals make decisions by automatically extracting actionable intelligence from large (unstructured) data (Musen et al., 2006; Antonio Palma-dos Reis, 1999). This paper focuses on the application of retrieval systems in a contact centers where the system assists agents while they are helping customers with problem resolution.

Currently, most contact center information retrieval use (web based) front-ends to search engines indexed with knowledge sources (Holland, 2005). Agents enter queries to retrieve documents related to the customer's problem. These sources are often incomplete as it is unlikely that all possible customer problems can be identified before product release. This is particularly true for recently released and frequently updated products. One approach, which we build on here, is to mine problems and resolutions from online discussion forums Yahoo! Answers[1] Ubuntu Forums[2] and Apple Support Communities[3]. While these often provide useful solutions within hours or days of a problem surfacing, they are semantically noisy (Gangadharaiah and Narayanaswamy, 2013).

Most contact centers and agents are evaluated based on the number of calls they handle over a period (Pinedo et al., 2000). As a result, queries entered by agents into the search engine are usually underspecified. This, together with noise in the database, results in a large number of documents being retrieved as relevant documents. This in turn, increases the cognitive load on agents, and reduces the effectiveness of the search system and the efficiency of the contact center. Our first task in this paper is to automatically make candidate suggestions that reduce the search space of relevant documents in a contact center application. The agent/user then interacts with the system by selecting one of the suggestions. This is used to expand the original query and the process can be repeated. We show that even one round of interaction, with a small set of suggestions, can lead to high quality solutions to user problems.

In query expansion, the classical approach is to automatically find suggestions either in the form of words, phrases or similar queries (Kelly et al., 2009; Feuer et al., 2007; Leung et al., 2008). These can be obtained either from query logs or based on their representativeness of the initial retrieved documents (Guo et al., 2008; Baeza-yates et al., 2004). The suggestions are then ranked either based on their frequencies or based on their similarity to the original query (Kelly et al., 2009; Leung et al., 2008). For example, if suggestions and queries are represented as term vectors (e.g.

[1] http://answers.yahoo.com/
[2] http://ubuntuforums.org/
[3] https://discussions.apple.com/

term frequency-inverse document frequency or tf-idf) their similarity may be determined using similarity measures such as cosine similarity or inverse of euclidean distance (Salton and McGill, 1983).

However, in question-answering and problem-resolution domains, and in contrast to traditional Information Retrieval, most often the query and the suggestions do not have many overlapping words. This leads to low similarity scores, even when the suggestion is highly relevant. Consider the representative example in Table 1, taken from our crawled dataset. Although the suggestions, "does not support file transfer", "connection not stable", "pairing failed" are highly relevant for the problem of "Bluetooth not working", their lexical similarity score is zero. The second task that this paper addresses is how to bridge this lexical chasm between the query and the suggestions. For this, we learn a measure of semantic-relatedness between the query and the suggestions rather than defining closeness based on lexical similarity.

Query	Bluetooth not working .
Suggestions	devices not discovered, bluetooth greyed out, bluetooth device did not respond, does not support file transfer, connection not stable, pairing failed

Table 1: Suggestions for the Query or customer's problem, "Bluetooth not working".

The primary contributions of this paper are that:

- We show how tensor methods can be used to learn measures of question-answer or problem-resolution similarity. In addition, we show that these learned measures can be used directly with well studied classification techniques like Support Vector Machines (SVMs) and Logistic Classifiers to classify whether suggestions are relevant. This results in substantially improved performance over using conventional similarity metrics.

- We show that along with the learned similarity metric, a data dependent Information Gain (which incorporates knowledge about the set of documents in the database) can be used as a feature to further boost accuracy.

- We demonstrate the efficacy of our approach on a complete end-to-end problem-resolution system, which includes crawled data from online forums and gold standard user interaction annotations.

2 System outline

As discussed in the Introduction, online discussion forums form a rich source of problems and their corresponding resolutions. Thread initiators or users of a product facing problems with their product post in these forums. Other users post possible solutions to the problem. At the same time, there is noise due to unstructured content, off-topic replies and other factors. Our interaction system has two phases, as shown in Figure 1. The offline phase attempts to reduce noise in the database, while the online phase assists users deal with the cognitive overload caused by a large set of retrieved documents. In our paper, threads form the documents indexed by the system.

The goals of the **offline phase** are two-fold. First, to reduce the aforementioned noise in the database, we succinctly represent each document (i.e., a thread in online discussion forums) by its *signature*, which is composed of *units* extracted from the first post of the underlying thread that best describe the problem discussed in the thread. Second, the system makes use of click-through data, where users clicked on relevant suggestions for their queries to build a relevancy model. As mentioned before, the primary challenge is to build a model that can identify units that are semantically similar to a given query.

In the **online phase**, the agent who acts as the mediator between the user and the Search Engine enters the user's/customer's query to retrieve relevant documents. From these retrieved documents, the system then obtains candidate suggestions and ranks these suggestions using the relevancy model built in the offline phase to further better understand the query and thereby reduce the space of documents retrieved. The user then selects the suggestion that is most relevant to his query. The retrieved documents are then filtered displaying only those documents that contain the selected suggestion in their signatures. The process continues until the user quits.

2.1 Signatures of documents

In the offline phase, every document (corresponding to a thread in online discussion forums) is represented by units that best describe a problem. We adopt the approach suggested in (Gangadharaiah and Narayanaswamy, 2013) to automatically generate these signatures from each discussion thread. We assume that the first post describes the user's problem, something we have found to be true in practice. From the dependency parse trees of the first posts, we extract three types of units (i) phrases (e.g., sync server), (ii) attribute-values (e.g., iOS, 4) and (iii) action-attribute tuples (e.g., sync server: failed). Phrases form good base problem descriptors. Attribute-value pairs provide configurational contexts to the problem. Action-attribute tuples, as suggested in (Gangadharaiah and Narayanaswamy, 2013), capture segments of the first post that indicate user wanting to perform an action ("I cannot hear notifications on bluetooth") or the problems caused by a user's action ("working great before I updated"). These make them particularly valuable features for problem-resolution and question-answering.

2.2 Representation of Queries and Suggestions

Queries are represented as term vectors using the term frequency-inverse document frequency (tf-idf) representation forming the query space. The term frequency is defined as the frequency with which word appears in the query and the inverse document frequency for a word is defined as the frequency of queries in which the word appeared. Similarly, units are represented as tf-idf term vectors from the suggestion space. Term frequency in the unit space is defined as the number of times a word appears in the unit and its inverse document frequency is defined in terms of the number of units in which the word appeared. Since the vocabulary used in the queries and documents are different, the representations for queries and units belong to different spaces of different dimensions.

For every query-unit pair, we learn a measure of similarity as explained in Section 4. Additionally, we use similarity features based on cosine similarity between the query and the unit under consideration. We also consider an additional feature based on information gain (Gangadharaiah and Narayanaswamy, 2013). In particular, if S represents the set all retrieved documents, S_1 is a subset of S ($S_1 \subseteq S$) containing a unit $unit_i$ and S_2 is a subset of S that does not contain $unit_i$, information gain with $unit_i$ is,

$$Gain(S, unit_i) = E(S) - \frac{|S_1|}{|S|}E(S_1) - \frac{|S_2|}{|S|}E(S_2) \quad (1)$$

$$E(S) = \sum_{k=1,\dots|S|} -p(doc_k)log_2p(doc_k). \quad (2)$$

The probability for each document is based on its rank in the retrieved of results,

$$p(doc_j) = \frac{\frac{1}{rank(doc_j)}}{\sum_{k=1,\dots|S|}\frac{1}{rank(doc_k)}}. \quad (3)$$

We crawled posts and threads from online forums for the products of interest, as detailed in Section 5.1, and these form the documents. We used trial interactions and retrievals to collect the click-though data, which we used as labeled data for similarity metric learning. In particular, labels indicate which candidate units were selected as relevant suggestions by a human annotator. We now explain our training (offline) and testing (online) phases that use this data in more detail.

2.3 Training

The labeled (click-through) data for training the relevance model is collected as follows. Annotators were given pairs of queries. Each pair is composed of an *underspecified* query and a *specific* query (Section 5.1 provides more information on the creation of these queries). An underspecified query is a query that reflects what a user/agent typically enters into the system, and the corresponding specific query is full-specified version of the underspecified query. Annotators were first asked to query the search engine with each underspecified query. We use the Lemur search engine (Strohman et al., 2004). From the resulting set of retrieved documents, the system uses the information gain criteria (as given in (1) below) to rank and display to the annotators the candidate suggestions (i.e., the units that appear in the signatures of the retrieved documents). Thus, our system is bootstrapped using the information gain criterion. The annotators then selects the candidate suggestion that is most relevant to the corresponding specific query. The interaction with the system continues until the annotators quit.

We then provide a class label for each unit based on the collected click-through information. In particular, if a unit $s \in \mathcal{S}(x)$ was clicked by a user for his query x, from the list $\mathcal{S}$ we provide a $+$ label to indicate that the unit is relevant suggestion for the query. Similarly, for all other units that are never clicked by users for x are labeled as $-$. This forms the training data for the system. Details on

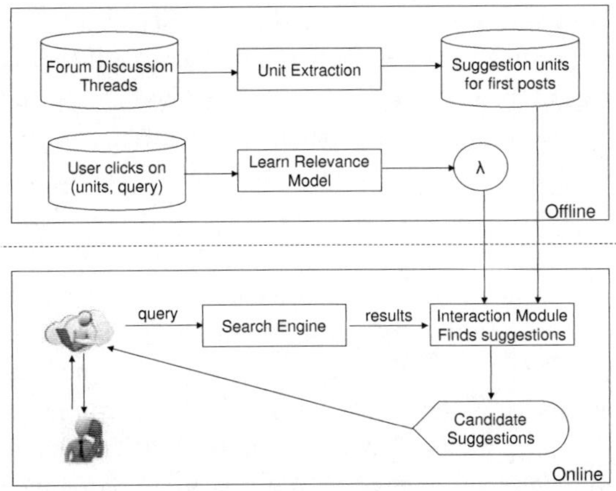

Figure 1: Outline of our interactive query refinement system for problem resolution

the feature extraction and how the model is created is given in Section 3.

2.4 Testing

In the online phase, the search engine retrieves documents for the user's query x'. Signatures for the retrieved documents form the initial space of candidate units. As done in training, for every pair of x' and unit the label is predicted using the model built in the training phase. Units that are predicted as $+$ are shown to the user. When a user clicks on his most relevant suggestion, the retrieved results are filtered to show only those documents that contain the suggestion (i.e., in its signature). This process continues until the user quits.

3 Model

We consider underspecified queries $x \in \mathbb{R}^{x_d}$ and units $y \in \mathbb{R}^{y_d}$. Given an underspecified query x we pass it through a search engine, resulting in a list of results $\mathcal{S}(x)$.

As explained in Section 2.3, our training data consists of labels $r(x, y) \in +1, -1$ for each under-specified query, $y \in \mathcal{S}(x)$. $r(x, y) = +1$ if the unit is labeled a relevant suggestion and $r(x, y) = -1$ if it is not labeled relevant. Units are relevant or not based on the final query, and not just y, a distinction we expand upon below.

At each time step, our system proposes a list $\mathcal{Z}(x)$ of possible query refinement suggestions z to the user. The user can select one or none of these suggestions. If the user selects z, only those documents that contain the suggestion (i.e., in its signature) are shown to the user, resulting in a filtered set of results, $\mathcal{S}(x + z)$.

This process can be repeated until a stopping criterion is reached. Stopping criterion include the size of the returned list is smaller than some number $|\mathcal{S}(x + z)| < N$, in which case all remaining documents are returned. Special cases include when only one document is returned $N = 1$. We will design query suggestions so that $|\mathcal{S}(x+z)| > 0$. Another criterion we use is to return all remaining documents after a certain maximum number of interactions or until the user quits.

4 Our Approach

We specify our algorithm using a tensor notation. We do this since tensors appear to subsume most of the methods applied in practice, where different algorithms use slightly different costs, losses and constraints. These ideas are strongly motivated by, but generalize to some extent, suggestions for this problem presented in (Elkan, 2010).

For our purposes, we consider tensors as multidimensional arrays, with the number of dimensions defined as the order of the tensor. An M order tensor $\mathbf{X} \in \mathbb{R}^{I_1 \times I_2 \ldots I_M}$. As such tensors subsume vectors (1st order tensors) and matrices (2nd order tensors). The vectorization of a tensor of order M is obtained by stacking elements from the M dimensions into a vector of length $I_1 \times I_2 \times \ldots \times I_M$ in the natural way.

The inner product of two tensors is defined as

$$\langle \mathbf{X}, \mathbf{W} \rangle = \sum_{i_1}^{I_1} \sum_{i_2}^{I_2} \ldots \sum_{i_M}^{I_M} x_{i_1} w_{i_1} x_{i_2} w_{i_2} \ldots x_{i_M} w_{i_M} \tag{4}$$

Analogous to the definition for vectors, the (Kharti-Rao) outer product $\mathbf{A} = \mathbf{X} \otimes \mathbf{W}$ of two tensors $\mathbf{X}$ and $\mathbf{W}$ has $A_{ij} = X_i W_j$ where i and j run over all elements of $\mathbf{X}$ and W. Thus, if $\mathbf{X}$ is of order M_X and $\mathbf{W}$ of order M_W, $\mathbf{A}$ is of order $M_A = M_X + M_W$.

The particular tensor we are interested in is a 2-D tensor (matrix) $\mathbf{X}$ which is the outer product of query and unit pairs (Feats). In particular, for a query x and unit y, $X_{i,j} = x_i y_j$.

Given this representation, standard classification and regression methods from the machine learning literature can often be extended to deal with tensors. In our work we consider two classifiers that have been successful in many applications, logistic regression and support vector machines (SVMs) (Bishop, 2006).

In the case of logistic regression, the conditional probability of a reward signal $r(\mathbf{X}) = r(x, y)$ is,

$$p(r(\mathbf{X}) = +1) = \frac{1}{1 + exp(-\langle \mathbf{X}, \mathbf{W} \rangle + b)} \quad (5)$$

The parameters $\mathbf{W}$ and b can be obtained by minimizing the log loss $\mathcal{L}_{reg}$ on the training data $\mathcal{D}$

$$\mathcal{L}_{reg}(\mathbf{W}, b) = \quad (6)$$
$$\sum_{(\mathbf{X}, r(\mathbf{X})) \in \mathcal{D}} \log(1 + exp(-r(\mathbf{X})\langle \mathbf{X}, \mathbf{W} \rangle + b)$$

For SVMs with the hinge loss we select parameters to minimize $\mathcal{L}_{hinge}$,

$$\mathcal{L}_{hinge}(\mathbf{W}, b) = ||\mathbf{X}||_F^2 + \quad (7)$$
$$\lambda \sum_{(\mathbf{X}, r(\mathbf{X})) \in \mathcal{D}} \max[0, 1 - (r(\mathbf{X})\langle \mathbf{X}, \mathbf{W} \rangle + b)]$$

where $||\mathbf{X}||_F$ is the Frobenius norm of tensor $\mathbf{X}$.

Given the number of parameters in our system $(\mathbf{W}, b)$ to limit overfitting, we have to regularize these parameters. We use regularizers of the form

$$\Omega(\mathbf{W}, b) = \lambda_W ||\mathbf{W}||_F \quad (8)$$

such regularizes have been successful in many large scale machine learning tasks including learning of high dimensional graphical models (Ravikumar et al., 2010) and link prediction (Menon and Elkan, 2011).

Thus, the final optimization problem we are faced with is of the form

$$\min_{\mathbf{W}, b} \mathcal{L}(\mathbf{W}, b) + \Omega(\mathbf{W}, b) \quad (9)$$

where $\mathcal{L}$ is $\mathcal{L}_{reg}$ or $\mathcal{L}_{hinge}$ as appropriate. Other losses, classifiers and regularizers may be used.

The advantage of tensors over their vectorized counterparts, that may be lost in the notation, is that they do not lose the information that the different dimensions can (and in our case do) lie in different spaces. In particular, in our case we use different features to represent queries and units (as discussed in Section 2.2) which are not of the same length, and as a result trivially do not lie in the same space.

Tensor methods also allow us to regularize the components of queries and units separately in different ways. This can be done for example by, i) forcing $\mathbf{W} = \mathbf{Q}_1\mathbf{Q}_2$, where $\mathbf{Q}_1$ and $\mathbf{Q}_2$ are constrained to be of fixed rank s ii) using trace or Frobenius norms on Q_1 and Q_2 for separate regularization as proxies for the rank iii) using different sparsity promoting norms on the rows of Q_1 and Q_2 iv) weighing these penalties differently for the two matrices in the final loss function. Note that by analogy to the vector case, we directly obtain generalization error guarantees for our methods.

We also discuss the advantage of the tensor representation above over a natural representation $\mathbf{X} = [x; y]$ i.e. $\mathbf{X}$ is the column vector obtained by stacking the query and unit representations. Note that in this representation, for logistic regression, while a change in the query x can change the probability for a unit $P(r(\mathbf{X}) = 1)$ it cannot change the relative probability of two different units. Thus, the ordering of all unit remains the same for all queries. This flaw has been pointed out in the literature in (Vert and Jacob, 2008) and (Bai et al., 2009), but was brought to our attention by (Elkan, 2010).

Finally, we note that by normalizing the query and unit vectors (x and y), and selecting $W = I$ (the identity matrix) we can recover the cosine similarity metric (Elkan, 2010). Thus, our representation is atleast as accurate and we show that learning the diagonal and off-diagonal components of $\mathbf{W}$ can substantially improve accuracy.

Additionally, for every (query,unit) we also compute information gain (IG) as given in (1), and the lexical similarity (Sim) in terms of cosine similarity between the query and the unit as additional features in the feature vectors.

5 Results and Discussion

To evaluate our system, we built and simulated a contact center information retrieval system for iPhone problem resolution.

5.1 Description of the Dataset

We collected data by crawling forum discussion threads from the Apple Discussion Forum, created during the period 2007-2011, resulting in about 147,000 discussion threads. The underspecified queries and specific queries were created as follows. Discussion threads were first clustered treating each discussion thread as a data point using a tf-idf representation. The thread nearest the centroid of the 60 largest clusters were marked as the 'most common' problems.

The first post is used as a proxy for the problem description. An annotator was asked to then create

Underspecified query "Safari not working"
1. safari:crashes
2. safari:cannot find:server
3. server:stopped responding
4. phone:freezes
5. update:failed

Table 2: Specific Queries generated with the underspecified Query, "Safari not working".

a short query (underspecified) from the first post of each of the 60 selected threads. These queries were given to the Lemur search engine (Strohman et al., 2004) to retrieve the 50 most similar threads from an index built on the entire set of 147,000 threads. The annotator manually analyzed the first posts of the retrieved threads to create contexts, resulting in a total 200 specific queries.

We give an example to illustrate the data creation in Table 2. From an under-specified query "Safari not working", the annotator found 5 specific queries. Two other annotators, were given these specific queries with the search engine's results from the corresponding under-specified query. They were asked to choose the most relevant results for the specific queries. The intersection of the choices of the annotators formed our 'gold standard' of relevant documents.

5.2 Results

We simulated a contact center retrieval systems (as in Figure 1) to evaluate the approach proposed in this paper. To evaluate the generality of our approach we conduct experiments with both SVMs and Logistic Regression. Due to lack of space we illustrate each result for only one kind of classifier.

5.2.1 Evaluating the Relevance Model

To measure the performance of the relevance model for predicting the class labels or for finding the most relevant units towards making the user's underspecified query more specific, we performed the following experiment. 4000 random query-unit pairs were picked from the training data, collected as explained in Section 2. Since most units are not relevant for a query, 90% of the pairs belonged to the $-$ class. On average, every specific query gave rise to 2.4 suggestions. Hence, predicting $-$ for all pairs still achieves an error rate of 10%. This data was then split into varying sizes of training and test sets. The relevancy model was then built on the training half and the classifiers were used to predict labels on the test

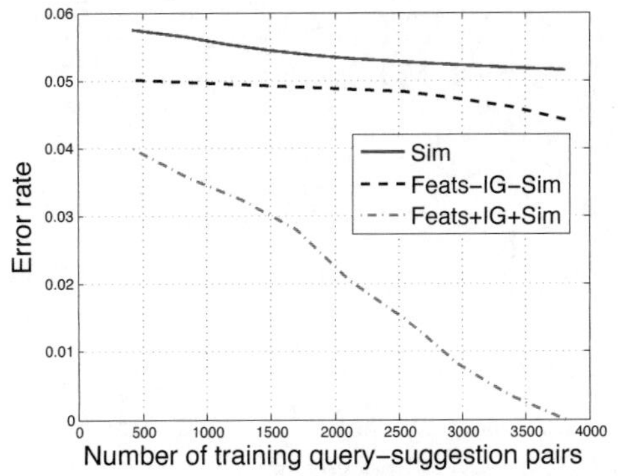

Figure 2: Performance with Logistic Regression using different features and various sizes of Training and Test sets. Feats-IG-Sim does not use cosine similarity (Sim) and information gain (IG). Feats+IG+Sim considers Sim and IG.

set. Figure 2 shows error rate obtained with logistic regression (a similar trend was observed with SVMs) on various sizes of the training data and test data. The plot shows that the model (Feats-IG-Sim and Feats+IG+Sim) performs significantly better at predicting the relevancy of units for underspecified queries when compared to just using cosine similarity (Sim) as a feature. Feats-IG-Sim does not make use of cosine similarity as a feature or the information gain feature while Feats+IG+Sim uses both these features for training the relevancy model and for predicting the relevancy of units. As expected the performance of the classifier improves as the size of the training data is increased.

5.2.2 Evaluating the Interaction Engine

We evaluate a complete system with both the user (the agent) and the search engine in the loop. We measure the value of the interactions by an analysis of which results 'rise to the top'. Users were given a specific query and its underspecified query along with the results obtained when the underspecified query was input to the search engine. They were presented with suggestions that were predicted $+$ for the underspecified query using SVMs. The user was asked to select the most appropriate suggestion that made the underspecified query more specific. This process continues until the user quits either because he is satisfied with the retrieved results or does not obtain relevant suggestions from the system. For example, for the underspecified query in Table 2, one of the predicted suggestions was, "server:stopped respond-

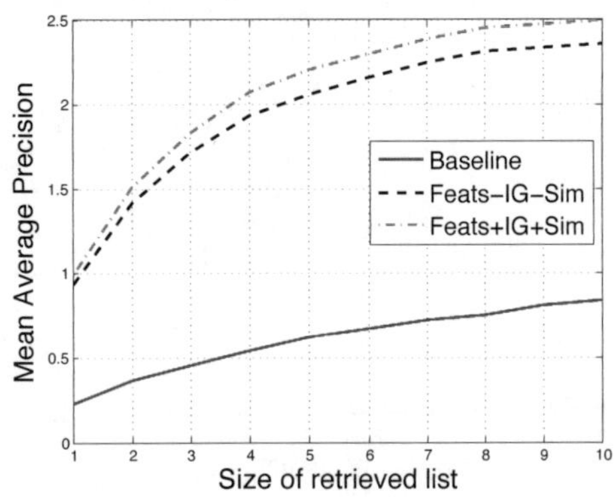

Figure 3: Comparison of the proposed approach with respect to the Baseline that does not involve interaction in terms of MAP at N.

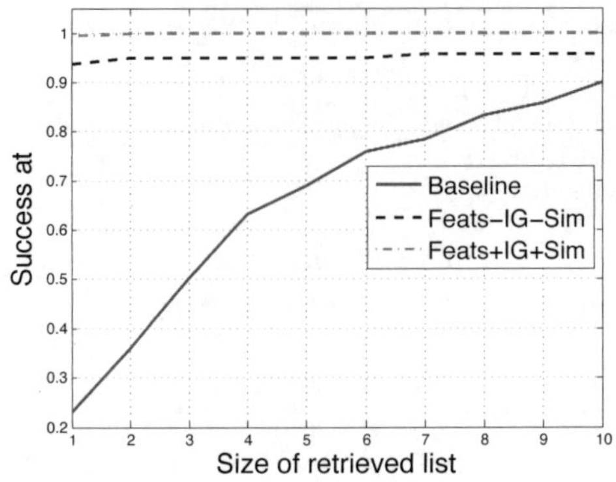

Figure 4: Comparison of the proposed approach with respect to the Baseline that does not involve interaction in terms of Success at N.

ing". If the user finds the suggestion relevant, he clicks on it. The selected suggestion then reduces the number of retrieved results. We then measured the relevance of the reduced result, with respect to the gold standard for that specific query, using metrics used in IR - MRR, Mean Average Precision (MAP) and Success at rank N.

Figures 3, 4 and Table 3 evaluate the results obtained with the interaction engine using Feats-IG-Sim and Feats+IG+Sim. We compared the performance of our algorithms with a Baseline that does not perform any interaction and is evaluated based on the retrieved results obtained with the underspecified queries. The models for each of the systems were trained using query-suggestion pairs collected from 100 specific queries (data collected as explained in Section 2). The remaining 100 specific queries were used for testing. We see that the suggestions predicted by the classifiers using the relevancy model indeed improves the performance of the baseline. Also, adding the IG and Sim feature further boosts the performance of the system.

Systems	MRR
Baseline	0.4218
Feats-IG-Sim	0.9449
Feats+IG+Sim	0.9968

Table 3: Comparison of the proposed approach with respect to the Baseline that does not involve interaction in terms of MRR.

5.3 Related Work

Learning affinities between queries an documents is a well studied area. (Liu, 2009) provides an excellent survey of these approaches. In these methods, there is a fixed feature function $\Phi(x, y)$ defined between any query-document pair. These features are then used, along with labeled training data, to learn the parameters of a model that can then be used to predict the relevance $r(x, y)$ of a new query-document pair. The output of the model can also be used to re-rank the results of a search engine. In contrast to this class of methods, we define and parameterize the Φ function and jointly optimize the parameters of the feature mapping and the machine learning re-ranking model.

Latent tensor methods for regression and classification have recently become popular in the image and signal processing domain. Most of these methods solve an optimization problem similar to our own (9), but add additional constraints limiting the rank of the learned matrix W either explicitly or implicit by defining $W = Q_1 Q_2^T$, and defining $Q_1 \in \mathbb{R}^{d_x \times d}$ and $Q_2 \in \mathbb{R}^{d_y \times d}$. This approach is used for example in (Pirsiavash et al., 2009) and more recently in (Tan et al., 2013) (Guo et al., 2012). While this reduces the number of parameters to be learned from $d_x d_y$ to $d(d_x + d_y)$ it makes the problem non-convex and introduces an additional parameter d that must be selected.

This approach of restricting the rank was recently suggested for information retrieval in (Wu et al., 2013). They look at a regression problem, using click-through rates as the reward function $r(x, y)$. In addition, (Wu et al., 2013) does not use an initial search engine and hence must learn an affinity function between all query-document pairs. In contrast to this, we learn a classification function that discriminates between the true and false positive documents that are deemed similar by the search engine. This has three beneficial effects : (i) it reduces the amount of labeled training data required and the imbalance between the positive and negative classes which can make learning difficult (He and Garcia, 2009) and (ii) allows us to build on the strengths of fast and strong existing search engines increasing accuracy and decreasing retrieval time and (iii) allows the learnt model to focus learning on the query-document pairs that are most problematic for the search engine.

Bilinear forms of tensor models without the rank restriction have recently been studied for link prediction (Menon and Elkan, 2011) and image processing (Kobayashi and Otsu, 2012). Since the applications are different, there is no preliminary search engine which retrieves results, making them ranking methods and ours a re-ranking approach. Related work in text IR includes (Beeferman and Berger, 2000), where two queries are considered semantically similar if their clicks lead to the same page. However, the probability that different queries lead to common clicks of the same URLs is very small, again increasing the training data required. Approaches in the past have also proposed techniques to automatically find suggestions either in the form of words, phrases (Kelly et al., 2009; Feuer et al., 2007; Baeza-yates et al., 2004) or similar queries (Leung et al., 2008) from query logs (Guo et al., 2008; Baeza-yates et al., 2004) or based on their probability of representing the initial retrieved documents (Kelly et al., 2009; Feuer et al., 2007). These suggestions are then ranked either based on their frequencies or based on their closeness to the query. Closeness is defined in terms of lexical similarity to the query. However, most often the query and the suggestions do not have any co-occurring words leading to low similarity scores, even when the suggestion is relevant.

(Gangadharaiah and Narayanaswamy, 2013) use information gain to rank candidate suggestions. However, the relevancy of the suggestions highly depends on the relevancy of the initial retrieved documents. Our work here addresses the question of how to bridge this lexical chasm between the query and the suggestions. For this, we use semantic-relatedness between the query and the suggestions as a measure of closeness rather than defining closeness based on lexical similarity. A related approach to handle this lexical gap by applying alignment techniques from Statistical Machine translation (Brown et al., 1993), in particular by building translation models for information retrieval (Berger and Lafferty, 1999; Riezler et al., 2007). These approaches require training data in the form of question-answer pairs, are again limited to words or phrases and are not intended for understanding the user's problem better through interaction, which is our focus.

6 Conclusions, Discussions and Future Work

We studied the problem of designing Information Retrieval systems for interactive problem resolution. We developed a system for bridging the large lexical gap between short, incomplete problem queries and documents in a database of resolutions. We showed that tensor representations are a useful tool to learn measures of semantic relatedness, beyond the cosine similarity metric. Our results show that with interaction, suggestions can be effective in pruning large sets of retrieved documents. We showed that our approach offers substantial improvement over systems that only use lexical similarities for retrieval and re-ranking, in an end-to-end problem-resolution domain.

In addition to the classification losses considered in this paper, we can also use another loss term based on ideas from recommender systems, in particular (Menon and Elkan, 2011). Consider the matrix $\mathbf{T}$ with all training queries as rows and all units as the columns. If we view the query refinement problem as a matrix completion problem, it is natural to assume that this matrix has low rank, so that $\mathbf{T}$ can be written as $\mathbf{T} = \mathbf{U}\Lambda\mathbf{V}^T$, where Λ is a diagonal matrix and parameter of our optimization. These can then be incorporated into the training process by appropriate changes to the cost and regularization terms.

Another benefit of the tensor representation is that it can easily be extended to incorporate other meta-information that may be available. For example, if context sensitive features, like the identity of the agent, are available these can be incorporated as another dimension in the tensor. While optimization over these higher dimensional tensors may be more computationally complex, the problems are still convex and can be solved efficiently. This is a direction of future research we are pursuing. Finally, exploring the power of information gain type features in larger database systems is of interest.

References

Fatemeh Zahedi Antonio Palma-dos Reis. 1999. Designing personalized intelligent financial decision support systems.

Ricardo Baeza-yates, Carlos Hurtado, and Marcelo Mendoza. 2004. Query recommendation using query logs in search engines. In *In International Workshop on Clustering Information over the Web (ClustWeb, in conjunction with EDBT), Creete*, pages 588–596. Springer.

Bing Bai, Jason Weston, David Grangier, Ronan Collobert, Kunihiko Sadamasa, Yanjun Qi, Corinna Cortes, and Mehryar Mohri. 2009. Polynomial semantic indexing. In *NIPS*, pages 64–72.

Doug Beeferman and Adam Berger. 2000. Agglomerative clustering of a search engine query log. In *Proceedings of the Sixth ACM SIGKDD International Conference on Knowledge Discovery and Data Mining*, KDD '00, pages 407–416, New York, NY, USA. ACM.

Adam Berger and John Lafferty. 1999. Information retrieval as statistical translation. In *Proceedings of the 22Nd Annual International ACM SIGIR Conference on Research and Development in Information Retrieval*, SIGIR '99, pages 222–229, New York, NY, USA. ACM.

Christopher M Bishop. 2006. Pattern recognition and machine learning.

Peter F. Brown, Vincent J. Della Pietra, Stephen A. Della Pietra, and Robert L. Mercer. 1993. The mathematics of statistical machine translation: Parameter estimation. *Comput. Linguist.*, 19(2):263–311, June.

Charles Elkan. 2010. Learning affinity with biliear models. *Unpublished Notes*.

Alan Feuer, Stefan Savev, and Javed A. Aslam. 2007. Evaluation of phrasal query suggestions. In *Proceedings of the Sixteenth ACM Conference on Conference on Information and Knowledge Management*, CIKM '07, pages 841–848, New York, NY, USA. ACM.

Rashmi Gangadharaiah and Balakrishnan Narayanaswamy. 2013. Natural language query refinement for problem resolution from crowdsourced semi-structured data. In *Proceedings of the Sixth International Joint Conference on Natural Language Processing*, pages 243–251, Nagoya, Japan, October. Asian Federation of Natural Language Processing.

Jiafeng Guo, Gu Xu, Hang Li, and Xueqi Cheng. 2008. A unified and discriminative model for query refinement. In Sung-Hyon Myaeng, Douglas W. Oard, Fabrizio Sebastiani, Tat-Seng Chua, and Mun-Kew Leong, editors, *SIGIR*, pages 379–386. ACM.

Weiwei Guo, Irene Kotsia, and Ioannis Patras. 2012. Tensor learning for regression. *Image Processing, IEEE Transactions on*, 21(2):816–827.

Haibo He and Edwardo A Garcia. 2009. Learning from imbalanced data. *Knowledge and Data Engineering, IEEE Transactions on*, 21(9):1263–1284.

Alexander Holland. 2005. Modeling uncertainty in decision support systems for customer call center. In *Computational Intelligence, Theory and Applications*, pages 763–770. Springer.

Diane Kelly, Karl Gyllstrom, and Earl W. Bailey. 2009. A comparison of query and term suggestion features for interactive searching. In *Proceedings of the 32Nd International ACM SIGIR Conference on Research and Development in Information Retrieval*, SIGIR '09, pages 371–378, New York, NY, USA. ACM.

Takumi Kobayashi and Nobuyuki Otsu. 2012. Efficient optimization for low-rank integrated bilinear classifiers. In *Computer Vision–ECCV 2012*, pages 474–487. Springer.

Kenneth Wai-Ting Leung, Wilfred Ng, and Dik Lun Lee. 2008. Personalized concept-based clustering of search engine queries. *IEEE Trans. on Knowl. and Data Eng.*, 20(11):1505–1518, November.

Tie-Yan Liu. 2009. Learning to rank for information retrieval. *Foundations and Trends in Information Retrieval*, 3(3):225–331.

Aditya Krishna Menon and Charles Elkan. 2011. Link prediction via matrix factorization. In *Machine Learning and Knowledge Discovery in Databases*, pages 437–452. Springer.

Mark A Musen, Yuval Shahar, and Edward H Shortliffe. 2006. Clinical decision-support systems.

Michael Pinedo, Sridhar Seshadri, and J George Shanthikumar. 2000. Call centers in financial services: strategies, technologies, and operations. In *Creating Value in Financial Services*, pages 357–388. Springer.

Hamed Pirsiavash, Deva Ramanan, and Charless Fowlkes. 2009. Bilinear classifiers for visual recognition. In *NIPS*, pages 1482–1490.

Pradeep Ravikumar, Martin J Wainwright, and John D Lafferty. 2010. High-dimensional ising model selection using 1-regularized logistic regression. *The Annals of Statistics*, 38(3):1287–1319.

Stefan Riezler, Alexander Vasserman, Ioannis Tsochantaridis, Vibhu Mittal, and Yi Liu. 2007. Statistical Machine Translation for Query Expansion in Answer Retrieval. In *Proceedings of the 45th Annual Meeting of the Association of Computational Linguistics*, pages 464–471, Prague, Czech Republic, June. Association for Computational Linguistics.

Gerard Salton and Michael J McGill. 1983. Introduction to modern information retrieval.

T. Strohman, D. Metzler, H. Turtle, and W. B. Croft. 2004. Indri: A language model-based search engine for complex queries. *Proceedings of the International Conference on Intelligence Analysis*.

Xu Tan, Yin Zhang, Siliang Tang, Jian Shao, Fei Wu, and Yueting Zhuang. 2013. Logistic tensor regression for classification. In *Intelligent Science and Intelligent Data Engineering*, pages 573–581. Springer.

Jean-Philippe Vert and Laurent Jacob. 2008. Machine learning for in silico virtual screening and chemical genomics: new strategies. *Combinatorial chemistry & high throughput screening*, 11(8):677.

Wei Wu, Zhengdong Lu, and Hang Li. 2013. Learning bilinear model for matching queries and documents. *The Journal of Machine Learning Research*, 14(1):2519–2548.

Aspectual Properties of Conversational Activities

Rebecca J. Passonneau and **Boxuan Guan** and **Cho Ho Yeung**
becky@ccls.columbia.edu and bg2469@columbia.edu and cy2277@columbia.edu
Columbia University, New York, NY, USA

Yuan Du
ydu@fb.com
Facebook, New York, NY, USA

Emma Conner
econner@oberlin.edu
Oberlin College, Oberlin, OH, USA

Abstract

Segmentation of spoken discourse into distinct conversational activities has been applied to broadcast news, meetings, monologs, and two-party dialogs. This paper considers the aspectual properties of discourse segments, meaning how they transpire in time. Classifiers were constructed to distinguish between segment boundaries and non-boundaries, where the sizes of utterance spans to represent data instances were varied, and the locations of segment boundaries relative to these instances. Classifier performance was better for representations that included the end of one discourse segment combined with the beginning of the next. In addition, classification accuracy was better for segments in which speakers accomplish goals with distinctive start and end points.

1 Introduction

People engage in dialogue to address a wide range of goals. It has long been observed that discourse can be structured into units that correspond to distinct goals and activities (Grosz and Sidner, 1986; Passonneau and Litman, 1997). This is conceptually distinct from structuring discourse into the topical units addressed in (Hearst, 1997). The ability to recognize where distinct activities occur in spoken discourse could support offline applications to spoken corpora such as search (Ward and Werner, 2013), summarization (Murray et al., 2005), and question answering. Further, a deeper understanding of the relation of conversational activities to observable features of utterance sequences could inform the design of interactive systems for online applications such as information gathering, service requests, tutoring, and companionship. Automatic identification of such units, however, has been difficult to achieve. This paper considers the *aspectual* properties of speakers' conversational activities, meaning how they transpire in time. We hypothesize that recognition of a transition to a new conversational activity depends on recognizing not only the start of a new activity but also the end of the preceding one, on the grounds that the relative contrast between endings and beginnings might matter as much or more than absolute characteristics consistent across all beginnings or all endings. We further hypothesize that transitions to certain kinds of conversational activity may be easier to detect than others.

Following Austin's view that speech constitutes action of different kinds (Austin, 1962), we assume that different kinds of communicative action have different ways of transpiring in time, just as other actions do. Conversational activities that address objective goals, for example, can have very well-demarcated beginnings and endings, as when two people choose a restaurant to go to for dinner. Conversational participants can, however, address goals that need not have a specific resolution, such as shared complaints about the lack of good Chinese restaurants. This distinction between different kinds of actions that speakers perform through their communicative behavior is analogous to the distinction in linguistic semantics pertaining to verbal aspect, between states, processes and transition events (or accomplishments and achievements) (Vendler, 1957) (Dowty, 1986). States (e.g., *being at a standstill*) have no perceptible change from moment to moment; processes (e.g., *walking*) have detectable differences in state from moment to moment with no clearly demarcated change of state during the process; transition events (e.g., *starting to walk; walking to the end of the block*) involve a transition from one state or process to another.

To investigate the aspectual properties of discourse segments, we constructed classifiers to detect discourse segment boundaries based on features of utterances. We considered the aspectual properties of discourse segments in two ways. First, to investigate the relative contribution of features from segment endings versus beginnings, we experimented with different sizes of utterance sequences, and different locations of segment boundaries relative to these sequences. Second, we considered different categories of segments, based on the speculation that segment transitions that are easier to recognize would be associated with conversational activities that have a well-demarcated event structure, in constrast to activities that involve goals to maintain or sustain aspects of interaction.

The following section describes related work in this area, as well as the difficulties in achieving good performance. Most work on identification of discourse segments (or other forms of discourse structure in spoken interaction) depends on a prior phase of annotation (e.g., (Galley et al., 2003; Passonneau and Litman, 1997)). We studied a corpus of eighty-two transcribed and annotated telephone dialogues between library patrons and librarians that had been annotated with units analogous to speech acts, and subsequently annotated with discourse segments comprised of these units. The annotation yielded eight distinct kinds of discourse segment, where a segment results from a linear segmentation of a discourse into strictly sequential units. (While the segmentation is sequential, the units can have hierarchical relations.) We found that classifiers to detect segment boundaries performed best with boundaries represented by features of sequences of utterances that spanned the end of one segment and the beginning of the next. Error analysis indicated that performance was better for boundaries that initiate conversational activities with clear beginnings and endings.

2 Related Work

Segmentation of spoken language interaction into distinct discourse units has been applied to meetings as well as to two-party discourse using acoustic features, lexical features, and very heterogeneous features. In our previous work, we used a very heterogeneous set of features to segment monologues into units that had been identified by annotators as corresonding to distinct intentional units (Passonneau and Litman, 1997). Text tiling (Hearst, 1997) has been applied to segmentation of meetings into distinct agenda segments using both prior and following context (Banerjee and Rudnicky, 2006). Results had high precision and low recall. We also find that recall is more challenging than precision. Topic modeling methods have also been applied to the identification of topical segments in speech (Purver et al., 2006) (Eisenstein and Barzilay, 2008), with improvements over earlier work on the ICSI meeting corpus (Galley et al., 2003) (Malioutov and Barzilay, 2006).

An analog of text tiling that uses acoustic patterns rather than lexical items has been applied to the segmentation of speech into stories using segmental dynamic time warping (SDTW) (Park and Glass, 2008). The method is based on the intuition of aligning utterances by similar acoustic patterns, possibly representing common words and phrases. Results on TDT2 Mandarin Broadcast News corpus were moderately good for short episodes with F=0.71 beating the baseline for lexical text tiling of 0.66, but poor on long episodes.

An alternative method of relying solely on acoustic information has been applied to importance prediction at a very fine granularity (Ward and Richart-Ruiz, 2013). Four basic classes of prosodic features derived from PCA were used (Ward and Vega, 2012): volume, pitch height, pitch range and speaking rate cross various widths of time intervals. The data was labeled by annotators using an importance scale of 1 to 5, and linear regression was used to predict the label for instances consisting of frames. The method performed well with a correlation of 0.82 and mean average error of 0.75 (5-fold cross validation).

The identification of different kinds of units in discourse is somewhat related to the notion of genre identification, e.g. (Obin et al., 2010) (Ries et al., 2000). Results from this area have been applied to segmentation of conversation by a combination of topic and style (Ries, 2002).

3 Data and Annotations

The corpus consists of recordings, transcripts and annotations on the transcripts of a set of 82 calls recorded in 2005 between patrons of the Andrew Heiskell Braille and Talking Book Library of New York City.[1] An annotation for dialog acts with a

[1]The audio files and transcripts are available for download from the Columbia University Data Commons. The annotations and raw features will be released in the near future.

reduced set of dialog act types and adjacency pair relations (Dialogue Function Units, DFUs) was developed, originally for comparison of dialogues across modalities (Hu et al., 2009). A subsequent phase of annotation at the discourse level that makes use of the dialog act annotation was later applied. This later annotation, referred to as Task Success and Cost Annotation (TSCA), was aimed at identifying individual dialog tasks analogous to those carried out by spoken dialog systems, to facilitate comparison of human-human dialog with human-machine dialog. Interannotator reliability of both annotations was measured using Krippendorff's alpha (Krippendorff, 1980) at levels of 0.66 and above for individual dialogues (Passonneau et al., 2011). The corpus consists of 24,760 words, or 302 words per dialog.

Briefly, the second phase of annotation involved grouping DFUs into larger sequences in which the participants continued to pursue a single coordinated activity, and labeling the large discourse units for their discourse function. The human annotation instructions avoided reference to overt signals of dialog structure. Rather, annotators were asked to judge the semantic and pragmatic functions of utterances. The annotations have been described in previous work (Hu et al., 2009; Passonneau et al., 2011); the annotation guidelines are available online.[2]

The location of a transition between one conversational activity and the next is represented as occurring between adjacent utterances. There are 9,340 utterance in the corpus, or 114 per dialog. About 10.6 percent of the utterances (994) start a new discourse unit. Within each unit, the speakers establish a conversational goal explicitly or implicitly, and continue to address the goal until it is achieved, suspended, or abandoned. The discourse segments were of the following seven categories, with an additional *Other category* for none of the above (examples from the corpus are shown after each segment category description; words in brackets represent overlapping talk of the two speakers):

- Conventional: The participants engage in conventionalized behavior, e.g., greetings (at the beginning of the call) or goodbyes (at the end of the call).

  Librarian: andrew heiskell library
  Librarian: how are you
  Patron: good morning
  Librarian: good morning

- Book-Request: The participants address a patron's request for a book, which can be a specific book that first needs to be identified, or which can be a non-specific request for a book fitting some criterion (e.g., a mystery the patron has not read before).

  Patron: do you have any fannie flagg stories
  Librarian: flag
  Patron: yeah
  Patron: F L A <Pause>
  Patron: A G G I think it is

- Inform: One of the participants provides the other with general information that does not support a Book Request, e.g., the patron provides identifying information so the librarian can pull up the patron's record.

  Patron: well I'll call him again then
  Patron: and I'll get the name [today]
  Librarian [talk] to him and call me back
  Patron: <pause> i- i'll call him
  Patron: and then i'll call you okay
  Librarian: okay

- Librarian-Proposal: The participants address the librarian's suggestion of a specific book or a kind of book that might meet the patron's desires.

  Librarian: I have ellis but not bret
  Patron: ah wa wa what do you have by him
  Librarian: by cose
  Librarian: C O S E
  Librarian: I have the rage of a privileged class
  Patron: that's all right

- Request-Action: One of the participants asks the other to perform an action, e.g., the patron asks that certain authors be added to the patron's list of preferences

  Patron: also <pause> uh
  Patron: <pause> of the favorite author list
  Librarian: mmhm
  Patron: would you um
  Patron: remove t jefferson parker
  Librarian: okay

[2]See links at `http://www1.ccls.columbia.edu/~Loqui/resources.html` for transcription guidelines, and annotation manuals.

- Information-Request: One of the participants seeks information from the other, e.g., the patron wants to know if

  Patron: this is the talking books right
  Librarian: yes
  Librarian: this is the library for the blind

- Sidebar: The librarian temporarily takes a call from another Patron only long enough to place the new caller on hold

  Librarian: hold on one second
  Librarian: Andrew Heiskell Library
  Librarian: please hold

- Other

Of these seven kinds of discourse units, Book-Requests and Librarian-Proposals are the most clearly delimited by beginning and ending points. At the beginning of a Book-Request, the patron establishes that she wants a book, and the end is identified by the mutual achievement of the librarian and patron of either a successful resolution, meaning the identification of a particular book in the library's collection that the patron will accept, or a failure of the current attempt, which often leads to a new revised book request. Librarian-Proposals are very parallel to Book-Requests; the difference is that the librarian makes a suggestion of a specific book or kind of book which must be identified for the patron, and which the patron then accepts or rejects.

4 Experiments

The experiments to automatically identify the locations of the annotated discourse units apply machine learning to instances consisting of utterance sequences that represent the two classes, presence versus absence of a boundary. We hyothesize that the enormous challenges for identifying discourse structure in human-machine dialogue can be better addressed through complementary reliance on semantics and interaction structure (behavioral cues), and each can reinforce the other. The main focus of the experiments reported here is on data representation to address the questions, what features of the context support the ability to segment a dialogue into conversational activity units, and how much context is necessary?

A disadvantage of the dataset is its relatively small size, especially given the extreme skew with

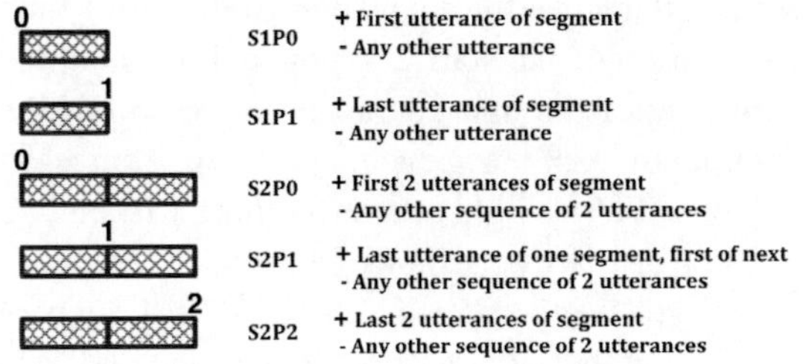

Figure 1: Schematic representation of instance spans and labels. Bars on the left show the number of utterances (size) and position of segment boundary (position) for five of the fourteen types of instances. Positive and negative labels are shown on the descriptions at the right.

the positive class consisting of only 10% of the instances. On the other hand, the small size made detailed annotation feasible, and the corpus is well-suited to our research question in that it represents naturally occurring, spontaneous human-human telephone discourse. Therefore. the manner in which the dialogs evolve over time is entirely natural. Our major question of interest is how much of the time-course of the discourse is required for a machine learner to identify the start of a new discourse unit. To examine this question, we vary two dimensions of the representation of the instances for learning. The first is the number of utterances around the location of the start of a new discourse unit. The second is the set of features to represent each instance, which as we will see below, affects to some degree how many utterances to include before and after the start of a new discourse unit.

Four machine learning methods were tested using the Weka toolkit (Hall et al., 2009): Naive Bayes, J48 Decision Trees, Logistic Regression and Multilayer Perceptron. Of these, J48 had the best and most consistent performance, which we speculate is due to a combination of the small size of the dataset, and non-linearity of the data. Because J48 is doing feature selection while building the tree, it can identify different threshholds for the same features, depending on the location in the tree. All results reported here are for J48.

4.1 Labels and Instance Spans

We refer to a sequence of utterances, and a potential location of the onset of a discourse unit relative to that sequence, as a *span*. We varied the number of utterances for each span from 1 to 4, and the location of the start of a new unit to be at the beginning of the first utterance, at the end of the last utterance, or between any pair of utterances in the span. For a single utterance, there will be two types of instances, as shown in Figure 1. Each instance type is represented as S<N>P<M> where N is the number of utterances in the span and M is how many utterances there are before the boundary. S1P0 denotes size 1 spans with the boundary at position 0; positively labeled instances represent the first utterance of a segment. S1P1 denotes size 1 spans with the boundary at position 1; positively labeled instances represent the last utterance of a segment. The experiments used all labelings for spans from size 1 to 4, yielding 14 types of instances. For multi-utterance spans that occur at the beginning or end of a discourse, dummy utterances are used to fill out the spans.

4.2 Features

We use three sets of features. A set we refer to as *discourse* features consists of a mixed set of acoustic features and lexicogrammatical features that have been associated with discourse structure, such as discourse cue words (Hirschberg and Litman, 1993). Table 1 lists the 35 discourse features. The second set is a bag-of-words (BOW) vector representation, and the third is the combination of the discourse and BOW features. We used alternative sets of features on the assumption that the performance of a machine learner across the different instance spans will vary, depending on the aspects of the utterance that the features capture. We see some expected differences in performance between the discourse features and BOW, with BOW benefitting more than the discourse features from longer spans. Unexpectedly, we see no gain in performance from the combination of both feature sets.

The discourse features consist of acoustic features, pause features, word and utterance length features, proper noun features and speaker change. The acoustic features and the (unfilled) pause location and duration features were extracted using Praat, a cross-platform tool for speech analysis. The features pertaining to filled pauses (e.g., *um, uh*) were extracted from the transcripts.

4.3 Conditions and Evaluation

The experimental conditions varied the feature set, the selection of training data versus testing data, and the fourteen kinds of instance spans and labels. Three feature sets consisted of the discourse features from Table 1 (discourse), bag-of-words (bow), and the combination of the two (combo). In all experiments, the data was randomly split into 75% for training, and 25% for testing, using two methods to select instances. In randomization by dialog, all utterances from a single dialog were kept together and 75% of the dialogs were selected for training. In randomization by utterance, 75% of all utterances were randomly selected for training, without regard to which dialog they came from. This was done to test the hypothesis that the bow representation would be more sensitive to changes of vocabulary across dialogs. The three feature sets, fourteen data representations and two randomization methods yield 84 experimental conditions.

While N-fold cross-validation is a popular method to estimate a classifier's prediction error, it is not a perfect substitute for isolating the training data from the test data (Ng, 1997). The cross-validation estimate of prediction error is relatively unbiased, but it can be highly variable (Efron and Tibshirani, 1997)(Rodriguez et al., 2010). To avoid the inherent risk of overfitting (Ng, 1997), one recommendation is to use cross-validation to compare models, and to reserve a test set to verify that a selected classifier has superior generalization (Rao and Fung, 2008). To assess whether performance measures of different models are genuinely different requires error bounds on the result, which is not done with cross-validation. We perform train-test splits of the data to minimize overfitting, and bootstrap confidence intervals for each classifier's accuracy (and other metrics) in order to measure the variance, and thereby assess whether the performance error bounds of two conditions are distinct.

5 Results

Given that for this data, the rate of segment boundary instances (positive labels) is about 10%, a baseline classifier that always predicts a non-segment will have about 90% overall accuracy. The baseline column in Table 2 shows the average accuracy that would be achieved by this simple baseline on the test data for a given run, along with the bootstrapped confidence interval for this baseline over the 50 runs. In the 84 experiments, the baseline ranged from 90% (+/- 1%) to 89% (+/-

		Interaction feature
1	Speaker	whether there is a speaker switch between preceding utterance and current utterance
		Acoustic features
2	Pitch_MIN	Minimum pitch of the utterance
3	Pitch_MAX	Maximum pitch of the utterance
4	Pitch_MEAN	Mean pitch of the utterance
5	Pitch_STDV	Standard deviation of the pitch of the utterance
6	Pitch_RANGE	Maximim pitch of the utterance less the minimum pitch
7	Pitch_CHANGE	Pitch_MEAN of the current utterance less the Pitch_MEAN of the preceding utterance
8	Intensity_MIN	Minimum intensity of the utterance
9	Intensity_MAX	Maximum intensity of the utterance
10	Intensity_MEAN	Mean intensity of the utterance
11	Intensity_STDV	Standard deviation of the intensity of the utterance
12	Intensity_RANGE	Intensity_MAX less Intensity_MIN
13	Intensity_CHANGE	Intensity_MEAN of the current utterance less Intensity_MEAN of preceding utterance
14	LR1	Utterance duration
15	LR1_Normalized	Utterance duration normalized by each speaker independently
		Lexical features
16	LR2_1	Word count
17	LR2_2	Word count normalized by speaker
18	LR3_1	Words per second
19	LR3_2	Words per second by speaker
20	LR4	Average word length
21	LR5	Maximum word length
22	LR6_1	Average frequency of characters in the utterance
23	LR6_2	Number of low frequency characters
24	IR	Number of content words
25	PN_1	Number of named entities
26	PN_2	Whether the utterance contains a new named entity
		Pause features
27	Pause_DURT	total duration of all pauses
28	Pause_RATIO	proportion utterance consisting of pauses
29	FP1	Presence of a filled pause at the beginning of an utterance
30	FP2	Presence of a filled pause at the end of an utterance
31	FP3	Presence of a filled pause in the middle of an utterance
32	P1	Presence of a pause tag at the beginning of an utterance
33	P2	Presence of a pause tag at the end of an utterance
34	P3	Presence of a pause tag in the middle of an utterance

Table 1: Discourse Features

1%). Crucially, however, the simple baseline will fail to identify any of the members of the positive class. Though it is difficult to beat the baseline on overall accuracy, the question addressed here is what level of accuracy is achieved on the positive class, while remaining relatively consistent with the baseline on overall accuracy. It should be noted that accuracy on the positive class is the same as *recall*, or *sensitivity* (the term used in the epidemiological literature). The worst performing classifier among the 84 (disc/utterance/ S1P4) achieves 83% (+/- 1%) accuracy overall, or below the baseline by 6%, with 11% accuracy on the positive class, 100% of which is a gain over the baseline. By this standard, the best classifier of the 84 conditions (bow/dial/S4P1) matches the baseline on overall accuracy, and achieves 50% (+/- 5%) accuracy on the positive class, which far exceeds the baseline. About half of the experimental conditions meet the baseline and achieve at least 25% accuracy on the positive class.

Overall accuracy, and accuracy on the positive class, measure prediction error, but can be supplemented with additional metrics that facilitate analysis of the nature and cost of error types. As a supplementary metric, we report average F-measure, the harmonic mean of recall and precision, due to its familiarity, and because it provides a sense of how often a classifier incorrectly predicts the positive class. An F-measure close to accuracy on the positive class indicates that precision is about the same as recall, while a relatively higher F-measure indicates that the precision is even higher than the F-measure, and the converse is true when the F-measure is lower than accuracy on the positive class. Table 2 shows 32 classifiers with the highest measures of accuracy, accuracy on the positive class, and F-measure. The confidence intervals for accuracy on the positive class and F-measure are rather wide, compared to those for overall accu-

Exp.	$\overline{Baseline}$ (sd)	$\overline{Acc}$ (sd)	$\overline{AccPos(Recall)}$ (sd)	$\overline{F}$ (sd)	$>_{Acc_{pos}}$	$> F$
bow/dial/S4P1	0.89 (+/-0.010)	0.89 (+/-0.009)	0.42 (+/-0.082)	0.28 (+/-0.054)	22	11
bow/dial/S4P2	0.90 (+/-0.013)	0.89 (+/-0.010)	0.39 (+/-0.071)	0.26 (+/-0.064)	22	3
bow/utterance/S1P0	0.90 (+/-0.004)	0.90 (+/-0.005)	0.51 (+/-0.051)	0.26 (+/-0.034)	30	11
bow/utterance/S4P0	0.89 (+/-0.005)	0.88 (+/-0.006)	0.43 (+/-0.049)	0.26 (+/-0.040)	23	10
disc/dial/S2P1	0.90 (+/-0.009)	0.87 (+/-0.009)	0.32 (+/-0.059)	0.26 (+/-0.037)	4	10
bow/utterance/S4P3	0.89 (+/-0.006)	0.88 (+/-0.005)	0.41 (+/-0.050)	0.25 (+/-0.027)	22	11
combo/dial/S3P2	0.89 (+/-0.011)	0.86 (+/-0.010)	0.31 (+/-0.048)	0.25 (+/-0.031)	7	10
disc/dial/S4P3	0.90 (+/-0.008)	0.86 (+/-0.009)	0.30 (+/-0.041)	0.25 (+/-0.030)	4	10
combo/dial/S3P1	0.89 (+/-0.010)	0.86 (+/-0.011)	0.31 (+/-0.059)	0.25 (+/-0.038)	3	10
combo/dial/S4P2	0.89 (+/-0.013)	0.86 (+/-0.012)	0.30 (+/-0.044)	0.25 (+/-0.031)	4	10
combo/dial/S2P1	0.89 (+/-0.012)	0.87 (+/-0.010)	0.32 (+/-0.054)	0.25 (+/-0.033)	7	10
combo/dial/S4P3	0.90 (+/-0.007)	0.87 (+/-0.008)	0.29 (+/-0.044)	0.25 (+/-0.035)	4	10
disc/dial/S3P2	0.90 (+/-0.008)	0.87 (+/-0.008)	0.29 (+/-0.047)	0.25 (+/-0.040)	3	10
bow/utterance/S4P1	0.90 (+/-0.005)	0.89 (+/-0.004)	0.40 (+/-0.053)	0.25 (+/-0.020)	22	10
bow/dial/S4P3	0.90 (+/-0.007)	0.89 (+/-0.009)	0.39 (+/-0.072)	0.25 (+/-0.035)	22	10
disc/dial/S4P2	0.90 (+/-0.009)	0.86 (+/-0.009)	0.28 (+/-0.042)	0.25 (+/-0.030)	0	10
bow/dial/S1P0	0.90 (+/-0.009)	0.89 (+/-0.009)	0.48 (+/-0.065)	0.24 (+/-0.045)	28	0
combo/dial/S4P1	0.90 (+/-0.010)	0.86 (+/-0.010)	0.28 (+/-0.045)	0.24 (+/-0.034)	0	9
disc/dial/S3P1	0.89 (+/-0.011)	0.86 (+/-0.010)	0.29 (+/-0.046)	0.24 (+/-0.033)	2	9
bow/dial/S4P0	0.90 (+/-0.009)	0.88 (+/-0.011)	0.37 (+/-0.031)	0.24 (+/-0.040)	22	0
disc/dial/S4P1	0.90 (+/-0.009)	0.86 (+/-0.008)	0.27 (+/-0.041)	0.23 (+/-0.032)	0	3
bow/utterance/S4P2	0.89 (+/-0.007)	0.88 (+/-0.010)	0.39 (+/-0.044)	0.23 (+/-0.033)	22	0
combo/utterance/S2P0	0.89 (+/-0.005)	0.86 (+/-0.009)	0.27 (+/-0.041)	0.21 (+/-0.029)	0	0
disc/dial/S2P0	0.89 (+/-0.010)	0.86 (+/-0.009)	0.27 (+/-0.047)	0.20 (+/-0.027)	0	0
disc/utterance/S2P0	0.90 (+/-0.006)	0.86 (+/-0.008)	0.26 (+/-0.032)	0.20 (+/-0.024)	0	0
combo/utterance/S1P0	0.89 (+/-0.005)	0.88 (+/-0.006)	0.31 (+/-0.041)	0.20 (+/-0.026)	10	0
combo/utterance/S3P0	0.90 (+/-0.005)	0.86 (+/-0.008)	0.25 (+/-0.038)	0.20 (+/-0.033)	0	0
disc/utterance/S4P3	0.89 (+/-0.006)	0.86 (+/-0.009)	0.24 (+/-0.043)	0.20 (+/-0.033)	0	0
combo/utterance/S2P1	0.89 (+/-0.006)	0.86 (+/-0.008)	0.26 (+/-0.036)	0.20 (+/-0.023)	0	0
disc/utterance/S2P1	0.89 (+/-0.005)	0.86 (+/-0.007)	0.26 (+/-0.032)	0.20 (+/-0.022)	0	0
combo/utterance/S4P1	0.89 (+/-0.006)	0.85 (+/-0.008)	0.24 (+/-0.033)	0.20 (+/-0.027)	0	0
disc/utterance/S4P0	0.89 (+/-0.006)	0.85 (+/-0.009)	0.24 (+/-0.034)	0.20 (+/-0.024)	0	0

Table 2: Classification performance (with standard deviations in parentheses) of the best 40% of 84 J48 models trained on 75% of the data and tested on the remaining 25%, with bootstrapped confidence intervals from 50 trials each.

racy. To draw comparisons among the classifiers that take into account this variance, the two rightmost columns of the table indicate for each classifier how many other classifiers in the same table the current classifier surpasses on mean accuracy of the positive class, or on mean F-measure. Here, to surpass another classifier means the lower bound of its confidence interval surpasses the upper bounds of other classifiers' confidence intervals.

Table 2 shows that there is no one classifier that surpasses all others on all measures. There are, however, some clear trends. Regarding the number of utterances spanned by each data instance, the table shows that of the 32 best performing classifiers, the majority (seventeen) have size 4 spans, and all but three have spans longer than a single utterance. This trend indicates that more context leads to better accuracy overall and better accuracy on the positive class. Regarding where the segment boundary is located relative to the span, the majority of cases (twenty-two) locate the boundary within the span, meaning that the span includes one or more of the final utterances of a segment and one or more of the initial utterances of the next segment. The remaining cases involve spans that include utterances only from the beginning of the segment. There are no cases of higher performing classifiers that use spans from segment endings. Among the classifiers in the top half of the table, the best performing bow classifiers surpass a larger number of the other classifiers on accuracy of the positive class. The best performing discourse or combination classifiers surpass a larger number of other classifiers on F-measure. This suggests that in general, the bow classifiers do better on recall and the classifiers with discourse features have higher precision.

The combination of BOW and discourse features has a performance that differs little from the discourse features alone, and does not do as well as BOW S4P1. This result was unexpected, and suggests that the bow and discourse feature sets often identify nearly the same set of discourse

Discourse, Rand Dial, S4P3		
Activity Type	TP %	FN %
Inform	7 (0.11)	56 (0.89)
Book Request	**18 (0.32)**	**40 (0.68)**
Librarian Proposal	4 (0.27)	11 (0.73)
Request-Action	0 (0.00)	6 (1.00)
Information-Request	6 (0.11)	47 (0.89)
Sidebar	1 (0.08)	11 (0.92)
Conventional	5 (0.17)	25 (0.83)
Total	37 (0.14)	230 (0.86)
BOW, Rand Dial, S4P2		
Inform	7 (0.10)	70 (0.90)
Book Request	14 (0.20)	57 (0.80)
Librarian Proposal	1 (0.05)	20 (0.95)
Request-Action	0 (0.00)	5 (1.00)
Information-Request	8 (0.16)	42 (0.84)
Sidebar	0 (0.00)	13 (1.00)
Conventional	6 (0.23)	29 (0.77)
Total	37 (0.14)	230 (0.86)

Table 3: Error Analysis of the Positive Class

boundaries. Since the initial utterances of a segment seem to have features with greater predictive power than the final utterances of a segment, and since discourse cue words tend to occur in the first utterance or so of a segment, it could be that discourse cue words explain the good performance of both sets of features. This could be tested in future work by restricting a BOW representation to words other than discourse cue words.

To pursue in more detail the factors that influence accuracy on the positive class (recall), we now turn to an error analysis of the kinds of discourse units associated with true positives versus false negatives of the classifier's confusion matrix. Table 3 presents the results of an error analysis of the two cells of the confusion matrix for a classifier's results on the positive class, the true positives and the false negatives. We looked at the breakdown of the seven kinds of discourse units to see whether there were differences in the likelihood of a correct identification of a boundary, depending on the kind of discourse unit in question. Results are drawn from classifiers learned under two conditions, S4P3 spans with discourse features randomized by dialogue (disc/dial/S4P3) and S4P3 spans with BOW features, randomized by dialogue (bow/dial/S4P3). (Results from other classifiers are very similar.) In both cases, Book-Requests have a much higher probability of being among the true positives (32% for discourse, 20% for BOW) than for the positive class overall (14%). Conventional discourse units, where the participants first make their greetings, or make their final good byes, are also correctly identified more often than the overall TP rate. Librarian Proposals are identified well by the model using the discourse features, but not by the one using the BOW features. We speculate that this is because Librarian Proposals typically present information that is new to the discourse: often, the librarian is making a suggestion to the patron based on information the librarian can see in the preference field of the patron's record, or in the patron's past borrowing behavior. We speculate that the vocabulary in Librarian Proposals may be too variable to be predictive. Information-Request units and Inform units are also relatively difficult to identify correctly.

6 Conclusion

The problem of identification of conversational activities is a difficult one for machine processing for many reasons. Like vision and speech, segmentation of the units is difficult because the units are not discrete, objective, components of perception, but instead are the result of abstraction. The experiments presented here consider a novel explanation for the difficulty of the task, which is that discourse units differ from each other regarding the manner in which they evolve in time. The results show that a data representation that includes utterances from both the end of one unit and the beginning of another improves performance. The transition between one conversational activity and another takes place over the course of several utterances, rather than occurring at an instant in time. Error analysis indicates further that discourse units that correspond to conversational activities with clear end points that can be achieved have a higher probability of being recognized correctly.

References

John L. Austin. 1962. *How to do Things with Words: The William James Lectures delivered at Harvard University in 1955*. Clarendon Press, Oxford.

Satanjeev Banerjee and Alexander I. Rudnicky. 2006. A texttiling based approach to topic boundary detection in meetings. Technical report, Department of Computer Science, Carnegie Mellon University.

David R. Dowty. 1986. The effects of aspectual class on the temporal structure of discourse: semantics or pragmatics? *Linguistics and Philosophy*, 9(1):37–61.

Bradley Efron and Robert Tibshirani. 1997. Improvements on cross-validation: The .632+ bootstrap method. *Journal of the American Statistical Association*, 92(438):548–560, June.

Jacob Eisenstein and Regina Barzilay. 2008. Bayesian unsupervised topic segmentation. In *Proceedings of the Conference on Empirical Methods in Natural Language Processing (EMNLP '08)*, pages 334–343. Association for Computational Linguistics.

Michel Galley, Kathleen McKeown, Eric Fosler-Lussier, and Hongyan Jing. 2003. Discourse segmentation of multi-party conversation. In *Proceedings of the 41st Annual Meeting on Association for Computational Linguistics*, pages 562–569, Stroudsburg, PA, USA. Association for Computational Linguistics.

Barbara J. Grosz and Candace L. Sidner. 1986. Attention, intentions, and the structure of discourse. *Computational Linguistics*, 12(3):175–204, July.

Mark Hall, Eibe Frank, Geoffrey Holmes, Bernhard Pfahringer, Peter Reutemann, and Ian H. Witten. 2009. The weka data mining software: An update. *SIGKDD Explorations*, 11(1):10–18.

Marti A. Hearst. 1997. Texttiling: segmenting text into multi-paragraph subtopic passages. *Computational Linguistics*, 23(1).

Julia Hirschberg and Diane Litman. 1993. Empirical studies on the disambiguation of cue phrases. *Computational Linguistics*, 19:501–530.

Jun Hu, Rebecca J. Passonneau, and Owen Rambow. 2009. Contrasting the interaction structure of an email and a telephone corpus: A machine learning approach to annotation of dialogue function units. In *Proceedings of the SIGDIAL 2009 Conference*, pages 357–366, London, UK, September. Association for Computational Linguistics.

Klaus Krippendorff. 1980. *Content Analysis: An Introduction to Its Methodology*. Sage Publications, Beverly Hills, CA.

Igor Malioutov and Regina Barzilay. 2006. Minimum cut model for spoken lecture segmentation. In *Proceedings of the 21st International Conference on Computational Linguistics and the 44th Annual Meeting of the Association for Computational Linguistics*, ACL-44, pages 25–32, Stroudsburg, PA, USA. Association for Computational Linguistics.

Gabriel Murray, Steve Renals, and Jean Carletta. 2005. Extractive summarization of meeting recordings. In *Proceedings of the 9th European Conference on Speech Communication and Technology*, pages 593–596.

Andrew Y. Ng. 1997. Preventing overfitting of cross-validation data. In *Proceedings of the Fourteenth International Conference on Machine Learning*, ICML '97, pages 245–253.

Nicolas Obin, Volker Dellwo, Anne Lacheret, and Xavier Rodet. 2010. Expectations for discourse genre identification: aprosodic study. In *Interspeech*, pages 3070–3073.

A.S. Park and J.R. Glass. 2008. Unsupervised pattern discovery in speech. *Audio, Speech, and Language Processing, IEEE Transactions on*, 16(1):186–197, Jan.

Rebecca J. Passonneau and Diane J. Litman. 1997. Discourse segmentation by human and automated means. *Computational Linguistics*, 23(1):103–139, March.

Rebecca J. Passonneau, Irene Alvarado, Phil Crone, and Simon Jerome. 2011. Paradise-style evaluation of a human-human library corpus. In *Proceedings of the SIGDIAL 2011 Conference*, pages 325–331, Portland, Oregon, June. Association for Computational Linguistics.

Matthew Purver, Thomas L. Griffiths, and Joshua B. Kording, Konrad P. andTenenbaum. 2006. Unsupervised topic modelling for multi-party spoken discourse. In *Proceedings of the 44th annual meeting of the Association for Computational Linguistics (ACL-44)*, pages 17–24. Association for Computational Linguistics.

R. Bharat Rao and Glenn Fung. 2008. On the dangers of cross-validation. an experimental evaluation. In *SDM*, pages 588–596. SIAM.

Klaus Ries, Lori Levin, Liza Valle, Alon Lavie, and Alex Waibel. 2000. Shallow discourse genre annotation in callhome spanish. In *Proceedings of International Conference on Language Resources and Evaluation (LREC)*. European Language Resources and Evaluation (ELRA).

Klaus Ries. 2002. Segmenting conversations by topic, initiative, and style. In AnniR. Coden, EricW. Brown, and Savitha Srinivasan, editors, *Information Retrieval Techniques for Speech Applications*, volume 2273 of *Lecture Notes in Computer Science*, pages 51–66. Springer Berlin Heidelberg.

J.D. Rodriguez, A. Perez, and J.A. Lozano. 2010. Sensitivity analysis of k-fold cross validation in prediction error estimation. *Pattern Analysis and Machine Intelligence, IEEE Transactions on*, 32(3):569–575, March.

Zeno Vendler. 1957. Verbs and times. *Philosophical Review*, 66(2):143–160.

Nigel G. Ward and Karen A. Richart-Ruiz. 2013. Patterns of importance variation in spoken dialog. In *SigDial*.

Nigel G. Ward and Alejandro Vega. 2012. A bottom-up exploration of the dimensions of dialog state in spoken interaction. In *SigDial*.

Nigel G. Ward and Steven D. Werner. 2013. Using dialog-activity similarity for spoken information retrieval. In *Interspeech*.

Detecting Inappropriate Clarification Requests in Spoken Dialogue Systems

Alex Liu[1], Rose Sloan[2], Mei-Vern Then[1], Svetlana Stoyanchev[3], Julia Hirschberg[1], Elizabeth Shriberg[4]
Columbia University[1], Yale University[2], AT&T Labs Research[3], SRI International[4]
{al3037@columbia.edu, rose.sloan@yale.edu, mt2837@columbia.edu, sveta@research.att.com, julia@cs.columbia.edu, elizabeth.shriberg@sri.com}

Abstract

Spoken Dialogue Systems ask for clarification when they think they have misunderstood users. Such requests may differ depending on the information the system believes it needs to clarify. However, when the error type or location is misidentified, clarification requests appear confusing or *inappropriate*. We describe a classifier that identifies inappropriate requests, trained on features extracted from user responses in laboratory studies. This classifier achieves 88.5% accuracy and .885 F-measure in detecting such requests.

1 Introduction

When Spoken Dialogue Systems (SDS) believe they have not understood a user, they generate requests for clarification. For example, in the following exchange, the System believes it has misunderstood the word *Washington* in the user's utterance and asks a clarification question, prompting the user to repeat the misrecognized word.

User: I'd like a ticket to *Washington.*
System: A ticket to where?
User: Washington.

Clarification requests may be generic or specific to the type and location of the information the system believes it has not recognized. **Targeted clarifications** focus on a specific part of an utterance, as in the system's question above. They use understood portions of an utterance (*"I'd like a ticket to"*) to query a misunderstood portion (*"Washington"*). Targeted clarification is a type of task-related request, which has been shown to be more effective and prevalent in human-human dialogues than more general clarification requests (Skantze, 2005). Such **generic clarifications** signal misunderstanding without identifying the type or location of the misunderstanding. They often take the form of a request to repeat or rephrase, e.g. *"please repeat"*, *"please rephrase"*, *"what did you say?"*.

Questions that address a particular type of misrecognition come in several varieties. Systems may ask reprise clarification questions, by repeating a recognized portion of an utterance (Ginzburg and Cooper, 2004; Purver, 2004). Systems may also request that users spell a word if they believe the misrecognized word is a proper name, especially one that is not in its vocabulary (OOV). They may ask the user to provide a synonym for OOV terms that are not proper names. Systems may also ask users to disambiguate homophones (e.g. "Did you mean 'right' as in correct or 'rite' as in a ritual?"). They may request confirmation explicitly (e.g. "I heard you say Washington. Is that correct?"), or implicitly, by repeating the recognized information while asking a follow-up query (e.g. "When do you want to go to Washington?"). Each request type may be appropriate in different circumstances. However, when systems make *inappropriate* requests to users, such as to rephrase a proper name or to confirm a statement that contains a misrecognized word, dialogues often go awry. Therefore, it is extremely important for systems to know when a request is *inappropriate*, so that they can provide a different clarification request or fall back to a more generic strategy.

In this work, we develop a data-driven method for detecting inappropriate clarification requests. We have defined a list of inappropriate request types and have collected a corpus of speaker responses to both appropriate and inappropriate requests under laboratory conditions. We use this corpus to train an inappropriate clarification classifier to be used by a system after a user responds to a system request, in order to determine whether the question was appropriate or not. In Section 2, we describe previous research on error handling in dialogue. We describe our data set in Section 3 and our approach in Section 4. We present our evaluation results in Section 5. We conclude in Section 6 and discuss future directions.

2 Related Work

Today's SDS use generic approaches to clarification, asking the user to repeat or rephrase an entire utterance when the system believes it has not been understood correctly. They use *confidence scores* on the ASR hypothesis to decide whether to accept, reject, or ask for clarification (Bohus and Rudnicky, 2005). Hypotheses with low scores may be confirmed and those with lower scores will trigger a generic request for repetition or rephrasing. Researchers have found that the formulation of system prompts has a significant effect on the success of SDS interaction. Goldberg et al. (2003) find that form of a clarification question affects user frustration and the consequent success of clarification subdialogue. In previous work, we explored the use of targeted reprise clarifications to improve naturalness (Stoyanchev et al., 2014).

Lendvai et al. (2002) apply machine learning methods to detect errors in human-machine dialogue, focusing on predicting when a user utterance causes a misunderstanding. Litman et al. (2006) identify user corrections of the system's recognition errors from speech prosody, ASR confidence scores, and the dialogue history. In contrast, we focus here on detecting when a **system** clarification request is the cause of dialogue problems. We employ only lexical features here, as well as the type of system request, to investigate user responses to a wide variety of system requests, and to identify system errors in request formulation from user reactions. In future work we will include acoustic and prosodic features as well.

3 Data

Our data consists of spoken answers to clarification requests collected at Columbia University using a simulated dialogue system in order to control recognition results and type of system response. The system displays a sentence and asks the user to read it. The system then issues a pre-prepared clarification request, which may be appropriate or inappropriate, to which the user responds. For example, in the following exchange, the system simulates a misunderstanding of the word *furor* by asking a targeted reprise clarification question.

User: We hope this won't create a *furor*.
System: Create a what?
User: A furor, an uproar.

The system issued six different types of clarification requests: confirmation; rephrase, spell, or disambiguate part of the utterance; targeted reprise clarification; and a targeted-reprise-rephrase combination. These request types were chosen based on the types of requests made by the SRI ThunderBOLT speech-to-speech translation system (Ayan and others, 2013). Confirmation questions simply ask the user to confirm an ASR hypothesis. Rephrase-part requests ask users to rephrase a specific part of an utterance which is played back to the user. Spell questions ask users to spell a word or phrase using the NATO alphabet. Disambiguate questions clarify ambiguous terms. Targeted reprise clarification questions make use of the recognized portion of an utterance to query the part that has been misrecognized based on the system's assessment. Targeted-reprise-rephrase requests are similar, with the additional request for the user to rephrase a portion of the utterance believed to have been misrecognized, which is played to the user.

Inappropriate requests in this study were defined as those that resulted from the ThunderBOLT system's incorrect identification of an error segment or an error type. For example, the clarification request *"Please say a different word for Afdhal"* is inappropriate since it asks for a rephrasal of a proper name. A request to spell a very long phrase is also identified as inappropriate since users have found this difficult, especially when using the NATO alphabet. Requests to disambiguate in the system provide two possible senses of the ambiguous word and are inappropriate when the correct sense is not one of the two provided. Targeted reprise clarification questions are inappropriate when the error segment is not correctly recognized and an errorful segment is included in the question (e.g. *"The okay I zoo would like what?"*). An appropriate question correctly identifies the error segment or ambiguous term and the error type. For example, the question *"I think 'Afdhal' is a name. Please spell it"*, would be appropriate when 'Afdhal' is OOV because it correctly targets the error and its type.

For each clarification request type, except for confirmation questions, which are always appropriate, we created one or more types of *inappropriate* requests for each of the conditions we observed in dialogues collected with the ThunderBOLT system. For example, when the system asks the user to rephrase a part of their utterance which the system believes to be a misrecognized non-proper-name, the question is appropriate when indeed that non-proper-name has been misrecognized. However, the request will be inappropriate when the hypothesized error segment played back to the user is a partial word, a proper name, an extended segment including a name, or a function word. We created instances of each of these conditions for our users to respond to in our experiment. A full list of the system question types and their appropriate and inappropriate conditions is provided in Table 3, in the Appendix. We prepared 228 clarification requests (84 appropriate and 144 inappropriate), 12 for each of the 19 categories listed in Table 3 in the Appendix, based on data in the TRANSTAC dataset (Akbacak and others, 2009). Our subjects were 17 native American English speakers, each of whom answered 114 requests. We recorded speakers' answers to 714 appropriate and 1224 inappropriate requests. As most request types have more than one inappropriate version, 63% of the requests in the data set are inappropriate.

4 Experiment

We used the Weka machine learning library (Witten and Eibe, 2005) to train classifiers to predict whether a clarification request was appropriate or inappropriate. Our features were extracted from transcripts of user utterances, and included lexical, syntactic, numeric, and features from the output of Linguistic Inquiry and Word Count (LIWC) (Pennebaker et al., 2007) as described in Table 1.

We included unigram and bigram features, excluding unigrams that appeared fewer than 3 times in the dataset (11% of the unigrams), and bigrams that appeared fewer than 2 times (25%), with thresholds set empirically. LIWC features were extracted using the LIWC 2007 software, which includes lexical categories, such as articles and negations, and psychological constructs, such as affect and cognition. In one version of the corpus, we replaced sequences of user spellings with the tag "SPELL" and disfluencies with the symbol "DISF". We used the Stanford POS tagger (Toutanova and others, 2003) to tag both the original corpus as well as the modified version. In the latter, we replaced the "SPELL" and "DISF" tags with the symbols themselves. We also mapped nine of the most frequent unigrams to their own POS classes, such as "no", "not", and "neither" to "NO" and "word" to "WORD". We then used counts of POS bigrams as a syntactic feature. Additionally, as we observed that responses to inappropriate requests contained a higher proportion of function words, we added this as a numeric feature. We also observed that average length of responses to inappropriate requests was greater than responses to appropriate ones, and we hypothesized this was in part due to inappropriate requests to spell long phrases. Therefore, we also used the length of the total spelling sequences, or the count of letters spelled out, as a numeric feature. We also added type of clarification request as a feature since some requests are less likely to be inappropriate than others. For example, we consider confirmation questions ("Did you say . . . ?") to always be appropriate.

Feature	Description
word_unigrams (Lexical)	Count of unigrams
word_bigrams (Lexical)	Count of bigrams
pos_bigrams (Syntactic)	Bigrams of POS assigned by Stanford tagger
liwc	LIWC Output
func_ratio	Proportion of function words in response
len_spell	Total length of spelling sequences in response
request_type	Type of request preceding response

Table 1: *Features used in Classification.*

5 Results

We report classification results using Weka's J48 decision tree classifier with 10-fold cross validation in Table 2, which outperformed JRip and LibSVM in our experiments. Compared to the majority baseline of 63.2% accuracy and .489 F-measure, our classifier which uses all of the features in Table 1 achieves a significant improvement, with an accuracy of 88.5% and an F-measure of .885. A baseline method that uses only system request type feature (Req. type baseline) achieves accuracy of 73.7% and F-measure of .686, which is significantly below the performance of the trained classifier. To identify the most important features in predicting inappropriate requests, we iteratively removed a single feature from the full feature set and re-evaluated prediction accuracy. Table 2 shows absolute decrease

Features	Acc (%)	P/R/F-Measure
Majority baseline	63.2 *	0.399/0.632/0.489
Req. type baseline	73.7 *	0.814/0.737/0.686
All Features	88.5	0.885/0.885/0.885
less request_type	−7.6 *	−0.076
less liwc	−2.3	−0.023
less pos_bigrams	−2.0	−0.020
less word_unigrams	−0.4	−0.004
less func_ratio	−0.1	−0.001
less len_spell	−0.05	−0.0005
less word_bigrams	+0.05	+0.0007

Table 2: *Classifying Inappropriate Requests: All Features vs. Baseline vs. Leave-One-Out Classifiers, where * indicates statistically significant difference from All Features* ($p < 0.01$)

in percentage points and in F-measure when each feature is removed in turn compared to the classifier trained on the full features set. We found that system request type was the most important feature, as performance decreased by 7.6 percentage points without it. This makes sense in light of the fact that the ratio of inappropriate to appropriate requests varied for the different request types represented in our dataset. The next most useful features were the output of LIWC and the POS bigrams. We had hypothesized that, since LIWC captures the presence of negations and assents, it could capture negative user responses to the system such as *yes* or *no*. As for the POS bigrams, we modified the POS tags to mark common words and included start and end markers in the bigrams because we hypothesized that the first words and last words in the responses might be particularly informative. Looking at the decision tree created with all our features, we find that the first five branches involve decisions regarding the unigrams "name" and "SPELL" (a collapsed spelling sequence), the ⟨START, "neither"⟩ bigram, the LIWC ingestion-word feature, and the type of request, in that order. Not only do these findings confirm our hypotheses, they also confirm that the unigrams "name", "SPELL", and "neither" which we had mapped to special POS classes are particularly useful.

After training our model, we used it to classify our entire dataset to see which responses it performed well on and which it tended to misclassify. Responses to targeted reprise and targeted-reprise-rephrase questions together accounted for around half of the misclassified instances. Many easily identifiable responses to inappropriate requests involved the user correcting the system, as in the following example:

User: You are going to need to dole out punishment.
System: I think this is a name: 'dole out punishment'. Please spell that name.
User: It is not a name, it is a phrase, dole out punishment.

However, when the users did **not** correct the system after an inappropriate request, their responses appeared no different from answers to appropriate requests. In the following example, the system misrecognizes "hyperbaric" and interprets it as the word "hyper" followed by an unknown phrase, but the user simply ignores the request and repeats.

User: We are going to put you in a hyperbaric chamber.
System: Put you in a high what? Please give me another word or phrase for 'perbaric'.
User: Hyperbaric chamber.

Many cases in which appropriate requests were misclassified as inappropriate involved users responding correctly to targeted or targeted-rephrase questions. We hypothesize that these are also due primarily to users ignoring the inappropriate system request and providing the information the system **should have** asked for. As a result, those cases make it difficult to distinguish between responses to appropriate and inappropriate targeted questions. Of course, users may be giving prosodic cues to indicate confusion or uncertainty or hyper-articulating in their responses. We will address the use of prosodic features in predicting inappropriate requests in future work.

6 Conclusions

In this work, we have addressed a novel task of identifying inappropriate clarification requests using features extracted from user responses. We collected responses to inappropriate clarification requests based on six request types in a simulated SDS environment. The classifier trained on this dataset detects inappropriate requests with accuracy of 88.5%, which is 25.3 percentage points above the majority baseline, and an F-measure of .885, which is .396 points above the majority F-measure. In future work, we will include acoustic and prosodic features as well as lexical features and we will evaluate the use of an inappropriate clarification request component in our speech-to-speech translation system.

References

M. Akbacak et al. 2009. Recent advances in SRI's IraqComm^{tm} Iraqi Arabic-English speech-to-speech translation system. In *ICASSP*, pages 4809–4812.

N. F. Ayan et al. 2013. "Can you give me another word for hyperbaric?": Improving speech translation using targeted clarification questions. In *Acoustics, Speech and Signal Processing (ICASSP), 2013 IEEE International Conference on*, pages 8391–8395. IEEE.

D. Bohus and A. I. Rudnicky. 2005. A principled approach for rejection threshold optimization in spoken dialog systems. In *INTERSPEECH*, pages 2781–2784.

J. Ginzburg and R. Cooper. 2004. Clarification, ellipsism and the nature of contextual updates. *Linguistics and Philosophy*, 27(3).

J. Goldberg, M. Ostendorf, and K. Kirchhoff. 2003. The impact of response wording in error correction subdialogs. In *ISCA Tutorial and Research Workshop on Error Handling in Spoken Dialogue Systems*.

P. Lendvai, A. van den Bosch, E. Krahmer, and M. Swerts. 2002. Improving machine-learned detection of miscommunications in human-machine dialogues through informed data splitting. In *Proceedings of the ESSLLI Workshop on Machine Learning Approaches in Computational Linguistics*, pages 1–15.

D. Litman, J. Hirschberg, and M. Swerts. 2006. Characterizing and predicting corrections in spoken dialogue systems. *Computational linguistics*, 32(3):417–438.

J. W. Pennebaker, C. K. Chung, M. Ireland, A. Gonzales, and R. J. Booth, 2007. *The development and psychometric properties of LIWC2007*. Austin, TX.

M. Purver. 2004. *The Theory and Use of Clarification Requests in Dialogue*. Ph.D. thesis, King's College, University of London.

G. Skantze. 2005. Exploring human error recovery strategies: Implications for spoken dialogue systems. *Speech Communication*, 45(2-3):325–341.

S. Stoyanchev, A. Liu, and J. Hirschberg. 2014. Towards natural clarification questions in dialogue systems. In *Proceedings of AISB2014*.

K. Toutanova et al. 2003. Feature-rich part-of-speech tagging with a cyclic dependency network. In *Proceedings of the 2003 Conference of the North American Chapter of the Association for Computational Linguistics on Human Language Technology - Volume 1*. Association for Computational Linguistics.

I. Witten and F. Eibe. 2005. *Data Mining: Practical machine learning tools and techniques*. Morgan Kaufmann, San Francisco, 2nd edition.

Appendix

ID	Simulation	Appro.	Example
1. Confirmation			
1	Correctly recognized utterance	yes	Did you say "place this on the pane"?
2	Misrecognized utterance	yes	Did you say "these are in um searches will cause the insurgents to priest buyer"?
2. Rephrase-part			
1	Full non-name word or phrase	yes	Please say a different word for "surmise".
2	Partial word	no	Please say a different word for "nouncing".
3	Name	no	Please say a different word for "Afdhal".
4	Extended segment including name	no	Please say a different word for "checkpoint at Betirma".
5	Function word	no	Please say a different word for "off over".
3. Disambiguate			
1	One choice is correct	yes	Did you mean fliers as in handouts or fliers as in pilots?
2	Neither choice is correct	no	Did you mean plane as in aircraft or plain as in simple?
3	Word being disambiguated was not said	no	Did you mean sight as in vision or site as in location?
4. Spell			
1	Name	yes	Please spell "Hadi Al Hemdani".
2	Non-name	no	I think this is a name: "eluding". Please spell that name.
3	Extended segment	no	Please spell "staff are stealing themselves".
5. Reprise			
1	Error segment correctly recognized and no other errors	yes	We will search some of the what?
2	Recognition error right before "what" word	no	Supplies of I see them what?
3	Recognition error which is not the last word before "what"	no	Ask if they are for eating for what?
6. Reprise rephrase			
1	No errors outside of the error segment	yes	Use a what? Please say another word for "bristled".
2	Error segment is a partial word	no	Are there any my what? Please say another word for "nors".
3	Error outside the targeted segment	no	Be a right is what? Please say another word for "rain".

Table 3: *Clarification Requests and Contexts in which they are Appropriate and Inappropriate.*

Using Ellipsis Detection and Word Similarity for Transformation of Spoken Language into Grammatically Valid Sentences

Manuel Giuliani
fortiss GmbH
Munich, Germany
giuliani@fortiss.org

Thomas Marschall
fortiss GmbH
Munich, Germany
marschat@in.tum.de

Amy Isard
University of Edinburgh
Edinburgh, UK
amyi@inf.ed.ac.uk

Abstract

When humans speak they often use grammatically incorrect sentences, which is a problem for grammar-based language processing methods, since they expect input that is valid for the grammar. We present two methods to transform spoken language into grammatically correct sentences. The first is an algorithm for automatic ellipsis detection, which finds ellipses in spoken sentences and searches in a combinatory categorial grammar for suitable words to fill the ellipses. The second method is an algorithm that computes the semantic similarity of two words using WordNet, which we use to find alternatives to words that are unknown to the grammar. In an evaluation, we show that the usage of these two methods leads to an increase of 38.64% more parseable sentences on a test set of spoken sentences that were collected during a human-robot interaction experiment.

Figure 1: The robot bartender of the JAMES project interacting with a customer.

1 Introduction

Computer systems that are designed to interact verbally with humans need to be able to recognise and understand human speech. In this paper we use as an example the robot bartender JAMES (Joint Action for Multimodal Embodied Social Systems),[1] shown in Figure 1. The robot is able to take drink orders from customers and to serve drinks. It is equipped with automatic speech recognition, to understand what the human is saying, and it has a grammar, to parse and process the spoken utterances.

The JAMES robot grammar was initially very restricted, and therefore during grammar development as well as during the user studies that we conducted (Foster et al., 2012; Giuliani et al., 2013; Keizer et al., 2013), we experienced situations in which the robot was not able to process the spoken input by humans, because they spoke sentences with grammatical structures that could not be parsed by the grammar, they used words that were not part of the grammar, or they left out words. We had for example cases where humans approached the robot and used a sentence with an ellipsis ("*I want Coke*", but the grammar expected a determiner in front of "*Coke*") or a sentence with a word that was unknown to the grammar ("*I need a water*", but "*need*" was not part of the grammar's word list). In these cases, the robot was unable to process and to respond to the spoken utterance by the human. Of course, these shortcomings can be overcome by extending the grammar, but even with a much more sophisticated grammar there will always be instances of unexpected language, and we believe that our approach can be very useful in extending the coverage of a grammar during testing or user studies.

Therefore, we present an approach to transform unparseable spoken language into sentences that a given grammar can parse. For ellipsis detection,

[1] http://www.james-project.eu

we present in Section 3.1 a novel algorithm that searches for ellipses in a sentence and computes candidate words to fill the ellipsis with words from a grammar. In Section 3.2, we show how we use WordNet (Miller, 1995) to find replacements for words that are not in the robot's grammar. In Section 4 we evaluate our approach with a test set of 211 spoken utterances that were recorded in a human-robot interaction (HRI) experiment, and the grammar for processing used in the same experiment.

2 Related Work

The work described in this paper draws on research and techniques from three main areas: the automatic detection of ellipses in sentences, calculation of semantic similarity between two words using WordNet, and spoken language processing. This section provides a summary of relevant work in these areas.

2.1 Ellipsis Detection

There is a wide range of research in ellipsis detection in written language, where different types of ellipses are widely defined, such as *gapping*, *stripping* or *verb phrase ellipsis* (Lappin, 1996). For example, an ellipsis occurs when a redundant word is left out of succeeding sentences, such as the words "*want to have*" in the sentence "*I want to have a water, and my friend a juice*", which are omitted in the second part of the sentence.

The detection of verb phrase ellipses (VPE) is a subfield of ellipsis detection that has received much attention. For VPE detection, researchers have used machine learning algorithms which were trained on grammar-parsed corpora, for example in the works of Hardt (1997), Nielsen (2004a), Nielsen (2004b), and Smith and Rauchas (2006). Other approaches for ellipsis detection rely on symbolic processing of sentences, which is similar to our work. Haddar and Hamadou (1998) present a method for ellipsis detection in the Arabic language, which is based on an augmented transition network grammar. Egg and Erk (2001) present a general approach for ellipsis detection and resolution that uses a language for partial description of λ-terms called Constraint Language for Lambda Structures.

2.2 WordNet-based Semantic Similarity Calculation

WordNet is used in many varied natural language processing applications, such as word sense disambiguation, determining the structure of texts, text summarisation and annotation, information extraction and retrieval, automatic indexing, lexical selection, and the automatic correction of word errors in text. In our work, we use WordNet to find similar or synonym words. In previous work, researchers have proposed several methods to generally compute the semantic relatedness of two words using WordNet. Budanitsky and Hirst (2006) review methods to determine semantic relatedness. Newer examples for WordNet-based calculation of semantic similarity are the works by Qin et al. (2009), Cai et al. (2010), Liu et al. (2012), and Wagh and Kolhe (2012).

2.3 Spoken Language Processing

Our work addresses the processing of spoken language, which differs from the processing of written language in that spoken language is more often elliptical and grammatically incorrect. Previous work in this area has attempted to address this issue at different levels of processing. Issar and Ward (1993) presented the CMU speech processing system that supports recognition for grammatically ill-formed sentences. Lavie (1996) presents GLR*, a grammar-based parser for spoken language, which ignores unparseable words and sentence parts and instead looks for the maximal subset of an input sentence that is covered by the grammar.

Other researchers in this area have designed grammar-based approaches for incremental spoken language processing: Brick and Scheutz (2007) present RISE, the robotic incremental semantic engine. RISE is able to process syntactic and semantic information incrementally and to integrate this information with perceptual and linguistic information. Kruijff et al. (2007) present an approach for incremental processing of situated dialogue in human-robot interaction, which maintains parallel interpretations of the current dialogue that are pruned by making use of the context information. Schlangen and Skantze (2009) describe a "general, abstract model of incremental dialogue processing", where their goal is to provide principles for designing new systems for incremental speech processing.

3 Approach

Our goal in this paper is to transform spoken utterances which cannot be parsed by our grammar into grammar-valid sentences. During this process, we have to make sure that the changes to the input sentence do not change its meaning. In this section, we show how we implement ellipsis detection and semantic similarity computation in order to achieve this goal. We present our ellipsis detection algorithm in Section 3.1. Section 3.2 explains our implementation of WordNet-based word similarity computation.

3.1 Ellipsis Detection Algorithm

We use the OpenCCG parser (White, 2006), which is based on Combinatory Categorial Grammar (Kruijff and Baldridge, 2004; Steedman, 2000), to parse the output of our speech recognition system. We use the properties of CCGs to solve a problem that often occurs during parsing of spoken language. In our evaluation (Section 4) we use a test set (Section 4.1) of spoken sentences that was collected during one of our human-robot interaction studies (Foster et al., 2012) and the CCG (Section 4.2) that was used in the same study. In the test set, we found that speakers leave out words. For example, one speaker said *I want water* to order a drink. The grammar used in the experiment assumed that every noun is specified by an article; the grammar was only able to parse the sentence *I want a water*. Just to remind you, of course this particular example could have been solved by rewriting the grammar, but at the time of running the experiment it was not possible to us to change the grammar. Furthermore, we argue that there will always be examples of the above described situation where experiment participants use grammatical structures or words that cannot be processed by the used grammar. Thus, we present an algorithm that automatically finds ellipses in sentences and suggests words from the grammar that could be used to fill the ellipses.

To illustrate our approach, we will use the example sentence *give me a water*. Example (1) shows the words of the example sentence with their assigned categories from the used CCG, and Example (2) shows the parsed sentence. In the examples, we use the category symbols s for sentence, n for noun, and np for noun phrase. In Example (2) the symbol > denotes the used CCG forward application combinator.

(1) *CCG lexicon entries*

a. *give* := s / np / np
b. *me* := np
c. *a* := np / n
d. *water* := n

(2) *Full parse of an example sentence*

```
 give      me    a     water
--------   --   ----   -----
s/np/np    np   np/n     n
                ------------>
                     np
----------->
   s/np
------------------------------>
               s
```

The algorithm consists of two parts: **(i)** search for ellipses in the sentence and selection of the most relevant ellipsis, and **(ii)** computation of the category for the word that will fill the chosen ellipsis.

(i) Ellipsis Search

In order to find the ellipsis in the sentence, our algorithm assumes that to the left and to the right of the ellipsis, the spoken utterance consists of sentence parts that the grammar can parse. In our example, these sentence parts would be *I want* to the left of the ellipsis and *water* to the right. In order to automatically find the sentence part to the right, we use the following algorithm, which we present in Listing 1 in a Java-style pseudo code: The algorithm uses the method tokenize() to split up the string that contains the utterance into an array of single words. It then iterates through the array and builds a new sentence of the words in the array, using the method buildString(). This sentence is then processed by the parser. If the parser finds a parse for the sentence, the algorithm returns the result. Otherwise it cuts off the first word of the sentence and repeats the procedure. This way, the algorithm searches for a parseable sentence part for the given utterance from the left to the right until it either finds the right-most parseable sentence part or there are no more words to parse. In order to find the left-most parseable sentence part, we implemented a method findParseReverse(), which parses sentence parts from right to left.

One has to consider that our method for ellipsis detection can falsely identify ellipses in certain sentence constellations. For example, if the word *like* in the sentence *I would like a water* is left out and given to our ellipsis detection algorithm, it would falsely find an ellipsis between *I* and *would*, and another ellipsis between *would*

Listing 1: Ellipsis detection algorithm.

```
Result findParse(String utterance) {
  words[] = tokenize(utterance);
  for (i = 0; i < words.length; i++) {
    String sentence = buildString(words[
        i], words.length);
    Result parse = parse(sentence);
    if (parse != null) {
      return parse;
    }
  }
  return null;
}
```

and *a*. The reason for the detection of the first ellipsis is that the categories for *I* and *would* cannot be combined together. *would* and *like* have to be parsed first to an auxiliary verb-verb construct. This construct can then be combined with the pronoun *I*. To overcome this problem, we first compute the category for each found ellipsis. Then we find a word for the ellipsis with the simplest category, which is either an atomic category or a functional category with fewer functors than the other found categories, add it to the original input sentence, and parse the output sentence. If the output sentence cannot be parsed, we repeat the step with the next found ellipsis.

(ii) Ellipsis Category Computation

After the algorithm has determined the ellipsis in an utterance, it computes the category of the word that will fill the ellipsis. The goal here is to find a category which the grammar needs to combine the sentence parts to the left and right of the ellipsis. For example, the left part of our example utterance *I want* has the category s/np and the right part *water* has the category n. Hence, the category for the missing word needs to be np/n, because it takes the category of the right sentence part as argument and produces the category np, which is the argument of the category of the left sentence part.

Figure 2 shows the processing sequence diagram of our algorithm for computing the category of an ellipsis. In the diagram, left and right stand for the categories of the sentence parts that are to the left and right of the ellipsis. The predicates symbolise functions: isEmpty(category) checks if a category is empty, atom(category) checks if a category is atomic, compl(category) checks if a category is complex and has a slash operator that faces toward the ellipsis. The predicate arg(category) returns the argument of a complex category. Rectangular boxes symbolise steps where the algorithm builds the result category for the missing word. The algorithm determines the category with the following rules:

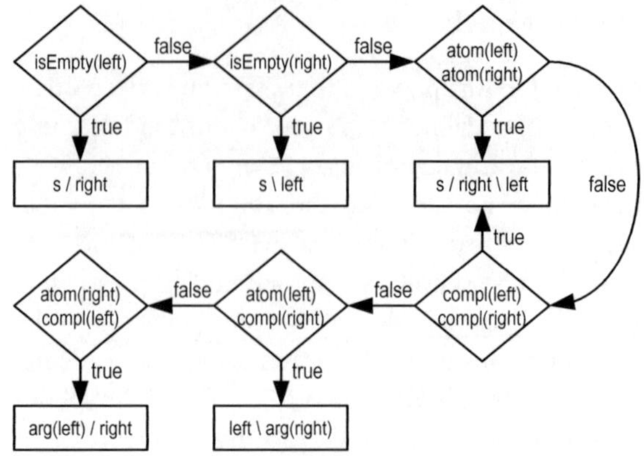

Figure 2: Processing sequence of the category computation algorithm.

- if the categories to the left or to the right of the ellipsis are empty, the ellipsis category is s/right or s\left, respectively,
- if the categories to the right and to the left of the ellipsis are atomic, the ellipsis category is s/right\left,
- if the categories to the right and to the left of the ellipsis are both complex and have a slash operator facing toward the ellipsis, the ellipsis category is s/right\left,
- if the category to the left of the ellipsis is atomic and to the right of the ellipsis is complex, the ellipsis category is left\arg(right),
- if the category to the right of the ellipsis is atomic and to the left of the ellipsis is complex, the ellipsis category is arg(left)\right.

After the computation of the ellipsis category, we use the OpenCCG grammar to select words to fill the ellipsis. This step is straightforward, because the grammar maintains a separate word list with corresponding categories. Here, we benefit from the usage of a categorial grammar, as the usage of a top-down grammar formalism would have meant a more complicated computation in this step.

3.2 WordNet-based Word Substitution

Spoken language is versatile and there are many ways to express one's intentions by using different expressions. Thus, in grammar-based spoken language processing it often happens that sentences cannot be parsed because of words that are not in the grammar. To overcome this problem, we use WordNet (Miller, 1995) to find semantically equivalent replacements for unknown words. WordNet arranges words in sets of synonyms called synsets which are connected to other synsets by a variety of relations, which differ for each word category. The most relevant relations for our work are: for nouns and verbs *hyperonyms* (e.g., drink is a hyperonym of juice) and *hyponyms* (e.g., juice is a hyponym of drink), and for adjectives we use the *similar to* relation.

Our implementation of word substitution executes two steps if a word is unknown to the grammar: (1) look-up of synonyms for the unknown words. The unknown word can be substituted with a semantically similar word directly, if the synset of the unknown word contains a word, which is known to the grammar. (2) Computation of similar words in the WordNet hyperonym/hyponym hierarchy. If the synset of the unknown word does not contain a substitution, we compute if one of the hyperonyms of the unknown word has a hyponym which is known to the grammar. Here, one has to be careful not to move too far away from the meaning of the unknown word in the WordNet tree, in order not to change the meaning of the originally spoken sentence. Also, the computation of the similar word should not take too much time. Therefore, in our implementation, we only substitute an unknown word with one of its hyperonym/hyponym neighbours when the substitution candidate is a direct hyponym of the direct hyperonym of the unknown word.

4 Evaluation

The goal of this evaluation is to measure how many spoken sentences that our grammar cannot parse can be processed after the transformation of the sentences with our methods. In Section 4.1 we present the test set of spoken sentences that we used in the evaluation. In Section 4.2 we give details of the used grammar. As mentioned above, both, the test set as well as the grammar, were taken from the human-robot interaction study reported by Foster et al. (2012). Section 4.3 summarises the details of the evaluation procedure. Finally, we present the evaluation results in Section 4.4 and discuss their meaning in Section 4.5.

4.1 Test Set

As test set for the evaluation, we used the spoken utterances from the participants of the human-robot interaction experiment reported by Foster et al. (2012). In the experiment, 31 participants were asked to order a drink from the robot bartender shown in Figure 1. The experiment consisted of three parts: in the first part, participants had to order drinks on their own, in the second and third part, participants were accompanied by a confederate in order to have a multi-party interaction with the robot. The spoken utterances in the test set were annotated by hand from video recordings of the 93 drink order sequences. Please refer to (Foster et al., 2012) for a detailed description of the experiment.

Table 1 shows an overview of the test set. In total, it contains 211 unique utterances; the experiment participants spoke 531 sentences of which some sentences were said repeatedly. We divided the test set into the following speech acts (Searle, 1965): Ordering (“*I would like a juice please.*”), Question (“*What do you have?*”), Greeting (“*Hello there.*”), Polite expression (“*Thank you.*”), Confirmation (“*Yes.*”), Other (“*I am thirsty.*”).

4.2 Grammar

The grammar that we used in this evaluation was also used in the robot bartender experiment (Foster et al., 2012). This grammar is limited in its scope, because the domain of the experiment—the robot hands out drinks to customers—was limited as well. Overall, the lexicon of the grammar contains 92 words, which are divided into the following part of speech classes: 42 verbs, 11 nouns, 10 greetings, 6 pronouns, 5 prepositions, 4 adverbs, 4 determiners, 3 quantifiers, 3 confirmations, 2 relative pronouns, 1 conjunction, 1 polite expression.

4.3 Procedure

For the evaluation, we implemented a programme that takes our test set and automatically parses each sentence with four different settings, which are also presented in Table 1: **(1)** parsing with the grammar only, **(2)** application of ellipsis detection and word filling before parsing, **(3)** application of WordNet similarity substitution before parsing, **(4)** application of a combination of both methods before parsing. Please note that for alternative **(4)** the sequence in which the methods

Speech act	No. utt	(1) CCG	(2) Ell. det.	(3) WordNet	(4) Ell. + WordNet
Ordering	143	34	16	-	1
Question	19	1	-	-	-
Greeting	18	4	1	-	-
Polite expression	14	1	-	-	-
Confirmation	5	4	-	-	-
Other	12	-	-	-	-
Total	211	44	17	-	1

Table 1: Overview for test set and evaluation. Column **No. utt** contains the number of test utterances per speech act. Column **(1) CCG** shows the number of utterances that were directly parsed by the grammar. Columns **(2) Ell. det.**, **(3) WordNet**, and **(4) Ell. + WordNet** show how many utterances were additionally parsed using the ellipsis detection , WordNet substitution, and combination of both modules.

are applied to a given sentence can make a difference to the parsing result. In this evaluation, we used both possible sequences: first ellipsis detection followed by WordNet substitution method or vice versa.

4.4 Results

Table 1 shows the result of the evaluation procedure. The grammar parses 44 sentences of the 211 test set sentences correctly. By using the ellipsis detection algorithm, 17 additional sentences are parsed. The usage of the WordNet substitution algorithm yields no additionally parsed sentences. The combination of both methods (in this case, first ellipsis detection, then WordNet substitution) leads to the correct parse of one additional sentence. None of the transformed sentences changed its meaning when compared to the original sentence.

4.5 Discussion

The evaluation results show that the application of our ellipsis detection algorithm leads to an increase of successfully parsed sentences of 38.64%. In the class of ordering sentences, which was the most relevant for the human-robot interaction experiment from which we used the evaluation test set, the number of successfully parsed sentences increases by 47.06%. Compared to this, the usage of WordNet substitution alone does not lead to an increase in parseable sentences. The one case in which the combination of ellipsis detection and WordNet substitution transformed an unparseable sentence into a grammatically valid sentence is interesting: here, the experiment participant said "*I need Coke.*" to order a drink from the robot. This sentence contained the word "*need*", which was not in the grammar. WordNet has the synonym "*want*" in the synset for the word "*need*". However, the sentence "*I want Coke.*" was also not parseable, because the grammar expected an article in front of every noun. The ellipsis detection algorithm was able to find the missing article in the sentence and filled it with an article "*a*" from the grammar, leading to a parseable sentence "*I want a Coke.*".

Although we see an increase in parsed sentences, 150 sentences of the test set were not transformed by our approach. Therefore, we made an analysis for the remaining utterances to find the main causes for this weak performance. We found that the following reasons cause problems for the grammar (with number of cases in brackets behind each reason):

- *Word missing in grammar (81).* The participant used a word that was not in the grammar. For example, users ordered drinks by saying "*One water, please.*" , but the grammar did not contain "*one*" as an article. This result shows that the WordNet similarity substitution has the potential to lead to a large increase in parseable sentences. However as mentioned above, there is a risk of changing the meaning of a sentence too much when allowing the replacement of words which are only vaguely similar to the unknown word.
- *Sentence structure (25).* Some participants said sentences that were either grammatically incorrect or had a sentence structure that was not encoded in the grammar. For example one participant tried to order a juice by saying "*Juice for me.*". Additionally, some participants asked questions ("*Do you have coke?*").

For the latter, please note that it was not part of the HRI experiment, from which we use the test set, that the experiment participants should be allowed to ask questions to the robot.

- *Unnecessary fill words (22).* Some experiment participants used unnecessary fill words that did not add meaning to the sentence, for example one participant said "*Oh come on, I only need water*" to order a drink.

- *Sentence not related to domain (22).* Some participants said sentences that were contrary to the given experiment instructions. For example, some participants asked questions to the robot ("*How old are you?*") and to the experimenter ("*Do I need to focus on the camera?*"), or complained about the robot's performance ("*You are not quite responsive right now.*"). Clearly, these sentences were out of the scope of the grammar.

5 Conclusion

We presented two methods for transforming spoken language into grammatically correct sentences. The first of these two approaches is an ellipsis detection, which automatically detects ellipses in sentences and looks up words in a grammar that can fill the ellipsis. Our ellipsis detection algorithm is based on the properties of the combinatory categorial grammar, which assigns categories to each word in the grammar and thus enables the algorithm to find suitable fill words by calculating the category of the ellipsis. The second approach for sentence transformation was a WordNet-based word similarity computation and substitution. Here, we used the synsets of WordNet to substitute words that are unknown to a given grammar with synonyms for these words. In an evaluation we showed that the usage of ellipsis detection leads to an increase of successfully parsed sentences of up to 47.06% for some speech acts. The usage of the WordNet similarity substitution does not increase the number of parsed sentences, although our analysis of the test set shows that unknown words are the most common reason that sentences cannot be parsed.

Our approach was specifically implemented to help circumventing problems during development and usage of grammars for spoken language processing in human-robot interaction experiments, and the example grammar was a very restricted one. However, we believe that our method can also be helpful with more extensive grammars, and for developers of dialogue systems in other areas, such as telephone-based information systems or offline versions of automatic smartphone assistants like Apple's Siri.

In the future, we will refine our methodology. In particular, the WordNet similarity substitution is too rigid in its current form. Here, we plan to loosen some of the constraints that we applied to our algorithm. We will systematically test how far away from a word one can look for suitable substitutes in the WordNet hierarchy, without losing the meaning of a sentence. Furthermore, we plan to add a dialogue history to our approach, which will provide an additional source of information—besides the grammar—to the ellipsis detection method. Finally, we plan to work with stop word lists to filter unnecessary fill words from the input sentences, since these proved also to be a reason for sentences to be unparseable.

Acknowledgements

This research was supported by the European Commission through the project JAMES (FP7-270435-STREP).

References

Timothy Brick and Matthias Scheutz. 2007. Incremental natural language processing for hri. In *Proceedings of the ACM/IEEE International Conference on Human-Robot Interaction*, pages 263–270. ACM New York, NY, USA.

Alexander Budanitsky and Graeme Hirst. 2006. Evaluating wordnet-based measures of lexical semantic relatedness. *Computational Linguistics*, 32(1):13–47.

Songmei Cai, Zhao Lu, and Junzhong Gu. 2010. An effective measure of semantic similarity. In *Advances in Wireless Networks and Information Systems*, pages 9–17. Springer.

Markus Egg and Katrin Erk. 2001. A compositional account of vp ellipsis. *Technology*, 3:5.

Mary Ellen Foster, Andre Gaschler, Manuel Giuliani, Amy Isard, Maria Pateraki, and Ronald P. A. Petrick. 2012. Two people walk into a bar: Dynamic multi-party social interaction with a robot agent. In *Proceedings of the 14th ACM International Conference on Multimodal Interaction (ICMI 2012)*, October.

Manuel Giuliani, Ronald P.A. Petrick, Mary Ellen Foster, Andre Gaschler, Amy Isard, Maria Pateraki, and Markos Sigalas. 2013. Comparing task-based and socially intelligent behaviour in a robot bartender. In *Proceedings of the 15th International Conference on Multimodal Interfaces (ICMI 2013)*, Sydney, Australia, December.

Kais Haddar and A Ben Hamadou. 1998. An ellipsis detection method based on a clause parser for the arabic language. In *Proceedings of the International Florida Artificial Intelligence Research Society FLAIRS98*, pages 270–274.

Daniel Hardt. 1997. An empirical approach to vp ellipsis. *Computational Linguistics*, 23(4):525–541.

Sunil Issar and Wayne Ward. 1993. Cmu's robust spoken language understanding system. In *Proceedings of the Third European Conference on Speech Communication and Technology (Eurospeech 1993)*.

Simon Keizer, Mary Ellen Foster, Oliver Lemon, Andre Gaschler, and Manuel Giuliani. 2013. Training and evaluation of an MDP model for social multiuser human-robot interaction. In *Proceedings of the SIGDIAL 2013 Conference*, pages 223–232, Metz, France, August.

Geert-Jan M. Kruijff and Jason Baldridge. 2004. Generalizing dimensionality in combinatory categorial grammar. In *Proceedings of the 20th International Conference on Computational Linguistics (COLING 2004)*, Geneva, Switzerland, August.

Geert-Jan M. Kruijff, Pierre Lison, Trevor Benjamin, Henrik Jacobsson, and Nick Hawes. 2007. Incremental, multi-level processing for comprehending situated dialogue in human-robot interaction. In Luis Seabra Lopes, Tony Belpaeme, and Stephen J. Cowley, editors, *Symposium on Language and Robots (LangRo 2007)*, Aveiro, Portugal, December.

Shalom Lappin. 1996. The interpretation of ellipsis. *The Handbook of Contemporary Semantic Theory*, 397:399.

Alon Lavie. 1996. *GLR*: A Robust Grammar-Focused Parser for Spontaneously Spoken Language*. Ph.D. thesis, Carnegie Mellon University.

Hongzhe Liu, Hong Bao, and De Xu. 2012. Concept vector for semantic similarity and relatedness based on wordnet structure. *Journal of Systems and Software*, 85(2):370–381.

George A. Miller. 1995. Wordnet: A lexical database for english. *Communications of the ACM*, 38(11):39–41.

Leif Arda Nielsen. 2004a. Verb phrase ellipsis detection using automatically parsed text. In *Proceedings of the 20th International Conference on Computational Linguistics*, page 1093. Association for Computational Linguistics.

Leif Arda Nielsen. 2004b. Verb phrase ellipsis detection using machine learning techniques. *Amsterdam Studies in the Theory and History of Linguistic Science*, page 317.

Peng Qin, Zhao Lu, Yu Yan, and Fang Wu. 2009. A new measure of word semantic similarity based on wordnet hierarchy and dag theory. In *Proceedings of the International Conference on Web Information Systems and Mining2009 (WISM 2009)*, pages 181–185. IEEE.

David Schlangen and Gabriel Skantze. 2009. A general, abstract model of incremental dialogue processing. In *Proceedings of the 12th Conference of the European Chapter of the Association for Computational Linguistics (EACL-09)*.

John R. Searle. 1965. What is a speech act? In Robert J. Stainton, editor, *Perspectives in the Philosophy of Language: A Concise Anthology*, pages 253–268.

Lindsey Smith and Sarah Rauchas. 2006. A machine-learning approach for the treatment of vp ellipsis. In *Proceedings of the Seventeenth Annual Symposium of the Pattern Recognition Association of South Africa*, November.

Mark Steedman. 2000. *The Syntactic Process*. MIT Press, Cambridge, MA, USA.

Kishor Wagh and Satish Kolhe. 2012. A new approach for measuring semantic similarity in ontology and its application in information retrieval. In *Multidisciplinary Trends in Artificial Intelligence*, pages 122–132. Springer.

Michael White. 2006. CCG chart realization from disjunctive inputs. In *Proceedings of the Fourth International Natural Language Generation Conference*, pages 12–19, Sydney, Australia, July. Association for Computational Linguistics.

SAWDUST: a Semi-Automated Wizard Dialogue Utterance Selection Tool for domain-independent large-domain dialogue

Sudeep Gandhe **David Traum**
University of Southern California, Institute for Creative Technologies
srgandhe@gmail.com, traum@ict.usc.edu

Abstract

We present a tool that allows human wizards to select appropriate response utterances for a given dialogue context from a set of utterances observed in a dialogue corpus. Such a tool can be used in Wizard-of-Oz studies and for collecting data which can be used for training and/or evaluating automatic dialogue models. We also propose to incorporate such automatic dialogue models back into the tool as an aid in selecting utterances from a large dialogue corpus. The tool allows a user to rank candidate utterances for selection according to these automatic models.

1 Motivation

Dialogue corpora play an increasingly important role as a resource for dialogue system creation. In addition to its traditional roles, such as training language models for speech recognition and natural language understanding, the dialogue corpora can be directly used for the *selection approach* to response formation (Gandhe and Traum, 2010). In the *selection* approach, the response is formulated by simply picking the appropriate utterance from a set of previously observed utterances. This approach is used in many wizard of oz systems, where the wizard presses a button to select an utterance, as well as in many automated dialogue systems (Leuski et al., 2006; Zukerman and Marom, 2006; Sellberg and Jönsson, 2008)

The resources required for the *selection* approach are a set of utterances to choose from and optionally, a set of pairs of ⟨context, response utterance⟩ to train automatic dialogue models. A wizard can generate such resources by performing two types of tasks. First is the traditional Wizard-of-Oz dialogue collection, where a wizard interacts with a user of the dialogue system. Here the wizard selects an appropriate response utterance for a context that is being updated in a dynamic fashion as the dialogue proceeds (*dynamic context setting*). The second task is geared towards gathering data for training/evaluating automatic dialogue models, where a wizard is required to select appropriate responses (perhaps more than one) for a context which is extracted from a human-human dialogue. The context does not change based on the wizard's choices (*static context setting*).

A wizard tool should help with the challenges presented by these tasks. A challenge for both of these tasks is that if the number of utterances in the corpus is large (e.g., more than the number of buttons that can be placed on a computer screen), it may be very difficult for a wizard to locate appropriate utterances. For the second task of creating human-verified training/evaluation data, tools like NPCEditor (Leuski and Traum, 2010) have been developed which, allow the tagging of a many to many relationships between contexts (approximated simply as input utterance) and responses. In other cases, a corpus of dialogues is used to acquire the set of selectable utterances, in which each context is followed by a single next utterance, and many utterances appear only once. This sparsity of data makes the selection task hard. Moreover, it may be the case that there are many possible continuations of a context or contexts in which an utterance may be appropriate (DeVault et al., 2011).

We address these needs with a semi-automated wizard tool that allows a wizard to engage in dynamic or static context utterance selection, select multiple responses, and use several kinds of search tools to locate promising utterances from a large set that can't all be displayed or remembered. In the next section we describe the tool and how it can be used. Then we describe how this tool was used to create evaluation data in the static context setting.

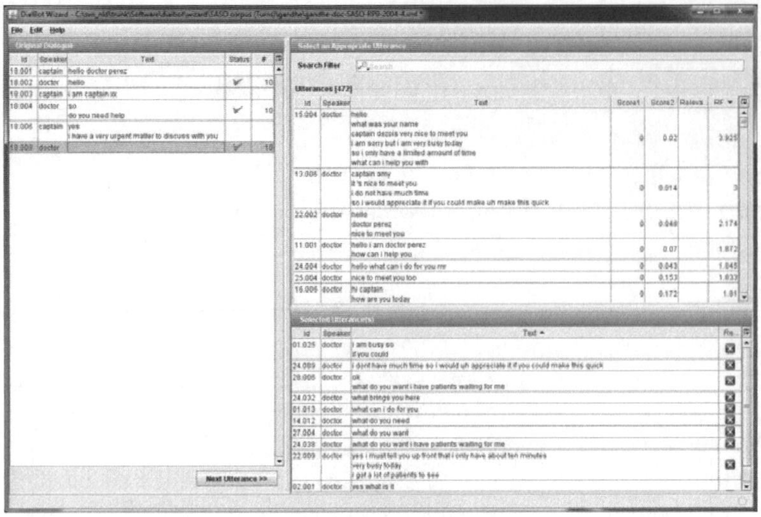

Figure 1: A screenshot of the interface for the wizard data collection in static context setting.

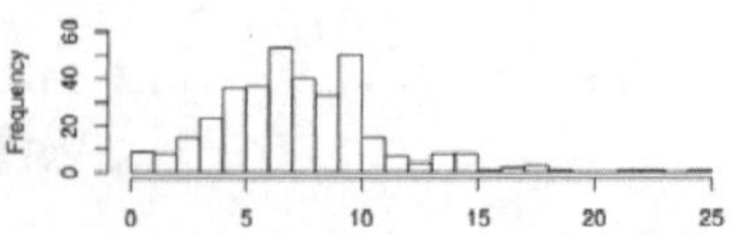

Figure 2: A Histogram for the number of selected appropriate responses.

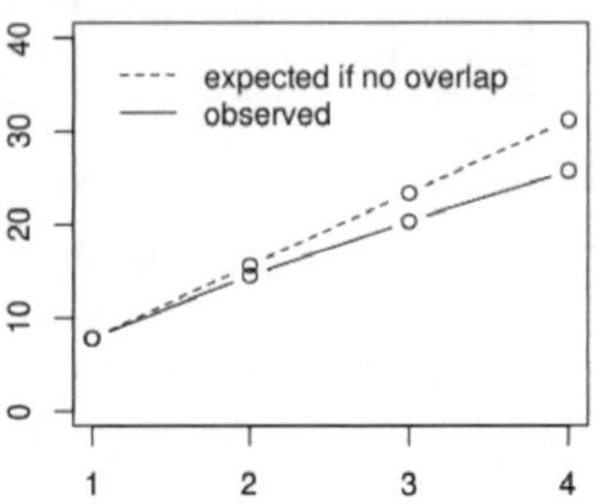

Figure 3: Avg. cardinality of the set for different values of $|R|$.

2 Wizard Tool

Our wizard tool consists of several different views (see figure 1), and is similar in some respects to the IORelator annotation tool (DeVault et al., 2010), but specialized to act as a wizard interface. The first view (left pane) is a dialogue context, that shows the recent history of the dialogue, before the wizard's decision point. The second view (top right pane) shows a list of possible utterances that can be selected from. This view can be ordered in several different ways, as described below. Finally, there is a view of selected utterances (bottom right pane). In the case of dynamic context, the wizard will probably only select one utterance and then a dialogue partner will respond with a new utterance that extends the previous context. In the case of static evaluation, however, used for training and/or evaluating automated selection algorithms, it is often helpful to select multiple utterances if more than one is appropriate.

To help wizards explore the set of all possible utterances, we provide the ability to rank the utterances by various automated scores. Our configuration used in the static context task uses *Score1* as the score calculated using one of the automatic dialogue models, specifically *Nearest Context* model (Gandhe and Traum, 2007) - this model orders candidate utterances from the corpus by the similarity of their previous two utterances to the current dialogue context. *Score2* is surface text similarity, computed as the METEOR score (Lavie and Denkowski, 2009) between the candidate utterance and the actual response utterance present at that location in original human-human dialogue (which is not available to the wizard). Wizards can also search the set of utterances for specific keywords and the third column, *Relevance*, shows the score for the search string entered by the wizards. The last column *RF* stands for relevance feedback and ranks the utterances by similarity to the utterances that have already been chosen by the wizard. This allows wizards to easily find paraphrases of already selected response utterances. Clicking the header of any of these columns will reorder the utterance list by the automated score, by relevance (assuming a search term has been entered) or by relevance feedback (assuming one or more utterances have already been chosen).

3 Evaluation

We evaluated the tool by having four human volunteers (wizards) use it in order to establish an upper baseline for human-level performance in the static context evaluation task described in (Gandhe and Traum, 2013). Wizards were instructed in how to use the search and relevance feedback features. In order to not bias the wizards, they were not told exactly what *score1* and *score2* indicate, but just that the scores can be useful in search.

Each wizard is presented with a set of utterances (U_{train}) ($|U_{train}| \approx 500$) and is asked to select a subset from these that will be appropriate as a response for the presented dialogue context. Each wizard was requested to select somewhere between 5 to 10 (at-least one) appropriate responses for each dialogue context extracted from five different human-human dialogues. There are a total of 89 dialogue contexts for the role that the wizards were to play. Figure 2 shows the histogram for the number of utterances selected as appropriate responses by the four wizards. As expected, wizards frequently chose multiple utterances as appropriate responses (mean = 7.80, min = 1, max = 25).

To get an idea about how much the wizards agree among themselves for this task, we calculated the overlap between the utterances selected by a specific wizard and the utterances selected by another wizard or a set of wizards. Let U_c^T be a set of utterances selected by a wizard T for a dialogue context c. Let R be a set of wizards ($T \notin R$) and U_c^R be the union of sets of utterances selected by the set of wizards (R) for the same context c. Then we define the following overlap measures,

$$\text{Precision}_c = \frac{|U_c^T \cap U_c^R|}{|U_c^T|} \quad \text{Recall}_c = \frac{|U_c^T \cap U_c^R|}{|U_c^R|}$$

$$\text{Jaccard}_c = \frac{|U_c^T \cap U_c^R|}{|U_c^T \cup U_c^R|} \quad \text{Dice}_c = \frac{2|U_c^T \cap U_c^R|}{|U_c^T| + |U_c^R|}$$

$$\text{Meteor}_c = \frac{1}{|U_c^T|} \sum_{u_t} \text{METEOR}\ (u_t, U_c^R) \quad \forall u_t \in U_c^T$$

We compute the average values of these overlap measures for all contexts and for all possible settings of test wizards and reference wizards. Table 1 shows the results with different values for the number of wizards used as reference.

#ref	Prec.	Rec.	Jacc.	Dice	Meteor
1	0.145	0.145	0.077	0.141	0.290
2	0.244	0.134	0.093	0.170	0.412
3	0.311	0.121	0.094	0.171	0.478

Table 1: Inter-wizard agreement

Precision can be interpreted as the probability that a response utterance selected by a wizard is also considered appropriate by at least one other wizard. Precision rapidly increases along with the number of reference wizards used. This happens because the size of the set U_c^R steadily increases with more reference wizards. Figure 3 shows this observed increase and the expected increase if there were no overlap between the wizards. The near-linear increase in $|U_c^R|$ suggests that selecting appropriate responses is a hard task and may require a lot more than four wizards to achieve convergence.

Subjectively, the wizards reported no major usability problems with the tool, and were able to use all four utterance ordering techniques to find appropriate utterances.

4 Future Work

Future work involves performing some formal evaluations comparing this tool to other tools (that are missing some of the features of this tool) in terms of amount of time taken to make selections and quality of the selections, using the same evaluation techniques as (Gandhe and Traum, 2013).

We also see a promising future for semi-automated selection, which blurs the line between a pure algorithmic response and pure wizard selection. Here the wizard can select appropriate responses, which can be used by algorithms as supervised training data, meanwhile the algorithms can be used to seed the wizard's selection.

References

David DeVault, Susan Robinson, and David Traum. 2010. IORelator: A graphical user interface to enable rapid semantic annotation for data-driven natural language understanding. In *Proc. of the 5th Joint ISO-ACL/SIGSEM Workshop on Interoperable Semantic Annotation (ISA-5)*.

David DeVault, Anton Leuski, and Kenji Sagae. 2011. An evaluation of alternative strategies for implementing dialogue policies using statistical classification and rules. In *Proceedings of the IJCNLP 2011*, Nov.

Sudeep Gandhe and David Traum. 2007. Creating spoken dialogue characters from corpora without annotations. In *Proceedings of Interspeech-07*, Antwerp, Belgium.

Sudeep Gandhe and David Traum. 2010. I've said it before, and I'll say it again: an empirical investigation of the upper bound of the selection approach to dialogue. In *Proceedings of the SIGDIAL '10*, Tokyo, Japan.

Sudeep Gandhe and David Traum. 2013. Surface text based dialogue models for virtual humans. In *Proceedings of the SIGDIAL 2013*, Metz, France.

A. Lavie and M. J. Denkowski. 2009. The meteor metric for automatic evaluation of machine translation. *Machine Translation*, 23:105–115.

Anton Leuski and David R. Traum. 2010. NPCEditor: A tool for building question-answering characters. In *Proceedings of LREC 2010*, Valletta, Malta.

Anton Leuski, Ronakkumar Patel, David Traum, and Brandon Kennedy. 2006. Building effective question answering characters. In *Proc. of SIGDIAL '06*, Australia.

Linus Sellberg and Arne Jönsson. 2008. Using random indexing to improve singular value decomposition for latent semantic analysis. In *Proceedings of LREC'08*, Morocco.

Ingrid Zukerman and Yuval Marom. 2006. A corpus-based approach to help-desk response generation. In *Computational Intelligence for Modelling, Control and Automation (CIMCA 2006), IAWTIC 2006*.

A Demonstration of Dialogue Processing in SimSensei Kiosk

Fabrizio Morbini, David DeVault, Kallirroi Georgila,
Ron Artstein, David Traum, Louis-Philippe Morency
USC Institute for Creative Technologies
12015 Waterfront Dr., Playa Vista, CA 90094
{morbini,devault,kgeorgila,artstein,traum,morency}@ict.usc.edu

Abstract

This demonstration highlights the dialogue processing in SimSensei Kiosk, a virtual human dialogue system that conducts interviews related to psychological distress conditions such as depression, anxiety, and post-traumatic stress disorder (PTSD). The dialogue processing in SimSensei Kiosk allows the system to conduct coherent spoken interviews of human users that are 15-25 minutes in length, and in which users feel comfortable talking and openly sharing information. We present the design of the individual dialogue components, and show examples of natural conversation flow between the system and users, including expressions of empathy, follow-up responses and continuation prompts, and turn-taking.

1 Introduction

This demonstration highlights the dialogue processing in SimSensei Kiosk, a virtual human dialogue system that conducts interviews related to psychological distress conditions such as depression, anxiety, and post-traumatic stress disorder (PTSD) (DeVault et al., 2014). SimSensei Kiosk has two main functions – a virtual human called Ellie (pictured in Figure 1), who converses with a user in a spoken, semi-structured interview, and a multimodal perception system which analyzes the user's behavior in real time to identify indicators of psychological distress.

The system has been designed and developed over two years using a series of face-to-face, Wizard-of-Oz, and automated system studies involving more than 350 human participants (Scherer et al., 2013; DeVault et al., 2013; DeVault et al., 2014). Agent design has been guided by two overarching goals: (1) the agent should make the user feel comfortable talking and openly sharing information, and at the same time (2) the agent should create interactional situations that support the automatic assessment of verbal and nonverbal behaviors correlated with psychological distress. During an interview, the agent presents a set of questions which have been shown in user testing to support these goals. Since the main interview questions and their order are mostly fixed, dialogue management concentrates on providing appropriate verbal feedback behaviors to keep the user engaged, maintain a natural and comfortable conversation flow, and elicit continuations and elaborations from the user.

Figure 1: Ellie, the virtual human interviewer in SimSensei Kiosk.

The agent is implemented using a modular architecture (Hartholt et al., 2013). Dialogue processing, which is the focus of this demonstration, is supported by individual modules for speech recognition, language understanding and dialogue management (see Section 2). The agent's language and speech are executed by selecting from pre-recorded audio clips. Additional agent modules include nonverbal behavior generation, which matches appropriately timed body movements to the agent's speech; character animation in a virtual 3D environment; and rendering in a game engine. The perception system analyzes audio and video in real time to identify features such as head position, gaze direction, smile intensity, and voice quality. DeVault et al. (2014) provides details on all the agent's modules.

2 Overview of Dialogue Processing

2.1 ASR and NLU components

Unlike many task-oriented dialogue domains, interview dialogues between SimSensei Kiosk and participants are naturally open-ended. People tend to respond to interview stimuli such as *"what's one of your most memorable experiences?"* with idiosyncratic stories and events from their lives. The variability in the vocabulary and content of participants' answers to such questions is so large that it makes the ASR task very challenging. Furthermore, continuous ASR is employed to ensure that participants feel comfortable interacting with the system without being distracted by having to use a push-to-talk microphone. The use of continuous ASR necessitates the development of specific policies for turn-taking (see Section 2.2). In this demonstration, voice activity detection and speech recognition are performed using PocketSphinx (Huggins-Daines et al., 2006).

Because of the open-ended participants' responses, for NLU, we cannot simply construct a small semantic ontology and expect to cover the majority of meanings that will be expressed by users. Thus, this is an application in which the dialogue policy needs to be able to create a sense of engagement, continuation, and empathy despite relatively shallow and limited understanding of user speech. SimSensei Kiosk currently uses 4 statistically trained utterance classifiers to capture different aspects of user utterance meaning.

The first NLU classifier identifies generic dialogue act types, including statements, yes-no questions, wh-questions, yes and no answers, and several others. This classifier is trained using the Switchboard DAMSL corpus (Jurafsky et al., 1997) using a maximum entropy model.

The second NLU classifier assigns positive, negative, or neutral valence to utterances, in order to guide Ellie's expression of empathy. We use SentiWordNet 3.0 (Baccianella et al., 2010), a lexical sentiment dictionary, to assign valence to individual words spoken by users (as recognized by the ASR); the valence assigned to an utterance is based primarily on the mean valence scores of the individual words in the utterance.

	Opening Rapport Building Phase
Ellie	*What are some things you really like about LA?* (top level question)
User	*I love the weather, I love the palm trees, I love the beaches, there's a lot to do here.*
	Diagnostic Phase
Ellie	*Have you noticed any changes in your behavior or thoughts lately?* (top level question)
User	*Yes.*
Ellie	*Can you tell me about that?* (continuation prompt)
User	*I'm having a lot more nightmares now uh can't sleep have haven't really been eating uh trying to eat... I have to force down food um just feeling like an emotional wreck.*
Ellie	*I'm sorry to hear that.* (empathy response)
Ellie	*What are you like when you don't sleep well?* (follow-up question)
User	*Irritable, emotional, it just adds to my overall stress um [long pause]*
Ellie	*What...* (Ellie speaks after the participant's long pause)
User	*Can't concentrate uh I uh...* (the participant starts speaking while Ellie is speaking)
Ellie	*I'm sorry please continue.* (Ellie realizes that she has interrupted the participant and apologizes)
	Positive Closing Phase
Ellie	*How would your best friend describe you?* (top level question)
User	*As caring, as fun because most of the time when I'm around my best friends I'm happy and I'm fun loving. I joke around with them a lot and uh I do better when I'm around my friends...*

Figure 2: Examples of Ellie's interview phases.

The third NLU classifier supports domain-specific small talk by recognizing a handful of specific anticipated responses to Ellie's rapport-building questions. For example, when Ellie asks users where they are from, this classifier detects the names of commonly mentioned cities and regions using keyphrase spotting.

The fourth NLU classifier identifies domain-specific dialogue acts, and supports Ellie's follow-up responses to specific questions, such as *"how close are you to your family?"*. This maximum entropy classifier is trained using face-to-face and Wizard-of-Oz data to detect specific responses such as assertions of closeness.

2.2 Dialogue Management

Ellie currently uses about 100 fixed utterances in total in the automated system. She employs 60 top level interview questions (e.g., *"do you travel a lot?"*), plus some follow-up questions (e.g., *"what do you enjoy about traveling?"*) and a range of backchannels (e.g., *"uh huh"*), empathy responses (e.g., *"that's great", "I'm sorry"*), and continuation prompts (e.g., *"tell me more about that"*).

The dialogue policy is implemented using the FLoReS dialogue manager (Morbini et al., 2012). The policy groups interview questions into three phases (opening rapport building, diagnostic, positive closing – ensuring that the participant leaves with positive feelings). Questions are generally asked in a fixed order, with some branching based on responses to specific questions.

Rule-based subpolicies determine what Ellie's follow-up responses will be for each of her top-level interview questions. The rules for follow-ups are defined in relation to the four NLU classifiers and the duration of user speech (measured in seconds). These rules trigger continuation prompts and empathy responses under specific conditions.

The turn-taking policy supports our design goal to encourage users to openly share information and to speak at length in response to Ellie's open-ended questions. In this domain, users often pause before or during their responses to think about their answers to Ellie's personal questions. The turn-taking policy is designed to provide ample time for users to consider their responses, and to let users take and keep the initiative as much as possible. Ellie's turn-taking decisions are based on thresholds for user pause duration, i.e., how much time the system should wait after the user has stopped speaking before Ellie starts speaking. These thresholds are tuned to the face-to-face and Wizard-of-Oz data to minimize Ellie's interruption rate, and are extended dynamically when Ellie detects that she has interrupted the participant. This is to take into account the fact that some people tend to use longer pauses than others.

Examples of the three interview phases and of Ellie's subdialogue policies (top level and follow-up questions, continuation prompts, empathy responses, and turn-taking) are given in Figure 2.

3 Demonstration Summary

The demonstration will feature a live interaction between Ellie and a participant, showing Ellie's real-time understanding and consequent policy actions. Live dialogues will highlight Ellie's strategies for questioning, follow-up continuation prompts, displays of empathy, and turn-taking, similar to the example in Figure 2. The demonstration will illustrate how these elements work together to enable Ellie to carry out extended interviews that also provide information relevant to the automatic assessment of indicators of distress.

Acknowledgments

The effort described here is supported by DARPA under contract W911NF-04-D-0005 and the U.S. Army. Any opinion, content or information presented does not necessarily reflect the position or the policy of the United States Government, and no official endorsement should be inferred.

References

S. Baccianella, A. Esuli, and F. Sebastiani. 2010. SentiWordNet 3.0: An enhanced lexical resource for sentiment analysis and opinion mining. In *Proceedings of LREC.*

D. DeVault, K. Georgila, R. Artstein, F. Morbini, D. Traum, S. Scherer, A. Rizzo, and L.-P. Morency. 2013. Verbal indicators of psychological distress in interactive dialogue with a virtual human. In *Proceedings of SIGDIAL.*

D. DeVault, R. Artstein, G. Benn, T. Dey, E. Fast, A. Gainer, K. Georgila, J. Gratch, A. Hartholt, M. Lhommet, G. Lucas, S. Marsella, F. Morbini, A. Nazarian, S. Scherer, G. Stratou, A. Suri, D. Traum, R. Wood, Y. Xu, A. Rizzo, and L.-P. Morency. 2014. SimSensei Kiosk: A virtual human interviewer for healthcare decision support. In *Proceedings of AAMAS.*

A. Hartholt, D. Traum, S. Marsella, A. Shapiro, G. Stratou, A. Leuski, L.-P. Morency, and J. Gratch. 2013. All together now, introducing the virtual human toolkit. In *Proceedings of IVA.*

D. Huggins-Daines, M. Kumar, A. Chan, A.W. Black, M. Ravishankar, and A.I. Rudnicky. 2006. PocketSphinx: A free, real-time continuous speech recognition system for hand-held devices. In *Proceedings of ICASSP.*

D. Jurafsky, E. Shriberg, and D. Biasca. 1997. Switchboard SWBD-DAMSL Shallow-Discourse-Function Annotation Coders Manual, Draft 13.

F. Morbini, D. DeVault, K. Sagae, J. Gerten, A. Nazarian, and D. Traum. 2012. FLoReS: A forward looking reward seeking dialogue manager. In *Proceedings of IWSDS.*

S. Scherer, G. Stratou, M. Mahmoud, J. Boberg, J. Gratch, A. Rizzo, and L.-P. Morency. 2013. Automatic behavior descriptors for psychological disorder analysis. In *Proceedings of IEEE Conference on Automatic Face and Gesture Recognition.*

MVA: The Multimodal Virtual Assistant

Michael Johnston[1], John Chen[1], Patrick Ehlen[2], Hyuckchul Jung[1], Jay Lieske[2], Aarthi Reddy[1], Ethan Selfridge[1], Svetlana Stoyanchev[1], Brant Vasilieff[2], Jay Wilpon[1]
AT&T Labs Research[1], AT&T[2]
{johnston,jchen,ehlen,hjung,jlieske,aarthi,
ethan,sveta,vasilieff,jgw}@research.att.com

Abstract

The Multimodal Virtual Assistant (MVA) is an application that enables users to plan an outing through an interactive multimodal dialog with a mobile device. MVA demonstrates how a cloud-based multimodal language processing infrastructure can support mobile multimodal interaction. This demonstration will highlight incremental recognition, multimodal speech and gesture input, contextually-aware language understanding, and the targeted clarification of potentially incorrect segments within user input.

1 Introduction

With the recent launch of virtual assistant applications such as Siri, Google Now, S-Voice, and Vlingo, spoken access to information and services on mobile devices has become commonplace. The Multimodal Virtual Assistant (MVA) project explores the application of *multimodal* dialog technology in the virtual assistant landscape. MVA departs from the existing paradigm for dialog-based mobile virtual assistants that display the unfolding dialog as a chat display. Instead, the MVA prototype situates the interaction directly within a touch-based interface that combines a map with visual information displays. Users can interact using combinations of speech and gesture inputs, and the interpretation of user commands depends on both map and GUI display manipulation and the physical location of the device.

MVA is a mobile application that allows users to plan a day or evening out with friends using natural language and gesture input. Users can search and browse over multiple interconnected domains, including music events, movie showings, and places to eat. They can specify multiple parameters in natural language, such as "Jazz concerts around San Francisco next Saturday". As users find interesting events and places, they can be collected together into plans and shared with others. The central components of the graphical user interface are a dynamic map showing business and event locations, and an information display showing the current recognition, system prompts, search result listing, or plans (Figure 1).

Figure 1: MVA User Interface

Spoken input begins when the user taps a microphone button on the display. As the user speaks, incremental speech recognition results appear. In addition to enabling voice input, the microphone button also activates the map as a drawing canvas, and enables the user to combine speech with drawing in coordinated multimodal commands. For example, a user might say, "Movies playing tonight in this area" while simultaneously outlining a relevant area on the map. Or a user may say, "Restaurants" while drawing a line down a specific street. MVA determines the intent and disambiguates concepts in the input in order to return relevant results. MVA then responds to user input multimodally, by updating the display and using speech synthesis to summarize results, provide feedback, or make requests for clarification and additional information.

2 Sample Interaction

In Figure 2 we present a sample of interaction from MVA that illustrates some of its capabilities. The user starts with a spoken natural language query where they specify some constraints: the type of music (*jazz*), location (*San Francisco*), and time (*tomorrow*). The system gets low confidence on the location, so it constructs a targeted clarification for clarifying only that constraint. The user repeats the location, and then the system searches for events meeting the user's constraints. The user then reviews the results, and follows on with a refinement: "What about blues?". Even though many parameters in this query are underspecified, the system applies contextually-aware natural language understanding and interprets this as "Blues concerts near San Francisco tomorrow". After selecting a concert, the user then searches for a restaurant nearby. The location of the concert remains salient. The user follows up with a multimodal query combining speech and gesture to search for similar restaurants in an adjoining area.

U:	"Jazz concerts near San Francisco tomorrow."
S:	"Where did you want to see jazz tomorrow?"
U:	"San Francisco."
S:	"I found 20 jazz concerts in San Francisco tomorrow." [*Zooms map to San Francisco and displays pins on map and list of results*]
U:	"What about blues?"
S:	"I found 20 blues concerts in San Francisco tomorrow."
U:	[*Clicks on a concert listing and adds it to the plan*]
U:	"Sushi restaurants near there."
S:	"I found 10 sushi restaurants."
U:	"What about here?" [*Circles adjoining area on map*]
S:	"I found 5 sushi restaurants in the area you indicated"

Figure 2: Sample Interaction

3 System Architecture

Figure 3 shows the underlying multimodal assistant architecture supporting the MVA app. The user interacts with a native iOS client. When the user taps the microphone icon, this initiates the flow of audio interleaved with gesture and context information streamed over a WebSocket connection to the platform.

This stream of interleaved data is handled at the server by a multimodal natural language processing pipeline. This fields incoming packets of data from the client, demuxes the incoming data stream, and sends audio, ink traces, and context information to three modules that operate in parallel. The audio is processed using the AT&T Watson^{SM} speech recognition engine (Goffin et al., 2005). Recognition is performed using a dynamic hierarchical language model (Gilbert et al., 2011) that combines a statistical N-gram language model with weighted sub-grammars. Ink traces are classified into gestures using a linear classifier. Speech recognition results serve as input to two NLU modules. A discriminative stochastic sequence tagger assigns tags to phrases within the input, and then the overall string with tags is assigned by a statistical intent classifier to one of a number of intents handled by the system e.g. *search(music_event), refine(location)*.

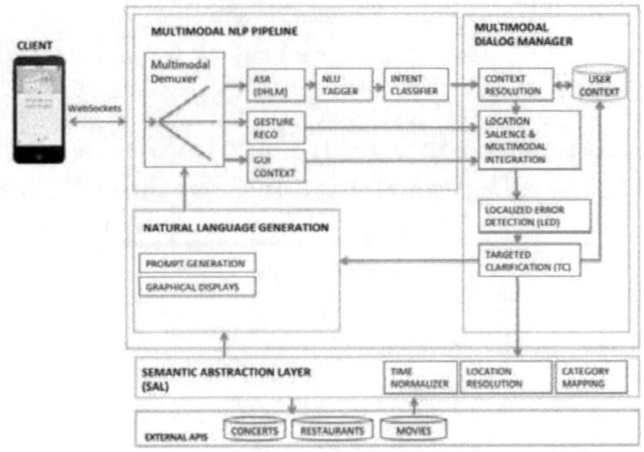

Figure 3: MVA Multimodal assistant Architecture

The NLU results are passed along with gesture recognition results and the GUI and device context to a multimodal dialog manager. The contextual resolution component determines if the input is a query refinement or correction. In either case, it retrieves the previous command from a user context store and combines the new content with the context through destructive unification (Ehlen and Johnston, 2012). A location salience component then applies to handle cases where a location is not specified verbally. This component uses a supervised classifier to select from among a series of candidate locations, including the gesture (if present), the current device location, or the current map location (Ehlen and Johnston, 2010).

The resolved semantic interpretation of the utterance is then passed to a Localized Error Detection (LED) module (Stoyanchev et al., 2012). The LED module contains two maximum entropy classifiers that independently predict whether a concept is present in the input, and whether a concept's current interpretation is correct. These classifiers use word scores, segment length, confusion networks and other recognition and context features. The LED module uses these classifiers to produce two probability distributions; one for presence and one for correctness. These distributions are then used by a Targeted Clarification component (TC) to either accept the input as is, reject all of the input, or ask a targeted clarification question (Stoyanchev et al., 2013). These decisions are currently made using thresholds tuned manually based on an initial corpus of user interaction with MVA. In the targeted clarification case, the input is passed to the natural language generation component for surface realization, and a prompt is passed back to the client for playback to the user. Critically, the TC component decides what to attempt to add to the common ground by explicit or implicit confirmation, and what to explicitly query from the user; e.g. "Where did you want to see jazz concerts?". The TC component also updates the context so that incoming responses from the user can be interpreted with respect to the context set up by the clarification.

Once a command is accepted by the multimodal dialog manager, it is passed to the *Semantic Abstraction Layer* (SAL) for execution. The SAL insulates natural language dialog capabilities from the specifics of any underlying external APIs that the system may use in order to respond to queries. A general purpose time normalization component projects relative time expressions like "tomorrow night" or "next week" onto a reference timeframe provided by the client context and estimates the intended time interval. A general purpose location resolution component maps from natural language expressions of locations such as city names and neighborhoods to specific geographic coordinates. These functions are handled by SAL—rather than relying on any time and location handling in the underlying information APIs—to provide consistency across application domains.

SAL also includes mechanisms for category mapping; the NLU component tags a portion of the utterance as a concept (e.g., a music genre or a cuisine) and SAL leverages this information to map a word sequence to generic domain-independent ontological representations/categories that are reusable across different backend APIs. Wrappers in SAL map from these categories, time, and location values to the specific query language syntax and values for each specific underlying API. In some cases, a single natural language query to MVA may require multiple API calls to complete, and this is captured in the wrapper. SAL also handles API format differences by mapping all API responses into a unified format. This unified format is then passed to our natural language generation component to be augmented with prompts, display text, and instructions to the client for updating the GUI. This combined specification of a multimodal presentation is passed to the interaction manager and routed back to the client to be presented to the user.

In addition to testing the capabilities of our multimodal assistant platform, MVA is designed as a testbed for running experiments with real users. Among other topics, we are planning experiments with MVA to evaluate methods of multimodal information presentation and natural language generation, error detection and error recovery.

Acknowledgements

Thanks to Mike Kai and to Deepak Talesra for their work on the MVA project.

References

Patrick Ehlen and Michael Johnston. 2010. Location grounding in multimodal local search. In *Proceedings of ICMI-MLMI*, pages 32–39.

Patrick Ehlen and Michael Johnston. 2012. Multimodal dialogue in mobile local search. In *Proceedings of ICMI*, pages 303–304.

Mazin Gilbert, Iker Arizmendi, Enrico Bocchieri, Diamantino Caseiro, Vincent Goffin, Andrej Ljolje, Mike Phillips, Chao Wang, and Jay G. Wilpon. 2011. Your mobile virtual assistant just got smarter! In *Proceedings of INTERSPEECH*, pages 1101–1104. ISCA.

Vincent Goffin, Cyril Allauzen, Enrico Bocchieri, Dilek Hakkani-Tur, Andrej Ljolje, S. Parthasarathy, Mazim Rahim, Giuseppe Riccardi, and Murat Saraclar. 2005. The AT&T WATSON speech recognizer. In *Proceedings of ICASSP*, pages 1033–1036, Philadelphia, PA, USA.

Svetlana Stoyanchev, Philipp Salletmayer, Jingbo Yang, and Julia Hirschberg. 2012. Localized detection of speech recognition errors. In *Proceedings of SLT*, pages 25–30.

Svetlana Stoyanchev, Alex Liu, and Julia Hirschberg. 2013. Modelling human clarification strategies. In *Proceedings of SIGDIAL 2013*, pages 137–141.

The PARLANCE Mobile Application for Interactive Search in English and Mandarin

Helen Hastie, Marie-Aude Aufaure*, Panos Alexopoulos,
Hugues Bouchard, Catherine Breslin, Heriberto Cuayáhuitl, Nina Dethlefs,
Milica Gašić, James Henderson, Oliver Lemon, Xingkun Liu, Peter Mika, Nesrine Ben Mustapha,
Tim Potter, Verena Rieser, Blaise Thomson, Pirros Tsiakoulis, Yves Vanrompay,
Boris Villazon-Terrazas, Majid Yazdani, Steve Young and Yanchao Yu

email: h.hastie@hw.ac.uk. See http://parlance-project.eu for full list of affiliations

Abstract

We demonstrate a mobile application in English and Mandarin to test and evaluate components of the PARLANCE dialogue system for interactive search under real-world conditions.

1 Introduction

With the advent of evaluations "in the wild", emphasis is being put on converting research prototypes into mobile applications that can be used for evaluation and data collection by real users downloading the application from the market place. This is the motivation behind the work demonstrated here where we present a modular framework whereby research components from the PARLANCE project (Hastie et al., 2013) can be plugged in, tested and evaluated in a mobile environment.

The goal of PARLANCE is to perform interactive search through speech in multiple languages. The domain for the demonstration system is interactive search for restaurants in Cambridge, UK for Mandarin and San Francisco, USA for English. The scenario is that Mandarin speaking tourists would be able to download the application and use it to learn about restaurants in English speaking towns and cities.

2 System Architecture

Here, we adopt a client-server approach as illustrated in Figure 1 for Mandarin and Figure 2 for English. The front end of the demonstration system is an Android application that calls the Google Automatic Speech Recognition (ASR) API and sends the recognized user utterance to a server running the Interaction Manager (IM), Spoken Language Understanding (SLU) and Natural Language Generation (NLG) components.

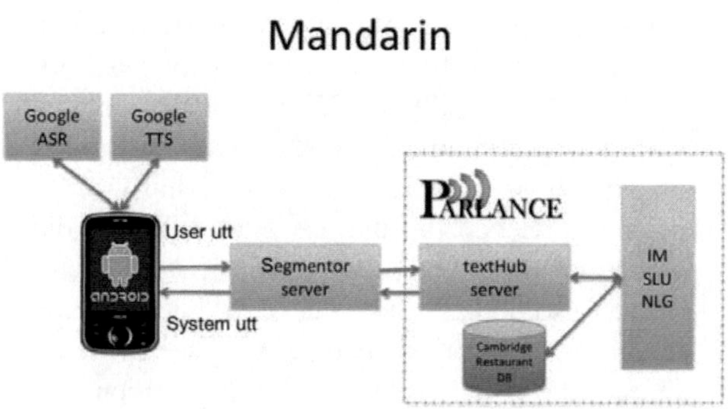

Figure 1: Overview of the PARLANCE Mandarin mobile application system architecture

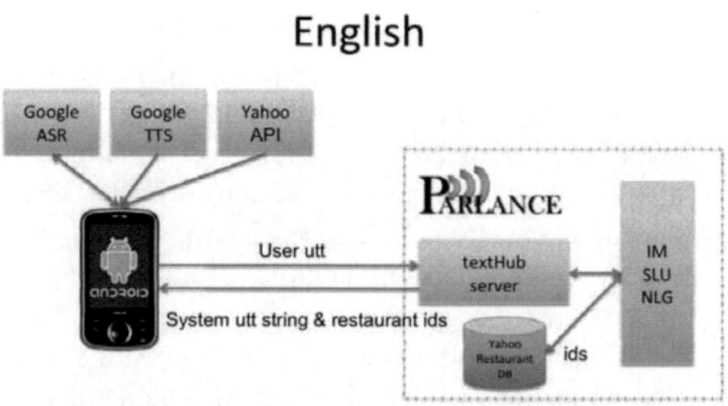

Figure 2: Overview of the PARLANCE English mobile application system architecture extended to use the Yahoo API to populate the application with additional restaurant information

When the user clicks the Start button, a dialogue session starts. The phone application first connects to the PARLANCE server (via the Java Socket Server) to get the initial system greeting which it speaks via the Google

*Authors are in alphabetical order

Text-To-Speech (TTS) API. After the system utterance finishes the recognizer starts to listen for user input to send to the SLU component. The SLU converts text into a semantic interpretation consisting of a set of triples of communicative function, attribute, and (optionally) value[1]. Probabilities can be associated with candidate interpretations to reflect uncertainty in either the ASR or SLU. The SLU then passes the semantic interpretation to the IM within the same server.

Chinese sentences are composed of strings of characters without any space to mark words as other languages do, for example:

```
Mandarin: 我想预订中国餐馆
English: I want to book a Chinese restaurant.
```

In order to correctly parse and understand Chinese sentences, Chinese word segmentations must be performed. To do this segmentation, we use the Stanford Chinese word segmentor[2], which relies on a linear-chain conditional random field (CRF) model and treats word segmentation as a binary decision task. The Java Socket Server then sends the segmented Chinese sentence to the SLU on the server.

The IM then selects a dialogue act, accesses the database and in the case of English passes back the list of restaurant identification numbers (ids) associated with the relevant restaurants. For the English demonstration system, these restaurants are displayed on the smart phone as seen in Figures 4 and 5. Finally, the NLG component decides how best to realise the restaurant descriptions and sends the string back to the phone application for the TTS to realise. The example output is illustrated in Figure 3 for Mandarin and Figure 4 for English.

As discussed above, the PARLANCE mobile application can be used as a test-bed for comparing alternative techniques for various components. Here we discuss two such components: IM and NLG.

[1]This has been implemented for English; Mandarin uses the rule-based Phoenix parser.

[2]http://nlp.stanford.edu/projects/chinese-nlp.shtml

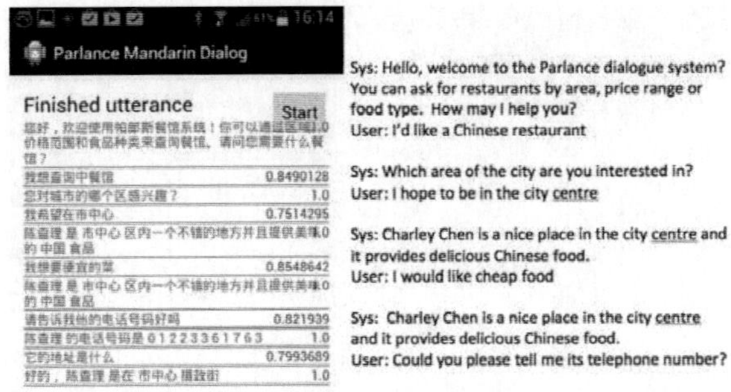

Figure 3: Screenshot and translation of the Mandarin system

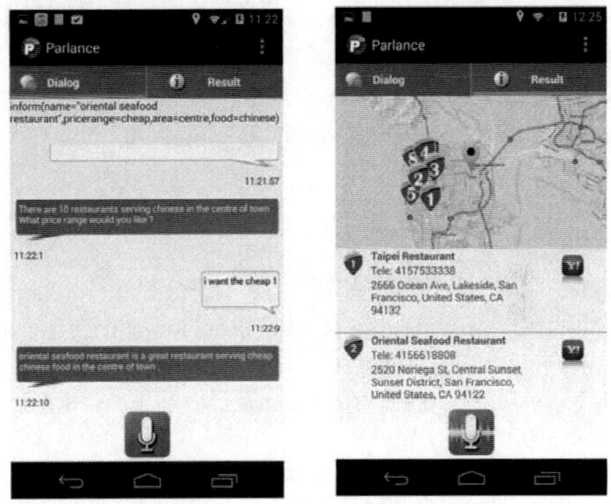

Figure 4: Screenshot of dialogue and the list of recommended restaurants shown on a map and in a list for English

2.1 Interaction Management

The PARLANCE Interaction Manager is based on the partially observable Markov decision process (POMDP) framework, where the system's decisions can be optimised via reinforcement learning. The model adopted for PARLANCE is the Bayesian Update of Dialogue State (BUDS) manager (Thomson and Young, 2010). This POMDP-based IM factors the dialogue state into conditionally dependent elements. Dependencies between these elements can be derived directly from the dialogue ontology. These elements are arranged into a dynamic Bayesian network which allows for their marginal probabilities to be updated during the dialogue, comprising the *belief state*. The belief state is then mapped into a smaller-scale summary space and the decisions are optimised using the natural actor critic algorithm. In the PARLANCE application, hand-crafted policies

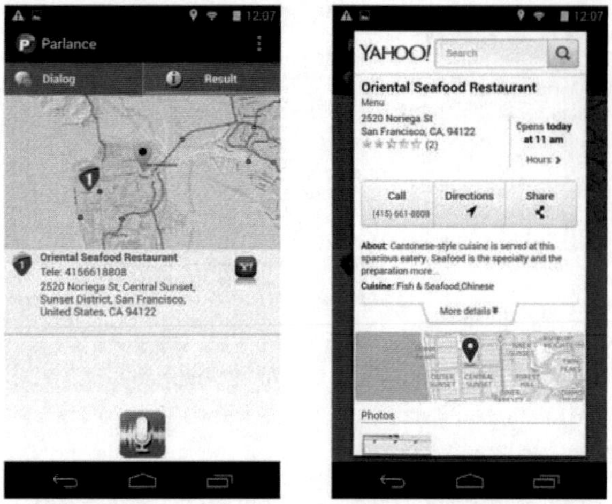

Figure 5: Screenshot of the recommended restaurant for the English application

can be compared to learned ones.

2.2 Natural Language Generation

As mentioned above, the server returns the string to be synthesised by the Google TTS API. This mobile framework allows for testing of alternative approaches to NLG. In particular, we are interested in comparing a surface realiser that uses CRFs against a template-based baseline. The CRFs take semantically annotated phrase structure trees as input, which it uses to keep track of rich linguistic contexts. Our approach has been compared with a number of competitive state-of-the art surface realizers (Dethlefs et al., 2013), and can be trained from example sentences with annotations of semantic slots.

2.3 Local Search and Knowledge Base

For the English system, the domain database is populated by the search Yahoo API (Bouchard and Mika, 2013) with restaurants in San Fransisco. These restaurant search results are returned based on their longitude and latitude within San Francisco for 5 main areas, 3 price categories and 52 cuisine types containing around 1,600 individual restaurants.

The Chinese database has been partially translated from an English database for restaurants in Cambridge, UK and search is based on 3 price categories, 5 areas and 35 cuisine types having a total of 157 restaurants. Due to the language-agnostic nature of the PARLANCE system, only the name and address fields needed to be translated.

3 Future Work

Investigating application side audio compression and audio streaming over a mobile internet connection would enable further assessment of the ASR and TTS components used in the original PARLANCE system (Hastie et al., 2013). This would allow for entire research systems to be plugged directly into the mobile interface without the use of third party ASR and TTS.

Future work also involves developing a feedback mechanism for evaluation purposes that does not put undue effort on the user and put them off using the application. In addition, this framework can be extended to leverage hyperlocal and social information of the user when displaying items of interest.

Acknowledgements

The research leading to this work was funded by the EC FP7 programme FP7/2011-14 under grant agreement no. 287615 (PARLANCE).

References

H. Bouchard and P. Mika. 2013. Interactive hyperlocal search API. Technical report, Yahoo Iberia, August.

N. Dethlefs, H. Hastie, H. Cuayáhuitl, and O. Lemon. 2013. Conditional Random Fields for Responsive Surface Realisation Using Global Features. In *Proceedings of the 51st Annual Meeting of the Association for Computational Linguistics (ACL)*, Sofia, Bulgaria.

H. Hastie, M.A. Aufaure, P. Alexopoulos, H. Cuayáhuitl, N. Dethlefs, M. Gasic, J. Henderson, O. Lemon, X. Liu, P. Mika, N. Ben Mustapha, V. Rieser, B. Thomson, P. Tsiakoulis, Y. Vanrompay, B. Villazon-Terrazas, and S. Young. 2013. Demonstration of the PARLANCE system: a data-driven incremental, spoken dialogue system for interactive search. In *Proceedings of the 14th Annual Meeting of the Special Interest Group on Discourse and Dialogue (SIGDIAL)*, Metz, France, August.

B. Thomson and S. Young. 2010. Bayesian update of dialogue state: A POMDP framework for spoken dialogue systems. *Computer Speech and Language*, 24(4):562–588.

The Second Dialog State Tracking Challenge

Matthew Henderson[1], **Blaise Thomson**[1] **and Jason Williams**[2]
[1]Department of Engineering, University of Cambridge, U.K.
[2]Microsoft Research, Redmond, WA, USA
mh521@eng.cam.ac.uk brmt2@eng.cam.ac.uk jason.williams@microsoft.com

Abstract

A spoken dialog system, while communicating with a user, must keep track of what the user wants from the system at each step. This process, termed *dialog state tracking*, is essential for a successful dialog system as it directly informs the system's actions. The first Dialog State Tracking Challenge allowed for evaluation of different dialog state tracking techniques, providing common testbeds and evaluation suites. This paper presents a second challenge, which continues this tradition and introduces some additional features – a new domain, changing user goals and a richer dialog state. The challenge received 31 entries from 9 research groups. The results suggest that while large improvements on a competitive baseline are possible, trackers are still prone to degradation in mismatched conditions. An investigation into ensemble learning demonstrates the most accurate tracking can be achieved by combining multiple trackers.

1 Introduction

Spoken language provides a medium of communication that is natural to users as well as hands- and eyes-free. Voice-based computer systems, called *spoken dialog systems*, allow users to interact using speech to achieve a goal. Efficient operation of a spoken dialog system requires a component that can track what has happened in a dialog, incorporating system outputs, user speech and context from previous turns. The building and evaluation of these trackers is an important field of research since the performance of dialog state tracking is important for the final performance of a complete system.

Until recently, it was difficult to compare approaches to state tracking because of the wide variety of metrics and corpora used for evaluation. The first dialog state tracking challenge (DSTC1) attempted to overcome this by defining a challenge task with standard test conditions, freely available corpora and open access (Williams et al., 2013). This paper presents the results of a second challenge, which continues in this tradition with the inclusion of additional features relevant to the research community.

Some key differences to the first challenge include:

- The domain is restaurant search instead of bus timetable information. This provides participants with a different category of interaction where there is a database of matching entities.
- Users' goals are permitted to change. In the first challenge, the user was assumed to always want a specific bus journey. In this challenge the user's goal can change. For example, they may want a 'Chinese' restaurant at the start of the dialog but change to wanting 'Italian' food by the end.
- The dialog state uses a richer representation than in DSTC1, including not only the slot/value attributes of the user goal, but also their search method, and what information they wanted the system to read out.

As well as presenting the results of the different state trackers, this paper attempts to obtain some insights into research progress by analysing their performance. This includes analyses of the predictive power of performance on the development set, the effects of tracking the dialog state using joint distributions, and the correlation between 1-best accuracy and overall quality of probability distributions output by trackers. An evaluation of the effects of ensemble learning is also performed.

The paper begins with an overview of the challenge in section 2. The labelling scheme and metrics used for evaluation are discussed in section 3 followed by a summary of the results of the challenge in section 4. An analysis of ensemble learning is presented in section 5. Section 6 concludes the paper.

2 Challenge overview

2.1 Problem statement

This section defines the problem of dialog state tracking as it is presented in the challenge. The challenge evaluates state tracking for dialogs where users search for restaurants by specifying constraints, and may ask for information such as the phone number. The dialog state is formulated in a manner which is general to information browsing tasks such as this.

Included with the data is an *ontology*[1], which gives details of all possible dialog states. The ontology includes a list of attributes termed *requestable slots* which the user may request, such as the food type or phone number. It also provides a list of *informable slots* which are attributes that may be provided as constraints. Each informable slot has a set of possible values. Table 1 gives details on the ontology used in DSTC2.

The dialog state at each turn consists of three components:

- The **goal constraint** for each *informable* slot. This is either an assignment of a value from the ontology which the user has specified as a constraint, or is a special value — either *Dontcare* which means the user has no preference, or *None* which means the user is yet to specify a valid goal for this slot.
- A set of **requested slots**, i.e. those slots whose values have been requested by the user, and should be informed by the system.
- An assignment of the current dialog **search method**. This is one of
  - *by constraints*, if the user is attempting to issue a constraint,
  - *by alternatives*, if the user is requesting alternative suitable venues,
  - *by name*, if the user is attempting to ask about a specific venue by its name,
  - *finished*, if the user wants to end the call
  - or *none* otherwise.

Note that in DSTC1, the set of dialog states was dependent on the hypotheses given by a Spoken Language Understanding component (SLU) (Williams et al., 2013), whereas here the state is labelled independently of any SLU (see section 3). Appendix B gives an example dialog with the state labelled at each turn.

A tracker must use information up to a given turn in the dialog, and output a probability distribution over dialog states for the turn. Trackers output separately the distributions for goal constraints, requested slots and the method. They may either report a joint distribution over the goal constraints, or supply marginal distributions and let the joint goal constraint distribution be calculated as a product of the marginals.

2.2 Challenge design

DSTC2 studies the problem of dialog state tracking as a corpus-based task, similar to DSTC1. The challenge task is to re-run dialog state tracking over a test corpus of dialogs.

A corpus-based challenge means all trackers are evaluated on the same dialogs, allowing direct comparison between trackers. There is also no need for teams to expend time and money in building an end-to-end system and getting users, meaning a low barrier to entry.

When a tracker is deployed, it will inevitably alter the performance of the dialog system it is part of, relative to any previously collected dialogs. In order to simulate this, and to penalise overfitting to known conditions, evaluation dialogs in the challenge are drawn from dialogs with a dialog manager which is not found in the training data.

2.3 Data

A large corpus of dialogs with various telephone-based dialog systems was collected using Amazon Mechanical Turk. The dialogs used in the challenge come from 6 conditions; all combinations of 3 dialog managers and 2 speech recognisers. There are roughly 500 dialogs in each condition, of average length 7.88 turns from 184 unique callers.

The 3 dialog managers are:

- **DM-HC**, a simple tracker maintaining a single top dialog state, and a hand-crafted policy
- **DM-POMDPHC**, a dynamic Bayesian network for tracking a distribution of dialog states, and a hand-crafted policy
- **DM-POMDP**, the same tracking method as DM-POMDPHC, with a policy learnt using

[1] Note that this ontology includes only the schema for dialog states and not the database entries

Slot	Requestable	Informable
area	yes	yes. 5 values; north, south, east, west, centre
food	yes	yes, 91 possible values
name	yes	yes, 113 possible values
pricerange	yes	yes, 3 possible values
addr	yes	no
phone	yes	no
postcode	yes	no
signature	yes	no

Table 1: Ontology used in DSTC2 for restaurant information. Counts do not include the special *Dontcare* value.

POMDP reinforcement learning

The 2 speech recognisers are:

- **ASR-degraded**, speech recogniser with artificially degraded statistical acoustic models
- **ASR-good**, full speech recogniser optimised for the domain

These give two acoustic conditions, the degraded model producing dialogs at higher error rates. The degraded models simulate in-car conditions and are described in Young et al. (2013).

The set of all calls with DM-POMDP, with both speech recognition configurations, constitutes the test set. All calls with the other two dialog managers are used for the training and development set. Specifically, the datasets are arranged as so:

- **dstc2_train**. Labelled dataset released in October 2013, with 1612 calls from DM-HC and DM-POMDPHC, and both ASR conditions.
- **dstc2_dev**. Labelled dataset released at the same time as dstc2_train, with 506 calls under the same conditions as dstc2_train. No caller in this set appears in dstc2_train.
- **dstc2_test**. Set used for evaluation. Released unlabelled at the beginning of the evaluation week. This consists of all 1117 dialogs with DM-POMDP.

Paid Amazon Mechanical Turkers were assigned tasks and asked to call the dialog systems. Callers were asked to find restaurants that matched particular constraints on the slots area, pricerange and food. To elicit more complex dialogs, including changing goals (goals in DSTC1 were always constant), the users were sometimes asked to find more than one restaurant. In cases where a matching restaurant did not exist they were required to seek an alternative, for example finding an Indian instead of an Italian restaurant.

A breakdown of the frequency of goal constraint changes is given in table 2, showing around 40% of all dialogs involved a change in goal constraint. The distribution of the goal constraints in

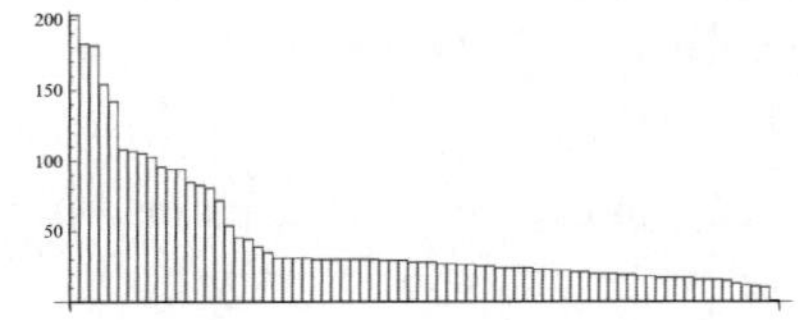

Figure 1: Histogram of values for the food constraint (excluding dontcare) in all data. The most frequent values are Indian, Chinese, Italian and European.

	Dataset		
	train	dev	test
area	2.9%	1.4%	3.8%
food	37.3%	34.0%	40.9%
name	0.0%	0.0%	0.0%
pricerange	1.7%	1.6%	3.1%
any	40.1%	37.0%	44.5%

Table 2: Percentage of dialogs which included a change in the goal constraint for each informable (and any slot). Barely any users asked for restaurants by name.

the data was reasonably uniform across the area and pricerange slots, but was skewed for food as shown in figure 1. The skew arises from the distribution of the restaurants in the system's database; many food types have very few matching venues.

Recently, researchers have started using word confusion networks for spoken language understanding (Henderson et al., 2012; Tür et al., 2013). Unfortunately, word confusion networks were not logged at the time of collecting the dialog data. In order to provide word confusion networks, ASR was run offline in batch mode on each dialog using similar models as the live system. This gives a second set of ASR results, labelled *batch*, which not only includes ASR N-best lists (as in *live* results), but also word confusion networks.

For each dataset and speech recogniser, table 3 gives the Word Error Rate on the top ASR hypothesis, and F-score for the top SLU hypothesis (calculated as in Henderson et al. (2012)). Note the batch ASR was always less accurate than the live.

		Live		Batch
Dataset	ASR	WER	F-score	WER
train	degraded	30.7%	72.4%	37.7%
	good	22.4%	78.7%	25.5%
	all	26.4%	75.7%	31.3%
dev	degraded	40.4%	67.3%	47.3%
	good	25.2%	75.2%	30.0%
	all	31.9%	71.6%	37.6%
test	degraded	33.6%	70.0%	41.1%
	good	23.5%	77.8%	27.1%
	all	28.7%	73.8%	34.3%

Table 3: Word Error Rate on the top hypothesis, and F-score on top SLU hypothesis.

3 Labelling and evaluation

The output of each tracker is a distribution over dialog states for each turn, as explained in section 2.1. To allow evaluation of the tracker output, the single correct dialog state at each turn is labelled.

Labelling of the dialog state is facilitated by first labelling each user utterance with its semantic representation, in the dialog act format described in Henderson et al. (2013) (some example semantic representations are given in appendix B). The semantic labelling was achieved by first crowdsourcing the transcription of the audio to text. Next a semantic decoder was run over the transcriptions, and the authors corrected the decoder's results by hand. Given the sequence of machine actions and user actions, both represented semantically, the true dialog state is computed deterministically using a simple set of rules.

Recall the dialog state is composed of multiple components; the goal constraint for each slot, the requested slots, and the method. Each of these is evaluated separately, by comparing the tracker output to the correct label. The joint over the goal constraints is evaluated in the same way, where the tracker may either explicitly enumerate and score its joint hypotheses, or let the joint be computed as the product of the distributions over the slots.

A bank of metrics which look at the tracker output and the correct labels are calculated in the evaluation. These metrics are a slightly expanded set of those calculated in DSTC1.

Denote an example probability distribution given by a tracker as $\mathbf{p}$ and the correct label to be i, so we have that the probability reported to the correct hypothesis is $\mathbf{p}_i$, and $\sum_j \mathbf{p}_j = 1$.

Accuracy measures the fraction of turns where the top hypothesis is correct, i.e. where $i = \arg\max_j \mathbf{p}_j$. **AvgP**, average probability, measures the mean score of the correct hypothesis, $\mathbf{p}_i$. This gives some idea of the quality of the score given to the correct hypothesis, ignoring the rest of the distribution. **Neglogp** is the mean negative logarithm of the score given to the correct hypothesis, $-\log \mathbf{p}_i$. Sometimes called the *negative log likelihood*, this is a standard score in machine learning tasks. **MRR** is the mean reciprocal rank of the top hypothesis, i.e. $\frac{1}{1+k}$ where $j_k = i$ and $\mathbf{p}_{j_0} \geq \mathbf{p}_{j_1} \geq \ldots$. This metric measures the quality of the ranking, without necessarily treating the scores as probabilities. **L2** measures the square of the l^2 norm between the distribution and the correct label, indicating quality of the whole reported distribution. It is calculated for one turn as $(1 - \mathbf{p}_i)^2 + \sum_{j \neq i} \mathbf{p}_j^2$. Two metrics, **Update precision** and **Update accuracy** measure the accuracy and precision of updates to the top scoring hypothesis from one turn to the next. For more details, see Higashinaka et al. (2004), which finds these metrics to be highly correlated with dialog success in their data.

Finally there is a set of measures relating to the receiver operating characteristic (ROC) curves, which measure the discrimination of the scores for the highest-ranked hypotheses. Two versions of ROC are computed, V1 and V2. V1 computes correct-accepts (CA), false accepts (FA) and false-rejects (FR) as fractions of *all* utterances. The V2 metrics consider fractions of correctly classified utterances, meaning the values always reach 100% regardless of the accuracy. V2 metrics measure discrimination independently of the accuracy, and are therefore only comparable between trackers with similar accuracies.

Several metrics are computed from the ROC statistics. **ROC V1 EER** computes the false acceptance rate at the point where false-accepts are equal to false-rejects. **ROC V1 CA05**, **ROC V1 CA10**, **ROC V1 CA20** and **ROC V2 CA05**, **ROC V2 CA10**, **ROC V2 CA20**, compute the correct acceptance rates for both versions of ROC at false-acceptance rates 0.05, 0.10, and 0.20.

Two *schedules* are used to decide which turns to include when computing each metric. **Schedule 1** includes every turn. **Schedule 2** only includes a turn if any SLU hypothesis up to and including the turn contains some information about the component of the dialog state in question, or if the correct label is not *None*. E.g. for a goal constraint, this is whether the slot has appeared with a value in any SLU hypothesis, an affirm/negate act has appeared after a system confirmation of the slot, or the user has in fact informed the slot regardless of the SLU.

The data is labelled using two schemes. The first, **scheme A**, is considered the standard labelling of the dialog state. Under this scheme, each component of the state is defined as the most recently asserted value given by the user. The *None* value is used to indicate that a value is yet to be given. Appendix B demonstrates labelling under scheme A.

A second labelling scheme, **scheme B**, is included in the evaluation, where labels are propagated backwards through the dialog. This labelling scheme is designed to assess whether a tracker is able to predict a user's intention before it has been stated. Under scheme B, the label at a current turn for a particular component of the dialog state is considered to be the next value which the user settles on, and is reset in the case of goal constraints if the slot value pair is given in a *canthelp* act by the system (i.e. the system has informed that this constraint is not satisfiable).

3.1 Featured metrics

All combinations of metrics, state components, schedules and labelling schemes give rise to 815 total metrics calculated per tracker in evaluation. Although each may have its particular motivation, many of the metrics will be highly correlated. From the results of DSTC1 it was found the metrics could be roughly split into 3 independent groups; one measuring 1-best quality (e.g. Acc), another measuring probability calibration (e.g. L2), and the last measuring discrimination (e.g. ROC metrics) (Williams et al., 2013).

By selecting a representative from each of these groups, the following were chosen as featured metrics:

- **Accuracy**, schedule 2, scheme A
- **L2 norm**, schedule 2, scheme A
- **ROC V2 CA 5**, schedule 2, scheme A

Accuracy is a particularly important measure for dialog management techniques which only consider the top dialog state hypothesis at each turn, while L2 is of more importance when multiple dialog states are considered in action selection. Note that the ROC metric is only comparable among systems operating at similar accuracies, and while L2 should be minimised, Accuracy and the ROC metric should be maximised.

Each of these, calculated for **joint goal constraints**, **search method** and **combined requested slots**, gives 9 metrics altogether which participants were advised to focus on optimizing.

3.2 Baseline trackers

Three baseline trackers were entered in the challenge, under the ID 'team0'. Source code for all the baseline systems is available on the DSTC website[2]. The first, 'team0.entry0', follows simple rules commonly used in spoken dialog systems. It gives a single hypothesis for each slot, whose value is the top scoring suggestion so far in the dialog. Note that this tracker does not account well for goal constraint changes; the hypothesised value for a slot will only change if a new value occurs with a higher confidence.

The *focus* baseline, 'team0.entry1', includes a simple model of changing goal constraints. Beliefs are updated for the goal constraint $s = v$, at turn t, $P\left(s=v\right)$, using the rule:

$$P\left(s=v\right)_t = q_t P\left(s=v\right)_{t-1} + SLU\left(s=v\right)_t$$

where $0 \leq SLU(s = v)_t \leq 1$ is the evidence for $s = v$ given by the SLU in turn t, and $q_t = \sum_{v'} SLU(s = v')_t \leq 1$.

Another baseline tracker, based on the tracker presented in Wang and Lemon (2013) is included in the evaluation, labelled 'team0.entry2'. This tracker uses a selection of domain independent rules to update the beliefs, similar to the focus baseline. One rule uses a learnt parameter called the noise adjustment, to adjust the SLU scores. Full details of this and all baseline trackers are provided on the DSTC website.

Finally, an oracle tracker is included under the label 'team0.entry3'. This reports the correct label with score 1 for each component of the dialog state, but only if it has been suggested in the dialog so far by the SLU. This gives an upper-bound for the performance of a tracker which uses only the SLU and its suggested hypotheses.

4 Results

Altogether 9 research teams participated in the challenge. Each team could submit a maximum of 5 trackers, and 31 trackers were submitted in total. Teams are identified by anonymous team numbers team1-9, and baseline systems are grouped under team0. Appendix A gives the results on the featured metrics for each entry submitted to the challenge. The full results, including tracker output, details of each tracker and scripts to run the evaluation are available on the DSTC2 website.

The table in appendix A specifies which of the inputs available were used for each tracker- from live ASR, live SLU and batch ASR. This facilitates comparisons between systems which used the same information.

A variety of techniques were used in the submitted trackers. Some participants provided short synopses, which are available in the download from the DSTC2 website. Full details on the trackers themselves are published at SIGdial 2014.

[2] http://camdial.org/~mh521/dstc/

For the "requested slot" task, some trackers outperformed the oracle tracker. This was possible because trackers could guess a slot was requested using dialog context, even if there was no mention of it in the SLU output.

Participants were asked to report the results of their trackers on the dstcs2_dev development set. Figure 2 gives some insight into how well performance on the development set predicted performance on the test set. Metrics are reported as percentage improvement relative to the focus baseline to normalise for the difficulty of the datasets; in general trackers achieved higher accuracies on the test set than on development. Figure 2 shows that the development set provided reasonable predictions, though in all cases improvement relative to the baseline was overestimated, sometimes drastically. This suggests that approaches to tracking have trouble with generalisation, underperforming in the mismatched conditions of the test set which used an unseen dialog manager.

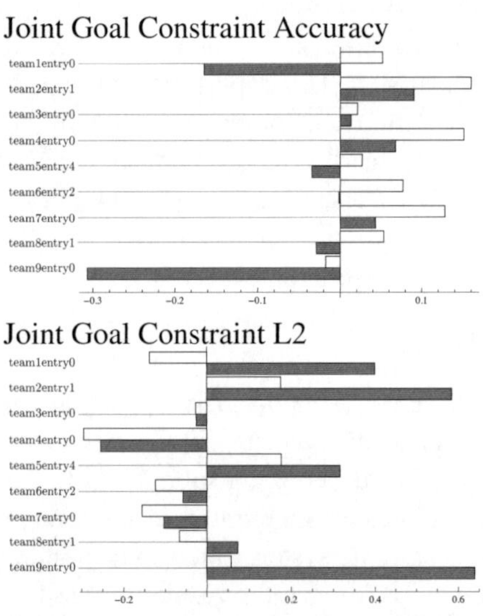

Figure 2: Performance relative to the focus baseline (percentage increase) for dev set (white) and test set (grey). Top entry for each team chosen based on joint goal constraint accuracy. A lower L2 score is better.

Recall from section 2, trackers could output joint distributions for goal constraints, or simply output one distribution for each slot and allow the joint to be calculated as the product. Two teams, team2 and team8, opted to output a joint distribution for some of their entries. Figure 3 compares performance on the test set for these trackers between the joint distributions they reported, and the joint calculated as the product. The entries from team2 were able to show an increase in the accuracy of the top joint goal constraint hypotheses, but seemingly at a cost in terms of the L2 score. Conversely the entries from team8, though operating at lower performance than the focus baseline, were able to show an improvement in L2 at a slight loss in accuracy. These results suggest that a tracking method is yet to be proposed which can, at least on this data, improve both accuracy and the L2 score of tracker output by reporting joint predictions of goal constraints.

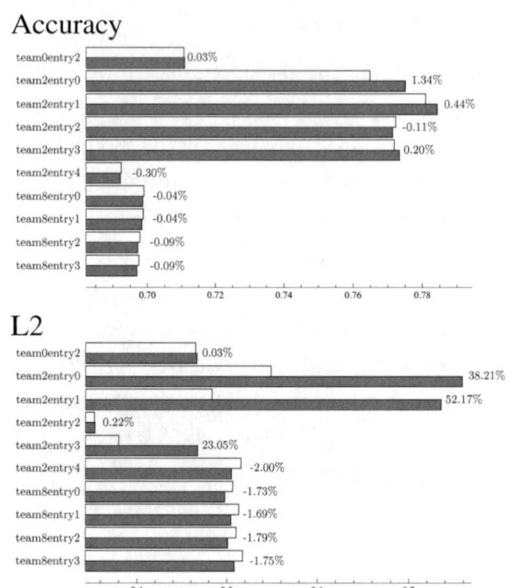

Figure 3: Influence of reporting a full joint distribution. White bar shows test set performance computing the goal constraints as a product of independent marginals; dark bar is performance with a full joint distribution. All entries which reported a full joint are shown. A lower L2 score is better.

It is of interest to investigate the correlation between accuracy and L2. Figure 4 plots these metrics for each tracker on joint goal constraints. We see that in general a lower L2 score correlates with a higher accuracy, but there are examples of high accuracy trackers which do poorly in terms of L2. This further justifies the reporting of these as two separate featured metrics.

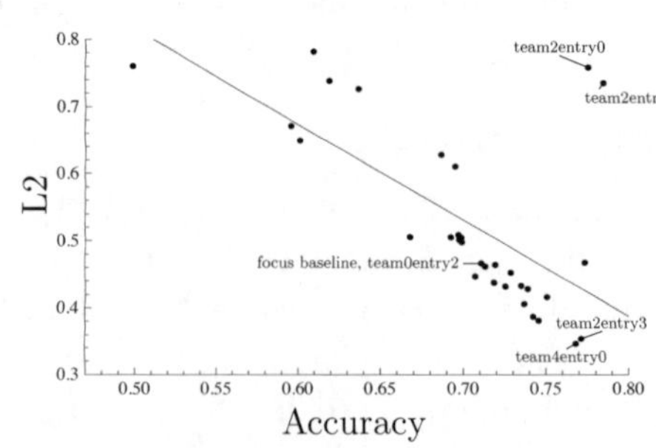

Figure 4: Scatterplot of joint goal constraint accuracy and joint goal constraint L2 for each entry. Plotted line is least-squares linear regression, $\text{L2} = 1.53 - 1.43\text{Accuracy}$

Tracker	Joint goal Acc.	Joint goal L2	Method Acc.	Method L2	Requested Acc.	Requested L2
Single best entry	0.784	0.346	**0.950**	**0.082**	0.978	0.035
Score averaging: top 2 entries	0.787	0.364-	0.945-	0.083	0.976	0.039-
Score averaging: top 5 entries	0.777	0.347	0.945	0.089-	0.976	0.038
Score averaging: top 10 entries	0.760-	0.364-	0.934-	0.108-	0.967-	0.056-
Score averaging: all entries	0.765-	0.362-	0.934-	0.103-	0.971-	0.052-
Stacking: top 2 entries	0.789	0.322+	0.949	0.085-	0.977	0.040-
Stacking: top 5 entries	0.795+	0.315+	0.949	0.084	0.978	0.037
Stacking: top 10 entries	0.796+	0.312+	0.949	0.083	0.979	0.035
Stacking: all entries	**0.798+**	**0.308+**	**0.950**	0.083	**0.980**	**0.034**

Table 4: Accuracy and L2 for Joint goal constraint, Method, and Requested slots for the single best tracker (by accuracy) in DSTC2, and various ensemble methods. "Top N entries" means the N entries with highest accuracies from distinct teams, where the baselines are included as a team. +/- indicates statistically significantly better/worse than the single best entry ($p < 0.01$), computed with McNemar's test for accuracy and the paired t-test for L2, both with Bonferroni correction for repeated tests.

5 Ensemble learning

The dialog state tracking challenge provides an opportunity to study *ensemble learning* – i.e. synthesizing the output of many trackers to improve performance beyond any single tracker. Here we consider two forms of ensemble learning: *score averaging* and *stacking*.

In score averaging, the final score of a class is computed as the mean of the scores output by all trackers for that class. One of score averaging's strengths is that it requires no additional training data beyond that used to train the constituent trackers. If each tracker's output is correct more than half the time, and if the errors made by trackers are not correlated, then score averaging is guaranteed to improve performance (since the majority vote will be correct in the limit). In (Lee and Eskenazi, 2013), score averaging (there called "system combination") has been applied to combine the output of four dialog state trackers. To help decorrelate errors, constituent trackers were trained on different subsets of data, and used different machine learning methods. The relative error rate reduction was 5.1% on the test set.

The second approach to ensemble learning is stacking (Wolpert, 1992). In stacking, the scores output by the constituent classifiers are fed to a *new* classifier that makes a final prediction. In other words, the output of each constituent classifier is viewed as a *feature*, and the new final classifier can learn the correlations and error patterns of each. For this reason, stacking often outperforms score averaging, particularly when errors are correlated. However, stacking requires a validation set for training the final classifier. In DSTC2, we only have access to trackers' output on the test set. Therefore, to estimate the performance of stacking, we perform cross-validation on the test set: the test set is divided into two folds. First, fold 1 is used for training the final classifier, and fold 2 is used for testing. Then the process is reversed. The two test outputs are then concatenated. Note that models are never trained and tested on the same data. A maximum entropy model (maxent) is used (details in (Metallinou et al., 2013)), which is common practice for stacking classifiers. In addition, maxent was found to yield best performance in DSTC1 (Lee and Eskenazi, 2013).

Table 4 reports accuracy and L2 for goal constraints, search method, and requested slots. For each ensemble method and each quantity (column) the table gives results for combining the top trackers from 2 or 5 distinct teams, for combining the top tracker from each team, and combining all trackers (including the baselines as a team). For example, the joint goal constraint ensemble with the top 2 entries was built from team2.entry1 & team4.entry0, and the method ensemble with the top 2 entries from team2.entry4 & team4.entry0.

Table 4 shows two interesting trends. The first is that score averaging does not improve performance, and performance declines as more trackers are combined, yielding a statistically significant decrease across all metrics. This suggests that the errors of the different trackers are correlated, which is unsurprising since they were trained on the same data. On the other hand, stacking yields a statistically significant improvement in accuracy for goal constraints, and doesn't degrade accuracy for the search method and requested slots. For stacking, the trend is that adding more trackers increases performance – for example, combining the best tracker from every team improves goal constraint accuracy from 78.4% to 79.8%.

For completeness, we note that the additional data could alternatively be used to improve the accuracy of a constituent classifier; given the constraints of the challenge, we can't assess the magnitude of that improvement, so it is an open question whether stacking is the *best* use of additional data. Also, the training and test conditions of the final stacking classifier are not mis-matched, whereas in practice they would be. Nonetheless, this result does suggest that, if additional data is available, stacking can be used to successfully combine multiple trackers and achieve performance better than the single best tracker.

6 Conclusions

DSTC2 continues the tradition of DSTC1 by providing a common testbed for dialog state tracking, introducing some additional features relevant to the research community– specifically a new domain, changing user goals and a richer dialog state. The data, evaluation scripts, and baseline trackers will remain available and open to the research community online.

Results from the previous challenge motivated the selection of a few metrics as *featured metrics*, which facilitate comparisons between trackers. Analysis of the performance on the matched development set and the mismatched test set suggests that there still appears to be limitations on generalisation, as found in DSTC1. The results also suggest there are limitations in exploiting correlations between slots, with few teams exploiting joint distributions and the effects of doing so being mixed. Investigating ensemble learning demonstrates the effectiveness of combining tracker outputs. Ensemble learning exploits the strengths of individual trackers to provide better quality output than any constituent tracker in the group.

A follow up challenge, DSTC3, will present the problem of adapting to a new domain with very few example dialogs. Future work should also verify that improvements in dialog state tracking translate to improvements in end-to-end dialog system performance. In this challenge, paid subjects were used as users with real information needs were not available. However, differences between these two user groups have been shown (Raux et al., 2005), so future studies should also test on real users.

Acknowledgements

The authors thank the advisory committee for their valuable input: Paul Crook, Maxine Eskenazi, Milica Gašić, Helen Hastie, Kee-Eung Kim, Sungjin Lee, Oliver Lemon, Olivier Pietquin, Joelle Pineau, Deepak Ramachandran, Brian Strope and Steve Young. The authors also thank Zhuoran Wang for providing a baseline tracker, and DJ Kim, Sungjin Lee & David Traum for comments on evaluation metrics. Finally, thanks to SIGdial for their endorsement, and to the participants for making the challenge a success.

References

Matthew Henderson, Milica Gašić, Blaise Thomson, Pirros Tsiakoulis, Kai Yu, and Steve Young. 2012. Discriminative Spoken Language Understanding Using Word Confusion Networks. In *Spoken Language Technology Workshop, 2012. IEEE.*

Matthew Henderson, Blaise Thomson, and Jason Williams. 2013. Dialog State Tracking Challenge 2 & 3 Handbook. camdial.org/~mh521/dstc/.

Ryuichiro Higashinaka, Noboru Miyazaki, Mikio Nakano, and Kiyoaki Aikawa. 2004. Evaluating discourse understanding in spoken dialogue systems. *ACM Trans. Speech Lang. Process.*, November.

Sungjin Lee and Maxine Eskenazi. 2013. Recipe for building robust spoken dialog state trackers: Dialog state tracking challenge system description. In *Proceedings of the SIGDIAL 2013 Conference.*

Angeliki Metallinou, Dan Bohus, and Jason D. Williams. 2013. Discriminative state tracking for spoken dialog systems. In *Proc Association for Computational Linguistics, Sofia.*

Antoine Raux, Brian Langner, Dan Bohus, Alan W Black, and Maxine Eskenazi. 2005. Let's go public! Taking a spoken dialog system to the real world.

Gökhan Tür, Anoop Deoras, and Dilek Hakkani-Tür. 2013. Semantic parsing using word confusion networks with conditional random fields. In *INTERSPEECH.*

Zhuoran Wang and Oliver Lemon. 2013. A simple and generic belief tracking mechanism for the dialog state tracking challenge: On the believability of observed information. In *Proceedings of the SIGDIAL 2013 Conference.*

Jason Williams, Antoine Raux, Deepak Ramachadran, and Alan Black. 2013. The Dialog State Tracking Challenge. In *Proceedings of the SIGDIAL 2013 Conference*, Metz, France, August.

David H. Wolpert. 1992. Stacked generalization. *Neural Networks*, 5:241–259.

Steve Young, Catherine Breslin, Milica Gašić, Matthew Henderson, Dongho Kim, Martin Szummer, Blaise Thomson, Pirros Tsiakoulis, and Eli Tzirkel Hancock. 2013. Evaluation of Statistical POMDP-based Dialogue Systems in Noisy Environment. In *Proceedings of IWSDS*, Napa, USA, January.

Appendix A: Featured results of evaluation

team	entry	Tracker Inputs: Live ASR	Tracker Inputs: Live SLU	Tracker Inputs: Batch ASR	Joint Goal Constraints: Acc	Joint Goal Constraints: L2	Joint Goal Constraints: ROC	Search Method: Acc	Search Method: L2	Search Method: ROC	Requested Slots: Acc	Requested Slots: L2	Requested Slots: ROC
0*	0		✓		0.619	0.738	0.000	0.879	0.209	0.000	0.884	0.196	0.000
	1		✓		0.719	0.464	0.000	0.867	0.210	0.349	0.879	0.206	0.000
	2		✓		0.711	0.466	0.000	0.897	0.158	0.000	0.884	0.201	0.000
	3		✓†		0.850	0.300	0.000	0.986	0.028	0.000	0.957	0.086	0.000
1	0		✓		0.601	0.649	0.064	0.904	0.155	0.187	0.960	0.073	0.000
	1		✓		0.596	0.671	0.036	0.877	0.204	0.397	0.957	0.081	0.000
2	0	✓	✓		0.775	0.758	0.063	0.944	0.092	0.306	0.954	0.073	0.383
	1	✓	✓	✓	**0.784**	0.735	0.065	0.947	0.087	0.355	0.957	0.068	0.446
	2	✓			0.668	0.505	0.249	0.944	0.095	0.499	0.972	0.043	0.300
	3	✓	✓	✓	0.771	0.354	0.313	0.947	0.093	0.294	0.941	0.090	0.262
	4	✓	✓	✓	0.773	0.467	0.140	**0.950**	**0.082**	0.351	0.968	0.050	0.497
3	0		✓		0.729	0.452	0.000	0.878	0.210	0.000	0.889	0.188	0.000
4	0	✓			0.768	**0.346**	0.365	0.940	0.095	0.452	**0.978**	**0.035**	0.525
	1	✓			0.746	0.381	0.383	0.939	0.097	0.423	0.977	0.038	0.490
	2		✓		0.742	0.387	0.345	0.922	0.124	0.447	0.957	0.069	0.340
	3		✓		0.737	0.406	0.321	0.922	0.125	0.406	0.957	0.073	0.385
5	0	✓	✓		0.686	0.628	0.000	0.889	0.221	0.000	0.868	0.264	0.000
	1	✓	✓		0.609	0.782	0.000	0.927	0.147	0.000	0.974	0.053	0.000
	2	✓	✓		0.637	0.726	0.000	0.927	0.147	0.000	0.974	0.053	0.000
	3	✓	✓		0.609	0.782	0.000	0.927	0.147	0.000	0.974	0.053	0.000
	4	✓	✓		0.695	0.610	0.000	0.927	0.147	0.000	0.974	0.053	0.000
6	0		✓		0.713	0.461	0.100	0.865	0.228	0.199	0.932	0.118	0.057
	1		✓		0.707	0.447	0.223	0.871	0.211	0.290	0.947	0.093	0.218
	2		✓		0.718	0.437	0.207	0.871	0.210	0.287	0.951	0.085	0.225
7	0	✓			0.750	0.416	0.081	0.936	0.105	0.237	0.970	0.056	0.000
	1	✓			0.739	0.428	0.159	0.921	0.161	0.554	0.970	0.056	0.000
	2	✓			0.750	0.416	0.081	0.929	0.117	0.379	0.971	0.054	0.000
	3	✓			0.725	0.432	0.105	0.936	0.105	0.237	0.972	0.047	0.000
	4		✓		0.735	0.433	0.086	0.910	0.140	0.280	0.946	0.089	0.190
8	0		✓		0.692	0.505	0.071	0.899	0.153	0.000	0.935	0.106	0.000
	1		✓		0.699	0.498	0.067	0.899	0.153	0.000	0.939	0.101	0.000
	2		✓		0.698	0.504	0.067	0.899	0.153	0.000	0.939	0.101	0.000
	3		✓		0.697	0.501	0.068	0.899	0.153	0.000	0.939	0.101	0.000
	4		✓		0.697	0.508	0.068	0.899	0.153	0.000	0.939	0.101	0.000
9	0		✓		0.499	0.760	0.000	0.857	0.229	0.000	0.905	0.149	0.000

* The entries under team0 are the baseline systems mentioned in section 3.2. † team0.entry3 is the oracle tracker, which uses the labels on the test set and limits itself to hypotheses suggested by the live SLU.

The top score in each column is indicated by bold-type. The ROC metric is only comparable for trackers operating at a similar accuracy, and so the highest values are not indicated.

Appendix B: Sample dialog, labels, and tracker output

Actual input and output	SLU hypotheses and scores	Labels	Example tracker output	Correct?
S: Which part of town? *request(area)*	0.2 inform(food=north_african) 0.1 inform(area=north)	area=north	0.2 food=north_african 0.1 area=north 0.7 ()	✗ ✓ ✗
U: The north uh area *inform(area=north)*		method=byconstraints	0.9 byconstraints 0.1 none	✓
		requested=()	0.0 phone 0.0 address	✓ ✓
S: Which part of town? *request(area)* U: A cheap place in the north *inform(area=north, pricerange=cheap)*	0.8 inform(area=north), inform(pricerange=cheap) 0.1 inform(area=north)	area=north pricerange=cheap	0.7 area=north pricerange=cheap 0.1 area=north food=north_african 0.2 ()	✓ ✗ ✗
		method=byconstraints	0.9 byconstraints 0.1 none	✓
		requested=()	0.0 phone 0.0 address	✓ ✓
S: Clown café is a cheap restaurant in the north part of town. U: Do you have any others like that, maybe in the south part of town? *reqalts(area=south)*	0.7 reqalts(area=south) 0.2 reqmore()	area=south pricerange=cheap	0.8 area=south pricerange=cheap 0.1 area=north pricerange=cheap 0.1 ()	✓ ✗ ✗
		method=byalternatives	0.6 byalternatives 0.2 byconstraints	✓
		requested=()	0.0 phone 0.0 address	✓ ✓
S: Galleria is a cheap restaurant in the south. U: What is their phone number and address? *request(phone), request(address)*	0.6 request(phone) 0.2 request(phone), request(address) 0.1 request(address)	area=south pricerange=cheap	0.9 area=south pricerange=cheap 0.1 area=north pricerange=cheap 0.0 ()	✓ ✗ ✗
		method=byalternatives	0.5 byconstraints 0.4 byalternatives	✗
		requested= (phone, address)	0.8 phone 0.3 address	✓ ✗

Example dialog illustrating DSTC2 data, labels, and evaluation procedure. The left column shows the actual system output and user input. The second column shows two SLU N-Best hypothesis and their scores. In practice, up to 10 SLU N-Best hypotheses are output. In the right 3 columns, the three shaded regions correspond to the three components of the dialog state output by a tracker at each turn. The blue region corresponds to the user's joint goal constraint; the red region to the user's search method; and the yellow region to the slots requested by the user. For space, only 2 of the 5 methods and 2 of the 8 requestable slots are shown. The third column shows the label (correct output) for each component. The fourth column shows example tracker output for each of these three quantities, and the fifth column indicates correctness. A goal constraint is correct if it exactly matches the label. Therefore, 0 or 1 of the output goal constraints is correct, and all the others are incorrect. Accuracy is determined by the correctness of the goal constraint with the highest tracker score. For search method, exactly one method is correct at each turn, so correctness is determined by comparing the maximum scoring method to the label. For requested slots, each slot can be requested (or not) in the same turn, so each requestable slot is separately marked as correct or incorrect. The quantity requested.all averages the correctness of all requested slots.

Optimizing Generative Dialog State Tracker via Cascading Gradient Descent

Byung-Jun Lee[1], **Woosang Lim**[1], **Daejoong Kim**[2], **Kee-Eung Kim**[1]
[1] Department of Computer Science, KAIST [2] LG Electronics

Abstract

For robust spoken dialog management, various dialog state tracking methods have been proposed. Although discriminative models are gaining popularity due to their superior performance, generative models based on the Partially Observable Markov Decision Process model still remain attractive since they provide an integrated framework for dialog state tracking and dialog policy optimization. Although a straightforward way to fit a generative model is to independently train the component probability models, we present a gradient descent algorithm that simultaneously train all the component models. We show that the resulting tracker performs competitively with other top-performing trackers that participated in DSTC2.

1 Introduction

Spoken dialog systems, a field rapidly growing with the spread of smart mobile devices, has to deal with challenges to become a primary user interface for natural interaction using conversations. One of the challenges is to maintain the state of the dialog in the conversational process, which is called *dialog state tracking*. The dialog state encapsulates the information needed to successfully finish the dialog, such as users' goal or requests, and thus it is an essential entity in spoken dialog systems. However, the error incurred by Automatic Speech Recognition (ASR) and Spoken Language Understanding (SLU) makes the true user utterance not directly observable, and this makes it difficult to figure out the true dialog state.

Various methods have been used to construct dialog state trackers. The traditional methods used in most commercial systems use hand-crafted rules that typically rely on the most likely result from SLU. However, these rule-based systems are prone to frequent errors as the most likely result is not always correct. Hence, these systems often drive the users to respond using simple keywords and to explicitly confirm everything they say, which is far from a natural conversational interaction. An accurate tracking of the dialog state is crucial for natural and efficient dialogs. On the other hand, modern methods take a statistical approach to calculate the posterior distribution over the dialog states using multiple results from SLU in order to overcome the error in the most likely SLU result.

Statistical dialog state trackers can be categorized into two approaches depending on how the posterior calculation is modeled. The *generative approach* uses the generative model that describes how the SLU results are generated from the hidden dialog state and uses the Bayes' rule to calculate the posterior. It has been a popular approach for statistical dialog state tracking, since it naturally fits into the Partially Observable Markov Decision Process (POMDP) (Williams and Young, 2007), an integrated model for dialog state tracking and dialog strategy optimization. In the POMDP point of view, the dialog state tracking is essentially belief monitoring, which is the task of calculating posterior distribution over the hidden state given the history of observations. Examples of the dialog state trackers that take the generative approach include (Young et al., 2010; Thomson and Young, 2010; Raux and Ma, 2011)

On the other hand, the *discriminative approach* directly models the posterior distribution. Since it avoids modeling of unnecessary aspects of the task, it typically achieves a better tracking accuracy compared to the generative approach. Examples of discriminative dialog state trackers include (Lee, 2013; Metallinou et al., 2013). However, their feature functions often refer to past observations, and it remains yet to be seen whether the discriminative approach can be successfully incorporated into POMDP or reinforcement learning (RL) for dialog strategy optimization.

This paper is concerned with the generative approach to dialog state tracking. In our earlier work (Kim et al., 2013), the optimization of the tracker was carried out independently for each component model (observation model, user action model, and belief refinement model) that comprised our tracker. This was not exactly a proper way to train the tracker for overall performance optimization. In this paper, we present an optimization method, which we call "cascading gradient descent", that trains component models simultaneously. We show that this approach yields a dialog state tracker that performs on par with the best ones that participated in the second Dialog State Tracking Challenge (DSTC2).

The rest of the paper is organized as follows: We briefly review the background of our work in section 2, and present our method in section 3. We then explain the DSTC2 dialog domain and the experimental settings in section 4, and discuss the results in section 5. Finally, we conclude the paper with the summary and the suggestion for future work in section 6.

2 Background and Related Work

The dialog state tracking is formalized as follows: In each turn of the dialog, the spoken dialog system executes system action a, and the user with goal g responds to the system with utterance u. The dialog state in each turn is defined $s = (u, g, h)$, where h is the dialog history encapsulating additional information needed for tracking the dialog state (Williams et al., 2005). The SLU processes the user utterance and generates the results as an N-best list $\boldsymbol{o} = [\langle \tilde{u}_1, f_1 \rangle, \ldots, \langle \tilde{u}_N, f_N \rangle]$, where $\tilde{u}_i$ is the hypothesized user utterance and f_i is its confidence score[1]. Without loss of generality, we assume that the last item in the N-best list is the null item $\langle \emptyset, 1 - \sum_{i=1}^{N-1} f_i \rangle$, representing the set of unrecognized user utterances. The statistical dialog state tracker maintains the probability distribution over states, called the *belief.*

2.1 Discriminative Dialog State Tracking

Dialog state trackers taking the discriminative approach calculates the belief via trained conditional models that represent the belief directly. *Maximum Entropy* is widely used for the discriminative approach, which formulates the belief as follows:

$$b'(g) = P(g|\boldsymbol{x}) = \eta \cdot exp(\boldsymbol{w}^T \boldsymbol{\phi}(\boldsymbol{x})) \qquad (1)$$

where η is the normalizing constant, $\boldsymbol{x} = (u_1, a_1, g_1, \ldots, u_t, a_t, g_t)$ is the history of user actions, system actions, and user goals up to the current dialog turn t, $\boldsymbol{\phi}(\cdot)$ is the vector of feature functions on $\boldsymbol{x}$, and finally, $\boldsymbol{w}$ is the set of model parameters to be learned from dialog data.

According to the formulation, the posterior computation has to be carried out for *all* possible user goals in order to obtain the normalizing constant η. This is not feasible for real dialog domains that have a large number of user goals (the DSTC2 dialog domain used on this paper has 371070 user goals).

Consequently, it is important for the discriminative approach to reduce the size of the state space. (Metallinou et al., 2013) adopts the idea behind the HIS model and confines the set of possible goals to those appeared in SLU results. (Lee, 2013) assumed conditional independence between dialog state components to address scalability, and used conditional random field.

2.2 Generative Dialog State Tracking

In contrast, the generative approach to the dialog state tracking calculates the belief using Bayes' rule, with the belief from the last turn b as a prior and the likelihood given the user utterance hypotheses $\Pr(\boldsymbol{o}|a, g, h)$. In the prior work (Williams et al., 2005), the likelihood is factored and some independence assumptions are made:

$$b'(g', h') = \eta \sum_u \Pr(\boldsymbol{o}|u) \Pr(u|g', a) \cdot \sum_h \Pr(h'|g', u, h, a) \sum_g \Pr(g'|g, a) b(g, h) \qquad (2)$$

where η is the normalizing constant and u is marginalized out in the belief.

Scalability became the important issue, just as in the generative approach. One way to reduce the amount of computation is to group the states into partitions, proposed as the Hidden Information State (HIS) model (Young et al., 2010). Beginning with one root partition with the probability of 1, partitions are split when the distinction is required by observations, i.e. a user utterance

[1] Here we assume that $\sum_{i=1}^{N-1} f_i \leq 1$, acting as a posterior of N-best list.

hypothesis from SLU. This confines the possible goal state to the values that have been appeared as SLU hypotheses, and provides scalability without a loss of accuracy when the coverage of N-best list is large enough to include the true utterance. Using the HIS model with an additional assumption that the user goal does not change (goal transition from one to another is 0), the belief update equation (2) is reformulated as follows:

$$b'(\psi', h') = \eta \sum_u \Pr(\boldsymbol{o}|u) \Pr(u|\psi', a) \cdot \sum_h \Pr(h'|\psi', u, h, a) \Pr(\psi'|\psi) b(\psi, h) \tag{3}$$

where ψ is a set of user goals that share the same belief. Each probability model in the above equation has a name: $\Pr(\boldsymbol{o}|u)$ is called the *observation model*, $\Pr(u|\psi', a)$ is called the *user action model*, $\Pr(\psi'|\psi)$ is called the *belief refinement model*, and $\Pr(h'|\psi', u, h, a)$ is called the *history model*.

In this paper, we used the last turn's belief of dialog states as history state and preserved its dependence in the observation model to improve performance. With the changes, observation model can distinguish user actions without their value. For example, *request alternative* user action may have the power of diminishing dominant partitions, and it can only be learnt by the dependence with partition confidence. The belief update formula used in this paper becomes:

$$b'(\psi') = \eta \sum_u \Pr(\boldsymbol{o}|u, a, h) \cdot \Pr(u|\psi', a) \Pr(\psi'|\psi) b(\psi) \tag{4}$$

Other approaches to cope with the scalability problem in dialog state tracking is to adopt factorized dynamic Bayesian network by making conditional independence assumptions among dialog state components, and use approximate inference algorithms such as loopy belief propagation (Thomson and Young, 2010) or blocked Gibbs sampling (Raux and Ma, 2011).

3 Cascading Gradient Descent

Although equation (4) is an elegant formulation of the dialog state tracking via Bayes rule, there has not been an integrated learning algorithm that simultaneously optimizes component probability models, i.e. the observation, the user action, and the belief refinement models. Our prior work (Kim et al., 2013) relied on independently training each component probability model, and then simply plugging them into (4). Since the independent optimization of component probability models does not lend itself to the optimization of overall dialog state tracking performance, we added an extra post-processing step called "belief transformation" in order to fine tune the results obtained from equation (4). Unfortunately, this effort generally resulted in overfitting to the training data. In this paper, we present an integrated learning algorithm that simultaneously optimizes the component probability models of the HIS model.

We start with defining an objective function which measures the error of the dialog state tracking:

$$E = \sum_{t=1}^{T} \sum_i \frac{1}{2} (b(\psi_i^t) - r_i^t)^2 \tag{5}$$

where t is the dialog turn, i is the partition index, r_i^t is the binary label with value 1 if and only if the partition ψ_i^t contains the true user goal. Note that our objective function coincides with the ℓ_2 performance metrics used in DSTC.

We then express component probability models as functions of features, which are parameterized by sets of weights, and rewrite equation (4):

$$b(\psi_i^t) = \eta^t \sum_{(u^t, f^t) \in \boldsymbol{o}^t} \Pr_{\boldsymbol{w}_\mathrm{O}}(u^t, f^t, a^t, b(\psi_i^{t-1})) \cdot \Pr_{\boldsymbol{w}_\mathrm{U}}(u^t|\psi_i^t, a^t) \Pr_{\boldsymbol{w}_\mathrm{R}}(\psi_i^t|\psi_i^{t-1}) b(\psi_i^{t-1}) \tag{6}$$

where $\boldsymbol{w}_\mathrm{O}$, $\boldsymbol{w}_\mathrm{U}$, and $\boldsymbol{w}_\mathrm{R}$ represent the set of parameters for the observation, the user action, and the belief refinement models, respectively.

Our learning method is basically a gradient descent. The gradient of E with respect to $\boldsymbol{w}_\mathrm{O}$ is derived as follows:

$$\frac{\partial E}{\partial \boldsymbol{w}_\mathrm{O}} = \sum_{t=1}^{T} \sum_i (b(\psi_i^t) - r_i^t) \frac{\partial b(\psi_i^t)}{\partial \boldsymbol{w}_\mathrm{O}}$$

By convenience, we define:

$$\begin{aligned} \delta_i^t &= \sum_{(u^t, f^t) \in \boldsymbol{o}^t} \Pr_{\boldsymbol{w}_\mathrm{O}}(u^t, f^t, a^t, b(\psi_i^{t-1})) \cdot \Pr_{\boldsymbol{w}_\mathrm{U}}(u^t|\psi_i^t, a^t) \Pr_{\boldsymbol{w}_\mathrm{R}}(\psi_i^t|\psi_i^{t-1}) b(\psi_i^{t-1}) \\ &= \sum_{(u^t, f^t) \in \boldsymbol{o}^t} p_\mathrm{O}^t p_\mathrm{U}^t p_\mathrm{R}^t b(\psi_i^{t-1}) \\ \eta^t &= (\sum_i \delta_i^t)^{-1}, \quad b(\psi_i^t) = \eta^t \delta_i^t \end{aligned}$$

and then obtain:

$$\frac{\partial b(\psi_i^t)}{\partial \boldsymbol{w}_{\mathrm{O}}} = \frac{\partial \delta_i^t}{\partial \boldsymbol{w}_{\mathrm{O}}} \cdot \eta^t + \frac{\partial \eta^t}{\partial \boldsymbol{w}_{\mathrm{O}}} \cdot \delta_i^t$$
$$= \frac{\partial \delta_i^t}{\partial \boldsymbol{w}_{\mathrm{O}}} \cdot \eta^t - b(\psi_i^t) \sum_{i'} \frac{\partial \delta_{i'}^t}{\partial \boldsymbol{w}_{\mathrm{O}}} \cdot \eta^t,$$

where

$$\frac{\partial \delta_i^t}{\partial \boldsymbol{w}_{\mathrm{O}}} = \Bigg(b(\psi_i^{t-1}) \sum_{(u^t, f^t) \in \boldsymbol{o}^t} \frac{\partial p_{\mathrm{O}}^t}{\partial \boldsymbol{w}_{\mathrm{O}}} p_{\mathrm{U}}^t p_{\mathrm{R}}^t$$
$$+ \frac{\partial b(\psi_i^{t-1})}{\partial \boldsymbol{w}_{\mathrm{O}}} \sum_{(u^t, f^t) \in \boldsymbol{o}^t} p_{\mathrm{O}}^t p_{\mathrm{U}}^t p_{\mathrm{R}}^t \Bigg).$$

Gradients for the parameters of other component probability models are derived similarly. We call our algorithm cascading gradient descent since the gradient $\frac{\partial b(\psi_i^t)}{\partial \boldsymbol{w}}$ requires computation of the gradient in the previous dialog turn $\frac{\partial b(\psi_i^{t-1})}{\partial \boldsymbol{w}}$, hence reflecting the temporal impact of the parameter change in throughout the dialog turns.

Once we obtain the gradients, we update the parameters using the gradient descent

$$\boldsymbol{w}_{\mathrm{O}}' = \boldsymbol{w}_{\mathrm{O}} - \alpha \left[\frac{\partial E}{\partial \boldsymbol{w}_{\mathrm{O}}} \right],$$
$$\boldsymbol{w}_{\mathrm{U}}' = \boldsymbol{w}_{\mathrm{U}} - \alpha \left[\frac{\partial E}{\partial \boldsymbol{w}_{\mathrm{U}}} \right],$$
$$\boldsymbol{w}_{\mathrm{R}}' = \boldsymbol{w}_{\mathrm{R}} - \alpha \left[\frac{\partial E}{\partial \boldsymbol{w}_{\mathrm{R}}} \right]$$

where α is the stepsize parameter. α is initially set to 0.5 and decreased by multiplying $\frac{1}{10}$ whenever the overall cost function increases.

4 Dialog State Tracking in the Restaurant Information Domain

This section describes the dialog domain used for the evaluation of our dialog tracker and the component probability models used for the domain. An instruction on how to obtain the dataset and a more detailed description on the dialog domain can be found in the DSTC2 summary paper (Henderson et al., 2014).

4.1 Task Description

We used the DSTC2 dialog domain in which the user queries the database of local restaurants. The dataset for the restaurant information domain were originally collected using Amazon Mechanical Turk. A usual dialog proceeds as follows: the user specifies the constraints (e.g. type of food, location, etc) or the name of restaurant he wants, and the system offers the name of a restaurant that qualifies the constraints. User then accepts the offer, and requests for additional information about accepted restaurant. The dialog ends when all the information requested by the user is provided.

The dialog state tracker should thereby clarify three types of information inside the state: goal, method, and requested. The goal state is composed of *name, pricerange, area, and food* slots, which is the information of the constraints that the user has. The method state represents what method user is using to accomplish his goal, whose value is one of the *none, by constraints, by alternatives, by name, or finished*. Lastly, the requested state represents the information currently requested by the user, such as the address, phone number, postal code, etc. In this paper, we restrict ourselves to tracking the goal states only, but our tracker can be easily extended to track others as well.

The dialog state tracker updates the belief turn by turn, receiving SLU N-best hypotheses each with an SLU confidence score in every turn. Despite the large number of states a dialog can have, in the most cases, the coverage of N-best hypotheses is enough to limit the consideration of possible goal state to values that has been observed in SLU hypotheses. Consequently, the task of the dialog state tracker is to generate a set of observed values and their confidence scores for each slot, with the confidence score corresponding to the posterior probability of the goal state being the true goal state. The dialog state tracker also maintains a special goal state, called *None*, which represents that the true goal state has not been observed. Its posterior probability is also computed together with the observed goal states as a part of the belief update. For the rest of this section, we describe the models chosen for each component probabilities.

4.2 Observation Model

The observation model that describes the generation of SLU result for the user utterance is defined as

$$\Pr(\mathbf{o} = \langle u^t, f^t \rangle | u, a, h) =$$
$$\eta_o \Pr_{\boldsymbol{w}_{\mathrm{O}}}(u^t, f^t, a^t, b(\psi_i^{t-1}))$$
$$= \eta_o \frac{1}{1 + \exp(-\boldsymbol{w}_{\mathrm{O}}^T \boldsymbol{\phi}_{\mathrm{O}}(u^t, f^t, a^t, b(\psi_i^{t-1})) - b_{\mathrm{O}})}$$

user action feature : 34	×	system action feature : 5	×	type of feature : 3	= 510
Inform action : 12 [food, pricerange, name, area] × [not_match, slot_match, value_match] % consistency check with system action		offer *or* inform		Bias tern (always 1)	
		canthelp *or* canthelp.exception			
Action with values : 8 [confirm, deny] × [food, pricerange, name, area]	×	expl-conf *or* impl-conf *or* request	×	Value of user confidence f^t	
Action without values : 14 [ack, affirm, bye, hello, negate, repeat, reqmore, reqalts, thankyou, request, null, confirm, deny, inform]		select		Value of last turn's confidence $b(\psi_i^{t-1})$	
		confirm-domain *or* welcomemsg			

Table 1: 510 features used in observation model are specified.

where $\phi_O(u^t, f^t, a^t, b(\psi_i^{t-1}))$ is the vector of features taken from the hypothesized user action u^t, its confidence score f^t generated from SLU, system action a^t, and the belief of partition we are dealing with $b(\psi_i^{t-1})$ from history state. Normalization constante η_o can be ignored since it is subsumed by overall normalization constant η. Feature details are specified in table 1.

4.3 User Action Model

Similar to the observation model, the user action model that predicts the user action given the previous system action and user goal is defined as

$$\Pr(u^t|\psi_i^t, a^t) = \Pr_{\boldsymbol{w}_\mathrm{U}}(u^t|\psi_i^t, a^t) = \frac{exp(\boldsymbol{w}_\mathrm{U}^T \phi_\mathrm{U}(u^t, \psi_i^t, a^t))}{\sum_u exp(\boldsymbol{w}_\mathrm{U}^T \phi_\mathrm{U}(u, \psi_i^t, a^t))}$$

where $\phi_\mathrm{U}(u^t, \psi_i^t, a^t) \in \{0,1\}^{322}$ is the vector of features taken from the (hypothesized) user action u^t, system action a^t, and the partition being updated ψ_i^t. Softmax function is used to normalize over possible user actions. Feature details are specified in table 2.

4.4 Belief Refinement Model

The belief refinement model predicts how the partition of the user goal will evolve at the next dialog turn. We defined it as a mixture of the empirical distribution and the uniform distribution obtained from the training data:

$$\Pr_{\boldsymbol{w}_\mathrm{R}}(\psi_i^t|\psi_i^{t-1}) = \frac{1}{1+\exp(-\boldsymbol{w}_\mathrm{R})} \frac{occurrence(\psi_i^t, \psi_i^{t-1})}{occurrence(\psi_i^{t-1})} + \left(1 - \frac{1}{1+\exp(-\boldsymbol{w}_\mathrm{R})}\right) \frac{|\psi_i^t|}{|\psi_i^{t-1}|}$$

where $occurrence(\psi_i^t, \psi_i^{t-1})$ is the number of consecutive dialog turns in the training data with user goals being consistent with ψ_i^{t-1} in the previous turn and ψ_i^t in the current turn, and $occurrence(\psi_i^{t-1})$ is defined similarly for a single turn only. The ratio of the two, which corresponds to the partition split probability used in (Young et al., 2010), is the first term in the mixture. On the other hand, if we use this empirical distribution only, we cannot deal with novel user goals that do not appear in the training data. Assuming that user goals are generated from the uniform distribution, the probability that the user goal is in a partition ψ is $\frac{|\psi|}{N}$ where $|\psi|$ is the number of user goals in the partition ψ, and N is the total number of user goals. The probability that ψ_i^t gets split from ψ_i^{t-1} is then $\frac{|\psi_i^t|}{|\psi_i^{t-1}|}$. Hence, we mix the two probabilities for the resulting model.

The mixture weight is the only parameter of the belief refinement model, which is learned as a part of the cascading gradient descent. Note that we use the sigmoid function in order to make the optimization unconstrained.

user action feature : 35	×	system action feature : 8	+	remaining actions: 42	= 322
Inform action : 24 [food, pricerange, name, area] × [not_match, slot_match, value_match] % consistency check with system action × [not_match, match] % consistency check with partition	×	[offer *or* inform, canthelp *or* canthelp.exception, expl-conf *or* impl-conf *or* request, select] × [not_match, match] % consistency check with partition	+	Confirm/deny action : 16 [confirm, deny] × [food, pricerange, name, area] × [not_match, match] % consistency check with partition	
Action without values : 11 [ack, affirm, bye, hello, negate, repeat, reqalts, reqmore, thankyou, request, null]				Remaining system action : 26 [confirm-domain *or* welcomemsg] × [24 inform actions, null, others] % corresponding user actions	

Table 2: 322 features used in user action model are specified.

5 Experimental Details

5.1 Datasets

The restaurant information domain used in DSTC2 is arranged into three datasets: *train, dev, test*. The first two datasets are labeled with the true user goals and user actions to optimize the dialog state tracker before submission. The half of the dialogs are created with artificially degraded speech recognizers, intended to better distinguish the performances of trackers. Details of each dataset are as below:

- **dstc2_train**: Composed of 1612 dialogs of 11405 turns, produced from two different dialog managers with a hand-crafted dialog policy.
- **dstc2_dev**: Composed of 506 dialogs of 3836 turns, produced from the dialog managers used in dstc2_train set. Most of dialog state trackers show lower performance on this dataset than others.
- **dstc2_test**: Composed of 1117 dialogs of 9689 turns, produced from the dialog policy trained by reinforcement learning, which is not used for the train and dev datasets.

We used both train and dev sets as the training data, as if they were one big dataset. Although the true labels for the test dataset were made public after the challenge, we did not use these labels in any way for optimizing our tracker.

5.2 Pre-training

One of the drawbacks in using gradient descent is convergence to a local optimum. We also observed this phenomena during the training of our dialog state tracker via cascading gradient descent. Randomized initialization of parameters is a common practice for gradient descent, but given the high-dimensionality of the parameter space, the randomized initialization had a limited effect in converging to a sufficiently good local optimum.

We adopted a pre-training phase where the parameters of each component model are optimized individually. Once the pre-training is done for each component model, we gathered the parameter values and took them as the initial parameter value for the cascading gradient descent. This pre-training phase helped tremendously converging to a good local optimum, and reduced the number of iterations as well. We pre-trained the parameters of each component model as follows:

- **Observation Model**: True user action labels in the training set are used as targets for the observation model. For every user action hypothesis in the N-best list, set the target value to 1 if the user action hypothesis is the true user action, and 0 otherwise. A simple gradient descent was used for pre-training.
- **User Action Model**: Although the user action and the system action labels are available, the partition of the user goals is not readily available. However, the latter can be easily obtained by running an unoptimized tracker. Thus, using the labels in the training set and the generated partitions, we set the target value to 1 if the user action hypothesis is the true user action and the partition is consistent with the true user action, and 0 oth-

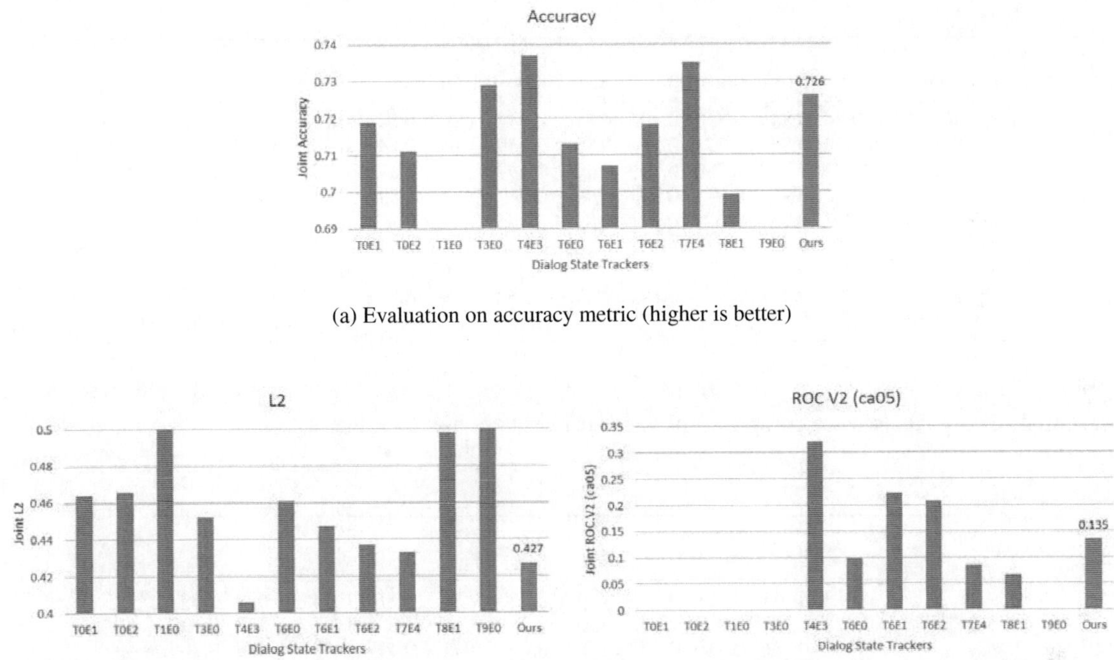

(a) Evaluation on accuracy metric (higher is better)

(b) Evaluation on L2 metric (lower is better)

(c) Evaluation on $ROC_{V2,ca05}$ metric (higher is better)

Figure 1: The overall results of proposed method. Each figure shows the evaluations over dstc2_test dataset by featured metrics (joint accuracy, joint l2, joint roc.v2) in DSTC2.

erwise. A simple gradient descent was also used for pre-training.

- **Belief Refinement Model**: Since there is only a single parameter for this model, we did not perform pre-training.

5.3 Results and Discussion

Table 3 shows the test set score of tracker implemented based on proposed algorithm, with the score of other trackers submitted to DSTC2. We tried 200 random initialised weights to train model with proposed algorithm, and learned model with the lowest training L2 error is picked to show the result on the test set. Because we only used live SLU and past data to track dialog state, other tracker results with the same condition are selected to compare with our tracker.

The implementation of our algorithm was not ready until the DSTC2 deadline. We participated as Team 8 using the old optimization method in (Kim et al., 2013). As shown in the table 3, the new algorithm shows a substantial improvement, achieving almost 15% decrease in the L2 error. Since both trackers are fine-tuned, this improvement seems to be originated from the new optimization algorithm.

For all three featured metrics used to evaluate, tracker constructed with our proposed method shows competitive performance. The key to excel baseline tracker was to discover the relation between user action and system action. For example, user actions that tell about the same slot system was talking about but giving different value are usually correcting wrong recognitions so far, which should significantly reduce the belief over state the system was tracking.

Due to the objective function that is designed to optimize L2 error, our tracker shows better performance at L2 error than the other metrics. For both all goal metric and joint goal metric, our tracker shows low L2 error when compared to other trackers while the rank of accuracy metric is not so high. When the fact that our method as a generative state tracker benefits from the ability to be easily incorporated into POMDP framework is considered, only similar performance to other trackers is satisfactory.

6 Conclusion

In this paper, we propose a simple method that optimizes overall parameters of generative state tracker using "Cascading Gradient Descent" al-

All goal

Team	0		1	3	4	6			7	8	9	Ours
Entry	1	2	0	0	3	0	1	2	4	1	0	
Accuracy	0.886	0.88	0.837	0.892	0.895	0.884	0.882	0.885	0.894	0.873	0.77	0.886
AvgP	0.865	0.852	0.778	0.856	0.853	0.789	0.833	0.843	0.862	0.827	0.782	0.846
L2	0.192	0.198	0.289	0.189	0.17	0.197	0.189	0.184	0.179	0.227	0.358	0.186
MRR	0.918	0.914	0.87	0.911	0.927	0.917	0.916	0.918	0.922	0.904	0.833	0.918
$\text{ROC}_{V1,ca05}$	0.777	0.767	0.0	0.778	0.842	0.773	0.786	0.809	0.806	0.635	0.0	0.805
$\text{ROC}_{V1,eer}$	0.139	0.133	0.0	0.119	0.103	0.135	0.123	0.116	0.116	0.163	0.219	0.120
$\text{ROC}_{V2,ca05}$	0.0	0.0	0.0	0.0	0.3	0.27	0.417	0.384	0.154	0.0	0.0	0.197
UpdateAcc	0.886	0.881	0.837	0.891	0.895	0.882	0.88	0.883	0.894	0.873	0.769	0.886
UpdatePrec	0.898	0.897	0.846	0.904	0.907	0.898	0.895	0.897	0.903	0.886	0.804	0.896

Table 3: Test set scores averaged over all goal slots of our proposed algorithm and other trackers are presented. The goal slots are composed of food, pricerange, name and area.

Joint goal

Team	0		1	3	4	6			7	8	9	Ours
Entry	1	2	0	0	3	0	1	2	4	1	0	
Accuracy	0.719	0.711	0.601	0.729	0.737	0.713	0.707	0.718	0.735	0.699	0.499	0.726
AvgP	0.678	0.66	0.503	0.659	0.636	0.54	0.619	0.638	0.673	0.583	0.522	0.658
L2	0.464	0.466	0.649	0.452	0.406	0.461	0.447	0.437	0.433	0.498	0.76	0.427
MRR	0.779	0.757	0.661	0.763	0.804	0.767	0.765	0.772	0.787	0.749	0.608	0.775
$\text{ROC}_{V1,ca05}$	0.332	0.316	0.096	0.32	0.461	0.324	0.395	0.432	0.349	0.22	0.0	0.438
$\text{ROC}_{V1,eer}$	0.256	0.254	0.382	0.249	0.208	0.281	0.241	0.226	0.243	0.299	0.313	0.218
$\text{ROC}_{V2,ca05}$	0.0	0.0	0.064	0.0	0.321	0.1	0.223	0.207	0.086	0.067	0.0	0.135
UpdateAcc	0.489	0.487	0.37	0.495	0.507	0.473	0.466	0.476	0.514	0.459	0.325	0.488
UpdatePrec	0.729	0.694	0.677	0.759	0.726	0.748	0.743	0.743	0.703	0.692	0.54	0.71

Table 4: Test set scores of joint goal slot of our proposed algorithm and other trackers are presented. The joint goal slot is a slot that is treated as correct when every goal slot is correct.

gorithm. Using proposed method on Hidden Information State model, we construct a tracker that performs competitively with DSTC2 participants, who mostly adopt discriminative approaches. Since generative approach has much more potential to be extended to more complex models or toward different domains such as DSTC3, our tracker has the advantage over the other trackers.

Hidden Information State (HIS) model with cascading gradient descent has far more steps of improvement remaining. Although history state in current paper only includes previous partition belief due to implementation convenience, utilizing additional history state is the key to improve performance even more. History state can include any information depending on how we define the state. The reason why the discriminative state tracking methods generally show good performance in terms of accuracy is rich set of potentially informative features, which can be employed by the history state.

In addition to the future improvements with history state, we can consider improving each probability models. In this paper, probability models are modeled with sigmoid function or softmax function over weighted features, which is in other words a neural network with no hidden layer. The model used in this paper can naturally developed by adding hidden layers, and ultimately deep learning techniques could be applicable. Applying deep learning techniques could help the history state to find out influential hidden features to employ.

Acknowledgments

This work was supported by the IT R&D program of MKE/KEIT. [10041678, The Original Technology Development of Interactive Intelligent Personal Assistant Software for the Information Service on multiple domains]

References

Matthew Henderson, Blaise Thomson, and Jason Williams. 2014. The second dialog state tracking challenge. In *Proceedings of the SIGdial 2014 Conference*, Baltimore, U.S.A., June.

Daejoong Kim, Jaedeug Choi, Kee-Eung Kim, Jungsu Lee, and Jinho Sohn. 2013. A specific analysis of a dialog state tracker in a challenge. In *Proceedings of the SIGDIAL 2013 Conference*, pages 462–466.

Sungjin Lee. 2013. Structured discriminative model for dialog state tracking. *Proceedings of the SIGDIAL 2013 Conference*, pages 442–451.

Angeliki Metallinou, Dan Bohus, and Jason D Williams. 2013. Discriminative state tracking for spoken dialog systems. In *Proceedings of the 51st Annual Meeting of the Association for Computational Linguastics*, pages 466–475.

Antoine Raux and Yi Ma. 2011. Efficient probabilistic tracking of user goal and dialog history for spoken dialog systems. In *INTERSPEECH*, pages 801–804.

Blaise Thomson and Steve Young. 2010. Bayesian update of dialogue state: A pomdp framework for spoken dialogue systems. *Computer Speech & Language*, 24(4):562–588.

Jason D Williams and Steve Young. 2007. Partially observable markov decision processes for spoken dialog systems. *Computer Speech & Language*, 21(2):393–422.

Jason D Williams, Pascal Poupart, and Steve Young. 2005. Factored partially observable markov decision processes for dialogue management. In *4th Workshop on Knowledge and Reasoning in Practical Dialog Systems, International Joint Conference on Artificial Intelligence (IJCAI)*, pages 76–82.

Steve Young, Milica Gašić, Simon Keizer, François Mairesse, Jost Schatzmann, Blaise Thomson, and Kai Yu. 2010. The hidden information state model: A practical framework for pomdp-based spoken dialogue management. *Computer Speech & Language*, 24(2):150–174.

Web-style ranking and SLU combination for dialog state tracking

Jason D. Williams
Microsoft Research, Redmond, WA, USA
jason.williams@microsoft.com

Abstract

In spoken dialog systems, statistical *state tracking* aims to improve robustness to speech recognition errors by tracking a posterior distribution over hidden dialog states. This paper introduces two novel methods for this task. First, we explain how state tracking is structurally similar to *web-style ranking*, enabling mature, powerful ranking algorithms to be applied. Second, we show how to use multiple spoken language understanding engines (SLUs) in state tracking — multiple SLUs can expand the set of dialog states being tracked, and give more information about each, thereby increasing both recall and precision of state tracking. We evaluate on the second Dialog State Tracking Challenge; together these two techniques yield highest accuracy in 2 of 3 tasks, including the most difficult and general task.

1 Introduction

Spoken dialog systems interact with users via natural language to help them achieve a goal. As the interaction progresses, the dialog manager maintains a representation of the state of the dialog in a process called *dialog state tracking* (Williams et al., 2013; Henderson et al., 2014). For example, in a restaurant search application, the dialog state might indicate that the user is looking for an inexpensive restaurant in the center of town. Dialog state tracking is difficult because errors in automatic speech recognition (ASR) and spoken language understanding (SLU) are common, and can cause the system to misunderstand the user's needs. At the same time, state tracking is crucial because the system relies on the estimated dialog state to choose actions – for example, which restaurants to present to the user.

Historically, commercial systems have used hand-crafted rules for state tracking, selecting the SLU result with the highest confidence score observed so far, and discarding alternatives. In contrast, statistical approaches compute a posterior *distribution* over many *hypotheses* for the dialog state, and in general these have been shown to be superior (Horvitz and Paek, 1999; Williams and Young, 2007; Young et al., 2009; Thomson and Young, 2010; Bohus and Rudnicky, 2006; Metallinou et al., 2013; Williams et al., 2013).

This paper makes two contributions to the task of statistical dialog state tracking. First, we show how to cast dialog state tracking as *web-style ranking*. Each dialog state can be viewed as a document, and each dialog turn can be viewed as a search instance. The benefit of this construction is that it enables a rich literature of powerful ranking algorithms to be applied. For example, the ranker we apply constructs a forest of decision trees, which — unlike existing work — automatically encodes conjunctions of low-level features. Conjunctions are attractive in dialog state tracking where relationships exist between low-level concepts like grounding and confidence score.

The second contribution is to incorporate the output of *multiple* spoken language understanding engines (SLUs) into dialog state tracking. Using more than one SLU can increase the number of dialog states being tracked, improving the chances of discovering the correct one. Moreover, additional SLUs supply more features, such as semantic confidence scores, improving accuracy.

This paper is organized as follows. First, section 2 states the problem formally and covers related work. Section 3 then lays out the data, features, and experimental design. Section 4 applies web-style ranking, and section 5 covers the usage of multiple SLUs. Section 6 extends the types of tracking tasks, section 7 compares performance to other entries in DSTC2, and section 8 briefly concludes.

2 Background

Statistical dialog state tracking can be formalized as follows. At each turn in the dialog, the state tracker maintains a set X of dialog state hypotheses $X = \{x_1, x_2, \ldots, x_N\}$. Each state hypothesis corresponds to a possible true state of the dialog. The posterior of a state x_i at a certain turn in the dialog is denoted $P(x_i)$.

Based on this posterior, the system takes an action a, the user provides an *utterance* in reply, and an automatic speech recognizer (ASR) converts the user's utterance into words. Since speech recognition is an error prone process, the speech recognizer outputs weighted alternatives, for example an N-best list or a word-confusion network. A *spoken language understanding* engine (SLU) then converts the ASR output into a meaning representation U for the user's utterance, where U can contain alternatives for the user's meaning, $U = \{u_1, \ldots, u_L\}$.

The state tracker then updates its internal state. This is done in three stages. First, a hand-written function G ingests the system's last action s, the meaning representation U, and the current set of states X, and yields a new set of possible states, $X' = G(s, U, X)$, where we denote the members of X' as $\{x'_1, x'_2, \ldots, x'_{N'}\}$. The number of elements in X' may be different than X, and typically the number of states increases as the dialog progresses, i.e. $N' > N$. In this work, G simply takes the Cartesian product of X and U. Second, for each new state hypothesis x'_i, a vector of J features is extracted, $\phi(x'_i) = [\phi_1(x'_i), \ldots, \phi_J(x'_i)]$. In the third stage, a scoring process takes all of the features for all of the new dialog states and scores them to produce the new distribution over dialog states, $P'(x'_i)$. This new distribution is used to choose another system action, and the whole process repeats.

Most early work cast dialog state tracking as a generative model in which hidden user goals generate observations in the form of SLU hypotheses (Horvitz and Paek, 1999; Williams and Young, 2007; Young et al., 2009; Thomson and Young, 2010). More recently, discriminatively trained direct models have been applied, and two studies on dialog data from two publicly deployed dialog systems suggest direct models yield better performance (Williams, 2012; Zilka et al., 2013). The methods introduced in this paper also use discriminative techniques.

One of the first approaches to direct models for dialog state tracking was to consider a small, fixed number of states and then apply a multinomial classifier (Bohus and Rudnicky, 2006). Since a multinomial classifier can make effective use of more features than a generative model, this approach improves precision, but can decrease recall by only considering a small number of states (e.g. 5 states). Another discriminative approach is to score each state using a binary model, then somehow combine the binary scores to form a distribution – see, for example (Henderson et al., 2013b) which used a binary neural network. This approach scales to many states, but unlike a multinomial classifier, each binary classifier isn't aware of its competitors, reducing accuracy. Also, when training a binary model in the conventional way, the training criteria is mis-matched, since the classifier is trained per hypothesis per timestep, but is evaluated only once per timestep.

Maximum entropy (*maxent*) models have been proposed which provide the strengths of both of these approaches (Metallinou et al., 2013). The probability of a dialog hypothesis x_i being correct ($y = i$) is computed as:

$$P(y = i|X, \lambda) = \frac{\exp(\sum_{j \in J} \lambda_j \phi_j(x_i))}{\sum_{x \in X} \exp(\sum_{j \in J} \lambda_j \phi_j(x))}. \tag{1}$$

Maximum entropy models yielded top performance in the first dialog state tracking challenge (Lee and Eskenazi, 2013). In this paper, we use maxent models as a baseline.

A key limitation with linear (and log-linear) models such as maximum entropy models is that they do not automatically build *conjunctions* of features. Conjunctions express conditional combinations of features such as whether the system attempted to confirm x *and* if "yes" was recognized *and* if the confidence score of "yes" is high. Conjunctions are important in dialog state tracking because they are often more discriminative than individual features. Moreover, in linear models for dialog state tracking, one weight is learned *per feature* (equation 1) (Metallinou et al., 2013). As a result, if a feature takes the same value for every dialog hypothesis at a given timestep, its contribution to every hypothesis will be the same, and it will therefore have no effect on the ranking. For example, features describing the current system action are identical for all state hypotheses. Concretely, if $\phi_j(x_i) = c$ for all i, then changing c causes no change in $P(y = i|X, \lambda)$ for all i.

Past work has shown that conjunctions improve dialog state tracking (Metallinou et al., 2013; Lee, 2013). However, past work has added conjunction *by hand*, and this doesn't scale: the number of possible conjunctions increases exponentially in the number of terms in the conjunction, and it's difficult to predict in advance which conjunctions will be useful. This paper introduces algorithms from web-style ranking as a mechanism for automatically building feature conjunctions.

In this paper we also use *score averaging*, a well-known machine learning technique for combining the output of several models, where each output class takes the average score assigned by all the models. Under certain assumptions — most importantly that errors are made independently — score averaging is guaranteed to exceed the performance of the best single model. Score averaging has been applied to dialog state tracking in previous work (Lee and Eskenazi, 2013). Here we use score averaging to maximize data use in cascaded models, and as a hedge against unlucky parameter settings.

3 Preliminaries

In this paper we use data and evaluation metrics from the second dialog state tracking challenge (DSTC2) (Henderson et al., 2014; Henderson et al., 2013a). Dialogs in DSTC2 are in the restaurant search domain. Users can search for restaurants in multiple ways, including via constraints, or by name. The system can offer restaurants that match, confirm user input, ask for additional constraints, etc.

There are three components to the hidden dialog state: user's **goal**, search **method**, and **requested slots**. The user's **goal** specifies the user's search constraints, and consists of 4 *slots*: area, pricerange, foodtype, and name. The number of values for the slots ranges from 4 to 113.[1] In DSTC2, trackers output scored lists for each slot, and also a scored list of joint hypotheses. For example, at a given timestep in a given dialog, three joint goal hypothesis might be (area=west,food=italian), (area=west), and (), where () means the user hasn't specified any constraints yet. Since tracking the joint user goal is the most general and most difficult task, we'll focus on this first, and return to the other tasks in section 6.

3.1 User goal features

For features, we broadly follow past work (Lee and Eskenazi, 2013; Lee, 2013; Metallinou et al., 2013). For a hypothesis x_i, *for each slot* the features encode 253 low-level quantities, such as: whether the slot value appears in this hypothesis; how many times the slot value has been observed; whether the slot value has been observed in this turn; functions of recognition metrics such as confidence score and position on N-best list; goal priors and confusion probabilities estimated on training data (Williams, 2012; Metallinou et al., 2013); results of confirmation attempts ("Italian food, is that right?"); output of the four rule-based baseline trackers; and the system act and its relation to the goal's slot value (e.g., whether the system act mentions this slot value).

Of these 253 features for each slot, 119 are the same for all values of that slot in a given turn, such as which system acts were observed in this turn. For these, we add 238 *conjunctions* with slot-specific features like confidence score, which makes these features useful to our maxent baseline. This results in a total of $253+238 = 491$ features per slot. The features for each of the 4 slots are concatenated together to yield $491 * 4 = 1964$ features per joint hypothesis.

3.2 Evaluation metrics

In DSTC2, there are 3 primary metrics for evaluation — accuracy of the top-scored hypothesis, the L2 probability quality, and an ROC measurement. The ROC measurement is only meaningful when compared across systems with similar accuracy; since our variants differ in accuracy, we omit ROC. However, note that *all* of the metrics, including ROC, for our final entries on the development set and test set are available for public download from the DSTC2 website.[2]

The DSTC2 corpus consists of three partitions: train, development, and test. Throughout sections 4-6, we report accuracy by training on the training set, and report accuracy on the development set and test set. The development set was available during development of the models, whereas the test set was not.

[1]Including a special "don't care" value.

[2]`camdial.org/~mh521/dstc/`

3.3 Baselines

We first compare to the four rule-based trackers provided by DSTC2. These were carefully designed by other research groups, and earlier versions of them scored very well in the first DSTC (Wang and Lemon, 2013). In each column in Tables 2 and 3, we report the best result from any rule-based tracker. We also compare to a maxent model as in Eq 1. Our implementation includes L1 and L2 regularization which was automatically tuned via cross-validation.

4 Web-style ranking

The ranking task is to order a set of N documents by relevance given a query. The input to a ranker is a query Q and set of documents $X = \{D_1, \ldots, D_N\}$, where each document is described in terms of features of that document and the query $\phi(D_i, Q)$. The output is a score for each document, where the highest score indicates the most relevant document. The overall objective is to order the documents by *relevance*, given the query. Training data indicates the relevance of example query/document pairs. Training labels are provided by judges, and relevance is typically described in terms of several levels, such as "excellent", "good", "fair", and "not relevant".

The application of ranking to dialog state tracking is straightforward: instead of ranking features of documents and queries $\phi(D_i, Q)$, we rank features of dialog states $\phi(X_i)$. For labeling, the correct dialog state is "relevant" and all other states are "not relevant".

Like dialog state tracking, ranking tasks often have features which are constant over all documents – particularly features of the query. This is one reason why ranking algorithms have incorporated methods for automatically building conjunctions. The specific algorithm we use here is lambdaMART (Wu et al., 2010; Burges, 2010). LambdaMART is a mature, scalable ranking algorithm: it has underpinned the winning entry in a community ranking challenge task (Chapelle and Chang, 2011), and is the foundation of the ranker in the Bing search engine. LambdaMART constructs a forest of M decision trees, where each tree consists of binary branches on features, and the leaf nodes are real values. Each binary branch specifies a threshold to apply to a single feature. For a forest of M trees, the score of a dialog state x is

$$F(x) = \sum_{m=1}^{M} \alpha_m f_m(x) \tag{2}$$

where α_m is the weight of tree m and $f_m(x)$ is the value of the leaf node obtained by evaluating decision tree m by features $[\phi_1(x), \ldots, \phi_J(x)]$. The training objective is to maximize ranking quality, which here means one-best accuracy. The decision trees are learned by regularized gradient descent, where trees are added successively to improve ranking quality – in our case, to maximize how often the correct dialog state is ranked first. The number of trees to create and the number of leaves per tree are tuning parameters. Through cross-validation, we found that 500 decision trees each with 32 leaves were the best settings. We use the same set of 1964 features for lambdaMART as was used for the maxent baseline.

Results are shown in row 3 of table 2 under "Joint goal". Ranking outperforms both baselines on both the development and training set. This result illustrates that automatically-constructed conjunctions do indeed improve accuracy in dialog state tracking. An example of a single tree computed by lambdaMART is shown in Appendix A. The complexity of this tree suggests that human designers would find it difficult to specify a tractable set of good conjunction features.

5 Multiple SLU engines

As described in the introduction, dialog state tracking typically proceeds in three stages: enumeration of the set of dialog states to score, feature extraction, and scoring. Incorporating the output of multiple SLUs requires changing the first two steps. Continuing with notation from section 2, with a single SLU output U, the enumeration step is $X' = G(s, U, X)$ — recall that U is a *set* of SLU hypotheses from an SLU engine. With multiple SLU engines we have K SLU outputs $U_1, \ldots, U_K$, and the enumeration step is thus $X' = G(s, U_1, \ldots, U_K, X)$. In our implementation, we simply take the union of all concepts on all SLU N-best lists and enumerate states as in the single SLU case – i.e., the Cartesian product of dialog states X with concepts on the SLU output.

The feature extraction step is modified to output features derived from all of the SLU engines. Concretely, if a feature $\phi_j(x)$ includes information from an SLU engine (such as confidence score or position on the N-best list), it is duplicated K times – i.e., once for each SLU engine. Additional binary features are added to encode whether each SLU engine has output the slot value of this dialog state. This allows for the situation that a slot value is not output by all SLU engines, in which case its confidence score, N-best list position, etc. will not be present from some SLU engines. Using two SLU engines on our data increases the number of features per joint goal from 1964 to 3140.

5.1 SLU Engines

We built two new SLU engines, broadly following (Henderson et al., 2012). Both consist of many binary classifiers. In the first engine **SLU1**, a binary classifier is estimated *for each slot/value pair*, and predicts the presence of that slot/value pair in the utterance. Similarly, a binary classifier is estimated for each user dialog act. Input features are word n-grams from the ASR N-best list. We only considered n-grams which were observed at least c times in the training data; infrequent n-grams were mapped to a special UNK feature. For binary classification we used decision trees, which marginally outperformed logistic regression, SVMs, and deep neural networks. Through cross-validation we set $n = 2$ and $c = 2$ – i.e., uni-grams and bi-grams which appear at least twice in the training data.

At runtime, the top SLU output on the N-best list is formed by taking the most likely combination of all the binary classifiers; the second SLU output is formed by taking the second most likely combination of all the binary classifiers; and so on, where only valid SLU combinations are considered. For example, the "bye" dialog act takes no arguments, so if "bye" and "food=italian" were the most likely combination, this combination would be skipped. Scores are formed by taking the product of all the binary classifiers, with some smoothing.

The second SLU engine **SLU2** is identical except that it also includes features from the word confusion network. Specifically, each word (unigram) appearing in the word confusion network is a feature. Bi-gram confusion network features did not improve performance.

If we train a new SLU engine and a ranker on the same data, this will introduce unwanted bias. Therefore, we divided the training data in half, and use the first half for training the SLU, and the second for training the ranker. Table 1 shows several evaluation metrics for each SLU engine, including the SLU included in the corpus, which we denote **SLU0**. SLU precision, recall, and F-measure are computed on the top hypotheses. Item cross-entropy (ICE) (Thomson et al., 2008) measures the quality of the scores for all the items on the SLU N-best list. Table 1 also shows joint goal accuracy by using SLU0, SLU1, or SLU2, for either a rule-based baseline or the ranking model. Overall, our SLU engines performed better on isolated SLU metrics, but did not yield better state tracking performance when used *instead* of the SLU results in the corpus.

5.2 Results with multiple SLU engines

Table 2, rows 4 and 7 show that an improvement in performance does results from using 2 SLU engines. In rows 4 and 7, the additional SLU engine is trained on the first half of the data, and the ranker is trained on the second half – we call this arrangement **Fold A**. To maximize use of the data, it's possible to train a second SLU/ranker pair by inverting the training data – i.e., train a second SLU on the second half, and a second ranker (using the second SLU) on the first half. We call this arrangement **Fold B**. These two configurations can be combined by running *both* trackers on test data, then averaging their scores. We call this arrangement **Fold AB**. If a hypothesis is output by only one configuration, it is assumed the other configuration output a zero score.

Table 2, rows 5 and 8 show that the fold AB configuration yields an additional performance gain.

5.3 Model averaging

A small further improvement is possible by averaging across multiple models (rankers) with different parameter settings. Since all of the models will be estimated on the same data, this is unlikely to make a large improvement, but it can hedge against an unlucky parameter setting, since the performance after averaging is usually close to the maximum.

To test this, we trained a second pair of ranking models, with a different number of leaves per tree (8 instead of 32). We then applied this second model, and averaged the scores between the two variants. Results are in Table 2, rows 6 and 9. Averaging scores across two parameter settings generally results in performance equal to or better than the maximum of the two models.

SLU source	Dev set: SLU Metrics Prec.	Recall	F-meas.	ICE	Goal track. acc. Rules	Ranking	Test set: SLU Metrics Prec.	Recall	F-meas.	ICE	Goal track. acc. Rules	Ranking
SLU0	**0.883**	0.666	0.759	2.185	**0.623**	**0.666**	**0.900**	0.691	0.782	1.955	**0.719**	**0.739**
SLU1	0.818	0.729	0.771	2.189	0.598	0.637	0.846	0.762	0.802	1.943	0.667	0.709
SLU2	0.844	**0.742**	**0.789**	**2.098**	0.605	0.658	0.870	**0.777**	**0.821**	**1.845**	0.685	0.734

Table 1: Performance of three SLU engines. SLU0 is the DSTC2 corpus; SLU1 is our engine with uni-grams and bi-grams of ASR results in the corpus; and SLU2 is SLU1 with the addition of unigram features from the word confusion network. Precision, Recall, F-measure, and ICE evaluate the quality of the SLU output, not state tracking. "ICE" is item-wise cross entropy — smaller numbers are better (Thomson et al., 2008). "Rules" indicates dialog state tracking accuracy for user joint goals by running the rule-based baseline tracker on the indicated SLU (alone); "Ranking" indicates joint goal accuracy of running a ranker trained on the indicated SLU (alone). For training, goal tracking results use the "Fold A" configuration (c.f. Section 5.2).

5.4 Joint goal tracking summary

The overall process used to train the joint goal tracker is summarized in Appendix B. For joint goal tracking, web-style ranking and multiple SLUs both yield improvements in accuracy on the development and test sets, with the improvement associated with multiple SLUs being larger. We also observe that ranking produces relatively poor L2 results. This can be attributed to its training objective, which explicitly maximizes 1-best accuracy without regard to the distribution of the scores. This is in contrast to maxent models which explicitly minimize the L2 loss. We examined the distribution of scores, and qualitatively the ranker is usually placing less mass on its top guess than maxent, and spreading more mass out among other (usually wrong) entries. We return to this in the future work section.

6 Fixed-size state components

DSTC2 consists of three tracking tasks: in addition to the user's goal, the user's search method and which slots they requested to hear were also tracked. These other two tasks were comparatively simpler because their domains are of a small, fixed size. Thus classical machine learning methods can be applied – i.e., ranking is not directly applicable to tracking the method and required slots. However, applying multiple SLU engines is still applicable.

The search **method** specifies how the user wants to search. There are 5 values: *by-constraints* such as area=west,food=italian, *by-name* such as "royal spice", *by-alternatives* as in "do you have any others like that?", *finished* when the user is done as in "thanks goodbye", and *none* when the method can't be determined. At each turn, exactly one of the 5 methods is active, so we view the method component as a standard multinomial classification task. For features, we use the score for each method output by each of the 4 rule-based baselines, and whether each of the methods is available according to the SLU results observed so far. We also take conjunctions for each method with: whether each system dialog act is present in the current turn, or has ever been used, and what slots they mentioned; and whether each slot has appeared in the SLU results from this turn, or any turn. In total there are 640 features for the method classifier (when using one SLU engine).

The **requested slots** are the pieces of information the user wants to hear in that turn. The user can request to hear a restaurant's area, food-type, name, price-range, address, phone number, postcode, and/or signature dish. The user can ask to hear any combination of slots in a turn – e.g., "tell me their address and phone number". Therefore we view each requested slot as a binary classification task, and estimate 8 binary classifiers, one for each requestable slot. Each requested slot takes as features: whether the slot could logically be requested at this turn in the dialog; whether the SLU output contained a "request" act and which slot was requested; the score output by each of the 4 rule-based baselines; whether each system dialog act is present in the current turn, or has ever been used, and what slots they mentioned; and whether each slot has appeared in the SLU results from this turn, or any turn. For each requestable slot's binary classifier, this results in 187 features (with one SLU engine).

For each of these tasks, we applied a maxent

					Joint goal				Search method				Requested slot			
				Model	Dev. set		Test set		Dev. set		Test set		Dev. set		Test set	
Row	SLU	Fold	Model	comb.	Acc.	L2	Acc.	L2	Acc.	L2	Acc.	L2	Acc.	L2	Acc.	L2
1	0	—	rules	N	0.623	0.601	0.719	**0.464**	0.860	0.217	0.897	0.158	0.903	0.155	0.884	0.196
2	0	all	maxent	N	0.649	**0.532**	0.692	0.480	0.890	0.177	0.909	0.143	0.952	0.078	0.967	0.054
3	0	all	*	N	0.666	0.739	0.739	0.721	—	—	—	—	—	—	—	—
4	0+1	A	*	N	0.686	0.770	0.757	0.766	0.912	0.144	0.936	0.104	0.960	0.062	0.976	0.039
5	0+1	AB	*	N	0.697	0.749	0.769	0.748	0.913	0.135	0.938	0.097	0.962	0.060	0.978	0.037
6	0+1	AB	**	Y	0.699	0.766	0.770	0.766	**0.916**	0.135	0.943	0.091	0.964	0.059	0.978	0.036
7	0+2	A	*	N	0.697	0.731	0.765	0.727	0.910	0.146	0.939	0.099	0.966	0.058	0.979	0.037
8	0+2	AB	*	N	**0.711**	0.725	0.778	0.721	0.913	0.133	0.943	0.092	**0.967**	0.058	**0.980**	**0.033**
9	0+2	AB	**	Y	0.710	0.742	**0.781**	0.739	0.915	**0.132**	**0.948**	**0.085**	**0.967**	**0.057**	**0.980**	**0.033**

Table 2: Summary of accuracy and L2 for the three tracking tasks, trained on the "train" set. In rows marked (*), joint goal accuracy used ranking, and the other two tasks used maxent. In rows marked (**), several model classes/parameter settings were used and combined with score averaging.

model; results for this and the best rule-based baseline are in the rows 1 and 2 of Table 2. We tried applying decision trees, but this did not improve performance (not shown) as it did for goal tracking. Note that in the goal tracking task, one weight is learned for each *feature* for any class (goal), whereas in standard multiclass and binary classification, one weight is learned for each *feature,class* pair.[3] Perhaps decision trees were not effective in increasing accuracy for method and requested slots because, compared to joint goal tracking, some conjunctions are implicitly included in linear models.

We then added a second SLU engine in the same manner as for goal tracking. This increased the number of features for the method task from 640 to 840, and from 187 to 217 for each binary requested slot classifier. Results are shown in Table 2; rows 4 and 7 show results with one fold, and rows 5 and 8 show results with both folds. Finally, we considered alternate model forms for each classifier, and then combined them with score averaging. For the method task, we used a second maximum entropy model with different regularization weights, and a multi-class decision tree. For the requested slot binary classifiers, we added a neural network classifier. As above, score averaging across different model classes can yield small gains (rows 6 and 9).

Overall, as with goal tracking, adding a second SLU engine resulted in a substantial increase in accuracy. Unlike goal tracking which used a ranker, the standard classification models used here are explicitly optimized for L2 performance and as a result achieved very good L2 performance.

[3]Plus a constant term per class.

7 Blind evaluation results

When preparing final entries for the DSTC2 blind evaluation, we not longer needed a separate development set, so our final models are trained on the combined training and development sets. In the DSTC2 results, we are team2. Our entry 0 and 1 use the process described above, including score averaging across multiple models. Entry0 used SLU0+1, and entry1 used SLU0+2. Entry3 used a maxent model on SLU0+2, but without model averaging since its parameters are set with cross-validation.[4]

Results are summarized in Table 3. For accuracy for the joint goal and method tasks, our entries had highest accuracy. After the evaluation, we learned that we were the only team to use features from the word confusion network (WCN). Comparing our entry0, which does not use WCN features, to the other teams shows that, given the same input data, our entries were still best for the joint goal and method tasks.

The blind evaluation results give a final opportunity to compare the maxent model with the ranking model: entry1 and entry3 both use SLU0+2, and score an identical set of dialog states using identical features. Joint goal accuracy is better for the ranking model. However, as noted above, L2 performance for the ranking model was substantially worse than for the maxent model.

After the blind evaluation, we realized that we had inadvertently omitted a key feature from the "requested" binary classifiers — whether the "request" dialog act appeared in the SLU results.

[4]The other entries team2.entry2 and team2.entry4 are not described in this paper. In brief, entry2 was based on a recurrent neural network, and entry4 was a combination of entries 1, 2, and 3.

model	Goal		Method		Requested		Requested*	
	Acc.	L2	Acc.	L2	Acc.	L2	Acc.	L2
Best baseline	0.719	0.464	0.897	0.158	0.884	0.196	0.884	0.196
Best DSTC2 result from another team	0.768	**0.346**	0.940	0.095	**0.978**	**0.035**	0.978	0.035
SLU0+1, AB, model comb. (entry0)	0.775	0.758	0.944	0.092	0.954	0.073	0.977	0.037
SLU0+2, AB, model comb. (entry1)	**0.784**	0.735	**0.947**	**0.087**	0.957	0.068	**0.980**	**0.034**
SLU0+2, AB, maxent (entry3)	0.771	0.354	**0.947**	0.093	0.941	0.090	0.979	0.040

Table 3: Final DSTC2 evaluation results, training on the combined "train" and "development" sets. In the results, we are team2. "Model comb." indicates score averaging over several model instances. For the "requested" task, our entry in DSTC2 inadvertently omitted a key feature, which decreased performance significantly. "Requested*" columns indicate results with this feature included. They were computed after the blind evaluation and are not part of the official DSTC2 results.

Therefore table 3 shows results with and without this feature. With the inclusion of this feature, the requested classifiers also achieved best accuracy and L2 scores, although we note that this is not part of the official DSTC2 results. (The results in the preceding sections of this paper included this feature.)

8 Conclusion

This paper has introduced two new methods for dialog state tracking. First, we have shown how to apply web-style ranking for scoring dialog state hypotheses. Ranking is attractive because it can construct a forest of decision trees which compute feature conjunctions, and because it optimizes directly for 1-best accuracy. Second, we have introduced the usage of multiple SLU engines. Using additional SLU engines is attractive because it both adds more possible dialog states to score (increasing recall), and adds features which help to discriminate the best states (increasing precision).

In experiments, using multiple SLU engines improved performance on all three of the tasks in the second dialog state tracking challenge. Maximum entropy models scored best in the previous dialog state tracking challenge; here we showed that web-style ranking improved accuracy over maxent when using either a single or multiple SLU engines. Thus, the two methods introduced here are additive: they each yield gains separately, and further gains in combination.

Comparing to other systems in the DSTC2 evaluation, these two techniques yielded highest accuracy in DSTC2 for 2 of 3 tasks. If we include a feature accidentally omitted from the third task, our methods yield highest accuracy for all three tasks. This experience highlights the importance of the manual task of extracting a set of informative features. Also, ranking improved accuracy, but yielded poor probability quality. For ranking, the L2 performance of ranking was among the worst in DSTC2. By contrast, for the method task, where standard classification could be applied, our entry yielded best L2 performance. The relative importance of L2 vs. accuracy in dialog state tracking is an open question.

In future work, we plan to investigate how to improve the L2 performance of ranking. One approach is to train a maxent model on the output of the ranker. On the test set, this yields an improvement in L2 score from 0.735 to 0.587, and simply clamping ranker's best guess to 1.0 and all others to 0.0 improves L2 to 0.431. This is a start, but not competitive with the best result in DSTC2 of 0.346. Also, techniques which avoid the extraction of manual features altogether would be ideal, particularly in light of experiences here.

Even so, for the difficult and general task of user goal tracking, the techniques here yielded a relative error rate reduction of 23% over the best baseline, and exceeded the accuracy of any other tracker in the second dialog state tracking challenge.

Acknowledgements

Thanks to Dan Bohus for making his maxent software available, to Andrzej Pastusiak for helpful guidance with lambdaMART, and to Geoff Zweig for several helpful conversations.

References

Dan Bohus and Alex Rudnicky. 2006. A 'K hypotheses + other' belief updating model. In *Proc American Association for Artificial Intelligence (AAAI) Workshop on Statistical and Empirical Approaches for Spoken Dialogue Systems, Boston*.

Christopher J.C. Burges. 2010. From ranknet to lambdarank to lambdamart: An overview. Technical Report MSR-TR-2010-82, Microsoft Research.

Olivier Chapelle and Yi Chang. 2011. Yahoo! learning to rank challenge. *JMLR Workshop and Conference Proceedings*, 14:1–24.

Matthew Henderson, Milica Gasic, Blaise Thomson, Pirros Tsiakoulis, Kai Yu, and Steve Young. 2012. Discriminative spoken language understanding using word confusion networks. In *Proc IEEE Workshop on Spoken Language Technologies (SLT), Miami, Florida, USA*.

Matthew Henderson, Blaise Thomson, and Jason D. Williams. 2013a. Handbook for the dialog state tracking challenge 2 & 3. Technical report, Cambridge University.

Matthew Henderson, Blaise Thomson, and Steve Young. 2013b. Deep neural network approach for the dialog state tracking challenge. In *Proceedings of the SIGDIAL 2013 Conference*, pages 467–471, Metz, France, August. Association for Computational Linguistics.

Matthew Henderson, Blaise Thomson, and Jason Williams. 2014. The second dialog state tracking challenge. In *Proceedings of the SIGdial 2014 Conference*, Baltimore, U.S.A., June.

Eric Horvitz and Tim Paek. 1999. A computational architecture for conversation. In *Proc 7th International Conference on User Modeling (UM), Banff, Canada*, pages 201–210.

Sungjin Lee and Maxine Eskenazi. 2013. Recipe for building robust spoken dialog state trackers: Dialog state tracking challenge system description. In *Proceedings of the SIGDIAL 2013 Conference*, pages 414–422, Metz, France, August. Association for Computational Linguistics.

Sungjin Lee. 2013. Structured discriminative model for dialog state tracking. In *Proceedings of the SIGDIAL 2013 Conference*, pages 442–451, Metz, France, August. Association for Computational Linguistics.

Angeliki Metallinou, Dan Bohus, and Jason D. Williams. 2013. Discriminative state tracking for spoken dialog systems. In *Proc Association for Computational Linguistics, Sofia*.

Blaise Thomson and Steve Young. 2010. Bayesian update of dialogue state: A POMDP framework for spoken dialogue systems. *Computer Speech and Language*, 24(4):562–588.

B Thomson, K Yu, M Gasic, S Keizer, F Mairesse, J Schatzmann, and S Young. 2008. Evaluating semantic-level confidence scores with multiple hypotheses. In *Proc Intl Conf on Spoken Language Processing (ICSLP), Brisbane, Australia*.

Zhuoran Wang and Oliver Lemon. 2013. A simple and generic belief tracking mechanism for the dialog state tracking challenge: On the believability of observed information. In *Proceedings of the SIGDIAL 2013 Conference*, pages 423–432, Metz, France, August. Association for Computational Linguistics.

Jason D Williams and Steve Young. 2007. Partially observable Markov decision processes for spoken dialog systems. *Computer Speech and Language*, 21(2):393–422.

Jason D. Williams, Antoine Raux, Deepak Ramachandran, and Alan Black. 2013. The dialog state tracking challenge. In *Proc SIGdial Workshop on Discourse and Dialogue, Metz, France*.

Jason D. Williams. 2012. Challenges and opportunities for state tracking in statistical spoken dialog systems: Results from two public deployments. *IEEE Journal of Selected Topics in Signal Processing, Special Issue on Advances in Spoken Dialogue Systems and Mobile Interface*, 6(8):959–970.

Qiang Wu, Christopher J. C. Burges, Krysta M. Svore, and Jianfeng Gao. 2010. Adapting boosting for information retrieval measures. *Journal of Information Retrieval*, 13(3):254–270.

Steve Young, Milica Gašić, Simon Keizer, François Mairesse, Jost Schatzmann, Blaise Thomson, and Kai Yu. 2009. The hidden information state model: a practical framework for POMDP-based spoken dialogue management. *Computer Speech and Language*, 24(2):150–174.

Lukas Zilka, David Marek, Matej Korvas, and Filip Jurcicek. 2013. Comparison of bayesian discriminative and generative models for dialogue state tracking. In *Proceedings of the SIGDIAL 2013 Conference*, pages 452–456, Metz, France, August. Association for Computational Linguistics.

Appendix A: Example decision tree

Figure 1 shows an example decision tree generated by lambdaMART. Note how the tree is able to combine features across different slots – for example, following the right-most path tests the scores of 3 different slots. Also, note how generally more positive evidence leads to higher scores.

Appendix B: Schematic of approach

Figure 2 shows a schematic diagram of our overall approach for training the state tracker (team2.entry0).

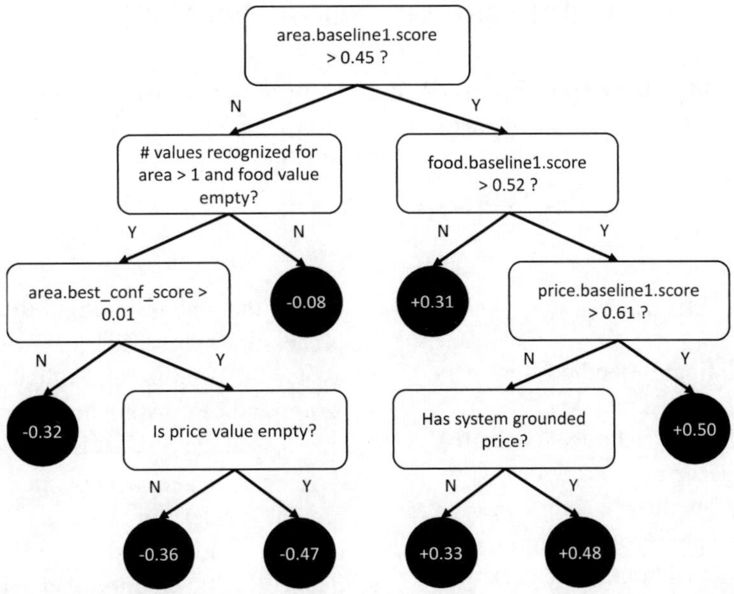

Figure 1: Appendix A: Example decision tree with 8 leaves generated by lambdaMART. Each non-terminal node contains a binary test; each terminal node contains a real value that linearly contributes to the score of the dialog state being evaluated. "baseline1" refers to the output of one of the rule-based baseline trackers, used in this classifier as an input feature.

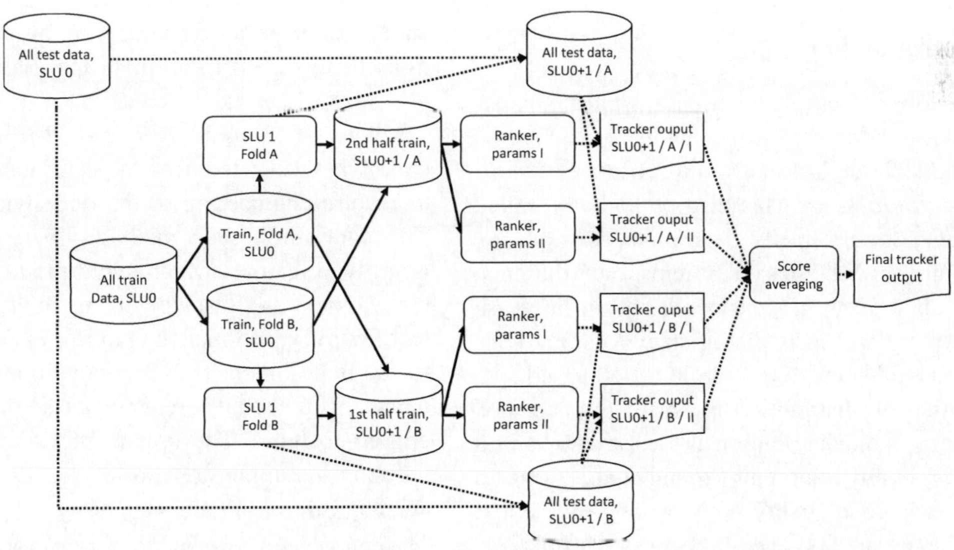

Figure 2: Appendix B: Schematic diagram of our overall approach for training the state tracker, using SLU1 (team2.entry0). Cylinders represent data, rectangles are models, and scripts are tracker output. Solid arrows are steps done at training time, and dotted arrows are steps done at test time. Approach for SLU2 (team2.entry1) is identical except that additional features are used in training the SLU models.

Word-Based Dialog State Tracking with Recurrent Neural Networks

Matthew Henderson, Blaise Thomson and Steve Young
Department of Engineering,
University of Cambridge, U.K.
{mh521, brmt2, sjy}@eng.cam.ac.uk

Abstract

Recently discriminative methods for tracking the state of a spoken dialog have been shown to outperform traditional generative models. This paper presents a new word-based tracking method which maps directly from the speech recognition results to the dialog state without using an explicit semantic decoder. The method is based on a recurrent neural network structure which is capable of generalising to unseen dialog state hypotheses, and which requires very little feature engineering. The method is evaluated on the second Dialog State Tracking Challenge (DSTC2) corpus and the results demonstrate consistently high performance across all of the metrics.

1 Introduction

While communicating with a user, statistical spoken dialog systems must maintain a distribution over possible dialog states in a process called *dialog state tracking*. This distribution, also called the *belief state*, directly determines the system's decisions. In MDP-based systems, only the most likely dialog state is considered and in this case the primary metric is dialog state accuracy (Bohus and Rudnicky, 2006). In POMDP-based systems, the full distribution is considered and then the shape of the distribution as measured by an L2 norm is equally important (Young et al., 2009). In both cases, good quality state tracking is essential to maintaining good overall system performance.

Typically, state tracking has assumed the output of a Spoken Language Understanding (SLU) component in the form of a semantic decoder, which maps the hypotheses from Automatic Speech Recognition (ASR) to a list of semantic hypotheses. This paper considers mapping directly from ASR hypotheses to an updated belief state at each turn in the dialog, omitting the intermediate SLU processing step. This *word-based* state tracking avoids the need for an explicit semantic representation and also avoids the possibility of information loss at the SLU stage.

Recurrent neural networks (RNNs) provide a natural model for state tracking in dialog, as they are able to model and classify dynamic sequences with complex behaviours from step to step. Whereas, most previous approaches to discriminative state tracking have adapted stationary classifiers to the temporal process of dialog (Bohus and Rudnicky, 2006; Lee and Eskenazi, 2013; Lee, 2013; Williams, 2013; Henderson et al., 2013b). One notable exception is Ren et al. (2013), which used conditional random fields to model the sequence temporally.

Currently proposed methods of discriminative state tracking require engineering of feature functions to represent the turn in the dialog (Ren et al., 2013; Lee and Eskenazi, 2013; Lee, 2013; Williams, 2013; Henderson et al., 2013b). It is unclear whether differences in performance are due to feature engineering or the underlying models. This paper proposes a method of using simple n-gram type features which avoid the need for feature engineering. Instead of using inputs with a select few very informative features, the approach is to use high-dimensional inputs with all the information to potentially reconstruct any such handcrafted feature. The impact of significantly increasing the dimensionality of the inputs is managed by careful initialisation of model parameters.

Accuracy on unseen or infrequent slot values is an important concern, particularly for discriminative classifiers which are prone to overfitting training data. This is addressed by structuring the recurrent neural network to include a component which is independent of the actual slot value in question. It thus learns general behaviours for specifying slots enabling it to successfully decode

ASR output which includes previously unseen slot values.

In summary, this paper presents a word-based approach to dialog state tracking using recurrent neural networks. The model is capable of generalising to unseen dialog state hypotheses, and requires very little feature engineering. The approach is evaluated in the second Dialog State Tracking Challenge (DSTC2) (Henderson et al., 2014) where it is shown to be extremely competitive, particularly in terms of the quality of its confidence scores.

Following a brief outline of DSTC2 in section 2, the definition of the model is given in section 3. Section 4 then gives details on the initialisation methods used for training. Finally results on the DSTC2 evaluation are given in 5.

2 The Second Dialog State Tracking Challenge

This section describes the domain and methodology of the second Dialog State Tracking Challenge (DSTC2). The challenge is based on a large corpus collected using a variety of telephone-based dialog systems in the domain of finding a restaurant in Cambridge. In all cases, the subjects were recruited using Amazon Mechanical Turk.

The data is split into a train, dev and test set. The train and dev sets were supplied with labels, and the test set was released unlabelled for a one week period. At the end of the week, all participants were required to submit their trackers' output on the test set, and the labels were revealed. A mis-match was ensured between training and testing conditions by choosing dialogs for the evaluation collected using a separate dialog manager. This emulates the mis-match a new tracker would encounter if it were actually deployed in an end-to-end system.

In summary, the datasets used are:

- **dstc2_train** - Labelled training consisting of 1612 dialogs with two dialog managers and two acoustic conditions.
- **dstc2_dev** - Labelled dataset consisting of 506 calls in the same conditions as dstc2_train, but with no caller in common.
- **dstc2_test** - Evaluation dataset consisting of 1117 dialogs collected using a dialog manager not seen in the labelled data.

In contrast with DSTC1, DSTC2 introduces dynamic user goals, tracking of requested slots and tracking the restaurant search method. A DSTC2 tracker must therefore report:

- **Goals**: A distribution over the user's goal for each slot. This is a distribution over the possible values for that slot, plus the special value *None*, which means no valid value has been mentioned yet.
- **Requested slots**: A reported probability for each requestable slot that has been requested by the user, and should be informed by the system.
- **Method**: A distribution over methods, which encodes how the user is trying to use the dialog system. E.g. 'by constraints', when the user is trying to constrain the search, and 'finished', when the user wants to end the dialog.

A tracker may report the goals as a joint over all slots, but in this paper the joint is reported as a product of the marginal distributions per slot.

Full details of the challenge are given in Henderson et al. (2013a), Henderson et al. (2014). The trackers presented in this paper are identified under 'team4' in the reported results.

3 Recurrent Neural Network Model

This section defines the RNN structure used for dialog state tracking. One such RNN is used per slot, taking the most recent dialog turn (user input plus last machine dialog act) as input, updating its internal memory and calculating an updated belief over the values for the slot. In what follows, the notation $\mathbf{a} \oplus \mathbf{b}$ is used to denote the concatenation of two vectors, $\mathbf{a}$ and $\mathbf{b}$. The ith component of the vector $\mathbf{a}$ is written $\mathbf{a}|_i$.

3.1 Feature Representation

Extracting n-grams from utterances and dialog acts provides the feature representations needed for input into the RNN. This process is very similar to the feature extraction described in Henderson et al. (2012), and is outlined in figure 1.

For n-gram features extracted from the ASR N-best list, unigram, bigram and trigram features are calculated for each hypothesis. These are then weighted by the N-best list probabilities and summed to give a single vector.

Dialog acts in this domain consist of a list of component acts of the form `acttype(slot=value)` where the `slot=value` pair is optional. The n-gram type features extracted from each such component act are 'acttype', 'slot', 'value', 'acttype slot', 'slot value' and 'acttype slot value', or just 'acttype' for the act acttype(). Each feature is given weight 1, and the features from individual component acts are summed.

To provide a contrast, trackers have also been implemented using the user dialog acts output by an SLU rather than directly from the ASR output. In this case, the SLU N-best dialog act list is encoded in the same way except that the n-grams from each hypothesis are weighted by the corresponding probabilities, and summed to give a single feature vector.

Consider a word-based tracker which takes an ASR N-best list and the last machine act as input for each turn, as shown in figure 1. A combined feature representation of both the ASR N-best list and the last machine act is obtained by concatenating the vectors. This means that in figure 1 the food feature from the ASR and the food feature from the machine act contribute to separate components of the final vector $\mathbf{f}$.

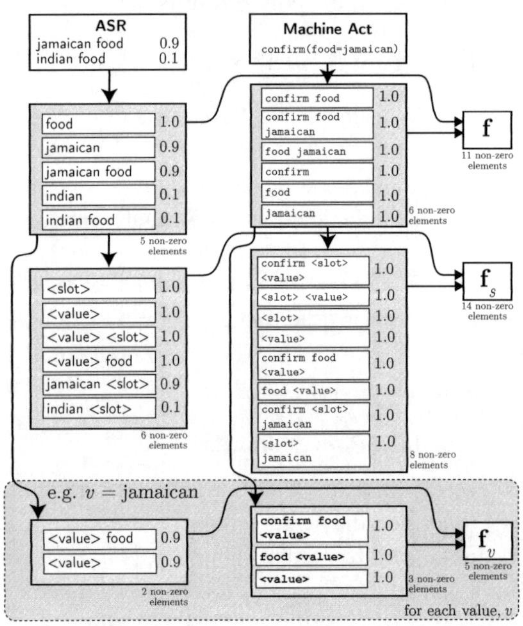

Figure 1: Example of feature extraction for one turn, giving $\mathbf{f}$, $\mathbf{f}_s$ and $\mathbf{f}_v$. Here s = food. For all $v \notin$ {indian, jamaican}, $\mathbf{f}_v = \mathbf{0}$.

Note that all the methods for tracking reported in DSTC1 required designing feature functions. For example, suggested feature functions included the SLU score in the current turn, the probability of an 'affirm' act when the value has been confirmed by the system, the output from baseline trackers etc. (e.g. Lee and Eskenazi (2013), Williams (2013), Henderson et al. (2013b)). In contrast, the approach described here is to present the model with all the information it would need to reconstruct any feature function that might be useful.

3.2 Generalisation to Unseen States

One key issue in applying machine learning to the task of dialog state tracking is being able to deal with states which have not been seen in training. For example, the system should be able to recognise any obscure food type which appears in the set of possible food types. A naïve neural network structure mapping n-gram features to an updated distribution for the food slot, with no tying of weights, would require separate examples of each of the food types to learn what n-grams are associated with each. In reality however n-grams like '<value> food' and 'serving <value>' are likely to correspond to the hypothesis food='<value>' for any food-type replacing '<value>'.

The approach taken here is to embed a network which learns a generic model of the updated belief of a slot-value assignment as a function of 'tagged' features, i.e. features which ignore the specific identity of a value. This can be considered as replacing all occurrences of a particular value with a tag like '<value>'. Figure 1 shows the process of creating the tagged feature vectors, $\mathbf{f}_s$ and $\mathbf{f}_v$ from the untagged vector $\mathbf{f}$.

3.3 Model Definition

In this section an RNN is described for tracking the goal for a given slot, s, throughout the sequence of a dialog. The RNN holds an internal memory, $\mathbf{m} \in \mathbb{R}^{N_{\text{mem}}}$ which is updated at each step. If there are N possible values for slot s, then the probability distribution output $\mathbf{p}$ is in $\mathbb{R}^{N+1}$, with the last component $\mathbf{p}|_N$ giving the probability of the *None* hypothesis. Figure 2 provides an overview of how $\mathbf{p}$ and $\mathbf{m}$ are updated in one turn to give the new belief and memory, $\mathbf{p}'$ and $\mathbf{m}'$.

One part of the neural network is used to learn a mapping from the untagged inputs, full memory and previous beliefs to a vector $\mathbf{h} \in \mathbb{R}^N$ which goes directly into the calculation of $\mathbf{p}'$:

$$\mathbf{h} = \text{NNet}\left(\mathbf{f} \oplus \mathbf{p} \oplus \mathbf{m}\right) \in \mathbb{R}^N$$

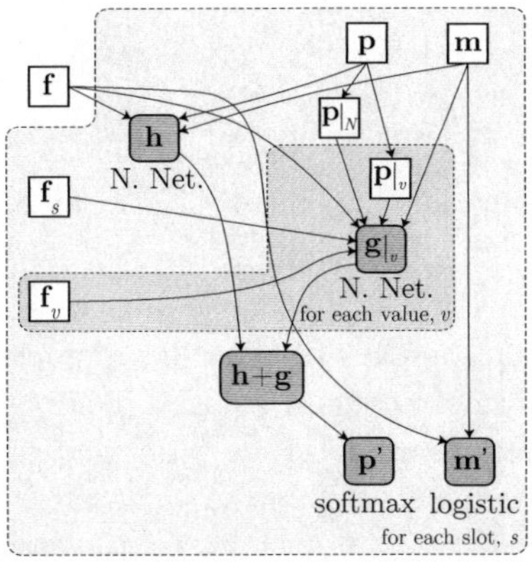

Figure 2: Calculation of $\mathbf{p}'$ and $\mathbf{m}'$ for one turn

where NNet(·) denotes a neural network function of the input. In this paper all such networks have one hidden layer with a sigmoidal activation function.

The sub-network for $\mathbf{h}$ requires examples of every value in training, and is prone to poor generalisation as explained in section 3.2. By including a second sub-network for $\mathbf{g}$ which takes tagged features as input, it is possible to exploit the observation that the string corresponding to a value in various contexts is likely to be good evidence for or against that value. For each value v, a component of $\mathbf{g}$ is calculated using the neural network:

$$\mathbf{g}|_v = \text{NNet}\begin{pmatrix} \mathbf{f} \oplus \mathbf{f}_s \oplus \mathbf{f}_v \oplus \\ \{\mathbf{p}|_v, \mathbf{p}|_N\} \oplus \mathbf{m} \end{pmatrix} \in \mathbb{R}$$

By using regularisation, the learning will prefer where possible to use the sub-network for $\mathbf{g}$ rather than learning the individual weights for each value required in the sub-network for $\mathbf{h}$. This sub-network is able to deal with unseen or infrequently seen dialog states, so long as the state can be tagged in the feature extraction. This model can also be shared across slots since $\mathbf{f}_s$ is included as an input, see section 4.2.

The sub-networks applied to tagged and untagged inputs are combined to give the new belief:

$$\mathbf{p}' = \text{softmax}\left([\mathbf{h} + \mathbf{g}] \oplus \{B\}\right) \in \mathbb{R}^{N+1}$$

where B is a parameter of the RNN, contributing to the *None* hypothesis. The contribution from $\mathbf{g}$ may be seen as accounting for general behaviour of tagged hypotheses, while $\mathbf{h}$ makes corrections due to correlations with untagged features and value specific behaviour e.g. special ways of expressing specific goals and fitting to specific ASR confusions.

Finally, the memory is updated according to the logistic regression:

$$\mathbf{m}' = \sigma\left(W_{m_0}\mathbf{f} + W_{m_1}\mathbf{m}\right) \in \mathbb{R}^{N_{\text{mem}}}$$

where the W_{m_i} are parameters of the RNN.

3.4 Requested Slots and Method

A similar RNN is used to track the requested slots. Here the v runs over all the requestable slots, and requestable slot names are tagged in the feature vectors $\mathbf{f}_v$. This allows the neural network calculating $\mathbf{g}$ to learn general patterns across slots just as in the case of goals. The equation for $\mathbf{p}'$ is changed to:

$$\mathbf{p}' = \sigma\left(\mathbf{h} + \mathbf{g}\right)$$

so each component of $\mathbf{p}'$ represents the probability (between 0 and 1) of a slot being requested.

For method classification, the same RNN structure as for a goal is used. No tagging of the feature vectors is used in the case of methods.

4 Training

The RNNs are trained using Stochastic Gradient Descent (SGD), maximizing the log probability of the sequences of observed beliefs in the training data (Bottou, 1991). Gradient clipping is used to avoid the problem of exploding gradients (Pascanu et al., 2012). A regularisation term is included, which penalises the $l2$ norm of all the parameters. It is found empirically to be beneficial to give more weight in the regularisation to the parameters used in the network calculating $\mathbf{h}$.

When using the ASR N-best list, $\mathbf{f}$ is typically of dimensionality around 3500. With so many weights to learn, it is important to initialise the parameters well before starting the SGD algorithm. Two initialisation techniques have been investigated, the denoising autoencoder and shared initialisation. These were evaluated by training trackers on the dstc2_train set, and evaluating on dstc2_dev (see table 1).

4.1 Denoising Autoencoder

The denoising autoencoder (dA), which provides an unsupervised method for learning meaningful

		Joint Goals		Method		Requested	
Shared init.	dA init.	Acc	L2	Acc	L2	Acc	L2
		0.686	0.477	0.913	0.147	0.963	0.059
	✓	0.688	0.466	0.915	0.144	0.962	0.059
✓		0.680	0.479	0.910	0.152	0.962	0.059
✓	✓	**0.696**	**0.463**	**0.915**	**0.144**	**0.965**	**0.057**
	Baseline:	0.612	0.632	0.830	0.266	0.894	0.174

Table 1: Performance on the dev set when varying initialisation techniques for word-based tracking. Acc denotes the accuracy of the most likely belief at each turn, and L2 denotes the squared $l2$ norm between the estimated belief distribution and correct (delta) distribution. For each row, 5 trackers are trained and then combined using score averaging. The final row shows the results for the *focus*-based baseline tracker (Henderson et al., 2014).

underlying representations of the input, has been found effective as an initialisation technique in deep learning (Vincent et al., 2008).

A dA is used to initialise the parameters of the RNN which multiply the high-dimensional input vector $\mathbf{f}$. The dA learns a matrix W_{dA} which reduces $\mathbf{f}$ to a lower dimensional vector such that the original vector may be recovered with minimal loss in the presence of noise.

For learning the dA, $\mathbf{f}$ is first mapped such that feature values lie between 0 and 1. The dA takes as input $\mathbf{f}_{\mathrm{noisy}}$, a noisy copy of $\mathbf{f}$ where each component is set to 0 with probability p. This is mapped to a lower dimensional hidden representation $\mathbf{h}$:

$$\mathbf{h} = \sigma\left(W_{\mathrm{dA}}\mathbf{f}_{\mathrm{noisy}} + b_0\right)$$

A reconstructed vector, $\mathbf{f}_{\mathrm{rec}}$, is then calculated as:

$$\mathbf{f}_{\mathrm{rec}} = \sigma\left(W_{\mathrm{dA}}^{\mathrm{T}}\mathbf{h} + b_1\right)$$

The cross-entropy between $\mathbf{f}$ and $\mathbf{f}_{\mathrm{rec}}$ is used as the objective function in gradient descent, with an added $l1$ regularisation term to ensure the learning of sparse weights. As the ASR features are likely to be very noisy, dense weights would be prone to overfitting the examples. [1]

When using W_{dA} to initialise weights in the RNN, training is observed to converge faster. Table 1 shows that dA initialisation leads to better solutions, particularly for tracking the goals.

4.2 Shared Initialisation

It is possible to train a slot-independent RNN, using training data from all slots, by not including $\mathbf{h}$ in the model (the dimensionality of $\mathbf{h}$ is dependent on the slot). In *shared initialisation*, such an RNN is trained for a few epochs, then the learnt parameters are used to initialise slot-dependent RNNs for each slot. This follows the shared initialisation procedure presented in Henderson et al. (2013b).

Table 1 suggests that shared initialisation when combined with dA initialisation gives the best performance.

4.3 Model Combination

In DSTC1, the most competitive results were achieved with model combination whereby the output of multiple trackers were combined to give more accurate classifications (Lee and Eskenazi, 2013). The technique for model combination used here is score averaging, where the final score for each component of the dialog state is computed as the mean of the scores output by all the trackers being combined. This is one of the simplest methods for model combination, and requires no extra training data. It is guaranteed to improve the accuracy if the outputs from the individual trackers are not correlated, and the individual trackers operate at an accuracy > 0.5.

Multiple runs of training the RNNs were found to give results with high variability and model combination provides a method to exploit this variability. In order to demonstrate the effect, 10 trackers with varying regularisation parameters were trained on dstc2_train and used to track dstc2_dev. Figure 3 shows the effects of combining these trackers in larger groups. The mean accuracy in the joint goals from combining m trackers is found to increase with m. The single output from combining all 10 trackers outperforms any single tracker in the group.

The approach taken for the DSTC2 challenge was therefore to train multiple trackers with vary-

[1] The state-of-the-art in dialog act classification with very similar data also uses sparse weights Chen et al. (2013).

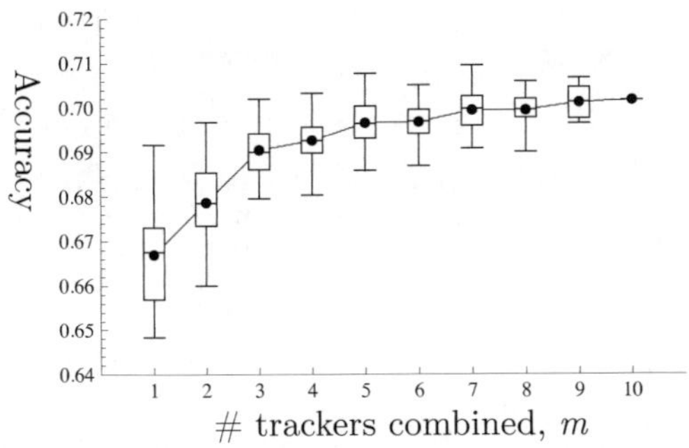

Figure 3: Joint goal accuracy on dstc2_dev from system combination. Ten total trackers are trained with varying regularisation parameters. For each $m = 1 \ldots 10$, all subsets of size m of the 10 trackers are used to generate ${}^{10}C_m$ combined results, which are plotted as a boxplot. Boxplots show minimum, maximum, the interquartile range and the median. The mean values are plotted as connected points.

ing model hyper-parameters (e.g. regularisation parameters, memory size) and combine their output using score averaging. Note that maintaining around 10 RNNs for each dialog state components is entirely feasible for a realtime system, as the RNN operations are quick to compute. An unoptimised Python implementation of the tracker including an RNN for each dialog state component is able to do state tracking at a rate of around 50 turns per second on an Intel® Core™ i7-970 3.2GHz processor.

5 Results

The strict blind evaluation procedure defined for the DSTC2 challenge was used to investigate the effect on performance of two contrasts. The first contrast compares word-based tracking and conventional tracking based on SLU output. The second contrast investigates the effect of including and omitting the sub-network for $\mathbf{h}$ in the RNN. Recall $\mathbf{h}$ is the part of the model that allows learning special behaviours for particular dialog state hypotheses, and correlations with untagged features. These two binary contrasts resulted in a total of 4 system variants being entered in the challenge.

Each system is the score-averaged combined output of 12 trackers trained with varying hyper-parameters (see section 4.3). The performance of the 4 entries on the featured metrics of the challenge are shown in table 2.

It should be noted that the live SLU used the word confusion network, not made available in the challenge. The word confusion network is known to provide stronger features than the N-best list for language understanding (Henderson et al., 2012; Tür et al., 2013), so the word-based trackers using N-best ASR features were at a disadvantage in that regard. Nevertheless, despite this handicap, the best results were obtained from word-based tracking directly on the ASR output, rather than using the confusion network generated SLU output. Including $\mathbf{h}$ always helps, though this is far more pronounced for the word-based trackers. Note that trackers which do not include $\mathbf{h}$ are value-independent and so are capable of handling new values at runtime.

The RNN trackers performed very competitively in the context of the challenge. Figure 4 visualises the performance of the four trackers relative to all the entries submitted to the challenge for the featured metrics. For full details of the evaluation metrics see Henderson et al. (2014). The box in this figure gives the entry IDs under which the results are reported in the DSTC (under the team ID '**team4**'). The word-based tracker including $\mathbf{h}$ ($\mathbf{h}$-ASR), was top for joint goals L2 as well as requested slots accuracy and L2. It was close to the top for the other featured metrics, following closely entries from team 2. The RNN trackers performed particularly well on measures assessing the quality of the scores such as L2.

There are hundreds of numbers reported in the DSTC2 evaluation, and it was found that the $\mathbf{h}$-ASR tracker ranked top on many of them. Considering L2, accuracy, average probability, equal error rate, log probability and mean reciprocal rank across all components of the the dialog state, these give a total of 318 metrics. The $\mathbf{h}$-ASR tracker ranked top of all trackers in the challenge in 89 of these metrics, more than any other tracker. The ASR tracker omitting $\mathbf{h}$ came second, ranking top in 33 of these metrics.

The trackers using SLU features ranked top in all of the featured metrics among the trackers which used only the SLU output.

6 Conclusions

The RNN framework presented in this paper provides very good performance in terms of both accuracy and the quality of reported probability distributions. Word-based tracking is shown to be one of the most competitive approaches submitted to DSTC2. By mapping straight from the ASR output to a belief update, it avoids any information

		Tracker Inputs		Joint Goals			Method			Requested		
entry	Include **h**	Live ASR	Live SLU	Acc	L2	ROC	Acc	L2	ROC	Acc	L2	ROC
0	✓	✓		**0.768**	**0.346**	0.365	**0.940**	**0.095**	0.452	**0.978**	**0.035**	0.525
1		✓		0.746	0.381	0.383	0.939	0.097	0.423	0.977	0.038	0.490
2	✓		✓	0.742	0.387	0.345	0.922	0.124	0.447	0.957	0.069	0.340
3			✓	0.737	0.406	0.321	0.922	0.125	0.406	0.957	0.073	0.385

Table 2: Featured metrics on the test set for the 4 RNN trackers entered to the challenge.

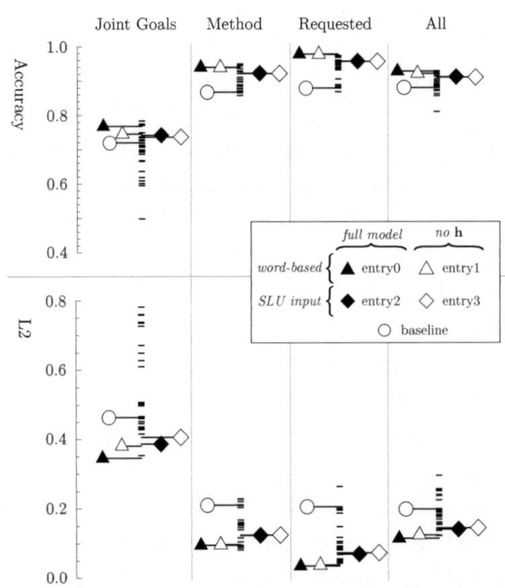

Figure 4: Relative performance of RNN trackers for featured metrics in DSTC2. Each dash is one of the 34 trackers evaluated in the challenge. Note a lower L2 is better. ROC metric is only comparable for systems of similar accuracies, so is not plotted. The *focus* baseline system is shown as a circle.

lost in the omitted SLU step.

In general, the RNN appears to be a promising model, which deals naturally with sequential input and outputs. High dimensional inputs are handled well, with little feature engineering, particularly when carefully initialised (e.g. as here using denoising autoencoders and shared initialisation).

Future work should include making joint predictions on components of the dialog state. In this paper each component was tracked using its own RNN. Though not presented in this paper, no improvement could be found by joining the RNNs. However, this may not be the case for other domains in which slot values are more highly correlated. The concept of tagging the feature functions allows for generalisation to unseen values and slots. This generalisation will be explored in future work, particularly for dialogs in more open-domains.

Acknowledgements

Matthew Henderson is a Google Doctoral Fellow.

References

Dan Bohus and Alex Rudnicky. 2006. A K-hypotheses+ Other Belief Updating Model. *Proc. of the AAAI Workshop on Statistical and Empirical Methods in Spoken Dialogue Systems.*

Léon Bottou. 1991. Stochastic gradient learning in neural networks. In *Proceedings of Neuro-Nîmes 91*, Nîmes, France. EC2.

Yun-Nung Chen, William Yang Wang, and Alexander I Rudnicky. 2013. An empirical investigation of sparse log-linear models for improved dialogue act classification. In *Acoustics, Speech and Signal Processing (ICASSP), 2013 IEEE International Conference on.*

Matthew Henderson, Milica Gašić, Blaise Thomson, Pirros Tsiakoulis, Kai Yu, and Steve Young. 2012. Discriminative Spoken Language Understanding Using Word Confusion Networks. In *Spoken Language Technology Workshop, 2012. IEEE.*

Matthew Henderson, Blaise Thomson, and Jason Williams. 2013a. Dialog State Tracking Challenge 2 & 3 Handbook. camdial.org/~mh521/dstc/.

Matthew Henderson, Blaise Thomson, and Steve Young. 2013b. Deep Neural Network Approach for the Dialog State Tracking Challenge. In *Proceedings of SIGdial*, Metz, France, August.

Matthew Henderson, Blaise Thomson, and Jason Williams. 2014. The second dialog state tracking challenge. In *Proceedings of the SIGdial 2014 Conference*, Baltimore, U.S.A., June.

Sungjin Lee and Maxine Eskenazi. 2013. Recipe for building robust spoken dialog state trackers: Dialog state tracking challenge system description. In *Proceedings of the SIGDIAL 2013 Conference*, Metz, France, August.

Sungjin Lee. 2013. Structured discriminative model for dialog state tracking. In *Proceedings of the SIGDIAL 2013 Conference*, Metz, France, August.

Razvan Pascanu, Tomas Mikolov, and Yoshua Bengio. 2012. Understanding the exploding gradient problem. *CoRR*.

Hang Ren, Weiqun Xu, Yan Zhang, and Yonghong Yan. 2013. Dialog state tracking using conditional random fields. In *Proceedings of the SIGDIAL 2013 Conference*, Metz, France, August.

Gökhan Tür, Anoop Deoras, and Dilek Hakkani-Tür. 2013. Semantic parsing using word confusion networks with conditional random fields. In *INTERSPEECH*.

Pascal Vincent, Hugo Larochelle, Yoshua Bengio, and Pierre-Antoine Manzagol. 2008. Extracting and composing robust features with denoising autoencoders. In *Proceedings of the 25th International Conference on Machine Learning*, Helsinki, Finland.

Jason Williams. 2013. Multi-domain learning and generalization in dialog state tracking. In *Proceedings of the SIGDIAL 2013 Conference*, Metz, France, August.

Steve Young, Milica Gašić, Simon Keizer, François Mairesse, Jost Schatzmann, Blaise Thomson, and Kai Yu. 2009. The Hidden Information State model: A practical framework for POMDP-based spoken dialogue management. *Computer Speech & Language*.

Comparative Error Analysis of Dialog State Tracking

Ronnie W. Smith
Department of Computer Science
East Carolina University
Greenville, North Carolina, 27834
rws@cs.ecu.edu

Abstract

A primary motivation of the Dialog State Tracking Challenge (DSTC) is to allow for direct comparisons between alternative approaches to dialog state tracking. While results from DSTC 1 mention performance limitations, an examination of the errors made by dialog state trackers was not discussed in depth. For the new challenge, DSTC 2, this paper describes several techniques for examining the errors made by the dialog state trackers in order to refine our understanding of the limitations of various approaches to the tracking process. The results indicate that no one approach is universally superior, and that different approaches yield different error type distributions. Furthermore, the results show that a pairwise comparative analysis of tracker performance is a useful tool for identifying dialogs where differential behavior is observed. These dialogs can provide a data source for a more careful analysis of the source of errors.

1 Introduction

The Dialog State Tracking Challenge (Henderson et al., 2013) provides a framework for comparison of different approaches to tracking dialog state within the context of an information-seeking dialog, specifically information about restaurants in the Cambridge, UK, area. The challenge makes available an annotated corpus that includes system logs from actual human-machine dialog interactions. These logs include information about the system dialog acts, the N-best speech recognition hypotheses, and the hypothesized interpretation (including confidence estimates) of the user's spoken utterances as provided by the dialog system's Spoken Language Understanding (SLU) module. Consequently, standalone algorithms for tracking the state of the dialog can be developed and tested. While performance as part of an actual dialog interaction cannot easily be evaluated (because differing results produced by different trackers may lead to different choices for system dialog acts in a real-time interaction), performance on a turn-by-turn basis can be evaluated and compared.

Results from the first challenge were presented in several papers at SIGDial 2013 (general reference Williams et al. (2013)) and highlighted several different approaches. These papers focused on comparative performance as well as a description of the various techniques for tracking dialog state that were employed. However, there was no detailed error analysis about tracker performance, either within or across trackers. Such analysis can help further our understanding of the sources and impact of dialog miscommunication. This paper presents such an analysis from the current Dialog State Tracking Challenge (DSTC 2) using the publicly available results of the challenge (`http://camdial.org/~mh521/dstc/`). This paper describes techniques for examining the following aspects of performance as it relates to tracking errors and their potential impact on effective communication in dialog.

- Estimating an upper bound on accuracy.
- Error distribution as a function of tracker—both globally and subdivided by acoustic model or attribute type.
- Pairwise comparative accuracy of trackers—for what types of dialogs does one tracker perform better than another?

Initial results based on application of these techniques are also presented.

2 Data Source: DSTC 2

DSTC 2 is based on corpora collected on dialogs about restaurant information for Cambridge, UK. Besides introducing a different domain from the original DSTC (that dealt with bus timetables) DSTC 2 is structured in such a way as to allow for the possibility of changing user goals and thus represents a more significant challenge for dialog state tracking. An overview of the current challenge and results can be found in Henderson et al. (2014).

2.1 Nature of Dialogs

Unlike the dialogs of the original DSTC that were based on actual uses of the bus timetable information system, the dialogs for DSTC 2 were collected in the more traditional experimental paradigm where system users were given a dialog scenario to follow. Example scenario descriptions extracted from two of the log files are given below.

- `Task 09825: You want to find a cheap restaurant and it should be in the south part of town. Make sure you get the address and phone number.`

- `Task 05454: You want to find an expensive restaurant and it should serve malaysian food. If there is no such venue how about korean type of food. Make sure you get the address and area of the venue.`

The basic structure of the dialogs has the following pattern.

1. Acquire from the user a set of constraints about the type of restaurant desired. Users may supply constraint information about area, food, name, and price range. This phase may require multiple iterations as user goals change.

2. Once the constraints have been acquired, provide information about one or more restaurants that satisfy the constraints. Users may request that additional attributes about a restaurant be provided (such as address and phone number).

2.2 Measuring Task Performance

Because of the complex nature of statistical dialog state tracking there are many different reasonable ways to measure tracker performance. Besides evaluating the accuracy of the 1-best hypothesis there are also a number of possible measures based on the quality of the estimate for dialog state (see Henderson et al. (2013) for details).

For the purpose of this paper the analysis will be based on tracker performance on accuracy (1-best quality) for the joint goal based on the four previously mentioned constraint attributes (area, food, name, and price range). The reason for this choice is that in an actual human-system dialog in an information-seeking domain, the dialog manager must choose an action based on the system's beliefs about the constraining attributes. While level of belief might positively influence when to engage in explicit or implicit confirmation, ultimate success depends on correct identification of values for the constraining attributes. Having too much confidence in inaccurate information has always been a major error source in dialog systems. Consequently, 1-best joint goal accuracy is the focus of study in this paper.

2.3 Description of Error Types

Since we are focused on joint goal accuracy, error type classification will be based on the following three types of possible deviations from the true joint goal label for a given turn.

1. Missing Attributes (MA) - these are situations where a value for an attribute has been specified in the actual data (e.g. "belgian" for the attribute "food"), but the dialog state tracker has no value for the attribute in the joint belief state.[1]

2. Extraneous Attributes (EA) - these are situations where the tracker has a value for the attribute in the joint belief state, but the attribute has not been mentioned in the actual dialog.

[1]The format of DSTC 2 allows for automatic compilation of the joint belief state by the scoring software. The probability mass for a given attribute that is not assigned to specific values for attributes is assigned to a special value *None*. If no value for the attribute has a probability estimate exceeding *None*, then no value for that attribute is included in the joint belief state. It is also possible for a dialog state tracker to explicitly provide a joint belief state. In DSTC 2 some systems do explicitly provide a joint belief state while others use the default.

3. False Attributes (FA) - these are situations where a value for an attribute has been specified in the actual data (e.g. "catalan" for the attribute "food"), but the dialog state tracker has a different value (such as "fusion" for "food").

For turns where there are errors, it is certainly possible that multiple errors occur, both multiple errors of a given type, and multiple errors of different types. This is taken into consideration as described next.

2.4 Recording Tracker Performance

For each tracker a data file consists of a sequence of tuples of the form ($Correct$,EA,MA,FA) that were generated for each turn for which there was a valid joint goal label.[2]. The meaning of each value in the tuple is given below.

- $Correct$ - has the value 1 if the tracker joint goal label is correct and 0 if it was incorrect.
- EA - a count of the number of different extraneous attributes that occurred in the turn. Will always be 0 if $Correct = 1$.
- MA - a count of the number of different missing attributes that occurred in the turn. Will always be 0 if $Correct = 1$.
- FA - a count of the number of different false attributes that occurred in the turn. Will always be 0 if $Correct = 1$.

Consequently, whenever $Correct$ is 1, the tuple will always be of the form (1,0,0,0). If $Correct$ is 0, at least one of the three following entries in the tuple will have a non-zero value.

These files were generated by modifying the scoring script provided by the DSTC organizing committee. The modification causes the necessary information to be output for each relevant turn. These data files represent the result of tracker performance on 1117 dialogs over a total of 9689 turns.

[2]In some cases at the start of dialogs, no SLU hypotheses have yet to mention any values for any of the joint goal attributes. As mentioned in Henderson et al. (2013), those turns are not included in the joint-goal accuracy evaluation. This occurred in a total of 201 turns over 193 dialogs.

2.5 Mapping Labels to Dialogs

Another modified version of the scoring script was used to iterate through the dialogs to produce a template that associates each of the 9689 labeled turns with the specific (dialog ID, turn within dialog) pair that the turn represents. This information was used in the error analysis process to identify specific dialogs for which tracking was not particularly accurate (see section 4).

2.6 Choice of Trackers

There were a total of 9 different teams that submitted a total of 31 trackers for DSTC 2. For this study, one tracker from each team is being used. The choice of tracker is the one that performed the best on 1-best joint goal accuracy, one of the overall "featured metrics" of the challenge (Henderson et al., 2013). Their performance on this metric ranged from 50.0% to 78.4%. Seven of the nine trackers had performance of better than 69%, while there were two performance outliers at 50% and 60%.

For purposes of this study, it seemed best to include a tracker from all groups since part of the intent of the challenge is to carefully examine the impact of different approaches to dialog state tracking. Based on the optional descriptions that teams submitted to the challenge, there were quite a variety of approaches taken (though not all teams provided a description). Some systems used the original SLU results. Other systems ignored the original SLU results and focused on the ASR hypotheses. Some systems created their own modified versions of the original SLU results. Modeling approaches included Maximum Entropy Markov model, Deep Neural Network model, rule-based models, Hidden Information State models, and conditional random fields. Hybrid approaches were used as well. A few more details about our submitted tracker will be provided in section 4.

One of the purposes of this study was to look at the distribution of errors based on the different types discussed in section 2.3, both in absolute and relative terms. Consequently, one intended investigation is to see if there is a difference in error type distribution depending on a number of parameters, including the approach used to dialog state tracking. Thus, examining the results from the top trackers of all teams can provide valuable information regardless of the absolute accuracy of the tracker. As it turned out, each tracker studied had multiple turns where it was the only tracker to provide a correct joint goal label. This happened on about 4% of all the turns. The number of turns for which a tracker was the only tracker to provide a correct joint goal label ranged from 5 to 89 and tended to follow the general ranking of accuracy (i.e., more accurate trackers tended to have more turns where it was the only tracker correct). However, it did not follow the relative rankings precisely.

3 Analysis: Global Tracker Performance

3.1 How much misunderstanding can be expected?

Another way to ask this question would be, "what error rate should be expected from a high performance tracker? For example, there were 21 dialogs consisting of 8 user turns or more where none of the trackers under study correctly represented the joint goal for any turn.

Looking more broadly, there were 1332 turns over the entire set of dialogs for which none of the trackers had a correct representation of the joint goal. Thus, if we could construct an "oracle" tracker that could always select the correct representation of the joint goal from among the nine trackers under study (when at least one of them had the correct representation), this would imply an error rate of 13.7%.[3] This contrasts with an error rate of 21.6% for the best performing tracker submitted as part of DSTC 2. If we look at tracker performance as a function of acoustic model (artificially degraded (A0), and optimized (A1)), the error rate estimate for the oracle tracker is 17.0% using model A0 and 10.3% using model A1.

3.2 Global Error Type Distribution

Using the classification of error types described in section 2.3: Extraneous Attributes (EA), Missing Attributes (MA), and False Attributes (FA), we can explore the distribution of error types as a function of the dialog tracker. Table 1 provides a summary view of the distributions over all the dialogs of the test set. For comparison, the baseline focus tracker provided by the DSTC 2 organizers (see Henderson et al. (2013)) and the HWU baseline tracker provided by Zhuoran Wang of Heriot-Watt University (see `http://camdial.org/~mh521/dstc/`) are also included. While trackers 1 and 9 are also presented for completeness, the main focus of the analysis is on trackers 2 through 8, the trackers with higher levels of performance on the featured metric of 1-best joint goal accuracy. Each row represents the relative distribution of errors by a given tracker. For example, for our tracker, tracker 3, there were 2629 turns (out of the total 9689 turns) where the tracker made one or more errors for the attributes of the joint goal. There were a total of 3075 different attribute errors of which 545 or 17.7% of the errors were of type EA, 1341 or 43.6% were of type MA, and 1189 or 38.7% of type FA. A visual representation of this information is provided in the Appendix in figure 1. Some general observations are the following.

- Other than tracker 5, the relative number of errors of type MA exceeded the relative number of errors of type FA. For attributes actually mentioned by the user, trackers in general were more likely to reject a correct hypothesis (leading to a type MA error) than accept an incorrect hypothesis (leading to a type FA error).

- Based on the brief description provided with submission of the tracker, tracker 5 uses a hybrid approach for tracking the different goals (one of the baseline trackers for the food attribute, but an n-best approach to the others). This approach seemed to lead to the acceptance of more spurious hypotheses than the other trackers (hence the higher EA rate). Tracker 8 also had a slightly higher error rate for EA. Its submission description indicates the combined use of several models, at least one of which used the training data for developing model parameters.

3.3 Error Type Distribution as a Function of Acoustic Model

Since publicly available spoken dialog systems cannot control the environment in which they are used, speech recognition rates can vary widely. One of the general goals of the DSTC is to evaluate tracker performance for varying levels of speech recognition accuracy. Hence the use in

[3]Note that this is not any sort of an absolute estimate. For example, if provided baseline trackers are included (one provided by the DSTC 2 organizers and another by Zhuoran Wang of Heriot-Watt University), the number of turns where no tracker correctly represents the joint goal reduces to 1325 turns.

	Total Errors		EA		MA		FA	
Tracker	# Turns	# Errors	Count	Percent	Count	Percent	Count	Percent
Focus	2720	3214	652	20.3%	1124	35.0%	1438	44.7%
HWU	2802	3352	601	17.9%	1526	45.5%	1225	36.6%
1	3865	4411	673	15.3%	2436	55.2%	1302	29.6%
2	2090	2432	451	18.5%	1177	48.4%	804	33.1%
3	2629	3075	545	17.7%	1341	43.6%	1189	38.7%
4	2246	2598	441	17.0%	1100	42.3%	1057	40.7%
5	2956	3618	947	26.2%	1218	33.7%	1453	40.2%
6	2730	3231	552	17.1%	1410	43.6%	1269	39.3%
7	2419	2791	446	16.0%	1205	43.2%	1140	40.8%
8	2920	3546	763	21.5%	1456	41.0%	1327	37.4%
9	4857	6183	781	12.6%	4222	68.3%	1180	19.1%

Table 1: Error Distribution: all dialogs

DSTC 2 of two acoustic models: model A1 which is a model optimized for the domain, and model A0 which has artificially degraded acoustic models (Henderson et al., 2013). For the test set, there were 542 dialogs yielding 4994 turns with joint goal labels for model A0, and 575 dialogs yielding 4695 turns with joint goal labels for model A1. It is unsurprising that the average number of turns in a dialog was shorter for the dialogs using the more accurate speech recognizer.

The previous table looked at the global behavior combining all the dialogs. An interesting question to examine is if the error distributions change as a function of acoustic model. Tables 2 and 3 give some insight into that question. Table 2, the results using the optimized model A1, unsurprisingly shows that when the speech signal is better and by implication the SLU confidence scores are stronger and more accurate, the relative rate of type FA errors declines while the relative rate of type MA errors increases (when compared to the overall results of Table 1). For errors of type EA it is about an even split—for some the relative number of EA errors decreases, and for some it increases. The results in Table 3 for the A0 model show the opposite trend for the relative errors of type MA compared to type FA.

3.4 Error Type Distribution as a Function of Attribute

While it is future work to do an exact count to determine the frequency with which the four different constraining attributes (area, food, name, and price range) are actually mentioned in the dialogs, it is clear from the data that the primary objects of conversation are area, food, and price range. This makes sense, since there are often alternative effective ways to access information about a restaurant other than to interact with a dialog system given that the name has already been determined by the user.[4] Consequently, for the remaining three attributes, an investigation into the relative distribution of errors as a function of attribute type within error type was conducted. The results are presented in Table 4. This table is looking at all the test data combined and not separating by acoustic model. Again the focus of discussion will be trackers 2 through 8. For brevity, the results for error type FA are omitted as they are pretty similar for all trackers.

> relative error rate for food >> than relative error rate for area >> than relative error rate for price range.

This follows naturally from the fact that there are 91 possible values for food, 5 possible values for area, and only 3 possible values for price range. Thus, there are many more possibilities for confusion for the value for the food attribute. When we examine the results in Table 4, there are a variety of interesting observations.

- Within error type EA, the only trackers for which the relative error rate for price range exceeds the relative error rate for area are trackers 5 and 7.
- Trackers 3 and 4 are more prone to have EA errors for the food attribute.

[4]One of the anonymous reviewers pointed out that the choice of scenarios used in the data collection process is also a factor.

Tracker	EA	MA	FA
1	12.4%	61.7%	25.9%
2	20.5%	53.4%	26.1%
3	16.1%	50.3%	33.7%
4	17.8%	45.7%	36.6%
5	25.7%	40.9%	33.4%
6	17.5%	49.9%	32.6%
7	15.0%	53.6%	31.5%
8	23.0%	43.0%	34.0%
9	11.6%	71.7%	16.7%

Table 2: Error Distribution: A1 dialogs

Tracker	EA	MA	FA
1	17.3%	50.5%	32.1%
2	17.5%	45.8%	36.6%
3	18.7%	39.8%	41.5%
4	16.5%	40.4%	43.0%
5	26.4%	29.9%	43.7%
6	16.8%	40.0%	43.2%
7	16.5%	37.4%	46.0%
8	20.6%	39.9%	39.5%
9	13.3%	65.8%	20.8%

Table 3: Error Distribution: A0 dialogs

- Trackers 2, 6, 7, and 8 all have a noticeable jump in the relative error rate for the food attribute for type MA errors over type EA errors. In contrast, trackers 3, 4, and 5 show a noticeable decrease.

What of course is missing from these observations is any conjecture of causality based on a careful analysis of individual tracker behavior. Given the lack of accessibility to the details of system implementations for all the trackers, other techniques of investigation are needed. The next section explores another potentially valuable technique—comparing the results of two trackers on a turn-by-turn basis, and using these results to identify particular dialogs that exhibit radically different outcomes in performance.

4 Analysis: Pairwise Comparative Accuracy

Another avenue of analysis is to directly compare the performance of two trackers. How do they differ in terms of the types of dialog situations that they handle effectively? We will examine these issues through comparison of the top performing tracker in the challenge (with respect to the featured metric 1-best joint goal accuracy) with our tracker entry, Pirate.[5]

4.1 Pirate methodology: what should dialog expectation mean?

The overarching philosophy behind the development of Pirate is simply the following.

> There is belief about what we think we know, but there should also be an expectation about what comes next if we are correct.

One of the first dialog systems to make use of a hierarchy of dialog expectations was the Circuit Fix-It Shop (Smith et al., 1995) which was also one of the first working dialog systems to be carefully and extensively evaluated (Smith and Gordon, 1997) and (Smith, 1998). However, at the time, the ability to make use of large corpora in system development was largely non-existent.[6]

Our approach in DSTC 2 for making use of the extensive training data combined the SLU hypotheses with confidence scores (interpreted as probabilities) with a simple statistical model of dialog expectation to create modified SLU confidence scores. The model of dialog expectation was based on a simple bigram model using frequency counts for (system dialog act, user speech act) pairs. This can be normalized into a probabilistic model that gives the probability of a user speech act given the context of the most recent system dialog act to which the user is responding. The equation used to modify SLU confidence scores is the following. Let $Prob(SLU)$ represent the confidence score (expressed as a probability) for the hypothesis SLU, and let $Val(SLU)$ represent the actual hypothesis (e.g. inform(food = belgian)).

$$Prob(SLUmod) = 0.7 * Prob(SLU) + 0.3 * Expct$$

where $Prob(SLU)$ is the original confidence score for the hypothesis, and $Expct$ is the probability of the occurrence of the speech act used

[5]The mascot name of East Carolina sports teams is the Pirates. In addition, the code development process for our tracker was based on modification of the simple baseline tracker provided by the DSTC 2 organizers.

[6]Moody (1988) used the Wizard-of-Oz paradigm to collect dialogs relevant to the Circuit Fix-It Shop domain as part of her research into the effects of restricted vocabulary on discourse structure, but the total number of dialogs was about 100. In contrast, DSTC 2 provided 1612 actual human-computer dialogs for the training set, 506 dialogs for the development set, and 1117 dialogs for the test set.

	EA			MA		
Tracker	Food	Price	Area	Food	Price	Area
1	41.2%	25.6%	29.9%	41.5%	36.7%	20.2%
2	29.5%	34.8%	35.7%	41.4%	26.6%	27.8%
3	36.0%	23.7%	33.0%	30.9%	34.1%	31.9%
4	44.4%	25.8%	27.7%	30.4%	35.4%	29.8%
5	32.2%	40.5%	27.0%	19.5%	34.0%	42.4%
6	28.8%	34.2%	37.0%	46.0%	27.7%	22.8%
7	26.7%	38.3%	31.4%	35.7%	33.1%	28.0%
8	28.3%	25.7%	44.2%	49.4%	28.9%	18.9%
9	28.3%	17.7%	34.3%	54.5%	17.8%	26.8%

Table 4: Error Distribution by Attribute

in the SLU hypothesis given the current system speech act (i.e., the probability that comes from the statistical model of dialog expectation). The 0.3 weighting factor was determined through trial and error to perform the best given the training data (basing performance on 1-best joint goal accuracy).[7]

After calculating the modified values, the scores are renormalized so that the confidence values sum to 1. Given the renormalized values for $Prob(SLUmod)$, dialog state was updated by using the following rules. Let $Val(HypCur)$ represent the current hypothesis in the dialog state for the value of an attribute, and its confidence score be denoted by $Prob(HypCur)$.

1. Increase $Prob(SLUmod)$ by $Prob(X)$ where $Val(X) == NULL$ (i.e. the default NULL hypothesis for the SLU), whenever $Prob(X)$ is < 0.5. Reset $Prob(X)$ to 0.

2. Replace $HypCur$ with the highest scoring $SLUmod$ for that attribute if the user speech act is an *inform*, and the following relationship holds.

   $$Prob(SLUmod) + Tol \geq Prob(HypCur)$$

   where Tol is an experimentally determined tolerance value (currently set at 0.1).

3. If the system speech act was a *canthelp* act that specifies particular attribute values (e.g. food = belgian), and the current chosen hypothesis ($SLUmod$) provides information about that attribute, overwrite the state information for the attribute listed in *canthelp* even if the confidence score is less.

The motivation for these rules comes from the assumption that the Gricean Cooperative Principle for conversation (Grice, 1975) applies to this dialog environment. Given this assumption, rule 1 is based on the belief that the human dialog participant is attempting to make an appropriate dialog contribution at every turn. Consequently when reasonable, we will augment the top hypothesized SLU's confidence score with any weight given to the NULL hypothesis. Rule 2 is based on the idea that an intended new contribution should replace a previous contribution and that some allowance should be made for "signal noise" in calculating SLU confidence. Rule 3 reflects the idea that when the system cannot provide assistance about a specified attribute value, any new information about the attribute should be considered a replacement.

The above rules are for updating choices for the individual attributes that are possible components of the goal state (area, food, name and price range). In our modeling of dialog state, we only maintain the top actual hypothesis for each attribute, For producing the joint goal, we used the default that the joint goal is the product of the marginal goals.[8]

With this fairly simple approach, Pirate had a 1-best joint goal accuracy of 72.9%. This accuracy rate exceeded the performance of all baseline trackers, and was 13th out of 31 for the trackers submitted.[9]

[7]For recent work using a Bayesian-based alternative for combining dialog history with the current utterance to calculate probabilities, see Raux and Ma (2011).

[8]Consequently, if our confidence score for the top hypothesis is < 0.5, that hypothesis will not be included in the joint goal, as the default "None" is associated with higher confidence.

[9]The set of 12 trackers that performed better is comprised of 4 trackers each from 3 other teams.

4.2 Comparison to the Best Performing Tracker

An entry from team2 achieved 78.4% accuracy on the 1-best joint goal accuracy metric. A comparative analysis was conducted whereby the performance of each tracker was compared on a turn-by-turn basis. Highlights of this analysis include the following.

- The two trackers were both correct 70.6% of the time and both incorrect 19.3% of the time.
- 7.8% of the time Pirate was incorrect when the team2 tracker was correct.
- 2.2% of the time, Pirate was correct when the team2 tracker was incorrect.

Further exploration examined performance within dialogs. It was discovered that there were 18 dialogs where Pirate was incorrect for at least 8 turns where the team2 tracker was correct. Furthermore, there were no turns in those dialogs where the team2 tracker was incorrect when Pirate was correct. Given that the team2 tracker performed several percentage points better overall, this is not surprising. What might be surprising is that there are 7 dialogs where the opposite was true, and Pirate performed better than the team2 tracker. An initial glance at an actual dialog from each situation indicated the following.

- While team2 did not offer a description of their methodology in their submission, it can be inferred that they used the original ASR hypotheses as part of its dialog state tracking. Pirate was unable to detect in the 2nd turn that the goal (area=dontcare) was being communicated because it did not show up in the SLU hypotheses. However, the top ASR hypothesis was "area". Integrating SLU with dialog context is known to be a good idea when technically feasible, and is borne out by this example. This missing attribute for goal state was propagated throughout all subsequent turns of the dialog. However, it should be noted that omitting an attribute where the correct value is "dontcare" is a somewhat benign error as discussed in the next example.
- The dialog reviewed where the team2 tracker had trouble that Pirate did not revolved around the fact that at an important moment in the dialog, the team2 tracker added an unstated hypothesis of the form (food=dontcare) to its joint goal. This was retained for the duration of the dialog. It can be readily argued that this is a benign error. If the user never explicitly gave a constraint about food (implying that $None$ is the correct value for the attribute), the dialog manager is not likely to make a wrong decision if it's basing its action instead on (food=dontcare).

Time constraints have prohibited further examination of the other dialogs, but clearly this is a fruitful area of exploration for understanding behavioral differences between approaches to dialog state tracking.

5 Conclusion

A primary motivation of the DSTC is to allow for direct comparisons between alternative approaches to dialog state tracking. The results from DSTC 1 focused on performance aspects without providing a detailed analysis of errors sources. This paper describes several techniques for examining the errors made by the dialog state trackers in order to refine our understanding of the limitations of various approaches to the tracking process.

Though the analysis at this point is incomplete, one immediate observation is that no one approach is universally superior to other approaches with respect to the performance metric 1-best joint goal accuracy. However, being able to carefully determine the conditions under which one approach outperforms another and determining if there are ways to combine alternative techniques into a more effective but sufficiently efficient tracking model is very much an unsolved problem. The results from this paper suggest that a careful analysis of errors can provide further insight into our knowledge about the difficult challenge of dialog state tracking. We would like to explore some of the trends observed with appropriate statistical tests as well as look more carefully at dialogs where pairwise comparative analysis indicates highly differential behavior.

Acknowledgments

The author would like to acknowledge the valuable work of East Carolina graduate student Ryan Dellana in developing several tools that assisted with compilation of the statistical based expectations as well as tools for generating selected transcripts from the DSTC 2 corpus. A special thanks goes to the organizers of the DSTC 2 challenge for making this work possible. Thanks also go to the anonymous reviewers for their constructive comments. Their suggestions have been very helpful in producing the final version of this paper.

References

H. P. Grice. 1975. Logic and conversation. In P. Cole and J.L. Morgan, editors, *Syntax and Semantics, Vol. 3: Speech Acts*, pages 41–58. Academic Press, New York.

M. Henderson, B. Thomson, and J. Williams, 2013. *Dialog State Tracking Challenge 2 & 3*. http://camdial.org/~mh521/dstc/downloads/handbook.pdf, accessed March 5, 2014.

M. Henderson, B. Thomson, and J. Williams. 2014. The second dialog state tracking challenge. In *Proceedings of the SIGdial 2014 Conference*, Philadelphia, U.S.A., June.

T. S. Moody. 1988. *The Effects of Restricted Vocabulary Size on Voice Interactive Discourse Structure*. Ph.D. thesis, North Carolina State University.

A. Raux and Y. Ma. 2011. Efficient probabilistic tracking of user goal and dialog history for spoken dialog systems. In *Proceedings of INTERSPEECH-2011*, pages 801–804.

R.W. Smith and S.A. Gordon. 1997. Effects of variable initiative on linguistic behavior in human-computer spoken natural language dialog. *Computational Linguistics*, 23:141–168.

R.W. Smith, D.R. Hipp, and A.W. Biermann. 1995. An architecture for voice dialog systems based on Prolog-style theorem-proving. *Computational Linguistics*, 21:281–320.

R.W. Smith. 1998. An evaluation of strategies for selectively verifying utterance meanings in spoken natural language dialog. *International Journal of Human-Computer Studies*, 48:627–647.

J. Williams, A. Raux, D. Ramachandran, and A. Black. 2013. The dialog state tracking challenge. In *Proceedings of the SIGDIAL 2013 Conference*, pages 404–413, Metz, France, August. Association for Computational Linguistics. http://www.aclweb.org/anthology/W13-4065.

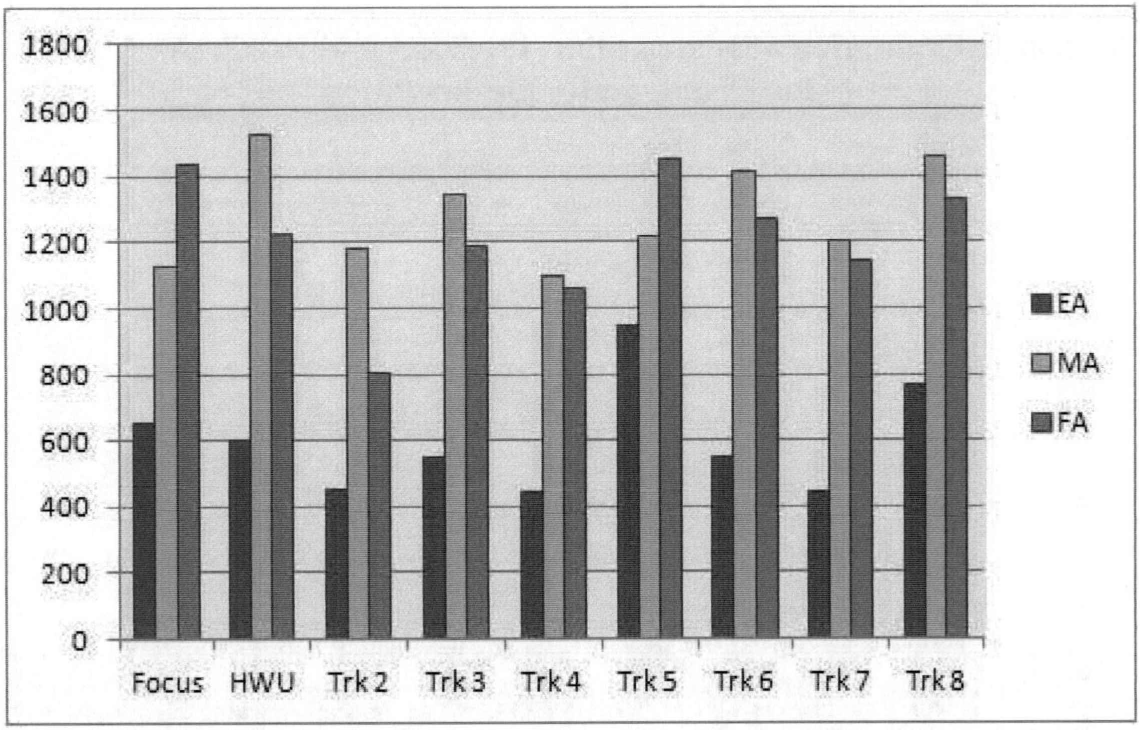

Figure 1: Error Distribution: all dialogs

Appendix

Figure 1 displays in a graphical fashion the error counts for the different types of missing attributes for the trackers listed in Table 1. For clarity, the data for trackers 1 and 9 are omitted. "Focus" is the baseline focus tracker provided by the DSTC 2 organizers (Henderson et al., 2013), and "HWU" is the baseline tracker provided by Zhuoran Wang (see `http://camdial.org/~mh521/dstc/`). "Trk 3" is our tracker, Pirate. As a reminder, the best overall performing tracker is the one labeled "Trk 2". One observation from the figure is that its best performance is in minimizing False Attribute (FA) errors.

Extrinsic Evaluation of Dialog State Tracking and Predictive Metrics for Dialog Policy Optimization

Sungjin Lee
Language Technologies Institute,
Carnegie Mellon University,
Pittsburgh, Pennsylvania, USA
sungjin.lee@cs.cmu.edu

Abstract

During the recent *Dialog State Tracking Challenge* (DSTC), a fundamental question was raised: *"Would better performance in dialog state tracking translate to better performance of the optimized policy by reinforcement learning?"* Also, during the challenge system evaluation, another non-trivial question arose: *"Which evaluation metric and schedule would best predict improvement in overall dialog performance?"* This paper aims to answer these questions by applying an off-policy reinforcement learning method to the output of each challenge system. The results give a positive answer to the first question. Thus the effort to separately improve the performance of dialog state tracking as carried out in the DSTC may be justified. The answer to the second question also draws several insightful conclusions on the characteristics of different evaluation metrics and schedules.

1 Introduction

Statistical approaches to spoken dialog management have proven very effective in gracefully dealing with noisy input due to *Automatic Speech Recognition* (ASR) and *Spoken Language Understanding* (SLU) error (Lee, 2013; Williams et al., 2013). Most recent advances in statistical dialog modeling have been based on the *Partially Observable Markov Decision Processes* (POMDP) framework which provides a principled way for sequential action planning under uncertainty (Young et al., 2013). In this approach, the task of dialog management is generally decomposed into two subtasks, i.e., dialog state tracking and dialog policy learning. The aim of dialog state tracking is to accurately estimate the true dialog state from noisy observations by incorporating patterns between turns and external knowledge as a dialog unfolds (Fig. 1). The dialog policy learning process then strives to select an optimal system action given the estimated dialog state.

Many dialog state tracking algorithms have been developed. Few studies, however, have reported the strengths and weaknesses of each method. Thus the *Dialog State Tracking Challenge* (DSTC) was organized to advance state-of-the-art technologies for dialog state tracking by allowing for reliable comparisons between different approaches using the same datasets (Williams et al., 2013). Thanks to the DSTC, we now have a better understanding of effective models, features and training methods we can use to create a dialog state tracker that is not only of superior performance but also very robust to realistic mismatches between development and deployment environments (Lee and Eskenazi, 2013).

Despite the fruitful results, it was largely limited to intrinsic evaluation, thus leaving an important question unanswered: "*Would the improved performance in dialog state tracking carry over to dialog policy optimization?*" Furthermore, there was no consensus on what and when to measure, resulting in a large set of metrics being evaluated with three different schedules. With this variety of metrics, it is not clear what the evaluation result means. Thus it is important to answer the question: "*Which metric best serves as a predictor to the improvement in dialog policy optimization*" since this is the ultimate goal, in terms of end-to-end dialog performance. The aim of this paper is to answer these two questions via corpus-based experiments. Similar to the rationale behind the DSTC, the corpus-based design allows us to

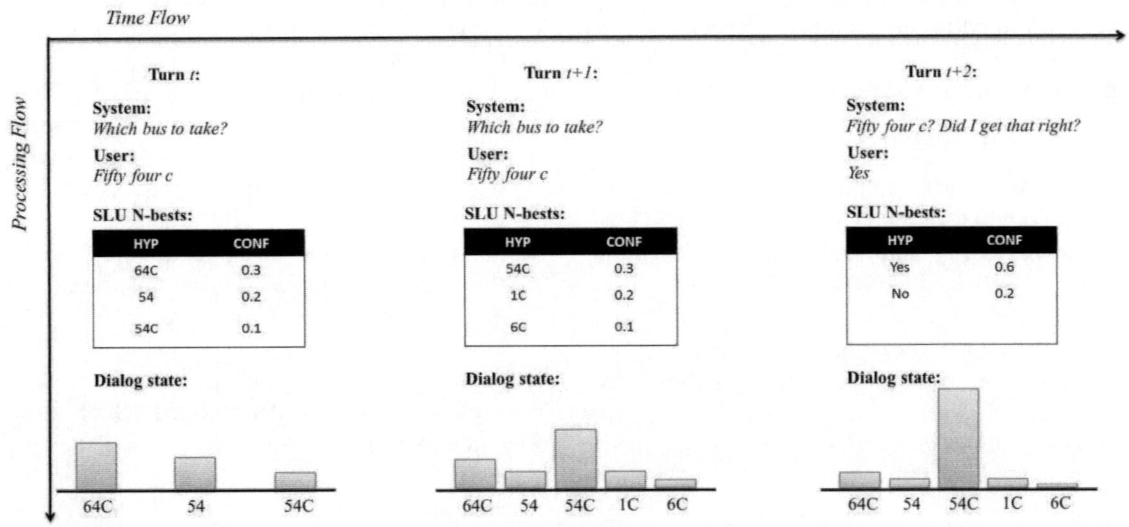

Figure 1: An example of dialog state tracking for the *Route* slot. At each turn the system asks for user's goal or attempts to confirm one of hypotheses. The user's utterance is recognized to output an N-best list. The SLU module generates semantic inputs to the dialog manager by parsing the N-best hypotheses. Each SLU hypothesis receives a confidence score. From the current turn's SLU hypotheses and all previous ones thus far, the dialog state tracker computes a probability distribution over a set of dialog state hypotheses. Note that the number of hypotheses in a dialog state can be different from the number of SLU hypotheses, e.g., at turn t+1, 3 and 5 respectively.

compare different trackers on the same data. We applied a sample efficient off-policy reinforcement learning (RL) method to the outputs of each tracker so that we may examine the relationship between the performance of dialog state tracking and that of the optimized policy as well as which metric shows the highest correlation with the performance of the optimized policy.

This paper is structured as follows. Section 2 briefly describes the DSTC and the metrics adopted in the challenge. Section 3 elaborates on the extrinsic evaluation method based on off-policy RL. Section 4 presents the extrinsic evaluation results and discusses its implication on metrics for dialog state tracking evaluation. Finally, Section 5 concludes with a brief summary and suggestions for future research.

2 DSTC Task and Evaluation Metrics

This section briefly describes the task for the DSTC and evaluation metrics. For more details, please refer to the DSTC manual[1].

[1] http://research.microsoft.com/apps/pubs/?id=169024

2.1 Task Description

DSTC data is taken from several different spoken dialog systems which all provided bus schedule information for Pittsburgh, Pennsylvania, USA (Raux et al., 2005) as part of the *Spoken Dialog Challenge* (Black et al., 2011). There are 9 slots which are evaluated: *route*, *from.desc*, *from.neighborhood*, *from.monument*, *to.desc*, *to.neighborhood*, *to.monument*, *date*, and *time*. Since both marginal and joint representations of dialog states are important for deciding dialog actions, the challenge takes both into consideration. Each joint representation is an assignment of values to all slots. Thus there are 9 marginal outputs and 1 joint output in total, which are all evaluated separately.

The dialog tracker receives the SLU N-best hypotheses for each user turn, each with a confidence score. In general, there are a large number of values for each slot, and the coverage of N-best hypotheses is good, thus the challenge confines its determination of whether a goal has been reached to slots and values that have been observed in an SLU output. By exploiting this aspect, the task of a dialog state tracker is to generate a set of observed slot and value pairs, with a score between 0 and 1. The sum of all scores is restricted to sum to 1.0. Thus 1.0 – total score is defined as the score of a special value *None* that indicates the user's goal has not yet appeared on any SLU output.

2.2 Evaluation Metrics

To evaluate tracker output, the correctness of each hypothesis is labeled at each turn. Then hypothesis scores and labels over the entire dialogs are collected to compute 11 metrics:

- **Accuracy** measures the ratio of states under evaluation where the top hypothesis is correct.
- **ROC.V1** computes the following quantity:

$$\mathrm{CA.V1}(s) = \frac{\mathrm{CA}(s)}{\mathrm{N}}$$

  where N is the total number of top hypotheses over the entire data and CA(s) denotes the number of correctly accepted top hypotheses with the threshold being set to s. Similarly FA denotes false-accepts and FR false-rejects. From these quantities, several metrics are derived. **ROC.V1.EER** computes FA.V1(s) where FA.V1(s) = FR.V1(s). The metrics **ROC.V1.CA05**, **ROC.V1.CA10**, and **ROC.V1.CA20** compute CA.V1(s) when FA.V1(s) = 0.05, 0.10, and 0.20 respectively. These metrics measure the quality of score via plotting accuracy with respect to false-accepts so that they may reflect not only accuracy but also discrimination.
- **ROC.V2** computes the conventional ROC quantity:

$$\mathrm{CA.V2}(s) = \frac{\mathrm{CA}(s)}{\mathrm{CA}(0)}$$

  ROC.V2.CA05, **ROC.V2.CA10**, and **ROC.V2.CA20** do the same as the V1 versions. These metrics measure the discrimination of the score for the top hypothesis independently of accuracy.

Note that Accuracy and ROC curves do not take into consideration non-top hypotheses while the following measures do.

- **L2** calculates the Euclidean distance between the vector consisting of the scores of all hypotheses and a zero vector with 1 in the position of the correct one. This measures the quality of tracker's output score as probability.
- **AvgP** indicates the averaged score of the correct hypothesis. Note that this measures the quality of the score of the correct hypothesis, ignoring the scores assigned to incorrect hypotheses.
- **MRR** denotes the mean reciprocal rank of the correct hypothesis. This measures the quality of rank instead of score.

As far as evaluation schedule is concerned, there are three schedules for determining which turns to include in each evaluation.

- **Schedule 1**: Include all turns. This schedule allows us to account for changes in concepts that are not in focus. But this makes across-concept comparison invalid since different concepts appear at different times in a dialog.
- **Schedule 2**: Include a turn for a given concept only if that concept either appears on the SLU N-Best list in that turn, or if the system's action references that concept in that turn. Unlike schedule 1, this schedule makes comparisons across concepts valid but cannot account for changes in concepts which are not in focus.
- **Schedule 3**: Include only the turn before the system starts over from the beginning, and the last turn of the dialog. This schedule does not consider what happens during a dialog.

3 Extrinsic Evaluation Using Off-Policy Reinforcement Learning

In this section, we present a corpus-based method for extrinsic evaluation of dialog state tracking. Thanks to the corpus-based design where outputs of various trackers with different characteristics are involved, it is possible to examine how the differences between trackers affect the performance of learned policies. The performance of a learned policy is measured by the expected return at the initial state of a dialog which is one of the common performance measures for episodic tasks.

3.1 Off-Policy RL on Fixed Data

To learn an optimal policy from fixed data, we applied a state-of-the-art kernelized off-policy RL method. Off-policy RL methods allows for optimization of a policy by observing how other policies behave. The policy used to control the system's behavior is called Behavior policy. As far as a specific algorithm is concerned, we have adopted *Least-Squares Temporal Difference* (LSTD) (Bradtke and Barto, 1996) for policy evaluation and *Least-Squares Policy Iteration* (LSPI) (Lagoudakis and Parr, 2003) for policy learning. LSTD and LSPI have been well known to be sample efficient, thus easily lending themselves to the application of RL to fixed data (Pietquin et al., 2011). LSPI is an instance of *Approximate Policy Iteration* where an approximated action-state value function (a.k.a Q function) is established for a current policy and an improved policy is formed by taking greedy actions with respect to the estimated Q function. The process of policy evaluation and improvement iterates until convergence. For value function approximation, in this work, we adopted the following linear approximation architecture:

$$\hat{Q}_\theta(s,a) = \theta^T \phi(s,a)$$

where θ is the set of parameters, $\phi(s,a)$ an activation vector of basis functions, s a state and a an action. Given a policy π_θ and a set of state transitions $\{(s_i, a_i, r_i, s_{i+1})_{1 \le i \le N}\}$, where r_i is the reward that the system would get from the environment by executing action a_i at state s_i, the approximated state-action value function $\hat{Q}_\theta$ is estimated by LSTD. The most important part of LSTD lies in the computation of the gradient of temporal difference:

$$\phi(s,a) - \gamma\phi(s', \pi(s'))$$

In LSPI, $\pi(s')$ takes the form of greedy policy:

$$\pi(s') = \underset{a'}{argmax}\, \hat{Q}_\theta(s', a')$$

It is however critical to take into consideration the inherent problem of insufficient exploration in fixed data to avoid overfitting (Henderson et al., 2008). Thus we confined the set of available actions at a given state to the ones that have an occurrence probability greater than some threshold δ:

$$\pi(s') = \underset{a',\ p(a'|s') > \delta}{argmax}\ \hat{Q}_\theta(s', a')$$

The conditional probability $p(a'|s')$ can be easily estimated by any conventional classification methods which provide posterior probability. In this study, we set δ to 0.1.

3.2 State Representation and Basis Function

In order to make the process of policy optimization tractable, the belief state is normally mapped to an abstract space by only taking crucial information for dialog action selection, e.g., the beliefs of the top and second hypotheses for a concept. Similarly, the action space is also mapped into a smaller space by only taking the predicate of an action. In this work, the simplified state includes the following elements:

- The scores of the top hypothesis for each concept with *None* excluded
- The scores of the second hypothesis for each concept with *None* excluded
- The scores assigned to *None* for each concept
- Binary indicators for a concept if there are hypotheses except *None*
- The values of the top hypothesis for each concept
- A binary indicator if the user affirms when the system asks a yes-no question for next bus

It has been shown that the rapid learning speed of recent approaches is partly attributed to the use of kernels as basis functions (Gasic et al., 2010; Lee and Eskenazi, 2012; Pietquin et al., 2011). Thus to make the best of the limited amount of data, we adopted a kernelized approach. Similar to previous studies, we used a product of kernel functions:

$$k(s,s') = k_c(s,s') \prod_{d \in D} k_d(s,s')$$

where $k_c(\cdot,\cdot)$ is responsible for a vector of continuous elements of a state and $k_d(\cdot,\cdot)$ for each discrete element. For the continuous elements, we adopted Gaussian kernels:

$$k_c(s,s') = h \cdot \exp\left(-\frac{\|s_c - s_c'\|}{2\sigma^2}\right)$$

where h governs the value at center, σ controls the width of the kernel and s_c represents the vector of continuous elements of a state. In the experiments, h and σ were set to 4 and 3, respectively. For a discrete element, we adopted delta kernel:

$$k_d(s, s') = \delta_{s_d}(s'_d)$$

where $\delta_x(x')$ returns one if $x = x'$, zero otherwise and s_d represents an element of a state.

As the number of data points increases, kernelized approaches commonly encounter severe computational problems. To address this issue, it is necessary to limit the active kernel functions being used for value function approximation. This sparsification process has to find out the sufficient number of kernels which keeps a good balance between computational tractability and approximation quality. We adopted a simple sparsification method which was commonly used in previous studies (Engel et al., 2004). The key intuition behind of the sparsification method is that there is a mapping $\psi(\cdot)$ to a *Hilbert* space in which the kernel function $k(x, x')$ is represented as the inner product of $\psi(x)$ and $\psi(x')$ by the Mercer's theorem. Thus the kernel-based representation of Q function can be restated as a plain linear equation in the *Hilbert* space:

$$\hat{Q}_\theta(p) = \sum_i \theta_i\, k(p, p'_i) = \langle \psi(p), \sum_i \theta_i \psi(p'_i) \rangle$$

where p denotes the pair of state and action. The term $\sum_i \theta_i \psi(p'_i)$ plays the role of the weight vector in the *Hilbert* space. Since this term takes the form of linear combination, we can safely remove any linearly dependent $\psi(p'_i)$ without changing the weighted sum by tuning θ. It is known that the linear dependence of $\psi(p)$ from the rest can be tested based on kernel functions as follows:

$$min_{\boldsymbol{a}}\, k(p_i, p_i) - \boldsymbol{k}_{\backslash p_i}(p_i)^T \boldsymbol{a} \le \nu \quad (1)$$

where $\boldsymbol{k}_{\backslash p_i} = [\ldots, k(p_i, p_{i-1}), k(p_i, p_{i+1}), \ldots]$ and ν is a sparsification threshold. When equation 1 is satisfied, p_i can be safely removed from the set of basis functions. Thus the sparsity can be controlled by changing ν. It can be shown that equation 1 is minimized when $\boldsymbol{a} = \boldsymbol{K}_{\backslash p_i}^{-1} \boldsymbol{k}_{\backslash p_i}(p_i)$, where $\boldsymbol{K}_{\backslash p_i}^{-1}$ is the Gram matrix excluding p_i. In the experiments, ν was set to 3.

	# Dialogs		# Turns	
	Training	Test	Training	Test
DS1	274	312	2594	2168
DS2	321	339	3394	2579
DS3	277	286	2221	1988
DS4	141	165	1060	979

Table 1: The DSTC test datasets (DS1-4) were evenly divided into two groups of datasets for off-policy RL training and test. To simplify the analysis, the dialogs that include *startover* and *canthelp* were excluded.

3.3 Reward Function

The reward function is defined following a common approach to form-filling, task-oriented systems:

- Every correct concept filled is rewarded 100
- Every incorrect concept filled is assigned -200
- Every empty concept is assigned -300 if the system terminated the session, -50 otherwise.
- At every turn, -20 is assigned

The reward structure is carefully designed such that the RL algorithm cannot find a way to maximize the expected return without achieving the user goal.

4 Experimental Setup

In order to see the relationship between the performance of dialog state tracking and that of the optimized policy, we applied the off-policy RL method presented in Section 3 to the outputs of each tracker for all four DSTC test datasets[2]. The summary statistics of the datasets are presented in Table 1. In addition, to quantify the impact of dialog state tracking on an end-to-end dialog, the performance of policies optimized by RL was compared with Behavior policies and another set of learned policies using supervised learning (SL). Note that Behavior policies were developed by experts in spoken dialog research. The use of a learned policy using supervised

[2] We took the entry from each team that achieved the highest ranks of that team in the largest number of evaluation metrics: entry2 for team3 and team6, entry3 for team8, entry4 for team9, and entry1 for the rest of the teams. We were not, however, able to process the tracker output of team2 due to its large size. This does not negatively impact the general results of this paper.

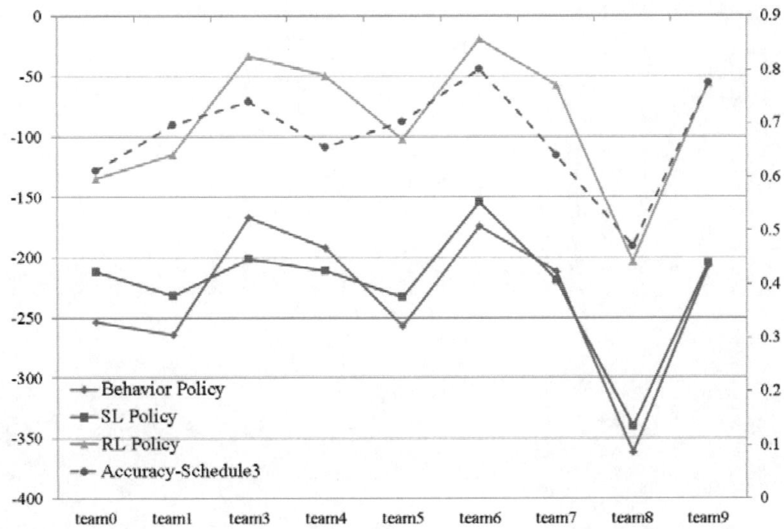

Figure 2: The left vertical axis is associated with the performance plots of RL, SL and Behavior policies for each team. The right vertical axis measures the accuracies of each team's tracker at the end of a dialog (schedule 3).

learning (Hurtado et al., 2005) is also one of the common methods of spoken dialog system development. We exploited the SVM method with the same kernel functions as defined in Section 3.2 except that the action element is not included. The posterior probability of the SVM model was also used for handling the insufficient exploration problem (in Section 3.1).

5 Results and Discussion

The comparative results between RL, SL and Behavior policies are plotted in Fig. 2. Despite the relatively superior performance of SL policies over Behavior policies, the performance improvement is neither large nor constant. This confirms that Behavior policies are very strong baselines which were designed by expert researchers. RL policies, however, consistently outperformed Behavior as well as SL policies, with a large performance gap. This result indicates that the policies learned by the proposed off-policy RL method are a lot closer to optimal ones than the hand-crafted policies created by human experts. Given that many state features are derived from the belief state, the large improvement in performance implies that the estimated belief state is indeed a good summary representation of a state, maintaining the *Markov* property between states. The *Markov* property is a crucial property for RL methods to approach to the optimal policy. On the other hand, most of the dialog state trackers surpassed the baseline tracker (team0) in the performance of RL policies. This result assures that the better the performance in dialog state tracking, the better a policy we can learn in the policy optimization stage. Given these two results, we can strongly assert that dialog state tracking plays a key role in enhancing end-to-end dialog performance.

Another interesting result worth noticing is that the performance of RL policies does not exactly align with the accuracy measured at the end of a dialog (Schedule 3) which would have been the best metric if the task were a one-time classification (Fig. 2). This misalignment therefore supports the speculation that accuracy-schedule3 might not be the most appropriate metric for predicting the effect of dialog state tracking on end-to-end dialog performance. In order to better understand *What To Measure* and *When To Measure* to predict end-to-end dialog performance, a correlation analysis was carried out between the performance of RL policies and that of the dialog state tracking measured by different metrics and schedules. The correlations are listed in descending order in Fig. 3. This result reveals several interesting insights for different metrics.

First, metrics which are intended to measure the quality of a tracker's score (e.g., L2 and AvgP) are more correlated than other metrics. This tendency can be understood as a consequence of the sequential decision-making nature of a dialog task. A dialog system can always initiate an additional turn, unless the user

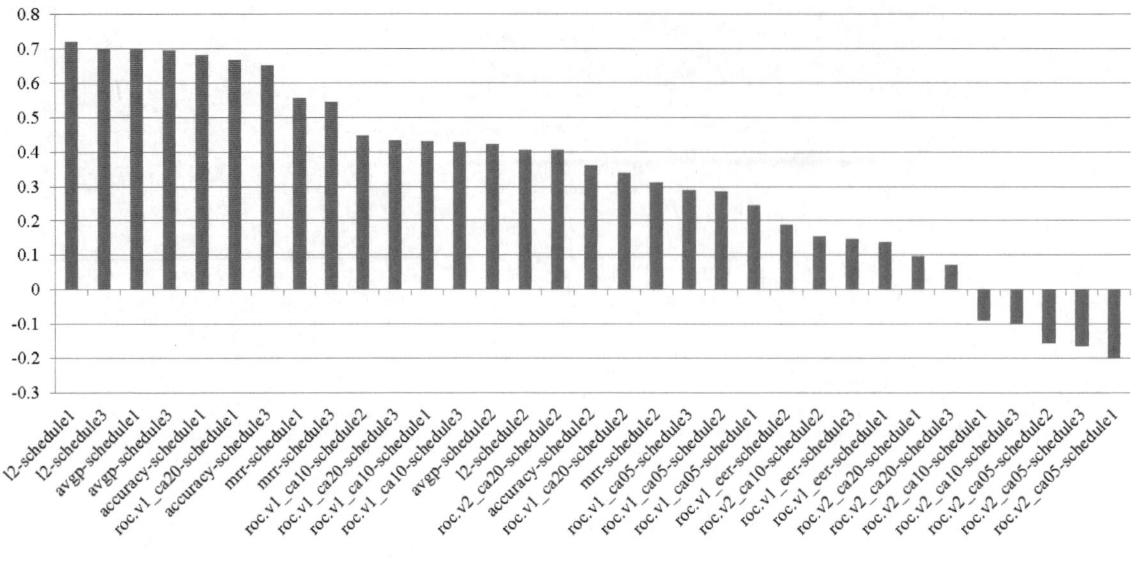

Figure 3: The correlations of each combination of metric and schedule with the performance of optimized polices.

terminates the session, to refine its belief state when there is no dominant hypothesis. Thus accurate estimation of the beliefs of all observed hypotheses is essential. This is why the evaluation of only the top hypothesis does not provide sufficient information.

Second, schedule1 and schedule3 showed a stronger correlation than schedule2. In fact schedule2 was more preferred in previous studies since it allows for a valid comparison of different concepts (Williams, 2013; Williams et al., 2013). This result can be explained by the fact that the best system action is selected by considering all of the concepts together. For example, when the system moves the conversation focus from one concept to another, the beliefs of the concepts that are not in focus are as important as the concept in focus. Thus evaluating all concepts at the same time is more suitable for predicting the performance of a sequential decision-making task involving multiple concepts in its state.

Finally, metrics for evaluating discrimination quality (measured by ROC.V2) have little correlation with end-to-end dialog performance. In order to understand this relatively unexpected result, we need to give deep thought to how the scores of a hypothesis are distributed during the session. For example, the score of a true hypothesis usually starts from a small value due to the uncertainty of ASR output and gets bigger every time positive evidence is observed. The score of a false hypothesis usually stays small or medium. This leads to a situation where both true and false hypotheses are pretty much mixed in the zone of small and medium scores without significant discrimination. It is, however, very important for a metric to reveal a difference between true and false hypotheses before their scores fully arrive at sufficient certainty since most additional turns are planned for hypotheses with a small or medium score. Thus general metrics evaluating discrimination alone are hardly appropriate for a tracking problem where the score develops gradually. Furthermore, the choice of threshold (i.e. FA = 0.05, 0.10, 0.20) was made to consider relatively unimportant regions where the true hypothesis is likely to have a higher score, meaning that no further turns need to be planned.

6 Conclusion

In this paper, we have presented a corpus-based study that attempts to answer two fundamental questions which, so far, have not been rigorously addressed: *"Would better performance in dialog state tracking translate to better performance of the optimized policy by RL?"* and *"Which evaluation metric and schedule would best predict improvement in overall dialog performance?"* The result supports a positive answer to the first question. Thus the effort to separately improve the performance of dialog state tracking as carried out in the recent held DSTC may be justified. As a way to address the second question, the correlations of different metrics and schedules with the performance of optimized policies were computed. The results revealed several insightful conclusions: 1) Metrics measuring score quality are more suitable for predicting the performance of an optimized policy. 2) Evaluation of all concepts at the same time is more appropriate for predicting the performance of a sequential decision making task involving multiple concepts in its state. 3) Metrics evaluating only discrimination (e.g., ROC.V2) are inappropriate for a tracking problem where the score gradually develops. Interesting extensions of this work include finding a composite measure of conventional metrics to obtain a better predictor. A data-driven composition may tell us the relative empirical importance of each metric. In spite of several factors which generalize our conclusions such as handling insufficient exploration, the use of separate test sets and various mismatches between test sets, it is still desirable to run different policies for live tests in the future. Also, since the use of an approximate policy evaluation method (e.g. LSTD) can introduce systemic errors, more deliberate experimental setups will be designed for a future study: 1) the application of different RL algorithms for training and test datasets 2) further experiments on different datasets, e.g., the datasets for DSTC2 (Henderson et al., 2014). Although the state representation adopted in this work is quite common for most systems that use a POMDP model, different state representations could possibly reveal new insights.

References

A. Black et al., 2011. Spoken dialog challenge 2010: Comparison of live and control test results. In Proceedings of SIGDIAL.

S. Bradtke and A. Barto, 1996. Linear Least-Squares algorithms for temporal difference learning. Machine Learning, 22, 1-3, 33-57.

Y. Engel, S. Mannor and R. Meir, 2004. The Kernel Recursive Least Squares Algorithm. IEEE Transactions on Signal Processing, 52:2275-2285.

M. Gasic and S. Young, 2011. Effective handling of dialogue state in the hidden information state POMDP-based dialogue manager. ACM Transactions on Speech and Language Processing, 7(3).

M. Gasic, F. Jurcicek, S. Keizer, F. Mairesse, B. Thomson, K. Yu and S. Young, 2010. Gaussian Processes for Fast Policy Optimisation of POMDP-based Dialogue Managers, In Proceedings of SIGDIAL, 2010.

J. Henderson, O. Lemon and K. Georgila, 2008. Hybrid reinforcement/supervised learning of dialogue policies from fixed data sets. Computational Linguistics, 34(4):487-511.

M. Henderson, B. Thomson and J. Williams, 2014. The Second Dialog State Tracking Challenge. In Proceedings of SIGDIAL, 2014.

L. Hurtado, D. Grial, E. Sanchis and E. Segarra, 2005. A Stochastic Approach to Dialog Management. In Proceedings of ASRU, 2005.

M. Lagoudakis and R. Parr, 2003. Least-squares policy iteration. Journal of Machine Learning Research 4, 1107-1149.

S. Lee, 2013. Structured Discriminative Model For Dialog State Tracking. In Proceedings of SIGDIAL, 2013.

S. Lee and M. Eskenazi, 2012. Incremental Sparse Bayesian Method for Online Dialog Strategy Learning. IEEE Journal of Selected Topics in Signal Processing, 6(8).

S. Lee and M. Eskenazi, 2013. Recipe For Building Robust Spoken Dialog State Trackers: Dialog State Tracking Challenge System Description. In Proceedings of SIGDIAL, 2013.

O. Pietquin, M. Geist, S. Chandramohan and H. Frezza-buet, 2011. Sample Efficient Batch Reinforcement Learning for Dialogue Management Optimization. ACM Transactions on Speech and Language Processing, 7(3).

O, Pietquin, M. Geist, and S. Chandramohan, 2011. Sample Efficient On-Line Learning of Optimal Dialogue Policies with Kalman Temporal Differences. In Proceedings of IJCAI, 2011.

A. Raux, B. Langner, D. Bohus, A. W Black, and M. Eskenazi, 2005. Let's Go Public! Taking a Spoken Dialog System to the Real World. In Proceedings of Interspeech.

J. Williams, 2013. Multi-domain learning and generalization in dialog state tracking. In Proceedings of SIGDIAL, 2013.

J. Williams, A. Raux, D. Ramachandran and A. Black, 2013. The Dialog State Tracking Challenge. In Proceedings of SIGDIAL, 2013.

S. Young, M. Gasic, B. Thomson and J. Williams 2013. POMDP-based Statistical Spoken Dialogue Systems: a Review. IEEE, 101(5):1160-1179.

The SJTU System for Dialog State Tracking Challenge 2

Kai Sun, Lu Chen, Su Zhu and Kai Yu
Department of Computer Science and Engineering, Shanghai Jiao Tong University
Shanghai, China
{accreator, chenlusz, paul2204, kai.yu}@sjtu.edu.cn

Abstract

Dialog state tracking challenge provides a common testbed for state tracking algorithms. This paper describes the SJTU system submitted to the second Dialogue State Tracking Challenge in detail. In the system, a statistical semantic parser is used to generate refined semantic hypotheses. A large number of features are then derived based on the semantic hypotheses and the dialogue log information. The final tracker is a combination of a rule-based model, a maximum entropy and a deep neural network model. The SJTU system significantly outperformed all the baselines and showed competitive performance in DSTC 2.

1 Introduction

Dialog state tracking is important because spoken dialog systems rely on it to choose proper actions as spoken dialog systems interact with users. However, due to automatic speech recognition (ASR) and spoken language understanding (SLU) errors, it is not easy for the dialog manager to maintain the true state of the dialog. In recent years, much research has been devoted to dialog state tracking. Many approaches have been applied to dialog state tracking, from rule-based to statistical models, from generative models to discriminative models (Wang and Lemon, 2013; Zilka et al., 2013; Henderson et al., 2013; Lee and Eskenazi, 2013). Recently, shared research tasks like the first Dialog State Tracking Challenge (DSTC 1) (Williams et al., 2013) have provided a common testbed and evaluation suite for dialog state tracking (Henderson et al., 2013).

Compared with DSTC 1 which is in the bus timetables domain, DSTC 2 introduces more complicated and dynamic dialog states, which may change through the dialog, in a new domain, i.e. restaurants domain (Henderson et al., 2014). For each turn, a tracker is supposed to output a set of distributions for each of the three components of the dialog state: *goals*, *method*, and *requested slots*. At a given turn, the goals consists of the user's true required value having been revealed for each slot in the dialog up until that turn; the method is the way the user is trying to interact with the system which may be *by name*, *by constraints*, *by alternatives* or *finished*; and the requested slots consist of the slots which have been requested by the user and not replied by the system. For evaluation in DSTC 2, 1-best quality measured by **accuracy**, probability calibration measured by **L2**, and discrimination measured by **ROC** are selected as featured metrics. Further details can be found in the DSTC 2 handbook (Henderson et al., 2013).

Previous research has demonstrated the effectiveness of rule-based (Zilka et al., 2013), maximum entropy (MaxEnt) (Lee and Eskenazi, 2013) and deep neural network (DNN) (Henderson et al., 2013) models separately. Motivated by this, the SJTU system employs a combination of a rule-based model, a MaxEnt and a DNN model. The three models were first trained (if necessary) on the training set and tested for each of the three components of the dialog state, i.e goals, method, and requested slots on the development set. Then, models with the best performance for each of the three components were selected to form a combined model. Finally, the combined model was retrained using both training set and development set. Additionally, as the live SLU was found not good enough with some information lost compared with the live ASR, a new semantic parser was implemented which took the live ASR as input and the SJTU system used the result from the new semantic parser instead of the live SLU.

The remainder of the paper is organized as follows. Section 2 describes the design of the new semantic parser. Section 3 presents the rule-based model. Section 4 describes the statistical models including the maximum entropy model and the deep neural network model. Section 5 shows and discusses the performance of the SJTU system. Finally, section 6 concludes the paper.

2 Semantic Parser

It was found that the live SLU provided by the organisers has poor quality. Hence, a new statistical semantic parser is trained to parse the live ASR hypotheses.

2.1 Semantic Tuple Classifier

The semantics of an utterance is represented in functor form called *dialogue act* consisting of a dialogue act type and a list of slot-value pairs, for example:

request(name,food=chinese)

where "request" is the dialogue *act type*,"name" is a *slot* requested and "food=chinese" is a *slot-value pair* which provides some information to the system. In DSTC 2, there are many different dialogue act types (e.g. "request", "inform", "deny", etc) and different slot-value pairs (e.g. "food=chinese", "pricerange=cheap", "area=center", etc), which are all called *semantic items*.

A semantic tuple (e.g. act type, type-slot pair, slot-value pair) classifier (STC) approach developed by Mairesse et al. (2009) is used in the SJTU system. It requires a set of SVMs to be trained on n-gram features from a given utterance: a multi-class SVM is used to predict the dialogue act type, and a binary SVM is used to predict the existence of each slot-value pair. Henderson et al. (2012) improved this method with converting the SVM outputs to probabilities, and approximating the probability of a dialogue-act d of type d-type$_j$ with a set of slot-value pairs S by:

$$P(d|u) = P(\text{d-type}_j|u) \prod_{sv \in S} P(sv|u) \prod_{sv \notin S} (1 - P(sv|u)) \quad (1)$$

where u denotes an utterance and sv runs over all possible slot-value pairs.

2.2 Dialogue Context Features

In addition to the n-gram feature used in the original STC parser, the dialogue context can be exploited to constrain the semantic parser. In DSTC 2, the dialogue context available contains the history information of user's ASR hypotheses, the system act and the other output of system (e.g. whether there is a barge-in from the user or not, the turn-index) and so on. In the SJTU system, the context features from the last system act (indicators for all act types and slot-value pairs on whether they appear), an indicator for "barge-in" and the reciprocal of turn-index are combined with the original n-gram feature to be the final feature vector.

2.3 Generating Confidence Scores

For testing and predicting the dialogue act, the semantic parser is applied to each of the top N ASR hypotheses h_i, and the set of results D_i with m_i distinct dialogue act hypotheses would be merged in following way:

$$P(d|o) = \sum_{i=1}^{N} \begin{cases} p(h_i|o)p(d|h_i) & \text{if } d \in D_i \\ 0 & \text{otherwise} \end{cases}$$

where o is the acoustic observation, d runs over each different dialogue act in $D_i, i = 1, ..., N$, $p(h_i|o)$ denotes the ASR posterior probability of the i-th hypothesis, $p(d|h_i)$ denotes the semantic posterior probability given the i-th ASR hypothesis as in equation (1). Finally, a normalization should be done to guarantee the sum of $P(d|o)$ to be one.

2.4 Implementation

The STCs-based semantic parser is implemented with linear kernel SVMs trained using the LibSVM package (Chang and Lin, 2011). The SVM misclassification cost parameters are optimised individually for each SVM classifier by performing cross-validations on the training data.

3 Rule-based Model

In this section, the rule-based model which is slightly different from the focus tracker (Henderson et al., 2013) and HWU tracker (Wang, 2013) is described. The idea of the rule-based model is to maintain beliefs based on basic probability operations and a few heuristic rules that can be observed on the training set. In the following the rule-based model for joint goals, method and requested slots are described in detail.

3.1 Joint Goals

For slot s, the i-th turn and value v, $p^+_{s,i,v}$ ($p^-_{s,i,v}$) is used to denote the sum of all the confidence scores assigned by the SLU to the user informing or affirming (denying or negating) the value of slot s is v. The belief of "the value of slot s being v in the i-th turn" denoted by $b_{s,i,v}$ is defined as follows.

- If $v \neq$ "$None$",

$$\begin{aligned} b_{s,i,v} &= (b_{s,i-1,v} + p^+_{s,i,v}(1 - b_{s,i-1,v})) \\ & \quad (1 - p^-_{s,i,v} - \sum_{v' \neq v} p^+_{s,i,v'}) \end{aligned}$$

- Otherwise,

$$b_{s,i,v} = 1 - \sum_{v' \neq \text{"}None\text{"}} b_{s,i,v'}$$

In particular, when $i = 0$, $b_{s,0,v} = 1$ if $v =$ "$None$", otherwise 0. The motivation here comes from HWU tracker (Wang, 2013) that only $p^+_{s,\cdot,v}$ positively contributes to the belief of slot s being v, and both $p^+_{s,\cdot,v'}$ ($v' \neq v$) and $p^-_{s,\cdot,v}$ contribute to the belief negatively.

3.2 Method

For the i-th turn, $p_{i,m}$ is used to denote the sum of all the confidence scores assigned by the SLU to method m. Then the belief of "the method being m in the i-th turn" denoted by $b_{i,m}$ is defined as follows.

- If $m \neq$ "$none$",

$$b_{i,m} = b_{i-1,m}(1 - \sum_{m' \neq \text{"}none\text{"}} p_{i,m'}) + p_{i,m}$$

- Otherwise,

$$b_{i,m} = 1 - \sum_{m' \neq \text{"}none\text{"}} b_{i,m'}$$

In particular, $b_{0,m} = 0$ when $i = 0$ and $m \neq$ "$none$". An explanation of the above formula is given by Zilka et al. (2013). The idea is also adopted by the focus tracker (Henderson et al., 2013).

3.3 Requested Slots

For the i-th turn and slot r, $p_{i,r}$ is used to denote the sum of all the confidence scores assigned by the SLU to r is one of the requested slots. Then the belief of "r being one of the requested slots in the i-th turn" denoted by $b_{i,r}$ is defined as follows.

- If $i = 1$, or system has at least one of the following actions: "canthelp", "offer", "reqmore", "confirm-domain", "expl-conf", "bye", "request",

$$b_{i,r} = p_{i,r}$$

- Otherwise,

$$b_{i,r} = b_{i-1,r}(1 - p_{i,r}) + p_{i,r}$$

This rule is a combination of the idea of HWU tracker (Wang, 2013) and an observation from the labelled data that once system has some certain actions, the statistics of requested slots from the past turn should be reset.

4 Statistical Model

In this section, two statistical models, one is the MaxEnt model, the other is the DNN model, are described.

4.1 Features

The performance of statistical models is highly dependent on the feature functions.

Joint Goals

For slot s, the i-th turn and value v, the feature functions designed for joint goals are listed below.

- $f_1 \triangleq inform(s,i,v)$ = the sum of all the scores assigned by the SLU to the user informing the value of slot s is v.
- $f_2 \triangleq affirm(s,i,v)$ = the sum of all the scores assigned by the SLU to the user affirming the value of slot s is v.
- $f_3 \triangleq pos(s,i,v) = inform(s,i,v) + affirm(s,i,v)$.
- $f_4 \triangleq deny(s,i,v)$ = the sum of all the scores assigned by the SLU to the user denying the value of slot s is v.
- $f_5 \triangleq negate(s,i,v)$ = the sum of all the scores assigned by the SLU to the user negating the value of slot s is v.

- $f_6 \triangleq neg(s,i,v) = deny(s,i,v) + negate(s,i,v)$.
- $f_7 \triangleq acc(s,i,v) = pos(s,i,v) - neg(s,i,v)$.
- $f_8 \triangleq rule(s,i,v)$ = the confidence score given by the rule-based model.
- $f_9 \triangleq rank\_inform(s,i,v)$ = the sum of all the reciprocal rank of the scores assigned by the SLU to the user informing the value of slot s is v, or 0 if informing v cannot be found in the SLU n-best list.
- $f_{10} \triangleq rank\_affirm(s,i,v)$ = the sum of all the reciprocal rank of the scores assigned by the SLU to the user affirming the value of slot s is v, or 0 if affirming v cannot be found in the SLU n-best list.
- $f_{11} \triangleq rank^{+}(s,i,v) = rank\_inform(s,i,v) + rank\_affirm(s,i,v)$.
- $f_{12} \triangleq rank\_deny(s,i,v)$ = the sum of all the reciprocal rank of the scores assigned by the SLU to the user denying the value of slot s is v, or 0 if denying v cannot be found in the SLU n-best list.
- $f_{13} \triangleq rank\_negate(s,i,v)$ = the sum of all the reciprocal rank of the scores assigned by the SLU to the user negating the value of slot s is v, or 0 if negating v cannot be found in the SLU n-best list.
- $f_{14} \triangleq rank^{-}(s,i,v) = rank\_deny(s,i,v) + rank\_negate(s,i,v)$.
- $f_{15} \triangleq rank(s,i,v) = rank^{+}(s,i,v) - rank^{-}(s,i,v)$.
- $f_{16} \triangleq max(s,i,v)$ = the largest score given by SLU to the user informing, affirming, denying, or negating the value of slot s is v from the 1-st turn.
- $f_{17} \triangleq rest(s,i,v)$ = 1 if v = "$None$", otherwise 0.
- $f_{18} \triangleq \overline{pos}(s,i,v) = \frac{\sum_{k=1\leq i} pos(s,k,v)}{i}$, which is the arithmetic mean of $pos(s,\cdot,v)$ from the 1-st turn to the i-th turn. Similarly, $f_{19} \triangleq \overline{neg}(s,i,v)$, $f_{20} \triangleq \overline{rank^{+}}(s,i,v)$ and $f_{21} \triangleq \overline{rank^{-}}(s,i,v)$ are defined.
- $\boldsymbol{f}_{22} \triangleq (f_{22,1}, f_{22,2}, \cdots, f_{22,10})$, where $f_{22,j} \triangleq bin\_pos(s,i,v,j) = \frac{tot_{pos}(s,i,v,j)}{Z}$, where $tot_{pos}(s,i,v,j)$ = the total number of slot-value pairs from the 1-st turn to the i-th turn with slot s and value v which will fall in the j-th bin if the range of confidence scores is divided into 10 bins, and $Z = \sum_{k\leq i, 1\leq j'\leq 10, v'} tot_{pos}(s,k,v',j')$, which is the normalization factor. Similarly, $\boldsymbol{f}_{23} \triangleq (f_{23,1}, f_{23,2}, \cdots, f_{23,10})$ where $f_{23,j} \triangleq bin\_neg(s,i,v,j)$ is defined.
- $\boldsymbol{f}_{24} \triangleq (f_{24,1}, f_{24,2}, \cdots, f_{24,10})$. Where $f_{24,j} \triangleq bin\_rule(s,i,v,j) = \frac{tot_{rule}(s,i,v,j)}{Z}$, where $tot_{rule}(s,i,v,j)$ = the total number of $rule(s,\cdot,v)$ from the 1-st turn to the i-th turn which will fall in the j-th bin if the range of $rule(\cdot,\cdot,\cdot)$ is divided into 10 bins, and $Z = \sum_{k\leq i, 1\leq j'\leq 10, v'} tot_{rule}(s,k,v',j')$, which is the normalization factor. Similarly, $\boldsymbol{f}_{25} \triangleq (f_{25,1}, f_{25,2}, \cdots, f_{25,10})$ where $f_{25,j} \triangleq bin\_rank(s,i,v,j)$, and $\boldsymbol{f}_{26} \triangleq (f_{26,1}, f_{26,2}, \cdots, f_{26,10})$ where $f_{26,j} \triangleq bin\_acc(s,i,v,j)$ are defined.
- $\boldsymbol{f}_{27} \triangleq (f_{27,1}, f_{27,2}, \cdots, f_{27,10})$. Where $f_{27,j} \triangleq bin\_max(s,i,v,j) = 1$ if $max(s,i,v)$ will fall in the j-th bin if the range of confidence scores is divided into 10 bins, otherwise 0.
- $\boldsymbol{f}_{28} \triangleq (f_{28,1}, f_{28,2}, \cdots, f_{28,17})$. Where $f_{28,j} \triangleq user\_acttype(s,i,v,u_j)$ = the sum of all the scores assigned by the SLU to the user act type being $u_j (1 \leq j \leq 17)$. There are a total of 17 different user act types described in the handbook of DSTC 2 (Henderson et al., 2013).
- $\boldsymbol{f}_{29} \triangleq (f_{29,1}, f_{29,2}, \cdots, f_{29,17})$. Where $f_{29,j} \triangleq machine\_acttype(s,i,v,m_j)$ = the number of occurrences of act type $m_j (1 \leq j \leq 17)$ in machine act. There are a total of 17 different machine act types described in the handbook of DSTC 2 (Henderson et al., 2013).
- $f_{30} \triangleq canthelp(s,i,v)$ = 1 if the system cannot offer a venue with the constrain $s = v$, otherwise 0.
- $f_{31} \triangleq slot\_confirmed(s,i,v)$ = 1 if the system has confirmed $s = v$, otherwise 0.

- $f_{32} \triangleq slot\_requested(s, i, v)$ = 1 if the system has requested the slot s, otherwise 0.
- $f_{33} \triangleq slot\_informed(s, i, v)$ = 1 if the system has informed $s = v$, otherwise 0.
- $f_{34} \triangleq bias(s, i, v)$ = 1.

In particular, all above feature function are 0 when $i \leq 0$.

Method

For the i-th turn and method m, the feature functions designed for method are listed below.

- $f_1 \triangleq slu(i, m)$ = the sum of all the scores assigned by the SLU to the method being m.
- $f_2 \triangleq rank(i, m)$ = the sum of all the reciprocal rank of the scores assigned by the SLU to the method being m.
- $f_3 \triangleq rule(i, m)$ = the confidence score given by the rule-based model.
- $f_4 \triangleq \overline{slu}(i, m) = \frac{\sum_{k=1}^{i} slu(k,m)}{i}$, which is the arithmetic mean of $slu(\cdot, m)$ from the 1-st turn to the i-th turn. Similarly, $f_5 \triangleq \overline{rank}(i, m)$ and $f_6 \triangleq \overline{rule}(i, m)$ are defined.
- $f_7 \triangleq score\_name(i)$ = the sum of all the scores assigned by the SLU to the user informing the value of slot $name$ is some value.
- $f_8 \triangleq venue\_offered(i)$ = 1 if at least one venue has been offered to the user by the system from the 1-st turn to the i-th turn, otherwise 0.
- $\boldsymbol{f_9} \triangleq (f_{9,1}, f_{9,2}, \cdots, f_{9,17})$. Where $f_{9,j} \triangleq user\_acttype(i, u_j)$ = the sum of all the scores assigned by the SLU to the user act type being $u_j (1 \leq j \leq 17)$.
- $f_{10} \triangleq bias(i)$ = 1.

In particular, all above feature function are 0 when $i \leq 0$.

Requested Slots

For the i-th turn and slot r, the feature functions designed for requested slots are listed below.

- $f_1 \triangleq slu(i, r)$ = the sum of all the scores assigned by the SLU to r being one of the requested slots.
- $f_2 \triangleq rank(i, r)$ = the sum of all the reciprocal rank of the scores assigned by the SLU to r being one of the requested slots.
- $f_3 \triangleq rule(i, r)$ = the confidence score given by the rule-based model.
- $f_4 \triangleq bias(i, r)$ = 1

In particular, all above feature function are 0 when $i \leq 0$.

4.2 Maximum Entropy Model

Total 6 MaxEnt models (Bohus and Rudnicky, 2006) are employed, four models for the joint goals, one for the method and one for the requested slots. The Maximum Entropy model is an efficient means that models the posterior of class y given the observations $\boldsymbol{x}$:

$$P(y|\boldsymbol{x}) = \frac{1}{Z(\boldsymbol{x})} \exp\left(\boldsymbol{\lambda}^T \boldsymbol{f}(y, \boldsymbol{x})\right)$$

Where $Z(\boldsymbol{x})$ is the normalization constant. $\boldsymbol{\lambda}$ is the parameter vector and $\boldsymbol{f}(y, \boldsymbol{x})$ is the feature vector.

The models for the joint goals are implemented for four informable slots (i.e. area, food, name and pricerange) separately. In the k-th turn, for every informable slot s and its value v, i.e. slot-value pair in SLU, the MaxEnt model for the corresponding slot is used to determine whether the value v for the slot s in the user goals is right or not. The input consists of 160 features [1] which are selected from the feature functions described in section 4.1 Joint Goals:

$$\{f_{34}\}_{i=k} \cup \bigcup_{k-2 \leq i \leq k} \{f_1, \cdots, f_{15}, \boldsymbol{f_{28}}, \cdots, f_{33}\}$$

Where i is the turn index . The output of the model is the confidence score that the value v for the slot s is right.

In the k-th turn, the model for the method is used to determine which way the user is trying to interact with the system. The input consists of 97 features which are selected from the feature func-

[1] For the feature function whose range is not 1 dimension, the number of features defined by the feature function is counted as the number of dimensions rather than 1. For example, the number of features defined by $\boldsymbol{f_{28}}$ is 17.

tions described in section 4.1 Method:

$$\{f_{10}\}_{i=k} \cup \bigcup_{k-3 \le i \le k} \{f_7, f_8, \boldsymbol{f_9}\}$$

$$\cup \bigcup_{\substack{m \\ k-3 \le i \le k}} \{f_3\}$$

and the output consists of five confidence scores that the method belongs to every one of the five ways (i.e. *by name*, *by constraints*, *by alternatives*, *finished* and *none*).

The model for the requested slots is used to determine whether the requestable slot r in the SLU "request(slot)" is truly requested by the user or not in the k-th turn. The input consists of 10 features which are selected from the feature functions described in section 4.1 Requested Slots:

$$\{f_4\}_{i=k} \cup \bigcup_{k-2 \le i \le k} \{f_1, f_2, f_3\}$$

and the output is the confidence score that r is truly requested by the user in this turn.

The parameters of the 6 MaxEnt models are optimised separately through maximizing the likelihood of the training data. The training process is stopped when the likelihood change is less than 10^{-4}.

4.3 Deep Neural Network Model

4 DNNs for joint goals (one for each slot), 1 for method and 1 for requested slots are employed. All of them have similar structure with Sigmoid for hidden layer activation and Softmax for output layer activation. As shown in figure 1, each DNN has 3 hidden layers and each layer has 64 nodes. DNNs take the feature set (which will be described in detail later) of a certain value of goal, method, or requested slots as the input, then output two values (donated by X and Y), through the hidden layer processing, and finally the confidence of the value can be got by $\frac{e^X}{e^X+e^Y}$.

For slot s, the k-th turn and value v, the feature set of goal consisting of 108 features is defined as:

$$\bigcup_{k-5 \le i \le k} \{f_3, f_6, f_7, f_8, f_{11}, f_{14}, f_{15}\}$$
$$\cup \{f_{18}, \cdots, f_{21}\}_{i=k-6}$$
$$\cup \{f_{16}, f_{17}, \boldsymbol{f_{22}}, \cdots, \boldsymbol{f_{27}}\}_{i=k}$$

For the k-th turn and method m, the feature set of method consisting of 15 features is defined as:

$$\bigcup_{k-3 \le i \le k} \{f_1, f_2, f_3\} \cup \{f_4, f_5, f_6\}_{i=k-4}$$

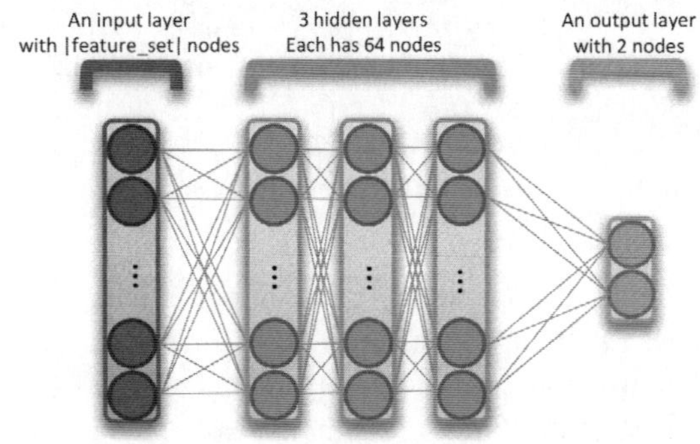

Figure 1: Structure of the DNN Model

For the k-th turn and slot r, the feature set of requested slots consisting of 12 features is defined as:

$$\bigcup_{k-3 \le i \le k} \{f_1, f_2, f_3\}$$

Bernoulli-Bernoulli RBM was applied to pretrain DNNs and Stochastic Gradient Descent with cross-entropy criterion to fine-tune DNNs. For the fine-tuning process, $3/4$ of the data was used for training and $1/4$ for validation.

5 Experiments

DSTC 2 provides a training dataset of 1612 dialogues (11677 utterances) and a development set of 506 dialogues (3934 utterances). The training data was first used to train the semantic parser and the MaxEnt and the DNN models for internal system development as shown in section 5.1 and 5.2. These systems were tested on the development data. Once the system setup and parameters were determined, the training and development set were combined together to train the final submitted system. The final system was then tested on the final evaluation data as shown in section 5.3.

5.1 Effect of the STC Semantic Parser

In DSTC 2, as the live semantic information was found to be poor, two new semantic parsers were then trained as described in section 2. One used the top ASR hypothesis n-gram features and the other one employed additional system feedback features (the last system act, "barge-in" and turn-index).

Table 1 shows the performance of two new semantic parser in terms of the precision, recall,

System	Precision	Recall	F-score	ICE
baseline	0.6659	0.8827	0.7591	2.1850
1-best	0.7265	0.8894	0.7997	1.4529
+ sys_fb	0.7327	0.8969	0.8065	1.3449

Table 1: Performance of semantic parsers with different features on the development set.

F-score of top dialogue act hypothesis and the Item Cross Entropy (ICE) (Thomson et al., 2008) which measures the overall quality of the confidences distribution of semantic items (the less the better). The baseline is the original live semantic hypotheses, "1-best" (row 3) represents the semantic parser trained on the top ASR hypothesis with n-gram feature, and "sys_fb" (row 4) represents the semantic parser added with the system feedback features. The STC semantic parsers significantly improve the quality of semantic hypotheses compared with baseline in the score of precision, recall, F-score and ICE. And the parser using context features (row 4) scored better than the other one (row 3).

The improved semantic parsers are expected to also yield better performance in dialogue state tracking. Hence, the parsers were used in focus baseline provided by the organiser. As shown in

	Joint Goals	Method	Requested
baseline	0.6121	0.8303	0.8936
1-best	0.6613	0.8764	0.8987
+ sys_fb	0.6765	0.8764	0.9297

Table 2: Results for focus baseline tracker with different parsers

table 2, the new parsers achieved consistent improvement on the accuracy of joint goals, method and requested slots. So the semantic hypotheses of parser using the system feedback features was used for later development.

5.2 Internal System Development

Table 3 shows the the results of rule-based model, the MaxEnt model and the DNN model on the development set. From the table we can see that the DNN model has the best performance for joint goals, the MaxEnt model has the best performance for method and the rule-based model has the best performance for requested slots. So the combined model is a combination of those three models, one for one of the three components where it has the best performance, that is, the rule-based model for requested slots, the MaxEnt model for method, and the DNN model for joint goals.

	Joint Goals	Method	Requested
Rule-based	0.6890	0.8955	0.9668
MaxEnt	0.6741	0.9079	0.9665
DNN	0.6906	0.8991	0.9661

Table 3: Performance of three tracking models

5.3 Evaluation Performance

The official results of the challenge are publicly available and the SJTU team is team 7. Entry 0, 1, 2, 3 of team 7 is the combined model, the rule-based model, the DNN model and the MaxEnt model respectively. They all used the new semantic parser based on live ASR hypotheses. Entry 4 of team 7 is also a combined model but it does not use the new semantic parser and takes the live SLU as input.

Table 4 shows the results on the final evaluation test set. As expected, the semantic parser does work, and the combined model has the best performance for joint goals and method, however, that is not true for requested slots. Notice that on the development set, the difference of the accuracy of requested slots among the 3 models is significantly smaller than that of joint goals and method. One reasonable explanation is that one cannot claim that the rule-based model has better performance for requested slots than the MaxEnt model and the DNN model only with an accuracy advantage less than 0.1%.

	Joint Goals	Method	Requested
Baseline	0.6191	0.8788	0.8842
Focus	0.7193	0.8670	0.8786
HWU	0.7108	0.8971	0.8844
HWU+	0.6662	0.8846	0.8830
Rule-based	0.7387	0.9207	0.9701
MaxEnt	0.7252	0.9357	0.9717
DNN	0.7503	0.9287	0.9710
Combined+	0.7503	0.9357	0.9701
Combined-	0.7346	0.9102	0.9458

Table 4: Accuracy of the combined model (Combined+) compared with the rule-based model, the MaxEnt model, the DNN model, the combined model without the new semantic parser (Combined-) and four baselines on the test set. Four baselines are the baseline tracker (Baseline), the focus tracker (Focus), the HWU tracker (HWU) and the HWU tracker with "original" flag set to (HWU+) respectively.

Figure 2 summaries the performance of the approach relative to all 31 entries in the DSTC 2.

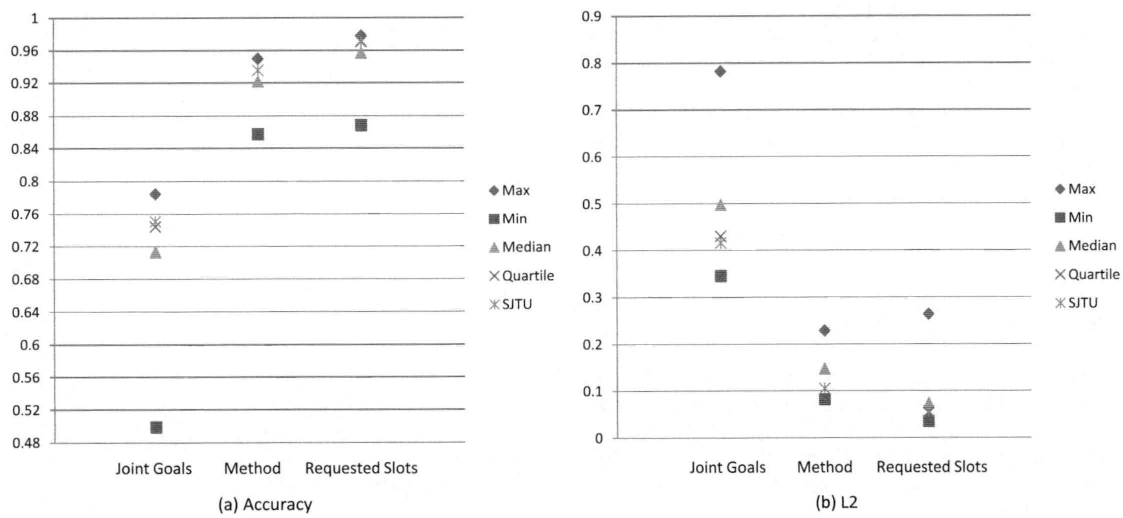

Figure 2: Performance of the combined model among 31 trackers. SJTU is the combined model (entry 0 of team 7).

As ROC metric is only comparable between systems of similar accuracy, only accuracy and L2 are compared. The results of the combined model is competitive for all the three components, especially for joint goals.

5.4 Post Evaluation Analysis

Two strategies and two kinds of features were added to the MaxEnt model for the requested slots after DSTC 2 based on some observations on the training set and development set. The first strategy is that the output for the requested slots of the first turn is set to empty by force. The second strategy is that the output of the confidence is additionally multiplied by $(1-C_f)$, where C_f denotes the confidence given by the MaxEnt model to the method of current turn being *finished*. As for the two kinds of features, one is the slot indicator and the other is the acttype-slot tuple. They are defined as [2]:

- $\boldsymbol{f}_5 \triangleq (f_{5,1}, f_{5,2}, \cdots, f_{5,8})$, where $f_{5,j} \triangleq slot\_indicator(i, r, s_j) = 1$ if the index of the slot r is j, i.e. $s_j = r$, otherwise 0.
- $\boldsymbol{f}_6 \triangleq (f_{6,1}, f_{6,2}, \cdots, f_{6,33})$, where $f_{6,j} \triangleq user\_act\_slot(i, r, t_j)$ = the sum of all the scores assigned by the SLU to the j-th user acttype-slot tuple t_j. The acttype-slot tuple is the combination of dialog act type and possible slot, e.g. $inform\text{-}food$, $confirm\text{-}area$. There are 33 user acttype-slot tuples.
- $\boldsymbol{f}_7 \triangleq (f_{7,1}, f_{7,2}, \cdots, f_{7,46})$, where $f_{7,j} \triangleq sys\_act\_slot(i, r, t_j)$ = the number of occurrences of the j-th machine acttype-slot tuple t_j in the dialog acts. There are 46 machine acttype-slot tuples.

With those strategies and features, the MaxEnt model achieved an accuracy of 0.9769 for the requested slots, which is significantly improved compared with the submitted system.

6 Conclusion

This paper describes the SJTU submission for DSTC 2 in detail. It is a combined system consisting of a rule-based model, a maximum entropy model and a deep neural network model with a STC semantic parser. The results show that the SJTU system is competitive and outperforms most of the other systems in DSTC 2 on test datasets. Post evaluation analysis reveal that there is still room for improvement by refining the features.

Acknowledgments

This work was supported by the Program for Professor of Special Appointment (Eastern Scholar) at Shanghai Institutions of Higher Learning and the China NSFC project No. 61222208.

References

Blaise Thomson, Kai Yu, Milica Gasic, Simon Keizer, Francois Mairesse, Jost Schatzmann and Steve

[2] The feature number is consistent with that in section 4.1.

Young. 2008. Evaluating semantic-level confidence scores with multiple hypotheses. In *INTERSPEECH*, pp. 1153-1156.

Chih-Chung Chang and Chih-Jen Lin. 2011. LIBSVM: a library for support vector machines. *ACM Transactions on Intelligent Systems and Technology (TIST)*, 2(3), 27.

Dan Bohus and Alex Rudnicky. 2006. A K-hypotheses + Other Belief Updating Model. In *Proc. of AAAI Workshop on Statistical and Empirical Approaches for Spoken Dialogue Systems.*

François Mairesse, Milica Gasic, Filip Jurcícek, Simon Keizer, Blaise Thomson, Kai Yu and Steve Young. 2009. Spoken language understanding from unaligned data using discriminative classification models. *Acoustics, Speech and Signal Processing, 2009. ICASSP 2009. IEEE International Conference on*, pp. 4749-4752. IEEE.

Jason Williams, Antoine Raux, Deepak Ramachandran and Alan Black. 2013. The Dialog State Tracking Challenge. In *SIGDIAL.*

Lukas Zilka, David Marek, Matej Korvas and Filip Jurcicek. 2013. Comparison of Bayesian Discriminative and Generative Models for Dialogue State Tracking. In *SIGDIAL.*

Matthew Henderson, Milica Gasic, Blaise Thomson, Pirros Tsiakoulis, Kai Yu and Steve Young. 2012. Discriminative spoken language understanding using word confusion networks. *Spoken Language Technology Workshop (SLT), 2012 IEEE*, pp. 176-181. IEEE.

Matthew Henderson, Blaise Thomson and Steve Young. 2013. Deep Neural Network Approach for the Dialog State Tracking Challenge. In *SIGDIAL.*

Matthew Henderson, Blaise Thomson and Jason Williams. 2013. Dialog State Tracking Challenge 2 & 3. Technical report, University of Cambridge.

Matthew Henderson, Blaise Thomson and Jason Williams. 2014. The Second Dialog State Tracking Challenge. In *SIGDIAL.*

Sungjin Lee and Maxine Eskenazi. 2013. Recipe For Building Robust Spoken Dialog State Trackers: Dialog State Tracking Challenge System Description. In *SIGDIAL.*

Zhuoran Wang and Oliver Lemon. 2013. A Simple and Generic Belief Tracking Mechanism for the Dialog State Tracking Challenge: On the believability of observed information. In *SIGDIAL.*

Zhuoran Wang. 2013. HWU Baseline Belief Tracker for DSTC 2 & 3. Technical report, Heriot-Watt University.

Markovian Discriminative Modeling for Dialog State Tracking

Hang Ren, Weiqun Xu, Yonghong Yan
The Key Laboratory of Speech Acoustics and Content Understanding
Institute of Acoustics, Chinese Academy of Sciences
21 North 4th Ring West Road, Beijing, China, 100190
{renhang, xuweiqun, yanyonghong}@hccl.ioa.ac.cn

Abstract

Discriminative dialog state tracking has become a hot topic in dialog research community recently. Compared to generative approach, it has the advantage of being able to handle arbitrary dependent features, which is very appealing. In this paper, we present our approach to the DSTC2 challenge. We propose to use discriminative Markovian models as a natural enhancement to the stationary discriminative models. The Markovian structure allows the incorporation of 'transitional' features, which can lead to more efficiency and flexibility in tracking user goal changes. Results on the DSTC2 dataset show considerable improvements over the baseline, and the effects of the Markovian dependency is tested empirically.

1 Introduction

Spoken dialog systems (SDS) have become much more popular these days, but still far from wide adoption. One of the most outstanding problems that affect user experience in an SDS is due to automatic speech recognition (ASR) and spoken language understanding (SLU) errors. While the advancement of ASR technology has a positive effect on SDS, it is possible to improve the SDS user experience by designing a module which explicitly handles ASR and SLU errors. With accurately estimated dialog state, the dialog manager could select more effective and flexible dialog actions, resulting in shorter dialogs and higher dialog success rate. Dialog state tracking is the task of identifying the correct dialog state (user action, user goal, etc.) from ASR and SLU outputs in the presence of errors. Commercial dialog systems these days usually use simple dialog state tracking strategies that only consider the most probable SLU output. Previous research shows that several errors in dialog state tracking can be rectified by considering the full N-best results from the ASR and SLU components (Williams, 2012). Thus it is very important to develop robust and practical dialog state tracking models.

In statistical dialog state tracking, models can be roughly divided into two major classes, i.e. generative and discriminative. Generative (Bayesian) dialog tracking models are prevalent in early studies due to its close relationship with the POMDP dialog management model (Young et al., 2013). Generative models generally use Dynamic Bayesian Networks to model the observation probability $P(O_t|S_t)$ and transition probability $P(S_t|S_{t-1})$, where O_t and S_t are observations and dialog state at turn t. In a discriminative model, the conditional probability $P(S_t|O_1^t)$ is modeled directly, where O_1^t is all the observations from turn 1 to t. One problem with the generative models is that the independent assumptions are always not realistic. For example, N-best hypotheses are often assumed independent of each other, which is flawed in realistic scenarios (Williams, 2012). Furthermore, it is intrinsically difficult for generative models to handle overlapping features, which prevents model designers from incorporating arbitrarily large feature set. Discriminative model does not suffer from the above problems as there is no need to make any assumptions about the probabilistic dependencies of the features. As a result. it is potentially able to handle much larger feature sets and to make more accurate predictions (Bohus and Rudnicky, 2006). Discriminative models also tend to be more data-driven, unlike generative models in which many sub-models parameters are heuristically tuned.

2 DSTC1 revisited

The first Dialog State Tracking Challenge (DSTC1) for the first time provided a common test bed for various state tracking methods, and several participants employed various discriminative models in the challenge. DSTC1 provided real user dialog corpora in the domain of bus route service to evaluate performance of various state tracking methods. In DSTC1 there are 9 teams with 27 submissions, where discriminative, generative and rule-based models are used in the challenge. Maximum entropy models (Lee and Eskenazi, 2013), conditional random fields (Lee, 2013) and neural networks (Henderson et al., 2013) are the most frequently used discriminative models, which gave competitive results on several metrics. It has been empirically analyzed that discriminative methods are especially advantageous when the ASR/SLU confidence scores are poorly estimated (Williams et al., 2013).

3 Discriminative modeling in dialog state tracking

In the design of a slot-filling or task-oriented dialog systems, dialog state tracking can be considered as a classification problem, i.e. assigning predefined *values* to a fixed number of *slots*. One major problem in the formulation is that in complex dialog scenarios the number of classes tends to be very big, resulting in extremely sparse training instances for each class. This sparsity affects the classification performance. A large prediction domain also leads to computation inefficiency which makes the model less practical. Usually we could focus only on the *on-list* hypotheses, which are the hypotheses appeared in the SLU results, and all the other values in the slot value set are grouped into a meta category `Other`. It is similar to the *partition* concept in HIS (Young et al., 2010), and by doing this we could reduce the number of classes to a reasonable size. We use $\mathcal{Y}_t$ to denote the prediction domain at turn t. Although the number of classes is reduced by focusing on the dynamically generated $\mathcal{Y}_t$, some classes will still suffer from the lack of training instances, and what is even worse is that a large portion of the classes will not have any training data, since in practical SDS deployment it is hard to collect a large dialog corpus. To handle the data sparseness problem, parameters are often shared across different slots, or even data sets, and by doing this the model complexity could be effectively controlled and the overfitting problem would be alleviated. Williams proposed to use various techniques from multi-domain learning to improve model performance (Williams, 2013), which could be taken as another way of parameter sharing.

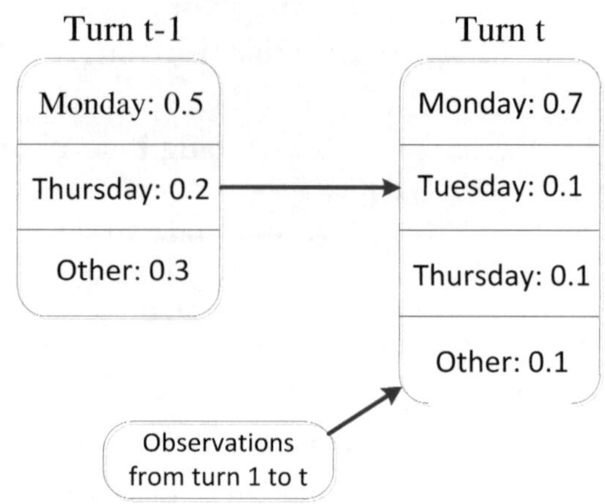

Figure 1: Markovian discriminative model dependency diagram. In this figure the dialog state is simplified to a single slot variable: *date*, the domain of the slot typically increases as dialog continues, which includes all the slot values appeared as SLU results. As indicated by the arrows, S_t depends on S_{t-1} and O_1^t. In stationary discriminative model, there's no dependency between adjacent turns indicated by the upper arrow.

3.1 Markovian discriminative model

A dialog can be naturally seen as a temporal sequence involving a user and an agent, where strong dependencies exist between adjacent turns. In typical task-oriented dialogs, users often change their goals when their original object cannot be satisfied. Even when the true user goal stays constant in a dialog session, the agent's perception of it will tend to evolve and be more accurate as the conversation proceeds, and thus the dialog state will often change. The states at adjacent turns are statistically correlated, and therefore it is important to leverage this natural temporal relationship in tracking dialog state. We enhance the stationary discriminative model in a similar way as described in (McCallum et al., 2000), by assuming Markovian dependency between adjacent turns.

Thus, the original probability $P(S_t|O_1^t)$ can be factored into the following form:

$$P(S_t|O_1^t) = \sum_{S_{t-1} \in \mathbf{S}} P(S_t|O_1^t, S_{t-1}) P(S_{t-1}|O_1^{t-1}) \quad (1)$$

The graphical model is shown is figure 1. Unlike stationary discriminative models, we model the *conditional transition* probability $P(S_t|O_1^t, S_{t-1})$ instead of $P(S_t|O_1^t)$ and the dialog state is updated according to equation 1 at each turn. The feature functions in the structured model can depend on the state of the previous turn, which we call *transitional* features.

It is worth noting that stationary discriminative model can include features built from dialog history (Metallinou et al., 2013). The major difference in utilizing this information from our approach is that by explicitly assuming the Markovian dependency, the structured model is able to exploit the whole probabilistic dialog state distribution of the previous turn. The previous dialog state S_{t-1} is inferred from previous dialog history O_1^{t-1}, which contains higher level hypotheses than the raw history features. Apart from that, the structured model can also use any stationary features built from O_1^t, which makes the stationary model a special case of the structured one.

3.2 Neural network classifier

We use the family of multi-layer neural networks to model the transition probability $P(S_t|O_1^{t-1}, S_{t-1})$. To allow for the use of the dynamic prediction domain, we utilize a forward network structure similar to (Henderson et al., 2013). Feature vectors for each class in $\mathcal{Y}_t$ are fed into the model and forwarded through several hidden layers for non-linear transformation in the hope that deeper layers may form higher abstraction of the raw inputs. The parameter vectors for each class are shared. For each feature vector the model generates a real score. The scores for all the classes in $\mathcal{Y}_t$ are then normalized using a softmax function resulting in valid probabilities.

$$y_i = W_{l-1} \cdot g_{l-1}(\dots g_1(W_1 \cdot X_i)\dots) \quad (2)$$

$$P_{\mathbf{Y}} = Softmax(y_1, \dots, y_{|\mathcal{Y}_t|}) \quad (3)$$

where g_1 to g_{l-1} are sigmoid functions, W_i is the weight matrix for linear transformation at layer i and $X_i = f(O_1^t, y_i)$ is the feature vector for class i. We also test maximum entropy models, which can be seen as a simple neural network without hidden layers:

$$P(\mathbf{Y} = y|O_1^t) = \frac{e^{\lambda \cdot f(O_1^t, y)}}{\sum_{y \in \mathcal{Y}} e^{\lambda \cdot f(O_1^t, y)}} \quad (4)$$

4 DSTC2 challenge

DSTC2 is the second round of Dialog State Tracking Challenge, and it provides dialog corpora collected from real human-machine dialogs in a restaurant domain. The corpora are split into labeled training and development sets and unlabeled test set. Test sets are collected from a SDS different from the training and development set to reflect the mismatch in real deployment. Unlike DSTC1, the user goal often changes in DSTC2 when the condition specified by the user cannot be met. For evaluation DSTC2 defined a number of metrics among which several featured metrics are selected. Besides tracking *user goals* (the values of each slot), two additional states *method* and *requested slots* are also defined, which track the method to query and the slots requested by users respectively. Further details about DSTC2 could be found in (Henderson et al., 2014).

5 Feature set

We briefly describe the feature set used in our system. We only use the live SLU information provided by the organizers, and no extra external data is used. The features used can be divided into two classes.

stationary features which only depend on the observations and the class (slot value) predicted at current turn in the form of $f(y_t, O_t)$.

transitional features that can also depends on the predicted class at the previous turn in the form of $f(y_t, y_{t-1}, O_t)$.

Stationary features include:

- SLU Scores: confidence scores of the current prediction binned into boolean values, raw scores are also added as real features.
- SLU Status: whether the prediction is denied, informed and confirmed in the current turn.
- Dialog history: whether the prediction has been denied, informed and confirmed in all the dialog turns until the current one.
- User/system action: The most probable user action and the machine action in the current turn.

The transitional features are as follows:

- Transition1: whether the predictions in the previous and the current turn are the same.

Name	Model Class	Hidden layers
Entry1	MEMM	–
Entry2	Structured NN	[50]
Entry3	Structured NN	[50, 30]
MLP	Stationary NN	[50, 30]

Table 1: Configurations of models. The model MLP uses the same structure as Entry3, but without the transitional features described in section 5. Number in brackets denotes the number of units used in each hidden layers.

- Transition2: joint feature of Transition1 in conjunction with the machine action in current turn, i.e. for each machine cation, Transision1 is replicated and only the one corresponding to the machine action at current turn is activated.

Transitional features are specific to Markovian models while stationary features can be used in any discriminative models.

6 Model training

Markovian models in various forms are tested to find the most appropriate structure for the task. Models for 'method' and 'state' are built separately using similar structured models.

When using the maximum entropy model to build the conditional probability, the Markovian model is equivalent to the maximum-entropy Markov model (MEMM) model introduced in (McCallum et al., 2000). More sophisticated neural networks with different configurations are used to fit the model to more complex patterns in the input features. In tracking the state 'goal', the joint distribution of slots is built assuming different slots are independent of each other. From the perspective of practical implementation, one advantage of the simpler MEMM model is that the training objective is convex. Thus the optimization routine is guaranteed to find the global optimum, while neural networks with hidden layers always have many local optima which require careful initialization of the parameters. LBFGS (Liu and Nocedal, 1989) is used in optimizing the batch log-likelihood objective and L1 and L2 regularizers are used to penalize the model from overfitting. We train the model on the training set, the development set is used for model selection and models produced at each training iteration are evaluated.

State	Tracker	ACC	L2	CA05
Goal	Baseline	0.619	0.738	0.000
	Entry1	0.707	0.447	**0.223**
	Entry2	0.713	**0.437**	0.207
	Entry3	**0.718**	0.461	0.100
	MLP	0.713	0.448	0.128
Method	Baseline	0.875	0.217	0.000
	Entry1	0.865	0.228	0.199
	Entry2	0.871	0.211	**0.290**
	Entry3	0.871	0.210	0.287
	MLP	**0.946**	**0.092**	0.000
Requested	Baseline	0.884	0.196	0.000
	Entry1	0.932	0.118	0.057
	Entry2	0.947	0.093	0.218
	Entry3	**0.951**	**0.085**	0.225
	MLP	0.863	0.231	**0.291**

Table 2: Evaluation results on the DSTC2 test set. ACC stands for accuracy, L2 measures the Euclidean distance between the predicted distribution and the ground truth vector with only the correct hypothesis set to 1. CA05 is the correct acceptance rate when false acceptance rate is 5%. Details of the metrics can be found in (Henderson et al., 2014). Except L2, the larger the scores, the better the performance.

In DSTC2 we submitted 3 trackers, an additional tracker without the transitional features is trained afterwards for comparison. Configurations of the models are described in table 1.

7 Experiments and part of the results

Featured metrics on the test set are shown in table 2. By most metrics our models are superior to the simple baseline. Especially in tracking user goals which is the most important state to track in DSTC2, the discriminative trackers show considerable performance gain. Judging from the performance of Entry1 to Entry3, we can conclude that the more complex 2-layer neural networks have better performance. Markovian neural networks can fit to the training instances with much more flexibility than the simple MEMM model. We have also trained a standard multi-layer neural network (MLP) model by disabling all the transitional features. By comparing the model 'Entry 3' and 'MLP', which share the same network structure, we explicitly test the effect of the Markovian structure. On the state 'goal' and 'requested', the Markovian model shows better tracking accuracies, which means that the Markovian structure has a positive effect on fitting the target. But in tracking the state 'method', the MLP model has the best performance among all the models compared. Thus although the log-likelihood increases considerably on the training set by adding the transitional features, the overfiting to the training set is more serious in tracking 'method'.

8 Conclusion

We described the models used in the DSTC2 challenge. We proposed a novel approach to enhancing the model capability of stationary discriminative models in dialog state tracking by assuming Markovian dependencies between adjacent turns. The results showed better performance than the simple baseline which uses the most probable hypothesis, and we empirically compared the models with and without the Markovian dependency. In future work, more discriminative models in different forms could be compared to evaluate their capability, and the effects of the Markovian structure and transitional features needs to be further studied.

Acknowledgments

We would like to thank the DSTC committee for their great efforts in organizing the challenge. We also thank the anonymous reviewers for their constructive comments.

This work is partially supported by the National Natural Science Foundation of China (Nos. 10925419, 90920302, 61072124, 11074275, 11161140319, 91120001), the Strategic Priority Research Program of the Chinese Academy of Sciences (Grant Nos. XDA06030100, XDA06030500), the National 863 Program (No. 2012AA012503) and the CAS Priority Deployment Project (No. KGZD-EW-103-2).

References

Dan Bohus and Alex Rudnicky. 2006. A k-hypotheses+ other belief updating model. In *Proc. of the AAAI Workshop on Statistical and Empirical Methods in Spoken Dialogue Systems*.

Matthew Henderson, Blaise Thomson, and Steve Young. 2013. Deep neural network approach for the dialog state tracking challenge. In *Proceedings of the SIGDIAL 2013 Conference*, pages 467–471, Metz, France, August. Association for Computational Linguistics.

Matthew Henderson, Blaise Thomson, and Jason Williams. 2014. The second dialog state tracking challenge. In *Proceedings of the SIGDIAL 2014 Conference*, Baltimore, U.S.A., June.

Sungjin Lee and Maxine Eskenazi. 2013. Recipe for building robust spoken dialog state trackers: Dialog state tracking challenge system description. In *Proceedings of the SIGDIAL 2013 Conference*, pages 414–422, Metz, France, August. Association for Computational Linguistics.

Sungjin Lee. 2013. Structured discriminative model for dialog state tracking. In *Proceedings of the SIGDIAL 2013 Conference*, pages 442–451, Metz, France, August. Association for Computational Linguistics.

Dong C Liu and Jorge Nocedal. 1989. On the limited memory bfgs method for large scale optimization. *Mathematical programming*, 45(1-3):503–528.

Andrew McCallum, Dayne Freitag, and Fernando C. N. Pereira. 2000. Maximum entropy markov models for information extraction and segmentation. In Pat Langley, editor, *ICML*, pages 591–598. Morgan Kaufmann.

Angeliki Metallinou, Dan Bohus, and Jason Williams. 2013. Discriminative state tracking for spoken dialog systems. In *Proceedings of the 51st Annual Meeting of the Association for Computational Linguistics*, pages 466–475, Sofia, Bulgaria, August. Association for Computational Linguistics.

Jason Williams, Antoine Raux, Deepak Ramachandran, and Alan Black. 2013. The dialog state tracking challenge. In *Proceedings of the SIGDIAL 2013 Conference*, page 404–413, Metz, France, August. Association for Computational Linguistics.

Jason Williams. 2012. A critical analysis of two statistical spoken dialog systems in public use. In *2012 IEEE Spoken Language Technology Workshop (SLT)*, pages 55–60.

Jason Williams. 2013. Multi-domain learning and generalization in dialog state tracking. In *Proceedings of the SIGDIAL 2013 Conference*, pages 433–441, Metz, France, August. Association for Computational Linguistics.

Steve Young, Milica Gašić, Simon Keizer, François Mairesse, Jost Schatzmann, Blaise Thomson, and Kai Yu. 2010. The hidden information state model: A practical framework for POMDP-based spoken dialogue management. *Computer Speech & Language*, 24(2):150–174.

Steve Young, Milica Gašić, Blaise Thomson, and Jason D Williams. 2013. Pomdp-based statistical spoken dialog systems: A review. *Proceedings of the IEEE*, 101(5):1160–1179.

Sequential Labeling for Tracking Dynamic Dialog States

Seokhwan Kim, Rafael E. Banchs
Human Language Technology Department
Institute for Infocomm Research
Singapore 138632
{kims,rembanchs}@i2r.a-star.edu.sg

Abstract

This paper presents a sequential labeling approach for tracking the dialog states for the cases of goal changes in a dialog session. The tracking models are trained using linear-chain conditional random fields with the features obtained from the results of SLU. The experimental results show that our proposed approach can improve the performances of the sub-tasks of the second dialog state tracking challenge.

1 Introduction

A dialog manager is one of the key components of a dialog system, which aims at determining the system actions to generate appropriate responses to users. To make the system capable of conducting a dialog in a more natural and effective manner, the dialog manager should take into account not only a given user utterance itself, but also the dialog state which represents various conversational situations obtained from the dialog session progress. Dialog state tracking is a sub-task of dialog management that analyzes and maintains this dialog state at each moment. The major obstacle to dialog state tracking is that the inputs to the tracker are likely to be noisy because of the errors produced by automatic speech recognition (ASR) and spoken language understanding (SLU) processes which are required to be performed prior to the tracking.

Thus, many researchers have focused on improving the robustness of dialog state trackers against ASR and SLU errors. The simplest ways to tackle this problem have been based on hand-crafted rules mainly on the confidence scores obtained from ASR and SLU modules (Nakano et al., 1999; Wang and Lemon, 2013). However, these approaches have the limitation that building the quality rules manually is expensive and, what is worse, the confidence scores could be unreliable and inconsistent in some cases.

The other direction of dialog state tracking approaches have utilized statistical machine learning techniques to obtain the distribution over a set of hypotheses. Although the most widely studied approaches have been based on generative models (Williams and Young, 2007; Williams, 2010; Young et al., 2010; Thomson and Young, 2010; Gašić and Young, 2011; Raux and Ma, 2011), recently, some researchers have reported that discriminative models (Bohus and Rudnicky, 2006; Lee, 2013; Zilka et al., 2013) achieved comparable, or even better, performances than generative models, especially in the tasks of the first dialog state tracking challenge (DSTC) (Williams et al., 2013).

This work focuses on the second phase of DSTC (Henderson et al., 2014). The major difference of DSTC 2 from the previous challenge is that user goals can be changed even in a single dialog session. This aspect can cause the limitations of the previous approaches assuming the fixed user goal for each session. To solve this dynamic state tracking problem, we propose a sequential labeling approach using linear-chain conditional random fields (CRFs) (Lafferty et al., 2001). This approach aims to improve the performances of the tracker in the case of goal changes by jointly performing prediction and segmentation of dialog states.

2 Problem Definition

A dialog state defined in DSTC 2 consists of the following three components: goals, method, and requested slots.

2.1 Goals Tracking

Goals represent the constraint values which are truly intended by a user at each moment. These values can be represented by using a slot filling

	Utterance	Goals	
		Food	Area
S_1	Hello, How may I help you?		
U_1	I need a Persian restaurant in the south part of town.	Persian	South
S_2	What kind of food would you like?		
U_2	Persian.	Persian	South
S_3	I'm sorry but there is no restaurant serving persian food		
U_3	How about Portuguese food?	Portuguese	South
S_4	Peking restaurant is a nice place in the south of town.		
U_4	Is that Portuguese?	Portuguese	South
S_5	Nandos is a nice place in the south of town serving tasty Portuguese food.		
U_5	Alright. Whats the phone number?	Portuguese	South
S_6	The phone number of nandos is 01223 327908 .		
U_6	And the address?	Portuguese	South
S_7	Sure, nandos is on Cambridge Leisure Park Clifton Way.		
U_7	Thank you good bye.		

Figure 1: Examples of user goals tracking on a dialog in the restaurant information domain

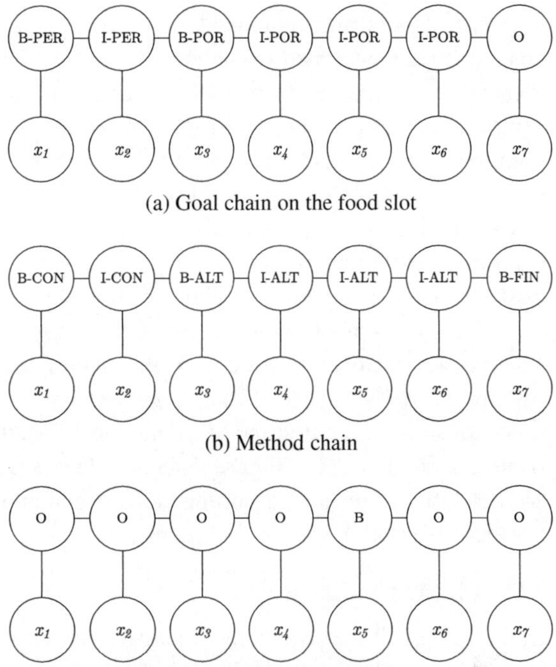

(c) Requested chain on the phone slot

Figure 2: Examples of dialog state tracking as sequential labeling with liner-chain CRFs

over the following four categories: area, food, name, and price range. Assuming the possible value set for each slot is fixed, this task can be considered to be a problem of finding the distributions over these hypotheses. While the previous challenge aims at identifying a single fixed goal for each session, the models for DSTC 2 should be able to handle goal changes during a session, as shown in Figure 1.

2.2 Method Tracking

Method tracking is performed by classifying the way of requesting information by a user into the following four categories: 'by constraints', 'by alternatives', 'by name', and 'finished'. The probability distribution over these four hypotheses is computed for each turn. For example, a methods sequence {byconstraints, byconstraints, byalternatives, byalternatives, byalternatives, byalternatives, finished} can be obtained for the dialog session in Figure 1.

2.3 Requested Slots Tracking

The other component for dialog state tracking is to specify the slots requested by a user. The tracker should output the binary distributions with the probabilities whether each slot is requested or not. Since the requestable slots are area, food, name, pricerange, addr, phone, postcode, and signature, eight different distributions are obtained at each turn. In the previous example dialog, 'phone' and 'addr' are requested in the 5th and 6th turns respectively.

3 Method

Although some discriminative approaches (Lee, 2013; Zilka et al., 2013; Lee and Eskenazi, 2013; Ren et al., 2013) have successfully applied to the dialog state tracking tasks of DSTC 1 by exploring various features, they have limited ability to perform the DSTC 2 tasks, because the previous models trained based on the features mostly extracted under the assumption that the user goal in a session is unchangeable. To overcome this limitation, we propose a sequential labeling approach using linear-chain CRFs for dynamic dialog state tracking.

3.1 Sequential Labeling of Dialog States

The goal of sequential labeling is to produce the most probable label sequence $\mathbf{y} = \{y_1, \cdots, y_n\}$ of a given input sequence $\mathbf{x} = \{x_1, \cdots, x_n\}$, where n is the length of the input sequence, $x_i \in \mathcal{X}$, $\mathcal{X}$ is the finite set of the input observation, $y_i \in \mathcal{Y}$, and $\mathcal{Y}$ is the set of output labels. The input sequence for dialog state tracking at a given turn t is defined as $\mathbf{x}_t = \{x_1, \cdots, x_t\}$, where x_i denotes the i-th turn in a given dialog session, then a tracker should be able to output a set of label sequences for every sub-task.

For the goals and requested slots tasks, a label sequence is assigned to each target slot, which means the number of output sequences for these sub-tasks are four and eight in total, respectively. On the other hand, only a single label sequence is defined for the method tracking task.

Due to discourse coherences in conversation, the same labels are likely to be located contiguously in a label sequence. To detect the boundaries of these label chunks, the BIO tagging scheme (Ramshaw and Marcus, 1999) is adopted for all the label sequences, which marks beginning of a chunk as 'B', continuing of a chunk as 'I', and outside a chunk as 'O'. Figure 2 shows the examples of label sequences according to this scheme for the input dialog session in Figure 1.

3.2 Linear Chain CRFs

In this work, all the sequential labeling tasks were performed by the tracking models trained using first-order linear-chain CRFs. Linear-chain CRFs are conditional probability distributions over the label sequences $\mathbf{y}$ conditioned on the input sequence $\mathbf{x}$, which are defined as follows:

$$p(\mathbf{y}|\mathbf{x}) = \frac{1}{Z(\mathbf{x})} \prod_{t=1}^{n} \Psi(y_t, y_{t-1}, \mathbf{x}),$$

$$\Psi(y_t, y_{t-1}, \mathbf{x}) = \Psi_1(y_t, \mathbf{x}) \cdot \Psi_2(y_t, y_{t-1}),$$

$$\Psi_1(y_t, \mathbf{x}) = \exp\left(\sum_k \lambda_k f_k(y_t, \mathbf{x})\right),$$

$$\Psi_2(y_t, y_{t-1}) = \exp\left(\sum_k \lambda_k f_k(y_t, y_{t-1})\right),$$

where $Z(\mathbf{x})$ is the normalization function which makes that the distribution sums to 1, $\{f_k\}$ is a set of feature functions for observation and transition, and $\{\lambda_k\}$ is a set of weight parameters which are learnt from data.

3.3 Features

To train the tracking models, a set of feature functions were defined based on the n-best list of user actions obtained from the live SLU results at a given turn and the system actions corresponding to the previous system output.

The most fundamental information to capture a user's intentions can be obtained from the SLU hypotheses with 'inform' action type. For each 'inform' action in the n-best SLU results, a feature function is defined as follows:

$$f_i(\text{inf}, s, v) = \begin{cases} \text{S}_i(\text{inf}, s, v), & \text{if inf}(s, v) \in \text{UA}_i, \\ 0, & \text{otherwise}, \end{cases}$$

where $\text{S}_i\,(a, s, v)$ is the confidence score of the hypothesis (a, s, v) assigned by SLU for the i-th turn, a is the action type, s is the target slot, v is its value, and UA_i is the n-best list of SLU results.

Similarly, the actions with 'confirm' and 'deny' types derive the corresponding feature functions defined as:

$$f_i(\text{con}, s, v) = \begin{cases} \text{S}_i(\text{con}, s, v), & \text{if con}(s, v) \in \text{UA}_i, \\ 0, & \text{otherwise}, \end{cases}$$

$$f_i(\text{den}, s, v) = \begin{cases} \text{S}_i(\text{den}, s, v), & \text{if den}(s, v) \in \text{UA}_i, \\ 0, & \text{otherwise}. \end{cases}$$

In contrast with the above action types, both 'affirm' and 'negate' don't specify any target slot and value information on the SLU results. The feature functions for these types are defined with (s, v) derived from the previous 'expl-conf' and 'impl-conf' system actions as follows:

$$f_i(\text{aff}, s, v) = \begin{cases} \max_j\left(\text{S}_{ij}(\text{aff})\right), & \text{if expl-conf}(s, v) \in \text{SA}_i, \\ & \text{or impl-conf}(s, v) \in \text{SA}_i \\ 0, & \text{otherwise}, \end{cases}$$

$$f_i(\text{neg}, s, v) = \begin{cases} \max_j\left(\text{S}_{ij}(\text{neg})\right), & \text{if expl-conf}(s, v) \in \text{SA}_i, \\ & \text{or impl-conf}(s, v) \in \text{SA}_i \\ 0, & \text{otherwise}, \end{cases}$$

where SA_i is the system actions at the i-th turn.

The user actions with 'request' and 'reqalts' could be able to play a crucial role to track the requested slots with the following functions:

$$f_i(\text{req}, s) = \begin{cases} \text{S}_i(\text{req}, s), & \text{if req}(s) \in \text{UA}_i, \\ 0, & \text{otherwise}, \end{cases}$$

$$f_i(\text{reqalts}, s) = \begin{cases} \text{S}_i(\text{reqalts}, s), & \text{if reqalts} \in \text{UA}_i, \\ 0, & \text{otherwise}. \end{cases}$$

The other function is to indicate whether the system is able to provide the information on (s, v) using the 'canthelp' actions as follows:

$$f_i(\text{canthelp}, s, v) = \begin{cases} 1, & \text{if canthelp}(s, v) \in SA_i, \\ 0, & \text{otherwise}. \end{cases}$$

		Dev set			Test set		
		Acc	L2	ROC	Acc	L2	ROC
Joint Goals	ME	0.638	0.551	**0.144**	0.596	0.671	0.036
	CRF	**0.644**	**0.545**	0.103	**0.601**	**0.649**	**0.064**
Method	ME	0.839	0.260	**0.398**	0.877	0.204	**0.397**
	CRF	**0.875**	**0.202**	0.181	**0.904**	**0.155**	0.187
Requested Slots	ME	**0.946**	**0.099**	0.000	0.957	0.081	0.000
	CRF	0.942	0.107	0.000	**0.960**	**0.073**	0.000

Table 1: Comparisons of dialog state tracking performances

4 Experiment

To demonstrate the effectiveness of our proposed sequential labeling approach for dialog state tracking, we performed experiments on the DSTC 2 dataset which consists of 3,235 dialog sessions on restaurant information domain which were collected using Amazon Mechanical Turk. The results of ASR and SLU are annotated for every turn in the dataset, as well as the gold standard annotations are also provided for evaluation. We used this dataset following the original division into training/development/test sets, which have 1,612/506/1,117 sessions, respectively.

Using this dataset, we trained two different types of models: one is based on CRFs for our proposed sequential labeling approach; and the other is a baseline using maximum entropy (ME) that performs the prediction for each individual turn separately from others in a given session. All the models for both approaches were trained on the training set with the same feature functions defined in Section 3.3 using MALLET [1] toolkit.

The trained models were used for predicting goals, method, and requested slots of each turn in the development and test sets, the results of which were then organized into a tracker output object defined as the input format to the evaluation script of DSTC 2. Since we omitted the joint goals distributions in the output, the evaluations on the joint goals were performed on the independent combinations of the slot distributions.

Among the various combinations of evaluation variables listed in the results of the evaluation script, the following three featured metrics were selected to report the performances of the tracker in this paper: Accuracy, L2 norm, and ROC CA 5. All these metrics were computed for the predicted joint goals, method and requested slots.

[1] http://mallet.cs.umass.edu/

Table 1 compares the performances of our proposed approach (CRF) and the baseline method (ME) for three sub-tasks on the development and test sets. The results indicate that our proposed sequential labeling approach achieved better performances than the baseline for most cases. Especially, CRF models produced better joint goals and method predictions in terms of accuracy and L2 norm on both development and test sets. For the requested slots task, our proposed approach failed to generate better results than the baseline on the development set. However, this situation was reversed on the test set, which means our proposed approach achieved better performances on all three sub-tasks on the test set in two of the three evaluation metrics.

5 Conclusions

This paper presented a sequential labeling approach for dialog state tracking. This approach aimed to solve the cases of goal changes using linear-chain CRFs. Experimental results show the merits of our proposed approach with the improved performances on all the sub-tasks of DSTC 2 compared to the baseline which doesn't consider sequential aspects.

However, these results are still not enough to be competitive with the other participants in the challenge. One possible reason is that our trackers were trained only on the very basic features in this work. If we discover more advanced features that help to track the proper dialog states, they can raise the overall performances further.

The other direction of our future work is to integrate these dialog state trackers with our existing dialog systems which accept the 1-best results of ASR and SLU as they are, then to see their impacts on the whole system level.

References

Dan Bohus and Alex Rudnicky. 2006. A k-hypotheses+ other belief updating model. In *Proc. of the AAAI Workshop on Statistical and Empirical Methods in Spoken Dialogue Systems*.

Milica Gašić and Steve Young. 2011. Effective handling of dialogue state in the hidden information state pomdp-based dialogue manager. *ACM Transactions on Speech and Language Processing (TSLP)*, 7(3):4.

Matthew Henderson, Blaise Thomson, and Jason Williams. 2014. The second dialog state tracking challenge. In *Proceedings of the SIGdial 2014 Conference*, Baltimore, U.S.A., June.

John Lafferty, Andrew McCallum, and Fernando CN Pereira. 2001. Conditional random fields: Probabilistic models for segmenting and labeling sequence data. In *Proceedings of ICML*, pages 282–289.

Sungjin Lee and Maxine Eskenazi. 2013. Recipe for building robust spoken dialog state trackers: Dialog state tracking challenge system description. In *Proceedings of the SIGDIAL 2013 Conference*, pages 414–422.

Sungjin Lee. 2013. Structured discriminative model for dialog state tracking. In *Proceedings of the SIGDIAL 2013 Conference*, pages 442–451.

Mikio Nakano, Noboru Miyazaki, Jun-ichi Hirasawa, Kohji Dohsaka, and Takeshi Kawabata. 1999. Understanding unsegmented user utterances in real-time spoken dialogue systems. In *Proceedings of the 37th annual meeting of the Association for Computational Linguistics on Computational Linguistics*, pages 200–207.

Lance A Ramshaw and Mitchell P Marcus. 1999. Text chunking using transformation-based learning. In *Natural language processing using very large corpora*, pages 157–176. Springer.

Antoine Raux and Yi Ma. 2011. Efficient probabilistic tracking of user goal and dialog history for spoken dialog systems. In *Proceedings of INTERSPEECH*, pages 801–804.

Hang Ren, Weiqun Xu, Yan Zhang, and Yonghong Yan. 2013. Dialog state tracking using conditional random fields. In *Proceedings of the SIGDIAL 2013 Conference*, pages 457–461.

Blaise Thomson and Steve Young. 2010. Bayesian update of dialogue state: A pomdp framework for spoken dialogue systems. *Computer Speech & Language*, 24(4):562–588.

Zhuoran Wang and Oliver Lemon. 2013. A simple and generic belief tracking mechanism for the dialog state tracking challenge: On the believability of observed information. In *Proceedings of the SIGDIAL 2013 Conference*, pages 423–432.

Jason D Williams and Steve Young. 2007. Partially observable markov decision processes for spoken dialog systems. *Computer Speech & Language*, 21(2):393–422.

Jason Williams, Antoine Raux, Deepak Ramachandran, and Alan Black. 2013. The dialog state tracking challenge. In *Proceedings of the SIGDIAL 2013 Conference*, pages 404–413.

Jason D Williams. 2010. Incremental partition recombination for efficient tracking of multiple dialog states. In *Acoustics Speech and Signal Processing (ICASSP), 2010 IEEE International Conference on*, pages 5382–5385. IEEE.

Steve Young, Milica Gašić, Simon Keizer, François Mairesse, Jost Schatzmann, Blaise Thomson, and Kai Yu. 2010. The hidden information state model: A practical framework for pomdp-based spoken dialogue management. *Computer Speech & Language*, 24(2):150–174.

Lukas Zilka, David Marek, Matej Korvas, and Filip Jurcicek. 2013. Comparison of bayesian discriminative and generative models for dialogue state tracking. In *Proceedings of the SIGDIAL 2013 Conference*, pages 452–456.

Author Index

Alexopoulos, Panos, 260
Artstein, Ron, 254
Ashok, Vikas, 123
Aufaure, Marie-Aude, 260

Banchs, Rafael E., 332
Ben Mustapha, Nesrine, 260
Berton, André, 12
Borodin, Yevgen, 123
Bouchard, Hugues, 260
Boye, Johan, 2
Boyer, Kristy, 41, 113
Breslin, Catherine, 260

Carenini, Giuseppe, 133
Chai, Joyce, 89
Chen, John, 257
Chen, Lu, 318
Cheng, Yu, 89
Chiba, Yuya, 74
Conner, Emma, 228
Corcoran, Thomas, 171
Cuayáhuitl, Heriberto, 260

Dethlefs, Nina, 260
DeVault, David, 254
Du, Yuan, 228
Dušek, Ondřej, 79

Efstathiou, Ioannis, 60
Ehlen, Patrick, 257
Ehrlich, Ute, 12
Elkan, Charles, 218
Ezen-Can, Aysu, 113

Fernández, Raquel, 151
Forbell, Eric, 69
Forbes-Riley, Katherine, 181

Gandhe, Sudeep, 251
Gangadharaiah, Rashmi, 218
Gašić, Milica, 260
Georgila, Kallirroi, 254
Girju, Roxana, 161
Giuliani, Manuel, 243
Guan, Boxuan, 228
Gupta, Rakesh, 22
Gustafson, Joakim, 2

Hastie, Helen, 260
Henderson, James, 260
Henderson, Matthew, 263, 292
Hirschberg, Julia, 238

Isard, Amy, 243
Ito, Akinori, 74
Ito, Masashi, 74

Jia, Yunyi, 89
Johnston, Michael, 257
Jung, Hyuckchul, 257
Jurčíček, Filip, 79, 108

Kawahara, Tatsuya, 32
Kennington, Casey, 84
Khouzaimi, Hatim, 98
Kim, Daejoong, 273
Kim, Kee-Eung, 273
Kim, Seokhwan, 332
Kousidis, Spyros, 84

Lane, Ian, 22
Laroche, Romain, 98
Lee, Byung-Jun, 273
Lee, Lillian, 141
Lee, Sungjin, 310
Lefevre, Fabrice, 98
Lemon, Oliver, 60, 260
Li, Junyi Jessy, 142, 199
Lieske, Jay, 257
Lim, Woosang, 273
Litman, Diane, 181
Liu, Alex, 238
Liu, Xingkun, 260

Marschall, Thomas, 243
Meena, Raveesh, 2
Mika, Peter, 260
Minker, Wolfgang, 51, 208
Misu, Teruhisa, 22

Morbini, Fabrizio, 69, 254
Morency, Louis-Philippe, 254

Narayanaswamy, Balakrishnan, 218
Nenkova, Ani, 142, 199
Nose, Takashi, 74
Nothdurft, Florian, 51
Nouri, Elnaz, 186

Oya, Tatsuro, 133

Pappu, Aasish, 194
Passonneau, Rebecca J., 228
Plátek, Ondřej, 79, 108
Potter, Tim, 260

Rahimtoroghi, Elahe, 171
Ramakrishnan, IV, 123
Raux, Antoine, 22
Reddy, Aarthi, 257
Reichel, Sven, 12
Ren, Hang, 327
Riaz, Mehwish, 161
Richter, Felix, 51
Rieser, Verena, 260
Rudnicky, Alexander, 194

Sagae, Kenji, 69
Schlangen, David, 84
Schlöder, Julian, 151
Selfridge, Ethan, 257
She, Lanbo, 89
Shriberg, Elizabeth, 238
Skantze, Gabriel, 2
Sloan, Rose, 238
Smith, Ronnie, 300
Sohn, Jasmin, 12
Stoyanchev, Svetlana, 123, 238, 257
Sun, Kai, 318
Swanson, Reid, 171

Then, Mei-Vern, 238
Thomson, Blaise, 260, 263, 292
Traum, David, 186, 251, 254
Tsiakoulis, Pirros, 260

Ultes, Stefan, 208

Vail, Alexandria, 41
Vanrompay, Yves, 260
Vasilieff, Brant, 257
Villazon-Terrazas, Boris, 260

Walker, Marilyn, 171
Weber, Michael, 12
Williams, Jason D, 263, 282
Wilpon, Jay, 257

Xi, Ning, 89
Xu, Weiqun, 327

Yan, Yonghong, 327
Yang, Shaohua, 89
Yazdani, Majid, 260
Yeung, Cho Ho, 228
Yoshino, Koichiro, 32
Young, Steve, 1, 260, 292
Yu, Kai, 318
Yu, Yanchao, 260

Zhu, Su, 318
Žilka, Lukáš, 79

Association for Computational Linguistics
209 N. Eighth Street
Stroudsburg, Pennsylvania 18360

CURRAN ASSOCIATES INC
proceedings.com